Lecture Notes in Computer Science 8168

Commenced Publication in 1973
Founding and Former Series Editors:
Gerhard Goos, Juris Hartmanis, and Jan van Leeuwen

Maria Simonetta Balsamo
William J. Knottenbelt Andrea Marin (Eds.)

Computer Performance Engineering

10th European Workshop, EPEW 2013
Venice, Italy, September 16-17, 2013
Proceedings

 Springer

Volume Editors

Maria Simonetta Balsamo
Università Ca' Foscari di Venezia
Dipartimento di Scienze Ambientali, Informatica e Statistica
via Torino 155, 30170 Venezia, Italy
E-mail: balsamo@dais.unive.it

William J. Knottenbelt
Imperial College London
Department of Computing
South Kensington Campus, London SW7 2AZ, UK
E-mail: wjk@doc.ic.ac.uk

Andrea Marin
Università Ca' Foscari di Venezia
Dipartimento di Scienze Ambientali, Informatica e Statistica
via Torino 155, 30170 Venezia, Italy
E-mail: marin@dais.unive.it

ISSN 0302-9743   e-ISSN 1611-3349
ISBN 978-3-642-40724-6   e-ISBN 978-3-642-40725-3
DOI 10.1007/978-3-642-40725-3
Springer Heidelberg New York Dordrecht London

Library of Congress Control Number: 2013946648

CR Subject Classification (1998): C.4, D.2.7-9, C.2.1-2, C.2.4, I.6.3-6, J.2

LNCS Sublibrary: SL 2 – Programming and Software Engineering

Typesetting: Camera-ready by author, data conversion by Scientific Publishing Services, Chennai, India

Printed on acid-free paper

Springer is part of Springer Science+Business Media (www.springer.com)

Preface

It is our great pleasure to present the proceedings of the 10th European Workshop on Performance Engineering (EPEW 2013) that took place in Venice. The purpose of this workshop series is to gather academic and industrial researchers working on all aspects of performance engineering. The program of EPEW 2013 comprises 16 full papers and 8 short papers selected from 33 submissions. Each paper was peer reviewed by at least three reviewers from the International Program Committee (IPC); after the collection of reviews the Program Committee members carefully discussed the quality of the papers for one week before deciding about the acceptance. We would like therefore to give a special thanks to all the members of the IPC for the excellent work in the reviewing process and the subsequent discussion panels during the selection process.

EPEW 2013 is honoured to have two distinguished keynote speakers: Vittorio Cortellessa from the University of L'Aquila and Claudio Palazzi from the University of Padova. We would like to express our gratitude for their participation.

Finally we would like to thank the University Ca' Foscari of Venice for hosting the workshop, the EasyChair team for having allowed us to use their conference system and Springer for the continued editorial support of this workshop series.

September 2013

Andrea Marin
Maria Simonetta Balsamo
William Knottenbelt

Organization

Program Committee

Gianfranco Balbo	Università di Torino, Italy
Simonetta Balsamo	Università Ca' Foscari Venezia, Italy
Marta Beltran	Rey Juan Carlos University, Spain
Marco Bernardo	Università di Urbino, Italy
Jeremy Bradley	Imperial College London, UK
Tadeusz Czachorski	IITiS PAN, Polish Academy of Sciences, Poland
Dieter Fiems	Ghent University, Belgium
Jean-Michel Fourneau	Universite de Versailles St Quentin, France
Stephen Gilmore	University of Edinburgh, UK
Richard Hayden	Imperial College London, UK
Andras Horvath	Università di Torino, Italy
Helen Karatza	Aristotle University of Thessaloniki, Greece
William Knottenbelt	Imperial College London, UK
Samuel Kounev	Karlsruhe Institute of Technology (KIT), Germany
Catalina M. Lladó	Universitat Illes Balears, Spain
Andrea Marin	Università Ca' Foscari Venezia, Italy
Dorina Petriu	Carleton University, Canada
Philipp Reinecke	HP Labs, Bristol, UK
Sabina Rossi	Università Ca' Foscari Venezia, Italy
Markus Siegle	Universität der Bundeswehr München, Germany
Mark Squillante	IBM Research, USA
Miklos Telek	Budapest University of Technology and Economics, Hungary
Nigel Thomas	Newcastle University, UK
Mirco Tribastone	Ludwig-Maximilians-Universität München, Germany
Petr Tuma	Charles University, Czech Republic
Maria Grazia Vigliotti	Imperial College London, UK
Jean-Marc Vincent	Laboratoire LIG, France
Katinka Wolter	Freie Universitaet zu Berlin, Germany

Additional Reviewers

Angius, Alessio	Dei Rossi, Gian-Luca
Beccuti, Marco	Galmés, Sebastià
Brosig, Fabian	Gouberman, Alexander

Guenther, Marcel
Jansen, David N.
Jones, Gareth
Krebs, Rouven
Milenkoski, Aleksandar
Noorshams, Qais

Riedl, Martin
Rota Bulò, Samuel
Shaw, Adrian L.
Tati, Bharath Siva Kumar
Tesei, Luca

Table of Contents

Invited Talks

Performance Antipatterns: State-of-Art and Future Perspectives   1
  Vittorio Cortellessa

Online Game Performance Engineering   7
  Claudio E. Palazzi

Full Papers

Stochastic Bounds and Histograms for Network Performance
Analysis   13
  *Farah Aït-Salaht, Hind Castel-Taleb, Jean-Michel Fourneau, and
  Nihal Pekergin*

Analytic Performance Modeling and Optimization of Live
VM Migration   28
  Arwa Aldhalaan and Daniel A. Menascé

Towards Supervisory Control of Generally-Distributed Discrete-Event
Systems   43
  Jasen Markovski

Tackling Truncation Errors in CSL Model Checking through Bounding
Semantics   58
  Yang Zhao and Gianfranco Ciardo

Automatic Performance Model Generation for Java Enterprise Edition
(EE) Applications   74
  Andreas Brunnert, Christian Vögele, and Helmut Krcmar

Canonical Representation of Discrete Order 2 MAP and RAP   89
  András Mészáros and Miklós Telek

Encoding Timed Models as Uniform Labeled Transition Systems   104
  Marco Bernardo and Luca Tesei

A Fast EM Algorithm for Fitting Marked Markovian Arrival Processes
with a New Special Structure   119
  Gábor Horváth and Hiroyuki Okamura

PMIF+: Extensions to Broaden the Scope of Supported Models   134
  Catalina M. Lladó and Connie U. Smith

Performance Regression Unit Testing: A Case Study   149
  *Vojtěch Horký, František Haas, Jaroslav Kotrč, Martin Lacina, and
  Petr Tůma*

Phase-Type Fitting Using HyperStar   164
  Philipp Reinecke, Tilman Krauß, and Katinka Wolter

Towards the Quantitative Evaluation of Phased Maintenance
Procedures Using Non-Markovian Regenerative Analysis   176
  *Laura Carnevali, Marco Paolieri, Kumiko Tadano, and
  Enrico Vicario*

Performance Enhancement by Means of Task Replication   191
  Peter G. Harrison and Zhan Qiu

Improving and Assessing the Efficiency of the MC4CSL^{TA} Model
Checker   206
  Elvio Gilberto Amparore and Susanna Donatelli

End-to-End Performance of Multi-core Systems in Cloud
Environments   221
  *Davide Cerotti, Marco Gribaudo, Pietro Piazzolla, and
  Giuseppe Serazzi*

Performance Analysis and Formal Verification of Cognitive Wireless
Networks   236
  Gian-Luca Dei Rossi, Lucia Gallina, and Sabina Rossi

Short papers

Sliding Hidden Markov Model for Evaluating Discrete Data   251
  Tiberiu Chis

Using Queuing Models for Large System Migration Scenarios – An
Industrial Case Study with IBM System z   263
  Robert Vaupel, Qais Noorshams, Samuel Kounev, and Ralf Reussner

Performance Evaluation for Collision Prevention Based on a Domain
Specific Language   276
  *Freek van den Berg, Anne Remke, Arjan Mooij, and
  Boudewijn Haverkort*

An Approximate Mean Value Analysis Approach for System
Management and Overload Control   288
  Vittoria De Nitto Personé and Andrea Di Lonardo

Modeling and Timing Simulation of Agilla Agents for WSN Applications
in Executable UML 300
    Luca Berardinelli, Antinisca Di Marco, Stefano Pace,
    Stefano Marchesani, and Luigi Pomante

Applying Model Differences to Automate Performance-Driven
Refactoring of Software Models 312
    Davide Arcelli, Vittorio Cortellessa, and Davide Di Ruscio

Reduction of Subtask Dispersion in Fork-Join Systems 325
    Iryna Tsimashenka and William J. Knottenbelt

SAT-Based Bounded Model Checking for RTECTL and Simply-Timed
Systems 337
    Bożena Woźna-Szcześniak, Agnieszka Zbrzezny, and
    Andrzej Zbrzezny

Author Index 351

Performance Antipatterns: State-of-Art and Future Perspectives

Vittorio Cortellessa

DISIM, University of L'Aquila, Italy
vittorio.cortellessa@univaq.it

Abstract. The problem of capturing performance problems is critical in the software design, mostly because the results of performance analysis (i.e. mean values, variances, and probability distributions) are difficult to be interpreted for providing feedback to software designers. Support to the interpretation of performance analysis results that helps to fill the gap between numbers and design alternatives is still lacking. The aim of this talk is to present the work that has been done in the last few years on filling such gap. The work is centered on software performance antipatterns, that are recurring solutions to common mistakes (i.e. bad practices) affecting performance. Such antipatterns can play a key role in the software performance domain, since they can be used in the investigation of performance problems as well as in the formulation of solutions in terms of design alternatives[1].

Keywords: Software Model, Performance Evaluation, Antipatterns, Feedback Generation, Design Alternatives.

1 The Context

The problem of interpreting the performance analysis results is still quite critical. A large gap exists between the representation of performance analysis results and the feedback expected by software architects. Additionally, the former usually contains numbers (e.g. mean response time, throughput variance, etc.), whereas the latter should embed architectural suggestions, i.e. design alternatives, useful to overcome performance problems (e.g. split a software component in two components and re-deploy one of them). Such activities are today exclusively based on the analysts' experience, and therefore their effectiveness often suffers of lack of automation.

Figure 1 schematically represents the typical steps that are executed to conduct a model-based performance analysis process. Rounded boxes in the figure represent operational steps whereas square boxes represent input/output data. Vertical lines divide the process in three different phases: in the *modeling* phase, an annotated software model is built; in the *performance analysis* phase, a performance model is obtained through model transformation, and such model is

---

[1] Most of the contents of this paper come from [1].

M.S. Balsamo, W.J. Knottenbelt, and A. Marin (Eds.): EPEW 2013, LNCS 8168, pp. 1–6, 2013.
© Springer-Verlag Berlin Heidelberg 2013

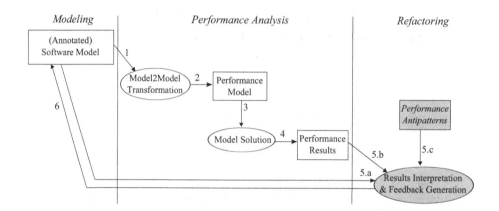

Fig. 1. Model-based software performance analysis process

solved to obtain the performance results of interest; in the *refactoring* phase, the performance results are interpreted and, if necessary, feedback is generated as refactoring actions on the original software model.

The modeling and performance analysis phases (i.e. arrows numbered from 1 through 4) represent the forward path from a software model all the way through the production of performance indices of interest. As outlined above, while in this path well-founded model-driven approaches have been introduced for inducing automation in all steps [2], there is a clear lack of automation in the backward path that shall bring the analysis results back to the software architecture.

The core step of the backward path is the shaded rounded box of Figure 1. Here, the performance analysis results have to be interpreted in order to detect, if any, performance problems. Once performance problems have been detected (with a certain accuracy) somewhere in the model, solutions have to be applied to remove those problems.

In Figure 1 the (annotated) software architectural model (label 5.a) and the performance results (label 5.b) are both inputs to the core step that searches problems in the model. The third input of this step represents the most promising elements that can drive this search, i.e. *performance antipatterns* (label 5.c). The main reference for performance antipatterns is the work done across the years by Smith and Williams [3] that have ultimately defined fourteen notation-independent antipatterns.

Figure 2 details the refactoring phase of Figure 1. In Figure 2, the core step of the backward path is split in two steps: (i) *detecting antipatterns* that provides the localization of the critical parts of software models, thus performing the results interpretation step; (ii) *solving antipatterns* that suggests the changes to be applied to the model under analysis, thus executing the feedback generation step.

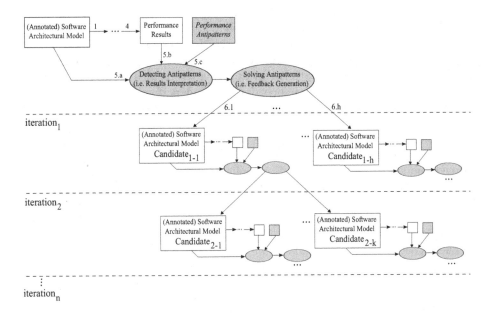

Fig. 2. Details of the refactoring phase across different iterations

Several *iteration*s can be conducted to find the software model that best fits the performance requirements, since several antipatterns may be detected in a model, and several refactoring actions may be available for solving each antipattern. At each iteration, the refactoring actions (labels 6.1 ... 6.h of Figure 2) aim at building a new software model (namely *Candidate*) that replaces the analyzed one. For example, $Candidate_{i-j}$ denotes the j-th candidate generated at the i-th iteration. Then, the detection and solution approach can be iteratively applied to all newly generated candidates to further improve the system, if necessary.

2   State-of-Art

A consistent amount of work has been done in the last few years around the management of performance antipatterns. For sake of space, the two most relevant examples are mentioned here below.

Williams et al. in [4] introduced the PASA (Performance Assessment of Software Architectures) approach. It aims at achieving good performance results through a deep understanding of the architectural features. This is the approach that firstly introduced the concept of antipatterns as support to the identification of performance problems in software architectural models as well as in the formulation of architectural alternatives. However, this approach is based on the interactions between software architects and performance experts, therefore its level of automation is still low.

Enterprise technologies and EJB performance antipatterns are analyzed by Parsons et al. in [5]: antipatterns are represented as sets of rules loaded into an engine. A rule-based performance diagnosis tool, named Performance Antipattern Detection (PAD), is presented. However, it deals with Component-Based Enterprise Systems, targeting only Enterprise Java Bean (EJB) applications. From the monitored data of running systems, it extracts the run-time system design and detects EJB antipatterns by applying the defined rules to it. Hence, the scope of [5] is restricted to such domain, and performance problems can neither be detected in other technology contexts nor in the early development stages.

Our research group has spent a quite large effort in the last few years around the problems of representing, detecting and solving performance antipatterns through model-driven techniques. Here below a summary of our main results.

The activity of *representing antipatterns* has been addressed in [6]: a structured description of the system elements that occur in the definition of antipatterns has been provided, and performance antipatterns have been modeled as logical predicates.

The activities of *detecting* and *solving antipatterns* have been implemented by defining the antipattern rules and actions with three modeling languages: (i) the UML and MARTE profile notation in [7], (ii) the PCM notation in [8], and the Aemilia notation in [9]. In [7] performance antipatterns have been automatically detected in UML models using OCL [10] queries, but their solution was not yet automated. In [8] a limited set of antipatterns has been automatically detected and solved in PCM models through a benchmark tool. In [9] the application of performance antipatterns to an ADL has been shown. These experiences led to investigate the expressiveness of modeling languages and to classify antipatterns in three categories: (i) detectable and solvable; (ii) semi-solvable (i.e. the antipattern solution is only achieved with refactoring actions to be manually performed); (iii) neither detectable nor solvable.

Instead of blindly moving among the antipattern solutions without eventually achieving the desired results, a technique to rank the antipatterns on the basis of their guilt for violated requirements has been defined in [11] [12].

A Performance Antipattern Modeling Language (PAML), i.e. a metamodel specifically tailored to describe antipatterns, has been introduced in [13,14], where it has been discussed how advanced model-driven techniques can be used to build an unifying notation-independent approach that addresses the problem of embedding antipatterns management across different modeling notations.

3   Future Perspectives

The work performed around antipatterns in the last few years brings evidence to the support they can provide to the identification and solution of performance problems. This research direction, however, still contains open issues that shall be addressed in the near future, as illustrated in what follows.

Accuracy of antipattern specification. The detection process may introduce false positive/negative instances of antipatterns, mostly due to the presence of thresholds in the antipattern specification. Potential sources to suitably tune the values of thresholds are: (i) the system requirements; (ii) the domain expert's knowledge; (iii) the evaluation of the system under analysis. However, threshold values inevitably introduce a degree of uncertainty and extensive experimentation must be done in this direction.

No Strict Guarantee of Performance Improvements. The solution of one or more antipatterns does not guarantee performance improvements in advance, because the entire process is based on heuristic evaluations. Applying a refactoring action results in a new software model, i.e. a candidate whose performance analysis will reveal if the action has been actually beneficial for the system under study.

Dependencies of Performance Requirements. The application of antipattern solutions leads the system to (probably) satisfy the performance requirements covered by such solutions. However, it may happen that a certain number of other requirements get worse. Hence, the new candidate model must take into account at each stage of the process all the requirements, also the previously satisfied ones.

Conflicts between Antipattern Solutions. The solution of a certain number of antipatterns cannot be unambiguously applied in case of incoherencies among their solutions. Even in cases of no explicit conflicts between antipattern solutions, coherency problems can be raised from the order of application of solutions. Criteria must be introduced to drive the application order of solutions in these cases.

Lack of Model Parameters. The application of antipattern-based approaches is not limited (in principle) along the software lifecycle, but it is obvious that an early usage is subject to lack of information because the system knowledge improves while the development process progresses. Both the software and the performance models may lack of parameters needed to apply this type of approach.

Influence of Other Software Layers. Oftenly a performance model comes from a (annotated) model that only contains information on the software application and the hardware platform. However, between these two layers there are other components, such as middleware and operating system, that should be considered because they can contain performance antipatterns.

Limitations from Requirements. The application of antipattern solutions can be restricted by functional or non-functional requirements. Example of functional requirements may be legacy components that cannot be split and redeployed whereas the antipattern solution requires of these actions. Example of non-functional requirements may be budget limitations that do not allow to adopt an antipattern solution due to its extremely high cost.

Ambiguity in Formalization. Finally, note that the formalization of antipatterns reflects our interpretation of the informal literature. Different formalizations of antipatterns can be originated by relying on different interpretations. This unavoidable gap is an open issue in this domain, and certainly requires a wider investigation to consolidate the formal definition of antipatterns.

Acknowledgments. This work has been supported by the European Office of Aerospace Research and Development, Grant/Cooperative Agreement Award no. FA8655-11-1-3055, on "Consistent evolution of software artifacts and non-functional models".

References

1. Cortellessa, V., Di Marco, A., Trubiani, C.: Software performance antipatterns: Modeling and analysis. In: Bernardo, M., Cortellessa, V., Pierantonio, A. (eds.) SFM 2012. LNCS, vol. 7320, pp. 290–335. Springer, Heidelberg (2012)
2. Balsamo, S., Di Marco, A., Inverardi, P., Simeoni, M.: Model-Based Performance Prediction in Software Development: A Survey. IEEE Trans. Software Eng. 30(5), 295–310 (2004)
3. Smith, C.U., Williams, L.G.: More New Software Antipatterns: Even More Ways to Shoot Yourself in the Foot. In: International Computer Measurement Group Conference, pp. 717–725 (2003)
4. Williams, L.G., Smith, C.U.: PASA(SM): An Architectural Approach to Fixing Software Performance Problems. In: International Computer Measurement Group Conference, Computer Measurement Group, pp. 307–320 (2002)
5. Parsons, T., Murphy, J.: Detecting Performance Antipatterns in Component Based Enterprise Systems. Journal of Object Technology 7, 55–91 (2008)
6. Cortellessa, V., Di Marco, A., Trubiani, C.: Performance Antipatterns as Logical Predicates. In: Calinescu, R., Paige, R.F., Kwiatkowska, M.Z. (eds.) ICECCS, pp. 146–156. IEEE Computer Society (2010)
7. Cortellessa, V., Di Marco, A., Eramo, R., Pierantonio, A., Trubiani, C.: Digging into UML models to remove performance antipatterns. In: ICSE Workshop Quovadis, pp. 9–16 (2010)
8. Trubiani, C., Koziolek, A.: Detection and solution of software performance antipatterns in palladio architectural models. In: International Conference on Performance Engineering (ICPE), pp. 19–30 (2011)
9. Cortellessa, V., de Sanctis, M., Marco, A.D., Trubiani, C.: Enabling performance antipatterns to arise from an adl-based software architecture. In: WICSA/ECSA, pp. 310–314 (2012)
10. Object Management Group (OMG): OCL 2.0 Specification, OMG Document formal/May 01, 2006 (2006)
11. Cortellessa, V., Martens, A., Reussner, R., Trubiani, C.: Towards the identification of "Guilty" performance antipatterns. In: WOSP/SIPEW International Conference on Performance Engineering, pp. 245–246 (2010)
12. Cortellessa, V., Martens, A., Reussner, R., Trubiani, C.: A Process to Effectively Identify "Guilty" Performance Antipatterns. In: Rosenblum, D.S., Taentzer, G. (eds.) FASE 2010. LNCS, vol. 6013, pp. 368–382. Springer, Heidelberg (2010)
13. Cortellessa, V., Di Marco, A., Eramo, R., Pierantonio, A., Trubiani, C.: Approaching the Model-Driven Generation of Feedback to Remove Software Performance Flaws. In: EUROMICRO-SEAA, pp. 162–169. IEEE Computer Society Press (2009)
14. Trubiani, C.: A model-based framework for software performance feedback. In: Dingel, J., Solberg, A. (eds.) MODELS 2010. LNCS, vol. 6627, pp. 19–34. Springer, Heidelberg (2011)

Online Game Performance Engineering

Claudio E. Palazzi

Department of Mathematics, University of Padova,
via Trieste 63, 35131 Padova, Italy
cpalazzi@math.unipd.it

Abstract. Interactive, massive online games are widely popular applications requiring specific solutions to ensure interactivity, consistency, network fairness, and scalability. The wireless revolution has further complicated this scenario by adding mobile players competing for network resources with other users. It is hence crucial to provide holistic solutions that enable a top quality online gaming experience regardless whether the player is wired, wireless, or even mobile. To this aim, we analyze how a high level of performance can be ensured through specific engineering of the game architecture, synchronization scheme, and game gateway.

Keywords: Interactivity, Online Games, Mobility, Performance.

1 Introduction

Internet-based entertainment applications such as online games play a major role in our everyday life with a persistent and accelerating growth that has now reached tens of millions of subscribers around the world. From a research point of view, they represent a very interesting and challenging topic especially when considering highly interactive mobile games, played in wireless environments, and involving a multitude of players simultaneously sharing the same virtual arena. In this context, main requirements involve interactivity, consistency, network fairness, and scalability; unfortunately, they are generally considered to be not compatible with each other, thus forcing online game providers to privilege just one or few of them when designing their game architecture. Instead, we show how a performance engineering approach may be adopted to design an online game architecture composed by holistic solutions able to simultaneously satisfy all classic requirements and even to leverage on the satisfaction of some of them to achieve the others as well.

In order to ensure optimal performance to players we need to split the problem into sub-parts which requires specific solutions applied by different subjects. In the following, with the help of Fig. 1, we explain the general division into sub-parts and the corresponding suggested approaches.

The first sub-part regards the core of the network topology, which represents the portion of the total connection path that can be handled by the online game service provider. In particular, the approach is based on the adoption of a hybrid architecture including solutions to support the communication and synchronization among game servers. Instead, the second sub-part regards the edge of the

M.S. Balsamo, W.J. Knottenbelt, and A. Marin (Eds.): EPEW 2013, LNCS 8168, pp. 7–12, 2013.

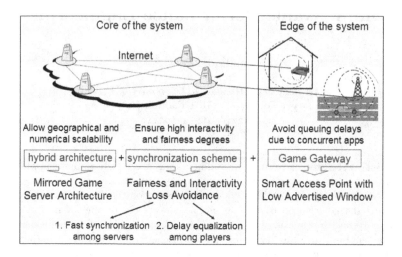

Fig. 1. Considered architecture for online game

network topology and is concerned with the links between game servers and their engaged players, thus including the last-mile wireless hop, which generally corresponds to the bottleneck of the connection and may be source of large queuing delays. To obtain a holistic solution, a viable approach is to proceed through successive steps and address the two sub-problems independently. Although the solutions discussed in this paper generate the best performance results when combined, they produce benefits even if singularly applied. In particular, for the first sub-part we propose to exploit a hybrid architecture combining both the advantages of client-server and peer-to-peer paradigms. This solution deploys over the network a constellation of Game State Servers (GSSs) that have to maintains a vision of the game state synchronized with each other [1]. Clearly, this requires an efficient event synchronization scheme among GSSs in order to guarantee a consistent and responsive evolution of the game state. To this aim, the semantics of the game can be put to good use in order to increase the interactivity degree provided to the player: discarding game events that are superseded by others can free network resources thus speeding up the delivery of fresh game events [2].

However, even if this scheme is proficient in maintaining a high degree of responsiveness among game servers, still problems may arise at the edges of the considered topology, where users in their homes or vehicles may be engaged in an online game through a Game Gateway which separates the wireless network from the rest of the Internet.

This represents the aforementioned second part of our problem. Concurrent traffic may generate queues that build up at the last (or first) link of the connection, thus delaying the game event delivery. This problem is worsened in case of players relying on wireless connectivity, as the wireless medium is generally shared by contemporary users who interfere with each other. In addition to the problem discussed above, TCP-based elastic flows (e.g., file download) can harm the performance of UDP-based real-time flows (e.g., online game) as TCP continuously probes the channel for more bandwidth, thus eventually generating queues, and hence delays, on the connection [3].

To address this issue, a Game Gateway between the wireless (home or vehicular) network and the game servers in Internet can take advantage of its knowledge about available wireless network resources and the on-going traffic in order to appropriately limit TCP's advertised windows so as to smoothen the network traffic progression and avoid queuing delays that would jeopardize the interactivity of online game applications and, in general, of any real-time application.

2 Main Requirements

Under a networking point of view, online games are characterized by main requirements which are intrinsically correlated: interactivity, consistency, fairness, and scalability. In particular, interactivity has a great impact even on the other requirements.

Interactivity (or responsiveness) refers to the delay between the generation of a game event in a node (i.e., a players' client or a game server) and the time at which other nodes receive that event. To ensure a pleasant experience to the player, the time elapsed from the game event generation at a certain node and its processing time at every other node participating in the same game session must remain under a certain interactivity threshold [4]. Unfortunately, variable congestion conditions in Internet may suddenly slow down the game fluency on the screen. Moreover, players in the same virtual arena could be so numerous that some game server may experience impulsive computational load and loose interactivity. These problems are obviously amplified when plunged into a wireless, mobile scenario.

Consistency regards having a simultaneous and homogeneous evolution of the game state at any nodes belonging to the system. Clearly, the easiest way to guarantee absolute consistency would be that of making the game proceed through discrete locksteps. Having a single move allowed for each player and synchronizing all the agents before moving toward the next round, for sure grants absolute consistency but, on the other hand, impairs the system interactivity. A trade-off between these two attributes needs thus to be found in order to develop a proficient game platform.

Fairness, or (network fairness), ensures that any player has the same chances of victory in the match, regardless of different network conditions. In this context, relative delays have to be considered as important as absolute ones. Simultaneous game evolution with identical speed should be guaranteed as much as possible to all participants. Furthermore, it has recently been demonstrated how increasing the interactivity degree of the game platform may lead also to improved fairness [5].

Scalability is related to the capability of the system in providing efficient support to a large community of players. Indeed, humans are social beings that enjoy the presence of others and the competition against real adversaries. Besides, it is primary interest of game companies to have huge revenues generated by a very high number of customers. Yet, especially in the case of fast-paced games, when the interactivity threshold cannot be met, scalability is sometimes sacrificed by denying the access to some users depending on their experienced delays. Therefore, by sustaining interactivity, one can also provide a higher scalability degree in terms of both the number and the geographic dispersion of players allowed to participate to the same virtual arena.

3   Smart Architecture: A Holistic Solution

In this section we describe in detail the main components of the proposed holistic solution as anticipated in Fig. 1. For the sake of clarity, we name this holistic solution *Smart Architecture*.

3.1   Fast Synchronization over a Hybrid Architecture

A mirrored game server architectures represents a hybrid solution efficiently embracing the positive aspects of both centralized client-server and fully distributed architectures [1]. Based on this approach, GSSs are interconnected in a peer-to-peer fashion over the Internet and contain replicas of the same game state view. Players communicate with their closest GSS through in a client-server fashion. Each GSS gathers all game events of its engaged players, updates the game state, and periodically forwards it to all its players and GSS peers.

The presence of multiple high performance GSSs helps in distributing the traffic over the system and reduces the processing burden at each node [6]. Moreover, having each player connected to a close GSS reduces the impact of the player-dependent access technology (e.g., dial-up, cable, DSL) on the total experienced delay. In this case, in fact, the communication among players results mainly deployed over links physically connecting GSSs, which can exploit the fastest available technology (e.g., optical fibers) to reduce latency. As a result, this architecture helps one in finding better solutions for the various tradeoff among interactivity, consistency, fairness, scalability, and continuity.

Even if synchronization is still required to ensure the global consistency of the game state held by the various servers, this requirement is made easier with respect to fully distributed architectures thanks to the lower number of involved nodes. Moreover smart solution can be devised to speed up this synchronization process. Indeed, taking inspiration from the Active Queue Management approach (e.g., RED, RIO [7]) in case of incipient congestion in best effort networks, the synchronization mechanism among GSSs could exploit the semantics of the game to discard few game packets to preempt interactivity loss when intense network traffic or excessive computational load is slowing down some GSS.

Indeed, during a game session some events can lose their significance as time passes, i.e., new actions may make the previous ones irrelevant. For example, where there is a rapid succession of movements performed by a single agent in a virtual world, the event representing the last destination supersedes the previous ones.

Discarding superseded events for processing fresher ones may be of great help for delay-affected GSSs, achieving high interactivity degree without compromising consistency.

For the sake of clarity, in the rest of the paper we refer to this synchronization mechanism able to discard game events as *Fast Synchronization* (FS).

To ensure an adequate playability degree even to fast and furious class of games a further dropping probability function is provided in order to discard even non-superseded game events when dropping all the superseded ones is not yet sufficient to maintain an adequate level of responsiveness. The two discarding functions are featured with specific parameters; they work independently one from the other and take action in sequence with the increasing of the game event GTDs at the GSSs. Dropping non-superseded events can be done without consistency-related consequences only for a category of games where little inconsistencies are not highly deleterious for players' fun (e.g., fast-paced games).

3.2 Game Gateway

Even when FS results proficient in maintaining a high degree of responsiveness among game servers (i.e., GSSs), problems may still arise at the edges of the considered topology, where users in their homes or along a street may be engaged in an online game through a Game Gateway. Concurrent traffic may generate queues that build up at the Game Gateway (or at the associated Access Point), thus delaying the game event delivery and wasting all the interactivity patrimony created by FS. The applications run in this context may vary and some of them may be particularly harmful toward real-time flows generated by online games. In particular, TCP-based FTP application for downloading files increases queuing delays to such an extent that interactivity may be completely jeopardized [3].

To this aim, we modify our Game Gateway to achieve best performance tradeoff for both elastic and real-time applications. To do so, the trick is to appropriately limit the advertised window for TCP flows so as to let them reach their expected bandwidth, but not more than that so as to not generate queues. This way, a solution to the tradeoff relationship existing between TCP throughput and real-time application delays can be found.

Needless to say, a technique that exploited existing features of standard protocols could be easily implemented in a real scenario. Moreover, an optimal tradeoff between throughput and low delays could be achieved by maintaining the sending rate (hence, the sending window) of TCP flows high enough to efficiently utilize all available bandwidth but, at the same time, limited in its growth so as to not utilize buffers. As a result, the throughput would be maximized by the absence of packet loss, while the delay would be minimized by the absence of queuing. This can be achieved through limiting the aggregate bandwidth utilized by TCP flows just below the total capacity of the bottleneck link diminished by the portion of the channel occupied by the simultaneous UDP-based real-time traffic.

This upper bound can be enforced to all TCP flows sharing the same wireless link by having the corresponding AP exploiting to this aim the TCP's advertised window. Simply, the actual sending window of a TCP flow is determined as the minimum between the congestion window and the advertised window; thereby, having the AP appropriately modifying the advertised window of passing-through TCP flows would limiting the factual sending rate of TCP flows.

4   Conclusion

Interactive, massive online games are very popular applications. Yet they also embody tough technical challenges related to interactivity, consistency, network fairness, and scalability, which require specific solutions. We have discussed the design of a holistic approach, including a hybrid game architecture, a synchronization scheme and a game gateway, able to satisfy these requirements, and ensure a top quality online gaming performance regardless whether the players are wired, wireless, or even mobile.

Acknowledgments. This work is partially supported by the MIUR/PRIN ALTERNET and the UNIPD/PRAT Web Squared projects.

References

1. Cronin, E., Kurc, A.R., Filstrup, B., Jamin, S.: An Efficient Synchronization Mechanism for Mirrored Game Architectures. Multimedia Tools and Applications 23, 7–30 (2004)
2. Palazzi, C.E., Ferretti, S., Cacciaguerra, S., Roccetti, M.: Interactivity-Loss Avoidance in Event Delivery Synchronization for Mirrored Game Architectures. IEEE Transactions on Multimedia 8, 847–879 (2006)
3. Palazzi, C.E., Ferretti, S., Roccetti, M., Pau, G., Gerla, M.: What's in that Magic Box? The Home Entertainment Center's Special Protocol Potion, Revealed. IEEE Transactions on Consumer Electronics 52, 1280–1288 (2006)
4. Pantel, L., Wolf, L.C.: On the Impact of Delay on Real-Time Multiplayer Games. In: 12th International Workshop on Network and Operating Systems Support for Digital Audio and Video, Miami, FL, USA (2002)
5. Palazzi, C.E., Ferretti, S., Cacciaguerra, S., Roccetti, M.: A RIO-like Technique for Interactivity Loss Avoidance in Fast-Paced Multiplayer Online Games. ACM Computers in Entertainment 3 (2005)
6. Safaei, F., Boustead, P., Nguyen, C.D., Brun, J., Dowlatshahi, M.: Latency Driven Distribution: Infrastructure Needs of Participatory Entertainment Applications. IEEE Communications Magazine 43, 106–112 (2005)
7. Clark, D.D., Fang, W.: Explicit Allocation of Best-Effort Packet Delivery Service. IEEE/ACM Transactions on Networking 6, 362–373 (1998)

Stochastic Bounds and Histograms
for Network Performance Analysis

Farah Aït-Salaht[1], Hind Castel-Taleb[2], Jean-Michel Fourneau[1],
and Nihal Pekergin[3]

[1] PRiSM, Univ. Versailles St Quentin, UMR CNRS 8144, Versailles France
{safa,jmf}@prism.uvsq.fr
[2] SAMOVAR, UMR 5157, Télécom Sud Paris, Evry, France
hind.Castel@it-sudparis.eu
[3] LACL, Univ. Paris Est-Créteil, France
nihal.pekergin@u-pec.fr

Abstract. Exact analysis of queueing networks under real traffic histograms becomes quickly intractable due to the state explosion. In this paper, we propose to apply the stochastic comparison method to derive performance measure bounds under histogram-based traffics. We apply an algorithm based on dynamic programming to derive bounding traffic histograms on reduced state spaces. We indeed obtain easier bounding stochastic processes providing stochastic upper and lower bounds on buffer occupancy histograms (queue length distributions) for finite queue models. We evaluate the proposed method under real traffic traces, and we compare the results with those obtained by an approximative method. Numerical results illustrate that the proposed method provides more accurate results with a tradeoff between computation time and accuracy. Moreover, the derived performance bounds are very relevant in network dimensioning.

Keywords: Network QoS, Histogram-based traffic models, Stochastic Comparison.

1 Introduction

Queueing-based models are very efficient modeling and evaluation tools for a variety of practical situations in telecommunication and computer network systems. The stochastic behavior prediction of queues gives a theoretical insight into the dynamics of these shared resources and how they can be designed to provide better utilization. The probability theory in queueing analysis plays a central role as it provides mathematical equations for performance measure computations such as queue length, response time, and server utilization. Most of the queueing theory is based on exponential assumption. However, this assumption can be applied only for certain applications as in telephone networks. In the Internet, several traffic traces are available, and are used to be approximated by a theoretical probability distribution (for example, the phase distribution).

M.S. Balsamo, W.J. Knottenbelt, and A. Marin (Eds.): EPEW 2013, LNCS 8168, pp. 13–27, 2013.
© Springer-Verlag Berlin Heidelberg 2013

Unfortunately, some problems arise: the accuracy of the model compared to the traffic, and the difficulty to exploit the model when the number of parameters is high. So most of the time, we must limit the number of parameters in the detriment of precision. Moreover, the exact analysis of the queueing network with the real traffic traces is in general impossible, as their sizes are too large to be used directly.

There has been a several amount of works on the Histogram-based approach for performance models. In the area of network calculus, the histogram model was introduced by Skelly et al [11] to model the video sources, to predict buffer occupancy distributions and cell loss rates for multiplexed streams. It was also applied by Kweon and Shin [8] to propose an implementation of statistical real-time communication in ATM networks using a modified version of the Traffic Controlled Rate-Monotonic Priority Scheduling (TCRM). These works used an analysis method based on a M/D/1/N queueing system. More recently, Hernández and al.[5–7] have proposed a new performance analysis to obtain buffer occupancy histograms. This new stochastic process called HBSP (Histogram Based Stochastic Process) works directly with histograms using a set of specific operators. The model is based on a basic histogram model (HD) as an input traffic which is supplied through finite capacity buffers with deterministic (D) service time distribution under First Come First Served (FCFS) policy. Considering a single node, the analysis method solves the HD/D/1/K queueing system, by reducing the state space of traffic trace into n subintervals (classes or bins) in order to avoid working with huge state spaces.

Another approach based on reducing the initial histogram in n subintervals has been presented by Tancrez and al.[14] in a slightly different context. The problem consists in building an upper (lower) bounding discrete distribution of a continuous distribution which models the service duration in a production line. They divide the support into n equal subintervals. Each of these subintervals of the continuous distribution is associated with one single point of the discrete one. This point is the upper limit (lower limit) of the interval and the probability mass of the sub-interval is associated to that point. As the production lines considered can be modeled by a decision free stochastic Petri-net, it is known since the seminal work of Baccelli et al. [3] that bounding the distribution of service times in the queues provides a bound on the end to end delay.

In this paper, we apply the stochastic bounding method for network performance analysis under histogram-based traffic. The goal is to generate bounding histograms with smaller sizes in order to make possible the analysis of the queueing network. We use the strong stochastic ordering (denoted $\leq_{st}$) [9]. We propose to use algorithmic techniques developed in [2] to obtain optimal lower and upper stochastic bounds of the buffer occupancy histogram. These algorithms allow to control the size of the model and compute the most accurate bound with respect to a given reward function. The bounding histograms are then used in the state evolution equations to derive bounds for performance measures both for a single queue and a tandem queueing network. To show the relevance of our work, we analyze systems with real traffic traces. We compare our bounds with the results under exact traffic traces and those obtained from the HBSP approximation method. The proposed method provides the most accurate results for blocking probability and mean buffer occupancy. Another important point is that HBSP only provides approximative results which are neither conservative nor optimistic. Our bounding approach gives, at the same time, upper and lower performance measures which could be used to check QoS constraints for network dimensioning.

This paper is organized as follows: in Section 2, we first describe the histogram traffic models, and the state evolution equations of the queuing model under study. Then, we explain the Histogram Buffer Stochastic Process (HBSP) method proposed by Hernandez and al. In Section 3, we introduce our approach based on the stochastic bounds to derive performance measure bounds. Finally in Section 4, we give numerical results based on real traffic measurements in order to study the accuracy of the bounds, compared to the exact results and those obtained by HBSP algorithm. These results are obtained for a single node analysis and also for a tandem queueing network.

2   Queueing Model Description

2.1   Histogram Traffic Model

Here a histogram describe a discrete distribution and its graphical representation. Figure 1 shows a plot of MAWI traffic trace [12] corresponding to a 1-hour trace of IP traffic of a 150 Mb/s transpacific line (samplepoint-F) for the 9th of January 2007 between 12:00 and 13:00. This traffic trace has an average rate of 109 Mb/s. Using a sampling period of T = 40 ms (25 samples per second), the resulting traffic trace has 90,000 frames (periods) and an average rate of $4.37\,Mb$ per frame, the corresponding histogram is given in Figure 2.

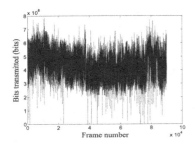

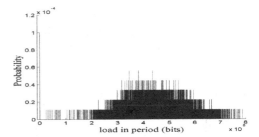

Fig. 1. MAWI traffic trace   **Fig. 2.** MAWI arrival load histogram

The arrival workload is characterized with the number of transmission units produced by the corresponding traffic source during a pre-established time period $T = 40\,ms$. Let $A(k)$ be a discrete random variable representing the amount of traffic entering to the system during the kth sampling interval (slot). We assume that the traffic is stationary and independently and identically distributed (iid). So, all random variables $A(k)$ follow the same distribution $\mathcal{A}$ characterized by a couple $(\mathbf{A}, p(\mathbf{A}))$, where $\mathbf{A}$ is the support and $p(\mathbf{A})$ is the corresponding probabilities.

2.2   State Evolution Equations

We denote by $Q(k)$ and $D(k)$ respectively random variables corresponding to buffer length and the output traffic (departure) during the kth slot (Figure 3).

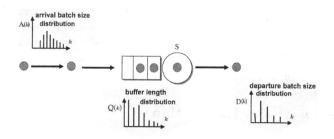

Fig. 3. Input and output parameters of a queueing model

Let B be the buffer size and S be the transmission (service) rate. We assume that the following sequence of events during a slot: acceptation of arrivals and then service. The queue or buffer length $Q(k)$ can be expressed with the following recursive formula:

$$Q(k) = \min(B, (Q(k-1) + A(k) - S)^{+}), \quad k \in \mathbb{N}. \tag{1}$$

where operator $(X)^{+} = \max(X, 0)$. As we assume a Tail Drop policy, the departure distribution is defined as follows:

$$D(k) = \min(S, Q(k-1)) + A(k)), \quad k \in \mathbb{N}. \tag{2}$$

The transmission channel utilization is defined as $\rho = \frac{E[A]}{S}$, where $E[A]$ is the average traffic. Equation 1 defines a Markov chain in discrete time (DTMC) if the arrivals $(A(k))$ are stationary and iid. As this chain is finite, it suffices to verify that the arrival process makes the chain irreducible and aperiodic thus ergodic. We give below some sufficient conditions to ensure both properties.

Proposition 1. *If the following conditions are satisfied, then the DTMC is ergodic:*

1. *there exists $i < S$ in the support of A such that $p(i) > 0$,*
2. *there exists $j > S$ in the support of A such that $p(j) > 0$,*
3. *$j = S + 1$ or $i = S - 1$.*

Proof. The first property implies that starting from state 0 we go back with a probability greater than or equal to $p(i)$. Indeed, if it arrives i customers, the buffer length before the services is i, as $i < S$, we return to state 0 after the end of service. So state 0 is aperiodic. In addition, the first property implies that the buffer length can be reduced to 0 by a sequence of transitions from one arrival of a batch of size $i < S$. So 0 is reachable from any states of the chain. Condition 2 implies that we can reach state B from state 0. Finally, the last condition implies that we can reach all states from 0 or B by jumps with amplitude 1 that are possible under assumptions 1 and 2.

We suppose in the following that the Markov chain is ergodic.

Let X (resp. Y) be a discrete random variable taking values in a set $\mathcal{G}_X$ (resp. $\mathcal{G}_Y$) of size $l_X > 1$ (resp. $l_Y > 1$).

Proposition 2. *The computation of the convolution of the distributions of two independent random variables generates a distribution with at most $l_X \times l_Y$ states. This computation requires $O(l_X \times l_Y)$ operation (+) using a naive approach and $O((l_X + l_Y)log(l_X + l_Y))$ for a Fast Fourier Transform (FFT) [10].*

The computation complexity depends on the size of the distributions and thus on the number of classes considered.

2.3 Histogram Reduction: HBSP Method

The Histogram Buffer Stochastic Process (HBSP) model is proposed by Hernández and al. [5–7]. Since working with a huge distribution can be cumbersome, the method suggests to reduce this size using n classes or bins. Consequently, if we have a range of $I = [0, N_{max}]$, then the interval size will be $l_A = N_{max}/n$. Using these intervals we define a binned process $\{A(t)\}$ that has a reduced state space $I' = \{0, \dots (n-1)\}$. A value a of I is mapped to i in I' such that $i = \lfloor \frac{a}{l_A} \rfloor$, which is also denoted by $i = class_A(a)$. Inversely, a value $i \in I'$ corresponds to the midpoint of interval i: $a = l_A \cdot i + l_A/2, a \in I$.

The traffic is assumed to be stationary, $\mathcal{A} = A(t), \forall t$, thus the time dependence of $A(t)$ is suppressed and replaced by a discrete random variable $\mathcal{A}$ which is defined by a couple of attributes $(\mathbf{A}, p(\mathbf{A}))$. Each attribute is a vector of size n, first vector is interval midpoints while the second gives the corresponding probabilities.

$$\mathcal{A} = (\mathbf{A}, p(\mathbf{A})) \quad \begin{cases} \mathbf{A} = \{a_i : i = 0 \dots n-1\}, \\ p(\mathbf{A}) = [p_\mathbf{A}(i) : i = 0 \dots n-1]. \end{cases}$$

The stochastic process of the evolution of HBSP model is based on the following recurrence relation:

$$Q(k) = \Phi_{\hat{S}}^{\hat{b}}(Q(k-1) \otimes \mathcal{A}). \tag{3}$$

where, $\hat{S} = class_\mathbf{A}(S)$ (resp. $\hat{b} = class_A(B)$), $\otimes$ is the convolution operator of distributions. $Q(k)$ denotes here the corresponding distribution and operator Φ limits buffer lengths so that they can not become negative and cannot overflow the corresponding class of buffer length. This operator is defined as follows:

$$\Phi_a^b(x) = \begin{cases} 0 \text{ , for } x < a, \\ x \text{ , for } a \leq x \leq b + a, \\ b \text{ , for } x \geq b + a. \end{cases} \tag{4}$$

Example 1. For the MAWI traffic trace with $n = 10$, the HBSP traffic is defined by $\mathcal{A} = (\mathbf{A}, p(\mathbf{A}))$ with $\mathbf{A} = \{0.3933, 1.1799, 1.9666, 2.7532, 3.5398, 4.3265, 5.1131, 5.8997, 6.6864, 7.4730\}$ Mb and $p(\mathbf{A}) = [0.0003, 0.0002, 0.0021, 0.0641, 0.2663, 0.3228, 0.2345, 0.0980, 0.0110, 0.0005]$ (Figure 4).

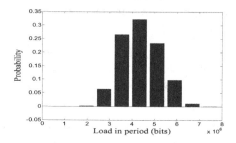

Fig. 4. Arrival workload histogram of MAWI traffic using 10 classes

3 Bounding Approach

We first present briefly the stochastic comparison method and we then present the proposed bounding algorithm for the reduction of the number of classes for a histogram. The application of this bounding approach for the network performance analysis will be given in the next section.

3.1 Stochastic Comparison

We refer to Stoyan's book ([9]) for theoretical issues of the stochastic comparison method. We consider state space $\mathcal{G} = \{1, 2, \ldots, n\}$ endowed with a total order denoted as $\leq$. Let X and Y be two discrete random variables taking values on $\mathcal{G}$, with cumulative probability distributions F_X and F_Y, and probability mass functions $\mathbf{d2}$ and $\mathbf{d1}$ ($\mathbf{d2}(i) = Prob(X = i)$, and $\mathbf{d1}(i) = Prob(Y = i)$, for $i = 1, 2, \ldots, n$). We give different manners to define the strong stochastic ordering $\leq_{st}$ for this case:

Definition 1.   – **generic definition:** $X \leq_{st} Y \Longleftrightarrow \mathbb{E}f(X) \leq \mathbb{E}f(Y)$,
   for all non decreasing functions $f : \mathcal{G} \to \mathbb{R}^+$ whenever expectations exist.
 – **cumulative probability distributions:**

$$X \leq_{st} Y \Leftrightarrow F_X(a) \geq F_Y(a), \ \forall a \in \mathcal{G}.$$

– **probability mass functions**

$$X \leq_{st} Y \Leftrightarrow \forall i, 1 \leq i \leq n, \ \sum_{k=i}^{n} d2(k) \leq \sum_{k=i}^{n} d1(k) \tag{5}$$

Notice that we use interchangeably $X \leq_{st} Y$ and d2 $\leq_{st}$ d1.

Example 2. We consider $\mathcal{G} = \{1, 2, \ldots, 7\}$, and two discrete random variables with $d2 = [0.1, 0.2, 0.1, 0.2, 0.05, 0.1, 0.25]$, and $d1 = [0, 0.25, 0.05, 0.1, 0.15, 0.15, 0.3]$. We can easily verify that $d2 \leq_{st} d1$: the probability mass of $d1$ is concentrated to higher states such as the probability cumulative distribution of $d1$ is always below the cumulative distribution of $d2$ (Figure. 5).

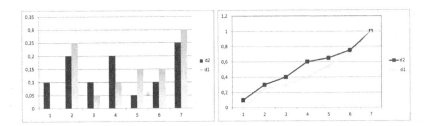

Fig. 5. $d2 \leq_{st} d1$: Their pmf (left) and their cumulative distribution functions (right)

3.2 Bounding Histogram Reduction

In order to reduce the computation complexity of evolution equations, we propose to apply the bounding approach to diminish the number of classes. The main advantage of this approach is the ability of computing bounds rather than approximations. Unlike approximation, the bounds allow us to check if QoS are satisfied or not. For a given distribution d, defined as a histogram with N classes, we build two bounding distribution $d1$ and $d2$ which are defined as histograms with $n < N$ classes. Moreover, $d1$ and $d2$ are constructed to be the closest with respect to a given reward function. Two algorithms are given in [2] to construct such bounds. More formally, for a given distribution d defined on $\mathcal{H}$ ($|\mathcal{H}| = N$), we compute bounding distributions $d1$ and $d2$ defined respectively on $\mathcal{H}^u$, $\mathcal{H}^l$ ($|\mathcal{H}^u| = n$, $|\mathcal{H}^l| = n$) such that:

1. $d2 \leq_{st} d \leq_{st} d1$,
2. $\sum_{i \in \mathcal{H}} r(i)d(i) - \sum_{i \in \mathcal{H}^l} r(i)d2(i)$ is minimal among the set of distributions on n states that are stochastically lower than d,
3. $\sum_{i \in \mathcal{H}^u} r(i)d1(i) - \sum_{i \in \mathcal{H}} r(i)d(i)$ is minimal among the set of distributions on n states that are stochastically upper than d.

$d1$ and $d2$ will be denoted as the optimal bounding distributions on n states according to reward r. We now present the bounding algorithm that will be used in this paper.

Optimal Algorithm Based on Dynamic Programming. We will transform our problem dealing with a discrete distribution into a graph theory problem. First, we consider the weighted graph $G = (V, E)$ such that:

- V is the set of vertices such that $V = \mathcal{H} \cup \{EndState\}$ where $EndState$ is a new state larger than all the states in $\mathcal{H}$.
- E is the set of arcs such that $(u, v) \in E$ if and only if $u < v$ or if $v = EndState$ and $u \in \mathcal{H}$. The weight of arc $e = (u, v)$, denoted by $\boldsymbol{w}(e)$, and it is defined as follows: $\boldsymbol{w}(e) = \begin{cases} \sum_{j \in \mathcal{H}: u < j < v} \boldsymbol{d}(j)(\boldsymbol{r}(j) - \boldsymbol{r}(u)) & \text{if } v \in \mathcal{H}, \\ \sum_{j \in \mathcal{H}: u < j} \boldsymbol{d}(j)(\boldsymbol{r}(j) - \boldsymbol{r}(u)) & \text{otherwise.} \end{cases}$

where $MinState$ denotes the minimal state of $\mathcal{H}$. A distribution is associated with a path. For the remaining, we focus on certain paths P provided with distribution $\boldsymbol{d}_P$ from state $MinState$ to state $EndState$ in graph G.

In fact, computing $\boldsymbol{d}_P$ is equivalent to compute a shortest path in G from state $MinState$ to state $EndState$ with n arcs. Such an algorithm based on dynamic programming with complexity $O(N^2 n)$ is given in [4].

Example 3. Let $\mathcal{A} = (\mathbf{A}, p(\mathbf{A}))$ be a discrete distribution with $\mathbf{A} = \{0, 2, 3, 5, 7\}$ and $p(\mathbf{A}) = [0.05, 0.3, 0.15, 0.2, 0.3]$. We aim to reduce the state space to $n = 3$ states and the reward function r is defined as follows: $\forall\, a_i \in \mathbf{A}$, $\boldsymbol{r}(a_i) = a_i$. The reward of the initial distribution, $R[\mathcal{A}] = \sum_{a_i \in \mathbf{A}} \boldsymbol{r}(a_i)\, p_{\mathbf{A}}(i) = 4.15$. The computation of the optimal upper bound $(\overline{\mathcal{A}})$ corresponds to explore all 3-hops paths from $EndState = 7$ such that $R[\overline{\mathcal{A}}] - R[\mathcal{A}]$ is minimal (see Figure 6). This can be done by applying the algorithm presented in [4]. The optimal upper bound is $\overline{\mathcal{A}} = (\overline{\mathbf{A}}, p(\overline{\mathbf{A}}))$ with $\overline{\mathbf{A}} = \{2, 5, 7\}$, $p(\overline{\mathbf{A}}) = [0.35, 0.35, 0.3]$ and $R[\overline{\mathcal{A}}] = 4.55$.

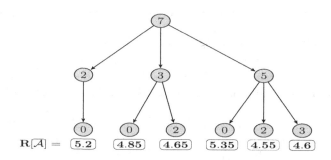

Fig. 6. Optimal upper bound histogram for $n = 3$ classes

3.3   Performance Measure Bounds

In this section, we prove that performance measures of the single node with bounding histograms provide bounds for exact performance measures. We compare the buffer length under the exact traffic histogram with that obtained under the bounding traffic histogram. The buffer length at slot k $(Q(k))$ under an input traffic $A(k)$ is given by Equation 1. Similarly, the buffer length of the same system under input arrival $\tilde{A}(k)$, denoted by $\tilde{Q}(k)$ is given as

$$\tilde{Q}(k) = \texttt{min}(B, (\tilde{Q}(k-1) + \tilde{A}(k) - S)^+), \quad k \in \mathbb{N}.$$

We have the following bounds, if the input arrivals are comparable in the sense of the $\leq_{st}$ order.

Proposition 3. *If $A(k) \leq_{st} \tilde{A}(k), \forall k \geq 0$, then $Q(k) \leq_{st} \tilde{Q}(k), \forall k \geq 0$.*

Proof. The proof is by induction: we suppose that $Q(k) \leq_{st} \tilde{Q}(k)$. We apply theorem 4.3.9 of Stoyan. As the function $\texttt{min}$ is an increasing function, and $A(k) \leq_{st} \tilde{A}(k)$, then we can deduce that $Q(k+1) \leq_{st} \tilde{Q}(k+1)$.

Similarly, it follows from Equation 2 that we have bounds on the departure processes.

Proposition 4. *If $A(k) \leq_{st} \tilde{A}(k), \forall k \geq 0$, then $D(k) \leq_{st} \tilde{D}(k), \forall k \geq 0$.*

We can now give the main theorem, by assuming that input arrivals $\tilde{A}(k)$ are bounds built as explained in subsection 3.2. We give here only the upper bounding case and the lower bounds can be similarly obtained.

Theorem 1. *Let $\mathcal{A}$ (resp. $\tilde{\mathcal{A}}$ be the stationary exact (resp. upper bounding) input histogram, and $\mathcal{Q}, \mathcal{D}$ (resp. $\tilde{\mathcal{Q}}, \tilde{\mathcal{D}}$) be the stationary buffer length and the departure processes under the exact $\mathcal{A}$, (resp. upper bounding $\tilde{\mathcal{A}}$) input arrival, then we have:*

$$\mathcal{Q} \leq_{st} \tilde{\mathcal{Q}} \quad and \quad \mathcal{D} \leq_{st} \tilde{\mathcal{D}}.$$

Proof. By construction $\mathcal{A} \leq_{st} \tilde{\mathcal{A}}$, and it follows from the above propositions that we have comparisons for all k, thus also for stationary processes when $k \to \infty$. Remark that by construction $\mathcal{Q}$ and $\mathcal{D}$ exist (due to the ergodicity assumption).

In the case when we consider a node in a tandem network, we have the same evolution equations as in the single node case, but the arrivals to a node are either external arrivals or the arrivals from the other nodes. By construction of histograms, we have bounding histograms for external arrivals. The internal arrivals are indeed the departure histograms of other nodes which are bounds. Therefore, we can also derive bounds for a node in a tandem network.

In order to compute the steady state distribution, we need an algorithm with a proved convergence test. Note that computing the difference between two successive distribution as [7] is not a correct test for convergence (see Stewart's book [13]). We propose the following algorithm based on the computation on a stochastic envelope Q^L and Q^U to prove the convergence.

Theorem 2. *Assume that the chain is ergodic and the steady state is π. We have*

$$Q^L(k) \leq_{st} Q^L(k+1) \leq_{st} \pi \leq_{st} Q^U(k+1) \leq_{st} Q^U(k).$$

Furthermore, the limit of $Q^L(k)$ and $Q^U(k)$ is π.

Algorithm 1. State evolution algorithm

1: $Q^U(0) = \delta_B$, (Dirac at state B).
2: $Q^L(0) = \delta_0$, (Dirac at state 0).
3: $k = 0$.
4: **repeat**
5:     $Q^U(k+1) = f(Q^U(k)) = \min(B, (Q^U(k) + \mathcal{A} - S)^+)$.
6:     $Q^L(k+1) = f(Q^L(k)) = \min(B, (Q^L(k) + \mathcal{A} - S)^+)$.
7: **until** $||Q^U(k+1) - Q^L(k+1)||_\infty < \epsilon$.

Proof. Remember that, for any non decreasing function f if $X \leq_{st} Y$ then, $f(X) \leq_{st} f(Y)$ [9]. Note that $\delta_0 \leq_{st} X$ is true for any distribution X defined on $\{0..B\}$. Therefore, $Q^L(0) \leq_{st} Q^L(1)$ and $f(Q^L(0)) \leq_{st} f(Q^L(1))$ because f is not deceasing. Thus $Q^L(1) \leq_{st} Q^L(2)$. By induction, we have $Q^L(k) \leq_{st} Q^L(k+1)$. The proof for $Q^U(k)$ is similar, noting that $X \leq_{st} \delta_B$ is true for any X.

As $Q^L(k) \leq_{st} \delta_B$ the sequence is bounded and increasing. Therefore, the limit exists. Similarly, the sequence of $Q^U(k)$ has a limit. Finally, by the ergodicity of the chain, both limits are equal and the iteration of Q^L, Q^U converges. Checking the difference between Q^L and Q^U provides a proved test of convergence.

4   Real Traffic Experiments

We compute the performance measures of interest under real traffic traces by applying three methods: exact computation, HBSP method and our method. We are interested in blocking probability, buffer occupancy histogram and mean buffer occupancy. We first, consider a single finite buffer case and then study a network of nodes. For all the experiments, we suppose that the stationarity is reached according to Algorithm 1 for $\epsilon = 10^{-6}$, reward function is defined by $r(a_i) = a_i$, $\forall a_i \in \mathbf{A}$. Real traffics are generally defined with large number of classes N. In order to accelerate the computation time of our bounds, we propose to reduce the initial size to n classes in two steps. First, we apply Tancrez's approach [14] to obtain bounds on N' ($n < N' < N$) states. In the following experiments we take N'=4000. In the second step, we apply our method to have bounding histograms on n states. The parameters considered in these experiments are taken from [7] to compare results.

4.1   Single Node

We first consider the single node under the MAWI traffic traces (Figure 1). We want to analyze the influence of the number of classes on the accuracy of the results. We set the mean transmission rate to $S = 110$ Mb/s and the buffer size to $B = 1$ Mb. We compute performance measures (Figure 7) for different number of bins (varying from 10 to 200). In each figure, we give the results computed by different methods: 1) exact result, 2) HBSP method, 3) Lower bound and 4) Upper bound. Obviously, when the number of bins increases the results become

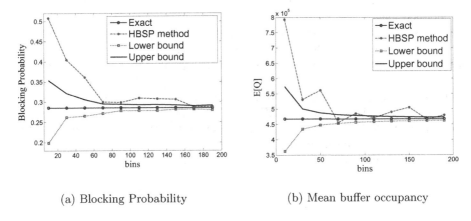

(a) Blocking Probability   (b) Mean buffer occupancy

Fig. 7. Number of classes vs Accuracy: QoS parameters using MAWI traffic trace

more accurate. But we must notice that the results provided by our bounds are very close to the exact ones.

We can remark that for small values of bins, HBSP method gives worse results. Moreover, we see clearly from Figure 7.b that HBSP method does not provide bounds. In Figure 8 we illustrate the cumulative probability distribution of buffer

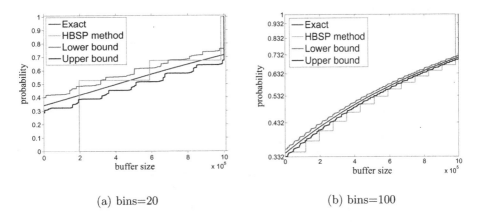

(a) bins=20   (b) bins=100

Fig. 8. Cumulative probability (cdf) of buffer occupancy under MAWI traffic trace

occupancy by taking number of bins equal to 20 or 100. Again, we see the HBSP method is not a bound and it does not provide a good approximation for small values of bins (bins=20). For bins equal to 100 all methods provide better results and our bounds are the most accurate ones. To get an idea of the execution times of the considered methods, we give the times for number of bins equal to 100. We find that the exact computations are obtained in 1897 seconds (s), the HBSP method in 0.007 s, the lower and upper bounds are respectively obtained in

0.35 s and 0.33 s. So, we remark that the HBSP method is the fastest one, but our bounds remain faster than the exact computation.

The second experiment is based on the CAIDA OC-48 traffic trace [1] collected in both directions of an OC48 link at the AMES Internet Exchange (AIX) on the 24th of April, 2003. The collected trace is one hour long with an average rate of $92\,Mb/s$. For our experiment, we take 5-minutes of packet header trace. Using a sampling period of T = 10 ms (100 samples per second), the resulting traffic trace has 30,000 frames and $E[\mathcal{A}] = 1.2885\,10^5\,bits$. We consider the relationship between buffer size and blocking probability (resp. mean buffer length) for bounding histograms, HBSP model and the exact result. The performance indices are calculated by varying the buffer size from $5.\,10^3\,bits$ to $10^5\,bits$.

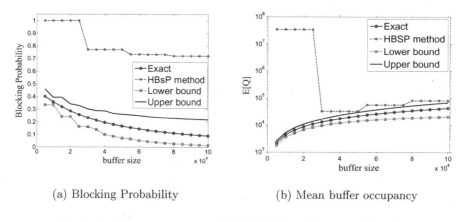

(a) Blocking Probability   (b) Mean buffer occupancy

Fig. 9. QoS parameters using CAIDA OC-48 traffic trace, bins=10

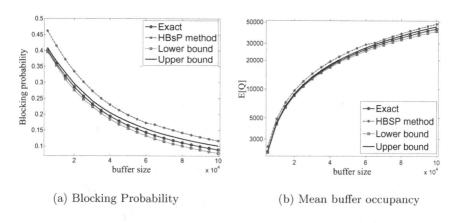

(a) Blocking Probability   (b) Mean buffer occupancy

Fig. 10. QoS parameters using CAIDA OC-48 traffic trace, bins=100

In Figure 9, we present the results with bins equal to 10 while Figure 10 presents the results with a number of bins equal to 100. When a number of bins equal to 10, the results obtained by HBSP method for blocking probability and mean buffer occupancy for small buffer sizes are not accurate. However, we see that the bounds are closer to the exact values. When the number of bins increases the accuracy of the HBSP method is improved and the bounds becomes very tight.

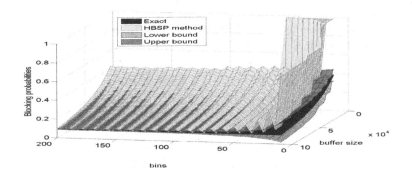

(a) Exact vs. approximate and bounding results

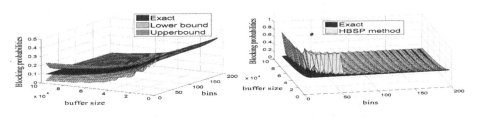

(b) Exact vs. bounding results   (c) Exact vs. HBSP results

Fig. 11. Blocking probability using CAIDA OC-48 traffic trace

In Figure 11, we give 3D representations to study the impact of the buffer size and the number of bins on blocking probabilities. We see from Figure 11.a that for small number of classes the HBSP method does not converge when buffer size is approximately less than 3.10^3 and gives less accurate results elsewhere. However, our bounds let us to provide fairly good coverage on the exact results. We notice also that when the number of classes increases, the used methods gives a closer results to the exact ones. Moreover, Figure 11.c illustrates well that the HBSP method does not provide bounds.

4.2   Queueing Network

In this section, we study a tandem queueing network with the MAWI traffic trace (Figure 2) as input arrival histogram. The network is defined by 3 service nodes having the following deterministic service rate: S_1=110 Mb/s, S_2=107.5 Mb/s and S_3=106.5 Mb/s. The buffers sizes are set to B_1=2 Mb, B_2=1 Mb and B_3=1 Mb. The analysis of the network is performed for two reductions 100 and 500 respectively on the input histogram of each queue (see Table 1).

We study as performance measures: blocking probability ($Prob(B)$), mean buffer length ($E[Q_i]_{i=\{1,2,3\}}$) and throughput (expected value of the departure histogram) ($E[D_i]_{i=\{1,2,3\}}$). We compute also mean transmission delays ($E[T_i]_{i=\{1...4\}}$) in each queue by using Little's theorem. In the last row, we present the execution time for the whole network analysis. These examples show that our method is fast even if it is slightly higher than HBSP. Moreover, we derive bounds which are more accurate than the results given by HBSP.

Table 1. Numerical results for the network using MAWI Traffic trace

	Bins		100			500		
		Exact	Lower b.	Upper b.	HBSP	Lower b.	Upper b.	HBSP
Queue 1	$Prob(B)$	0.1818	0.1714	0.1937	0.2147	0.1798	0.1846	0.1854
	$E[Q_1]$	938529	908137	969289	1019260	931778	945367	950271
	$E[D_1] \cdot 10^6$	4.26185	4.25076	4.27272	4.24416	4.25954	4.26416	4.26055
	$E[T_1]$	0.2202	0.2136	0.2269	0.2402	0.2188	0.2217	0.2230
Queue 2	$Prob(B)$	0.1735	0.1200	0.2052	0.1551	0.1481	0.1809	0.1559
	$E[Q_2]$	488719	425739	524331	468094	464797	497174	474322
	$E[D_2] \cdot 10^6$	4.24692	4.23377	4.25604	4.23441	4.24325	4.24903	4.24776
	$E[T_2]$	0.1151	0.1006	0.1232	0.1105	0.1095	0.1170	0.1117
Queue 3	$Prob(B)$	0.1635	0.0782	0.2379	$1.18 \cdot 10^{-6}$	0.1286	0.1799	0.2223
	$E[Q_3]$	505240	388396	585229	39418.4	463092	524231	564428
	$E[D_3] \cdot 10^6$	4.2408	4.22816	4.24768	4.23441	4.23732	4.2425	4.23809
	$E[T_3]$	0.1191	0.0919	0.1378	0.0093	0.1093	0.1236	0.1332
Ex. Time (s)		21868	2.20	2.16	0.13	14.57	18.21	0.28

5   Conclusions

Performance analysis of communication networks under general traffic is very difficult and sometimes impossible by simulation and queueing theory. We propose in this paper to develop a formalism based on stochastic bounds in order to reduce the size of the traffic histograms. We apply an algorithm based on dynamic programming to define bounding histograms. We analyze the performance of tandem queueing networks. We consider real traffic traces and derive bounds on different performance measures as blocking probabilities and buffer occupancy. We compare our results with the system under the exact traffic trace, and those obtained from the HBSP approximation. We show clearly that our results are more accurate and can be obtained within very interesting execution times. The more important point is the fact that we derive stochastic bounds which provide guarantee for non decreasing rewards. We will extend the theory in the near future to deal with non stationary flows.

References

1. Caida, traces of oc48 link at ames internet exchange (aix), accessed via datcat - internet data measurement catalog (April 24, 2003), http://imdc.datacat.org
2. Aït-Salaht, F., Cohen, J., Castel-Taleb, H., Fourneau, J.M., Pekergin, N.: Accuracy vs. complexity: the stochastic bound approach. In: 11th International Workshop on Disrete Event Systems, pp. 343–348 (2012)
3. Baccelli, F., Cohen, G., Olsder, G.J., Quadrat, J.-P.: Synchronization and Linearity: An Algebra for Discrete Event Systems. Willey, New York (1992)
4. Guérin, R., Orda, A.: Computing shortest paths for any number of hops. IEEE/ACM Trans. Netw. 10(5), 613–620 (2002)
5. Hernández-Orallo, E., Vila-Carbó, J.: Network performance analysis based on histogram workload models. In: MASCOTS, pp. 209–216 (2007)
6. Hernández-Orallo, E., Vila-Carbó, J.: Web server performance analysis using histogram workload models. Computer Networks 53(15), 2727–2739 (2009)
7. Hernández-Orallo, E., Vila-Carbó, J.: Network queue and loss analysis using histogram-based traffic models. Computer Communications 33(2), 190–201 (2010)
8. Kweon, S.-K., Shin, K.G.: Real-time transport of mpeg video with a statistically guaranteed loss ratio in atm networks. IEEE Transactions on Parallel and Distributed Systems, 12–4 (2001)
9. Muller, A., Stoyan, D.: Comparison Methods for Stochastic Models and Risks. Wiley, New York (2002)
10. Robertson, J.P.: The computation of aggregate loss distributions. In: Proceedings of the Casualty Actuarial Society, pp. 57–133 (1992)
11. Skelly, P., Schwartz, M., Dixit, S.S.: A histogram-based model for video traffic behavior in an atm multiplexer. IEEE/ACM Trans. Netw. 1(4), 446–459 (1993)
12. Sony, K.C., Cho, K.: Traffic data repository at the wide project. In: Proceedings of USENIX 2000 Annual Technical Conference: FREENIX Track, pp. 263–270 (2000)
13. Stewart, W.J.: Introduction to the numerical Solution of Markov Chains. Princeton University Press, New Jersey (1995)
14. Tancrez, J.-S., Semal, P., Chevalier, P.: Histogram based bounds and approximations for production lines. European Journal of Operational Research 197(3), 1133–1141 (2009)

Analytic Performance Modeling and Optimization of Live VM Migration

Arwa Aldhalaan[1] and Daniel A. Menascé[2]

[1] Volgenau School of Engineering, George Mason University,
Fairfax, VA 22030, USA
aaldhala@gmu.edu
[2] Department of Computer Science, George Mason University,
Fairfax, VA 22030, USA
menasce@gmu.edu

Abstract. Earlier virtual machine (VM) migration techniques consisted of stop-and-copy: the VM was stopped, its address space was copied to a different physical machine, and the VM was restarted at that machine. Recent VM hypervisors support live VM migration, which allows pages to be copied while the VM is running. If any copied page is dirtied (i.e., modified), it has to be copied again. The process stops when a fraction α of the pages need to be copied. Then, the VM is stopped and the remaining pages are copied. This paper derives a model to compute the downtime, total number of pages copied, and network utilization due to VM migration, as a function of α and other parameters under uniform and non-uniform dirtying rates. The paper also presents a non-linear optimization model to find the value of α that minimizes the downtime subject to network utilization constraints.

Keywords: VM Migration, Live VM Migration, Performance Modeling, Optimization.

1 Introduction

Cloud computing is based on largely distributed virtual environments that provide Infrastructure-as-a-Service (IaaS) services to consumers allowing them to lease computing resources that scale to their needs. These services rely on virtualization as an important technology that facilitates dynamic resource management to meet Service Level Agreements (SLA) of disparate applications sharing the same computing and networking platform. Virtualization platforms provide support for entire virtual machines (VM) to be migrated from one physical machine to another should the need arise. Earlier techniques relied on stop-and-copy approaches by which the VM was stopped and its address space copied over the network to a different physical machine before the VM was restarted at the target machine. This technique could lead to long VM downtimes. More recently, VM hypervisors started to offer live VM migration approaches that allow pages of the address space to be copied while the VM is running. If any copied page

M.S. Balsamo, W.J. Knottenbelt, and A. Marin (Eds.): EPEW 2013, LNCS 8168, pp. 28–42, 2013.

is dirtied (i.e., modified), it has to be copied again. The process stops when a fraction α of the pages need to be copied. Then, the VM is stopped and these remaining pages are copied.

The main contributions of this paper are: (1) analytic performance models to compute the VM downtime, the total number of pages copied during migration, and network utilization due to VM migration, as a function of α and other system parameters; (2) analytic performance models for the case in which a fraction of the pages of the address space are *hot* pages (i.e., have a higher dirtying rate than the other pages); and (3) a non-linear optimization model to find the value of α that minimizes the VM downtime subject to constraints on network utilization.

The rest of the paper is organized as follows. Section 2 provides some background on VM migration and introduces the problem statement. Then, sections 3 and 4 provide the analytic model for the cases in which all pages have the same dirtying rate and the case in which some pages ("hot pages") have a higher dirtying rate than the rest of the pages. In section 6, the optimization problem is described. The results of the experiments are discussed in Section 7. Section 8 discusses related work. Finally, Section 9 concludes the paper.

2   Background and Problem Statement

Live migration is the process of migrating the contents of a VM's memory from one physical host (source VM) to another (target VM), while the VM is executing. The goal is to minimize both the downtime (the period during which the VM's execution is stopped) and total migration time (the duration of end-to-end migration, from the moment the migration is initiated until the source VM is discarded) [1].

In contrast to live migration, *stop and copy* [1,2] is considered the simplest VM migration technique, which involves suspending the source VM, copying all its memory pages to the target VM, and then starting this new target VM. Although this approach can be easy to implement and control, it can cause long periods of VM downtime and total migration time especially with practical applications and large memory size VMs. Thus, leading to performance degradation and unacceptable VM outage.

The live migration approach discussed in this paper uses the *pre-copy* based migration [1,3] in which memory pages are copied from the source VM to the target VM iteratively. While the source VM continues to execute, the migration process starts by copying all pages at the first round, and then copying at each subsequent round i the modified or dirtied pages on round $i - 1$. *Dirty pages* are memory pages that have been modified during the migration process while the source VM is still running. The hypervisor tracks the dirty pages at each iteration in order to re-send them. This iterative process continues for a fixed number of iterations, or until a small working set size is reached. After that, the source VM is stopped and the downtime phase starts in order to transfer the remaining active memory contents of the source VM. However, since most of the source VM's memory contents were already transferred during the pre-copy phase, the downtime is significantly reduced, except for some special cases.

Current virtual machine software supports live migration of VMs that can be migrated with very short downtimes (depending on the workload) ranging from tens of milliseconds to a few seconds [4]. Examples of such support is present in VMWare [5] and Xen [6], an open source virtual machine monitor (VMM) allowing multiple commodity operating systems to share conventional hardware.

Many parameters can affect the performance of the live migration process such as the size and number of memory pages, dirtying rate, and network bandwidth. In this paper we analytically model and optimize the parameters of the problem stated above. Our model quantitatively predicts the performance of this live migration process. The goal of our optimization is to minimize the VM's downtime subject to some resource constraint. In other words, the goal is to determine the optimal point at which the pre-copy phase should stop to provide the lowest VM downtime subject to the resource constraint. We also took into consideration the concept of hot pages which is the set of pages that get updated very frequently.

3   Analytic Model of Live Migration with Uniform Dirtying Rate

Let us define the following:

- P_s: number of memory pages currently on VM s ($0 \leq j \leq P_s$, $j \in \mathbb{N}$).
- s: source VM selected to be migrated.
- t: the newly instantiated VM as target.
- B: available network bandwidth, in KB/sec, between source VM s and target VM t.
- S: size of a page in KB.
- τ: time to transmit a page over the network. $\tau = S/B$.
- n: last iteration number during which pages are migrated before downtime. It is a threshold to stop the migration process. It can either be a fixed number of iterations, or a number of iterations until a small working set size is reached ($0 \leq i \leq n$, $i \in \mathbb{N}$).
- D: memory dirtying rate in pages/sec.
- ρ: network utilization during live migration. $\rho = D \cdot \tau$.
- $P(i)$: number of pages copied during iteration i. Note that $P(0) = P_s$ because the entire address space is copied during the first iteration.
- $T(i)$: time spent in each iteration i. Note that $T(0) = P(0) \cdot \tau = P_s \cdot \tau$.
- U_{net}: utilization of the network due to VM migration.

The number of pages copied from VM s to VM t at a given iteration i is equal to the number of pages dirtied during the previous iteration. Thus,

$$P(i) = D \cdot T(i-1). \tag{1}$$

The time spent at iteration i is equal to the time spent transmitting the number of pages that need to be transferred at that iteration. So,

$$T(i) = P(i) \cdot \tau. \tag{2}$$

Using Eq. (1) in Eq. (2) we obtain the following recursive expression for $T(i)$.

$$T(i) = T(i-1) \cdot D \cdot \tau = T(i-1) \cdot \rho \tag{3}$$

Solving the recursion in Eq. (3) and noting that $T(0) = P_s \cdot \tau$ provides us with the following closed form expression for $T(i)$.

$$T(i) = P_s \cdot D^i \cdot \tau^{i+1} = P_s \cdot \tau \cdot \rho^i \quad \text{for } i \geq 0. \tag{4}$$

Then, using Eq. (4) in Eq. (1) gives us a closed form expression for $P(i)$:

$$P(i) = P_s \cdot \rho^i \quad \text{for } i \geq 0. \tag{5}$$

Because $P(i) \leq P_s$ for $i \geq 0$, Eq. (5) implies that $\rho \leq 1$. We will assume throughout the paper that $\rho < 1$ as our steady state condition.

Pages will be copied while the source VM is live during iterations 0 to n. Then, the VM is taken down and all pages that were dirtied during iteration n, i.e., $P(n+1)$ pages have to be copied. Thus, using Eq. (5), the VM downtime, defined as T_{down}, can be computed as

$$T_{\text{down}} = P(n+1) \cdot \tau = P_s \cdot \tau \cdot \rho^{n+1}. \tag{6}$$

The time during which pages are being copied and the VM is up, $T_{\text{pre-copy}}$, is

$$T_{\text{pre-copy}} = \sum_{i=0}^{n} T(i) = \sum_{i=0}^{n} P_s \cdot \tau \cdot \rho^i = P_s \cdot \tau \cdot \frac{1 - \rho^{n+1}}{1 - \rho}. \tag{7}$$

The total VM migration time is then the sum of the durations of all iterations during the pre-copy phase (i.e., iterations from 0 to n) plus the downtime. Thus,

$$\begin{aligned}
T_{\text{total}} &= T_{\text{pre-copy}} + T_{down} \\
&= P_s \cdot \tau \cdot \frac{1 - \rho^{n+1}}{1 - \rho} + P_s \cdot \tau \cdot \rho^{n+1} = P_s \cdot \tau \cdot \left[\frac{1 - \rho^{n+2}}{1 - \rho} \right].
\end{aligned} \tag{8}$$

If the value of the threshold n is defined as the number of iterations such that at most αP_s pages (with $\alpha < 1$) need to be migrated, we can write that

$$P(n+1) = P_s \cdot \rho^{n+1} \leq \alpha P_s. \tag{9}$$

Applying natural logarithms to both sides and noting that $D \cdot \tau < 1$, we obtain

$$n \geq \left\lceil \frac{\ln \alpha}{\ln \rho} - 1 \right\rceil. \tag{10}$$

Given that we want to use the smallest number of iterations such that at most αP_s pages need to be migrated,

$$n = \left\lceil \frac{\ln \alpha}{\ln \rho} - 1 \right\rceil. \tag{11}$$

Since n must be ≥ 0, it follows that $\alpha \leq \rho$. Note that n is independent of the size of the address space of the source VM.

The total number of pages migrated up to iteration i can be obtained as

$$NMP(i) = P_s \sum_{j=0}^{i} \rho^j = P_s \cdot \frac{1 - \rho^{i+1}}{1 - \rho} \tag{12}$$

and the total number of pages migrated P_{TotalMig} is then

$$P_{\text{TotalMig}} = \lceil NMP(n) + \alpha \cdot P_s \rceil = \left\lceil P_s \left(\frac{1 - \rho^{n+1}}{1 - \rho} + \alpha \right) \right\rceil. \tag{13}$$

We now define the gain G in downtime as the ratio between the downtime without live migration and with live migration. The downtime without live migration is equal to the time to copy the entire address space, i.e., $P_s \cdot \tau$. Thus, using Eq. (6), we obtain

$$G = \frac{P_s \cdot \tau}{T_{\text{down}}} = \frac{P_s \cdot \tau}{P_s \cdot \rho^{n+1} \cdot \tau} = \frac{1}{\rho^{n+1}}. \tag{14}$$

Because $\rho < 1$, $G > 1$, which means that the downtime without live migration is higher than that using live migration by a factor equal to ρ^{n+1}. It is interesting to note that the gain is independent of the size of the address space of the source VM.

The utilization of the network, U_{net}, due to VM migration can be computed as follows. During live copying, the network utilization is ρ. During the period in which the VM is down, the network utilization due to the copying of αP_s pages is $[\alpha \cdot P_s \cdot (S/B)]/T_{\text{down}} = (\alpha \cdot P_s \cdot \tau)/T_{\text{down}}$. The fraction of time live copying is taking place is $T_{\text{pre-copy}}/(T_{\text{down}} + T_{\text{pre-copy}})$ and the fraction of time copying is taking place when the VM goes down is $T_{\text{down}}/(T_{\text{down}} + T_{\text{pre-copy}})$. Thus, the average network utilization due to VM migration is

$$U_{\text{net}} = \rho \cdot \frac{T_{\text{pre-copy}}}{T_{\text{down}} + T_{\text{pre-copy}}} + \frac{\alpha \cdot P_s \cdot \tau}{T_{\text{down}}} \cdot \frac{T_{\text{down}}}{T_{\text{down}} + T_{\text{pre-copy}}} \tag{15}$$

Using Eqs. (6) and (7) in Eq. (15) and doing some algebraic manipulation provides

$$U_{\text{net}} = \frac{\rho - \rho^{n+2} + \alpha(1 - \rho)}{1 - \rho^{n+2}}. \tag{16}$$

Note that the utilization U_{net} does not depend on P_s.

4   Analytic Model of Live Migration with Hot Pages

Most programs exhibit a locality of reference such that a relatively small number of pages have a much higher percentage of being modified than others. We call them *hot pages* as in [1]. We define some additional notation for this case.

- β: fraction of hot pages in the address space of the source VM s.
- D_{nh}: dirtying rate of the non-hot pages.
- D_h: dirtying rate of the hot pages. $D_h > D_{nh}$.

We show in what follows how the model in the previous section can be adapted for the following two situations: (1) Hot I: all pages, including hot pages, are migrated during pre-copy and (2) Hot II: hot pages are not copied during pre-copy; instead, they are copied when the VM is taken down.

Figure 1 shows how the ratio HG (for Hot page Gain) varies with β for three values of α (10%, 40%, and 70%). This ratio is defined as the VM downtime under Hot I divided by the VM downtime under Hot II. The curves show that for the two smallest values of α, the VM downtime is smaller when hot pages are migrated during pre-copy than when they are only migrated when the VM is down. Also, the ratio decreases as β increases, i.e., as there are more hot pages in the address space of the V.M. For the large value of α (70%), the situation reverses, i.e., the downtime for the case when hot pages are only copied when the VM is down is always smaller then when hot pages are copied during pre-copy. The intuitive explanation is that Hot I copies hot pages during pre-copy. Thus, lower values of α imply in more iterations and more opportunities for the hot pages to be copied during pre-copy, and consequently, less down-time. For higher values of α, there will be less hot pages copied during pre-copy under Hot I, and Hot II will have a smaller downtime. The two following subsections provide models that quantify the tradeoffs between these two alternatives.

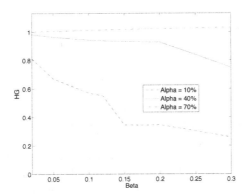

Fig. 1. HG vs. β for three values of α (10% bottom, 40% center, and 70% top) and for $P_s = 4096$ bytes

4.1 Model of Copying Hot Pages during the Pre-copy Phase

In this case, we can just use the results derived in the previous section by replacing D by the effective dirtying rate, $D_{\text{effective}}$.

$$D_{\text{effective}} = D_{nh}(1 - \beta) + D_h \cdot \beta. \tag{17}$$

We define ρ_{eff} as $D_{\text{effective}} \cdot \tau$. Then, T_{down} becomes

$$T_{\text{down}} = P_s \cdot \tau \cdot \rho_{\text{eff}}^{n+1}. \tag{18}$$

where

$$n = \left\lceil \frac{\ln \alpha}{\ln \rho_{\text{eff}}} - 1 \right\rceil \tag{19}$$

The duration of the pre-copy phase is

$$T_{\text{pre-copy}} = P_s \cdot \tau \cdot \frac{1 - \rho_{\text{eff}}^{n+1}}{1 - \rho_{\text{eff}}}. \tag{20}$$

The total number of pages migrated is

$$P_{\text{TotalMig}} = \left\lceil P_s \left(\frac{1 - \rho_{\text{eff}}^{n+1}}{1 - \rho_{\text{eff}}} + \alpha \right) \right\rceil. \tag{21}$$

Therefore, the gain G in this case is computed

$$G = \frac{1}{\rho_{\text{eff}}^{n+1}}. \tag{22}$$

The network utilization due to VM migration is

$$U_{\text{net}} = \frac{\rho_{\text{eff}} - \rho_{\text{eff}}^{n+2} + \alpha(1 - \rho_{\text{eff}})}{1 - \rho_{\text{eff}}^{n+2}}. \tag{23}$$

Note that the utilization U_{net} depends on β through ρ_{eff}, which depends on $D_{\text{effective}}$. Also, as in the uniform dirtying rate case, U_{net} does not depend on P_s.

4.2 Model of Copying Hot Pages during the Downtime Phase

In this case, we can adapt the results in the previous section as follows. The value of P_s has to be replaced by $P_s(1 - \beta)$ because only a fraction $(1 - \beta)$ of the address space participates in the live migration. The dirtying rate has to be replaced by the dirtying rate of the non-hot pages, D_{nh}. When the VM is taken down, the hot pages as well as the non-hot pages dirtied during iteration n have to be copied. We define ρ_{nh} as $D_{nh} \cdot \tau$. Thus, T_{down} becomes

$$T_{\text{down}} = P(n + 1) \cdot \tau + P_s \cdot \beta \cdot \tau \tag{24}$$
$$= P_s \cdot (1 - \beta) \cdot \rho_{nh}^{n+1} \cdot \tau + P_s \cdot \beta \cdot \tau$$
$$= P_s \cdot \tau \left[(1 - \beta)\rho_{nh}^{n+1} + \beta \right] \tag{25}$$

where

$$n = \left\lceil \frac{\ln \alpha}{\ln \rho_{nh}} - 1 \right\rceil . \tag{26}$$

The total time spent in the pre-copy phase is

$$T_{\text{pre-copy}} = P_s \cdot (1 - \beta) \cdot \tau \cdot \frac{1 - \rho_{nh}^{n+1}}{1 - \rho_{nh}} . \tag{27}$$

The total number of pages migrated is

$$
\begin{aligned}
P_{\text{TotalMig}} &= \left\lceil P(n+1) + (\alpha + \beta)P_s \right\rceil \\
&= \left\lceil P_s(1-\beta)\left(\frac{1-\rho_{nh}^{n+1}}{1-\rho_{nh}}\right) + (\alpha+\beta)P_s \right\rceil \\
&= \left\lceil P_s \left[(1-\beta)\left(\frac{1-\rho_{nh}^{n+1}}{1-\rho_{nh}}\right) + (\alpha+\beta) \right] \right\rceil . \tag{28}
\end{aligned}
$$

Therefore, the gain G in this case is computed as

$$G = \frac{P_s \cdot \tau}{T_{\text{down}}} = \frac{P_s \cdot \tau}{P_s \cdot \tau \left[(1-\beta)\rho_{nh}^{n+1} + \beta \right]} = \frac{1}{(1-\beta)\rho_{nh}^{n+1} + \beta} . \tag{29}$$

The network utilization due to VM migration is computed similarly to Eq. (15), namely

$$U_{\text{net}} = \rho_{nh} \frac{T_{\text{pre-copy}}}{T_{\text{down}} + T_{\text{pre-copy}}} + \frac{(\alpha + \beta) \cdot P_s \cdot \tau}{T_{\text{down}}} \frac{T_{\text{down}}}{T_{\text{down}} + T_{\text{pre-copy}}} \tag{30}$$

Using Eqs. (25) and (27) in (30), we obtain

$$U_{\text{net}} = \frac{(1-\beta)(\rho_{nh} - \rho_{nh}^{n+2}) + (\alpha+\beta)(1-\rho_{nh})}{(1-\beta)(1-\rho_{nh}^{n+2}) + \beta(1-\rho_{nh})} . \tag{31}$$

Note that, as expected, the above expression has the same form as that for the uniform case when $\beta = 0$.

5   Summary of Results

Table 1 shows all the equations derived in the previous sections. These equations allow us to draw some important conclusions. First, as α increases, n decreases, and T_{down} increases in all three cases. Second, T_{down} increases with P_s in all cases. Third, P_{TotalMig} is not monotonically increasing or decreasing with α because the terms $1 - \rho^{n+1}$, $1 - \rho_{\text{eff}}^{n+1}$, and $1 - \rho_{nh}^{n+1}$ decrease as α increases (thus making P_{TotalMig} decrease) but the term α that appears as a multiplier of P_s makes P_{TotalMig} increase with α. The gain G is always greater than one and decreases with α. The network utilization due to live migration does not depend on the size of the source VM's address space.

6   Optimizing Live Migration Parameters

An interesting optimization problem is that of finding the value of α that minimizes the VM downtime subject to some constraints such as keeping the network utilization due to VM migration below a certain limit. We note that $T_{\text{down}} = f(\alpha)$ and $U_{\text{net}} = g(\alpha)$ where the specific functions f and g for each of the three cases are given by Table 1. Then, the optimization problem can be written as

$$\text{Minimize } T_{\text{down}} = f(\alpha)$$
$$\text{subject to } U_{\text{net}}(\alpha) \leq U_{\text{net}}^{\max}.$$

This is a non-linear optimization problem that we solve using methods included in MATLAB.

Table 1. Summary of performance model results

Uniform Dirtying Rate
$\rho = D \cdot \tau$
$T_{\text{down}} = P_s \cdot \tau \cdot \rho^{n+1}$; $n = \left\lceil \frac{\ln \alpha}{\ln \rho} - 1 \right\rceil$
$P_{\text{TotalMig}} = \left\lceil P_s \left(\frac{1-\rho^{n+1}}{1-\rho} + \alpha \right) \right\rceil$
$G = \frac{1}{\rho^{n+1}}$; $U_{\text{net}} = \frac{\rho - \rho^{n+2} + \alpha(1-\rho)}{1-\rho^{n+2}}$
Condition: $\alpha \leq \rho < 1$
Hot Pages Copied During the Pre-Copy Phase
$D_{\text{effective}} = D_{nh}(1-\beta) + D_h \cdot \beta$
$\rho_{\text{eff}} = D_{\text{effective}} \cdot \tau$
$T_{\text{down}} = P_s \cdot \tau \cdot \rho_{\text{eff}}^{n+1}$; $n = \left\lceil \frac{\ln \alpha}{\ln \rho_{\text{eff}}} - 1 \right\rceil$
$P_{\text{TotalMig}} = \left\lceil P_s \left(\frac{1-\rho_{\text{eff}}^{n+1}}{1-\rho_{\text{eff}}} + \alpha \right) \right\rceil$
$G = \frac{1}{\rho_{\text{eff}}^{n+1}}$; $U_{\text{net}} = \frac{\rho_{\text{eff}} - \rho_{\text{eff}}^{n+2} + \alpha(1-\rho_{\text{eff}})}{1-\rho_{\text{eff}}^{n+2}}$
Conditions: $\alpha \leq \rho_{\text{eff}} < 1$, $\beta < 1$
Hot Pages Copied During the Downtime Phase
$\rho_{nh} = D_{nh} \cdot \tau$
$T_{\text{down}} = P_s \cdot \tau \left[(1-\beta)\rho_{nh}^{n+1} + \beta \right]$; $n = \left\lceil \frac{\ln \alpha}{\ln \rho_{nh}} - 1 \right\rceil$
$P_{\text{TotalMig}} = \left\lceil P_s \left[(1-\beta) \left(\frac{1-\rho_{nh}^{n+1}}{1-\rho_{nh}} \right) + (\alpha + \beta) \right] \right\rceil$
$G = \frac{1}{(1-\beta)\rho_{nh}^{n+1} + \beta}$; $U_{\text{net}} = \frac{(1-\beta)(\rho_{nh} - \rho_{nh}^{n+2}) + (\alpha+\beta)(1-\rho_{nh})}{(1-\beta)(1-\rho_{nh}^{n+2}) + \beta(1-\rho_{nh})}$
Conditions: $\alpha \leq \rho_{nh} < 1$, $\beta < 1$

7   Numerical Results

Table 2 shows the parameters used in the experiments reported here. Figure 2(a) shows the variation of the VM downtime in seconds, T_{down}, with α for the four

Table 2. Parameter values used in the experiments

Parameter	Value	Parameter	Value
P_s	4096, 8192, 16384, and 32768	D_{nh}	1.8 pages/sec
B	60 KB/sec	D_h	4 pages/sec
S	16 KB	β	10%
D	2 pages/sec	$U_{\text{net}}^{\max}$	40%

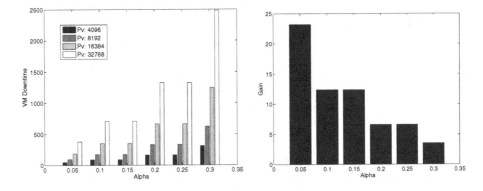

Fig. 2. (a) T_{down} in seconds vs. α for different values of P_s (4 KB, 8KB, 16KB, and 32KB); (b) Gain vs. α for the uniform dirtying rate case

values of P_s shown in Table 2 for the case of uniform dirtying rate. As predicted by the equations, the downtime increases (or stays the same) with α because more pages will have to be copied when the VM is taken down. The reason that T_{down} may not increase at times with α is that the increase in α may not be enough to increase the number of pages to be copied. The figure shows that, for the parameters used, larger values of α can create very large (and intolerable) downtimes, especially for large address spaces. For example, if one wanted to keep the downtime below 500 sec, one could use any of the values of α shown in the figure for $P_s = 4096$ pages, $\alpha \in \{0.05, 0.1, 0.15\}$ for $P_s \in \{4096, 8192, 16384\}$, and $\alpha = 0.05$ for $P_s = 32768$. Thus, the formulation presented in this paper would allow a hypervisor to dynamically determine the value of the parameter α for a given set of parameters.

Figure 2(b) shows the variation of the gain G with α. As predicted, the gain decreases or stays the same as α increases. For a small value of α such as 0.05, the downtime in the stop and copy case is 23 times higher than in live migration for the parameters used.

Figure 3(a) shows the variation of the total number of pages migrated during the entire VM migration copy including the pages copied while the VM is up and those copied while the VM is down. Clearly, larger address spaces will generate more pages being copied. As pointed out before, P_{TotalMig} is not monotonically

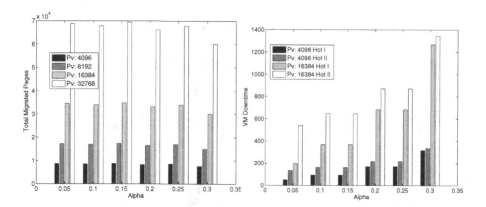

Fig. 3. (a) P_{TotalMig} vs. α for different values of P_s (4 KB, 8KB, 16KB, and 32KB) for the uniform dirtying rate; (b) T_{down} in seconds vs. α for the two cases of hot pages (hot pages copied during the pre-copy phase (case Hot I) and hot pages copied when the VM is taken down (case Hot II)) for two values of P_s (4 KB and 16KB)

increasing or decreasing with α. This is because as α increases, more pages will have to be copied when the VM goes down, but less iterations, and therefore less pages will be copied when the VM is up. This effect is more pronounced for the case of larger address spaces.

Figure 3(b) shows the variation of the VM down time, in seconds, versus α for the two cases of hot page migration and for two sizes of the address space. The figure shows that for the same type of hot page migration, the downtime increases as the size of the address space increases. The figure also shows that, for the parameters used, the VM downtime is smaller for the case in which hot pages are migrated while the VM is up.

Figure 4(a) shows the variation of the gain G versus α for the two cases of hot pages and for two values of P_s. In both cases, the gain decreases or stays the same as α increases. However, for the parameters used, the gain is higher when hot pages are migrated when the VM is up because this case has a lower downtime as seen in Fig. 3(b).

Figure 4(b) shows the total number of migrated pages for the two cases of hot page migration and two values of P_s. The figure shows that in the case in which hot pages are copied while the VM is up, more pages end up being copied resulting in more overall network traffic.

We ran the optimization problem described in section 6 for a network utilization constraint $U_{\text{net}}^{\max} = 40\%$ and for the three cases described above. The results are shown in Table 3. The table shows the value of α that minimizes the downtime T_{down} and that does not violate $U_{\text{net}}^{\max}$. For the same value of P_s the uniform case provides a lower downtime than Hot I, which provides a lower downtime than Hot II.

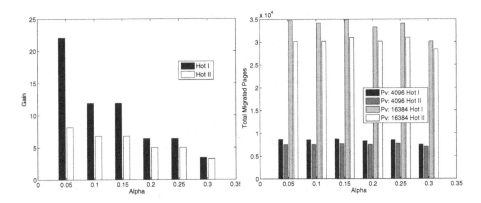

Fig. 4. (a) Gain vs. α for the two cases of hot pages (hot pages copied during the pre-copy phase (case Hot I) and hot pages copied when the VM is taken down (case Hot II)) for two values of P_s (4 KB and 16KB); (b) P_{TotalMig} vs. α for the two cases of hot pages (hot pages copied during the pre-copy phase (case Hot I) and hot pages copied when the VM is taken down (case Hot II)) for two values of P_s (4 KB and 16KB)

8   Related Work

Live migration has been an essential topic in cloud computing environments which is studied in a variety of contexts. In particular, providing methods and approaches to enhance the performance of live VM migration, and thus providing a more reliable distributed virtual environments. In [1], the authors studied and described the live migration of entire OS instances, and provided the design issues involved in live migration including minimizing downtime, minimizing total migration time, and ensuring that migration does not disrupt active services in the network.

The authors in [7] carried out a performance analysis of virtualized environments and examined the performance overhead in VMware ESX and Citrix XenServer virtualized environments. They created regression-based models for virtualized CPU and memory performance in order to predict the performance when migrating applications. In [8], the authors provided a live migration performance and energy model. The model's primary goal is to determine which VM should be migrated within a server farm with minimum migration cost. In their experiment, they specify the most dirtied memory pages as hot pages for their workloads. They use linear regression technology, and show that migration is an I/O intensive application. Another performance model of concurrent live migration is proposed in [9]. The authors experimentally collect performance of a virtualized system. Then, they constructed a performance model representing the performance characteristics of live migration using PRISM, a probabilistic model checker. In [10], a self-adaptive resource allocation method based on online architecture-level performance prediction models is proposed. Their method

Table 3. Optimization Results

	P_s	Optimal α	T_{down}	U_{net}
Uniform	4096	0.152	88	0.394
	8192	0.152	177	0.394
	16384	0.152	353	0.394
	32768	0.152	707	0.394
Hot I	4096	0.156	92	0.399
	8192	0.156	184	0.399
	16384	0.156	368	0.399
	32768	0.156	736	0.399
Hot II	4096	0.480	336	0.400
	8192	0.480	671	0.400
	16384	0.480	1340	0.400
	32768	0.480	2690	0.400

takes considers cloud dynamics triggered by variations in application workload. The authors of [11] propose a memory page selection in order to choose the memory pages to transfer during VM live migration. Their approach is based on the probability density function of the changes made by virtual machines on memory pages. This approach can help reduce the live migration downtime.

The behavior of iterative pre-copy live migration for memory intensive applications has been studied in [12], which proposes an optimized pre-copy strategy that dynamically adapts to the memory change rate in order to guarantee convergence. Their proposed algorithm, which is implemented in KVM, detects memory update patterns and terminates migration when improvements in downtime are unlikely to occur. A simulator based on Xen's migration algorithm is designed in [13] to characterize the downtime and total migration time. However, their simulation model is based on dynamic information collected during pre-copying iterations. Thus, it is hard to use it for a prior migration decision before the migration begins. In [14], the authors propose a framework for automatic machine scaling that meets consumer performance requirements and minimizes the number of provisioned virtual machines. This optimization reduces the cost resulting from over-provisioning and the performance issues related to under-provisioning.

In contrast, none of the above works provide an optimization model with the goal to minimize the VM's downtime subject to constraints such as network utilization. Our proposed model is a detailed analytical model of the pre-copy based live VM migration, and includes the case of hot pages in the prediction and estimation of VM's downtime, total migration time, number of iterations needed before downtime, gain, and network utilization.

9   Conclusion

This paper presented analytic models to estimate the time needed to perform live migration of a VM machine. Three cases were considered: uniform page dirtying rate, hot pages being copied during the pre-copy phase, and hot pages copied only during the VM's downtime. The pre-copy phase continues until no more than a fraction α of the pages copied during the pre-copy phase need to be copied. The value of α is an important parameter because as its value increases, the VM's downtime increases. However, at the same time, lower values of α generate higher network utilization due to VM migration. The performance of VMs not being migrated may be degraded due to high network utilization caused by VM migration.

For that reason, the paper presents a non-linear optimization problem that finds the value of α that minimizes the VM downtime subject to network utilization constraints. As future work, this optimization model can be implemented and tested in an open-source VMM hypervisor such as Xen. The analytic models presented here can be used to predict the performance of a specific VM's live migration before starting the migration process. This way, a cloud provider can select the VM with the least cost for migration in a large environment while satisfying Service Level Agreements. The optimization model can be extended by adding energy consumption constraints associated with the use of resources during VM migration.

As part of future work, there are several ongoing research activities related to this paper. The first, is to validate the model in an experimental setting. This paper made some simplifying assumptions such as constant page dirtying rate and a constant network bandwidth. Experiments with real systems will allow us to assess the impact of these assumptions. Nevertheless, we believe that this is the first paper to address this problem and the first to provide a closed form solution to the problem. Secondly, we intend to extend the model to the case in which more than one VM is being migrated at the same time. Related and interesting problems include the optimal selection of which VM to migrate first in order to minimize the impact on running applications while not exceeding some thresholds in terms of maximum migration time and/or downtime.

Acknowledgements. The work of D. Menascé is partially supported by NIST grant 70NANB12H277.

References

1. Clark, C., Fraser, K., Hand, S., Hansen, J.G., Jul, E., Limpach, C., Pratt, I., Warfield, A.: Live migration of virtual machines. In: Proc. 2nd Symp. Networked Systems Design & Implementation, vol. 2, pp. 273–286. USENIX Association (2005)
2. Isci, C., Liu, J., Abali, B., Kephart, J., Kouloheris, J.: Improving server utilization using fast virtual machine migration. IBM J. Research and Development 55(6), 4:1–4:12 (2011)
3. Theimer, M.M., Lantz, K.A., Cheriton, D.R.: Preemptable remote execution facilities for the v-system. In: Proc. 10th ACM Symp. Operating System Principles, pp. 2–12. ACM (1985)

4. Hacking, S., Hudzia, B.: Improving the live migration process of large enterprise applications. In: Proc. 3rd Intl. Workshop on Virtualization Technologies in Distributed Computing, pp. 51–58. ACM (2009)

5. Nelson, M., Lim, B.H., Hutchins, G.: Fast transparent migration for virtual machines. In: Proc. USENIX Annual Technical Conf. ATEC 2005, pp. 391–394. USENIX Association (2005)

6. Barham, P., Dragovic, B., Fraser, K., Hand, S., Harris, T., Ho, A., Neugebauer, R., Pratt, I., Warfield, A.: Xen and the art of virtualization. ACM SIGOPS Operating Systems Review 37(5), 164–177 (2003)

7. Huber, N., von Quast, M., Hauck, M., Kounev, S.: Evaluating and modeling virtualization performance overhead for cloud environments. In: Intl. Conf. Cloud Computing and Service Science (CLOSER 2011), Noordwijkerhout, The Netherlands (2011)

8. Liu, H., Xu, C.Z., Jin, H., Gong, J., Liao, X.: Performance and energy modeling for live migration of virtual machines. In: Proc. 20th Intl. Symp. High Performance Distributed Computing, pp. 171–182. ACM (2011)

9. Kikuchi, S., Matsumoto, Y.: Performance modeling of concurrent live migration operations in cloud computing systems using prism probabilistic model checker. In: 2011 IEEE Intl. Conf. Cloud Computing, pp. 49–56. IEEE (2011)

10. Huber, N., Brosig, F., Kounev, S.: Model-based self-adaptive resource allocation in virtualized environments. In: Proc. 6th International Symp. Software Engineering for Adaptive and Self-Managing Systems, pp. 90–99. ACM (2011)

11. Moghaddam, F.F., Cheriet, M.: Decreasing live virtual machine migration downtime using a memory page selection based on memory change pdf. In: 2010 Intl. Conf. Networking, Sensing and Control, pp. 355–359. IEEE (2010)

12. Ibrahim, K.Z., Hofmeyr, S., Iancu, C., Roman, E.: Optimized pre-copy live migration for memory intensive applications. In: Proc. 2011 Intl. Conf. High Performance Computing, Networking, Storage and Analysis, p. 40. ACM (2011)

13. Akoush, S., Sohan, R., Rice, A., Moore, A.W., Hopper, A.: Predicting the performance of virtual machine migration. In: 2010 IEEE Intl. Symp. Modeling, Analysis & Simulation of Computer and Telecommunication Systems, pp. 37–46. IEEE (2010)

14. Beltran, M., Guzman, A.: An automatic machine scaling solution for cloud systems. In: 19th Intl. Conf. High Performance Computing (HiPC), pp. 1–10. IEEE (2012)

Towards Supervisory Control
of Generally-Distributed Discrete-Event Systems

Jasen Markovski*

Department of Mechanical Engineering,
Eindhoven University of Technology,
Den Dolech 2, 5612AZ, Eindhoven, The Netherlands
j.markovski@tue.nl

Abstract. We develop a process-theoretic approach for generally-distributed discrete-event systems with unrestricted nondeterminism that is geared towards supervisory control. Supervisory control theory deals with synthesis of models of supervisory controllers that ensure safe and nonblocking behavior of the supervised system. The models are synthesized based on a model of the uncontrolled system and a formalization of the control requirements. Even though there exist extensions of supervisory control theory for timed and Markovian discrete-event systems, there are hardly any investigations of supervisory control of discrete-event systems with generally-distributed delays. General distributions provide for (convenient) modeling of important real-world phenomena that cannot be consistently modeled by means of real time or Markovian (exponentially-distributed) delays, like heavy-tail or uniformly distributed processes. Our theory relies on a behavioral preorder termed partial bisimulation, for which we provide a suitable extension. Based on the proposed theory we provide for an appropriate abstraction of the stochastic behavior, which enables us to employ standard supervisory controller synthesis tools. The synthesized supervisor can, thereafter, be coupled with the stochastic model of the unsupervised system and abstracted to a generalized semi-Markov process for the purpose of analysis and simulation.

1 Introduction

Supervisory control theory deals with automated synthesis of models of supervisory controllers that ensure safe functioning of the supervised system by coordinating the discrete-event behavior of its distributed components [37,13]. The theory was prompted by the ever-increasing complexity of control software for high-tech systems and the difficulties experienced in applying traditional software engineering methodology [27]. Namely, the control requirements that the control software should implement change frequently during the design process, leading to an excessive number of (re)coding-testing iterations, posing great challenges for software developers.

---
* Supported by Dutch NWO project: ProThOS, no. 600.065.120.11N124.

M.S. Balsamo, W.J. Knottenbelt, and A. Marin (Eds.): EPEW 2013, LNCS 8168, pp. 43–57, 2013.
© Springer-Verlag Berlin Heidelberg 2013

Supervisory controllers coordinate high level system behavior by receiving sensor signals from ongoing activities, make a decision on allowed activities, and send back control signals to the hardware actuators. A standard assumption is that the controller reacts sufficiently fast on machine input, which enables the modeling of the supervisory control feedback loop as a pair of synchronizing processes [37,13]. The model of the supervisory controller is referred to as supervisor, which is synthesized automatically based on formal models of the unsupervised system, referred to as plant, and the model of the control requirements. The synchronization of the plant and the supervisor, referred to as supervised plant, models the supervisory control loop. The supervisor disables or enables events in the plant by synchronizing or not synchronizing with them, respectively. In addition, supervised plants must satisfy the control requirements, which model the allowed (or safe) system behavior.

1.1   Generally-Distributed Delays

Like most formal approaches, supervisory control theory focused on qualitative aspects of discrete-event systems, subsequently being extended with quantitative aspects like time [8,39], probability [36,19], and Markovian delays [24,26]. In this paper, we focus on an extension with generally-distributed (continuous) stochastic delays. Stochastic delays are a generalization of timed delays, as their duration is obtained by sampling from some continuous probability distribution. We note that even though Markovian phase-type distributions [35] can be employed to approximate many general distributions, for the most part this approach leads to large Markov processes and it is not compositional. Moreover, important distributions, like heavy-tail, uniform, normal, and deterministic delays cannot be satisfactorily approximated in most cases. The use of general distributions is also prompted by the need to mix timed (deterministic) and stochastic delays, as the former model timeouts, which are often employed in modeling high-tech systems in order to raise exception, prevent failures, or validate user input, whereas the latter are needed to model uncertainties in arrival and processing times. Unfortunately, such combinations cannot be directly fitted in any of the separate frameworks that deal with real or Markovian time.

The main issue when dealing with generally-distributed delays is the problem of compositionality, which arises due to the fact that the generally-distributed delays are not memoryless (unless they are exponentially-distributed) [23], i.e., the distribution of the remainder of the stochastic delay changes as time progresses. To this end, we adapt the approach of [16,11] to a supervisory control theory setting, whereas the stochastic delays are represented by means of stochastic clocks. The events can be guarded by sets of clocks, which need to expire before the event becomes enabled.

We provide for start-termination semantics, introduced in [9] for general distributions, which allows for an interleaving (compositional) semantics of the parallel composition. Let P and Q be two processes, guarded by the clocks c and d, informally denoted by $c : P$ and $d : Q$, such that the clocks are reset by c^+ and d^+ and expire on c^- and d^-, respectively. Intuitively, we can then expand the parallel composition $P \parallel Q$ of P and Q and represent it as:

$$c \colon P \parallel d \colon Q = c^+.c^-.P \parallel d^+.d^-.Q = \{c^+, d^+\}.(c^-.P \parallel d^-.Q),$$

where the events of setting (c^+, d^+) and expiration (c^-, d^-) of the clock guards are interleaved. We note that this approach differs from the probabilistic pre-selection policy for generalized semi-Markov processes of [21], which is not compositional in its original form, for suitable extensions see [9].

The proposed start-termination approach is, however, in accordance with timed [4] and Markovian semantics [23], where a race condition is imposed and the timed and stochastic delays, respectively. The induced race is won by the delay with the minimal sample as it expires first. Unlike the standard Markovian setting, which relies on the memoryless property of the exponential distribution, in the setting with general distributions, we have to deal with the additional complication of the residual samples of the stochastic clocks that do not expire.

1.2 Motivation and Contributions

The need and potential of supervisory control for generally-distributed discrete-event systems has been recognized early [28], but little exists beyond this preliminary investigation. We can distinguish between several approaches that deal with Markovian delays, which is among the closest related work. Early approaches extend performance evaluation with control actions that can choose between multiple future Markovian processes, leading to the development of Markov decision processes [23]. The control problem there is to derive schedulers of the control actions in order to satisfy some performance requirements, typically executed by employing dynamic programming techniques [15]. Novel approaches employ temporal logic specifications of the performance properties and apply extensions of stochastic model checking algorithms [5,12] or stochastic games [14]. In the supervisory control community, an orthogonal approach is generally adopted, where existing language-based models are extended with Markovian delays [19,26,36]. These approaches require redefinition of the performance metrics in order to fit into the trace-based semantics.

We note that the roles of the supervisory control is to ensure safety of the supervised system, whereas the role of the performance analysis is to determine or validate the performance of the system. All of the above techniques attempt to do this simultaneously or partially ignore one component. Recent approaches [33,30] propose to decouple the ascertainment of safety properties from the performance evaluation of the system. The work of [33] relies on the memoryless property of the exponential delays in order to syntactically manipulate them without ruining compositionality of Interactive Markov chains [22], which orthogonally extend labeled transition systems with exponential delays. A more general approach is adopted in [30], where discrete-time probabilistic (Markovian) delays are abstracted from, enabling synthesis of pure discrete-event models using standard synthesis tools [2]. The resulting model of the supervised system is thereafter analyzed as a discrete-time Markov chain using probabilistic model checking [25].

We find this work to be an appropriate basis to handle a more general setting and, in this paper, we extend all of our previous work that depends on untimed models, purely timed models, or models comprising memoryless distributions to (continuous) generally-distributed delays.

To synthesize supervisory controllers for generally-distributed discrete-event systems, we propose to first abstract from the stochastic behavior and to synthesize a supervisor for the resulting nondeterministic discrete-event system. We show that such a supervisor is also viable for the stochastic model of the system, as the discrete-event supervisor does not make a decision based on passage of time, but based on the history of observed events. To be able to support unrestricted nondeterminism and to provide for suitable abstractions from the stochastic behavior, we rely on a process-theoretic approach to supervisory control theory [3]. This approach advocates the use of the behavioral preorder partial bisimulation, which is employed to characterize the notion of controllability, which states when some process can be considered as a model of a supervisory controller for a given unsupervised system. The notion is employed to provide a refinement relation between the original and the supervised system. The latter is a restriction of the former, where the restriction is implemented by the use of a supervisor under several structural assumptions of supervisory control [37,13], specified and discussed below in section 3. We provide for an appropriate extension of the behavioral preorder for the setting with generally-distributed stochastic delays and make a proposal for a synthesis-centric model-based systems engineering framework.

The remainder of this paper is structured as follows. Section 2 introduces an extension of nondeterministic finite automata with generally-distributed stochastic delays and defines a suitable notion of synchronous parallel composition. In Section 3 we discuss the extension of partial bisimulation and its application in supervisory control theory of generally-distributed discrete-event systems. Thereafter, we abstract from the stochastic behavior and show that the resulting supervisory controllers are viable for control requirements that restrict the discrete-event behavior of the system.

2   Stochastic Nondeterministic Finite Automata

We introduce the notion of stochastic (nondeterministic) finite automata that can model generally-distributed discrete-event systems with unrestricted nondeterminism. These automata combine several approaches from prominent stochastic process algebras with generally-distributed delays, like GSMPA [10], SPADES [17], IGSMP [9], NMSPA [29], and MODEST [7], and they are geared towards supervisory control theory.

With respect to the sampling of the stochastic clocks we can distinguish between two execution policies: A race condition [17,29,7], which enables the action transitions guarded by the clocks that expire first, and (2) pre-selection policy [10,9], which preselects the clocks by making a probabilistic choice. The former is the policy that conforms to timed [4] and Markovian semantics [23], whereas the latter is the execution policy of generalized semi-Markov process-es [21]. A combination of these execution policies is applied for generalized stochastic Petri nets, which comprise exponential delays and immediate proba-bilistic choices and where multiple transitions can be enabled and taken at the same time [1]. In this paper, we opt for the race condition policy as we intend to employ the generally-distributed delays to model both deterministic timed and stochastic delays [32].

We implement the start-termination semantics [9] by employing resetting of clocks and their expiration in the vein of [16], where transition guards depend on the latter in order to implement the race condition. As we can no longer rely on the memoryless property, we need a mechanism for keeping track of the clock samples as the residual sample and distribution of the stochastic clocks depend on the delay since the last clock reset. We decide to keep track of residual clock lifetimes as we are dealing with delayable events that depend on the expiration of the clocks that guard them.

2.1 Syntax

By E we denote the set of events that model the activities of the system. By G we denote the set of generally-distributed stochastic clocks, where for each clock $c \in \mathsf{G}$, by F_c we denote its continuous probability distribution function with a positive real support, i.e., the probability $P(c \leq t)$ for some $t \in \mathbb{R}$. We note that we require that the support of the distribution is in the positive reals since we are dealing with clocks that denote duration of time. By $t \in F_c$ we denote that $t \in \mathbb{R}_{>0}$ is a sample from the distribution F_c, with cumulative probability $F_c(t)$. By $\Sigma = \mathbb{R}^{\mathsf{G}}$ we denote the set of residual sample functions $\sigma \colon \mathsf{G} \to \mathbb{R}$. We note that the residual samples can become negative when the sample expires, but the guard needs to wait for another sample with a longer duration if the guard comprises multiple clocks. Initially, every sample is take from the respective clock distribution.

Definition 1. *A stochastic (nondeterministic) finite automaton A as a tuple $A = (S, E, C, \longrightarrow, \gamma, \rho, (s_0, \sigma_0))$, where S denotes a finite set of states; $E \subseteq \mathsf{E}$ denotes a finite set of events; $C \subseteq \mathsf{G}$ denotes a finite set of clocks that guard the transitions of the automaton; $\longrightarrow \in S \times E \times S$ is a transition relation that is labeled by the events of E; $\gamma \colon \longrightarrow \to 2^C$ is a clock guard function that specifies the guards of the transitions; $\rho \colon 2^S \to C$ is the clock reset function; and $(s_0, \sigma_0) \in S \times \Sigma$ is the initial state.*

We employ infix notation and write $s \xrightarrow{e} s'$ for $(s, e, s') \in \longrightarrow$. If the set of clocks of a stochastic finite automaton is empty, then it reduces to a standard nondeterministic finite automaton as employed in supervisory control theory [13]. We emphasize, however, that the behavioral relation that we employ in this paper does not rely solely on language inclusion or equality as in the original setting of [37,13] and that the branching structure of the automaton is of equal importance, as for (bi)simulation semantics [20]. If the transition relation is deterministic, i.e., for every $e \in E$ and $s, s' \in S$, it holds that if $s \overset{e}{\longmapsto} s'$ and $s \overset{e}{\longmapsto} s''$, then $s' = s''$, then stochastic finite automata specify a class of generalized semi-Markov processes, where the pre-selection probabilistic choice is induced by the race condition [21,23,32].

2.2 Operational Semantics

The dynamics of the stochastic finite automaton A is given by the instantiated labeled transition relation $\longrightarrow \subseteq (S \times \Sigma) \times E \times \mathbb{R}_{>0} \times (S \times \Sigma)$, where the clock reset function ρ samples the clocks from their respective distributions with a positive support. We note that initially all clocks receive a positive sample that eventually expires. By (s, σ) we denote that the automaton is residing in state $s \in S$, where the samples of the clocks are given by $\sigma \in \Sigma$.

We introduce some auxiliary notation. By $\mathrm{dom}(f)$ we denote the domain of the function f, whereas by $f|_C$ we denote the restriction of the function f to the domain $C \subseteq \mathrm{dom}(f)$, i.e., $f|_C = \{x \mapsto f(x) \mid x \in \mathrm{dom}(f) \cap C\}$. Also, we introduce the notation $f\{f_1\} \ldots \{f_n\}$, where $f \colon A \to B$ and $f_i \colon A \rightharpoonup B$ for $1 \leq i \leq n$ are partial functions with mutually disjoint domains, i.e., $\mathrm{dom}(f_i) \cap \mathrm{dom}(f_j) = \emptyset$ for $i \neq j$. For every $x \in A$, we have that $f\{f_1\} \ldots \{f_n\}(x) = f_j(x)$, if there exists some j such that $1 \leq j \leq n$ and $x \in \mathrm{dom}(f_j)$, or $f\{f_1\} \ldots \{f_n\}(x) = f(x)$, otherwise. Finally, by $\sigma - d$, we denote the function $(\sigma - d)(c) = \sigma(c) - d$ for $\sigma \in \Sigma$ and $d \in \mathbb{R}$.

Now, we capture the dynamics of (s, σ) by the operational rule (1), coupled with the probability distribution when sampling from the stochastic clocks, as given below:

$$\frac{s \overset{e}{\longmapsto} s', \ d \in \mathbb{R}_{>0}, \ \sigma(c) - d \leq 0 \text{ for all } c \in \gamma(s, e, s')}{(s, \sigma) \overset{e,d}{\longrightarrow} (s', (\sigma - d)\{\{c \mapsto d_c \mid d_c \in F_c, c \in \rho(s')\}\})}. \tag{1}$$

Rule (1) states that an instantiated labeled transition is possible after a passage of time of duration $d \in \mathbb{R}_{>0}$, provided that all samples from the clocks guarding that labeled transitions have expired. In that case, the residual samples of the remaining clocks must be updated by decrementing them for d, with the exception of the clocks that are reset in the target state $s' \in S$, identified by $\rho(s')$. The stochastic clocks that are reset in the target state s' sample from their respective distributions with cumulative probability distribution $\prod_{c \in \rho(s')} F_c(d_c)$, where $d_c \in \mathbb{R}_{>0}$ for $c \in \rho(s)$ are the fresh clocks samples. We note that in case the automaton does not comprise any stochastic clocks, then the transition relations $\longrightarrow$ and $\longmapsto$ coincide, where the (then unspecified) time duration in $\longrightarrow$ denotes the waiting time of the delayable transition.

2.3 Synchronous Parallel Composition

We define a CSP-like synchronous composition of two stochastic finite automata in the vein of [37,13] that synchronizes on transitions labeled with common events and interleaves on the other transitions. We note that, in general, the parallel composition of systems with stochastic clocks can be defined as a composition of dependent or independent systems [32,16]. The systems are considered as dependent when the clocks with the same name in two different components must admit the same samples, whereas independent systems with clocks with the same name admit different samples (with probability 1 when their distributions are continuous), but the samples are taken from the same probability distribution. Both approaches can lead to conflicting situations that can spoil the compositional semantics [32], but these conflicts can be promptly resolved by means of α-conversion, i.e., consistent renaming of conflicting clock names in one of the components [16]. For the sake of clarity and compactness of presentation, we do not dwell on this issue, and we assume that components of the unsupervised system have been correctly modeled and all potential conflicts have been resolved by employing the techniques proposed in [16,32]. Moreover, the coupling of the supervisory controller and the system cannot introduce any conflicts because the supervisory controller does not comprise stochastic behavior, so this issue is not of high importance for the setting of supervisory control.

Definition 2. *Let $A_i = (S_i, E_i, C_i, \longmapsto_i, \gamma_i, \rho_i, (s_{0i}, \sigma_{0i}))$ for $i \in \{1,2\}$ be two stochastic finite automata such that $\sigma_{01}\{\sigma_{02}\} = \sigma_{02}\{\sigma_{01}\}$. The synchronous parallel composition of A_1 and A_2 is defined by the stochastic finite automaton $A_1 \parallel A_2 = (S_1 \times S_2, E_1 \cup E_2, C_1 \cup C_2, \longmapsto, \gamma, \rho, (s_0, \sigma_0))$, where*

$$- \longmapsto \text{ is given by } (s_1, s_2) \stackrel{e}{\longmapsto} \begin{cases} (s_1', s_2), & \text{if } s_1 \stackrel{e}{\longmapsto}_1 s_1', e \in E_1 \setminus E_2 \\ (s_1, s_2'), & \text{if } s_2 \stackrel{e}{\longmapsto}_2 s_2', e \in E_2 \setminus E_1 \\ (s_1', s_2'), & \text{if } s_1 \stackrel{e}{\longmapsto}_1 s_1', s_2 \stackrel{e}{\longmapsto}_2 s_2', e \in E_1 \cap E_2, \end{cases}$$

$$- \gamma(((s_1, s_2), e, (s_1', s_2'))) = \begin{cases} \gamma(s_1, e, s_1'), & \text{if } e \in E_1 \setminus E_2 \\ \gamma(s_2, e, s_2'), & \text{if } e \in E_2 \setminus E_1 \\ \gamma(s_1, e, s_1') \cap \gamma(s_2, e, s_2'), & \text{if } e \in E_1 \cap E_2, \end{cases}$$

$$- \rho((s_1, s_2)) = \rho(s_1) \cup \rho(s_2),$$

$$- s_0 = (s_{01}, s_{02}) \text{ and } \sigma_0 = \sigma_{01}\{\sigma_{02}\} = \sigma_{02}\{\sigma_{01}\}.$$

We note that Definition 2 of the synchronous composition of stochastic finite automata is given in terms of automata and not in terms of the underlying labeled transition system, as in [34]. Moreover, it is not difficult to observe that the same synchronization can be achieved on the level of labeled transition systems by requiring that exhibited duration of the samples of the synchronizing event coincides. This can also be observed in the operational rule (1), as if $(s, \sigma) \stackrel{e,d}{\longrightarrow} (s', \sigma')$, then there always exists $d' > d$ and $s'' \in \Sigma$ such that $(s, \sigma) \stackrel{e,d'}{\longrightarrow} (s', \sigma'')$. The latter holds as an arbitrary passage of time is allowed to pass due to the delayable labeled transitions, once the corresponding transitions are enabled by successful evaluation of the transition guards that depend on expiration of clocks. Finally, we note that the proposed parallel composition is commutative and associative, which follows directly from the symmetry of the definition and the associativity of the parallel composition of nondeterministic finite automata [13].

3   Controllability

Standardly, we model the activities of the unsupervised system by means of events. Depending on the type of activities that these events model, the events are traditionally split into controllable and uncontrollable events. The former can be disabled by the supervisor to preclude potentially dangerous behavior and they typically model interaction with actuators of the system. The latter cannot be disabled by the supervisor and they usually model user interaction or sensory information. Thus, we split the set of events E to sets of controllable events W and uncontrollable events U, such that $E = W \cup U$ and $W \cap U = \emptyset$.

3.1   Plant, Supervisor, and Supervised Plant

The plant is typically given by a set of concurrently running components. For the purpose of the discussion in this section and without loss of generality, we can assume that the composition of the plant components is modeled by stochastic finite automaton $P = (S_P, E_P, C_P, \longmapsto_P, \gamma_P, \rho_P, (s_{0P}, \sigma_{0P}))$, which defines its complete behavior. We note that we employ this behavior to define the needed notions, whereas some synthesis techniques employ modularity in the plant to increase computation efficiency [13].

Unlike the plant, which may comprise stochastic behavior, the supervisor should be given as a deterministic pure discrete-event process, i.e., a deterministic finite automaton [18,13,3]. The deterministic nature of the supervisor is also insinuated by the role of the supervisory controller that sends unambiguous control signals to the system under control based on the observed history of activities [37]. As a consequence, the event set of the supervisor is included in the event set of the plant, which is enforced by the proposed refinement relation. Furthermore, the supervisor comprises no stochastic behavior, implying that its transitions are not guarded by stochastic clocks. This leads to the following form of a supervisor $S = (S_S, E_S, \emptyset, \longmapsto_S, \emptyset, \emptyset, (s_{0S}, \emptyset))$. We note that if the supervisor is not monolithic, e.g., supervisors for distributed or hierarchical supervision [13], then it comprises multiple deterministic discrete-event components, with the same form as S, which ultimately synchronize to form the complete supervisor behavior, again with the same form as S.

The coupling of the plant and the supervisor is given by the parallel composition $P \parallel S$. We note that this parallel composition is always well-defined as the supervisor does not comprise any stochastic behavior. It makes observations with respect to the discrete-event plant behavior, typically relying on sensory information. Based upon the observed history of events, it makes a decision on which events are allowed to be carried out safely.

3.2   Partial Bisimulation

To capture that the uncontrollable events in the reachable states of the plant cannot be disabled by the supervisor, we employ the behavioral relation termed partial bisimulation as a refinement between the original plant P and the supervised plant $P \parallel S$. This relation was originally introduced in [38] to capture the notion of controllability for languages formed by deterministic finite automata in a coalgebraic setting. It was lifted to a process theory for supervisory control of nondeterministic discrete-event systems in [3]. Here, we extend this notion for stochastic finite automata. Intuitively, partial bisimulation states that the controllable events in the supervised plant should be simulated (in the sense of [20]) in the original plant, implying that they existed in the first place and that they have not been artificially introduced by the supervisor. The uncontrollable events, however, must be bisimulated (again in the sense of [20]) meaning that they have not been disabled by the supervisor, nor that additional events have been introduced. Thus, this definition of controllability preserves the branching behavior of the system up to (bi)simulation.

The relation is parameterized by a so-called bisimulation event set $B \subseteq \mathsf{E}$. The main idea is that the bisimulation event set plays the role of the uncontrollable events that must always be enabled both in the original and the supervised plant for all reachable states. We note that partial bisimulation sits on the top of the spectrum as the finest preorder relation suitable to capture controllability of nondeterministic systems [3]. For deterministic systems, controllability defined by means of partial bisimulation reduces to the standard notion of language-based controllability of [37,13]. The stochastic clocks can be treated modulo α-conversion, i.e., renaming of clock names in different components with the same distribution, along the lines of [32,16]. We note, however, that the supervisor does not comprise any clocks, so we can directly relate the stochastic finite automata that represent the original and the supervised plant, without having to instantiate the underlying labeled transition systems. This provides for a succinct and compact characterization of a supervisor.

Definition 3. *Let $A_i = (S_i, E_i, C_i, \longmapsto_i, \gamma_i, \rho_i, (s_{0i}, \sigma_{0i}))$ for $i \in \{1, 2\}$ be two stochastic finite automata. A relation $R \subseteq S_1 \times S_2$ is said to be a stochastic partial bisimulation with respect to a bisimulation action set $B \subseteq E_2$, if for all $(s_1, s_2) \in R$, it holds that:*

1. *if $s_1 \overset{e}{\longmapsto} s_1'$ for some $e \in E_1$ and $s_1' \in S_1$, then there exists $s_2' \in S_2$ such that $s_2 \overset{e}{\longmapsto} s_2'$, $\gamma(s_1, e, s_1') = \gamma(s_2, e, s_2')$, and $(s_1', s_2') \in R$;*
2. *if $s_2 \overset{b}{\longrightarrow} s_2'$ for some $b \in B$ and $s_2' \in S_2$, then there exists $s_1' \in S_1$ such that $s_1 \overset{b}{\longrightarrow} s_1'$, $\gamma(s_1, b, s_1') = \gamma(s_2, b, s_2')$, and $(s_1', s_2') \in R$; and*
3. *$\rho(s_1) = \rho(s_2)$.*

If R is a stochastic partial bisimulation relation such that $(s_{01}, s_{02}) \in R$ and $\sigma_{01}|_{(C_1 \cap C_2)} = \sigma_{02}|_{(C_1 \cap C_2)}$, then A_1 is partially bisimilar to A_2 with respect to B, and we write $A_1 \leq_B A_2$. If $A_2 \leq_B A_1$ holds as well, we write $A_1 =_B A_2$.

We note that due to condition 1), it must hold that $E_1 \subseteq E_2$, whereas due to condition 2) it holds that $B \subseteq E_1$. It is not difficult to show that stochastic partial bisimilarity is a preorder relation as partial bisimulation is a preorder relation [3] and the stochastic clocks are directly preserved. Moreover, it is shown that partial bisimilarity is the greatest partial bisimulation preorder [38] and we obtain the same result due to preservation of the stochastic clocks. We note that if $B = \mathsf{E}$, then stochastic partial bisimulation equivalence $=_\mathsf{E}$ reduces to the bisimulation of [16,32], where no α-conversion between clocks with the same distribution is allowed. For exponential distributions $=_\mathsf{E}$, reduces to strong Markovian bisimulation [22]. Furthermore, we note that when the finite automata comprise no stochastic clocks, then stochastic partial bisimulation preorder and equivalence reduce to partial bisimulation preorder and equivalence, respectively [3]. In that case, partial bisimulation preorder and equivalence further reduce to (strong) bisimulation equivalence [20], if $B = \mathsf{E}$, and strong simulation preorder and equivalence, respectively, if $B = \emptyset$.

3.3   A Process-Theoretic Approach

Now, we can express the notion of a supervisor from above by requiring that the supervised plant is partially bisimulated by the original plant with respect to the uncontrollable events, i.e., we require that

$$P \parallel S \leq_U P \tag{2}$$

where $U = E_P \cap \mathsf{U}$. If P is a deterministic non-stochastic discrete-event system, then it can be straightforwardly shown, cf. [3], that (2) reduces to standard language controllability of [37,13].

In addition to equation (2), the supervised plant must satisfy the control requirements, i.e., its behavior must be within the allowed behavior. Here, we separate the concerns of controllability and optimality, i.e., first we treat controllability and after synthesizing a supervisor, we aim to choose the most optimal supervisor by scheduling controllable events, e.g., by employing dynamic programming techniques from control theory for Markov decision processes or discrete-event simulation [21].

To be able to relate the discrete-event control requirements and the stochastic supervised plant, we need to abstract from the stochastic behavior in the latter. For this purpose, given an automaton $A = (S, E, C, \longrightarrow, \gamma, \rho, (s_0, \sigma_0))$, we define the corresponding time-abstracted automaton $\overline{A}$ as $\overline{A} = (S, E, \emptyset, \longrightarrow, \emptyset, \emptyset, (s_0, \emptyset))$. It is straightforwardly observed that $\overline{\overline{A}} = \overline{A}$ and also for every non-stochastic finite automaton N it holds that $\overline{N} = N$. The latter directly implies that for the supervisor it holds that $\overline{S} = S$. Intuitively, the time abstraction replaces the probabilistic choices induced by the sampling of the stochastic clocks, with nondeterministic choices of the enabled labeled transitions, removing the transition guards and always enabling the labeled transitions, which eliminates all dependencies of the observed passage of time and, thus, effectively abstracting from it.

Since we desire that the control requirements only concern the functional aspects of the stochastic plant, they are specified as a non-stochastic finite automaton $R = (S_R, E_R, \emptyset, \longrightarrow_R, \emptyset, \emptyset, (s_{0R}, \emptyset))$ that defines the allowed behavior of the plant, implying that $\overline{R} = R$. Again, the control requirements can be given as a set of parallel synchronizing processes, ultimately resulting in the non-stochastic finite automaton R. Moreover, we have that E_R is not necessarily related to E_P as event-based control requirements are typically specified separately from the plant model, but for reasonable sets of control requirements it would hold that $E_R \subseteq E_P$. To specify that the behavior of the time-abstracted supervised plant, given by $\overline{P \parallel S}$, is allowed by the control requirements, we employ the equivalent of language inclusion for branching processes, i.e., simulation preorder [20]. Consequently, in addition to equation (2), we require that

$$\overline{P \parallel S} \leq_\emptyset R. \tag{3}$$

Equation (3) states that the traces of the supervised plant are restricted by the allowed traces of the control requirements, while preserving the branching structure of the supervised plant. Together with equation (2), these conditions characterize the notion of a supervisor for stochastic finite automata with respect to a set of (functional) event-based control requirements.

4   Towards Supervisor Synthesis

In controllability condition expressed by equation (3), the relation between the plant, the supervisor, and the control requirements is given in terms of time abstracted processes. The following lemma states the compositionality of the time abstraction.

Lemma 1. *Let $A_i = (S_i, E_i, C_i, \longmapsto_i, \gamma_i, \rho_i, (s_{0i}, \sigma_{0i}))$ for $i \in \{1, 2\}$ be stochastic finite automata. If $\sigma_{01}|_{(C_1 \cap C_2)} = \sigma_{02}|_{(C_1 \cap C_2)}$, then $\overline{A_1 \parallel A_2} = \overline{A_1} \parallel \overline{A_2}$.*

Proof. By definition $\overline{A_i} = (S_i, E_i, \emptyset, \longmapsto_i, \emptyset, \emptyset, (s_{0i}, \emptyset))$ for $i \in \{1, 2\}$. Then $\overline{A_1} \parallel \overline{A_2} = (S_1 \times S_2, E_1 \cup E_2, \longmapsto, \emptyset, \emptyset, ((s_{01}, s_{02}), \emptyset))$ by Definition 2. Due to the assumption that $\sigma_{01}|_{(C_1 \cap C_2)} = \sigma_{02}|_{(C_1 \cap C_2)}$, we have that $A_1 \parallel A_2$ is well-defined and we obtain $A_1 \parallel A_2 = (S_1 \times S_2, E_1 \cup E_2, C_1 \cup C_2, \longmapsto, \gamma, \rho, ((s_{01}, s_{02}), \sigma_{01}\{\sigma_{02}\}))$, where $\longmapsto$ is given by Definition 2. Now, $\overline{A_1 \parallel A_2} = (S_1 \times S_2, E_1 \cup E_2, \longmapsto, \emptyset, \emptyset, ((s_{01}, s_{02}), \emptyset))$ coinciding with $\overline{A_1} \parallel \overline{A_2}$.

Lemma 1 enables us to rewrite equation (3) as

$$\overline{P} \parallel S \leq_\emptyset R, \tag{4}$$

by employing Lemma 1 to derive $\overline{P \parallel S} = \overline{P} \parallel \overline{S}$ and having in mind that $\overline{S} = S$. This insinuates that the supervisor S can be synthesized based on the time-abstracted plant, instead of the original stochastic model.

4.1   Time-Abstracted Supervisors

It remains to be shown that every supervisor for the original plant P is a supervisor for the time-abstracted plant $\overline{P}$, and vice versa.

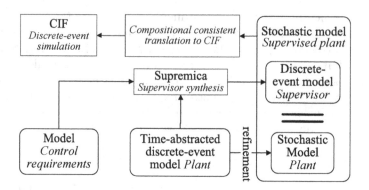

Fig. 1. Core of the model-based systems engineering framework

Theorem 1. *Let a stochastic plant P be given by $P = (S_P, E_P, C_P, \longmapsto_P, \gamma_P,$ $\rho_P, (s_{0P}, \sigma_{0P}))$ and $S = (S_S, E_S, \emptyset, \longmapsto_S, \emptyset, \emptyset, (s_{0S}, \emptyset))$ be a deterministic supervisor. Then, we have that $P \parallel S \leq_U P$ if and only if $\overline{P \parallel S} \leq_U \overline{P}$ for $U = \mathsf{U} \cap E_P$.*

Proof. By employing Lemma 1, we have that $\overline{P \parallel S} = \overline{P} \parallel \overline{S} = \overline{P} \parallel S$. As $P \parallel S \leq_U P$ holds, there exists a stochastic partial bisimulation Q, such that $((s_{0P}, s_{0S}), s_{0P}) \in Q$. We show that Q is a (non)stochastic partial bisimulation that relates $\overline{P} \parallel S$ and $\overline{P}$. We note that the states and transitions of P and $\overline{P}$ are the same, which makes Q a well-defined relation between the states of $\overline{P}$ and S. Now, suppose that $((p, s), q) \in Q$, where $p, q \in S_P$ and $s \in S_S$. Let us suppose that $(p, s) \overset{e}{\longmapsto} (p', s')$ for some $e \in \mathsf{E}$, $p' \in E_P$, and $s' \in E_S$. Then by condition 1) for stochastic partial bisimulation, we have that $q \longmapsto_P q'$ for some $q' \in S_P$ such that $\gamma(((p, s), e, (p', s'))) = \gamma((q, e, q'))$ and $((p', s'), q') \in Q$. As $\overline{P}$ and S are non-stochastic processes, implying that the γ functions are empty, and the definition of the labeled transition of the parallel composition coincides, we immediately obtain that condition 1) is satisfied for $\overline{P} \parallel S$ and $\overline{P}$. Analogously, we can show that condition 2) is satisfied as well. Condition 3) that relates the reset functions is trivially satisfied as the reset functions are also empty. For the other direction, the arguments are symmetrical, as we employ the same stochastic partial bisimulation relation Q to relate the processes at hand, which completes the proof.

Theorem 1 enables us to decouple the supervisory controller synthesis procedure from the analysis or simulation of the underlying performance model, i.e., the induced generalized semi-Markov process. A direct consequence is that we can employ standard synthesis tools, like TCT [37] or Supremica [2] for supervisory controller synthesis, effectively ensuring safety of the control design.

4.2   A Model-Based Systems Engineering Framework

We cast the proposal for supervisory control of generally-distributed discrete-event systems in a model-based systems engineering framework, which core is depicted in Fig. 1. The proposed framework aims to extend previous frameworks of [40,31] with stochastic modeling of the supervised plant. We refer to [40,31] for details regarding the complete modeling process and formalization of the control requirements. Here, we assume that the formalization of the control requirements and the modeling and time abstraction of the stochastic plant are successfully completed, by employing the results of Theorem 1.

We employ the synthesis tool Supremica [2] to synthesize a supervisory controller based on the control requirements and time-abstracted plant model. By coupling the synthesized supervisor and the stochastic plant we obtain the stochastic supervised plant. We interface the synthesis tool Supremica with the simulation environment of the modeling language CIF [6], which is capable of modeling hybrid systems with stochastic clocks. We employ only a part of the CIF language, most importantly: synchronizing actions, which behavior in the parallel composition is CSP-like as given by Definition 2, stochastic clocks, which are reset and expire in a compatible manner with respect to Definition 1, and deterministic trajectories, which are extensions of timed delays to represent hybrid time, but we employ them only to keep track of passage of time as specified by operational rule (1).

The framework depicted in Fig. 1 effectively decouples the synthesis of the supervisor and the analysis of the stochastic behavior of the supervised system. Thus, we are able to employ effective specialized tool for the corresponding tasks, relying on the results of Theorem 1.

5   Concluding Remarks

We developed a process-theoretic approach towards supervisory control theory for generally-distributed discrete-event systems. The proposed theory supports unrestricted nondeterminism and it is based on a stochastic extension of the behavioral preorder partial bisimulation with general distributions. We decoupled the treatment of controllability from the analysis of the underlying performance model by abstracting from the stochastic behavior in the original system. The result enables synthesis of supervisors for the time-abstracted variant of the system using standard synthesis tools, effectively ensuring safe functioning of the supervised system. Subsequently, we employ the synthesized supervisor to derive a model of the supervised system, which quantitative behavior can be analyzed, e.g., by employing discrete-event simulation. We casted the modeling processes in a model-based systems engineering framework that employs state-of-the-art tools for the specialized tasks. We employ Supremica to synthesize a supervisor based on the time-abstracted model and the simulation environment of the stochastic hybrid language CIF to provide for subsequent quantitative analysis. As future work, we schedule extension of several industrial case studies with generally-distributed delays, which were previously modeled either by timed or Markovian discrete-event models. The introduction of general distribution should provide for a more precise modeling of timeouts and general stochastic arrival and processing times.

References

1. Ajmone Marsan, M., Balbo, G., Conte, G., Donatelli, S., Franceschinis, G.: Modelling with Generalized Stochastic Petri Nets. Wiley (1995)
2. Akesson, K., Fabian, M., Flordal, H., Malik, R.: Supremica - an integrated environment for verification, synthesis and simulation of discrete event systems. In: Proceedings of WODES 2006, pp. 384–385. IEEE (2006)
3. Baeten, J.C.M., van Beek, D.A., Luttik, B., Markovski, J., Rooda, J.E.: A process-theoretic approach to supervisory control theory. In: Proceedings of ACC 2011. IEEE (2011), http://se.wtb.tue.nl
4. Baeten, J.C.M., Middelburg, C.A.: Process Algebra with Timing. Springer (2002)
5. Baier, C., Größer, M., Leucker, M., Bollig, B., Ciesinski, F.: Controller synthesis for probabilistic systems. In: Proceedings of IFIP TCS 2004, pp. 493–506. Kluwer (2004)
6. van Beek, D.A., Reniers, M.A., Schiffelers, R.R.H., Rooda, J.E.: Foundations of a compositional interchange format for hybrid systems. In: Bemporad, A., Bicchi, A., Buttazzo, G. (eds.) HSCC 2007. LNCS, vol. 4416, pp. 587–600. Springer, Heidelberg (2007)
7. Bohnenkamp, H.C., D'Argenio, P.R., Hermanns, H., Katoen, J.-P.: MODEST: A compositional modeling formalism for hard and softly timed systems. IEEE Transactions on Software Engineering 32, 812–830 (2006)
8. Brandin, B., Wonham, W.: Supervisory control of timed discrete-event systems. IEEE Transactions on Automatic Control 39(2), 329–342 (1994)
9. Bravetti, M.: Specification and Analysis of Stochastic Real-time Systems. Ph.D. thesis, Università di Bologna (2002)
10. Bravetti, M., Bernardo, M., Gorrieri, R.: From EMPA to GSMPA: Allowing for general distributions. In: Proceedings of PAPM 1997, pp. 17–33. Enschede (1997)
11. Bravetti, M., D'Argenio, P.R.: Tutte le algebre insieme: Concepts, discussions and relations of stochastic process algebras with general distributions. In: Baier, C., Haverkort, B.R., Hermanns, H., Katoen, J.-P., Siegle, M. (eds.) Validation of Stochastic Systems. LNCS, vol. 2925, pp. 44–88. Springer, Heidelberg (2004)
12. Brázdil, T., Forejt, V.: Strategy synthesis for Markov decision processes and branching-time logics. In: Caires, L., Vasconcelos, V.T. (eds.) CONCUR 2007. LNCS, vol. 4703, pp. 428–444. Springer, Heidelberg (2007)
13. Cassandras, C., Lafortune, S.: Introduction to discrete event systems. Kluwer Academic Publishers (2004)
14. Chatterjee, K., Jurdziński, M., Henzinger, T.A.: Simple stochastic parity games. In: Baaz, M., Makowsky, J.A. (eds.) CSL 2003. LNCS, vol. 2803, pp. 100–113. Springer, Heidelberg (2003)
15. Chen, T., Han, T., Lu, J.: On the markovian randomized strategy of controller for markov decision processes. In: Wang, L., Jiao, L., Shi, G., Li, X., Liu, J. (eds.) FSKD 2006. LNCS (LNAI), vol. 4223, pp. 149–158. Springer, Heidelberg (2006)
16. D'Argenio, P.R., Katoen, J.-P.: A theory of stochastic systems, part I: Stochastic automata. Information and Computation 203(1), 1–38 (2005)
17. D'Argenio, P.R., Katoen, J.-P.: A theory of stochastic systems, part II: Process algebra. Information and Computation 203(1), 39–74 (2005)
18. Fabian, M., Lennartson, B.: On non-deterministic supervisory control. Proceedings of the 35th IEEE Decision and Control 2, 2213–2218 (1996)
19. Garg, V.K., Kumar, R., Marcus, S.I.: A probabilistic language formalism for stochastic discrete-event systems. IEEE Transactions on Automatic Control 44(2), 280–293 (1999)

20. Glabbeek, R.J.V.: The linear time–branching time spectrum I. In: Handbook of Process Algebra, pp. 3–99 (2001)
21. Glynn, P.W.: A GSMP formalism for discrete event systems. Proceedings of the IEEE 77(1), 14–23 (1989)
22. Hermanns, H. (ed.): Interactive Markov Chains. LNCS, vol. 2428. Springer, Heidelberg (2002)
23. Howard, R.A.: Dynamic Probabilistic Systems, vols. 1 & 2. John F. Wiley & Sons (1971)
24. Kumar, R., Garg, V.K.: Control of stochastic discrete event systems: Synthesis. In: Proceedings of CDC 1998, vol. 3, pp. 3299–3304. IEEE (1998)
25. Kwiatkowska, M., Norman, G., Parker, D.: PRISM: probabilistic model checking for performance and reliability analysis. SIGMETRICS Performance Evaluation Review 36(4), 40–45 (2009)
26. Kwong, R.H., Zhu, L.: Performance analysis and control of stochastic discrete event systems. In: Francis, B.A., Tannenbaum, A.R. (eds.) Feedback Control, Nonlinear Systems, and Complexity. LNCIS, vol. 202, pp. 114–130. Springer, Heidelberg (1995)
27. Leveson, N.G.: The challenge of building process-control software. IEEE Software 7(6), 55–62 (1990)
28. Lin, F., Yao, D.: Generalized semi-Markov process: a view through supervisory control. In: Proceedings of CDC 1998, pp. 1075–1076. IEEE (1989)
29. López, N., Núñez, M.: NMSPA: A non-Markovian model for stochastic processes. In: Proceedings of ICDS 2000, pp. 33–40. IEEE (2000)
30. Markovski, J.: Towards optimal supervisory control of discrete-time stochastic discrete-event processes with data. In: Proceedings ACSD 2013. IEEE (to appear, 2013)
31. Markovski, J., van Beek, D.A., Theunissen, R.J.M., Jacobs, K.G.M., Rooda, J.E.: A state-based framework for supervisory control synthesis and verification. In: Proceedings of CDC 2010. IEEE (2010) (to appear)
32. Markovski, J., D'Argenio, P.R., Baeten, J.C.M., Vink, E.P.: Reconciling real and stochastic time: the need for probabilistic refinement. Formal Aspects of Computing 24, 497–518 (2012)
33. Markovski, J., Reniers, M.: Verifying performance of supervised plants. In: Proceedings of ACSD 2012, pp. 52–61. IEEE (2012)
34. Miremadi, S., Akesson, K., Lennartson, B.: Extraction and representation of a supervisor using guards in extended finite automata. In: Proceedings of WODES 2008, pp. 193–199. IEEE (2008)
35. Neuts, M.F.: Matrix-geometric solutions in stochastic models, an algorithmic approach. John Hopkins University Press (1981)
36. Pantelic, V., Postma, S.M., Lawford, M.: Probabilistic supervisory control of probabilistic discrete event systems. IEEE Transactions on Automatic Control 54(8), 2013–2018 (2009)
37. Ramadge, P.J., Wonham, W.M.: Supervisory control of a class of discrete event processes. SIAM Journal on Control and Optimization 25(1), 206–230 (1987)
38. Rutten, J.J.M.M.: Coalgebra, concurrency, and control. SEN Report R-9921, Center for Mathematics and Computer Science, Amsterdam, The Netherlands (1999)
39. Saadatpoor, A., Ma, C., Wonham, W.M.: Supervisory control of timed state tree structures, pp. 477–482. IEEE (2008)
40. Schiffelers, R.R.H., Theunissen, R.J.M., Beek, D.A.V., Rooda, J.E.: Model-based engineering of supervisory controllers using CIF. Electronic Communications of the EASST 21, 1–10 (2009)

Tackling Truncation Errors in CSL Model Checking through Bounding Semantics

Yang Zhao and Gianfranco Ciardo

Department of Computer Science and Engineering
University of California, Riverside
{zhaoy,ciardo}@cs.ucr.edu

Abstract. Model checking aims to give exact answers to queries about a model's execution but, in probabilistic model checking, ensuring exact answers might be difficult. Numerical iterative methods are heavily used in probabilistic model checking and errors caused by truncation may affect correctness. To tackle truncation errors, we investigate the bounding semantics of *continuous stochastic logic* for Markov chains. We first focus on analyzing truncation errors for model-checking the time-bounded or unbounded Until operator and propose new algorithms to generate lower and upper bounds. Then, we study the bounding semantics for a subset of nested CSL formulas. We demonstrate result on two models.

1 Introduction

To support dependability and performance analysis, model checking [3] has been extended to address quantitative properties of probabilistic models such as continuous-time Markov chains (CTMCs). While traditional model checking studies the existence of counterexamples to given properties and provides a "true" or "false" answer, probabilistic model checking needs to compute real-valued probabilities of the temporal behaviors being investigated.

Continuous Stochastic Logic (CSL) [1] with semantics similar to Computational Tree Logic (CTL) [7], is the most widely discussed logic in probabilistic model checking. Unlike CTL, where the result is obtained by exploring the state space, the set of states corresponding to a CSL formula is generated by comparing real values obtained from a numerical analysis of a CTMC against some given threshold. Errors and approximations in this analysis are inevitable, and may propagate to the resulting set of states. For example, if we seek the set of states with probability ≤ 0.5 (with respect to some condition) and the computed probability on a state is between 0.49 and 0.51, it is not clear whether this state belongs to the result. No matter how high a precision we request in the numerical analysis, such cases can never be ruled out. Thus, the correctness of CSL results may not be guaranteed due to numerical errors, especially under resource constraints (runtime, memory). In other words, the exact semantics of CSL, defined as a resulting set of states, is not practically achievable even if CSL has been shown to be decidable in principle (using rational number representations) [1].

M.S. Balsamo, W.J. Knottenbelt, and A. Marin (Eds.): EPEW 2013, LNCS 8168, pp. 58–73, 2013.
© Springer-Verlag Berlin Heidelberg 2013

Worse yet, due to the inability to compute an exact result for a given CSL formula, nested CSL formulas are even more difficult to handle in the current CSL model-checking framework. While a nested CTL formula can be evaluated by simply following its syntax tree from leaf nodes to the root, the corresponding approach for nested CSL formulas can only be proposed after we are able to handle errors in CSL model checking.

We propose a solution to the above problems by defining the result of a CSL formula using bounds (sets). The lower bound contains states that "must" satisfy the threshold on the probability, while the upper bound also includes states that "might" satisfy the threshold, based on the given precision of the numerical analysis. We focus on the error introduced in the truncation of the iteration and modify the CSL model checking algorithm to provide and support our new CSL semantics with bounds. The proposed algorithms handle nested CSL formulas by taking into account uncertainty in the subformulas.

Using lower and upper bounds to handle model checking uncertainty is not a new idea. In the probabilistic setting, [8] and [11] discuss the application of three-value logic, which reflects a similar idea as our lower and upper bounds. The main difference between our paper and these previous works is the source of uncertainty. In [8] and [11], uncertainty comes from abstracting models, while in this paper we discuss the inherent uncertainty arising from the numerical analysis employed in CSL model checking itself. The proposed bounding semantics and techniques for nested CSL formulas also apply to the problem settings in [8] and [11], where abstraction on Markov chains is carried out.

The rest of the paper is structured as follows. Section 2 reviews CTMCs, CSL, and existing algorithms. Section 3 presents new algorithms to generate bounds on the exact result. Section 4 introduces an approach to handle nested CSL formulas. Section 5 applies our new techniques to two nontrivial cases. Section 6 concludes the paper and points to future work.

2   Preliminaries and Notation

A CTMC is a Markov process defined on a discrete state space.

Definition 1. A (labeled) CTMC $\mathcal{M}$ is a tuple $(\mathcal{S}, \mathbf{R}, \mathit{Init}, \mathcal{A}, L)$ where:

- $\mathcal{S}$ is the *state space* (a set of states) which we assume finite. In the following, $\mathcal{X}, \mathcal{Y} \subseteq \mathcal{S}$ denote sets of states and $\mathbf{s}, \mathbf{i}, \mathbf{j} \in \mathcal{S}$ denote states.
- $\mathbf{R} : \mathcal{S} \times \mathcal{S} \to \mathbb{R}^{\geq 0}$ is the *transition rate matrix*, where $\forall \mathbf{i}, R_{\mathbf{i},\mathbf{i}} = 0$. If state $\mathbf{i}$ is absorbing, the *exit* rate $E(\mathbf{i}) = \sum_{\mathbf{j} \in \mathcal{S}} R_{\mathbf{i},\mathbf{j}}$ is 0, the CTMC cannot leave it. Otherwise, $\mathcal{M}$ remains in $\mathbf{i}$ for a duration that is exponentially distributed with rate $E(\mathbf{i})$, then it moves to state $\mathbf{j}$ with probability $R_{\mathbf{i},\mathbf{j}}/E(\mathbf{i})$.
- $\mathit{Init} : \mathcal{S} \to [0, 1]$ is the *initial distribution*. $\mathit{Init}(\mathbf{i})$ is the probability that $\mathcal{M}$ is state $\mathbf{i}$ at time 0, thus $\sum_{\mathbf{i} \in \mathcal{S}} \mathit{Init}(\mathbf{i}) = 1$.
- $\mathcal{A}$ is a set of *atomic propositions*.
- $L : \mathcal{S} \to 2^{\mathcal{A}}$ is a *labeling*. $L(\mathbf{i})$ are the atomic propositions holding in state $\mathbf{i}$. In the following, ϕ, ψ denote propositions and we let $\mathit{Sat}(\phi) = \{\mathbf{i} \in \mathcal{S} | \phi \in L(\mathbf{i})\}$.
- An ordinary CTMC is similarly defined, without the $\mathcal{A}$ and L components.

We then define vector $\boldsymbol{\pi}(t) : \mathcal{S} \to [0,1]$ such that $\pi_{\mathbf{i}}(t)$ is the probability that $\mathcal{M}$ is in state $\mathbf{i}$ at time $t \geq 0$, thus $\sum_{\mathbf{i} \in \mathcal{S}} \pi_{\mathbf{i}}(t) = 1$. The evolution of $\mathcal{M}$ is described by the system of differential equations

$$d\boldsymbol{\pi}(t)/dt = \boldsymbol{\pi}(t)\mathbf{Q} \text{ with initial conditions } \forall \mathbf{i} \in \mathcal{S}, \pi_{\mathbf{i}}(0) = Init(\mathbf{i}), \qquad (1)$$

where the *infinitesimal generator matrix* $\mathbf{Q}$ satisfies $Q_{\mathbf{i},\mathbf{j}} = R_{\mathbf{i},\mathbf{j}}$ for $\mathbf{i} \neq \mathbf{j}$ and $Q_{\mathbf{i},\mathbf{i}} = -E(\mathbf{i})$. Since $\mathcal{S}$ is finite, there is a *steady-state vector* describing the long-term behavior of $\mathcal{M}$, $\boldsymbol{\pi}(\infty) = \lim_{t \to \infty} \boldsymbol{\pi}(t)$, which might depend on $Init$.

While $\boldsymbol{\pi}(t)$ describes the probability distribution of $\mathcal{M}$ at time t starting from a given initial distribution at time $t = 0$, model checking often requires us to "go backwards": given a "target" state $\mathbf{j}$, we need to compute vector $\boldsymbol{\nu}(\mathbf{j}, t) : \mathcal{S} \to [0,1]$, where $\nu_{\mathbf{i}}(\mathbf{j}, t)$ is the probability of reaching $\mathbf{j}$ at time t starting from state $\mathbf{i}$ at time 0, so that, if $Init(\mathbf{i}) = 1$, then $\nu_{\mathbf{i}}(\mathbf{j}, t) = \pi_{\mathbf{j}}(t)$. Note that $\boldsymbol{\nu}(\mathbf{j}, t)$ is not a probability distribution but a vector of probabilities, i.e., its elements do not sum to 1 in general. Finally, define $\boldsymbol{\nu}(\mathcal{X}, t) = \sum_{\mathbf{j} \in \mathcal{X}} \boldsymbol{\nu}(\mathbf{j}, t)$.

Instead of solving Eq. 1, we often calculate $\boldsymbol{\pi}$ or $\boldsymbol{\nu}$ using uniformization [10].

Definition 2. Given $\mathcal{M} = (\mathcal{S}, \mathbf{R}, Init)$ and a rate $q \geq max_{\mathbf{i} \in \mathcal{S}}\{E(\mathbf{i})\}$, the *uniformization* of $\mathcal{M}$ is a discrete-time Markov chain (DTMC) $\mathcal{M}_{unif} = (\mathcal{S}, \mathbf{P}, Init)$, where $P_{\mathbf{i},\mathbf{j}} = R_{\mathbf{i},\mathbf{j}}/q$ for $\mathbf{i} \neq \mathbf{j}$ and $P_{\mathbf{i},\mathbf{i}} = 1 - \sum_{\mathbf{j} \in \mathcal{S} \setminus \{\mathbf{i}\}} P_{\mathbf{i},\mathbf{j}}$.

Then, $\boldsymbol{\pi}(t) = \sum_{k=0}^{\infty} \boldsymbol{\pi}(0)\mathbf{P}^k \cdot Poisson[k]$, where $Poisson[k] = e^{-qt}(qt)^k/k!$ is the kth element of the Poisson distribution with parameter qt (in the rest of this paper, the parameter for $Poisson$ is assumed to be qt). For $\boldsymbol{\nu}(\mathcal{X}, t)$, there is instead the "backward solution" [12]: $\boldsymbol{\nu}(\mathcal{X}, t) = \sum_{k=0}^{\infty} \mathbf{P}^k \boldsymbol{\delta}^{\mathcal{X}} \cdot Poisson[k]$, where $\boldsymbol{\delta}^{\mathcal{X}} : \mathcal{S} \to \{0,1\}$ is the indicator vector satisfying $\delta_{\mathbf{i}}^{\mathcal{X}} = 1$ iff $\mathbf{i} \in \mathcal{X}$.

2.1   CSL

Continuous stochastic logic (CSL) [1] extends CTL to probability and timing aspects. It has two temporal operators, U ("until") and X ("next"), and it replaces the CTL path quantifiers E and A with probabilistic operators referring to the steady-state or transient behavior of the CTMC.

A run of $\mathcal{M}$ is an infinite timed path σ: $(\mathbf{i}_0, t_0) \to (\mathbf{i}_1, t_1) \to \cdots$, where $\mathbf{i}_k$ is the state entered at time t_k and $t_0 = 0$. Let $\sigma[k]$ be $\mathbf{i}_k$, and $\tau[k] = t_{k+1} - t_k$ be the length of the kth sojourn time, in $\sigma[k]$. The state of $\mathcal{M}$ at time t is $\sigma@t = \sigma[k]$ iff $t_k \leq t < t_{k+1}$.

In this paper, we focus on a subset of CSL. Let $p \in [0,1]$ be a probability, $\bowtie$ be one of $\{\leq, <, \geq, >\}$, and I be a time interval of the following types:

- time-bounded: $[0, t], t > 0$;
- unbounded: $[0, \infty)$, so that $\mathsf{X}^{[0,\infty)}$ and $\mathsf{U}^{[0,\infty)}$ are simply written as X and U;
- point-interval: $[t, t], t \geq 0$;
- general interval: $[t, t'], t' > t > 0$.

The syntax of this subset of CSL over the set of atomic propositions $\mathcal{A}$ is defined inductively as follows:

- Each atomic proposition $\phi \in \mathcal{A}$ is a CSL formula.
- If $\mathcal{F}_1$ and $\mathcal{F}_2$ are CSL formulas, so are the following formulas:
  - $\neg \mathcal{F}_1$, $\mathcal{F}_1 \lor \mathcal{F}_2$, and $\mathcal{F}_1 \land \mathcal{F}_2$,
  - $\mathbb{P}_{\bowtie p}(\mathsf{X}^I \mathcal{F}_1)$,
  - $\mathbb{P}_{\bowtie p}(\mathcal{F}_1 \mathsf{U}^I \mathcal{F}_2)$.

Like in CTL, CSL formulas define properties for states, and we write $\mathbf{i} \models \mathcal{F}$ if state $\mathbf{i}$ satisfies CSL formula $\mathcal{F}$. Given CSL formulas $\mathcal{F}_1$ and $\mathcal{F}_2$, $\mathsf{X}^I \mathcal{F}_2$ and $\mathcal{F}_1 \mathsf{U}^I \mathcal{F}_2$ are path formulas defining a set of paths as follows:

- $\sigma \models \mathsf{X}^I \mathcal{F}_2$ iff $\sigma[1] \models \mathcal{F}_2$ and $\tau[0] \in I$.
- $\sigma \models \mathcal{F}_1 \mathsf{U}^I \mathcal{F}_2$ iff $\exists t \in I.(\sigma@t \models \mathcal{F}_2 \land (\forall t' \in [0,t).\sigma@t' \models \mathcal{F}_1))$.

Let Φ be a path formula and $Prob(\mathbf{i}, \Phi)$ be the cumulative probability of all paths in $\{\sigma \mid \sigma[0] = \mathbf{i} \land \sigma \models \Phi\}$ (see [2, Sect. 2.3] for details about the probability of a set of paths, the next subsection only describes how to compute it). Then, $\mathbf{i} \models \mathbb{P}_{\bowtie p}(\Phi)$ iff $Prob(\mathbf{i}, \Phi) \bowtie p$. Again, we use bold letter notation $\mathbf{Prob}(\Phi)$ to denote the vector describing $Prob(\mathbf{i}, \Phi)$ for each $\mathbf{i} \in \mathcal{S}$.

A CSL formula $\mathcal{F}$ evaluates to a set of states $\{\mathbf{i} \mid \mathbf{i} \models \mathcal{F}\}$ as follows:

- $eval(\psi) = Sat(\psi)$
- $eval(\neg \mathcal{F}) = \mathcal{S} \backslash eval(\mathcal{F})$
- $eval(\mathcal{F}_1 \land \mathcal{F}_2) = eval(\mathcal{F}_1) \cap eval(\mathcal{F}_2)$
- $eval(\mathcal{F}_1 \lor \mathcal{F}_2) = eval(\mathcal{F}_1) \cup eval(\mathcal{F}_2)$
- $eval(\mathbb{P}_{\bowtie p}(\mathsf{X}^I \mathcal{F})) = \mathbb{P}_{\bowtie p}\mathbf{Prob}(\mathsf{X}^I \mathcal{F}) \triangleq \{\mathbf{i} \mid Prob(\mathbf{i}, \mathsf{X}^I \mathcal{F}) \bowtie p\}$
- $eval(\mathbb{P}_{\bowtie p}(\mathcal{F}_1 \mathsf{U}^I \mathcal{F}_2)) = \mathbb{P}_{\bowtie p}\mathbf{Prob}(\mathcal{F}_1 \mathsf{U}^I \mathcal{F}_2) \triangleq \{\mathbf{i} \mid Prob(\mathbf{i}, \mathcal{F}_1 \mathsf{U}^I \mathcal{F}_2) \bowtie p\}$

Compared with the original definition of CSL [1], we do not allow "multiple until" formulas of the form $\mathcal{F}_1 \mathsf{U}^{I_1} \mathcal{F}_2 \mathsf{U}^{I_2} \cdots \mathcal{F}_k$ and only study "binary until" formulas of the form $\mathcal{F}_1 \mathsf{U}^I \mathcal{F}_2$, like in [2]. Also, we do not consider the stationary operator $\mathbb{S}_{\bowtie p}$, nor we discuss the X^I operator (the algorithm for X^I does not result in truncation errors so that the exact solution, ignoring rounding errors, is always available). We mainly focus on the time-bounded and unbounded until operator since the other two types of interval for the until operator can be tackled using a similar technique.

2.2 Model Checking CSL

We now review model checking algorithms for the until operator. The key step is to calculate the vector $\mathbf{Prob}(\phi \mathsf{U}^I \psi)$.

Define the conversion of $\mathcal{M} = (\mathcal{S}, \mathbf{R}, Init)$ into $\mathcal{M}^{\mathcal{X}} = (\mathcal{S}, \mathbf{R}^{\mathcal{X}}, Init)$, where states in $\mathcal{X}$ are absorbing, and into the uniformized DTMC $\mathcal{M}^{\mathcal{X}}_{unif} = (\mathcal{S}, \mathbf{P}^{\mathcal{X}}, Init)$ according to the uniformizing rate q, $q > \max_{\mathbf{i} \in \mathcal{S}} E(\mathbf{i})$, as follows:

$ProbVector \ BoundedUntil(qt, StateSet \ \mathcal{Y}, StateSet \ \mathcal{Z}, float \ \varepsilon)$ is

1 Build $\mathbf{P}$ for $\mathcal{M}_{unif}^{\mathcal{S}_0 \cup \mathcal{S}_1}$ with uniformizing rate q ; $\bullet \mathcal{S}_1 = \mathcal{Z}, \mathcal{S}_0 = \mathcal{S}\backslash\mathsf{E}(\mathcal{Y}\cup\mathcal{Z})$
2 $p, L_\varepsilon, R_\varepsilon \leftarrow FoxGlynn(qt, \varepsilon)$; $\bullet$ Poisson probability, left and right bound w.r.t ε
3 $\boldsymbol{\nu} \leftarrow \mathbf{0}$; $\mathbf{b} \leftarrow \boldsymbol{\delta}^{\mathcal{Z}}$ $\bullet \delta_{\mathbf{i}}^{\mathcal{Z}} = 1$ iff $\mathbf{i} \in \mathcal{Z}$
4 for $k = 0$ to R_ε do
5   if $k \geq L_\varepsilon$ then $\boldsymbol{\nu} \leftarrow \boldsymbol{\nu} + p[k] \cdot \mathbf{b}$;
6    $\mathbf{b} \leftarrow \mathbf{P} \cdot \mathbf{b}$;
7 endfor;
8 return $\boldsymbol{\nu}$;

Fig. 1. Backward computation of the probability vector for $\mathcal{Y}\mathsf{U}^{[0,t]}\mathcal{Z}$

$$R_{\mathbf{i},\mathbf{j}}^{\mathcal{X}} = R_{\mathbf{i},\mathbf{j}} \quad \text{and} \quad P_{\mathbf{i},\mathbf{j}}^{\mathcal{X}} = R_{\mathbf{i},\mathbf{j}}/q \text{ if } \mathbf{i} \neq \mathbf{j} \text{ else } 1 - E(\mathbf{i})/q \quad \text{if } \mathbf{i} \notin \mathcal{X}$$
$$R_{\mathbf{i},\mathbf{j}}^{\mathcal{X}} = 0 \quad \text{and} \quad P_{\mathbf{i},\mathbf{j}}^{\mathcal{X}} = 0 \quad \text{if } \mathbf{i} \neq \mathbf{j} \text{ else } 0^1 \quad \text{if } \mathbf{i} \in \mathcal{X}$$

(in the following, we write $\mathbf{P}$ instead of $\mathbf{P}^{\mathcal{X}}$ when $\mathcal{X}$ is clear from the context).

We first discuss the time-bounded until and the unbounded until operators. Before numerical analysis, we partition $\mathcal{S}$ into three sets of states:

$$\mathcal{S}_1 = \{\mathbf{i} \in \mathcal{S} \mid \mathbf{i} \models \psi\} \quad \mathcal{S}_0 = \{\mathbf{i} \in \mathcal{S} \mid \mathbf{i} \nvDash \mathsf{E}\phi\mathsf{U}\psi\} \quad \mathcal{S}_? = \{\mathbf{i} \in \mathcal{S} \mid \mathbf{i} \models (\mathsf{E}\phi\mathsf{U}\psi) \setminus \mathcal{S}_1\}$$

where $\mathsf{E}\phi\mathsf{U}\psi$ is a CTL formula describing a set of states $\mathbf{i}_0$ from which there exists a finite path $\mathbf{i}_0 \to \mathbf{i}_1 \to \cdots \to \mathbf{i}_k$ where $\mathbf{i}_k \models \psi$ and $\forall l \geq 0 \wedge l < k, \mathbf{i}_l \models \phi$. For states that do not satisfy $\mathsf{E}\phi\mathsf{U}\psi$, the probability is 0 for sure, while for states satisfying ψ, this probability is 1. Thus, we have

$$\mathbf{i} \in \mathcal{S}_1 \Rightarrow \forall t > 0, Prob(\mathbf{i}, \phi\mathsf{U}^{[0,t]}\psi) = 1; \quad \mathbf{i} \in \mathcal{S}_0 \Rightarrow \forall t > 0, Prob(\mathbf{i}, \phi\mathsf{U}^{[0,t]}\psi) = 0$$

and we only need to calculate the probabilities for states in $\mathcal{S}_?$.

Computing the probability vector $\mathbf{Prob}(\phi\mathsf{U}^{[0,t]}\psi)$ on $\mathcal{M}$ is equivalent to computing $\boldsymbol{\nu}(\mathcal{S}_1, t)$ on $\mathcal{M}^{\mathcal{S}_0 \cup \mathcal{S}_1}$, which we can do using transient analysis, if $t < \infty$, or steady-state analysis, if $t = \infty$, as follows.

Time-Bounded U. We can employ uniformization to calculate $\boldsymbol{\nu}(\mathcal{S}_1, t)$. A backward approach [12] (its pseudo-code is shown in Fig. 1) is more desirable, as it directly returns the vector $\boldsymbol{\nu}(\mathcal{S}_1, t)$.

Unbounded U. $\mathbf{Prob}(\phi\mathsf{U}\psi) = \boldsymbol{\nu}(\mathcal{S}_1)$ where $\boldsymbol{\nu}(\mathcal{S}_1) = \lim_{t \to \infty} \boldsymbol{\nu}(\mathcal{S}_1, t)$ is the solution of the linear system (where, from now on, we let $\boldsymbol{\delta}^\psi$ mean $\boldsymbol{\delta}^{Sat(\psi)}$):

$$\mathbf{P} \cdot \boldsymbol{\nu} + \boldsymbol{\delta}^\psi = \boldsymbol{\nu}. \tag{2}$$

Given the potentially huge state space, direct methods, such as Gaussian elimination, do not scale, thus iterative methods are normally employed. For example, assuming some order "$\prec$" on the states, the Gauss-Seidel iteration

$$\nu_{\mathbf{i}}^{(k+1)} = \left(\sum_{\mathbf{j} \prec \mathbf{i}} P_{\mathbf{i},\mathbf{j}} \nu_{\mathbf{j}}^{(k+1)} + \sum_{\mathbf{j} \succ \mathbf{i}} P_{\mathbf{i},\mathbf{j}} \nu_{\mathbf{j}}^{(k)} + \delta_{\mathbf{i}}^\psi \right) / (1 - P_{\mathbf{i},\mathbf{i}}) \tag{3}$$

can be used to converge to a (numerically close) answer.

---

[1] $P_{\mathbf{i},\mathbf{i}}$ should be 1 for absorbing state $\mathbf{i}$, but we set it to 0 here to simplify Equation 2.

Point-Interval and General Interval U. The algorithms for both operators employ transient analysis, similar to that for time-bounded U. For $\mathbb{P}_{\bowtie p}(\phi \mathsf{U}^{[t,t]}\psi)$, we redefine ψ as $\psi \wedge \phi$, since the probability of moving from $Sat(\phi)$ to $Sat(\psi \wedge \neg \phi)$ exactly at time t is obviously 0. We can then generate $\mathcal{M}_{unif}^{Sat(\neg \phi)}$ and obtain the desired $\mathbf{Prob}(\phi \mathsf{U}^{[t,t]}\psi)$ as the vector $\boldsymbol{\nu}(Sat(\psi),t)$ computed for $\mathcal{M}_{unif}^{Sat(\neg \phi)}$.

$\mathbb{P}_{\bowtie p}(\phi \mathsf{U}^{[t,t']}\psi)$ requires two rounds of transient analysis: first we generate $\mathcal{M}_{unif}^{Sat(\neg \phi \vee \psi)}$ and compute $\boldsymbol{\nu}_{last}(Sat(\psi),t'-t)$, the probability of reaching ψ states within the last $t'-t$ time units starting from each state; then we generate $\mathcal{M}_{unif}^{Sat(\neg \phi)}$ with $\mathbf{P} = \mathbf{P}^{Sat(\neg \phi)}$ and compute:

$$\sum_{k=L_\varepsilon}^{R_\varepsilon} \mathbf{P}^k \boldsymbol{\nu}_{last}(Sat(\psi),t'-t) \cdot Poisson[k]$$

which is a backward transient analysis similar to that in Fig. 1 but starting from the probability vector $\boldsymbol{\nu}_{last}(Sat(\psi),t'-t)$ instead of $\boldsymbol{\delta}^\psi$.

3   Bounding the Probability in CSL Model Checking

We now introduce our numerical technique to tackle truncation errors and generate bounds when computing the U^I operator. Sections 3.1 and 3.2 focus on the time-bounded and unbounded U operators, respectively, and exploit the monotonic property of the probability vector being computed. Section 3.3 briefly introduces how to handle the point-interval and general interval U operators.

3.1   Time-Bounded Until

Given $\mathcal{M}$ and formula $\mathbb{P}_{\bowtie p}(\phi \mathsf{U}^{[0,t]}\psi)$, we first compute the partition $\{S_0, S_1, S_?\}$, then apply the conversion of Section 2.1 to obtain CTMC $\mathcal{M}^{S_0 \cup S_1}$. Consequently, $\mathbf{Prob}(\phi \mathsf{U}^{[0,t]}\psi)$ for $\mathcal{M}$ equals $\boldsymbol{\nu}(S_1,t)$ for $\mathcal{M}^{S_0 \cup S_1}$. The following equality

$$\boldsymbol{\nu}(S_?,t) + \boldsymbol{\nu}(S_1,t) + \boldsymbol{\nu}(S_0,t) = \mathbf{1} \qquad \text{where } \mathbf{1} \text{ is a vector of 1's}$$

holds at any time $t \geq 0$, since the state of $\mathcal{M}^{S_0 \cup S_1}$ is in one of S_1, S_0, or $S_?$. From now on, let the l and u superscripts indicate lower and upper bounds on the corresponding quantities, respectively. Then, if we can compute $\boldsymbol{\nu}^l(S_1,t)$, $\boldsymbol{\nu}^l(S_?,t)$, and $\boldsymbol{\nu}^l(S_0,t)$, we can let $\boldsymbol{\nu}^u(S_1,t) = \mathbf{1} - \boldsymbol{\nu}^l(S_?,t) - \boldsymbol{\nu}^l(S_0,t)$.

In the traditional use of uniformization, $\boldsymbol{\nu}(S_1,t)$ is calculated by truncating an infinite sum:

$$\sum_{k=0}^{\infty} \mathbf{P}^k \boldsymbol{\delta}^\psi \cdot Poisson[k] \approx \sum_{k=L_\varepsilon}^{R_\varepsilon} \mathbf{P}^k \boldsymbol{\delta}^\psi \cdot p[k].$$

We compute the approximate Poisson probability $p[k] \approx Poisson[k]$ for $L_\varepsilon \leq k \leq R_\varepsilon$ using the Fox-Glynn algorithm [9], which first finds the left and right

$\{L_\varepsilon, R_\varepsilon, p^l[L_\varepsilon, ..., R_\varepsilon]\}$ $FoxGlynnLB(qt, \varepsilon)$ is

```
1  m ← ⌊qt⌋;
2  L_ε, R_ε, w[m] ← Finder(λ, ε);
3  w[L_ε, ..., R_ε] ← ComputeWeight(L_ε, R_ε, w[m]);
4  W ← sumup(w[L_ε, ..., R_ε]);
5  W ← W/(1 − ε);                    • Upper bound on overall weight
6  p^l[L_ε, ..., R_ε] ← w[L_ε, ..., R_ε]/W;   • Lower bound on Poisson probabilities
7  return L_ε, R_ε, p^l[L_ε, ..., R_ε]
```

Fig. 2. Modified Fox-Glynn algorithm for lower bounds on Poisson probabilities

truncation points L_ε and R_ε that ensure $\sum_{k=L_\varepsilon}^{R_\varepsilon} Poisson[k] \geq 1 - \varepsilon$, where ε is the specified acceptable truncation error, then computes $p[k]$ based on the recurrence

$$p[k-1] \cdot qt = p[k] \cdot k \qquad \text{with normalization} \qquad \sum_{k=L_\varepsilon}^{R_\varepsilon} p[k] = 1 \qquad (4)$$

which results in $p[k] > Poisson[k]$. To calculate a lower bound $\boldsymbol{\nu}^l(\mathcal{S}_1, t)$, we first need to obtain a lower bound $p^l[k]$ for the Poisson probability $Poisson[k]$, thus we substitute the normalization in Equation 4 with

$$\sum_{k=L_\varepsilon}^{R_\varepsilon} p^l[k] = 1 - \varepsilon. \qquad (5)$$

Fig. 2 shows the pseudo-code of our modified Fox-Glynn algorithm generating lower bounds for the Poisson probabilities. We then have

$$\boldsymbol{\nu}^l(\mathcal{S}_1, t) = \sum_{k=L_\varepsilon}^{R_\varepsilon} \mathbf{P}^k \boldsymbol{\delta}^\psi \cdot p^l[k] < \sum_{k=0}^{\infty} \mathbf{P}^k \boldsymbol{\delta}^\psi \cdot Poisson[k] = \boldsymbol{\nu}(\mathcal{S}_1, t).$$

We could compute $\boldsymbol{\nu}^l(\mathcal{S}_?, t)$ and $\boldsymbol{\nu}^l(\mathcal{S}_0, t)$ with the same technique, but for $\boldsymbol{\nu}^u(\mathcal{S}_1, t)$ we do not need to do that. Considering Eq. 5, we have

$$\boldsymbol{\nu}^l(\mathcal{S}_?, t) + \boldsymbol{\nu}^l(\mathcal{S}_1, t) + \boldsymbol{\nu}^l(\mathcal{S}_0, t) = (1-\varepsilon) \cdot \mathbf{1} \quad \text{and} \quad \boldsymbol{\nu}^l(\mathcal{S}_?, t) + \boldsymbol{\nu}(\mathcal{S}_1, t) + \boldsymbol{\nu}^l(\mathcal{S}_0, t) \leq 1,$$

which means that we can define the upper bound

$$\boldsymbol{\nu}^u(\mathcal{S}_1, t) = \boldsymbol{\nu}^l(\mathcal{S}_1, t) + \varepsilon \cdot \mathbf{1} = 1 - \boldsymbol{\nu}^l(\mathcal{S}_?, t) - \boldsymbol{\nu}^l(\mathcal{S}_0, t) \geq \boldsymbol{\nu}(\mathcal{S}_1, t).$$

By adjusting ε, we can obtain arbitrarily tight bounds.

3.2 Unbounded Until

Again, we first build $\mathcal{M}^{\mathcal{S}_0 \cup \mathcal{S}_1}$ so that $\mathbf{Prob}(\phi \mathsf{U} \psi)$ in $\mathcal{M}$ equals $\boldsymbol{\nu}(\mathcal{S}_1)$ (recall that $\boldsymbol{\nu}(\mathcal{S}_1) = \lim_{t \to \infty} \boldsymbol{\nu}(\mathcal{S}_1, t)$) in $\mathcal{M}^{\mathcal{S}_0 \cup \mathcal{S}_1}$. Eventually, $\mathcal{M}^{\mathcal{S}_0 \cup \mathcal{S}_1}$ will be absorbed in $\mathcal{S}_0$ or $\mathcal{S}_1$, thus

$$\boldsymbol{\nu}(\mathcal{S}_1) + \boldsymbol{\nu}(\mathcal{S}_0) = 1.$$

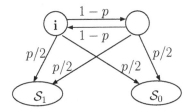

Fig. 3. An example of computing $\nu(\mathcal{S}_1)$

Hence, as long as we obtain the lower bounds $\nu^l(\mathcal{S}_1)$ and $\nu^l(\mathcal{S}_0)$, we can define the upper bound $\nu^u(\mathcal{S}_1) = 1 - \nu^l(\mathcal{S}_0)$.

$\nu(\mathcal{S}_1)$ is the solution ν of the linear system $\mathbf{P}\nu + \delta^\psi = \nu$, which can be solved using Gauss-Seidel (see Eq. 3). A practical criterion to terminate the iteration is $||\nu^{(k+1)} - \nu^{(k)}|| < \varepsilon$, where ε is again a parameter expressing the error tolerance. However, this criterion does not guarantee that the result is close to the actual solution, thus the error is *not* predictable from ε. Fig. 3 shows a simple example, $\mathcal{S}_?$ contains two states and we compute $\nu_i(\mathcal{S}_1)$. It is clear that $\nu_i(\mathcal{S}_1) = 0.5$ for any p, since the two top states are bisimilar. However, if $p \ll \varepsilon$, a naïve convergence test stops the iteration at $\nu_i(\mathcal{S}_1) = p/2$, which is far from the actual result.

If we initialize $\nu^{(0)}$ to be the zero vector, the following theorem holds (Theorem 5.8 in [4]).

Theorem: If $\nu^{(0)} = \mathbf{0}$, $\nu^{(k+1)} \geq \nu^{(k)}$ for all $k \geq 0$.

This theorem holds for the most widely used iterative methods such as Power, Jacobi, Gauss-Seidel, and SOR. It guarantees that the computed ν using one of these iterative methods naturally gives a lower bound $\nu^l(\mathcal{S}_1)$. We can similarly compute the lower bound $\nu^l(\mathcal{S}_0)$ with a second numerical solution, and let $\nu^u(\mathcal{S}_1) = 1 - \nu^l(\mathcal{S}_0)$.

Unlike the case of time-bounded until, it is difficult to predict the distance between $\nu^l(\mathcal{S}_1)$ and $\nu^u(\mathcal{S}_1)$, since there is no simple relation between ε and $||\nu^u - \nu^l||$. However, $||\nu^u - \nu^l||$ provides a much better criterion for convergence check. Still, in the example of Fig. 3 with $p \ll \varepsilon$, a naïve convergence test stops the iteration at $\nu_i(\mathcal{S}_1) = p/2$, and we obtain the bounds $\nu_i^l(\mathcal{S}_1) = p/2$ and $\nu_i^u(\mathcal{S}_1) = 1 - p/2$, which alert us that there is still a huge uncertainty in the result, thus the iteration should proceed further (with a smaller ε).

3.3   Point-Interval and General Interval Until

In both cases, we employ the analysis of Section 3.1. For $\mathbb{P}_{\bowtie p}(\phi \mathsf{U}^{[t,t]}\psi)$, where ψ implies ϕ, we generate $\mathcal{M}_{unif}^{Sat(\neg\phi)}$ and compute $[\nu^l(Sat(\psi), t), \nu^u(Sat(\psi), t)]$ as the bounds for $\mathbf{Prob}(\phi \mathsf{U}^{[t,t]}\psi)$.

Bounding the probability for $\phi \mathsf{U}^{[t,t']}\psi$ requires multiple transient analysis rounds. We first compute $[\nu_{last}^l(Sat(\psi), t'-t), \nu_{last}^u(Sat(\psi), t'-t)]$ in $\mathcal{M}_{unif}^{Sat(\neg\phi\vee\psi)}$.

---

bound *UntilBounds(interval I, StateSet Y, StateSet Z, float ε)* is

1   if $I = [0,t]$ then
2   Build $\mathbf{P}$ for $\mathcal{M}_{unif}^{\mathcal{S}_0 \cup \mathcal{S}_1}$ for uniformizing rate q;   • $\mathcal{S}_1 = \mathcal{Z}, \mathcal{S}_0 = \mathcal{S} \backslash \mathsf{E}(\mathcal{Y} \cup \mathcal{Z})$
3       $\boldsymbol{\nu}^l = BoundedUntil(qt, \mathcal{Y}, \mathcal{Z}, \varepsilon)$; • *Replace FoxGlynn by FoxGlynnLB in Fig. 2*
4       $\boldsymbol{\nu}^u = \boldsymbol{\nu}^l + \varepsilon \cdot \mathbf{1}$;
5   elseif $I = [0, \infty)$ then
6   Build $\mathbf{P}$ for $\mathcal{M}_{unif}^{\mathcal{S}_0 \cup \mathcal{S}_1}$ for uniformizing rate q;
7       $\boldsymbol{\nu}^l \leftarrow GaussSeidel(\mathbf{P}, \boldsymbol{\delta}^{\mathcal{S}_1}, \varepsilon)$; $\boldsymbol{\nu}^u \leftarrow \mathbf{1} - GaussSeidel(\mathbf{P}, \boldsymbol{\delta}^{\mathcal{S}_0}, \varepsilon)$;
8   elseif $I = [t,t]$ then
9   Build $\mathbf{P}$ for $\mathcal{M}_{unif}^{\mathcal{S} \backslash \mathcal{Y}}$ for uniformizing rate q;
10     $\boldsymbol{\nu}^l = BoundedUntil(qt, \mathcal{Y}, \mathcal{Z}, \varepsilon)$; $\boldsymbol{\nu}^u = \boldsymbol{\nu}^l + \varepsilon \cdot \mathbf{1}$;
11   elseif $I = [t,t']$ then
12    $\cdots$ • *See Section 3.3*
13   endif
14   return $\mathbb{P}_{\bowtie p}[\boldsymbol{\nu}^l, \boldsymbol{\nu}^u]$;

Fig. 4. Model checking algorithm for U^I generating bounds

Then in $\mathcal{M}_{unif}^{Sat(\neg\phi)}$,

$$\sum_{k=L_\varepsilon}^{R_\varepsilon} \mathbf{P}^k \boldsymbol{\nu}_{last}^l(Sat(\psi), t'-t) \cdot p^l[k]$$

gives the bound $\mathbf{Prob}^l(\phi \mathsf{U}^{[t,t']} \psi)$. The upper bound can be computed by considering that any path is described by exactly one of these path formulas:

$$\phi \mathsf{U}^{[0,t]}(\neg\phi) \qquad \phi \mathsf{U}^{[t,t']}\psi \qquad \phi \mathsf{U}^{[t,t']}(\neg\psi \wedge \neg\phi) \qquad \phi \mathsf{U}^{[t',t']}(\phi \wedge \neg\psi)$$

so that we can obtain $\mathbf{Prob}^u(\phi \mathsf{U}^{[t,t']} \psi)$ by

$$\mathbf{1} - (\mathbf{Prob}^l(\phi \mathsf{U}^{[0,t]}(\neg\phi)) + \mathbf{Prob}^l(\phi \mathsf{U}^{[t,t']}(\neg\psi \wedge \neg\phi)) + \mathbf{Prob}^l(\phi \mathsf{U}^{[t',t']}(\phi \wedge \neg\psi))).$$

To summarize the above discussion, Fig. 4 depicts the algorithm for U^I, which returns a pair of "lower and upper sets" $[\mathcal{X}^l, \mathcal{X}^u]$ satisfying $\mathcal{X}^l \subseteq \mathcal{X} \subseteq \mathcal{X}^u$, where $\mathcal{X}$ is the set satisfying the until formula.

4 Semantics for CSL Formulas with Bounds

This section addresses nested CSL formulas under our semantics with bounds. To accommodate the bounds generated by the above algorithms, we need to redefine the semantics of CSL. Specifically, we replace the exact set of states with the lower and upper bounds of this set.

Definition 3. The evaluation of a CSL state formula $\mathscr{F}$ returns a pair of state sets $[eval^l(\mathscr{F}), eval^u(\mathscr{F})]$ satisfying $eval^l(\mathscr{F}) \subseteq eval(\mathscr{F}) \subseteq eval^u(\mathscr{F})$.

  – $eval(\psi) = [Sat(\psi), Sat(\psi)]$

- $eval(\neg\mathscr{F}) = [\mathcal{S}\backslash eval^u(\mathscr{F}),\mathcal{S}\backslash eval^l(\mathscr{F})]$
- $eval(\mathscr{F}_1 \wedge \mathscr{F}_2) = [eval^l(\mathscr{F}_1) \cap eval^l(\mathscr{F}_2), eval^u(\mathscr{F}_1) \cap eval^u(\mathscr{F}_2)].$
- $eval(\mathscr{F}_1 \vee \mathscr{F}_2) = [eval^l(\mathscr{F}_1) \cup eval^l(\mathscr{F}_2), eval^u(\mathscr{F}_1) \cup eval^u(\mathscr{F}_2)]$
- $eval(\mathbb{P}_{\geq p}(\mathsf{X}^I\mathscr{F})) = [\mathbb{P}_{\geq p}\mathbf{Prob}(\mathsf{X}^I eval^l(\mathscr{F})),\mathbb{P}_{\geq p}\mathbf{Prob}(\mathsf{X}^I eval^u(\mathscr{F}))]$
- $eval(\mathbb{P}_{\leq p}(\mathsf{X}^I\mathscr{F})) = [\mathbb{P}_{\leq p}\mathbf{Prob}[\mathsf{X}^I eval^u(\mathscr{F})],\mathbb{P}_{\leq p}\mathbf{Prob}(\mathsf{X}^I eval^l(\mathscr{F}))]$
- $eval(\mathbb{P}_{\geq p}(\mathscr{F}_1\mathsf{U}^I\mathscr{F}_2)) =$
  $[\mathbb{P}_{\geq p}\mathbf{Prob}^l(eval^l(\mathscr{F}_1)\mathsf{U}^I eval^l(\mathscr{F}_2)),\mathbb{P}_{\geq p}\mathbf{Prob}^u(eval^u(\mathscr{F}_1)\mathsf{U}^I eval^u(\mathscr{F}_2))]$
- $eval(\mathbb{P}_{\leq p}(\mathscr{F}_1\mathsf{U}^I\mathscr{F}_2)) =$
  $[\mathbb{P}_{\leq p}\mathbf{Prob}^u(eval^u(\mathscr{F}_1)\mathsf{U}^I eval^u(\mathscr{F}_2)),\mathbb{P}_{\leq p}\mathbf{Prob}^l(eval^l(\mathscr{F}_1)\mathsf{U}^I eval^l(\mathscr{F}_2))]$

For the evaluation of nested formulas, we can still follow the syntax tree order from leaves to the root, and always enforce a high precision (small ε) when evaluating each subformula. The drawback of this approach is the potentially high and unnecessary cost. Instead, we can start from a low precision, and, if the resulting bounds are not tight enough, refine by incrementally increasing the precision for evaluating each level of subformula. The merit of this approach is the possibility of focusing the expensive numerical analysis efforts on the important subformulas. However, depending on the order in which we refine subformulas, this may result in unnecessarily going back and forth between the evaluation of outer and inner subformulas.

We propose the framework in Fig. 5 to evaluate nested CSL formulas and we only consider the evaluation of $\mathbb{P}_{\bowtie p}(\mathscr{F}_1\mathsf{U}^I\mathscr{F}_2)$ since the evaluation of $\mathbb{P}_{\bowtie p}(\mathsf{X}^I\mathscr{F})$ can be simply reduced to that of $\mathscr{F}$. *Eval* is the top-level function to evaluate the U^I operator, and all subformulas are assumed to be of the form $\mathbb{P}_{\bowtie p}(\mathscr{F}_1\mathsf{U}^I\mathscr{F}_2)$. We first evaluate with an initial precision and invoke Function *EvalError*, which evaluates the whole formula with error parameter ε. For the refinement, we give two different orders: *RefineTopDown* and *RefineBottomUp*. The former first increases the precision for evaluating the top-level formula, then, when it does not further tighten the resulting bounds, it refines the results from subformulas; the latter instead first refines subformulas, then the top-level formula. As the following case studies show, these two orders of refinement generally result in different costs to eventually reach sufficiently tight bounds.

5   Case Studies

For the experiments, we use our tool SMART [5] (Stochastic Model checking Analyzer for Reliability and Timing). SMART takes in a stochastic Petri net and generates the underlying CTMC. In our previous work, SMART has been developed as an analyzer and model checker [6] for stochastic Petri nets. Our recent work extends the capability of SMART to CSL model checking. The CSL model checking engine in SMART employs EV*MDDs to store the rate matrix [16], and uses a new two-phase symbolic algorithm to perform the Gauss-Seidel iteration [17].

We consider two models, for an embedded system and for the Advanced Airspace Concept (AAC) system. The embedded system model is described in [15] and also released as an example with PRISM [13]. The AAC system

---

bound $Eval(\mathbb{P}_{\bowtie p}(\mathscr{F}_1 \mathsf{U}^I \mathscr{F}_2))$ is

1   $\varepsilon \leftarrow InitialValue$;
2   $[\mathcal{X}^l, \mathcal{X}^u] \leftarrow EvalError(\mathbb{P}_{\bowtie p}(\mathscr{F}_1 \mathsf{U}^I \mathscr{F}_2), \varepsilon)$;
3   while $|\mathcal{X}^u| - |\mathcal{X}^l| > acceptable$ do
4      $[\mathcal{X}^l, \mathcal{X}^u] \leftarrow RefineTopDown/RefineBottomUp(\mathscr{F}_1 \mathsf{U}^I \mathscr{F}_2)$;
5   endwhile;
6   return $[\mathcal{X}^l, \mathcal{X}^u]$;

---

bound $EvalError(\mathscr{F}, \varepsilon)$ is

1   if $\mathscr{F}$ in form $\mathbb{P}_{\bowtie p}(\mathscr{F}_1 \mathsf{U}^I \mathscr{F}_2)$;
2      $[\mathcal{Y}^l, \mathcal{Y}^u] \leftarrow EvalError(\mathscr{F}_1, \varepsilon)$; $[\mathcal{Z}^l, \mathcal{Z}^u] \leftarrow EvalError(\mathscr{F}_2, \varepsilon)$;
3      $[\mathcal{X}^l, \mathcal{X}^u] \leftarrow$ bounds from $UntilBounds(I, \mathcal{Y}^l, \mathcal{Z}^l, \varepsilon), UntilBounds(I, \mathcal{Y}^u, \mathcal{Z}^u, \varepsilon)$;
4   else if $\mathscr{F}$ in form ϕ or $\neg\phi$ • *base case, atomic proposition*
5      $\mathcal{X}^l, \mathcal{X}^u \leftarrow Sat(\phi)$ or $\mathcal{S} \backslash Sat(\phi)$
6   else if $\mathscr{F}$ in form $\mathscr{F}_1 \vee \mathscr{F}_2$ or $\mathscr{F}_1 \wedge \mathscr{F}_2$
7      $[\mathcal{Y}^l, \mathcal{Y}^u] \leftarrow EvalError(\mathscr{F}_1, \varepsilon)$; $[\mathcal{Z}^l, \mathcal{Z}^u] \leftarrow EvalError(\mathscr{F}_2, \varepsilon)$;
8      $[\mathcal{X}^l, \mathcal{X}^u] \leftarrow [\mathcal{Y}^l \vee \mathcal{Z}^l, \mathcal{Y}^u \vee \mathcal{Z}^u]$ or $[\mathcal{Y}^l \wedge \mathcal{Z}^l, \mathcal{Y}^u \wedge \mathcal{Z}^u]$;
9   endif
10 Set $[\mathcal{X}^l, \mathcal{X}^u]$ and ε as CurrentResult and CurrentPrecision for $\mathscr{F}$;
11 return $[\mathcal{X}^l, \mathcal{X}^u]$;

---

bound $RefineTopDown(\mathbb{P}_{\bowtie p}(\mathscr{F}_1 \mathsf{U}^I \mathscr{F}_2))$ is

1   $\varepsilon \leftarrow$ CurrentPrecision for $\mathbb{P}_{\bowtie p}(\mathscr{F}_1 \mathsf{U}^I \mathscr{F}_2)$;
2   Reduce ε;
3   $[\mathcal{Y}^l, \mathcal{Y}^u] \leftarrow$ CurrentResult for $(\mathscr{F}_1)$;
4   $[\mathcal{Z}^l, \mathcal{Z}^u] \leftarrow$ CurrentResult for $(\mathscr{F}_2)$;
5   $oldbound \leftarrow$ CurrentResult for $\mathbb{P}_{\bowtie p}(\mathscr{F}_1 \mathsf{U}^I \mathscr{F}_2)$;
6   repeat
7      $[\mathcal{X}^l, \mathcal{X}^u] \leftarrow$ bounds from $UntilBounds(I, \mathcal{Y}^l, \mathcal{Z}^l, \varepsilon), UntilBounds(I, \mathcal{Y}^u, \mathcal{Z}^u, \varepsilon)$;
8   if $oldbound = [\mathcal{X}^l, \mathcal{X}^u]$ then
9         $[\mathcal{Y}^l, \mathcal{Y}^u] \leftarrow RefineTopDown(\mathscr{F}_1)$; $[\mathcal{Z}^l, \mathcal{Z}^u] \leftarrow RefineTopDown(\mathscr{F}_2)$;
10   else
11       $oldbound \leftarrow [\mathcal{X}^l, \mathcal{X}^u]$;
12   Reduce ε;
13   endif
14 until $|\mathcal{X}^u| - |\mathcal{X}^l| \leq acceptable$;
15 Set $[\mathcal{X}^l, \mathcal{X}^u]$ and ε as CurrentResult and CurrentPrecision for $\mathscr{F}$;
16 return $[\mathcal{X}^l, \mathcal{X}^u]$;

---

bound $RefineBottomUp(\mathbb{P}_{\bowtie p}(\mathscr{F}_1 \mathsf{U}^I \mathscr{F}_2))$ is

1   $\varepsilon \leftarrow$ CurrentPrecision for $\mathbb{P}_{\bowtie p}(\mathscr{F}_1 \mathsf{U}^I \mathscr{F}_2)$;
2   $[\mathcal{Y}^l, \mathcal{Y}^u] \leftarrow RefineBottomUp(\mathscr{F}_1)$; $[\mathcal{Z}^l, \mathcal{Z}^u] \leftarrow RefineBottomUp(\mathscr{F}_2)$;
3   $oldbound \leftarrow$ CurrentResult for $\mathbb{P}_{\bowtie p}(\mathscr{F}_1 \mathsf{U}^I \mathscr{F}_2)$;
4   repeat
5      $[\mathcal{X}^l, \mathcal{X}^u] \leftarrow$ bounds from $UntilBounds(I, \mathcal{Y}^l, \mathcal{Z}^l, \varepsilon), UntilBounds(I, \mathcal{Y}^u, \mathcal{Z}^u, \varepsilon)$;
6   if $oldbound = [\mathcal{X}^l, \mathcal{X}^u]$ then
7   Reduce ε;
8   else
9       $oldbound \leftarrow [\mathcal{X}^l, \mathcal{X}^u]$;
10     $[\mathcal{Y}^l, \mathcal{Y}^u] \leftarrow RefineBottomUp(\mathscr{F}_1)$; $[\mathcal{Z}^l, \mathcal{Z}^u] \leftarrow RefineBottomUp(\mathscr{F}_2)$;
11   endif
12 until $|\mathcal{X}^u| - |\mathcal{X}^l| \leq acceptable$;
13 Set $[\mathcal{X}^l, \mathcal{X}^u]$ and ε as CurrentResult and CurrentPrecision for $\mathscr{F}$;
14 return $[\mathcal{X}^l, \mathcal{X}^u]$;

Fig. 5. Algorithm for the evaluation of nested CSL formulas

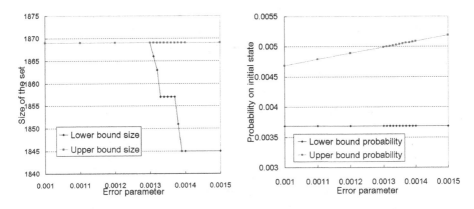

Fig. 6. Embedded system bounded until: size of lower and upper bound sets satisfying the formula (left) and probability bounds for the initial state (right)

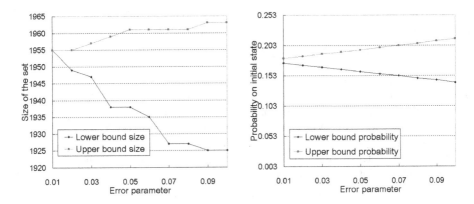

Fig. 7. Embedded system unbounded until: size of lower and upper bound sets satisfying the formula (left) and probability bounds for the initial state (right)

model describes the reliability in an airspace control protocol which was recently proposed; [18] provides the details about this protocol and also discusses the model-checking scheme for this system. We demonstrate the algorithms in Section 3 for non-nested CSL formulas, then show preliminary results on nested CSL formulas. Source code of the models and CSL formulas is available at [14].

Embedded System. This system consists of a main processor, an input processor, an output processor, two actuators, and three sensors, each associated with a failure rate. The main processor maintains a count of the number of retries when receiving data from sensors or sending data to actuators and, if the count exceeds a threshold, the entire system fails. More details about this model are available in [15].

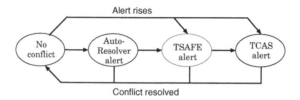

Fig. 8. High-level state transition of the AAC system

Table 1. Results for Formula 7 using top-down refinement

$\varepsilon_d = \varepsilon_n$	$|\mathcal{D}^l|$	$|\mathcal{D}^u|$	$|\mathcal{X}^l|$	$|\mathcal{X}^u|$	$\nu_{s_0}^l$	$\nu_{s_0}^u$
0.01	480	2160	224	1532	0.0439	0.0539
0.005	480	1392	224	1532	0.0441	0.0491
0.001	480	576	1532	1532	0.0443	0.0453
0.0005	480	576	1532	1532	0.0443	0.0448
0.0001	480	480	1532	1532	0.0443	0.0444

First, we check the time-bounded until property "the system runs without failure until the count reaches threshold 3 within 12 hours", written as:

$$[\mathcal{X}^l, \mathcal{X}^u] := \mathbb{P}_{\leq 0.005}[Normal \ \mathsf{U}^{[0, 12 \times 3600]} \ InOutFail].$$

For initial state s_0, the calculated probability bounds are $[\nu_{s_0}^l, \nu_{s_0}^u]$, In Fig. 6, the horizontal axis represents the error parameter ε. The left of Fig. 6 shows the size of $\mathcal{X}^l$ and $\mathcal{X}^u$ while the right shows $\nu_{s_0}^l$ and $\nu_{s_0}^u$; as we discussed, $\nu_{s_0}^u - \nu_{s_0}^l = \varepsilon$. When $\varepsilon \leq 0.0013$, we obtain an exact result for this formula, i.e., $\mathcal{X}^l = \mathcal{X}^u$.

We then check the unbounded until formula "the embedded system eventually fails with probability ≤ 0.2", written as:

$$[\mathcal{X}^l, \mathcal{X}^u] := \mathbb{P}_{\leq 0.2}[Normal \ \mathsf{U} \ InOutFail].$$

Again, the left of Fig. 7 shows the size of $\mathcal{X}^l$ and $\mathcal{X}^u$ while the right shows $\nu_{s_0}^l$ and $\nu_{s_0}^u$. In general $\nu_{s_0}^u - \nu_{s_0}^l$ does not have a simple relation with ε, but, in this case, it decreases almost linearly as ε decreases, which is desirable.

Advanced Airspace Concept (AAC). This model depicts conflict detection and resolution between a pair of aircraft. To ensure safe separation between aircraft, the AAC system provides three subsystems: AutoResolver, TSAFE, and TCAS, which can detect and resolve potential future conflicts. To resolve a detected conflict, a resolution is calculated automatically and sent to the pilot of the involved aircraft. The pilot is then responsible for executing the most urgent resolution first. Fig. 8 shows the high-level state transition in the AAC system for a pair of aircraft.

First, we define "dangerous states" to be those where a TSAFE alert rises and, with probability greater than 0.05 it will not be resolved within 3 minutes (180 seconds). Dangerous states can be described using the CSL formula:

$$[\mathcal{D}^l, \mathcal{D}^u] := TSAFEalert \wedge \mathbb{P}_{\leq 0.95}[TSAFEalert \ \mathsf{U}^{[0, 180]} \ \neg TSAFEalert]. \tag{6}$$

Table 2. Results for Formula 8

ε_d	ε_n	$\|\mathcal{D}^l\|$	$\|\mathcal{D}^u\|$	$\|\mathcal{X}^l\|$	$\|\mathcal{X}^u\|$	$\nu_{s_0}^l$	$\nu_{s_0}^u$
0.1	0.1	432	2160	224	5453	0.000	0.1400
	0.01	432	2160	5453	5453	0.000	0.0539

Then, we study the probability that, from a state without TSAFE alert on, the system reaches dangerous states within 5 minutes (300 seconds).

$$[\mathcal{X}^l,\mathcal{X}^u]:=\mathbb{P}_{\leq 0.01}[\neg TSAFEalert \; \mathsf{U}^{[0,300]} \; [\mathcal{D}^l,\mathcal{D}^u]]. \tag{7}$$

We use ε_d and ε_n to denote the error parameters for Formula 6 and 7, respectively. For this experiment, we keep refining the bound $[\mathcal{X}^l,\mathcal{X}^u]$ until $\mathcal{X}^l = \mathcal{X}^u$ (of course, in practice this might be neither achievable nor necessary). We first try to evaluate Formula 7 employing top-down refinement, and obtain the results in Table 1. For each row, we also tried to refine by just reducing ε_n, but this did not generate tighter bounds $[\mathcal{X}^l,\mathcal{X}^u]$ than those listed. In the first two rows, $[\mathcal{D}^l,\mathcal{D}^u]$ is too loose to obtain an exact result for the outer formula; from the third row, instead, while there is still uncertainty in the result of the inner subformula, $[\mathcal{D}^l,\mathcal{D}^u]$ is tight enough to generate an exact result for the nested formula. Thus, the model checking procedure could stop at $\varepsilon_d = \varepsilon_n = 0.001$.

We also study the formula using a larger probability threshold:

$$[\mathcal{X}^l,\mathcal{X}^u]:=\mathbb{P}_{\leq 0.1}[\neg TSAFEalert \; \mathsf{U}^{[0,300]} \; [\mathcal{D}^l,\mathcal{D}^u]]. \tag{8}$$

We start from $\varepsilon_d = \varepsilon_n = 0.1$ and refine. Using the bottom-up approach, we should first refine the subformula to tighter bounds, then go back to the top level. From Fig. 1, we know that $\varepsilon_d = 0.0001$ ensures an exact result for the subformula. However, Table 2 shows, refining the top-level formula directly produces an exact result, so it is in fact unnecessary to refine the subformula. This is because the probability threshold $\mathbb{P}_{\leq 0.1}$ is so slack that a precise evaluation on the top-level is sufficient to get an exact result even with very loose bounds on the subformula.

We can see that finding a scheme for nested formula requires us to identify the "bottleneck" of the precision for the final result. For Formula 7, the bottleneck lies in the inner formula, while for Formula 8 the bottleneck lies in the outer formula. However, it is difficult to come up with the best general scheme without several trials, thus finding good heuristics for efficient evaluation of nested CSL formulas is an interesting future work.

6 Conclusion

Since iterative methods are widely utilized in CSL model checking, truncation errors must be considered to ensure correctness of the results. In this paper, we investigated a bounding semantics of CSL formulas with the U^I operator. We first improved the CSL model checking algorithm by providing lower and upper bounds, to support the bounding semantics. Then, we applied the bounding semantics to nested CSL formulas and studied approaches for their evaluations. We demonstrated the new algorithms on two case studies. The results show that, for nested CSL formulas, appropriately scheduling the precision on different subformulas could achieve tight bounds and even exact results, with less computational cost. However, finding a "best" scheme is nontrivial. Thus we believe that finding good heuristics to guide the evaluation of nested CSL formulas is a promising future line of investigation.

References

1. Aziz, A., Sanwal, K., Singhal, V., Brayton, R.: Verifying continuous time Markov chains. In: Alur, R., Henzinger, T.A. (eds.) CAV 1996. LNCS, vol. 1102, pp. 269–276. Springer, Heidelberg (1996)
2. Baier, C., Haverkort, B., Hermanns, H., Katoen, J.-P.: Model checking algorithms for continuous-time Markov chains. IEEE Trans. Softw. Eng. 29(6), 524–541 (2003)
3. Baier, C., Katoen, J.-P.: Principles of Model Checking. MIT Press (2008)
4. Berman, A., Plemmons, R.: Nonnegative Matrices in the Mathematical Sciences. SIAM (1979)
5. Ciardo, G., Jones, R.L., Miner, A.S., Siminiceanu, R.: Logical and stochastic modeling with SMART. Perf. Eval. 63, 578–608 (2006)
6. Ciardo, G., Zhao, Y., Jin, X.: Ten years of saturation: A Petri Net perspective. In: Jensen, K., Donatelli, S., Kleijn, J. (eds.) Transactions on Petri Nets and Other Models of Concurrency V. LNCS, vol. 6900, pp. 51–95. Springer, Heidelberg (2012)
7. Clarke, E.M., Grumberg, O., Peled, D.A.: Model Checking. MIT Press (1999)
8. Fecher, H., Leucker, M., Wolf, V.: Don't know in probabilistic systems. In: Valmari, A. (ed.) SPIN 2006. LNCS, vol. 3925, pp. 71–88. Springer, Heidelberg (2006)
9. Fox, B.L., Glynn, P.W.: Computing Poisson Probabilities. Comm. ACM 31(4), 440–445 (1988)
10. Grassmann, W.K.: Finding transient solutions in Markovian event systems through randomization. In: Numerical Solution of Markov Chains, pp. 357–371. Marcel Dekker, Inc. (1991)
11. Katoen, J.-P., Klink, D., Leucker, M., Wolf, V.: Three-Valued abstraction for continuous-time Markov chains. In: Damm, W., Hermanns, H. (eds.) CAV 2007. LNCS, vol. 4590, pp. 311–324. Springer, Heidelberg (2007)
12. Katoen, J.-P., Kwiatkowska, M., Norman, G., Parker, D.: Faster and symbolic CTMC model checking. In: de Luca, L., Gilmore, S. (eds.) PROBMIV 2001, PAPM-PROBMIV 2001, and PAPM 2001. LNCS, vol. 2165, pp. 23–38. Springer, Heidelberg (2001)
13. Kwiatkowska, M., Norman, G., Parker, D.: PRISM 4.0: Verification of probabilistic real-time systems. In: Gopalakrishnan, G., Qadeer, S. (eds.) CAV 2011. LNCS, vol. 6806, pp. 585–591. Springer, Heidelberg (2011)
14. Models in this paper, http://www.cs.ucr.edu/~zhaoy/EPEW2013.html
15. Muppala, J.K., Ciardo, G., Trivedi, K.S.: Stochastic reward nets for reliability prediction. Communications in Reliability, Maintainability and Serviceability 1(2), 9–20 (1994)

16. Wan, M., Ciardo, G., Miner, A.S.: Approximate steady-state analysis of large Markov models based on the structure of their decision diagram encoding. Perf. Eval. 68, 463–486 (2011)
17. Zhao, Y., Ciardo, G.: A two-phase Gauss-Seidel algorithm for steady-state solution of structured CTMCs encoded with EVMDDs. In: Proc. QEST, London, UK, pp. 74–83. IEEE Comp. Soc. Press (September 2012)
18. Zhao, Y., Rozier, K.Y.: Formal specification and verification of a coordination protocol for an automated air traffic control system. In: Proc. AVoCS. Electronic Communications of the EASST. European Association of Software Science and Technology, vol. 53 (2012)

Automatic Performance Model Generation for Java Enterprise Edition (EE) Applications

Andreas Brunnert[1], Christian Vögele[1], and Helmut Krcmar[2]

[1] Fortiss GmbH, Guerickestrasse 25, 80805 München, Germany
{brunnert,voegele}@fortiss.org
[2] Technische Universität München, Boltzmannstr. 3, 85748 Garching, Germany
krcmar@in.tum.de

Abstract. The effort required to create performance models for enterprise applications is often out of proportion compared to their benefits. This work aims to reduce this effort by introducing an approach to automatically generate component-based performance models for running Java EE applications. The approach is applicable for all Java EE server products as it relies on standardized component types and interfaces to gather the required data for modeling an application. The feasibility of the approach and the accuracy of the generated performance models are evaluated in a case study using a SPECjEnterprise2010 industry standard benchmark deployment. Simulations based on a generated performance model of this reference deployment show a prediction error of 1 to 20 % for response time and of less than 10 % for CPU utilization and throughput.

Keywords: Performance Evaluation, Performance Modeling, Palladio Component Model, Java Enterprise Edition, Enterprise Applications.

1 Introduction

Performance modeling of software systems has been a research topic for several decades [1]. Even though the flexibility of a performance evaluation using performance models would be beneficial for many industry software projects [2,3], they are not in widespread use as of today [4,5]. One of the key challenges is the effort required to create representative performance models that often outweighs their benefits [6].

Many recently introduced performance modeling approaches focus on the evaluation of component-based software systems such as modern enterprise applications [4]. The performance evaluation of such enterprise applications is especially challenging as they are used by several hundred or thousand users concurrently with varying workloads. Component-based performance modeling languages [4] have already simplified the modeling process because component-based enterprise applications can be represented in these models using the same components they are composed of [7]. Additionally, different aspects that influence the performance of a component (such as the deployment platform or the usage

M.S. Balsamo, W.J. Knottenbelt, and A. Marin (Eds.): EPEW 2013, LNCS 8168, pp. 74–88, 2013.
© Springer-Verlag Berlin Heidelberg 2013

profile) can be modeled separately. This is a huge step forward regarding the applicability in practice compared to performance models using abstract notations such as layered queuing networks or queuing petri nets [1]. Tools emerged for these component-based performance modeling languages that help to make performance modeling a lot more accessible to practitioners [8]. Unfortunately, there are still some challenging questions left during the model creation process that need to be answered by researchers and practitioners alike:

1. Which components should be represented?
2. Which component relationships should be represented?
3. What data needs to be collected to parametrize a performance model?
4. How can the required data be collected?
5. How can the required data be processed and added to a performance model?

Answering these questions requires a lot of experience in the software engineering as well as in the performance modeling process. General guidelines to answer these questions for different software development domains would therefore help to simplify the modeling process. The automated performance model generation approach proposed in this work answers these questions for Java Enterprise Edition (EE) applications. The Java EE specification [9] defines the component types an application needs to be composed of and a runtime environment for hosting Java EE applications that is consistently available across Java EE server products. Therefore, the suggested performance model generation approach is designed in a way that it can be applied for Java EE applications running on all Java EE server products that are compliant with the specification.

2 Automatic Performance Model Generation

The performance model generation is executed in three different steps which are shown in figure 1: First of all, the data to create a performance model is collected from a running Java EE application (1.); afterwards the data is preprocessed (2.) to aggregate the required information. Finally, the aggregated data is used to generate a component-based performance model (3.). These three steps are explained below.

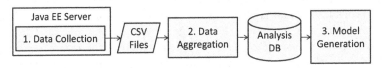

Fig. 1. Performance Model Generation Process

2.1 Data Collection

One of the main challenges when representing enterprise applications in performance models is choosing an appropriate level of detail for the model elements.

This decision directly influences the data required to create a performance model. Wu and Woodside [7] suggest that software systems that are assembled by predefined components should be represented using the same components in a performance model. Following this suggestion, the approach presented in this work uses component types defined in the Java EE specification to construct a performance model. The Java EE specification [9] defines the main application component types as Applets, Application Clients, Enterprise JavaBeans (EJB) and web components (i.e. Servlets, JavaServer Pages (JSP)). Complex Java EE applications are typically composed of a combination of such application component types. As Applets and Application Clients are executed outside of a Java EE server runtime, the remainder of this paper focuses on EJBs and web components. Using this level of detail for modeling Java EE applications comes along with the advantage that users of such performance models can easily map their findings to real application components and thus solve performance issues more easily. Furthermore, interfaces defined in the Java EE specification can be used to collect the required performance model parameters automatically. To parametrize a component-based performance model that contains all EJB and web components of a Java EE application as model elements, the following data needs to be collected:

1. EJB and web component names
2. EJB and web component operation names accessible to other components
3. EJB and web component relationships on the level of component operations
4. Resource demands for all EJB and web component operations

The data collection is described first for Servlets and JSPs. For these component types the Java EE specification defines Servlet filters that are always invoked before and after a Servlet or JSP is called [9]. Each request-response cycle of a Servlet or JSP invocation is assigned to exactly one thread at a time. This enables a very fine-grained data collection for all web components of an application.

The basic logic of the Servlet filter for collecting the required data can be found in listing 1. The *doFilter* method of the *PerformanceMonitoringFilter* is invoked whenever a Servlet or JSP is called. Before forwarding the current request to the Servlet or JSP (using *chain.doFilter*) the resource demand that the current thread has consumed so far is stored in a temporary variable (*startRD*). Once the request processing is completed, the updated resource demand for the current thread is stored in the *stopRD* variable. By subtracting the corresponding stop and start values, the resource demand for the current request can be calculated afterwards. As of today, the *PerformanceMonitoringFilter* can be configured to collect the central processing unit (CPU) demand in nanoseconds (ns) and the allocated bytes in the heap for the current thread. By default, only the CPU demand is collected. The *storeDemand* method stores the resource demands of the current invocation in multiple comma-separated value (CSV) files (one file per thread) for further analysis. Additionally, the Servlet path is stored as the component name and a configurable request parameter that is passed to the JSP or Servlet is stored as operation name for the current invocation.

The CPU demand in nanoseconds (ns) for the current thread is collected using the *getCurrentThreadCpuTime()* method provided by the *java.lang.management.ThreadMXBean* of the Java Virtual Machine (JVM). An approximation of the bytes allocated in the Java heap by the current thread can be acquired by using the *getThreadAllocatedBytes()* method of the *com.sun.management.-ThreadMXBean*. It is important to note, that even though the returned values of the *getCurrentThreadCpuTime()* method are of nanosecond precision, the accuracy of this method varies on different operating systems [10]. Typical Windows operating systems provide an accuracy of 10 milliseconds (ms), whereas some UNIX based operating systems provide an accuracy of 1 ns [10]. In consequence, if a high accuracy is required, this measurement approach is only feasible on these systems.

Listing 1. Basic Servlet filter logic

```
public class PerformanceMonitoringFilter implements Filter {
  public void doFilter(req, res, chain){
    ResourceDemand startRD = getCurrentThreadResourceDemand();
    chain.doFilter(req, res);
    ResourceDemand stopRD = getCurrentThreadResourceDemand();
    storeDemand(startResourceDemand, stopResourceDemand);
  }
}
```

Similar to a Servlet filter, an EJB interceptor can be applied to filter all calls to specific or all EJBs of an application. Such an EJB interceptor is used to gather the resource demand of single method invocations for different EJBs in a system [11]. The basic logic of the EJB interceptor is similar to the one of the Servlet filter: an *intercept* method is called for each invocation of an EJB method and stores the resource demands of the request processing thread before and after the invocation of the EJB method. Afterwards, the EJB interceptor also stores the data in multiple CSV files (one file per thread) for further analysis. The EJB class name is used as the component name and the called EJB method name passed to the *intercept* method as component operation name.

Multiple nested Servlet filter and EJB interceptor invocations can occur within one request-response cycle. It is therefore important to mention that the resource demand measurements of the first filters (or interceptors) in the chain already contain the resource demand measurements of the filters and interceptors that get called afterwards. To differentiate these demands afterwards, a request in the system needs to be uniquely identifiable. For that purpose, the filter or interceptor that gets called first, generates a unique transaction identifier (ID). The transaction ID is used in subsequent filter or interceptor invocations in the same thread to identify a request. Using this ID allows to track the resource usage of different components for single transactions in the system. In addition to this transaction ID, the Servlet filter and the EJB interceptor track the call-stack depth. The call-stack depth defines the amount of filters and interceptors that are nested within one request, to recreate the execution flow during the data analysis. Using an additional call-order attribute for each operation invocation during one thread execution, the different invocations can be ordered according to their execution sequence. Therefore, each entry of the CSV files contains the following information: transaction ID; call-order; call-stack depth; Servlet, JSP or EJB name; EJB method name or the selected Servlet/JSP request parameter; startCPUTime; stopCPUTime; startHeapByteAllocation; stopHeapByteAllocation; time stamp of the data collection. It is therefore possible to extract the application components, their relationships as well as their resource demand from this data.

The file operations are optimized by using different caches and output files for each thread to reduce the Servlet filter and the EJB interceptor impact on the monitored system. To assess the influence of the monitoring code on the measurement results, test runs to collect the CPU demand for a reference system are performed twice. In the first run only the CPU demands for components that started transactions (without any sub-measurements) are collected. In the second run the same values are measured while all Servlet filters or EJB interceptors are active. Comparing the results shows that each Servlet filter or EJB interceptor invocation results in a mean CPU demand overhead of 0.03 ms. This overhead is always included in the CPU demand measurements of the calling component.

2.2   Data Aggregation

The CSV files that are generated during the data collection phase are used as the input for a data aggregation component. The purpose of this component is to pre-process the data to reduce the model generation time afterwards.

All the pre-processed data is stored in a relational database (DB) called *analysis DB* to allow for a more flexible access to the collected data. As explained in the previous section, each entry in the CSV files represents a single component invocation. Therefore, the first step in the data aggregation process is to extract the existing components of the Java EE application from the CSV files. The component names found in this data are stored in a specific table in the database. At the same time, the existing component operations (EJB methods or Servlet/JSP request parameters) are extracted from the data. Component operations are stored in a separate database table. While searching for the existing components and their operations, the component invocations are stored in another database table. The component invocations are associated with the component names and operations they belong to. Additionally, the data aggregation component associates all component invocations with the transactions they are involved in based on the transaction ID in the log files. This data model simplifies the model generation process as component relationships can be easily identified on the level of single component operations.

2.3   Model Generation

The data stored in the *analysis DB* is used to generate a component-based performance model based on the available information. The Palladio Component Model (PCM) is used as the meta model for the generated models. PCM is described by Reussner et al. [8] as a software component model for business information systems to enable model-driven quality of service (QoS, i.e. performance) predictions. A software system is represented in PCM by several model types which can reference each other [8]. The most important model within PCM is called repository model. This model contains the basic components of a software system and their relationships. These components are assembled in a system model to represent an application. The user interactions with the system are described in a usage model. The other two models in PCM are the resource environment and allocation models. The purpose of the resource environment model is to specify available resource containers (i.e. servers) with their associated hardware resources (i.e. CPU cores). The allocation model specifies the mapping of components to resource containers. To take these different model types into account, the model generation process is divided in three sub-tasks:

1. PCM repository model generation
2. Associating resource demands with the PCM repository model components
3. Generating the system, resource environment and allocation models

PCM Repository Model Generation. First of all, a PCM repository model is generated to represent the Java EE application components and their relationships. The component relationships are represented in a repository model using interfaces. Each component can *provide* an interface to offer operations to other components and *require* interfaces from other components to access their operations (see figure 2(a)). As the component relationships are stored in the *analysis DB* on the level of single component operations, the generated component interfaces contain all externally accessible operations of a component. Internal component operations are not represented in the model.

The behavior of the component operations is specified in so called Resource Demanding Service Effect Specifications (RDSEFF). RDSEFFs are behavior descriptions of single component operations similar to activity diagrams in the Unified Modeling Language (UML) [12]. Input- or output-parameters of the component operations are not represented to simplify the model and because they are not available in the *analysis DB*. However, as these parameters can have great influence on the component performance, the probabilities of different execution flows (caused by different input- or output-parameters) are represented in the individual RDSEFFs. These probabilities are represented as so called probability branches in each RDSEFF [8]. An example for such a probability branch can be found in figure 2(b). The RDSEFF of the *operationA* of *ComponentA* contains a probability branch with two execution flows. One execution flow is executed with 30 % probability whereas the second execution flow is executed with 70 % probability.

To calculate the probability of each execution flow, the transactions in the *analysis DB* are first of all grouped by the component operation that was invoked first (i.e. by the user or external systems). In a second step, the execution flows that have been started by a specific component operation are grouped by the order in which they call external component operations. The total amount of transactions started by a specific component operation and the amount of transactions for each external component operation call order allow to calculate the probability of each execution flow. The second grouping does not consider the amount of times an external component operation was called in a row. To account for such invocation count variations, these values are represented as loop probabilities in the corresponding execution flows. An example for such a loop probability can be found in figure 2(b): In the execution flow with 70 % probability, the external *operationC* of *ComponentB* is called one time in 40 % of the cases and two times in the other 60 %.

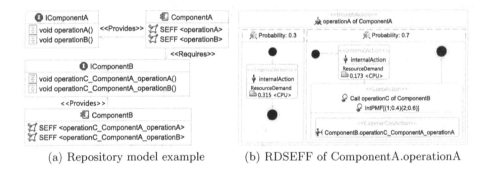

(a) Repository model example   (b) RDSEFF of ComponentA.operationA

Fig. 2. PCM repository model elements

A component operation can be included in execution flows that have been started by different component operations. To simplify the RDSEFFs, a new interface operation and a corresponding RDSEFF is created for each execution flow a component operation is involved in. The naming pattern for the new operation is as follows: *[operation name]_[component initially called]_[operation name initially called]*. For example, in figure 2(a), the *operationC* of *ComponentB* is called in an execution flow started from *operationA* and also in a flow started from *operationB* of *ComponentA*. The model generation code therefore generates two services for this operation: *operationC_ComponentA_operationA* and *operationC_ComponentA_operationB*.

Associating Resource Demands. The resource demand of a component operation is also stored in the corresponding RDSEFF. As representing memory is not directly supported by the PCM meta model without further extensions, the model generation currently only uses the CPU demand logged in the data collection step. As explained in section 2.1, the CPU demand of a component invocation already contains the CPU demands of all sub-invocations. Therefore, each transaction is processed in reverse order to calculate and remove the CPU demand of all external calls from the current operation. As the external calls vary between each execution flow, the CPU demand values are calculated separately for each of the flows in a probability branch. The mean CPU demand in ms for each execution flow is then assigned to the component operation. In the example in figure 2(b), one execution flow of *operationA* consumes 0.315 ms CPU time whereas the other flow consumes 0.173 ms.

Generating the Remaining PCM Models. When the repository model generation is completed, a system model is generated to represent a Java EE application that contains all repository model components. The automatic model generation specifies all interfaces that are not required by other components as externally accessible interfaces of the system. Thus, the model generation assumes that end-users or external systems interacting with a Java EE application have invoked the operations contained in these interfaces. Component operations that are not contained in these interfaces are not accessible outside of the generated system (i.e. not accessible from the usage model).

The resource environment and the allocation models are also generated automatically. The resource environment model is generated to define a reference system for the CPU demand values specified in the RDSEFFs. This is necessary to ensure that the CPU demand values are interpreted as ms values. The allocation model maps the system model components to the resource container in the resource environment model. Currently, only one server (resource container) with a single CPU core is generated in the resource environment and all components are mapped to this resource container. The resource environment model should therefore be configured according to the required setup (i.e. number of CPU cores) before it is used for a performance evaluation. The only PCM model that is not automatically generated is the usage model.

3   Evaluation

To evaluate the feasibility of the suggested performance model generation approach, a performance model for a SPECjEnterprise2010[1] industry standard benchmark deployment is generated using a software prototype that implements the approach [13]. SPECjEnterprise2010 specifies a Java EE application, a workload as well as a dataset that needs to be used for a performance test execution. The tests are therefore easily reproducible. Using the SPECjEnterprise2010 applications and predefined workloads performance tests are executed and a performance model is derived. Afterwards, workloads using varying amounts of users are executed both as a simulation using the performance model and on a real system to compare the results. This quantitative validation ensures that the automatically generated performance model provides a solid base for the performance evaluation.

---

[1] SPECjEnterprise is a trademark of the Standard Performance Evaluation Corp. (SPEC). The SPECjEnterprise2010 results or findings in this publication have not been reviewed or accepted by SPEC, therefore no comparison nor performance inference can be made against any published SPEC result. The official web site for SPECjEnterprise2010 is located at http://www.spec.org/osg/Enterprise2010.

3.1   SPECjEnterprise2010 Industry Benchmark Deployment

The business case for the SPECjEnterprise2010 application is a scenario that incorporates Supply Chain Management (SCM), Manufacturing and Customer Relationship Management (CRM) for an automobile manufacturer [13]. Following these key functional areas, the application is divided into three major parts: the Supplier domain for the SCM, the Manufacturing domain and the Orders domain for the CRM. The analysis in this paper focuses on the Orders domain. The communication between the domains is also not examined in this paper. The SPECjEnterprise2010 Orders domain is used as reference application for the case study because it is fully compliant to the Java EE specification and therefore portable across different application server products. This portability is a rare characteristic for such a complex Java EE application that already uses a lot of common technologies within the Java EE technology stack. Furthermore, the SPECjEnterprise2010 Orders domain is slightly different compared to the other domains as it represents a complete application intended to be used by end-users. The other two domains are mainly intended to be used by other applications as (web-)services.

Application Architecture. The Orders domain is a Java EE web application implemented using Servlets and JSPs [9] as key technologies. Apart from these technologies the Orders domain uses stateless EJBs and the Java Persistence API (JPA) [9] to implement an E-Commerce catalog and a shopping cart for automobile dealers [13]. The setup for the Orders domain consists of a System Under Test (SUT) on which the Orders domain application components are deployed and a Benchmark Driver used for generating load on the system (see figure 3(a)). A relational DB is the persistence layer of the Orders domain application. The automobile dealers access the web application over the Hypertext Transfer Protocol (HTTP) using their web browsers to order and sell cars. The execution flow of the Orders domain application can be described in four steps: Each HTTP request of the automobile dealers is processed by a Servlet (1.) which determines the type of request and executes the business logic while calling one or more stateless EJBs (2.). Afterwards, the request is forwarded to a JSP to render the view (4.). The stateless EJBs interact with JPA Entities (3.) which represent the application model that is persisted in a relational database.

System Topology. The SUT is deployed on a virtualized hardware environment exclusively used for the SPECjEnterprise2010 benchmarks performed for this paper. Two IBM System X3755M3 servers with 256 gigabyte (GB) random-access memory (RAM) and four AMD Opteron 6172 Processors with 12 cores and a 2.1 GHz frequency each are virtualized using the VMWare ESXi 5.0.0 (build 469512) hypervisor. The SUT is represented by a single virtual machine (VM) with four virtual CPU cores, 40 GB RAM and openSUSE 12.3 64 bit as operating system. The runtime for the Orders domain application components is a JBoss Application Server (AS) 7.1.1 in the Java EE 6.0 full profile and an

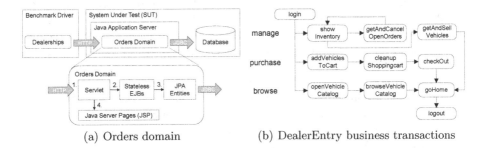

(a) Orders domain   (b) DealerEntry business transactions

Fig. 3. SPECjEnterprise2010

Apache Derby DB in version 10.9.1.0 as persistence layer. The JBoss AS and the
Apache Derby DB are executed within a 64 bit Java OpenJDK Server VM in
version 1.7.0 (IcedTea7 2.3.8, build 23.7-b01). The database is therefore included
in the server JVM. A different virtual machine is used for the Benchmark Driver.
SPECjEnterprise2010 uses the Faban Harness and Benchmark Framework [14]
to generate load on the SUT. To avoid influences on the system performance by
the load generation, the Benchmark Driver VM is placed on a different hardware server than the SUT VM. Both servers are connected by a gigabit ethernet
connection. The workloads that are generated by the Benchmark Driver will be
explained in the next section.

Workload Description. The automobile dealers can perform three different
business transactions: browse, manage and purchase. The dealers interact with
the Orders domain application by browsing the catalog of available cars (browse),
purchasing new cars (purchase) and managing their inventory by selling vehicles or cancel orders (manage). The main steps for each of these transactions
are shown in figure 3(b). These transactions are implemented in the SPEC-
jEnterprise2010 benchmark by the DealerEntry application that executes the
corresponding transactions on the SUT [13]. This application specifies the probability for each transaction and its single steps during a single DealerEntry
execution. Each transaction starts with a login of an automobile dealer, whose
identity is randomly selected. While the automobile dealer is logged in, the user
can perform multiple browse, purchase and manage operations with a specific
probability. After a specified time interval the user logs out of the application.

3.2   Automatic Performance Model Generation

A moderate load (~55 % CPU utilization) is generated on the SUT to gather
the required data for the model generation using the data collection approach
outlined earlier. The load is generated for 30 minutes while only data collected
between a five minute ramp up and a five minute ramp down phase is stored in
the *analysis DB*. As the database is included within the server JVM, these measurements already contain the database CPU demands. Afterwards, a software

prototype that implements the performance model generation process is used to generate a component-based performance model based on this data. The generated PCM repository model of the Orders domain application is shown in figure 4. Following the application architecture, the generated model contains a controller Servlet component (*app*), several EJB components (*CustomerSession, ItemBrowserSession, LargeOrderSenderSession* and *OrderSession*) and different JSP components to render the view (*dealerinventory.jsp, error.jsp, order.jsp, purchase.jsp, shoppingcart.jsp, SpecJhome.jsp* and *welcome.jsp*). The main entry point for the user is the *app* Servlet that dispatches the calls to the other components. Which component operations are called by the different *app* Servlet operations can be seen in the generated operation names of the other components.

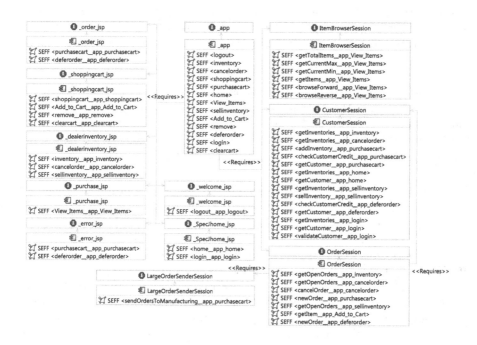

Fig. 4. Simplified performance model of the Orders domain application

In the generated resource environment model the CPU core count is set to four according to the SUT configuration. The repository-, system- and allocation models that are generated automatically are not changed manually. The usage model is modeled manually following the DealerEntry application source code.

3.3   Measurement and Simulation Results in Comparison

PCM models can be taken as the input for a simulation engine to predict and evaluate the application performance for different workloads or resource environments. The standard simulation engine for PCM models is SimuCom which uses model-2-text transformations to translate PCM models into Java code, that is compiled and executed to start a simulation [15]. To evaluate the accuracy of the model introduced in the previous section this simulation engine is used to predict the application performance from low (~40 % CPU utilization) to high load conditions (~90 % CPU utilization). The simulation results are compared with measurement data of the real system under the same load conditions. To generate low load on the system, the different tests start with 500 parallel dealer clients and then gradually increase in steps of 100 until high load conditions with 1100 parallel dealer clients are reached.

The comparison includes the throughput and response time of the browse, manage and purchase transactions as well as the CPU utilization of the SUT. The instrumentation to gather the CPU demand for the different application components is removed from the real system for the tests. Each simulation and test run on the real system lasted 30 minutes. To avoid influences of warm up effects and varying user counts, only data between a five minute ramp up and a five minute ramp down phase is included in the following comparison. The measured and simulated values within this 20 minute phase are used for the calculation of the mean response time and mean CPU utilization values without further filtering. During the test the CPU demand of the real system is collected using the system activity reporter (SAR). The throughput data for the different business transactions is taken from the reports generated by the Faban harness for each test run. Even though the Faban harness also reports response times for the business transactions, they cannot be compared with the simulation results as the network overhead between the Benchmark Driver VM and the SUT VM is not represented in the automatically generated performance model. Therefore, the response time values for the real system are gathered using a Servlet filter by logging the response times for each of the operations processed by the controller Servlet of the Orders domain application. The mean response times for the different Servlet operations are used to calculate the business transaction response time according to their distribution in the business transactions of the DealerEntry application. This approach enables the comparison of the simulated business transaction response times with those of the real system.

The measured and simulated results are shown in table 1. For each load condition specified by the number of clients (C) the table contains the following data per business transaction (T): Measured Mean Response Time (MMRT), Simulated Mean Response Time (SMRT), Response Time Error (RTE), Measured Throughput (MT), Simulated Throughput (ST), Throughput Error (TE), Measured (MCPU) and Simulated (SCPU) Mean CPU Utilization and the CPU Utilization Error (CPUE). The simulation predicts the mean response time of the business transactions with an error of mostly 7 to 17 %. Only the browse and manage transactions have a prediction error of 20 % for a load of 1100 concurrent dealer clients. As the performance model is solely based on the components CPU demand, external effects like input/output operations are one possible reason for the deviation in high load conditions. The throughput of the system is predicted

Table 1. Measured and simulated results

C	T	MMRT	SMRT	RTE	MT	ST	TE	MCPU	SCPU	CPUE
500	B	52.08 ms	57.49 ms	10.38 %	30,065	30,343	0.92 %			
	M	12.27 ms	13.54 ms	10.34 %	15,081	15,099	0.12 %	43.71 %	39.65 %	9.28 %
	P	22.18 ms	23.76 ms	7.13 %	15,105	14,991	0.75 %			
600	B	52.94 ms	57.76 ms	9.10 %	36,325	36,349	0.07 %			
	M	12.41 ms	13.62 ms	9.75 %	18,085	18,093	0.04 %	51.93 %	47.50 %	8.52 %
	P	22.28 ms	24.06 ms	7.97 %	18,223	18,100	0.67 %			
700	B	56.10 ms	60.49 ms	7.83 %	42,262	42,496	0.55 %			
	M	12.42 ms	14.24 ms	14.70 %	21,381	21,194	0.87 %	60.47 %	55.40 %	8.38 %
	P	23.18 ms	24.97 ms	7.72 %	21,131	20,923	0.98 %			
800	B	59.55 ms	64.38 ms	8.11 %	48,623	48,243	0.78 %			
	M	13.15 ms	15.21 ms	15.64 %	24,532	24,227	1.24 %	68.78 %	63.11 %	8.25 %
	P	24.42 ms	26.67 ms	9.21 %	24,159	24,149	0.04 %			
900	B	65.43 ms	65.74 ms	0.48 %	54,231	54,350	0.22 %			
	M	14.08 ms	15.53 ms	10.32 %	27,487	27,171	1.15 %	75.67 %	71.04 %	6.11 %
	P	26.33 ms	27.28 ms	3.60 %	26,752	27,085	1.24 %			
1000	B	84.02 ms	80.54 ms	4.14 %	60,658	60,312	0.57 %			
	M	16.20 ms	18.97 ms	17.12 %	30,231	30,203	0.09 %	83.70 %	78.88 %	5.76 %
	P	32.57 ms	33.53 ms	2.95 %	29,938	30,049	0.37 %			
1100	B	140.81 ms	113.02 ms	19.73 %	66,563	66,364	0.30 %			
	M	22.32 ms	26.69 ms	19.57 %	33,269	33,146	0.37 %	90.94 %	86.61 %	4.76 %
	P	51.90 ms	47.13 ms	9.20 %	33,384	32,820	1.69 %			

with an error below 2 %. This high accuracy can be explained by the fact that the average think time of 9.9 s between all dealer client requests is much higher than the average execution time of a business transaction, which is at maximum 140.81 ms (see table 1). Therefore, prediction errors of the response times have a low impact on the predicted number of executed transactions. A prediction error of less than 10 % is achieved for the CPU utilization. The simulated mean CPU utilization is constantly below the measured mean CPU utilization. This is expected, as the simulated data represents the CPU utilization of the JBoss AS process whereas the measured data represents the CPU utilization of the whole system. Thus, the measured CPU utilization of the SUT also contains other processes running on the operating system. Additionally, the CPU demand of the garbage collector and other JVM activities that are not executed within the request processing threads is not included in the model.

4   Related Work

Several approaches to evaluate the performance of Java EE (or similar component-based) applications using performance models have already been discussed by Kounev [6]. Extending the previous work, Kounev [16] shows how to apply model-based performance analysis to large-scale Java EE applications. Using the SPECjAppServer2002 [17] industrial benchmark, Kounev analyzes the applicability of analytical performance models for Java EE applications with realistic complexity. The author extends his work in [6,18] by using Queuing Petri Nets [19] to evaluate the performance of a SPECjAppServer2004 industrial benchmark [17] deployment. In these works, Kounev models the system manually as a number of server nodes without detailing single components of the application or differentiating between single applications running within a server. Therefore, the models can evaluate the performance of the whole system but do not provide sufficient detail to evaluate an application or its components.

Brosig et al. [20] show that they are able to semi-automatically extract Palladio Component Models (PCM) for Java EE applications using a SPECjEnterprise2010 deployment as case study. The authors define methods for an automatic identification of connections between single runtime components based on monitoring data of a WebLogic Application Server. Unfortunately, the identification of an appropriate granularity level for modeling the components is still left to the user. Their approach also requires a manual calculation and distribution of the CPU demands to the application components based on the overall utilization and throughput of the system.

5   Conclusion and Future Work

This paper introduced an approach to generate component-based performance models for Java EE applications automatically. The approach is applicable for Java EE applications running on server products that are compliant with the Java EE specification. Using the approach does not require detailed knowledge about the application architecture as the performance model components are based on component types·defined in the Java EE specification. It is also not required to have detailed knowledge about the performance modeling process as the generation process already answers the questions raised in the beginning. These characteristics reduce the effort required to create performance models and thus make them better applicable in practice.

Future work for this approach includes case studies for other applications and Java EE server products. Additionally, the approach needs to be extended to work with distributed systems. A key requirement for this extension is the possibility to uniquely identify transactions across multiple server instances. Especially if the approach should work with Java EE components typically used as back-ends such as web-services or message driven beans. Other external systems should be represented using black box approaches to reduce the need to collect data outside of Java EE runtime environments. Representing the heap demand in the generated models is another challenge that needs to be addressed.

References

1. Balsamo, S., Di Marco, A., Inverardi, P., Simeoni, M.: Model-based performance prediction in software development: A survey. IEEE Transactions on Software Engineering 30(5), 295–310 (2004)

2. Woodside, M., Franks, G., Petriu, D.C.: The future of software performance engineering. In: Future of Software Engineering (FOSE), pp. 171–187 (2007)
3. Smith, C.U.: Introduction to software performance engineering: Origins and outstanding problems. In: Bernardo, M., Hillston, J. (eds.) SFM 2007. LNCS, vol. 4486, pp. 395–428. Springer, Heidelberg (2007)
4. Koziolek, H.: Performance evaluation of component-based software systems: A survey. Performance Evaluation 67(8), 634–658 (2010)
5. Mayer, M., Gradl, S., Schreiber, V., Wittges, H., Krcmar, H.: A survey on performance modelling and simulation of sap enterprise resource planning systems. In: The 10th International Conference on Modeling and Applied Simulation, pp. 347–352. Diptem Universitá di Genoa (2011)
6. Kounev, S.: Performance Engineering of Distributed Component-Based Systems - Benchmarking, Modeling and Performance Prediction. Shaker Verlag. Ph.D. Thesis, Technische Universität Darmstadt, Germany, Aachen, Germany (2005)
7. Wu, X., Woodside, M.: Performance modeling from software components. SIGSOFT Softw. Eng. Notes 29(1), 290–301 (2004)
8. Reussner, R., Becker, S., Happe, J., Koziolek, H., Krogmann, K., Kuperberg, M.: The Palladio component model. Universität Karlsruhe (2007)
9. Shannon, B.: Java platform, enterprise edition (java ee) specification, v5 (2006)
10. Kuperberg, M.: Quantifying and Predicting the Influence of Execution Platform on Software Component Performance. The Karlsruhe Series on Software Design and Quality. KIT Scientific Publishing, Karlsruhe (2011)
11. DeMichiel, L., Keith, M.: Jsr 220: Enterprise javabeans, version 3.0 - ejb 3.0 simplified api (2006)
12. Krogmann, K.: Reconstruction of Software Component Architectures and Behaviour Models using Static and Dynamic Analysis. The Karlsruhe Series on Software Design and Quality. KIT Scientific Publishing, Karlsruhe (2010)
13. SPEC: Specjenterprise2010 (2012),
   http://www.spec.org/jEnterprise2010/ (accessed at April 07, 2012)
14. Faban: Faban harness and benchmark framework (2012),
   http://java.net/projects/faban/ (accessed at September 17, 2012)
15. Becker, S.: Coupled Model Transformations for QoS Enabled Component-Based Software Design. Karlsruhe Series on Software Quality. Universitätsverlag Karlsruhe (2008)
16. Kounev, S., Buchmann, A.: Performance modeling and evaluation of large-scale j2ee applications. In: Proceedings of the 29th International Conference of the Computer Measurement Group on Resource Management and Performance Evaluation of Enterprise Computing Systems (CMG), Dallas, Texas, USA, pp. 273–283 (2003)
17. SPEC: Spec jappserver development page (2002),
   http://www.spec.org/osg/jAppServer/ (accessed at September 02, 2012)
18. Kounev, S.: Performance modeling and evaluation of distributed component-based systems using queueing petri nets. IEEE Transactions on Software Engineering 32(7), 486–502 (2006)
19. Bause, F.: 'qn + pn= qpn' - combining queueing networks and petri nets. Technical report, Dept. of Computer Science, University of Dortmund (1993)
20. Brosig, F., Huber, N., Kounev, S.: Automated extraction of architecture-level performance models of distributed component-based systems. In: 26th IEEE/ACM International Conference on Automated Software Engineering (ASE), pp. 183–192 (2011)

Canonical Representation of Discrete Order 2 MAP and RAP

András Mészáros[1,3] and Miklós Telek[1,2]

[1] Budapest University of Technology and Economics
[2] MTA-BME Information Systems Research Group
[3] Inter-University Center for Telecommunications and Informatics Debrecen
{meszarosa,telek}@hit.bme.hu

Abstract. Matrix-geometric distributions (MG) and discrete (time) rational arrival processes (DRAP) are natural extensions of discrete phase-type distributions (DPH) and discrete Markov arrival processes (DMAP) respectively. However, the exact relation of the Markovian classes and their non-Markovian counterparts and the boundaries of these classes are not known yet. It has been shown that for the order two case the MG and DPH classes are equivalent. In this paper we prove that the equivalence holds for the order two DMAPs and DRAPs as well. We prove this equivalence by introducing a Markovian canonical form for order two DRAPs and by showing, that this canonical form can indeed be used to describe the whole order two DRAP class.

Keywords: discrete Markov arrival process, discrete rational arrival process, canonical representation.

1 Introduction

Stochastic models with underlying Markov chains have been widely used since the introduction of matrix analytic methods [1], which allow efficient numerical analysis of such stochastic models. Relaxing the limitations of stochastic processes with underlying Markov chains, non-Markovian generalizations of these processes, matrix exponential distributions (ME) [2] and continuous rational arrival processes (CRAP) [3], have been introduced. More recently it has turned out that these non-Markovian generalizations inherit the applicability of the efficient numerical procedures for their analysis [4]. Due to the nice computational properties, parameter estimation (fitting) and moments matching of CMAP and CRAP processes have gained significant attention [5,6]. The order two models (the lowest order non-trivial models) allow explicit analytical treatment. For order two continuous processes the canonical representation and the moments matching were investigated in [7]. It was shown that order two CMAP $\equiv$ order two CRAP. In this paper we investigate the discrete counterparts of these processes and introduce a canonical representation for the order two DRAP class, we prove that the order two DMAP $\equiv$ order two DRAP relation also holds, and we present explicit moments and correlation matching formulas.

M.S. Balsamo, W.J. Knottenbelt, and A. Marin (Eds.): EPEW 2013, LNCS 8168, pp. 89–103, 2013.
© Springer-Verlag Berlin Heidelberg 2013

The rest of the paper is organized as follows. In Section 2 we survey the necessary definitions and essential properties of existing Markov chain driven stochastic processes and their non-Markovian generalizations. Unfortunately, we need to introduce a lot of concepts in this section, which makes it rather dense. The next section focuses on the special properties of the order 2 class of these processes. The main result of the paper, the canonical representation of order 2 DMAP and DRAP processes, is presented in Section 4. Finally, explicit moments and correlation matching formulas are provided in Section 5.

2 Markov Chain Driven Point Processes in Discrete and Continuous Time and Their Non-Markovian Generalizations

The following subsections summarize the main properties of simple stochastic models with a background discrete state Markov chain and their non-Markovian generalizations. If the background chain is a discrete time Markov chain we obtain discrete (time) stochastic models and if it is a continuous time Markov chain we obtain continuous (time) stochastic models. The main focus of the paper is on the discrete models, but some results are related to their continuous counterparts and that is why we introduce both of them.

2.1 Discrete Phase Type and Matrix Geometric Distributions

The following stochastic models define discrete distributions on the positive integers.

Definition 1. *Let $\mathcal{X}$ be a discrete random variable on $\mathbb{N}^+$ with probability mass function (pmf)*

$$P_{\mathcal{X}}(i) = Pr(\mathcal{X} = i) = \alpha \boldsymbol{A}^{i-1}(\mathbb{1} - \boldsymbol{A}\mathbb{1}) \ \ \forall i \in \mathbb{N}^+, \tag{1}$$

where α is a row vector of size n, $\boldsymbol{A}$ is a square matrix of size $n \times n$, and $\mathbb{1}$ is the column vector of ones of size n. If the pmf has this matrix geometric form, then we say that $\mathcal{X}$ is matrix geometrically distributed with representation $\alpha, \boldsymbol{A}$, or shortly, MG($\alpha, \boldsymbol{A}$) distributed.

In this and the subsequent models the scalar quantity is obtained as a product of a row vector, a given number of square matrices and a column vector. In the sequel we refer to the row vector as initial vector and to the column vector as closing vector. It is an important consequence of Definition 1 that α and $\boldsymbol{A}$ have to be such that (1) is non-negative.

Definition 2. *If $\mathcal{X}$ is an MG($\alpha, \boldsymbol{A}$) distributed random variable, where α and $\boldsymbol{A}$ have the following properties:*

– $\alpha_i \geq 0$,

$-\ A_{ij} \geq 0,\ \boldsymbol{A}\mathbb{1} \leq \mathbb{1},$

then we say that $\mathcal{X}$ is discrete phase type distributed with representation $\alpha, \boldsymbol{A}$, or shortly, $DPH(\alpha, \boldsymbol{A})$ distributed.

The vector-matrix representations satisfying the conditions of Definition 2 are called Markovian.

In this paper we focus on distributions on the positive integers, consequently, $\alpha\mathbb{1} = 1$. The cumulative density function (cdf), the moment generating function, and the factorial moments of $\mathcal{X}$ are

$$F_{\mathcal{X}}(i) = Pr(\mathcal{X} \leq i) = 1 - \alpha \boldsymbol{A}^i \mathbb{1}, \tag{2}$$

$$\mathcal{F}_{\mathcal{X}}(z) = E(z^{\mathcal{X}}) = z\alpha(\boldsymbol{I} - z\boldsymbol{A})^{-1}(\mathbb{1} - \boldsymbol{A}\mathbb{1}), \tag{3}$$

$$f_n = E(\mathcal{X}(\mathcal{X}-1)\ldots(\mathcal{X}-n+1)) = \frac{d^n}{dz^n}\mathcal{F}_{\mathcal{X}}(z)|_{z=1} = n!\alpha(\boldsymbol{I} - \boldsymbol{A})^{-n}\boldsymbol{A}^{n-1}\mathbb{1}. \tag{4}$$

2.2 Discrete Markov Arrival Process and Discrete Rational Arrival Process

Let $\mathcal{X}(t)$ be a point process on $\mathbb{N}^+$ with joint probability mass function of inter-event times $P_{\mathcal{X}}(x_0, x_1, \ldots, x_k)$ for $k = 1, 2, \ldots$ and $x_0, \ldots, x_k \in \mathbb{N}^+$.

Definition 3. *$\mathcal{X}(t)$ is called a rational arrival process if there exists a finite $(\boldsymbol{H_0}, \boldsymbol{H_1})$ square matrix pair such that $(\boldsymbol{H_0} + \boldsymbol{H_1})\mathbb{1} = \mathbb{1}$,*

$$\underline{\pi}(\boldsymbol{I} - \boldsymbol{H_0})^{-1}\boldsymbol{H_1} = \underline{\pi}, \quad \underline{\pi}\mathbb{1} = \mathbb{1} \tag{5}$$

has a unique solution and

$$P_{\mathcal{X}(t)}(x_0, x_1, \ldots, x_k) = \underline{\pi}\boldsymbol{H_0}^{x_0-1}\boldsymbol{H_1}\boldsymbol{H_0}^{x_1-1}\boldsymbol{H_1}\ldots\boldsymbol{H_0}^{x_k-1}\boldsymbol{H_1}\mathbb{1}, \tag{6}$$

In this case we say that $\mathcal{X}(t)$ is a discrete rational arrival process with representation $(\boldsymbol{H_0}, \boldsymbol{H_1})$, or shortly, $DRAP(\boldsymbol{H_0}, \boldsymbol{H_1})$.

The size of the $\boldsymbol{H_0}$ and $\boldsymbol{H_1}$ matrices is also referred to as the order of the associated process. An important consequence of Definition 3 is that $\boldsymbol{H_0}$ and $\boldsymbol{H_1}$ have to be such that (6) is always non-negative.

Definition 4. *If $\mathcal{X}(t)$ is a $DRAP(\boldsymbol{H_0}, \boldsymbol{H_1})$, where $\boldsymbol{H_0}$ and $\boldsymbol{H_1}$ are non-negative, we say that $\mathcal{X}(t)$ is a Discrete Markov arrival process with representation $(\boldsymbol{H_0}, \boldsymbol{H_1})$, or shortly, $DMAP(\boldsymbol{H_0}, \boldsymbol{H_1})$.*

The matrix pairs satisfying the conditions of Definition 4 are called Markovian and the matrix pairs violating Definition 4 are called non-Markovian.

Definition 5. *The correlation parameter, γ, of a $DRAP(\boldsymbol{H_0}, \boldsymbol{H_1})$ is the eigenvalue of $(\boldsymbol{I} - \boldsymbol{H_0})^{-1}\boldsymbol{H_1}$ with the second largest absolute value.*

One of the eigenvalues of $(I - H_0)^{-1}H_1$ is 1, because $(H_0 + H_1)\mathbb{1} = \mathbb{1}$, and the other eigenvalues are on the unit disk. If γ is real, it is between -1 and 1. This parameter is especially important in case of order 2 DRAPs, as their ρ_k lag-k autocorrelation coefficient can be given as $\rho_k = \gamma^k c_0$, where c_0 depends only on the stationary inter-arrival time distribution of the process.

In general, a DMAP has infinitely many different Markovian and non-Markovian representations (matrix pairs, that fulfill (6)). One way to get a different representation of a DMAP(D_0, D_1) with the same size is the application of the similarity transformation

$$H_0 = T^{-1}D_0T, \quad H_1 = T^{-1}D_1T, \tag{7}$$

where T is an arbitrary non-singular matrix for which $T\mathbb{1} = \mathbb{1}$. The (stationary) marginal distribution of the inter-event time of DRAP(H_0, H_1) is MG(π, H_0), where π is the unique solution of (5).

2.3   Continuous Phase Type and Matrix Exponential Distributions

The continuous counterparts of the above introduced models are defined as follows.

Definition 6. *Let $\mathcal{X}$ be a continuous random variable with support on $\mathbb{R}^+$ and cumulative distribution function (cdf)*

$$F_X(x) = Pr(\mathcal{X} < x) = 1 - \alpha e^{Ax}\mathbb{1},$$

where α is a row vector of size n, A is a square matrix of size $n \times n$, and $\mathbb{1}$ is the column vector of ones of size n. In this case, we say that $\mathcal{X}$ is matrix exponentially distributed with representation α, A, or shortly, ME(α, A) distributed.

Definition 7. *If $\mathcal{X}$ is an ME(α, A) distributed random variable, where α and A have the following properties:*

- *$\alpha_i \geq 0$, $\alpha\mathbb{1} = 1$ (there is no probability mass at $x = 0$),*
- *$A_{ii} < 0$, $A_{ij} \geq 0$ for $i \neq j$, $A\mathbb{1} \leq 0$,*

we say that $\mathcal{X}$ is phase type distributed with representation α, A, or shortly, CPH(α, A) distributed.

The vector-matrix representations satisfying the conditions of Definition 7 are called Markovian.

The probability density function (pdf), the Laplace transform, and the moments of $\mathcal{X}$ are

$$f_X(x) = -\alpha e^{Ax}A\mathbb{1}, \tag{8}$$

$$f_X^*(s) = E(e^{-s\mathcal{X}}) = -\alpha(sI - A)^{-1}A\mathbb{1}, \tag{9}$$

$$\mu_n = E(\mathcal{X}^n) = n!\alpha(-A)^{-n}\mathbb{1}. \tag{10}$$

2.4   Continuous Markov Arrival Process and Continuous Rational Arrival Process

Let $\mathcal{X}(t)$ be a point process on $\mathbb{R}^+$ with joint probability density function of inter-event times $f(x_0, x_1, \ldots, x_k)$ for $k = 1, 2, \ldots$.

Definition 8. *$\mathcal{X}(t)$ is called a rational arrival process if there exists a finite (H_0, H_1) square matrix pair such that $(H_0 + H_1)\mathbb{1} = 0$,*

$$\underline{\pi}(-H_0)^{-1}H_1 = \underline{\pi}, \quad \underline{\pi}\mathbb{1} = \mathbb{1}, \tag{11}$$

has a unique solution, and

$$f(x_0, x_1, \ldots, x_k) = \underline{\pi}e^{H_0 x_0} H_1 e^{H_0 x_1} H_1 \cdots e^{H_0 x_k} H_1 \mathbb{1}. \tag{12}$$

In this case we say that $\mathcal{X}(t)$ is a rational arrival process with representation (H_0, H_1), or shortly, RAP(H_0, H_1).

Definition 9. *If $\mathcal{X}(t)$ is a RAP(H_0, H_1), where H_0 and H_1 have the following properties:*

- *$H_{1ij} \geq 0$,*
- *$H_{0ii} < 0$, $H_{0ij} \geq 0$ for $i \neq j$, $H_0\mathbb{1} \leq 0$,*

we say that $\mathcal{X}(t)$ is a Markov arrival process with representation (H_0, H_1), or shortly, MAP(H_0, H_1).

Similar to the discrete case, the representations satisfying the conditions of Definition 9 are called Markovian and similarity transformations generate different representations of the same process.

3   Some Properties of Order 2 DPH and MG Distributions

In this section we summarize some recent results concerning the canonical representation of order 2 DPH and MG distributions (DPH(2) and MG(2), respectively) from [8], which are going to be utilized in the subsequent sections. Matrix A of an order 2 MG distribution has two (not necessarily distinct) real eigenvalues, out of which at least one is positive. The cases when both eigenvalues of A are positive can always be represented with an acyclic Markovian canonical representation, whose properties are studied in [9]. The cases when one of the eigenvalues is negative can always be represented with a cyclic Markovian canonical representation as it is summarized below.

Theorem 1. *[8] The pmf of an MG(2) distribution has one of the following two forms*

- *different eigenvalues:*

$$p_i = a_1 s_1^{i-1} + a_2 s_2^{i-1}, \tag{13}$$

where s_1, s_2 are real, $0 < s_1 < 1$, $s_1 > |s_2|$, $a_2 = (1 - s_2)\left(1 - \frac{a_1}{1 - s_1}\right)$ and a_1 is such that

- if $s_2 > 0$, then $0 \le a_1 \le \frac{(1-s_1)(1-s_2)}{s_1-s_2}$ and
- if $s_2 < 0$, then $\frac{(1-s_1)(1-s_2)s_2}{(1-s_2)s_2-(1-s_1)s_1} \le a_1 \le \frac{(1-s_1)(1-s_2)}{s_1-s_2}$,

- *identical eigenvalues:*

$$p_i = (a_1(i-1) + a_2)s^{i-1}, \tag{14}$$

where s is real $0 < s < 1$, and a_1, a_2 are such that $0 < a_1 \le \frac{(1-s)^2}{s}$ and $a_2 = \frac{(1-s)^2 - a_1 s}{1-s}$.

Theorem 2. *[9] If $\mathcal{X}$ is $MG(2)$ distributed with two distinct positive eigenvalues $(0 < s_2 < s_1 < 1)$, it can be represented as $DPH(\alpha, \boldsymbol{A})$, where*

$$\alpha = \left[\frac{a_1(s_1 - s_2)}{(s_1 - 1)(s_2 - 1)}, \frac{a_1 + a_2}{1 - s_2} \right], \qquad \boldsymbol{A} = \left[\begin{array}{cc} s_1 & 1-s_1 \\ 0 & s_2 \end{array} \right].$$

Theorem 3. *[8] If $\mathcal{X}$ is $MG(2)$ distributed with a dominant positive and a negative eigenvalue ($s_2 < 0 < s_1 < 1$ and $s_1 + s_2 > 0$), it can be represented as $DPH(\alpha, \boldsymbol{A})$, where*

$$\alpha = \left[\frac{a_1 s_1 + a_2 s_2}{(s_1 - 1)(s_2 - 1)}, \frac{(a_1 + a_2)(1 - s_1 - s_2)}{(s_1 - 1)(s_2 - 1)} \right], \qquad \boldsymbol{A} = \left[\begin{array}{cc} 1 - \beta_1 & \beta_1 \\ \beta_2 & 0 \end{array} \right],$$

$\beta_1 = 1 - s_1 - s_2$ and $\beta_2 = \frac{s_1 s_2}{s_1 + s_2 - 1}$.

Theorem 4. *[9] If $\mathcal{X}$ is $MG(2)$ distributed with two identical eigenvalues ($0 < s = s_2 = s_1 < 1$), it can be represented as $DPH(\alpha, \boldsymbol{A})$, where*

$$\alpha = \left[\frac{a_1 s}{(1 - s)^2}, \frac{a_2}{1 - s} \right], \qquad \boldsymbol{A} = \left[\begin{array}{cc} s & 1-s \\ 0 & s \end{array} \right].$$

There are several interesting consequences of Theorem 1 – 4. First of all

$$DPH(2) \equiv MG(2),$$

that is all $MG(2)$ can be represented with a Markovian vector-matrix pair. Further more

$$ADPH(2) \equiv MG(2) \text{ with positive eigenvalues,}$$

where $ADPH(2)$ denotes the subclass of $DPH(2)$ with acyclic matrix $\boldsymbol{A}$.

The canonical representation of the stochastic models introduced in Section 2 is a convenient Markovian representation that takes Cumani's acyclic canonical form [10] if possible and contains the maximal number of zero elements. In some cases these principles completely define the canonical representation, while additional criteria are applied in other cases. The representations in Theorem 2 – 4 are recommended as canonical representations in [8,9].

The $ADPH(2)$ canonical forms (Theorem 2 and 4) have an interesting relation with the Cumani's canonical form of CPH distributions. If $MG(\gamma, \boldsymbol{G})$ is a $MG(2)$

with positive eigenvalues then vector γ and matrix $G - I$ define a ME(2) distribution, ME($\gamma, G - I$). Let PH(δ, D) be the Cumani's acyclic canonical form of ME($\gamma, G - I$), which always exists [9]. Vector δ and matrix $D + I$ define the canonical representation of MG(γ, G) according to Theorem 2 or 4. That is

$$\mathrm{MG}(\gamma, G) \stackrel{D \Rightarrow C}{=} \mathrm{ME}(\gamma, G - I) \equiv \mathrm{CPH}(\underbrace{\gamma T}_{\delta}, \underbrace{T^{-1}(G - I)T}_{D})$$

$$\stackrel{C \Rightarrow D}{=} \mathrm{DPH}(\gamma T, T^{-1}(G - I)T + I) \equiv \mathrm{DPH}(\gamma T, T^{-1}GT), \quad (15)$$

where the eigenvalues of G and $T^{-1}GT$ are between in $(0, 1)$ and the eigenvalues of D are in $(-1, 0)$. Note that the similarity transformation $T^{-1}GT$ maintains the eigenvalue structure of G.

4   Canonical Representation of DRAP(2) Processes

The main goal of this paper is to define Markovian canonical forms for order 2 DRAP processes.

The DRAP(2) processes are defined by 4 parameters [11], e.g. the first 3 factorial moments of the stationary inter-arrival time distribution, f_1, f_2, f_3, and the correlation parameter, γ. D_0 and D_1 of size 2×2 has a total of 8 elements (free parameters). The $(D_0 + D_1)\mathbb{1} = \mathbb{1}$ constraint reduces the number of free parameters to 6. If additionally, two elements of the representation are set to 0 then the obtained (canonical) representation characterizes the process exactly with 4 parameters.

4.1   Canonical Forms of CMAP(2)

The last paragraph of the previous section discusses the relation of the discrete and continuous distributions. We are going to utilize a similar relation between DMAP(2) and CMAP(2). To this end we summarize the canonical representation of CMAP(2) from [7].

Theorem 5. *[7] If the correlation parameter of the order 2 CRAP(H_0, H_1) is*

- *non-negative, then it can be represented in the following Markovian canonical form*

$$D_0 = \begin{bmatrix} -\lambda_1 & (1-a)\lambda_1 \\ 0 & -\lambda_2 \end{bmatrix}, \quad D_1 = \begin{bmatrix} a\lambda_1 & 0 \\ (1-b)\lambda_2 & b\lambda_2 \end{bmatrix}.$$

where $0 < \lambda_1 \leq \lambda_2$, $0 \leq a, b \leq 1$, $\min\{a, b\} \neq 1$, $\gamma = ab$ and the associated embedded stationary vector is $\pi = \begin{bmatrix} \frac{1-b}{1-ab} & \frac{b-ab}{1-ab} \end{bmatrix}$,

- *negative, then it can be represented in the following Markovian canonical form*

$$D_0 = \begin{bmatrix} -\lambda_1 & (1-a)\lambda_1 \\ 0 & -\lambda_2 \end{bmatrix}, \quad D_1 = \begin{bmatrix} 0 & a\lambda_1 \\ b\lambda_2 & (1-b)\lambda_2 \end{bmatrix},$$

where $0 < \lambda_1 \leq \lambda_2$, $0 \leq a \leq 1$, $0 < b \leq 1$, $\gamma = -ab$ and the associated embedded stationary vector is $\pi = \begin{bmatrix} \frac{b}{1+ab} & 1 - \frac{b}{1+ab} \end{bmatrix}$.

4.2   Canonical Forms of DMAP(2) with Positive Eigenvalues

Theorem 6. *If the eigenvalues of H_0 are positive and the correlation parameter of the order 2 DRAP(H_0, H_1) is*

- *non-negative, then it can be represented in the following Markovian canonical form*

$$D_0 = \begin{bmatrix} 1 - \lambda_1 & (1-a)\lambda_1 \\ 0 & 1 - \lambda_2 \end{bmatrix}, \quad D_1 = \begin{bmatrix} a\lambda_1 & 0 \\ (1-b)\lambda_2 & b\lambda_2 \end{bmatrix}. \quad (16)$$

where $0 < \lambda_1 \leq \lambda_2$, $0 \leq a,b < 1$, $\gamma = ab$ and the associated embedded stationary vector is $\pi = \left[\frac{1-b}{1-ab} \; \frac{b-ab}{1-ab} \right]$,

- *negative, then it can be represented in the following Markovian canonical form*

$$D_0 = \begin{bmatrix} 1 - \lambda_1 & (1-a)\lambda_1 \\ 0 & 1 - \lambda_2 \end{bmatrix}, \quad D_1 = \begin{bmatrix} 0 & a\lambda_1 \\ b\lambda_2 & (1-b)\lambda_2 \end{bmatrix}, \quad (17)$$

where $0 < \lambda_1 \leq \lambda_2$, $s_1 = 1 - \lambda_1$, $s_2 = 1 - \lambda_2$, $0 \leq a \leq 1$, $0 < b \leq 1$, $\gamma = -ab$ and the associated embedded stationary vector is $\pi = \left[\frac{b}{1+ab} \; 1 - \frac{b}{1+ab} \right]$.

Proof. Practically the same approach is applied here as in (15). The detailed proof of the theorem follows the same pattern as the proof of Theorem 5 in [7] which we omit here because we focus on the proof of Theorem 7, the related theorem with negative eigenvalues.

4.3   Canonical Forms of DMAP(2) with a Negative Eigenvalue

Theorem 7. *If one eigenvalue of H_0 is negative and the γ correlation parameter of the order 2 DRAP(H_0, H_1) is*

- *non-negative, then it can be represented in the following Markovian canonical form*

$$D_0 = \begin{bmatrix} 1 - \beta_1 & a\beta_1 \\ \frac{1}{a}\beta_2 & 0 \end{bmatrix}, D_1 = \begin{bmatrix} (1-a)\beta_1 & 0 \\ (1-\frac{1}{a}\beta_2)b & (1-\frac{1}{a}\beta_2)(1-b) \end{bmatrix}, \quad (18)$$

- *negative, then it can be represented in the following Markovian canonical form*

$$D_0 = \begin{bmatrix} 1 - \beta_1 & a\beta_1 \\ \frac{1}{a}\beta_2 & 0 \end{bmatrix}, D_1 = \begin{bmatrix} 0 & (1-a)\beta_1 \\ (1-\frac{1}{a}\beta_2)b & (1-\frac{1}{a}\beta_2)(1-b) \end{bmatrix}, \quad (19)$$

where the eigenvalues are such that $s_2 < 0 < s_1 < 1$, $s_1 + s_2 > 0$, the relation of the parameters and the eigenvalues is $\beta_1 = 1 - s_1 - s_2$, $\beta_2 = \frac{s_1 s_2}{s_1 + s_2 - 1}$, $0 \leq b < 1$ and $\beta_2 \leq a \leq \min\left(1, b\frac{1-s_2}{1-s_1}\right)$ in case of $\gamma \geq 0$ or $\beta_2 \leq a \leq 1$ in case of $\gamma < 0$,

The correlation parameter and the first coordinate of the embedded stationary probability vectors (the unique solution of (5))

– of (18) are

$$\gamma = (1-a)(1-b)\left(1 + \frac{1-a}{a}\frac{s_1 s_2}{1-s_1-s_2+s_1 s_2}\right),\qquad(20)$$

$$\pi_1 = \frac{1 - \frac{1}{1-a}\gamma}{1-\gamma},\qquad(21)$$

– of (19) are

$$\gamma = -(1-a)b\left(1 + \frac{1-a}{a}\frac{s_1 s_2}{1-s_1-s_2+s_1 s_2}\right),\qquad(22)$$

$$\pi_1 = 1 - \frac{1 + \frac{a}{1-a}\gamma}{1-\gamma}.\qquad(23)$$

We prove the theorem by considering the full flexibility of the DRAP(2) class with a negative eigenvalue and showing that the canonical forms of Theorem 7 cover this whole set of processes. To this end we first investigate the flexibility of the DRAP(2) class.

Constraints of the DRAP(2) Class. We investigate the flexibility of the DRAP(2) class based on the following representation

$$\boldsymbol{H_0} = \begin{bmatrix} s_1 & 0 \\ 0 & s_2 \end{bmatrix}, \boldsymbol{H_1} = \begin{bmatrix} a_1 + (1-a_1-s_1)\gamma & (1-a_1-s_1)(1-\gamma) \\ \frac{a_1(1-s_2)(1-\gamma)}{1-s_1} & \frac{(1-s_2)(1-a_1-s_1+a_1\gamma)}{1-s_1} \end{bmatrix},\qquad(24)$$

where s_1 is the positive, s_2 is the negative eigenvalue, γ is the correlation parameter and a_1 is the parameter that characterizes the stationary inter-arrival distribution together with the eigenvalues according to (13). With this representation the first coordinate of the embedded stationary vector is $\pi_1 = \frac{a_1}{1-s_1}$.

For a given pair of eigenvalues, $s_1 > 0$ and $s_2 < 0$, Theorem 1 defines the limits of a_1. According to these limits the first coordinate of any embedded vector of DRAP($\boldsymbol{H_0}, \boldsymbol{H_1}$) should be bounded by

$$\frac{(1-s_2)s_2}{(1-s_2)s_2-(1-s_1)s_1} \le x \le \frac{(1-s_2)(1-s_2)}{s_1-s_2}.\qquad(25)$$

Function $U_n(x)$ describes the effect of an n long inter-arrival period on the first coordinate of the embedded vector.

$$U_n(x) = \frac{(x, 1-x)\boldsymbol{H_0}^{n-1}\boldsymbol{H_1}}{(x, 1-x)\boldsymbol{H_0}^{n-1}\boldsymbol{H_1}\mathbb{1}}(1, 0)^T.\qquad(26)$$

If the embedded vector is $(x, 1-x)$ at an arrival instance and the next inter-arrival is n time unit long, the embedded vector is going to be $(U_n(x), 1-U_n(x))$ at the next arrival instance. In case of DMAPs the embedded vector represents the probability distribution of the background Markov chain at arrivals, but in case of DRAPs it does not have any probabilistic interpretations. H_0 and H_1 has to be such that starting from the stationary embedded vector π for any series of inter-arrival times the first coordinate of the embedded vector satisfy (25). Based on this property we define simple constraints.

- *long series of* 1 *time unit long inter-arrivals:*
  $U_1(x) = x$ has to have a real solution between the bounds in (25), because if $U_1(x)$ would be larger (smaller) than x between the bounds then a series of one time unit long inter-arrivals would increase (decrease) the first coordinate above the upper (below the lower) limit (cf. Figure 1). This constraint results in

  $$\gamma \leq \frac{(\sqrt{c_1} - \sqrt{c_2})^2}{(c_3 - a_1 s_2)^2}. \tag{27}$$

- *a long series of* 1 *time unit long inter-arrivals, then a* 2 *time unit long inter-arrival:*
  If $\gamma > 0$, then $U_1(x)$ is a shifted negative hyperbolic function which increases monotonously between the bounds in (25). If $U_1(x) = x$ has two solutions, w_1, w_2 ($w_1 < w_2$), then w_1 is stable and w_2 is unstable, which means that starting from $x < w_1$ or $w_1 < x < w_2$ and having a long series of 1 time unit long inter-arrivals the first coordinate converges to w_1, while starting from $x > w_2$ and having a long series of 1 time unit long inter-arrivals the first coordinate diverges. Consequently a long series of 1 time unit long inter-arrivals and a 2 time unit long inter-arrival keep the first coordinate between the bounds if $U_2(w_1) \leq w_2$ holds. This constraint results in

  $$\gamma \leq \frac{s_1 s_2 c_2 - c_1(1 - s_1 - s_2) - \sqrt{s_1 s_2 c_1 c_2 (s_1 + s_2)^2}}{c_4 c_5}. \tag{28}$$

- *long series of* 2 *time unit long inter-arrivals:*
  Similar to the first constraint $U_2(x) = x$ has to have a real solution which results in

  $$\gamma \geq \frac{(\sqrt{s_1 s_2 c_2} + \sqrt{c_6})^2}{c_4{}^2}. \tag{29}$$

- *a long series of* 1 *time unit long inter-arrivals:*
  If $\gamma < 0$ then $U_1(x)$ is a shifted hyperbolic function which decreases monotonously between the bounds in (25). $U_1(x) = x$ has to have a stable real solution (w_1) between the bounds in (25), which holds if $\frac{d}{dx}U_1(x)|_{x=w_1} > -1$ (cf. Figure 2) (in case of a long series of 1 time unit long inter-arrivals the first coordinate converge to w_1). This constraint results in

  $$\gamma \geq \frac{s_2(1 - a_1 - s_1) + a_1 s_1}{(c_3 - a_1 s_1)^2}. \tag{30}$$

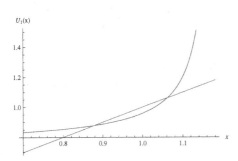

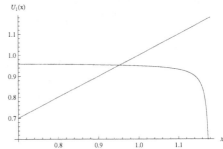

Fig. 1. The $U_1(x)$ function when $s_1 = 0.8, s_2 = -0.3, a_1 = 0.19, \gamma = 0.17$

Fig. 2. The $U_1(x)$ function when $s_1 = 0.8, s_2 = -0.3, a_1 = 0.19, \gamma = -0.012$

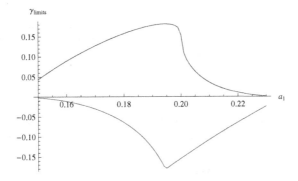

Fig. 3. The upper and lower γ limits as a function of a_1 when $s_1 = 0.8, s_2 = -0.3$

In the above expressions the auxiliary variables are

$$
\begin{aligned}
c_1 &= -a_1(s_1 - s_2)^2(1 - a_1 - s_1), \\
c_2 &= (1 - s_1)^3(1 - s_2), \\
c_3 &= 1 - s_1(2 - a_1 - s_1), \\
c_4 &= s_1(1 - s1)(1 - a_1 - s_1) + a_1 s_2(1 - s_2), \\
c_5 &= (a_1(s_1 - s_2) + s_2(1 - s_1)^2), \\
c_6 &= -a_1(1 - a_1 - s_1)(s_1(1 - s_1) - s_2(1 - s_2))^2.
\end{aligned}
\tag{31}
$$

We summarize the results of this subsection in the following theorem.

Theorem 8. *For DRAP(H_0, H_1) defined in (24) with $0 < s_1 < 1$, $-s_1 < s_2 < 0$ and a1 satisfying Theorem 1 the correlation parameter satisfies the inequalities (27) - (30).*

Theorem 8 defines only some bounds of the set of DRAP(2) processes, but the subsequent analysis of the canonical DMAP(2) proves that these bounds are tight.

Constraints of the Set of Canonical DMAP(2) Processes. Having the bounds of the DRAP(2) class from Theorem 8 we are ready to prove Theorem 7.

Proof. (Theorem 7) First we need to relate the variables of the canonical representation with the parameters used for characterizing the DMAP(2) processes. The relation of β_1, β_2 with s_1, s_2 is

$$s_{1,2} = \frac{1}{2}(1 - \beta_1 \pm \sqrt{(1 - \beta_1)^2 + 4\beta_1\beta_2}) \tag{32}$$

The relation of s_1, s_2, a_1, γ with a and b can be obtained from (20) and (21) for the first canonical form and form (22) and (23) for the second canonical form.
    If $\gamma > 0$, then

$$a = \frac{g_1 + \sqrt{g_1^2 - g_2}}{2e_1}, \quad b = 1 - \frac{a\gamma(1 - s_1 - s_2 + s_1 s_2)}{(1 - a)(a(1 - s_1 - s_2) + s_1 s_2)}, \tag{33}$$

where

$$\begin{aligned}
e_1 &= (1 - s_1)(1 - s_1 - s_2)^2, \\
e_2 &= (1 - s_1 - s_2)(a_1(s_1 - s_2)(1 - \gamma) - s_1(1 - s_1)), \\
e_3 &= \gamma(1 - s_1)^2, \\
g_1 &= e_1 + e_2 - e_3(1 - s_1 - s_2), \\
g_2 &= 4e_1(e_2 + e_3 s_1)
\end{aligned} \tag{34}$$

and if $\gamma < 0$, then

$$a = \frac{g_3 - \sqrt{g_3^2 + g_4}}{g_5}, \quad b = 1 - \frac{a\gamma(1 - s_1 - s_2 - s_1 s_2)}{(1 - a)(a(1 - s_1 - s_2) + s_1 s_2)}, \tag{35}$$

where

$$\begin{aligned}
e_6 &= a_1(s1 - s2)(1 - \gamma), \\
e_7 &= (1 - s_1)(s_2(1 - \gamma) - (1 - s_1 - s_2)\gamma), \\
e_8 &= (1 - s_1 - s_2)(1 - s_1)s_2, \\
g_3 &= -(1 - s_1 - s_2)e_6 + e_7 s_1 - e_8, \\
g_4 &= 4(e_6 + e_7)e_8 s_1, \\
g_5 &= -2(1 - s_1 - s_2)(e_6 + e_7).
\end{aligned} \tag{36}$$

Based on these relations the constraints of the canonical DMAP(2) processes can be obtained using the fact that all the elements of D_0 and D_1 have to be non-negative real numbers. That is a is real, $\beta_2 \le a \le 1$ and $0 \le b \le 1$. a is real when the expression under the square root sign in (33) for $\gamma > 0$ and in (33) for $\gamma < 0$ is non-negative. All together these constrains result in 5 inequalities for $\gamma > 0$ and 5 for $\gamma < 0$. Out of these the following ones are relevant.

- Case $\gamma > 0$:
  - a is real when $g_1^2 - g_2 \geq 0$ which translates to (27),
  - the inequality $b \leq 1$ translates to (28),
- Case $\gamma < 0$:
  - a is real when $g_3^2 + g_4 \geq 0$ which translates to (29),
  - the inequality $b \leq 0$ translates to (30).

We neglect the details of the other derivations here.

5   Explicit Moments and Correlation Matching with the Canonical Forms

One of the most important applications of the introduced canonical forms is the moments and correlation matching of DMAP(2) processes. Using the different canonical forms ((16) - (19)) we can obtain analytical formulas for their 4 characterizing parameters the first 3 factorial moments (f_1, f_2, f_3) and the correlation parameter (γ). Obviously, the different canonical forms result in different equations.

The moments and correlation matching requires the inverse of the computation of these parameters, that is the appropriate canonical form and its parameters have to be found for a given f_1, f_2, f_3 and γ. Unfortunately, based on f_1, f_2, f_3 it is not obvious how to decide if the eigenvalues are positive or one of them is negative and consequently, it is not trivial to decide which canonical form needs to be used. However, for any given set of f_1, f_2, f_3 and γ parameters at most one canonical form gives a Markovian representation. In the following we present methods to obtain the different canonical DMAP(2) from f_1, f_2, f_3 and γ. These methods consist of two steps. The first step is the calculation of the representation of the stationary inter-arrival time, i.e., α and A of Theorem 2 and 3 using the first three factorial moments, the second step is the computation of the parameters associated with γ.

Transformation to DMAP(2) Canonical Form with Positive Eigenvalues. As in the previous section we will first consider the DMAP(2) canonical form with positive eigenvalues ((16) and (17)). In this case the first step is based on Table 3 in [9]. the s_1 and s_2 elements of matrix A and vector α can be calculated as

$$\alpha = [p, 1-p], \; p = \frac{-z(h_3 - 6f_1h_1) + \sqrt{h_4}}{zh_3 + \sqrt{h_4}},$$

$$s_1 = 1 - \frac{h_3 - z\sqrt{h_4}}{h_2}, \; s_2 = 1 - \frac{h_3 + z\sqrt{h_4}}{h_2},$$

where

$$h_1 = 2f_1^2 - 2f_1 - f_2, \; h_2 = 3f_2^2 - 2f_1f_3,$$

$$h_3 = 3f_1f_2 - 6(f_1 + f_2 - f_1^2) - f_3, \; h_4 = h_3^2 - 6h_1h_2, \; z = \frac{h_2}{|h_2|}.$$

The second step is the calculation of a, b of Theorem 6. If $\gamma = 0$, then $a = 1$, $b = 0$. If $\gamma > 0$, then a and b can be computed using

$$a = \frac{d_1 - \sqrt{d_2}}{2(1 - s_1)}, \quad b = \frac{d_1 + \sqrt{d_2}}{2(1 - s_2)},$$

with

$$d_1 = 1 - s_2 - p(1 - s_2)(1 - \gamma) + (1 - s_1)\gamma, \quad d_2 = d_1^2 - 4(1 - s_1)(1 - s_2)\gamma.$$

If $\gamma \leq 0$, then

$$a = \frac{-\gamma(1 - s_2)}{p(1 - s_2)(1 - \gamma) - \gamma(1 - s_1)}, \quad b = \frac{p(1 - s_2)(1 - \gamma) - \gamma(1 - s_1)}{1 - s_2}.$$

Transformation to Canonical Form with a Negative Eigenvalue. For the DMAP(2) canonical form with a negative eigenvalue the β_1, β_2 parameters and the α vector can be calculated using

$$\beta_1 = \frac{12f_1^2 - 3f_2(4 + f_2) - 2f_3 + 2f_1(-6 + 3f_2 + f_3)}{(3f_2^2 - 2f_1f_3)}$$

$$\beta_2 = \frac{-3f_2(2 - 2f_1 + f_2) + 2(-1 + f_1)f_3}{12f_1^2 - 3f_2(4 + f_2) - 2f_3 + 2f_1(-6 + 3f_2 + f_3)}$$

$$p = \frac{\beta_1 - f_1\beta_1 + \beta_2 + f_1\beta_1\beta_2}{-1 + \beta_2}, \quad \alpha = [p, 1 - p].$$

From β_1 and β_2 the eigenvalues s_1 and s_2 are obtained by (32). In the second step a, b of Theorem 7 are calculated. If $\gamma = 0$ then $a = 1$, $b = 0$ stands again. Otherwise

$$a = \frac{k_1 + \sqrt{k_1^2 - k_2}}{2\beta_1}, \quad b = 1 - \frac{a\gamma(1 - \beta_2)}{(1 - a)(a - \beta_2)}, \quad \text{if } \gamma > 0,$$

$$a = \frac{k_3 + \sqrt{k_3^2 + 4\beta_2 k_4}}{2k_4}, \quad b = -\frac{a\gamma(1 - \beta_2)}{(1 - a)(a - \beta_2)}, \quad \text{if } \gamma < 0,$$

where

$$k_1 = (1 - \gamma)(p + \beta_1 + \beta_2 - p\beta_2) - 1 + \beta_1, \quad k_2 = 4\beta_1(k_1 - \beta_1 + \gamma - \beta_2\gamma),$$
$$k_3 = (1 - \gamma)(-p(1 - \beta_2) - 2\beta_2) - \gamma(1 - \beta_1), \quad k_4 = k_3 + \beta_2 + \gamma - \beta_2\gamma.$$

6   Conclusions

We have investigated the properties of order 2 DMAP and DRAP processes and found that some of their properties are identical with the ones of order 2 CMAP and CRAP, specifically the subset of order 2 DMAP and DRAP processes with positive eigenvalues can be mapped to the class of order 2 CMAP and

CRAP, while the subset of order 2 DMAP and DRAP processes with one negative eigenvalue differs from the order 2 CMAP and CRAP and requires a different treatment. We showed that the whole set of order 2 DMAP and DRAP cannot be represented with acyclic Markovian D_0 matrix, which was the case with order 2 CMAP and CRAP, but allowing cyclic representations as well the whole order 2 DRAP class can be represented with Markovian matrices.

We proposed a minimal (contains exactly 4 parameters) Markovian canonical representation of order 2 DMAPs and DRAPs. This canonical representation can be used efficiently for fitting, because the limits of the parameters are known a priori. Additionally, we presented simple explicit procedures for moments and correlation matching of canonical DMAP(2)s.

Acknowledgement. The authors gratefully acknowledge the support of the TÁMOP-4.2.2C-11/1/KONV-2012-0001 and the OTKA K101150 projects.

References

1. Neuts, M.F.: Matrix-Geometric Solutions in Stochastic Models: An Algorithmic Approach. Dover (1981)
2. Bladt, M., Neuts, M.F.: Matrix-exponential distributions: Calculus and interpretations via flows. Stochastic Models 19(1), 113–124 (2003)
3. Asmussen, S., Bladt, M.: Point processes with finite-dimensional conditional probabilities. Stochastic Processes and their Application 82, 127–142 (1999)
4. Bean, N., Nielsen, B.: Quasi-birth-and-death processes with rational arrival process components. Stochastic Models 26(3), 309–334 (2010)
5. Buchholz, P., Kemper, P., Kriege, J.: Multi-class Markovian arrival processes and their parameter fitting. Performance Evaluation 67(11), 1092–1106 (2010)
6. Mitchell, K., van de Liefvoort, A.: Approximation models of feed-forward g/g/1/n queueing networks with correlated arrivals. Perform. Eval. 51(2-4), 137–152 (2003)
7. Bodrog, L., Heindl, A., Horváth, G., Telek, M.: A Markovian canonical form of second-order matrix-exponential processes. European Journal of Operation Research 190, 459–477 (2008)
8. Papp, J., Telek, M.: Canonical representation of discrete phase type distributions of order 2 and 3. In: Proc. of UK Performance Evaluation Workshop, UKPEW 2013 (2013)
9. Telek, M., Heindl, A.: Matching moments for acyclic discrete and continuous phase-type distributions of second order. International Journal of Simulation Systems, Science & Technology 3(3-4), 47–57 (2002); Special Issue on: Analytical & Stochastic Modelling Techniques
10. Cumani, A.: On the canonical representation of homogeneous Markov processes modelling failure-time distributions. Microelectronics and Reliability 22, 583–602 (1982)
11. Telek, M., Horváth, G.: A minimal representation of Markov arrival processes and a moments matching method. Performance Evaluation 64(9-12), 1153–1168 (2007)

Encoding Timed Models
as Uniform Labeled Transition Systems*

Marco Bernardo[1] and Luca Tesei[2]

[1] Dipartimento di Scienze di Base e Fondamenti, Università di Urbino, Italy
[2] Scuola di Scienze e Tecnologie, Università di Camerino, Italy

Abstract. We provide a unifying view of timed models such as timed automata, probabilistic timed automata, and Markov automata. The timed models and their bisimulation semantics are encoded in the framework of uniform labeled transition systems. In this unifying framework, we show that the timed bisimilarities present in the literature can be re-obtained and that a new bisimilarity, of which we exhibit the modal logic characterization, can be introduced for timed models including probabilities. We finally highlight similarities and differences among the models.

1 Introduction

Several extensions of classical automata have been proposed in the last twenty years to model timed aspects of the behavior of systems and to support the verification of hard and soft real-time constraints. The first of these extensions is given by timed automata (TA) [1]. They are equipped with clock variables that measure the passage of time within states, while transitions are instantaneous, may be subject to clock-based guards, and may reset the value of some clocks.

A subsequent extension is that of probabilistic timed automata (PTA) [12]. They are TA where the destination of every transition is a function that associates with each state the probability of being the target state. This allows for the representation both of nondeterministic choices and of probabilistic choices, and enables the investigation of properties such as the probability of executing certain activities within a given deadline is not lower than a given threshold.

The semantics of a TA/PTA can be defined in terms of a variant of labeled transition system (LTS) [11] together with a notion of bisimulation [8]. The characteristic of the underlying variant of LTS is that of having uncountably many states, as any of these states essentially corresponds to a pair composed of a TA/PTA state and a vector of clock values each taken from $\mathbb{R}_{\geq 0}$.

A more recent extension is constituted by Markov automata (MA) [7], in which the probabilistic flavor of PTA transitions is retained, while temporal aspects are described through exponentially distributed random variables rather than deterministic quantities. Since exponential distributions enjoy the memoryless property, an MA no longer needs clocks and hence can be directly viewed as a variant of LTS whose states correspond to the MA states.

* Work partially supported by the MIUR-PRIN Project CINA and the European Commission FP7-ICT-FET Proactive Project TOPDRIM (grant agreement no. 318121).

M.S. Balsamo, W.J. Knottenbelt, and A. Marin (Eds.): EPEW 2013, LNCS 8168, pp. 104–118, 2013.

In order to emphasize similarities and differences among the various models, in this paper we provide a unifying view of TA, PTA, and MA by encoding all of them as uniform labeled transition systems (ULTRAS) [4]. This is a recently developed framework that has proven to be well suited for uniformly representing different models – ranging from LTS models to discrete-/continuous-time Markov chains and Markov decision processes without/with internal nondeterminism – together with their behavioral equivalences.

The paper is organized as follows. In Sect. 2, we recall the notion of ULTRAS and we extend it in order to deal with uncountable state spaces. In Sect. 3, we encode as ULTRAS the variant of LTS underlying TA and we show that the corresponding bisimilarity in [16,20] coincides with a suitable instance of the bisimilarity for ULTRAS. In Sect. 4, we reuse the same encoding to handle TA. In Sect. 5, we encode as ULTRAS the variant of LTS underlying PTA and we show that two different bisimilarities can be defined: the one in [19] and a new one for which we exhibit a modal logic characterization. In Sects. 6 and 7, we reuse almost the same encoding to handle PTA and MA, respectively. Finally, in Sect. 8 we draw some conclusions about the considered timed models.

2   Revisiting the Definition of ULTRAS

The definition of ULTRAS given in [4] was based on a set of states and a set of transition-labeling actions that are at most countable. When dealing with TA and PTA models whose time domain is $\mathbb{R}_{\geq 0}$, the underlying LTS models turn out to have *uncountably* many states and actions. Therefore, we need to extend the definition of ULTRAS by admitting uncountable sets of states and actions, in a way that preserves the results in [4].

Every ULTRAS is parameterized with respect to a set D, whose values are interpreted as different degrees of *one-step reachability*, and a preorder $\sqsubseteq_D$ equipped with minimum $\perp_D$, which denotes *unreachability*. In this paper, we consider the set $[S \to D]_{cs}$ of *countable-support* functions from a set S to D, i.e., the set of functions $\mathcal{D} : S \to D$ whose support $supp(\mathcal{D}) = \{s \in S \mid \mathcal{D}(s) \neq \perp_D\}$ is at most countable. As in [4], when S is a set of states, every element $\mathcal{D}$ of $[S \to D]_{cs}$ is interpreted as a *next-state distribution function* and $supp(\mathcal{D})$ represents the set of reachable states.

Definition 1. *Let $(D, \sqsubseteq_D, \perp_D)$ be a preordered set equipped with a minimum. A* uniform labeled transition system *on $(D, \sqsubseteq_D, \perp_D)$, or D-ULTRAS for short, is a triple $\mathcal{U} = (S, A, \longrightarrow)$ where S is a possibly uncountable set of states, A is a possibly uncountable set of actions, and $\longrightarrow \subseteq S \times A \times [S \to D]_{cs}$ is a transition relation. We say that the D-ULTRAS $\mathcal{U}$ is* functional *iff $\longrightarrow$ is a total function from $S \times A$ to $[S \to D]_{cs}$.* ∎

Every transition $(s, a, \mathcal{D})$ is written $s \xrightarrow{a} \mathcal{D}$, where $\mathcal{D}(s')$ is a D-value quantifying the degree of reachability of s' from s via that transition and $\mathcal{D}(s') = \perp_D$ means that s' is not reachable with that transition. If the D-ULTRAS is functional, we shall write $\mathcal{D}_{s,a}(s')$ to denote the same D-value.

A D-ULTRAS can be depicted as a directed graph-like structure in which vertices represent states and action-labeled edges represent action-labeled transitions. Given a transition $s \xrightarrow{a} \mathcal{D}$, the corresponding a-labeled edge goes from the vertex representing s to a set of vertices linked by a dashed line, each of which represents a state $s' \in supp(\mathcal{D})$ and is labeled with $\mathcal{D}(s')$. Should $\mathcal{D}(s') = \perp_D$ for all states s' – which may happen when the considered D-ULTRAS is functional – the transition would not be depicted at all. A $\mathbb{B}$-ULTRAS is shown on the right-hand side of Fig. 1, where $\mathbb{B} = \{\perp, \top\}$ is the support set of the Boolean algebra, $\perp$ (false) denotes unreachability, $\top$ (true) denotes reachability, and $\perp \sqsubseteq_{\mathbb{B}} \top$.

In [4], various equivalences were defined over ULTRAS and shown to coincide in most cases with those appeared in the literature of nondeterministic, probabilistic, stochastic, and mixed models. Since in this paper we focus on bisimilarity, we shall recall only the definition of bisimilarity for ULTRAS. This definition, like the one of the other equivalences, is parameterized with respect to a measure function that expresses the degree of *multi-step reachability* of a set of states in terms of values taken from a preordered set equipped with minimum. In the following, we call *trace* an element α of A^* and we denote by ε the empty trace, by "$|\_|$" the operation that computes the length of a trace, and by "$\_ \circ \_$" the operation that concatenates two traces.

Definition 2. *Let* $\mathcal{U} = (S, A, \longrightarrow)$ *be a* D-ULTRAS, $n \in \mathbb{N}$, $s_i \in S$ *for* $0 \leq i \leq n$, *and* $a_i \in A$ *for* $1 \leq i \leq n$. *We say that* $s_0 \xrightarrow{a_1} s_1 \xrightarrow{a_2} s_2 \ldots s_{n-1} \xrightarrow{a_n} s_n$ *is a computation of* $\mathcal{U}$ *of length* n *that goes from* s_0 *to* s_n *and is labeled with trace* $a_1 a_2 \ldots a_n$ *iff for all* $i = 1, \ldots, n$ *there exists a transition* $s_{i-1} \xrightarrow{a_i} \mathcal{D}_i$ *such that* $s_i \in supp(\mathcal{D}_i)$. ∎

Definition 3. *Let* $\mathcal{U} = (S, A, \longrightarrow)$ *be a* D-ULTRAS *and* $(M, \sqsubseteq_M, \perp_M)$ *be a preordered set equipped with a minimum. A* measure function *on* $(M, \sqsubseteq_M, \perp_M)$ *for* $\mathcal{U}$, *or* M-measure function for $\mathcal{U}$, *is a function* $\mathcal{M}_M : S \times A^* \times 2^S \to M$ *such that the value of* $\mathcal{M}_M(s, \alpha, S')$ *is defined by induction on* $|\alpha|$ *and depends only on the reachability of a state in* S' *from state* s *through computations labeled with trace* α. ∎

Definition 4. *Let* $\mathcal{U} = (S, A, \longrightarrow)$ *be a* D-ULTRAS *and* $\mathcal{M}_M$ *be an* M-measure function for $\mathcal{U}$. *An equivalence relation* $\mathcal{B}$ *over* S *is an* $\mathcal{M}_M$-bisimulation *iff, whenever* $(s_1, s_2) \in \mathcal{B}$, *then for all actions* $a \in A$ *and groups of equivalence classes* $\mathcal{G} \in 2^{S/\mathcal{B}}$ *it holds that:*
$$\mathcal{M}_M(s_1, a, \bigcup \mathcal{G}) = \mathcal{M}_M(s_2, a, \bigcup \mathcal{G})$$
where $\bigcup \mathcal{G}$ *is the union of all the equivalence classes in* $\mathcal{G}$. *We say that* $s_1, s_2 \in S$ *are* $\mathcal{M}_M$-bisimilar, *written* $s_1 \sim_{B,\mathcal{M}_M} s_2$, *iff there exists an* $\mathcal{M}_M$-bisimulation $\mathcal{B}$ *over* S *such that* $(s_1, s_2) \in \mathcal{B}$. ∎

The preordered structure $(M, \sqsubseteq_M, \perp_M)$ for multi-step reachability used in the definition of the equivalence does *not* necessarily coincide with the preordered structure $(D, \sqsubseteq_D, \perp_D)$ for one-step reachability used in the definition of the model. In [4], various cases were illustrated that demonstrate the necessity of keeping the two structures separate to retrieve certain equivalences.

The definition of bisimilarity is given in the style of [14], i.e., it requires a bisimulation to be an equivalence relation. However, it deals with arbitrary *groups of equivalence classes* rather than only with individual equivalence classes. As shown in [4], working with groups of equivalence classes provides an adequate support to models in which nondeterminism and quantitative aspects coexist. In particular, it gives rise to new probabilistic bisimulation equivalences that have interesting logical characterizations (see the references in [4]).

3   Encoding Timed LTS Models

Timed processes can be represented as models enriched with timing information. Following the orthogonal-time approach[1] of [16], we consider an extension of LTS called timed labeled transition system (TLTS). In this model, functional aspects (i.e., process activities assumed to be instantaneous) are separate from temporal aspects (i.e., time passing) by means of two distinct transition relations: one labeled with actions and the other labeled with amounts of time. Since we are interested in TLTS models obtained from TA, we shall consider $\mathbb{R}_{\geq 0}$ as time domain and allow for uncountably many states and actions.

Definition 5. *A* timed labeled transition system (TLTS) *is a quadruple* $(S, A, \longrightarrow, \rightsquigarrow)$ *where* S *is a possibly uncountable set of states,* A *is a possibly uncountable set of actions, and:*

- $\longrightarrow \subseteq S \times A \times S$ *is an action-transition relation such that for all* $s \in S$ *and* $a \in A$ *it holds that* $\{s' \in S \mid (s, a, s') \in \longrightarrow\}$ *is at most countable.*
- $\rightsquigarrow \subseteq S \times \mathbb{R}_{\geq 0} \times S$ *is a time-transition relation satisfying* $(s, 0, s) \in \rightsquigarrow$ *[0-delay],* $(s, t, s'_1) \in \rightsquigarrow \wedge (s, t, s'_2) \in \rightsquigarrow \implies s'_1 = s'_2$ *[time determinism], and* $(s, t_1, s') \in \rightsquigarrow \wedge (s', t_2, s'') \in \rightsquigarrow \implies (s, t_1 + t_2, s'') \in \rightsquigarrow$ *[time additivity].* ∎

Every action-transition (s, a, s') is written $s \xrightarrow{a} s'$ and means that s can reach s' by executing action a, whilst every time-transition (s, t, s') is written $s \xrightarrow{t} s'$ and means that s can evolve into s' after an amount of time equal to t.

Following [20], we can merge the two transition relations into a single one by adding a special time-elapsing action $\epsilon(t)$ for every $t \in \mathbb{R}_{\geq 0}$. With this in mind, it is immediate to see that a TLTS can be encoded as a functional $\mathbb{B}$-ULTRAS.

Definition 6. *Let* $(S, A, \longrightarrow, \rightsquigarrow)$ *be a TLTS. Its corresponding functional* $\mathbb{B}$-ULTRAS $\mathcal{U} = (S, A_{\mathcal{U}}, \longrightarrow_{\mathcal{U}})$ *is defined by letting:*

- $A_{\mathcal{U}} = A \cup \{\epsilon(t) \mid t \in \mathbb{R}_{\geq 0}\}.$
- $s \xrightarrow{a}_{\mathcal{U}} \mathcal{D}_{s,a}$ *for all* $s \in S$ *and* $a \in A_{\mathcal{U}}.$
- $\mathcal{D}_{s,a}(s') = \begin{cases} \top & \text{if } a \in A \text{ and } s \xrightarrow{a} s', \text{ or } a = \epsilon(t) \text{ and } s \xrightarrow{t} s' \\ \bot & \text{otherwise} \end{cases}$
  for all $s' \in S.$ ∎

---

[1] As opposed to the integrated-time approach, in which process activities are assumed to be durational: see [6,3] for an overview of both approaches in different settings.

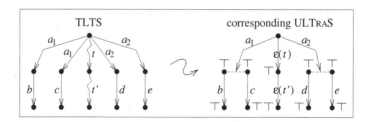

Fig. 1. Translation of a TLTS exhibiting both external and internal nondeterminism

If a TLTS state has a certain number of *differently labeled* outgoing action-transitions, then those transitions are retained in the corresponding functional $\mathbb{B}$-ULTRAS. In other words, *external nondeterminism* in the original model is preserved by the resulting model. In contrast, *internal nondeterminism* is encoded within the target countable-support functions of the transitions of the resulting model. Indeed, if a TLTS state has several *identically labeled* outgoing action-transitions, then a single transition is generated in the corresponding functional $\mathbb{B}$-ULTRAS, in which several states are assigned $\top$ as reachability value. The encoding of both forms of nondeterminism is exemplified in Fig. 1.

A notion of bisimilarity for timed processes was introduced in [16,20], where the congruence property and an equational characterization were also studied. The decidability of timed bisimilarity was established in [5].

Definition 7. Let $(S, A, \longrightarrow, \rightsquigarrow)$ be a TLTS. A relation $\mathcal{B}$ over S is a timed bisimulation iff, whenever $(s_1, s_2) \in \mathcal{B}$, then for all actions $a \in A$ and amounts of time $t \in \mathbb{R}_{\geq 0}$ it holds that:

- For each $s_1 \xrightarrow{a} s_1'$ (resp. $s_2 \xrightarrow{a} s_2'$) there exists $s_2 \xrightarrow{a} s_2'$ (resp. $s_1 \xrightarrow{a} s_1'$) such that $(s_1', s_2') \in \mathcal{B}$.
- For each $s_1 \xrightarrow{t} s_1'$ (resp. $s_2 \xrightarrow{t} s_2'$) there exists $s_2 \xrightarrow{t} s_2'$ (resp. $s_1 \xrightarrow{t} s_1'$) such that $(s_1', s_2') \in \mathcal{B}$.

We say that $s_1, s_2 \in S$ are timed bisimilar, written $s_1 \sim_{\text{TB}} s_2$, iff there exists a timed bisimulation $\mathcal{B}$ over S such that $(s_1, s_2) \in \mathcal{B}$. ■

Timed bisimilarity over TLTS models is captured by $\sim_{\text{B},\mathcal{M}_\mathbb{B}}$ over the corresponding functional $\mathbb{B}$-ULTRAS models, where measure function $\mathcal{M}_\mathbb{B}$ is defined in Table 1. When $\alpha = a \circ \alpha'$, the measure function considers each possible next state s' by examining whether it is reachable from s via a ($\mathcal{D}_{s,a}(s')$) and it can reach a state in S' via α' ($\mathcal{M}_\mathbb{B}(s', \alpha', S')$). If this is the case for at least one of the possible next states s', then $\mathcal{M}_\mathbb{B}(s, \alpha, S') = \top$, otherwise $\mathcal{M}_\mathbb{B}(s, \alpha, S') = \bot$. Note that, for TLTS models, the preordered structure of the corresponding ULTRAS models coincides with the preordered structure of the measure function.

Theorem 1. Let $(S, A, \longrightarrow, \rightsquigarrow)$ be a TLTS and $\mathcal{U} = (S, A_\mathcal{U}, \longrightarrow_\mathcal{U})$ be the corresponding functional $\mathbb{B}$-ULTRAS. For all $s_1, s_2 \in S$:

$$s_1 \sim_{\text{TB}} s_2 \iff s_1 \sim_{\text{B},\mathcal{M}_\mathbb{B}} s_2$$

■

Table 1. Measure function for functional $\mathbb{B}$-ULTRAS models representing TLTS models

$$\mathcal{M}_{\mathbb{B}}(s, \alpha, S') = \begin{cases} \bigvee_{s' \in S} \mathcal{D}_{s,a}(s') \wedge \mathcal{M}_{\mathbb{B}}(s', \alpha', S') & \text{if } \alpha = a \circ \alpha' \\ \top & \text{if } \alpha = \varepsilon \text{ and } s \in S' \\ \bot & \text{if } \alpha = \varepsilon \text{ and } s \notin S' \end{cases}$$

4   Encoding Timed Automata

Timed automata (TA) [1] extend classical automata by introducing *clock variables*, or simply clocks, that measure the passage of time. They all advance at the same speed and take values in $\mathbb{R}_{\geq 0}$. A *clock valuation* $\nu \in \mathcal{V}_{\mathcal{X}}$ over a finite set of clocks $\mathcal{X}$ is a total function from $\mathcal{X}$ to $\mathbb{R}_{\geq 0}$. Given a valuation ν and a delay $t \in \mathbb{R}_{\geq 0}$, we let $\nu + t$ denote the valuation mapping each clock $x \in \mathcal{X}$ into $\nu(x) + t$. A *reset* γ is a set of clocks in $\mathcal{X}$ whose value is set back to zero. For a valuation ν and a reset γ, we let $\nu \backslash \gamma(x) = 0$ if $x \in \gamma$ and $\nu \backslash \gamma(x) = \nu(x)$ if $x \notin \gamma$.

In TA, time elapses in states, called *locations*, as long as *invariant conditions* associated with the locations themselves hold. These are constraints on the values of the clocks through which notions such as urgency or laziness of actions can be expressed [9]. In contrast, the execution of an action transition is considered instantaneous. Transitions are *guarded*, i.e., enabled/disabled, by constraints on the values of the clocks, and can reset the value of some clocks.

The set $\Psi_{\mathcal{X}}$ of *clock constraints* over a finite set of clocks $\mathcal{X}$ is defined by the following grammar: $\psi ::= x \# c \mid \psi \wedge \psi$ where $x \in \mathcal{X}$, $c \in \mathbb{N}$, and $\# \in \{<, >, \leq, \geq, =\}$. Clock constraints are assessed over clock valuations. The satisfaction of a clock constraint ψ by a valuation ν, denoted by $\nu \models \psi$, is defined as follows: (i) $\nu \models x \# c$ iff $\nu(x) \# c$, (ii) $\nu \models \psi_1 \wedge \psi_2$ iff $\nu \models \psi_1$ and $\nu \models \psi_2$. The given syntax for constraints is minimal; the so-called diagonal clock constraints of the form $x - y \# c$ can be simulated by using more locations and the constraints of the given form [2]. An invariant condition is a clock constraint with the property of being *past-closed*, i.e., for all valuations ν and delays $t \in \mathbb{R}_{\geq 0}$ it holds that $\nu + t \models \psi \Longrightarrow \nu \models \psi$.

Definition 8. *A* timed automaton (TA) *is a tuple* $(L, A, \mathcal{X}, I, \longrightarrow)$ *where* L *is a finite set of locations,* A *is a set of actions,* $\mathcal{X}$ *is a finite set of clocks,* I *is a function mapping each location into an invariant condition, and* $\longrightarrow \subseteq L \times \Psi_{\mathcal{X}} \times A \times 2^{\mathcal{X}} \times L$ *is a transition relation.* ∎

Every transition is written $\ell \xrightarrow{\psi, a, \gamma} \ell'$ where ℓ is the source location, ψ is the guard, a is the action label, γ is the clock reset, and ℓ' is the target location.

The semantics of a TA is given in terms of a TLTS. Thus, it is natural to encode a TA as a functional $\mathbb{B}$-ULTRAS generated by using the same conditions defining the TA semantics.

Definition 9. *Let* $(L, A, \mathcal{X}, I, \longrightarrow)$ *be a TA. Its corresponding functional* $\mathbb{B}$-ULTRAS $\mathcal{U} = (S, A_{\mathcal{U}}, \longrightarrow_{\mathcal{U}})$ *is defined by letting:*

- $S = \{(\ell, \nu) \in L \times \mathcal{V}_\chi \mid \nu \models I(\ell)\}$.
- $A_\mathcal{U} = A \cup \{\epsilon(t) \mid t \in \mathbb{R}_{\geq 0}\}$.
- $(\ell, \nu) \overset{a}{\longrightarrow}_\mathcal{U} \mathcal{D}_{(\ell,\nu),a}$ for all $(\ell, \nu) \in S$ and $a \in A_\mathcal{U}$.

- $\mathcal{D}_{(\ell,\nu),a}(\ell', \nu') = \begin{cases} \top & \text{if } a \in A,\ \ell \overset{\psi,a,\gamma}{\longrightarrow} \ell',\ \nu \models \psi,\ \nu' = \nu \backslash \gamma,\ \nu' \models I(\ell') \\ \top & \text{if } a = \epsilon(t),\ \ell' = \ell,\ \nu' = \nu + t,\ \nu' \models I(\ell') \\ \bot & \text{otherwise} \end{cases}$

  for all $(\ell', \nu') \in S$.   ■

Timed bisimilarity over TA models is defined in terms of the underlying TLTS models. Therefore, we can reuse both Def. 7 and Table 1, so that Thm. 1 also applies to functional $\mathbb{B}$-ULTRAS models corresponding to TA models.

5   Encoding Probabilistic Timed LTS Models

A probabilistic extension of the TLTS model (PTLTS) was introduced in [19]. Following the simple probabilistic automaton model of [18], the action-transition relation is transformed into a probabilistic action-transition relation. This means that a PTLTS action transition, instead of leading to a single target state, has a *probability distribution over target states* assigning each such state the probability of being reached. Therefore, the choice among several outgoing action transitions from the same state is *nondeterministic*, whereas the choice of the target state for the selected transition is *probabilistic*. Given a possibly uncountable set S, we denote by $Distr_{cs}(S)$ the set of probability distributions $\mathcal{D}$ over S whose support $supp(\mathcal{D}) = \{s \in S \mid \mathcal{D}(s) > 0\}$ is at most countable.

While in [19] there is a single transition relation and hence each transition is also labeled with the duration of the corresponding action, here we stick to the orthogonal-time approach and hence keep using two transition relations: a probabilistic one labeled with actions and a deterministic one labeled with amounts of time. We prefer to do so for two reasons. Firstly, this allows us to use a consistent notation and model structure throughout the paper. Secondly, separating functional aspects from time aspects simplifies the development of weak behavioral equivalences, as has been shown in the deterministic time case [20,17,13] and in the stochastic time case [10,7].

Definition 10. *A probabilistic timed labeled transition system (PTLTS) is a quadruple* $(S, A, \longrightarrow, \rightsquigarrow)$ *where S is a possibly uncountable set of states, A is a possibly uncountable set of actions, and:*

- $\longrightarrow \subseteq S \times A \times Distr_{cs}(S)$ *is a probabilistic action-transition relation.*
- $\rightsquigarrow \subseteq S \times \mathbb{R}_{\geq 0} \times S$ *is a time-transition relation satisfying 0-delay, time determinism, and time additivity.*   ■

Every action-transition $(s, a, \mathcal{D})$ is written $s \overset{a}{\longrightarrow} \mathcal{D}$ – which is already in the ULTRAS transition format – whilst every time-transition (s, t, s') is written $s \overset{t}{\rightsquigarrow} s'$. As in the TLTS case, we can merge the two transition relations into a single one by adding a special time-elapsing action $\epsilon(t)$ for every $t \in \mathbb{R}_{\geq 0}$, such that

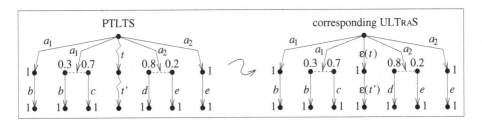

Fig. 2. Translation of a PTLTS exhibiting both external and internal nondeterminism

the target distributions of the transitions labeled with such actions concentrate all the probability mass into a single state. At this point, it is straightforward to encode a PTLTS as an $\mathbb{R}_{[0,1]}$-ULTRAS, which relies on the usual ordering for real numbers – with 0 denoting unreachability – and is not necessarily functional due to the coexistence of probability and internal nondeterminism [4]. In the following, given $s \in S$ we denote by δ_s the Dirac distribution for s, where $\delta_s(s) = 1$ and $\delta_s(s') = 0$ for all $s' \in S \setminus \{s\}$.

Definition 11. *Let* $(S, A, \longrightarrow, \rightsquigarrow)$ *be a PTLTS. Its corresponding* $\mathbb{R}_{[0,1]}$*-ULTRAS* $\mathcal{U} = (S, A_{\mathcal{U}}, \longrightarrow_{\mathcal{U}})$ *is defined by letting:*

- $A_{\mathcal{U}} = A \cup \{\epsilon(t) \mid t \in \mathbb{R}_{\geq 0}\}$.
- $s \xrightarrow{a}_{\mathcal{U}} \mathcal{D}$ *for each* $s \xrightarrow{a} \mathcal{D}$.
- $s \xrightarrow{\epsilon(t)}_{\mathcal{U}} \delta_{s'}$ *for each* $s \xrightarrow{t} s'$. ∎

Different from the TLTS encoding, both external nondeterminism and internal nondeterminism in the original PTLTS are preserved in the corresponding $\mathbb{R}_{[0,1]}$-ULTRAS. This is exemplified in Fig. 2.

A notion of bisimilarity for probabilistic timed processes was introduced in [19], where a modal logic characterization and a decision procedure were also studied. Below, we reformulate the definition in the orthogonal-time framework and we let $\mathcal{D}(C) = \sum_{s \in C} \mathcal{D}(s)$ for $\mathcal{D} \in \mathit{Distr}_{cs}(S)$ and $C \subseteq S$.

Definition 12. *Let* $(S, A, \longrightarrow, \rightsquigarrow)$ *be a PTLTS. An equivalence relation* $\mathcal{B}$ *over* S *is a* probabilistic timed bisimulation *iff, whenever* $(s_1, s_2) \in \mathcal{B}$, *then for all actions* $a \in A$ *and amounts of time* $t \in \mathbb{R}_{\geq 0}$ *it holds that:*L

- *For each* $s_1 \xrightarrow{a} \mathcal{D}_1$ *there exists* $s_2 \xrightarrow{a} \mathcal{D}_2$ *such that for all equivalence classes* $C \in S/\mathcal{B}$ *it holds that* $\mathcal{D}_1(C) = \mathcal{D}_2(C)$.
- *For each* $s_1 \xrightarrow{t} s_1'$ *there exists* $s_2 \xrightarrow{t} s_2'$ *such that* $(s_1', s_2') \in \mathcal{B}$.

We say that $s_1, s_2 \in S$ *are* probabilistic timed bisimilar, *written* $s_1 \sim_{\mathrm{PTB}} s_2$, *iff there exists a probabilistic timed bisimulation* $\mathcal{B}$ *over* S *such that* $(s_1, s_2) \in \mathcal{B}$. ∎

It is relatively easy to see that the relation $\sim_{\mathrm{PTB}}$ coincides with the following bisimulation equivalence defined over $\mathbb{R}_{[0,1]}$-ULTRAS models corresponding to

Table 2. Measure function for $\mathbb{R}_{[0,1]}$-ULTRAS models representing PTLTS models

$$
\mathcal{M}_{2^{\mathbb{R}_{[0,1]}}}(s,\alpha,S') = \begin{cases} \displaystyle\bigcup_{s \xrightarrow{a}_{\mathcal{D}}} \{ \sum_{s'\in S} \mathcal{D}(s') \cdot p_{s'} \mid p_{s'} \in \mathcal{M}_{2^{\mathbb{R}_{[0,1]}}}(s',\alpha',S') \} \\ \qquad\qquad\qquad \text{if } \alpha = a \circ \alpha' \text{ and there exists } s \xrightarrow{a} \mathcal{D} \\[2ex] \{1\} \qquad\qquad\quad \text{if } \alpha = \varepsilon \text{ and } s \in S' \\[2ex] \{0\} \qquad\qquad\quad \text{if } \alpha = a \circ \alpha' \text{ and there is no } s \xrightarrow{a} \mathcal{D} \\ \qquad\qquad\qquad \text{or } \alpha = \varepsilon \text{ and } s \notin S' \end{cases}
$$

PTLTS models. The equivalence below is called *group-distribution* bisimilarity because it compares *entire distributions* of reaching groups of equivalence classes. Given two related states, for each transition of one of the two states there must exist an equally labeled transition of the other state such that, *for every group of equivalence classes*, the two transitions have the same probability of reaching a state in that group. In other words, the two transitions must be *fully matching*, i.e., they must match with respect to all groups.

Definition 13. *Let* $\mathcal{U} = (S, A_{\mathcal{U}}, \longrightarrow_{\mathcal{U}})$ *be the* $\mathbb{R}_{[0,1]}$-ULTRAS *corresponding to a PTLTS* $(S, A, \longrightarrow, \rightsquigarrow)$. *An equivalence relation* $\mathcal{B}$ *over* S *is a* probabilistic timed group-distribution bisimulation *iff, whenever* $(s_1, s_2) \in \mathcal{B}$, *then for all actions* $a \in A_{\mathcal{U}}$ *it holds that:*

- *For each* $s_1 \xrightarrow{a}_{\mathcal{U}} \mathcal{D}_1$ *there exists* $s_2 \xrightarrow{a}_{\mathcal{U}} \mathcal{D}_2$ *such that* for all groups of equivalence classes $\mathcal{G} \in 2^{S/\mathcal{B}}$ *it holds that* $\mathcal{D}_1(\bigcup \mathcal{G}) = \mathcal{D}_2(\bigcup \mathcal{G})$.

We say that $s_1, s_2 \in S$ *are* probabilistic timed group-distribution bisimilar, *written* $s_1 \sim_{\text{PTB,dis}} s_2$, *iff there exists a probabilistic timed group-distribution bisimulation* $\mathcal{B}$ *over* S *such that* $(s_1, s_2) \in \mathcal{B}$. ∎

Theorem 2. *Let* $(S, A, \longrightarrow, \rightsquigarrow)$ *be a PTLTS and* $\mathcal{U} = (S, A_{\mathcal{U}}, \longrightarrow_{\mathcal{U}})$ *be the corresponding* $\mathbb{R}_{[0,1]}$-ULTRAS. *For all* $s_1, s_2 \in S$:
$$s_1 \sim_{\text{PTB}} s_2 \iff s_1 \sim_{\text{PTB,dis}} s_2$$
∎

The relation $\sim_{\text{PTB}}$ over PTLTS models has been expressed as $\sim_{\text{PTB,dis}}$ in the ULTRAS setting, but cannot be captured by any instantiation of the general bisimilarity for ULTRAS given in Def. 4. In the case of probabilistic timed processes, a natural measure function is the one defined in Table 2. Denoting by $2^{\mathbb{R}_{[0,1]}}$ the set of *nonempty* subsets of $\mathbb{R}_{[0,1]}$, this measure function associates a suitable element of $2^{\mathbb{R}_{[0,1]}}$ with every triple composed of a source state s, a trace α, and a set of destination states S'. The set $\mathcal{M}_{2^{\mathbb{R}_{[0,1]}}}(s, \alpha, S')$ contains for each possible way of resolving nondeterminism the probability of performing a computation that is labeled with trace α and leads to a state in S' from state s. It is worth pointing out that, while the considered ULTRAS models are based on the preordered structure $(\mathbb{R}_{[0,1]}, \leq, 0)$, the measure function relies on the different preordered structure $(2^{\mathbb{R}_{[0,1]}}, \sqsubseteq, \{0\})$ where $R_1 \sqsubseteq R_2$ means $\inf R_1 \leq \inf R_2$ and $|R_1| \leq |R_2|$ (the latter condition ensures $\{0\}$ being the minimum).

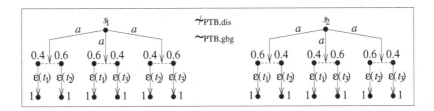

Fig. 3. Counterexample showing that $\sim_{\text{PTB,gbg}}$ is strictly coarser than $\sim_{\text{PTB,dis}}$

The resulting bisimilarity $\sim_{\text{B},\mathcal{M}_{2,\,[0,1]}^{\mathbb{R}}}$ captures the following equivalence that we call *group-by-group* bisimilarity because it considers *a single group of equivalence classes at a time*. Technically speaking, this amounts to anticipating the quantification over groups (underlined in Def. 13) with respect to the quantification over transitions. In this way, a transition departing from one of two related states is allowed to be matched, with respect to the probabilities of reaching different groups, by several different transitions departing from the other state. In other words, *partially matching* transitions are allowed.

Definition 14. *Let* $\mathcal{U} = (S, A_{\mathcal{U}}, \longrightarrow_{\mathcal{U}})$ *be the* $\mathbb{R}_{[0,1]}$-*ULTRAS corresponding to a PTLTS* $(S, A, \longrightarrow, \rightsquigarrow)$. *An equivalence relation* $\mathcal{B}$ *over* S *is a* probabilistic timed group-by-group bisimulation *iff, whenever* $(s_1, s_2) \in \mathcal{B}$, *then for all actions* $a \in A_{\mathcal{U}}$ *and* <u>*for all groups of equivalence classes*</u> $\mathcal{G} \in 2^{S/\mathcal{B}}$ *it holds that:*

- *For each* $s_1 \xrightarrow{a}_{\mathcal{U}} \mathcal{D}_1$ *there exists* $s_2 \xrightarrow{a}_{\mathcal{U}} \mathcal{D}_2$ *such that* $\mathcal{D}_1(\bigcup \mathcal{G}) = \mathcal{D}_2(\bigcup \mathcal{G})$.

We say that $s_1, s_2 \in S$ *are* probabilistic timed group-by-group bisimilar, *written* $s_1 \sim_{\text{PTB,gbg}} s_2$, *iff there exists a probabilistic timed group-by-group bisimulation* $\mathcal{B}$ *over* S *such that* $(s_1, s_2) \in \mathcal{B}$. ∎

Theorem 3. *Let* $\mathcal{U} = (S, A_{\mathcal{U}}, \longrightarrow_{\mathcal{U}})$ *be the* $\mathbb{R}_{[0,1]}$-*ULTRAS corresponding to a PTLTS* $(S, A, \longrightarrow, \rightsquigarrow)$. *For all* $s_1, s_2 \in S$:

$$s_1 \sim_{\text{PTB,gbg}} s_2 \iff s_1 \sim_{\text{B},\mathcal{M}_{2,\,[0,1]}^{\mathbb{R}}} s_2$$ ∎

In presence of internal nondeterminism, $\sim_{\text{PTB,gbg}}$ strictly contains $\sim_{\text{PTB,dis}}$, as shown in Fig. 3. Indicating states with the actions they enable, it holds that $s_1 \not\sim_{\text{PTB,dis}} s_2$ because the group distribution of the leftmost a-transition of s_1 – which assigns probability 1 to each group containing both the $\epsilon(t_1)$-state and the $\epsilon(t_2)$-state, probability 0.4 to each group containing the $\epsilon(t_1)$-state but not the $\epsilon(t_2)$-state, probability 0.6 to each group containing the $\epsilon(t_2)$-state but not the $\epsilon(t_1)$-state, and probability 0 to any other group – is not matched by the group distribution of any of the three a-transitions of s_2. In contrast, $s_1 \sim_{\text{PTB,gbg}} s_2$. For instance, the leftmost a-transition of s_1 is matched by the leftmost a-transition of s_2 with respect to every group containing both the $\epsilon(t_1)$-state and the $\epsilon(t_2)$-state, the central a-transition of s_2 with respect to every group containing the $\epsilon(t_1)$-state but not the $\epsilon(t_2)$-state, and the rightmost a-transition of s_2 with respect to every group containing the $\epsilon(t_2)$-state but not the $\epsilon(t_1)$-state.

Theorem 4. *Let $\mathcal{U} = (S, A_{\mathcal{U}}, \longrightarrow_{\mathcal{U}})$ be the $\mathbb{R}_{[0,1]}$-ULTRaS corresponding to a PTLTS $(S, A, \longrightarrow, \rightsquigarrow)$. For all $s_1, s_2 \in S$:*

$$s_1 \sim_{\text{PTB,dis}} s_2 \implies s_1 \sim_{\text{PTB,gbg}} s_2 \qquad\blacksquare$$

We conclude by exhibiting a modal logic characterization of $\sim_{\text{PTB,gbg}}$ (and hence of $\sim_{B,\mathcal{M}_{2,\ast}^{\mathbb{R}_{[0,1]}}}$). Unlike the characterization of $\sim_{\text{PTB}}$ (i.e., $\sim_{\text{PTB,dis}}$) provided in [19], which relies on an expressive probabilistic extension of HML [8] interpreted over state distributions, here it is sufficient to consider the interval-based variant IPML of the probabilistic modal logic in [14] with the following syntax: $\phi ::= \text{true} \mid \neg\phi \mid \phi \wedge \phi \mid \langle a \rangle_{[p_1,p_2]}\phi$ where $a \in A_{\mathcal{U}}$ and $p_1, p_2 \in \mathbb{R}_{[0,1]}$ such that $p_1 \leq p_2$. A state $s \in S$ belongs to the set $\mathcal{M}[\![\langle a \rangle_{[p_1,p_2]}\phi]\!]$ of states satisfying $\langle a \rangle_{[p_1,p_2]}\phi$ iff there exists $s \xrightarrow{a}_{\mathcal{U}} \mathcal{D}$ such that $p_1 \leq \mathcal{D}(\mathcal{M}[\![\phi]\!]) \leq p_2$.

Theorem 5. *Let $\mathcal{U} = (S, A_{\mathcal{U}}, \longrightarrow_{\mathcal{U}})$ be the $\mathbb{R}_{[0,1]}$-ULTRaS corresponding to a PTLTS $(S, A, \longrightarrow, \rightsquigarrow)$. For all $s_1, s_2 \in S$ it holds that $s_1 \sim_{\text{PTB,gbg}} s_2$ iff s_1 and s_2 satisfy the same formulae of IPML.* $\qquad\blacksquare$

6   Encoding Probabilistic Timed Automata

Probabilistic timed automata (PTA) [12] extend TA with probabilities. While the passage of time remains deterministic, the target of each action transition becomes a probability distribution. The approach is exactly the one described in Sect. 5 for moving from TLTS models to PTLTS models.

Definition 15. *A probabilistic timed automaton (PTA) is a tuple $(L, A, \mathcal{X}, I, \longrightarrow)$ where L is a finite set of locations, A is a set of actions, $\mathcal{X}$ is a finite set of clocks, I is a function mapping each location into an invariant condition, and $\longrightarrow \subseteq L \times \Psi_{\mathcal{X}} \times A \times Distr_{cs}(2^{\mathcal{X}} \times L)$ is a transition relation.* $\qquad\blacksquare$

Every transition is written $\ell \xrightarrow{\psi,a} \mathcal{D}$ where $\mathcal{D}$ is the probability distribution assigning each pair (γ, ℓ') the probability of being reached via that transition.

Like for TA, the semantics of a PTA is given in terms of a PTLTS. Following the same approach used in Sect. 4, we thus encode a PTA as an $\mathbb{R}_{[0,1]}$-ULTRaS generated by using the same conditions defining the PTA semantics.

Definition 16. *Let $(L, A, \mathcal{X}, I, \longrightarrow)$ be a PTA. Its corresponding $\mathbb{R}_{[0,1]}$-ULTRaS $\mathcal{U} = (S, A_{\mathcal{U}}, \longrightarrow_{\mathcal{U}})$ is defined by letting:*

- *$S = \{(\ell, \nu) \in L \times V_{\mathcal{X}} \mid \nu \models I(\ell)\}$.*
- *$A_{\mathcal{U}} = A \cup \{\epsilon(t) \mid t \in \mathbb{R}_{\geq 0}\}$.*
- *$(\ell, \nu) \xrightarrow{a}_{\mathcal{U}} \mathcal{D}$ for each $\ell \xrightarrow{\psi,a} \mathcal{D}'$ such that $\nu \models \psi$, where for all $(\ell', \nu') \in S$ $\mathcal{D}(\ell', \nu') = \sum_{\gamma \in reset(\nu,\nu')} \mathcal{D}'(\gamma, \ell')$ with $reset(\nu, \nu') = \{\gamma \in 2^{\mathcal{X}} \mid \nu \backslash \gamma = \nu'\}$.*
- *$(\ell, \nu) \xrightarrow{\epsilon(t)}_{\mathcal{U}} \delta_{(\ell', \nu')}$ for $\ell' = \ell$, $\nu' = \nu + t$, $\nu' \models I(\ell')$.* $\qquad\blacksquare$

Similar to TA models, probabilistic timed bisimilarity over PTA models is defined in terms of the underlying PTLTS models. Therefore, we can reuse Defs. 12, 13, and 14 as well as Table 2, so that Thms. 2, 3, 4, and 5 also apply to $\mathbb{R}_{[0,1]}$-ULTRaS corresponding to PTA models.

7   Encoding Markov Automata

So far, we have considered timed models in which temporal aspects are described as fixed amounts of time. In other words, in these models the passage of time is represented *deterministically*. However, in many situations there are fluctuations in the time that elapses between instantaneous activities. When these fluctuations are quantifiable, the passage of time can be represented *stochastically*.

Due to the simplicity of their mathematical treatment, *exponentially distributed random variables* are mostly used for a stochastic representation of time. Given one such variable X with parameter $\lambda \in \mathbb{R}_{>0}$, the probability that a duration sampled from X is at most $t \in \mathbb{R}_{\geq 0}$ is given by $\Pr\{X \leq t\} = 1 - \mathrm{e}^{-\lambda \cdot t}$. The parameter λ is said the *rate* of X; its reciprocal is the expected value of X.

If several alternative exponentially distributed delays can elapse from a state, the *race policy* is adopted; the delay that elapses is the one sampling the least duration. It can be shown that the following property $\mathcal{RP}$ holds in that state: the sojourn time is exponentially distributed with rate given by the sum of the rates of the various delays, with the probability of selecting each such delay being proportional to its rate.

The recently introduced model of Markov automata (MA) [7] can be viewed as a variant of PTA models in which time passing is described through exponentially distributed random variables. An important property of any of these variables is that it enjoys the *memoryless property*; even if we know that a certain amount of time has already elapsed, the residual time is still quantified by the same exponentially distributed random variable. As a consequence, in this setting there is *no need for clocks* and hence Markov automata can actually be viewed as a variant of PTLTS models, with exponentially distributed delays (uniquely identified by their rates) in place of deterministic delays.

Definition 17. *A* Markov automaton (MA) *is a quadruple* $(S, A, \longrightarrow, \rightsquigarrow)$ *where* S *is a possibly uncountable set of states, A is a possibly uncountable set of actions, and:*

- $\longrightarrow \subseteq S \times A \times Distr_{cs}(S)$ *is a probabilistic action-transition relation.*
- $\rightsquigarrow \subseteq S \times \mathbb{R}_{>0} \times S$ *is a bounded time-transition relation, i.e., for all $s \in S$ it holds that $\{s' \in S \mid \exists \lambda \in \mathbb{R}_{>0}. (s, \lambda, s') \in \rightsquigarrow\}$ is at most countable and* $\sum_{(s,\lambda,s') \in \rightsquigarrow} \lambda < \infty$. ■

Similar to the PTLTS case, every action-transition $(s, a, \mathcal{D})$ is written $s \xrightarrow{a} \mathcal{D}$, every time-transition (s, λ, s') is written $s \overset{\lambda}{\rightsquigarrow} s'$, and we can merge the two transition relations into a single one by adding a special time-elapsing action $\epsilon(\lambda)$ for every $\lambda \in \mathbb{R}_{>0}$. Following the transformation sketched in [7], it is straightforward to encode an MA as a not necessarily functional $\mathbb{R}_{[0,1]}$-ULTRAS, in which the race policy is represented based on $\mathcal{RP}$. For each state having outgoing time-transitions, we generate a single time-elapsing transition – instead of one such transition for each original delay – such that its rate λ is the sum of the rates identifying the original delays and its target distribution assigns to every state a probability proportional to the rate at which that state can be reached.

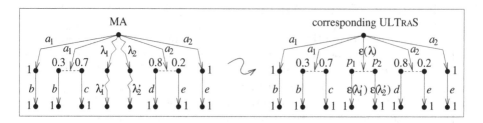

Fig. 4. Translation of an MA ($\lambda = \lambda_1 + \lambda_2$, $p_1 = \lambda_1/\lambda$, $p_2 = \lambda_2/\lambda$)

Definition 18. *Let $(S, A, \longrightarrow, \rightsquigarrow)$ be an MA. Its corresponding $\mathbb{R}_{[0,1]}$-ULTRAS $\mathcal{U} = (S, A_{\mathcal{U}}, \longrightarrow_{\mathcal{U}})$ is defined by letting:*

- $A_{\mathcal{U}} = A \cup \{\epsilon(\lambda) \mid \lambda \in \mathbb{R}_{>0}\}$.
- $s \xrightarrow{a}_{\mathcal{U}} \mathcal{D}$ *for each* $s \xrightarrow{a} \mathcal{D}$.
- $s \xrightarrow{\epsilon(\lambda)}_{\mathcal{U}} \mathcal{D}$ *for all* $s \in S$ *having outgoing time-transitions, where* $\lambda = \sum_{s \rightsquigarrow \lambda' s'} \lambda'$ *and* $\mathcal{D}(s') = \sum_{s \rightsquigarrow \lambda' s'} \lambda'/\lambda$ *for all* $s' \in S$. ∎

Nondeterministic choices over actions, probabilistic choices over states, and the race policy for exponentially distributed delays in the original MA are preserved in the corresponding $\mathbb{R}_{[0,1]}$-ULTRAS. This is exemplified in Fig. 4.

A notion of bisimilarity for probabilistic exponentially-timed processes was introduced in [7]. Below, we reformulate the definition in terms of the two distinct transition relations.

Definition 19. *Let $(S, A, \longrightarrow, \rightsquigarrow)$ be an MA. An equivalence relation $\mathcal{B}$ over S is a probabilistic exponentially-timed bisimulation iff, whenever $(s_1, s_2) \in \mathcal{B}$, then for all actions $a \in A$ and rates $\lambda \in \mathbb{R}_{>0}$ it holds that:*

- *For each $s_1 \xrightarrow{a} \mathcal{D}_1$ there exists $s_2 \xrightarrow{a} \mathcal{D}_2$ such that for all equivalence classes $C \in S/\mathcal{B}$ it holds that $\mathcal{D}_1(C) = \mathcal{D}_2(C)$.*
- *If s_1 has outgoing time-transitions, then s_2 has outgoing time-transitions too and for all equivalence classes $C \in S/\mathcal{B}$ it holds that:*
$$\sum_{s_1 \rightsquigarrow \lambda s_1' \in C} \lambda = \sum_{s_2 \rightsquigarrow \lambda s_2' \in C} \lambda$$

We say that $s_1, s_2 \in S$ are probabilistic exponentially-timed bisimilar, written $s_1 \sim_{\text{PEB}} s_2$, iff there exists a probabilistic exponentially-timed bisimulation $\mathcal{B}$ over S such that $(s_1, s_2) \in \mathcal{B}$. ∎

The relation $\sim_{\text{PEB}}$ over MA models coincides with the relation $\sim_{\text{PTB,dis}}$ over $\mathbb{R}_{[0,1]}$-ULTRAS models given in Def. 13. As a consequence, all the subsequent definitions and results in Sect. 5 also apply to $\mathbb{R}_{[0,1]}$-ULTRAS models corresponding to MA models.

Theorem 6. *Let $(S, A, \longrightarrow, \rightsquigarrow)$ be an MA and $\mathcal{U} = (S, A_{\mathcal{U}}, \longrightarrow_{\mathcal{U}})$ be the corresponding $\mathbb{R}_{[0,1]}$-ULTRAS. For all $s_1, s_2 \in S$:*
$$s_1 \sim_{\text{PEB}} s_2 \iff s_1 \sim_{\text{PTB,dis}} s_2$$
∎

8   Discussion and Conclusions

In this paper, widely used timed models such as TA [1] (together with their underlying semantic model TLTS), PTA [12] (with their underlying PTLTS), and MA [7] have been put in a unifying view by encoding them in the ULTRaS framework [4] and by examining their bisimulation semantics [16,20,19,7].

As immediate results of this work, we have been able to re-obtain the already existing timed bisimilarities and, most notably, to give new contributions. In particular, by naturally instantiating the ULTRaS general bisimilarity definition to the case of deterministically timed models – i.e., TLTS and TA – we have retrieved the same timed bisimilarity introduced in the literature (Thm. 1). Instead, when time is mixed with probability – i.e., for PTLTS, PTA, and MA models – we have found that the bisimilarities present in the literature, although expressible within the ULTRaS framework (Thms. 2 and 6), are different from the one that can be naturally obtained from ULTRaS. This has led us to introduce a new bisimilarity for those models (Def. 14 and Thm. 3), which we have called *group-by-group* and shown to be coarser than the original one (Thm. 4). Moreover, we have exhibited a modal logic characterization for the group-by-group bisimilarity by using an interval-based variant of the logic in [14] (Thm. 5), while the original bisimilarity needs a much more expressive logic [19].

The ULTRaS-based encodings permit also more general considerations about the studied models. Firstly, the transition relation of the ULTRaS corresponding to a TA is functional and based on $\mathbb{B}$, whilst in the case of a PTA/MA it is not a function (because internal nondeterminism cannot be mixed with probabilities in the target state distributions of transitions) and it is necessarily based on $\mathbb{R}_{[0,1]}$. This stresses the higher expressivity of PTA/MA compared to TA with regard to describing state reachability. Furthermore, it evidences a structural analogy between PTA and MA that has not been addressed so far in the literature.

Secondly, the quantitative information related to time in TA/PTA/MA can be made disappear to a large extent, while quantitative information related to probabilities in PTA/MA cannot be abstracted. This underlines an important difference between time and probability. Time elapses independent of the occurrence of events and hence its passage can be viewed as an event in its own, which can thus be represented like the other events. Probabilities, instead, are inherently associated with the occurrence of events and must therefore be explicitly represented as event attributes.

Indeed, in our encodings time passing has been represented through special actions that encompass the duration/rate of delays. A purely qualitative representation of time based on a single special action ϵ is also possible and was used, for instance, in the construction of the region/zone graph and in the notion of time-abstract bisimilarity [15]. This supports a compact description of the state space of the ULTRaS corresponding to a TA/PTA, which is uncountable while this is not necessarily the case for an MA. The reason is the inherent difference between deterministic time, which needs the concrete representation of all possible delays, and exponentially distributed time, for which a symbolic representation based on rates is sufficient thanks to the memoryless property.

A natural continuation of our work is to investigate trace and testing equivalences by applying their general definitions in [4] to the considered timed models.

References

1. Alur, R., Dill, D.L.: A theory of timed automata. Theoretical Computer Science 126, 183–235 (1994)
2. Bérard, B., Petit, A., Diekert, V., Gastin, P.: Characterization of the expressive power of silent transitions in timed automata. Fundamenta Informaticae 36, 145–182 (1998)
3. Bernardo, M.: On the expressiveness of Markovian process calculi with durational and durationless actions. In: Proc. of GANDALF 2010. EPTCS, vol. 25, pp. 199–213 (2010)
4. Bernardo, M., De Nicola, R., Loreti, M.: A uniform framework for modeling nondeterministic, probabilistic, stochastic, or mixed processes and their behavioral equivalences. Information and Computation 225, 29–82 (2013)
5. Cerans, K.: Decidability of bisimulation equivalences for parallel timer processes. In: Probst, D.K., von Bochmann, G. (eds.) CAV 1992. LNCS, vol. 663, pp. 302–315. Springer, Heidelberg (1993)
6. Corradini, F.: Absolute versus relative time in process algebras. Information and Computation 156, 122–172 (2000)
7. Eisentraut, C., Hermanns, H., Zhang, L.: On probabilistic automata in continuous time. In: Proc. of LICS 2010, pp. 342–351. IEEE-CS Press (2010)
8. Hennessy, M., Milner, R.: Algebraic laws for nondeterminism and concurrency. Journal of the ACM 32, 137–162 (1985)
9. Henzinger, T.A., Nicollin, X., Sifakis, J., Yovine, S.: Symbolic model checking for real-time systems. Information and Computation 111, 193–244 (1994)
10. Hermanns, H.: Interactive Markov Chains. LNCS, vol. 2428. Springer, Heidelberg (2002)
11. Keller, R.M.: Formal verification of parallel programs. Communications of the ACM 19, 371–384 (1976)
12. Kwiatkowska, M., Norman, G., Segala, R., Sproston, J.: Automatic verification of real-time systems with discrete probability distributions. Theoretical Computer Science 282, 101–150 (2002)
13. Lanotte, R., Maggiolo-Schettini, A., Troina, A.: Weak bisimulation for probabilistic timed automata. Theoretical Computer Science 411, 4291–4322 (2010)
14. Larsen, K.G., Skou, A.: Bisimulation through probabilistic testing. Information and Computation 94, 1–28 (1991)
15. Larsen, K.G., Yi, W.: Time abstracted bisimulation: Implicit specifications and decidability. In: Main, M.G., Melton, A.C., Mislove, M.W., Schmidt, D., Brookes, S.D. (eds.) MFPS 1993. LNCS, vol. 802, pp. 160–176. Springer, Heidelberg (1994)
16. Moller, F., Tofts, C.: A temporal calculus of communicating systems. In: Baeten, J.C.M., Klop, J.W. (eds.) CONCUR 1990. LNCS, vol. 458, pp. 401–415. Springer, Heidelberg (1990)
17. Moller, F., Tofts, C.: Behavioural abstraction in TCCS. In: Kuich, W. (ed.) ICALP 1992. LNCS, vol. 623, pp. 559–570. Springer, Heidelberg (1992)
18. Segala, R.: Modeling and Verification of Randomized Distributed Real-Time Systems. PhD Thesis (1995)
19. Sproston, J., Troina, A.: Simulation and bisimulation for probabilistic timed automata. In: Chatterjee, K., Henzinger, T.A. (eds.) FORMATS 2010. LNCS, vol. 6246, pp. 213–227. Springer, Heidelberg (2010)
20. Yi, W.: CCS + Time = An Interleaving Model for Real Time Systems. In: Leach Albert, J., Monien, B., Rodríguez-Artalejo, M. (eds.) ICALP 1991. LNCS, vol. 510, pp. 217–228. Springer, Heidelberg (1991)

A Fast EM Algorithm for Fitting Marked Markovian Arrival Processes with a New Special Structure

Gábor Horváth[1,2,3] and Hiroyuki Okamura[4]

[1] Budapest University of Technology and Economics
Department of Networked Systems and Services
[2] MTA-BME Information Systems Research Group
[3] Inter-University Center of Telecommunications and Informatics,
Debrecen 1521 Budapest, Hungary
ghorvath@hit.bme.hu
[4] Department of Information Engineering
Graduate School of Engineering, Hiroshima University
1-4-1 Kagamiyama, Higashi-Hiroshima 739–8527, Japan
okamu@rel.hiroshima-u.ac.jp

Abstract. This paper presents an EM algorithm for fitting traces with Markovian arrival processes (MAPs). The proposed algorithm operates on a special subclass of MAPs. This special structure enables the efficient implementation of the EM algorithm; it is more orders of magnitudes faster than methods operating on the general MAP class while providing similar or better likelihood values. An other important feature of the algorithm is that it is able to fit multi-class traces with marked Markovian arrival processes as well. Several numerical examples demonstrate the efficiency of the procedure.

1 Introduction

Phase-type (PH) distributions and Markovian arrival processes (MAPs) play an important role in the performance and reliability analysis as they allow to describe a wide class of distributions and processes with Markovian techniques. The solutions of various queueing systems, failure models, etc. incorporating PH distributions and MAPs are typically numerically tractable.

However, the applicability of these models depends on how well the load of the system is represented, thus, how efficient the PH fitting and/or MAP fitting methods are when the empirical properties of the system are approximated.

Several fitting algorithms exist for PH distributions. As for correlated processes, the maturity of MAP fitting methods is a bit behind to the maturity of the PH fitting methods. There are several MAP fitting methods that aim to maximize the likelihood, all of them are based on the EM (expectation-maximization) algorithm. However, EM based MAP fitting algorithms have some distinct drawbacks that limit their practical usability. These algorithms suffer from slow convergence, high per-iteration computational effort and the final result is overly

M.S. Balsamo, W.J. Knottenbelt, and A. Marin (Eds.): EPEW 2013, LNCS 8168, pp. 119–133, 2013.

dependent on the initial guess. As in case of PH fitting methods, it turned out that basing the fitting on a special MAP structure has a beneficial effect on both the convergence speed and the per-iteration computational effort. It is even typical that results obtained by fitting with general MAP structures are worse than those obtained by fitting with specialized structures [16].

The development of fitting procedures for the multi-type extension of MAPs, called MMAPs (marked Markovian arrival processes) is in initial stages, only a few solutions are available. In this paper we introduce a new special MMAP structure which enables a fast implementation of the EM algorithm. This special structure resembles to the ER-CHMM structure introduced for the single-class case in [16], but it is more general.

The rest of the paper is organized as follows. Section 2 introduces the notations and basic properties of marked Markovian arrival processes. We provide an overview on the available MAP and MMAP fitting methods in Section 3. The proposed MMAP structure and the corresponding EM algorithm is presented in Section 4. The numerical experiments are detailed in Section 5, finally, Section 6 concludes the paper.

2   Marked Markovian Arrival Processes

In a Markovian Arrival Process (MAP, [15]) there is a background process (also referred to as phase process) given by a continuous time Markov chain with generator matrix denoted by D. Some of the transitions in this Markov chain are accompanied by an arrival event; the corresponding transition rates are the entries of matrix D_1. The transition rates of the background process not accompanied by an arrival event are the entries of matrix D_0. For the sum of these matrices we have $D = D_0 + D_1$ (we assume that D defines an irreducible Markov chain throughout this paper).

Marked Markovian arrival processes (MMAPs, [11]) are the multi-class extensions to MAPs, where the arrival events are tagged (marked) with the *class* of the arrivals. A MMAP distinguishing C different classes of arrival events is given by a set of matrices $D_c, c = 0, \ldots, C$, where D_0 describes the transition rates not accompanied by an arrival and D_c the ones accompanied by a type c arrival. The generator of the background Markov process is $D = \sum_{c=0}^{C} D_c$. Furthermore, we can introduce the embedded phase process at arrivals and obtain matrices $P^{(c)} = (-D_0)^{-1} D_c$ whose i,jth entry is the joint probability of the phase and the type of the next arrival given the phase at the previous arrival. The stationary phase probability vector at arrival instants, $\underline{\pi}$, is then the unique solution of $\underline{\pi} P = \underline{\pi}, \underline{\pi} \mathbb{1} = 1$ with $P = \sum_{c=1}^{C} P^{(c)}$ ($\mathbb{1}$ denotes a column vector of ones of appropriate size).

Let us denote the random variable representing the inter-arrival time between the $i - 1$th and ith arrivals by $\mathcal{X}_i$, and the type of the ith arrival by $\mathcal{C}_i = \{1, \ldots, C\}$. The joint probability density function (pdf) that the consecutive inter-arrival times are $x_1, x_2, \ldots, x_K$ and the corresponding arrival classes are $c_1, c_2, \ldots, c_K$ can be expressed by

$$f(x_1, c_1, x_2, c_2, \ldots, x_K, c_K) = \underline{\pi} e^{\boldsymbol{D_0} x_1} \boldsymbol{D_{c_1}} e^{\boldsymbol{D_0} x_2} \boldsymbol{D_{c_2}} \cdots e^{\boldsymbol{D_0} x_K} \boldsymbol{D_{c_K}} \mathbb{1}, \qquad (1)$$

which we will use several times in the sequel.

3   MAP and MMAP Fitting Methods

The MAP and MMAP fitting methods published in the literature can be classified to two categories. There are methods that are based on fitting statistical quantities of the trace (like moments, auto-correlations, etc.), while other methods aim to maximize the likelihood.

A purely moment matching based solution is described in [19], where a rational arrival process is constructed based on the marginal moments and the lag-1 joint moments of the trace. The resulting rational arrival process is transformed to a MAP in the second phase of the algorithm. This method has been generalized to MMAPs in [12]. A drawback of this approach is that it may happen that the result does not have a Markovian representation, or does not even define a valid stochastic process. An other popular framework falling into this category has been introduced in [13], where the MAP fitting is performed in two steps: the fitting of the marginal distribution and the fitting of the correlations. For the first step any PH fitting method can be applied, while for the second step several different solutions appeared. In [13] the target of fitting is the lag-k auto-correlation function, in [7] and [3] it is the lag-1 joint moments. The procedure in [6] is a MMAP fitting method based on marginal and joint moment fitting. The KPC procedure published in [8] follows a different approach, it achieves impressive results by combining small MAPs for fitting the moments, the auto-correlations and the bi-correlations of the trace.

Another family of MAP fitting methods aim to find a MAP or a MMAP that maximizes the likelihood of the measurement trace. The EM algorithm ([9]) is an iterative framework, which is a popular choice to implement likelihood maximization. Rydén [18] discussed an EM algorithm for a subclass of MAPs called MMPP (Markov modulated Poisson process), and it could naturally be extended to the general MAP parameter estimation. Buchholz [5] presented an improved EM algorithm in terms of computation speed for the general MAP class to analyze real trace data. The EM algorithms for the general MAP with multiple arrival types (or batches), i.e., the general MMAPs, were proposed in [4] and [14]. Okamura and Dohi [16] discussed the maximum likelihood estimation for the generalized structure.

4   Fitting Traces with MMAPs Having a Special Structure

4.1   Motivation

A major drawback of EM-algorithm based MAP fitting methods is that they are slow if the number of measurements to fit is large. A large number of iterations are required till convergence, and the per-iteration computational effort is also significant.

In case of EM-algorithm based phase-type (PH) distribution fitting methods the solution for this issue has been recognized for a long time. It turned out that fitting with sub-classes of PH distributions like hyper-exponential [10], hyper-Erlang [20], or acyclic PH distributions [17] is more efficient than fitting with the general PH class [2].

The computational effort of EM-algorithm based MAP fitting methods can be reduced in the same way, however identifying sub-classes of MAPs is far less trivial than it was in case of PH distributions. A possible sub-class of MAPs has been introduced in [13], where the proposed structure consists of a set of *component PH distributions* and a *transition probability matrix* that determines which component generates the next inter-arrival time given the current one, it is a kind of Markov-modulated PH distributions. (The procedure itself combines the moment matching and maximum likelihood estimation). Okamura and Dohi [16] provided a fast EM-based MAP fitting algorithm for the same structure, and found that it gives high likelihood values while the execution time is much lower compared with fitting by general MAPs. They found the case when the component PH distributions are Erlang distributions (called ER-CHMM) especially beneficial.

In this paper, our aim is to improve the ER-CHMM structure based EM-algorithm for fitting traces from several aspects:

- We generalize it to fit multi-type (marked) arrival processes as well.
- We introduce a structure that is more general than ER-CHMM, while the computational complexity remains relatively low.
- We present an improved method to optimize the discrete (shape) parameters of the structure.

4.2   The Definition of the Special Structure Used for Fitting

In this section we define the special MMAP structure on which our fitting procedure is based on.

This special MMAP process is a generalization of the ER-CHMM structure. Similar to ER-CHMM, we have M branches with branch i consisting of r_i states connected in a row with the same transition rates λ_i. However, in our case these branches do not represent Erlang distributions, as not all states of the branch are traversed before generating an arrival. When a branch is selected to generate the next inter-arrival time, the initial state of the branch is determined by a probability vector.

Let us assign a two-dimensional identifier to the phases: phase (i, n) identifies state n in branch i.

The parameters characterizing this process are

- the rate and the shape parameters of the branches, denoted by λ_i and r_i, $i = 1, \ldots, M$, $\sum_{i=1}^{M} r_i = N$, respectively;

– probabilities $p_{i,(j,m)}^{(c)}$ with $c = 1, \ldots, C, \ i, j = 1, \ldots, M, \ m = 1, \ldots, r_j$. $p_{i,(j,m)}^{(c)}$ represents the probability that the next phase just after the arrival is (j, m) given that the previous arrival has been generated by branch i resulting in a type c arrival. Note that the ER-CHMM structure is obtained if $p_{i,(j,m)}^{(c)} = 0$ for $m > 1$.

According to the definition matrix $\boldsymbol{D_0}$ is given by

$$
\boldsymbol{D_0} =
\begin{bmatrix}
-\lambda_1 & \lambda_1 & & & & & & & \\
 & \ddots & \ddots & & & & & & \\
 & & -\lambda_1 & & & & & & \\
 & & & -\lambda_2 & \lambda_2 & & & & \\
 & & & & \ddots & \ddots & & & \\
 & & & & & -\lambda_2 & & & \\
 & & & & & & \ddots & & \\
 & & & & & & & -\lambda_M & \lambda_M \\
 & & & & & & & & \ddots & \ddots \\
 & & & & & & & & & -\lambda_M
\end{bmatrix}
\begin{matrix} \left.\vphantom{\begin{matrix}a\\a\\a\end{matrix}}\right\} r_1 \\ \left.\vphantom{\begin{matrix}a\\a\\a\end{matrix}}\right\} r_2 \\ \left.\vphantom{\begin{matrix}a\\a\\a\end{matrix}}\right\} r_M \end{matrix}
\tag{2}
$$

and matrices $\boldsymbol{D_c}, c = 1, \ldots, C$ are

$$
\boldsymbol{D_c} =
\begin{bmatrix}
0 & \cdots & 0 & 0 & \cdots & 0 & & 0 & \cdots & 0 \\
\lambda_1 p_{1,(1,1)}^{(c)} & \cdots & \lambda_1 p_{1,(1,r_1)}^{(c)} & \lambda_1 p_{1,(2,1)}^{(c)} & \cdots & \lambda_1 p_{1,(2,r_2)}^{(c)} & \cdots & \lambda_1 p_{1,(M,1)}^{(c)} & \cdots & \lambda_1 p_{1,(M,r_M)}^{(c)} \\
0 & \cdots & 0 & 0 & \cdots & 0 & & 0 & \cdots & 0 \\
\lambda_2 p_{2,(1,1)}^{(c)} & \cdots & \lambda_2 p_{2,(1,r_1)}^{(c)} & \lambda_2 p_{2,(2,1)}^{(c)} & \cdots & \lambda_2 p_{2,(2,r_2)}^{(c)} & \cdots & \lambda_2 p_{2,(M,1)}^{(c)} & \cdots & \lambda_2 p_{2,(M,r_M)}^{(c)} \\
\vdots & & \vdots & \vdots & & \vdots & \vdots & \vdots & & \vdots \\
0 & \cdots & 0 & 0 & \cdots & 0 & & 0 & \cdots & 0 \\
\lambda_M p_{M,(1,1)}^{(c)} & \cdots & \lambda_M p_{M,(1,r_1)}^{(c)} & \lambda_M p_{M,(2,1)}^{(c)} & \cdots & \lambda_M p_{M,(2,r_2)}^{(c)} & \cdots & \lambda_M p_{M,(M,1)}^{(c)} & \cdots & \lambda_M p_{M,(M,r_M)}^{(c)}
\end{bmatrix}
\begin{matrix} \left.\vphantom{\begin{matrix}a\\a\\a\end{matrix}}\right\} r_1 \\ \left.\vphantom{\begin{matrix}a\\a\end{matrix}}\right\} r_2 \\ \\ \left.\vphantom{\begin{matrix}a\\a\end{matrix}}\right\} r_M \end{matrix}
\tag{3}
$$

By construction, the entries of matrix $\boldsymbol{P}^{(c)} = [u_{(i,n),(j,m)}^{(c)}, i, j = 1, \ldots, M, n = 1, \ldots, r_i, m = 1, \ldots, r_j]$ describing the transition probabilities of phases embedded just after arrival instants corresponding to type c arrivals are given by

$$
u_{(i,n),(j,m)}^{(c)} = p_{i,(j,m)}^{(c)}.
\tag{4}
$$

The stationary distribution of the phases right after arrivals is the unique solution of the linear system

$$
\underline{\pi} = \underline{\pi} \sum_{c=1}^{C} \boldsymbol{P}^{(c)}, \quad \underline{\pi} \mathbb{1} = 1,
\tag{5}
$$

which can be partitioned according to the two-dimensional phase numbering as $\underline{\pi} = [\pi_{(i,n)}, i = 1, \ldots, M, n = 1, \ldots, r_i]$.

Given that the MMAP is in state (i, n) just after arrivals the density of the inter-arrival times is

$$f_{(i,n)}(x) = \frac{(\lambda_i x)^{r_i - n}}{(r_i - n)!} \lambda_i e^{-\lambda_i x}, \tag{6}$$

from which the marginal distribution of the arrival process is obtained by un-conditioning yielding

$$f(x) = \sum_{i=1}^{M} \sum_{n=1}^{r_i} \pi_{(i,n)} f_{(i,n)}(x). \tag{7}$$

4.3   The EM Algorithm

Let us denote the trace data by $\mathcal{X} = \{x_1, c_1, x_2, c_2 \ldots, x_K, c_K\}$, where $x_k \in \mathbb{R}$ is the kth inter-arrival time and $c_k \in \mathbb{N}$ is the type of the kth arrival. In this section we assume that the shape parameters of the branches given by vector $\underline{r} = (r_1, \ldots, r_M)$ is fixed. Our goal is to maximize the likelihood for the trace data

$$L(\Theta(\underline{r})|\mathcal{X}) = \underline{\pi} e^{\boldsymbol{D}_0 x_1} \boldsymbol{D}_{c_1} e^{\boldsymbol{D}_0 x_2} \boldsymbol{D}_{c_2} \ldots e^{\boldsymbol{D}_0 x_K} \boldsymbol{D}_{c_K} \mathbb{1}, \tag{8}$$

where the parameters defining our MAP are $\Theta(\underline{r}) = \{\lambda_i, p_{i,(j,m)}\}$, from which matrices $\boldsymbol{D}_c, c = 0, \ldots, C$ are derived by (2) and (3).

Let the (i, n)th entry of row vector $\underline{a}[k] = (a_{(i,n)}[k], i = 1, \ldots, M, n = 1, \ldots, r_i)$ denote the likelihood of phase (i, n) after observing $x_1, c_1, x_2, c_2, \ldots, x_k, c_k$. This vector will be referred to as forward likelihood vector in the sequel and can be obtained recursively by

$$\underline{a}[0] = \underline{\pi}, \quad \underline{a}[k] = \underline{a}[k-1] \cdot e^{\boldsymbol{D}_0 x_k} \boldsymbol{D}_{c_k}. \tag{9}$$

Similarly, we can define backward likelihood vectors $\underline{b}[k] = (b_{(i,n)}[k])$ as

$$\underline{b}[K] = \mathbb{1}, \quad \underline{b}[k] = e^{\boldsymbol{D}_0 x_k} \boldsymbol{D}_{c_k} \underline{b}[k+1]. \tag{10}$$

The likelihood is then given by

$$L(\Theta(\underline{r})|\mathcal{X}) = \underline{a}[k] \cdot \underline{b}[k+1], \tag{11}$$

for any $k = 0, \ldots, K - 1$.

Due to the special structure the forward and backward likelihood vectors can be expressed in a simpler way as

$$a_{(i,n)}[k] = \sum_{j=1}^{M} \sum_{m=1}^{r_j} a_{(j,m)}[k-1] \cdot f_{(j,m)}(x_k) \cdot u_{(j,m),(i,n)}^{(c_k)}, \tag{12}$$

$$b_{(j,m)}[k] = \sum_{i=1}^{M} \sum_{n=1}^{r_i} f_{(j,m)}(x_k) \cdot u_{(j,m),(i,n)}^{(c_k)} \cdot b_{(i,n)}[k+1]. \tag{13}$$

Note that as opposed to (9) and (10), (12) and (13) does not involve matrix exponential operations, which will be a significant gain in speed.

According to the EM approach we consider the data $\mathcal{X}$ to be incomplete, and assume that there is an unobserved data $\mathcal{Y}$ which, together with $\mathcal{X}$, forms the complete data. In our case the values of the unobserved data $\mathcal{Y} = \{y_1, z_1 \ldots, y_K, z_K\}$ inform us which branch generates the kth data item of $\mathcal{X}$ ($y_k \in \{1, \ldots, M\}$) and which was the initial state of branch y_k when generating the kth inter-arrival time ($z_k \in \{1, \ldots r_{y_k}\}$).

Given the unobserved data $\mathcal{Y}$, it is possible to obtain maximum likelihood estimates (MLE) for λ_i and p_{ij}. Let us start with λ_i. Since the inter-arrival times are independent given the unobserved data we can express the log-likelihood of parameters $\lambda_1, \ldots, \lambda_M$ as

$$\log L(\lambda_1, \ldots, \lambda_M | \mathcal{X}, \mathcal{Y}, \underline{r}) = \sum_{k=1}^{K} \log \left(f_{(y_k, z_k)}(x_k) \right). \tag{14}$$

To obtain MLE for λ_i we need to find the maximum of (14) by solving

$$\frac{\partial}{\partial \lambda_i} \sum_{k=1}^{K} I_{\{y_k=i\}} \log \left(\sum_{n=1}^{r_i} I_{\{z_k=n\}} f_{(i,n)}(x_k) \right) = 0, \tag{15}$$

that gives

$$\hat{\lambda}_i = \frac{\sum_{k=1}^{K} \sum_{n=1}^{r_i} n \cdot I_{\{y_k=i, z_k=n\}}}{\sum_{k=1}^{K} x_k I_{\{y_k=i\}}}. \tag{16}$$

To obtain MLE for probabilities $\hat{p}_{i,(j,m)}^{(c)}$ we apply [1] yielding

$$\hat{p}_{i,(j,m)}^{(c)} = \frac{\sum_{k=1}^{K-1} I_{\{c_k=c, y_k=i, y_{k+1}=j, z_{k+1}=m\}}}{\sum_{k=1}^{K-1} I_{\{y_k=i\}}}. \tag{17}$$

In the *E-step* of the EM algorithm the expected values of the unobserved variables are computed:

$$
\begin{aligned}
q_{(i,n),(j,m)}^{(c)}[k] &= P(c_k = c, y_k = i, z_k = n, y_{k+1} = j, z_{k+1} = m | \hat{\Theta}(\underline{r}), \mathcal{X}) \\
&= \frac{P(c_k = c, y_k = i, z_k = n, y_{k+1} = j, z_{k+1} = m, \mathcal{X} | \hat{\Theta}(\underline{r}))}{P(\mathcal{X} | \hat{\Theta}(\underline{r}))} \\
&= \frac{a_{(i,n)}[k-1] \cdot f_{(i,n)}(x_k) \cdot u_{(i,n),(j,m)}^{(c)} \cdot b_{(j,m)}[k+1]}{P(\mathcal{X} | \hat{\Theta}(\underline{r}))},
\end{aligned}
\tag{18}
$$

$$q_{(i,n)}[k] = \frac{P(y_k = i, z_k = n, \mathcal{X} | \hat{\Theta}(\underline{r}))}{P(\mathcal{X} | \hat{\Theta}(\underline{r}))} = \frac{a_{(i,n)}[k-1] \cdot b_{(i,n)}[k]}{P(\mathcal{X} | \hat{\Theta}(\underline{r}))}, \tag{19}$$

where $\hat{\Theta}(\underline{r})$ are the estimates of the parameters $\Theta(\underline{r})$.

Algorithm 1. Pseudo-code of the proposed EM algorithm

1: **procedure** HEM-FIT($x_k, \lambda_i, r_i, p_{i,(j,m)}^{(c)}$)
2:   $LogLi \leftarrow -\infty$
3:   **while** $(LogLi - oLogLi)/LogLi > \epsilon$ **do**
4:     Obtain vector $\underline{\pi}$ by (5)
5:     **for** $k = 1$ **to** K **do**
6:       Compute and store conditional densities $f_{(i,n)}(x_k)$ by (6)
7:     **end for**
8:     **for** $k = 0$ **to** K **do**
9:       Compute and store forward likelihood vectors $\underline{a}[k]$ by (12)
10:    **end for**
11:    **for** $k = K$ **downto** 1 **do**
12:      Compute and store backward likelihood vectors $\underline{b}[k]$ by (13)
13:    **end for**
14:    **for** $i = 1$ **to** M **do**
15:      Compute new estimate for λ_i by (20)
16:    **end for**
17:    **for** $c = 1$ **to** C, $i = 1$ **to** M, $j = 1$ **to** M **do**
18:      **for** $m = 1$ **to** r_j **do**
19:        Compute new estimate for $p_{i,(j,m)}^{(c)}$ by (21)
20:      **end for**
21:    **end for**
22:    $oLogLi \leftarrow LogLi$
23:    $LogLi \leftarrow \underline{\pi} \cdot \underline{b}[0]$
24: **end while**
25: **return** $(\lambda_i, p_{i,(j,m)}^{(c)}), i, j = 1, \ldots, M, m = 1, \ldots, r_j, c = 1, \ldots, C)$
26: **end procedure**

In the *M-step* the new estimates of Θ (denoted by $\hat{\Theta}(\underline{r})$) are computed which maximize the expected likelihood function. From (17) it follows that

$$\hat{\lambda}_i = \frac{\sum_{k=1}^{K} \sum_{n=1}^{r_i} n \cdot q_{(i,n)}[k]}{\sum_{k=1}^{K} x_k \sum_{n=1}^{r_i} q_{(i,n)}[k]} = \frac{\sum_{k=1}^{K} \sum_{n=1}^{r_i} n \cdot a_{(i,n)}[k-1] \cdot b_{(i,n)}[k]}{\sum_{k=1}^{K} x_k \sum_{n=1}^{r_i} a_{(i,n)}[k-1] \cdot b_{(i,n)}[k]}, \quad (20)$$

$$\hat{p}_{i,(j,m)}^{(c)} = \frac{\sum_{k=1}^{K-1} \sum_{n=1}^{r_i} q_{(i,n),(j,m)}^{(c)}[k]}{\sum_{k=1}^{K-1} \sum_{n=1}^{r_i} q_{(i,n)}[k]}$$

$$= \frac{\sum_{k=1}^{K-1} \sum_{n=1}^{r_i} a_{(i,n)}[k-1] \cdot f_{(i,n)}(x_k) \cdot u_{(i,n),(j,m)}^{(c)} \cdot b_{(j,m)}[k+1]}{\sum_{k=1}^{K-1} \sum_{n=1}^{r_i} a_{(i,n)}[k-1] \cdot b_{(i,n)}[k]}. \quad (21)$$

The pseudo-code of the EM algorithm is depicted in Algorithm 1. The input of the algorithm is the trace and the initial guesses for probabilities $p_{i,(j,m)}^{(c)}$ and the shape and rate parameters of the branches. The outputs of the algorithm are the optimized values of these parameters.

For the initial guesses we apply the k-means algorithm as suggested in [16].

4.4 Optimization of the Shape Parameters

To make the algorithm more user friendly, it is possible to optimize the shape parameter vector $\underline{r} = (r_1, \ldots, r_M)$ as well. In this case the user has to enter just a single parameter: the size of the MAP he/she wants (N). The problem to determine the parameter N is addressed by statistical argument such as information criterion, but this is out of scope of this report.

The set of possible $\underline{r}$ vectors is given by

$$\mathcal{H}_N = \left\{ (r_1, \ldots, r_M); \sum_{m=1}^{M} r_i = N, 1 \leq M \leq N, 1 \leq r_1 \leq \cdots \leq r_M \right\}, \quad (22)$$

Note that the last condition $1 \leq r_1 \leq \cdots \leq r_M$ is based on the fact that each pair of any two values r_i and r_j is commutative; for example, $\underline{r} = (1, 2, 1)$ and $\underline{r} = (1, 1, 2)$ are supposed to be same.

Then the maximum likelihood estimates (MLEs) of shape parameters are given by the solution of the following maximization problem:

$$\hat{\underline{r}} = \underset{\underline{r} \in \mathcal{H}_N}{\operatorname{argmax}} L(\underline{r}, \hat{\Theta}(\underline{r}) | \mathcal{X}), \quad (23)$$

Since the shape parameters are restricted to an integer, (23) is essentially an integer programming, i.e., the combinational problem over a set $\mathcal{H}_N$.

A possible straight-forward solution of this optimization problem is to execute the presented EM algorithm with *all possible shape parameter vectors* $\underline{r} \in \mathcal{H}_N$, which can make the fitting very slow, since the cardinality of $\mathcal{H}_N$ increases exponentially as N grows.

Thummler et al. [20] presented a heuristic method that tries to predict promising combinations of shape parameters by doing a few iterations of the EM algorithm which is called the *progressive preselection*. This method first considers all vectors $\underline{r} \in \mathcal{H}_N$. Then the EM algorithm is started for each of the vectors with loose convergence conditions ($\epsilon = 10^{-2}$, usually requiring only a few iterations). The results are sorted according to the likelihood values, and half of the vectors (the worst performing ones) are dropped. Then further EM iterations are applied with the remaining vectors with tighter convergence conditions, the worst performing ones are dropped, and so on, till only a single vector $\underline{r}$ remains. While this approach is fast, it does not guarantee that it finds the optimal $\underline{r}$ at the end. The reason is that the optimal $\underline{r}$ can be dropped during the pre-selection steps if it converges slower to the optimum, which happened frequently in our numerical investigations if the convergence conditions corresponding to the preselection phases are not set adequately.

This paper presents an alternative approach to find the best combination of shape parameters with an *incremental approach*. The idea behind the method is to search only the neighborhood of a shape parameter vector. For a given sum of shape parameters N, we consider the following sets:

$$\tilde{\mathcal{H}}_k = \left\{ (r_1, \ldots, r_N); \sum_{m=1}^{N} r_i = k, 0 \leq r_1 \leq \cdots \leq r_N \right\}, \quad k = 1, \ldots, N. \quad (24)$$

The set $\tilde{\mathcal{H}}_k$ is essentially same as $\mathcal{H}_k$ in Eq. (22). Note that r_i is allowed to be 0 in $\tilde{\mathcal{H}}_k$ and that the length of all the elements of $\tilde{\mathcal{H}}_k$, $k = 1, \ldots, N$, becomes N. For all the elements in $\bigcup_{k=1}^{N} \tilde{\mathcal{H}}_k$, we define the following distance:

$$D(\underline{r}_i, \underline{r}_j) = \sum_{n=1}^{N} |r_{i,n} - r_{j,n}|, \quad \underline{r}_i, \underline{r}_j \in \bigcup_{k=1}^{N} \tilde{\mathcal{H}}_k, \tag{25}$$

where $\underline{r}_i = (r_{i,1}, \ldots, r_{i,N})$ and $\underline{r}_j = (r_{j,1}, \ldots, r_{j,N})$. According to the above distance, neighborhood of $\underline{r}$ is defined as follows.

$$\mathcal{N}(\underline{r}) = \left\{ \underline{r}'; D(\underline{r}, \underline{r}') = 1, \underline{r}' \in \bigcup_{k=1}^{N} \tilde{\mathcal{H}}_k \right\}. \tag{26}$$

For instance, if $N = 4$ the neighborhood of the vector $\underline{r} = (0, 0, 1, 2)$ is

$$\mathcal{N}(\underline{r}) = \{(0,0,0,2), (0,0,1,1), (0,1,1,2), (0,0,2,2), (0,0,1,3)\}. \tag{27}$$

Observe that if $\underline{r} \in \tilde{\mathcal{H}}_k$, then a member of $\mathcal{N}(\underline{r})$ is a member of either $\tilde{\mathcal{H}}_{k-1}$ or $\tilde{\mathcal{H}}_{k+1}$.

Based on the above insights, we propose an algorithm based on the local search to find the MLE of shape parameter vector in Algorithm 2. In the algorithm, $L(\underline{r})$ means the log-likelihood function of $\underline{r}$. From the argument of degree of freedom in statistics, the maximum of log-likelihood functions in $\tilde{\mathcal{H}}_k$ is a non-decreasing function with respect to k. Then the algorithm searches for the maximum value in neighborhood with the direction from which k increases, and provides the (local) maximum of log-likelihood functions in the set $\tilde{\mathcal{H}}_N$. If the assumption that the neighborhood of the maximum of log-likelihood functions in $\tilde{\mathcal{H}}_k$ includes the shape parameter vector maximizing the log-likelihood function in $\tilde{\mathcal{H}}_{k-1}$ holds, the algorithm finds the global maximum of log-likelihood functions in $\tilde{\mathcal{H}}_N$. Although it is difficult to prove that this assumption holds for any situation, the assumption is expected to hold for many practical situation. The time complexity of Algorithm 2 is $O(N^{1.5})$, because the maximum size of neighborhood of $\mathcal{N}(\underline{r})$, $\underline{r} \in \tilde{\mathcal{H}}_k$ is proportional to a square of k. Since the size of $\mathcal{H}_N$ is given by a function of the factorial of N, the proposed method is applicable even for a large N.

5   Numerical Experiments

In this section we present two numerical examples to examine how effective our enhanced EM algorithm is.

5.1   Fitting Single-Class Trace

In the first example we intend to fit a well-known traffic trace, the BC-pAug89 trace[1] that is frequently used as a benchmark in several papers. It consist of the

---

[1] Downloaded from `http://ita.ee.lbl.gov/html/contrib/BC.html`

Algorithm 2. Incremental search for the best shape parameters

---

1: $\underline{r} \leftarrow (0,\ldots,0,1)$
2: **for** $k = 2 : N$ **do**
3:      $L_{max} \leftarrow -\infty$
4:      **for** $\underline{r}' \in \mathcal{N}(\underline{r}) \bigcap \tilde{\mathcal{H}}_k$ **do**
5:          **if** $L(\underline{r}') > L_{max}$ **then**
6:              $\underline{r}_{max} \leftarrow \underline{r}'$
7:              $L_{max} \leftarrow L(\underline{r}')$
8:          **end if**
9:      **end for**
10:     $\underline{r} \leftarrow \underline{r}_{max}$
11: **end for**

---

inter-arrival times of one million packet arrivals measured on an Ethernet network. This trace does not distinguish multiple arrival types, thus we are applying single-class MAP fitting in this example. We are investigating two questions:

- How capable the proposed special MAP structure is when fitting the trace with the EM algorithm.
- How efficient the proposed heuristic method called "Incremental" is in optimizing the shape parameters $r_1, \ldots, r_M$.

The following MAP fitting methods are involved into the comparison.

- The EM-algorithm introduced in [5][2].
- The EM-algorithm published in [16] which operates on the general class of MAPs.
- The EM-algorithm operating on the ER-CHMM structure ([16]).
- The EM-algorithm operating on the special MAP structure proposed by this paper.

The latter two procedures are included in our new MAP/MMAP fitting tool called SPEM-FIT[3]. This open-source tool has been implemented in C++ and is able to utilize the multiple cores of modern CPUs. It supports three different methods to optimize the shape parameters, namely "progressive preselection" (referred to as "PreSel" in the sequel), enumerating all possible configurations and selecting the best one (referred to as "All"), and the new incremental method proposed in this paper ("Incr").

The likelihood values obtained when fitting with MAPs of different sizes are depicted in Figure 1. (The likelihood values in this section are all log-likelihoods divided by the length of the trace). The corresponding execution times are shown in Figure 2. We note that method "Buchholz" and "Okamura-Dohi" stopped before convergence when the maximum number of iterations has been reached (that is 1000 for "Buchholz", and 3000 for "Okamura-Dohi").

---

[2] We would like to thank Peter Buchholz and Jan Kriege for providing the implementation of the algorithm and for guidance on the usage.

[3] It can be downloaded from `https://bitbucket.org/ghorvath78/spemfit`

When examining the execution times it is striking how slow the methods operating on the general MAP class are. Observe that these methods pick a single initial guess and apply several EM iterations on it, while in case of ER-CHMM and the proposed structure the execution times include the optimization of the shape parameters as well, they are still 1, 2, or even 3 orders of magnitudes faster. While being faster, they are also able to achieve as high or higher likelihood values than the EM algorithms working with general MAPs.

Table 1. Log-likelihood values obtained with different methods

Method	4	6	8	10	12
Buchhoz	−0.8033	−0.7957	−0.7929	n/a	n/a
Okamura-Dohi	−0.8002	−0.76345	−0.75512	−0.728709	−0.725897
ER-CHMM (All)	−0.80079	−0.77634	−0.74766	−0.72598	−0.715183
ER-CHMM (PreSel)	−0.800787	−0.776342	−0.747659	−0.723873	−0.715183
ER-CHMM (Incr)	−0.80079	−0.77936	−0.74766	−0.7314	−0.715183
Our (All)	−0.80051	−0.76494	−0.74173	−0.72813	−0.71399
Our (PreSel)	−0.800506	−0.764944	−0.741738	−0.727968	−0.713967
Our (Incr)	−0.80051	−0.76494	−0.74173	−0.72813	−0.71402

Based on the numerical results it is possible evaluate how the different components of our refined EM algorithm perform. With the proposed MAP structure it is possible to obtain higher likelihood values in most of the cases, although the execution time increases as well (which is straight forward as it has more parameters to optimize than the ER-CHMM). Regarding the optimization of the shape parameters we found that the "Incremental" procedure was able to find the optimum in the majority of the cases. With a small number of states "All" turned out to be faster than "Incremental", but from 8 states on "Incremental" catches up and the its speed advantage grows with increasing number of states.

Table 2. Fitting times obtained with different methods (in seconds)

Method	4	6	8	10	12
Buchhoz	33571	57703	103162	n/a	n/a
Okamura-Dohi	11172	17407	32896	60726	82773
ER-CHMM (All)	24	213	388	795	1954
ER-CHMM (PreSel)	25	94	113	337	582
ER-CHMM (Incr)	34	103	331	596	867
Our (All)	98	247	1026	2434	6179
Our (PreSel)	91	234	328	982	2257
Our (Incr)	139	450	1040	1988	3415

Regarding the "PreSel" heuristic, that does not guarantee finding the optimum, performs very well in this example. We note however, that fine-tuning the thresholds used by this method is a hard task. If the thresholds are too loose, the procedure will be fast but it may drop candidates prematurely, potentially loosing the one that could provide the best result at the end. At the other hand, too tight thresholds make the progressive pre-selection practically equivalent to the "All" method. We selected the appropriate thresholds based on a large number of numerical experiments with several traces, however, these thresholds are not universal.

5.2   Fitting Multi-class Trace

To examine the behavior of the proposed enhancements further, we made a multi-class trace from the BC-pAug89 trace according to the packet sizes. Arrivals with packet sizes between 1 and 759 are marked as class-1 arrivals, while arrivals of larger packets are considered as class-2 arrivals. As we do not have the implementations of EM algorithms for MMAPs published in the past, we compare the multi-class generalization of the ER-CHMM structure (our procedure with $p_{i,(j,m)}^{(c)} = 0$ for $m > 1$) and the proposed more general MMAP structure in this Section.

Table 3. Log-likelihood values obtained by using the two special structures

Vector r	ER-CHMM	Proposed	Vector r	ER-CHMM	Proposed
(1, 7)	-1.29603	-1.35266	(1, 1, 2, 4)	-1.00136	-0.997126
(2, 6)	-1.51657	-1.21412	(1, 1, 3, 3)	-1.02608	-0.997745
(3, 5)	-1.70301	-1.21671	(1, 2, 2, 3)	-1.03497	-1.10369
(4, 4)	-1.72712	-1.51611	(2, 2, 2, 2)	-1.05739	-1.04147
(1, 1, 6)	-1.11458	-1.11355	(1, 1, 1, 1, 4)	-1.05193	-1.05193
(1, 2, 5)	-1.18571	-1.12161	(1, 1, 1, 2, 3)	-1.01446	-1.09347
(1, 3, 4)	-1.21068	-1.15472	(1, 1, 2, 2, 2)	-1.05179	-1.03403
(2, 2, 4)	-1.19233	-1.17741	(1, 1, 1, 1, 1, 3)	-1.0743	-1.06969
(2, 3, 3)	-1.23412	-1.13608	(1, 1, 1, 1, 2, 2)	-1.04512	-1.09436
(1, 1, 1, 5)	-1.04259	-1.11015	(1, 1, 1, 1, 1, 1, 2)	-1.11112	-1.1638

Table 3 shows the log-likelihood values obtained by using the two special structures with all possible shape parameter configurations providing 8 states in total. Examining the results we can observe that the more general structure is able to achieve a significant improvement if there are several branches having a high shape parameter. If the shape parameter is low in most of the branches (or in the dominating branches having high steady state probability), the ER-CHMM performs better, as it has fewer parameters to optimize. In this particular example the optimal shape parameter vector is $(1, 1, 2, 4)$, where the proposed new structure wins by a slight margin.

Finally, Figure 1 compares the best results obtained with various MMAP sizes, showing that the EM algorithm with the proposed structure provides slightly better log-likelihood values, but the difference is marginal. With other traces, where the optimal shape parameters are higher, we expect the difference to be higher.

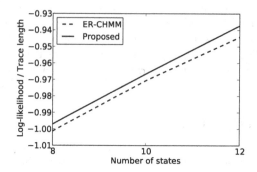

Fig. 1. Log-likelihood values obtained with different MMAP sizes

6   Conclusion

This paper presents several improvements on the EM algorithm based MAP fitting methods. As recognized in numerous past papers, the key idea to make MAP fitting efficient is to apply a special MAP structure instead of the general MAP class. We followed the same path in this paper. We generalized the ER-CHMM structure introduced in [16], developed a method to find the optimal shape parameters of this structure, finally, our method is able to fit multi-class traces as well. The proposed MAP structure is able to improve the log-likelihood values of the results of fitting in most of the cases investigated in the numerical experiments. The gain depends on the nature of the trace. In our numerical example the improvement is slight, but, since the execution time of the fitting is reasonable, it is still worth taking the advantage of this more general structure. With the procedure introduced to find the optimal shape parameters it is possible to avoid trying out all possible combinations, which is beneficial on the fitting times as well.

Acknowledgment. This work was supported by the Hungarian Government through the TAMOP-4.2.2C-11/1/KONV-2012- 0001 and the OTKA K101150 projects, and by the János Bolyai Research Scholarship of the Hungarian Academy of Sciences.

References

1. Anderson, T.W., Goodman, L.A.: Statistical inference about Markov chains. The Annals of Mathematical Statistics, 89–110 (1957)
2. Asmussen, S., Nerman, O., Olsson, M.: Fitting phase-type distributions via the EM algorithm. Scandinavian Journal of Statistics, 419–441 (1996)
3. Bause, F., Horváth, G.: Fitting Markovian Arrival Processes by Incorporating Correlation into Phase Type Renewal Processes. In: 2010 Seventh International Conference on the Quantitative Evaluation of Systems (QEST), pp. 97–106. IEEE (2010)

4. Breuer, L.: An EM algorithm for batch Markovian arrival processes and its comparison to a simpler estimation procedure. Annals of Operations Research 112(1-4), 123–138 (2002)
5. Buchholz, P.: An EM-algorithm for MAP fitting from real traffic data. In: Kemper, P., Sanders, W.H. (eds.) TOOLS 2003. LNCS, vol. 2794, pp. 218–236. Springer, Heidelberg (2003)
6. Buchholz, P., Kemper, P., Kriege, J.: Multi-class Markovian arrival processes and their parameter fitting. Performance Evaluation 67(11), 1092–1106 (2010)
7. Buchholz, P., Kriege, J.: A heuristic approach for fitting MAPs to moments and joint moments. In: Sixth International Conference on the Quantitative Evaluation of Systems, QEST 2009, pp. 53–62. IEEE (2009)
8. Casale, G., Zhang, E.Z., Smirni, E.: KPC-toolbox: Simple yet effective trace fitting using Markovian arrival processes. In: Fifth International Conference on Quantitative Evaluation of Systems, QEST 2008, pp. 83–92. IEEE (2008)
9. Dempster, A.P., Laird, N.M., Rubin, D.B.: Maximum likelihood from incomplete data via the EM algorithm. Journal of the Royal Statistical Society. Series B (Methodological), 1–38 (1977)
10. El Abdouni Khayari, R., Sadre, R., Haverkort, B.R.: Fitting world-wide web request traces with the EM-algorithm. Performance Evaluation 52(2), 175–191 (2003)
11. He, Q., Neuts, M.F.: Markov chains with marked transitions. Stochastic Processes and their Applications 74, 37–52 (1998)
12. Horváth, A., Horváth, G., Telek, M.: A traffic based decomposition of two-class queueing networks with priority service. Computer Networks 53(8), 1235–1248 (2009)
13. Horváth, G., Buchholz, P., Telek, M.: A MAP fitting approach with independent approximation of the inter-arrival time distribution and the lag correlation. In: Second International Conference on the Quantitative Evaluation of Systems, pp. 124–133. IEEE (2005)
14. Klemm, A., Lindemann, C., Lohmann, M.: Modeling IP traffic using the batch Markovian arrival process. Performance Evaluation 54(2), 149–173 (2003)
15. Latouche, G., Ramaswami, V.: Introduction to matrix analytic methods in stochastic modeling. Society for Industrial and Applied Mathematics, vol. 5 (1987)
16. Okamura, H., Dohi, T.: Faster maximum likelihood estimation algorithms for Markovian arrival processes. In: Sixth International Conference on the Quantitative Evaluation of Systems, QEST 2009, pp. 73–82. IEEE (2009)
17. Okamura, H., Dohi, T., Trivedi, K.S.: A refined EM algorithm for PH distributions. Performance Evaluation 68(10), 938–954 (2011)
18. Rydén, T.: An EM algorithm for estimation in Markov-modulated Poisson processes. Computational Statistics & Data Analysis 21(4), 431–447 (1996)
19. Telek, M., Horváth, G.: A minimal representation of Markov arrival processes and a moments matching method. Performance Evaluation 64(9), 1153–1168 (2007)
20. Thummler, A., Buchholz, P., Telek, M.: A novel approach for phase-type fitting with the EM algorithm. IEEE Transactions on Dependable and Secure Computing 3(3), 245–258 (2006)

PMIF+: Extensions to Broaden the Scope of Supported Models

Catalina M. Lladó[1] and Connie U. Smith[2]

[1] Universitat de les Illes Balears. Departament de Ciències Matemàtiques
i Informàtica. Ctra de Valldemossa, Km. 7.6, 07071 Palma de Mallorca, Spain
`cllado@uib.es`
[2] Performance Engineering Services, P.O. Box 2640,
Santa Fe, New Mexico, 87504-2640 USA
`www.spe-ed.com`

Abstract. The performance model interchange format (PMIF) is a common representation for data that reduces the number of custom interfaces required to move performance models among modeling tools. In order to manage the research scope, the initial version of PMIF was limited to Queueing Network Models (QNM) that can be solved by efficient, exact solution algorithms. The overall model interoperability approach has now been demonstrated to be viable. This paper broadens the scope of PMIF to represent models that can be solved with additional methods such as analytical approximations or simulation solutions. It presents the extensions considered, shows alternatives for representing them with a meta-model, describes the PMIF+ extended meta-model and its validation.

1 Introduction

A Performance Model Interchange Format (PMIF) to move models among tools that support the Queueing Network Model (QNM) paradigm was first proposed in 1995 [20]. That version was subsequently revised (PMIF 2), implemented using XML, and many case studies established proof of concept [16]. Other model interchange formats and extensions have been proposed. Examples include: CSM - Core Scenario Model for representing Layered Queueing Network (LQN) models [22]; MARTE - Modeling and Analysis of Real Time Embedded Systems is a profile associated with OMGs Unified Modeling Language (UML) and Systems Modeling Language (SysML) containing a Performance Analysis Model (PAM) for representing performance features in systems; S-PMIF - Software Performance Model Interchange Format for exchanging information among software design tools and software performance engineering tools [12]; Palladio Component Model (PCM) - for representing software architecture with respect to structure, behavior, resource usage, execution environment and usage profile [6]; KLAPER - Kernel Language for Performance and Reliability analysis of component based models [9]; EX-SE - Experiment Schema Extension for specifying the experiments to run with the models [18]. An extensive discussion of this and

M.S. Balsamo, W.J. Knottenbelt, and A. Marin (Eds.): EPEW 2013, LNCS 8168, pp. 134–148, 2013.
© Springer-Verlag Berlin Heidelberg 2013

other related work is covered in [15].[1] We used this related work in determining features to be included in these PMIF extensions.

MIFs require minor extensions to tool functions (import and export) or an external translator to convert tool-specific file formats to/from interchange formats. They enable easy comparison of results from multiple tools, and the use of tools best suited to the task without laborious and error prone manual translations.

The contents of the PMIF meta-model resulted from a taxonomy of the terminology used for QNM in performance tools and performance textbooks, and of the features provided by available tools for solving performance models [20]. A wide variety of features and terms were considered, as well as feedback from researchers in the performance field, to ensure that PMIF adequately described the information requirements.

The initial PMIF was restricted to QNM that can be solved by efficient, exact solution algorithms; this scope let us explore the end-to-end process of creating models, exchanging them among multiple tools, running experiments, and comparing solutions. PMIF and the overall model interoperability approach have been demonstrated to be viable and it is time to broaden the scope to support performance models that cannot be solved with efficient, exact solution algorithms. This paper extends PMIF to represent models that can be solved with additional methods such as analytical approximations or simulation solutions. We call this version PMIF+.

The next section discusses the requirements for selecting features to be supported and the candidate extensions. Section 3 discusses the alternatives for representing the extensions with a meta-model and the approach we selected. Section 4 presents the PMIF+ meta-model and how it represents the selected features. Section 5 expounds the validation, and the final section presents conclusions.

2   Requirements for the Selection of Extensions

Our earlier work examined representative QNM tools, meta-models, and techniques, proposed a set of features to be added, and sought community feedback [17]. We examined features in tools and techniques that allow models to be solved with approximate analytical and/or simulation techniques. A table showed features supported by the following:

- Performance Engineering Book [19] - advanced model solution features for Software Performance Engineering
- CSIM [3] - a powerful process-oriented simulation tool (also used by the *SPE-ED* tool for advanced model solution features)
- Qnap [14] - a classic, full-featured QNM solver with both analytic and simulation solution capabilities

---

[1] This paper assumes familiarity with PMIF2 and QNM solution techniques.

- Java Modelling Tools (JMT) [7] - a recent QNM tool that incorporates features for modeling current systems
- CSM/LQN [4] - a formal definition of the information requirements for Layered Queueing Networks
- KLAPER [10] - a metamodel and language for evaluating system performance

The first requirement for the selection of PMIF Extensions is stability. MIFs must be relatively stable to be viable; frequent changes would affect all tools using the MIFs. On the other hand, MIFs must evolve with technology changes. Changes to the PMIF meta-model should be infrequent and should limit the affect on existing tools to the extent possible. The original PMIF was based on concepts embodied in two earlier model interchange formats: the Electronic Data Interchange Format (EDIF) for VLSI designs [2] and the Case Data Interchange Format (CDIF) for software design interchange (also based on EDIF) [5]. Creators of EDIF envisioned the need to extend the model interchange formats (and thus the meta-models) and addressed it by providing for a concept of *levels* that add functionality at each successive level. Tools can continue to support a lower level without change, or may opt to modify interfaces to support additional functionality and/or other changes. Future work should use the newest version, even for the basic level. Tools may support different levels of the interchange format by specifying the meta-model (i.e., name) they use.

Creators of EDIF also addressed stability by giving ownership to a standards organization that managed changes. Using a standards organization to manage the contents of performance model interchange formats should be considered after stakeholders have established a viable version that meets essential needs.

For stability, the features we considered are those supported by commercial tools or popular open source tools. We do not specifically address features of more theoretical performance modeling results such as negative customers or triggers. Theoretical features should be represented in a different meta-model until they become well-established, are generally supported by tools, and are regularly used by practitioners.

In selecting the features for this level, we sought to add functions in a way that older models specified according to the PMIF would still be valid according to the PMIF+ meta-model. This increases stability because older model instances would not need to be updated.

Ideally the features selected for the PMIF extensions would include all the features listed below; however, supporting some of these features can be difficult depending on the modeling tools used. For example, classic techniques and tools support primitives for modeling computer systems such as waiting for and setting events. Events can then be used to model various types of synchronization among workloads. More modern tools and techniques provide higher level constructs for features common in todays computer systems, such as getting and putting data in buffers. There may not be a primitive called buffer in a classic tool; buffer behavior must be implemented using the lower-level primitives.

The PMIF extensions should support available features going forward, so we sought a mechanism to address both the newer features and the classic ones.

The EDIF philosophy is to import/export everything and to make appropriate substitutions for features that tools cannot handle. So tools can replace features they do not support by mapping them onto their own primitives.

Best practices in Service Oriented Architectures as defined by [8] suggest generalizing the definition of context dependent settings. In particular, the Validation Abstraction pattern suggests replacing constraints in meta-models with more general specifications. So, for example, rather than using an enumerated type explicitly defining queue scheduling disciplines, the pattern suggests defining it as a string. That allows tools to defer attribute validation and makes the interchange format evolution easier because meta-models do not have to be changed for every new queue scheduling discipline. The downside is that tools must be prepared to handle a situation when a feature is specified that the tool does not support. For example, if an unsupported queue scheduling discipline is specified, the tool could reject the model and return an error, or substitute another supported queue scheduling discipline and report the substitution.

As a consequence, the features considered for extending the scope of models supported by PMIF are as follows:

- Wait/Queue/Set Event - An Event may be *Set* or *Cleared*. Workloads may *Wait* or *Queue* for an event to be *Set*. When an event is *Set*, all waiting workloads and one queued workload may proceed.
- Allocate/Deallocate Resource - When access to a passive resource is restricted, a workload may request access and wait in a queue until the resource is *Allocated*. When access to the resource is no longer needed the workload *Deallocates* the resource. A scheduling policy determines the next workload to receive the Allocation.
- Create/Destroy Token - A Token is a special type of passive resource. In addition to Allocate/Deallocate, it is possible to dynamically *Create* and *Destroy* the token.
- Get/Put Buffer - A Buffer is another special type of passive resource, with a specified initial size (therefore it uses Get/Put operations instead of Allocate/Deallocate). *Get* requests the specified quantity from the Buffer and waits until it is available. *Put* adds the specified quantity to the Buffer and waits if there is insufficient space.
- Send/Receive Message - A mailbox is a container for holding messages. A workload can *Send* a message to a mailbox. A workload can *Receive* a message from a mailbox; if the mailbox is empty, the workload waits until the next message is *Sent* to that mailbox.
- Call/Accept/Return Synchronization Point - A workload may *Call* another workload and wait for the called workload to signal that it has completed the request; the called workload *Accepts* the request and *Returns* to the waiting workload.
- Fork/Split/Join Workload - A workload may *Fork* or *Split* into one or more child workloads that execute concurrently. Forked workloads later *Join*; the

parent workload waits until all child workloads *Join*, then the parent workload resumes execution. *Split* workloads do not join, they eventually complete and leave the system.

- Phase Change - A workload may have distinct execution characteristics such as routing, resource consumption, or passive resource usage. A *Phase* identifier distinguishes the behavior specifications; phases may *Change* at specific execution points, and execution output metrics may be associated with Phases.
- Priority - Workloads may have a Priority that controls queue scheduling. A higher priority workload is ahead of a lower priority one. For equal priorities the scheduling is usually first-come, first-served. Priorities may be changed during execution.
- Allocate/Deallocate/Add Memory - Memory is a special kind of resource, with an initial quantity. A workload can request allocation of a specific amount of memory and may queue if it is not available. *Allocate* requests a specified amount of a memory, the workload must wait if it is not available. *Deallocate* releases the specified amount of the specified memory; the waiting workloads which will fit are allocated, but a lower priority workload cannot go ahead of a higher priority one. *Add* increases the amount of a specified Memory.
- External Resource - represents resource usage outside the modeled system. It is usually represented by a delay server if at all, needs no explicit representation in the meta-model, and is not addressed further.
- Sub-model - represents a collection of queues/servers that may be grouped together. It may represent hierarchy in the system where the collection is represented at a higher level of detail by a single queue that represents the behavior of the collection. Sub-models may be useful for approximate solution techniques, and/or for aggregating execution output metrics.
- Compute - represents a point in execution where statistics may be calculated and used in execution behavior specifications.
- User-written Subroutine - is a mechanism for specifying customized execution behavior in a tool-dependent manner. It is usually written in a language recognized by a simulation tool or compiled code that may be called at a specified point in execution.
- Interrupt - is a mechanism for halting the execution of a workload and specifying alternate behavior.
- Arrival and Service Distributions - a broader set of stochastic distributions can be used when solving models with simulation and approximation methods.
- Queue Scheduling Disciplines - additional disciplines can be used to determine the next workload selected from a queue.

We have omitted several simulation run control features that were included in our earlier proposal such as reset counters, re-running a simulation, specification of stopping conditions, etc. We propose that these features logically belong in the Experiment specifications [18]. Future work will augment the Experiment and output specifications for the extended models.

Several features in the list are difficult to represent and implement. Compute statements, User-written subroutines and Interrupt have no simple substitution for tools without these capabilities. These features are not widely supported by tools, and in our experience are used infrequently. Therefore, they are omitted from this level of the PMIF+ meta-model. Sub-models are useful abstractions of processing details. Some theoretical model approximations have been proposed in the literature for solving sub-models with particular properties and substituting the calculated solution in higher level models. Sub-models are not yet established well enough to propose a general semantic that could be used in multiple tools. We have also deferred sub-models for a future level of PMIF+.

3   Meta-model Representations of PMIF Extensions

We considered two approaches for representing the new features. The first approach is derived from Information Process Graphs (IPGs) [13,19], a graphical representation of performance models. IPGs use special nodes to represent points in execution where special behavior occurs such as waiting for an event. The second approach defines service requests (*ServiceRequestPlus*) for the new features. A combination of active and passive service requests can be made at any node. The two approaches, their advantages and disadvantages are described first, then the meta-model of the selected approach is presented in Section 4.

IPGs were first supported by performance modeling tools such as the Performance Analyst Workbench (PAWS) developed by a company then called Scientific and Engineering Software (both the tool and the company have since changed names and ownership and that tool is no longer available). IPGs were subsequently used to explain advanced modeling features for performance engineering in [19].

The primary advantages of IPGs are: facilitating the visualization of performance model details, and representing most of the performance aspects of computer systems. Figure 1 shows an excerpt of a meta-model of the IPG-based approach. It adds a *SpecialServer* abstract node that may be Phase change, Allocate, Release, Fork, Join, etc. A *SpecialServiceRequest* provides specifications for the behavior at each of the nodes. *Workloads* can visit the *SpecialServer* with normal routing specifications.

One disadvantage of this approach is that it is difficult to determine from the textual representation (in xmi format) what the model represents, and what is the sequence of processing steps. The model representation also tends to be verbose because the extra nodes require extra specifications to route *Workloads* to the *SpecialServer* nodes and then to regular *Servers* for normal processing. Another disadvantage of IPGs is that they do not explicitly represent some higher-level features that are common in today's computer systems such as buffers and message passing. They do, however, provide low level primitives that allow the representation of those features as well as more complex behavior.

The second approach does not require a *SpecialServer* for each of the new features; Instead any *Server* may have one or more *ServiceRequestPlus* with an

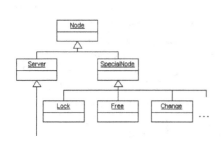

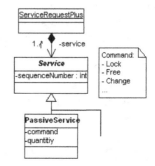

Fig. 1. IPG-based approach   **Fig. 2.** *ServiceRequestPlus* approach

optional *sequenceNumber* that specifies the order of execution when ordering is required. Figure 2 shows an excerpt of the meta-model for this approach. With this approach *PassiveService* requests specify the *Command* such as allocate/deallocate, specify the quantity, and reference the *PassiveEntity*. Several requests can be made at any node.

The primary advantage of this approach is that the extra features added with PMIF+ do not invalidate models that were specified with the meta-model version of the regular PMIF models. Thus it is not necessary to add an EDIF-like "level of support" for these new features, the newer meta-model can be used for both new and original features. Another advantage is that it is much easier to add new features to support. It is usually only necessary to add new commands; new features do not also need a new type of node with a new type of service request for the node. We were able to add many new features such as buffers and mailboxes that were not in the original IPGs. Also, multiple *ServiceRequestPlus* can be combined without having to move to another type of node, and for those cases it is easier to understand the processing steps in the model. The focus is on the processing steps required rather than on the node where they occur. The resulting model may also be less verbose.

The primary disadvantage is that there is no specified graphical depiction for models that correspond to this meta-model. The purpose of the meta-model, however, is not its depiction but the specification of semantic details sufficient for its solution. A minor inconvenience also occurs in some models when it is necessary to create a *Server* just to have a place to specify *ServiceRequestPlus* when no *ActiveService* is required.

We adopted the second approach with the *ServiceRequestPlus*. The ease of adding features and the ability to use the new meta-model for original models outweigh the benefit of the graphical depiction of the other version of the meta-model. Most of the extensions adopted in Section 2 have similar behavior: they request a passive resource, may have to wait for it, then release it which may cause it to be given to another waiting workload. The Fork/Join, however, causes additional workloads to begin parallel execution and the parent workload needs a place to wait for their completion that does not block the execution of other workloads. Therefore we created a Fork/Join node for that purpose, but use the *ServiceRequestPlus* approach for all the other extensions.

We have also developed specific enumerations of scheduling policies and probability distributions (shown in the next section) that we consider to be part of PMIF+. For a specific implementation, it is possible to instead use the Validation Abstraction pattern [8] by substituting a "string" type rather than using our *SchedulingPolicy* and *Distribution* types. We thought it is best to define in the PMIF+ meta-model the options that could be in a PMIF+ model.

4   PMIF+ Meta-model

The PMIF+ meta-model for the approach adopted is in Figure 3. Elements that are added for PMIF+ are yellow and original features are green (shaded gray if viewed in black and white).

A *QueueingNetworkModel*[2] is composed of: one or more *Nodes*, one or more *Workloads*, one or more *ServiceRequests*, and zero or more *PassiveEntities*. Several types of *Nodes* may be used in constructing a *QueueingNetworkModel*:

- *Server* represents a component of the execution environment that provides some active processing service. A *Server* may be a *WorkUnitServer* that executes a fixed amount of work (processing service) for each *Workload* that makes a request for service.
- *NonServerNode* represents nodes that show topology of the model, but do not provide service. The *Server* has an extended schedulingPolicy as shown in Figure 3. There are three types of *NonServerNodes*
  - *SourceNode* represents the origin of an *OpenWorkload*
  - *SinkNode* represents the exit point of an *OpenWorkload*
  - *ForkJoin* represents a component of the execution environment that handles Fork and Join operations. When the *willJoin* attribute is true, it is a Fork and the parent waits for all children (*ForkWorkloads*, see below) to complete and return to the same node to do the Join. When *willJoin* is false, it is a Split; the parent continues execution and the child workloads exit the system upon completion.

A *Server* provides service for one or more *Workloads*. A *Workload* represents a collection of transactions or jobs that make similar *ServiceRequests* from *Servers* and may have a priority. There are several types of *Workloads*:

- *OpenWorkload* represents a workload with a potentially infinite population where transactions arrive from the outside world, receive service, and exit. The population of the *OpenWorkload* at any point in time is variable.
- *ClosedWorkload* represents a workload with a fixed population that circulates among the *Servers*. A closed workload has a *ThinkDevice* or independent delay node characterized by its thinkTime (average interval of time that elapses between the completion of a transaction or job and the submission of the next transaction or job).

---

[2] We opted not to change the name to *QueueingNetworkModelPlus* so that previous models are still compatible with this meta-model.

- *ForkWorkload* represents a child workload with a maximum population that is created by its parent at a point in execution (at a *ForkJoin* node).
- *Workload* represents a different Phase for an already existing workload that can be any of the above.

Upon arrival or creation, *OpenWorkloads*, *ClosedWorkloads*, and *ForkWorkloads transitFirst* to other *Nodes* with a specified probability.

A service request associates the *Workloads* with *Servers*. A *ServiceRequest* specifies the average *TimeService*, *DemandService*, *WorkUnitService* or a *ServiceRequestPlus* provided for each *Workload* that visits the *Server*. The different types of *ServiceRequest* are:

- *TimeServiceRequest* specifies the average service time and number of visits provided for each *Workload* that visits the *Server*.
- *DemandServiceRequest* specifies the average service demand (service time multiplied by number of visits) provided for each *Workload* that visits the *Server*.
- *WorkUnitServiceRequest* specifies the average number of visits requested by each *Workload* that visits a *WorkUnitServer*.
- *ServiceRequestPlus* specifies a combination of active and passive service requests that can be made at any node with an optional *sequenceNumber* which specifies the order of execution of these requests when ordering is required.

   Note that sequence numbers are increasing but need not be consecutive. *PassiveService* requests specify the *command*, the quantity, and reference the *PassiveEntity*. Table 1 shows the different options for *PassiveEntity* with the associated *commands*, as described in Section 2. Some of the commands are shared with different *PassiveEntities*.

   Note that *PassiveService* does not normally block the server, it only blocks the workload. It has an optional attribute, *blocksServer* which is set to *True* when the server needs also to be blocked. *ActiveService* requests specify a service time similar to the *TimeServiceRequest*. They may use a special *ProbabilityDistribution* or a load dependent service time. The latter is specified as a string which will be interpreted by the tool.

Table 1. *ServiceRequestPlus* attribute options

Pas. Entity	Commands	Pas. Entity	Commands
timer	start/stop	event	wait/queue/set/clear
mailbox	send/receive	buffer	get/put/create/destroy
resource	allocate/deallocate	memory	allocate/deallocate/add
token	wait/queue/create/destroy	syncpoint	callreturn/accept/return

Upon completion of the *ServiceRequest*, the *Workload Transits* to other *Nodes* with a specified probability. A *Transit* may be a *TransitPlus* that specifies that the *Workload* changes to a *newWorkload* and/or specifies a type of dependent

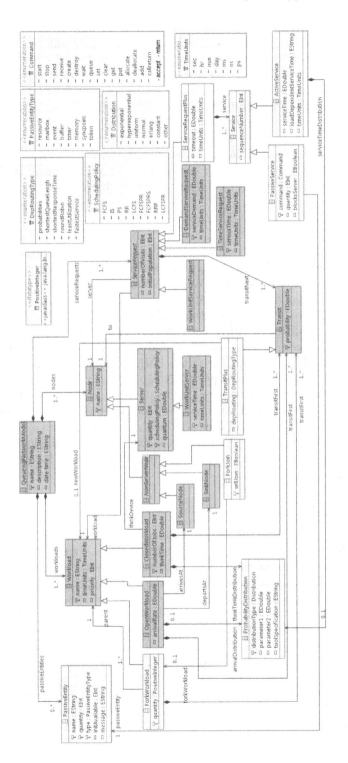

Fig. 3. PMIF+ meta-model

routing (shown in Figure 3). The Phase change feature from Section 2 can be represented by allowing workloads to change to another workload using the *newWorkload* specification. This represents phase-change behavior with simpler specifications. The *newWorkload* specification may also be used to change the priority of a *Workload*.

The specification of a *ProbabilityDistribution* different from Exponential (which is the default) is allowed for *arrivalRate* of *OpenWorkload*, *thinkTime* of *Closed-Workload* and *serviceTime* of *ActiveService* (so a *SeviceRequestPlus* needs to be specified in this case). The *ProbabilityDistribution* specification indicates the *distributionType* and two parameters for the distribution values. There is also an optional *toolSpecification* for the case of a tool specific distribution.

5   Validation

We have validated the PMIF+ meta-model by constructing test models of all features, then creating and solving those models in two very different modeling tools: Qnap [14], and *SPE-ED* [21]. We have also created and solved a more complex model of an actual system that uses several of the new features in combination and compared simulation results. This confirms that it is feasible to represent and solve all the included features, that we have defined the features correctly with all necessary data specified, and that it is feasible to automatically translate models that conform to the PMIF+ meta-model into different modeling tools. It is beyond the scope of this paper to cover all these examples. Instead, we have selected two examples that require solutions with analytical approximations or simulation and illustrate common behavior patterns: requiring exclusive access to a resource and waiting if it is not available, and a Fork/Join example. The subsections below explain the examples, discuss implementation differences in the two tools, and present results from the two tools for comparison and validation.

5.1   Fork/Join Examples

We start with a simple Fork/Join example that has two versions. It has an open workload, which does some work at CPUA and then Forks. Version 1 (V1) Forks into 3 different workloads (1 child each), each of them going to a specific CPU (CPU1, CPU2, CPU3), and when all finish the Join happens, and the parent workload leaves the system. Version 2 (V2) Forks into 1 workload with 3 children who go to CPU1, CPU2 or CPU3 with probability 1/3, and again when all 3 children finish the parent workload leaves the system.

The model conforming to the PMIF+ ecore meta-model is created in Eclipse [1] with the *Create Dynamic Instance* command. This ensures that the model instance conforms to the meta-model, that all required attributes are specified, and that there is a way of specifying all necessary parameters. An excerpt of the xmi specification for V1 is as follows (we include only one of the three *ForkWorkloads*, only one of the *Servers*, and one of the *ServiceRequests* specifications since the others are similar):

```
<workloads  xsi:type="csqnmm:OpenWorkload"  name="C1"  arrivalRate="1.0"
              arrivesAt="//@nodes.6"  departsAt="//@nodes.5">
  <transitFirst  to="//@nodes.0"  probability="1.0"/>
</workloads>
<workloads  xsi:type="csqnmm:ForkWorkload"  name="ForkC1"  quantity="1"
              parent="//@workloads.3">
  <transitFirst  to="//@nodes.1"  probability="1.0"/>
</workloads> ...
<nodes  xsi:type="csqnmm:Server"  name="CPUA"/> ...
<nodes  xsi:type="csqnmm:ForkJoin"  name="ForkNode"  forkWorkload=
       "//@workloads.0_//@workloads.1_//@workloads.2"  willJoin="true"/>

<serviceRequests  xsi:type="csqnmm:TimeServiceRequest"  server="//@nodes.1"
              workload="//@workloads.0"  serviceTime="0.4"> ...
```

V2 needs only 1 *forkWorkload* specification, with 3 different *Transits*, each of them equally likely. The complete specification of all the examples can be found at `dmi.uib.es/~cllado/mifs/`.

The Fork/Join implementation in Qnap is fairly straightforward. Workloads are translated to Classes and the ForkJoin node is translated into two queues with infinite server scheduling and service time 0. The Fork happens at one queue with a Qnap *Split* operation; and the Join happens at the other queue with a Qnap *Match*.

The *SPE-ED* implementation uses a table-driven simulation using the process-oriented CSIM [11] for the simulation engine. The Fork is implemented by creating new processes. They execute in a different address space than the parent, so the create command passes a pointer to an event, and each child sets the event to true when it reaches the Join point. The parent process waits until all child processes have set the event then it proceeds.

The results for Qnap and *SPE-ED* are in Table 2. Note that in V2, even though the child workloads are equally likely to visit CPU1-3, probabilistically they will sometimes end up going to the same CPU, which is reflected in the Response and Residence Time results. This difference lets us test both types of Fork/Join and confirm that the models have been correctly implemented.

Table 2. Fork/Join Results

Example	Response	Residence Time				Utilization			
		CPUA	CPU1	CPU2	CPU3	CPUA	CPU1	CPU2	CPU3
ForkJoinV1									
Qnap	1.829	0.6696	0.6655	0.6673	0.6659	0.4011	0.3999	0.4001	0.4000
SPE-ED	1.827	0.6662	0.6647	0.6686	0.6667	0.4002	0.3994	0.4006	0.4001
ForkJoinV2									
Qnap	2.182	0.6641	1.002	0.9961	1.004	0.4000	0.4002	0.3992	0.3999
SPE-ED	2.085	0.6676	0.8932	0.8901	0.8942	0.3996	0.4009	0.4004	0.4009

5.2 Buffer Example

This example represents the other general type of passive resource behavior: requesting a passive resource, possibly waiting, then releasing it which may schedule another waiting workload. It uses two different ProbabilityDistributions, and buffers for synchronization between processes, which is supported differently in the two tools.

The example has a pipe and filter architectural style. Data arrives from an external source at a constant arrival rate of 1 unit per second, it is processed by the first (open) workload, GetIm, then *put* in a buffer. The second (closed) workload, Spatial, after a thinkTime of 0, begins with a *get* from that buffer, when the data arrives Spatial processes it, then *puts* it to another buffer, and the cycle repeats. Three other "downstream" closed workloads, Temporal, Threshold, Paths, do the same. Each workload executes on its own processor so the workloads can execute in parallel. Workloads may have to wait on a *get* for data to arrive in the buffer, or at a *put* if there is not space in the buffer because a downstream process has not yet processed earlier data.

The following shows an excerpt of the xmi specification with a *ServiceRequestPlus* for one of the workloads at its CPU. The get/put commands are specified (on different buffers) as *PassiveServices* as well as an *ActiveService* which is a *Normal* service time distribution.

```
<serviceRequests xsi:type="csqnmm:ServiceRequestPlus"
                  server="//@nodes.4" workload="//@workloads.1">
  <transitNext to="//@nodes.3" probability="1.0"/>
  <service xsi:type="csqnmm:PassiveService" sequenceNumber="1"
           command="get" passiveEntity="//@passiveEntities.0"/>
  <service xsi:type="csqnmm:PassiveService" sequenceNumber="3"
           command="put" passiveEntity="//@passiveEntities.1"/>
  <service xsi:type="csqnmm:ActiveService" sequenceNumber="2">
    <serviceTimeDistribution distributionType="normal"
         parameter1="0.279" parameter2="1.0E-5"/> ...
```

The Buffer implementation in Qnap is easily done with Semaphores, which consist of a queue and a counter. The counter is the number of pass grants available if positive, and the number of customers waiting if negative. The workload that puts data to the buffer produces a pass grant for the semaphore, and the workload that gets data from the buffer asks the semaphore for a pass grant and it waits if the value of the counter is ≤ 0.

The implementation in *SPE-ED* is also easy. CSIM has a buffer type that is declared and a size specified; operations sendRequest and receiveRequest have the desired semantics and CSIM manages the waiting/activation of processes when appropriate. Both constant and normal probability distributions (and others) are supported by CSIM.

The results are shown in Table 3. Because of the constant arrival rate, and normal service time distribution, the results are identical except for the precision reported thus confirming that the models have been correctly implemented.

Table 3. Buffer Results

Example	Latency	Response Time				
		GetIm	Spatial	Temporal	Threshold	Paths
Qnap	0,4864	0.0869	0.2792	0.1110	0.0090	0.0003
SPE-ED	0.486	0.087	0.279	0.111	0.009	0.000

6   Conclusions

This paper presents extensions to PMIF to relax the constraint that specified models must be solvable with efficient, exact solution algorithms. It describes the features that were considered, their semantics, and the requirements for the selection of extensions. Most extensions are included and we provided reasons for excluding some. Contributions of this work include:

- A powerful set of extensions that can represent and analyze the performance of most if not all types of systems
- An easily extendable approach - it is easy to add passive entities and commands for new behavior
- One meta-model that can be used for both efficient, exact solutions and simulation or approximate solutions
- One meta-model that can be supported by both classic tools with modeling primitives (e.g., semaphores) and newer tools that directly support new features (e.g., buffers)
- An approach that supports both automatic transformation (e.g., ATL/Acceleo) of models to tool-specific input and automatic generation of code to support the meta-model with an import/export interface
- A flexible approach that allows tools to select features that they will support, when they will make substitutions for something similar they support, and when they will not attempt to solve models because they include features that they do not wish to handle (e.g., some dependent routing specifications)
- It is relatively easy to understand models that conform to PMIF+ (as illustrated in the validation section).

Future work will implement and test additional case studies that combine different sets of features. Then we will adapt the companion specifications for output and experiments for PMIF+ and include additional simulation control features in the experiment specification. We will also develop ATL transformations and/or import/export interfaces for Qnap, *SPE-ED*, and other tools. Finally, we also envision to work on a model to model transformation from PMIF+ to Petri Nets.

Acknowledgments. This work is partially funded by the TIN2010-16345 project of the *Ministerio de Educacion y Ciencia*, Spain. Smith's early participation was sponsored by US Air Force Contract FA8750-11-C-0059; the contract ended before this work was completed.

References

1. Eclipse modeling project, `http://www.eclipse.org/modeling`
2. EDIF, Electronic Design Interchange Format,
   `http://en.wikipedia.org/wiki/EDIF`
3. Mesquite software, `http://www.mesquite.com`

4. Puma project: Core scenario model, http://www.sce.carleton.ca/rads/puma/
5. Electronics Industries Association. CDIF - CASE Data Interchange Format Overview, EIA/IS-106 (1994)
6. Becker, S., Koziolek, H., Reussner, R.: The palladio component model for model-driven performance prediction. J. Syst. Softw. 82(1), 3–22 (2009)
7. Bertoli, M., Casale, G., Serazzi, G.: Jmt: performance engineering tools for system modeling. SIGMETRICS Perform. Eval. Rev. 36(4), 10–15 (2009)
8. Erl, T.: SOA Design Patterns. Prentice Hall (2009)
9. Grassi, V., Mirandola, R., Sabetta, A.: From design to analysis models: A kernel language for performance and reliability analysis of component-based systems. In: Proc. of the Fifth International Workshop on Software and Performance (WOSP), pp. 25–36 (July 2005)
10. Grassi, V., Mirandola, R., Randazzo, E., Sabetta, A.: Klaper: An intermediate language for model-driven predictive analysis of performance and reliability. In: Rausch, A., Reussner, R., Mirandola, R., Plášil, F. (eds.) The Common Component Modeling Example. LNCS, vol. 5153, pp. 327–356. Springer, Heidelberg (2008)
11. Mesquite Software Inc., http://www.mesquite.com
12. Moreno, G.A., Smith, C.U.: Performance analysis of real-time component architectures: An enhanced model interchange approach. Performance Evaluation, Special Issue on Software and Performance 67, 612–633 (2010)
13. Neuse, D.M., Browne, J.C.: Graphical tools for software system performance engineering. In: Proc. Computer Measurement Group, Washington, D.C. (1983)
14. Simulog. Modline 2.0 qnap2 9.3: Reference manual (1996)
15. Smith, C.U., Lladó, C.M.: Model interoperability for performance engineering: Survey of milestones and evolution. In: Hummel, K.A., Hlavacs, H., Gansterer, W. (eds.) PERFORM 2010 (Haring Festschrift). LNCS, vol. 6821, pp. 10–23. Springer, Heidelberg (2011)
16. Smith, C.U., Lladó, C.M., Puigjaner, R.: Performance Model Interchange Format (PMIF 2): A comprehensive approach to queueing network model interoperability. Performance Evaluation 67(7), 548–568 (2010)
17. Smith, C.U., Lladó, C.M., Puigjaner, R.: Pmif extensions: Increasing the scope of supported models. In: Proc. of the 1st Joint WOSP/SIPEW International Conference on Performance Engineering (ICPE), pp. 255–256 (Jannuary 2010)
18. Smith, C.U., Lladó, C.M., Puigjaner, R.: Model interchange format specifications for experiments, output and results. The Computer Journal (2011)
19. Smith, C.U.: Performance Engineering of Software Systems. Addison-Wesley (1990)
20. Smith, C.U., Williams, L.G.: A performance model interchange format. Journal of Systems and Software 49(1), 63–80 (1999)
21. SPE-ED. LS Computer Technology Inc. Performance Engineering Services Division, www.spe-ed.com
22. Woodside, C.M., Petriu, D.C., Petriu, D.B., Shen, H., Israr, T., Merseguer, J.: Performance by unified model analysis (PUMA). In: Proc. of the Fifth International Workshop on Software and Performance (WOSP), pp. 1–12 (July 2005)

Performance Regression Unit Testing: A Case Study

Vojtěch Horký, František Haas, Jaroslav Kotrč, Martin Lacina, and Petr Tůma

Department of Distributed and Dependable Systems
Charles University in Prague, Faculty of Mathematics and Physics
Malostranské náměstí 25, 118 00 Prague 1, Czech Republic
{horky,tuma}@d3s.mff.cuni.cz

Abstract. Including performance tests as a part of unit testing is technically more difficult than including functional tests – besides the usual challenges of performance measurement, specifying and testing the correctness conditions is also more complex. In earlier work, we have proposed a formalism for expressing these conditions, the Stochastic Performance Logic. In this paper, we evaluate our formalism in the context of performance unit testing of JDOM, an open source project for working with XML data. We focus on the ability to capture and test developer assumptions and on the practical behavior of the built in hypothesis testing when the formal assumptions of the tests are not met.

Keywords: Stochastic Performance Logic, regression testing, performance testing, unit testing, performance evaluation.

1 Introduction

Software testing is an established part of the software development process. Besides *functional testing*, where the correctness of the implementation with respect to functional requirements is assessed, it is also possible to employ *performance testing*, that is, to assess the temporal behavior of the implementation. This paper deals with performance testing during the software development process.

In general terms, the goal of performance testing is making sure that the system under test executes fast enough. What exactly is fast enough, however, depends on the context in which the performance testing is performed. When evaluating the end-to-end performance of a complete software system or a reasonably large component, the performance requirements are often derived from the application function or from the user expectations. Examples of such requirements include the time limit for decoding a frame in a video stream, determined from the frame rate, or the time limit for serving a web page in an interactive application, determined from the studies of user attention span. Importantly, these requirements can be naturally expressed in terms of absolute time limits.

The software development process, however, also employs testing before large system components are available. In a process called *unit testing*, individual

M.S. Balsamo, W.J. Knottenbelt, and A. Marin (Eds.): EPEW 2013, LNCS 8168, pp. 149–163, 2013.
© Springer-Verlag Berlin Heidelberg 2013

functions are evaluated alone. In this context, performance testing against absolute time limits is much less practical. To begin with, it is difficult to determine how fast an individual function or method should execute when the overall system performance, rather than the unit performance, remains the ultimate criterion. It is also difficult to scale the absolute time limits to reflect their platform dependence. Hence, unit testing of performance requirements is rare.

Working on our long term goal of unit testing of performance, we have argued [2] that it is often reasonable to express performance requirements as relative time limits, using the execution time of similar functions or methods as the baseline. For example, memory-bound methods can be compared with the memory copy operation. Analogously, processor-bound methods can be compared with a baseline computation. In the same work, we have also introduced the Stochastic Performance Logic (SPL), a mathematical formalism for expressing and evaluating such performance requirements. Our previous work focused on introducing the SPL formalism on a theoretical level, here we evaluate the use of SPL for unit testing of performance on a case study.

The paper proceeds with Section 2, which introduces various aspects of our environment for unit testing of performance in Java – it outlines the formalism for specifying the performance test criteria, explains the test construction, discusses the test workload, and summarizes the implemented test tool features. Following that, Section 3 introduces the case study we use to evaluate our environment. Section 4 discusses detailed technical issues related to the case study, including portability, sensitivity to execution time changes and overall test duration. Section 5 presents the related work. Section 6 concludes the paper.

2   SPL Unit Testing Environment

As suggested in the introduction, absolute time limits are not suitable criteria in unit testing of performance. The complexity of the contemporary software development platforms all but prevents developers from estimating the expected performance of individual functions or methods while coding. It is possible to measure the implementation after initial coding and derive the time limit from the observed performance, but such approach is evidently time consuming and error prone.

Even if the absolute time limits were somehow deduced, their portability becomes an issue. Platform dependent factors such as processor speed or cache size directly impact observed performance. A time limit that is tuned on a particular processor – that is, one loose enough to reliably accept the correct implementation but strict enough to be sensitive to performance regressions – would likely trigger erroneous test failures on a slower platform and miss performance regressions on a faster platform.

An alternative to the absolute time limits is comparing the performance of the tested function to the performance of a reasonably similar baseline function [2]. Comparison to a properly chosen baseline function can be both more intuitive and more portable – for example, the developer can relate the performance of a binary tree search function on a tree of certain size to the performance of a linked list search function on a list of logarithmically smaller size. Working with the assumption that the list search time is a linear function of the list size, the developer thus asserts that the tree search time should be a logarithmic function of the tree size, and that a single step in traversing the tree should be similar to a single step in traversing the list. Both are reasonable assertions that would be difficult to express using absolute time limits. Furthermore, the performance of both the tree search and the list search is likely to change in a similar manner when the test is carried over to a different platform, making the comparison somewhat portable. Although such portability is certainly not absolute, it represents an improvement over the absolute time limits as well.

The obvious challenge is choosing an appropriate baseline function. When testing an initial implementation of a function, trial and error remains the obvious – but not very efficient – method. In the context of unit testing, however, tests are also constructed to detect regressions, in which case an earlier version of the same function is an obvious baseline candidate. Using relative time limits, the developer can easily assert that the current version of a function should not be slower than an earlier version of known sufficient performance, or that the current version of a function should be faster than an earlier version it is meant to improve upon.

Because the performance of a function is likely to change between invocations, a test must collect multiple observations. A time limit can then be interpreted in multiple ways – for example, as a limit that no single invocation should exceed, or as a limit that an average of all invocations should not exceed. To introduce the necessary rigor into the interpretation of the criteria specification, we have introduced the Stochastic Performance Logic (SPL) [2], a many-sorted first-order logic with operators for comparing performance of multiple functions against each other. Example (1) uses SPL to assert that the mean execution time of the encryption function encrypt() will not exceed the mean execution time of the memory copy function memcopy by more than a factor of 200 when used on inputs of sizes 1024, 16384 and 65536.

$$\forall n \in \{1024, 16384, 65536\} : Perf_{\text{encrypt}}(n) <_{p(id, \lambda x.200x)} Perf_{\text{memcopy}}(n) \quad (1)$$

In the SPL notation, $Perf(n)$ stands for the execution time on input of size n, $<_{p(id, \lambda x.200x)}$ denotes comparison after transforming the left operand by an identity function and the right operand by a lambda function that multiplies the execution time by a constant. An important property of SPL is that the execution times, $Perf_{\text{encrypt}}(n)$ and $Perf_{\text{memcopy}}(n)$ in Example (1), are not treated as numbers but as random variables parametrized by the function argument size. Evaluating an SPL formula then amounts to statistical hypothesis testing on observations collected during testing. The proposed interpretation relies on Welch's t-test [17] for hypothesis testing, as discussed later.

For sake of brevity, we limit our introduction to SPL to this example. The reader is invited to check [2] for additional details.

2.1 Performance Test Construction

For unit testing to be efficient, the process of test construction must remain simple. In functional testing, a test is often as simple as a method invocation and a test assertion. Listing 1 illustrates that in performance testing, even a simple test is more complex.

```
Random rnd = new Random();
long durations[] = new long[SAMPLE_COUNT];
for (long i = 0; i < SAMPLE_COUNT; i++) {
  int param = rnd.nextInt();
  long start = System.nanoTime();
  testedMethod(param);
  long end = System.nanoTime();
  durations[i] = end - start;
}
assertMeanLessThan(durations, 3.5);
```

Listing 1. Hypothetical performance test

Although Listing 1 tests performance of a simple method with an argument of a primitive type, the amount of boilerplate dealing with test iteration and time measurement is fairly high. We therefore adopt a test construction approach where the iteration and measurement code is provided by the environment and the test code only specifies the method to be invoked and the assertion to be tested.

As another concern, we want to keep the testing and the tested code close to each other – we believe this simplifies maintenance especially when the tested code changes and the testing code must follow suit. Our environment for unit testing of performance allows tests to be specified in annotations of the tested methods as illustrated in Listing 2 ; it is also possible to specify the test separately if necessary.

Listing 2 uses a library method as a baseline for comparison. Besides comparing with another method in the same project, our environment also supports comparing with methods from different versions of the same project and with methods from different projects.

2.2 Performance Test Workload

To invoke the tested method, the test needs to provide it with input arguments, which in essence define the workload to be tested. Depending on circumstances, functional tests would use few typical inputs to assess method correctness under common workload, and many additional inputs to assess handling of corner cases or to test against repeated occurrence of earlier errors. In contrast, performance

```
@SPL(
  methods = "javaSort=java.util.Arrays#sort(long[])",
  generators = "data=SPL:LongUniform('0;1000')",
  formula = "for ( i {100, 1000, 10000} ) "
    + "SELF[data](i) <=(2, 1) javaSort[data](i)"
)
public void fasterSort(long[] data) {
  // Tested method ...
}
```

The method specification identifies code to compare performance to. The generator provides integer arrays to sort, as discussed later in text. The formula states that fasterSort should be at least two times faster than javaSort.

Listing 2. Performance test specified in annotations

tests would focus on performance under common workload, which is usually considered more important than performance in corner cases.

Another difference concerns the number of inputs required. Functional tests can often test an assertion after a single method invocation. Performance tests require multiple method invocations to collect a representative set of observations. Inputs to those invocations should be of similar properties to be perceived as one workload, but at the same time, they should be randomized to avoid introducing systematic measurement bias. Listing 2 provides an example of addressing this requirement by using arrays of equal size but different random content for each sort invocation.

Given the difference between input arguments to functional and performance tests, we have decided to rely on separate input argument generators in our environment. Each test specifies the generator to use, which can be a custom generator or a predefined generator provided by our environment, such as the random array generator.

2.3   Tool Features Overview

To conclude the overview of our environment for unit testing of performance, we briefly list the features of the implemented tools, also available for download at [16].

At the core of the tools is a command line utility to execute the tests. The utility scans a given project and locates and executes the tests specified using the annotations. The results are provided in the form of an HTML report with a quick overview and a detailed information for each test including visualization of measurements. An example report fragment is displayed in Figure 1. The utility can cooperate with both Git and Subversion to fetch particular project versions used as baselines, it can also use SSH to execute the measurements on a remote host, which can help improve measurement stability.

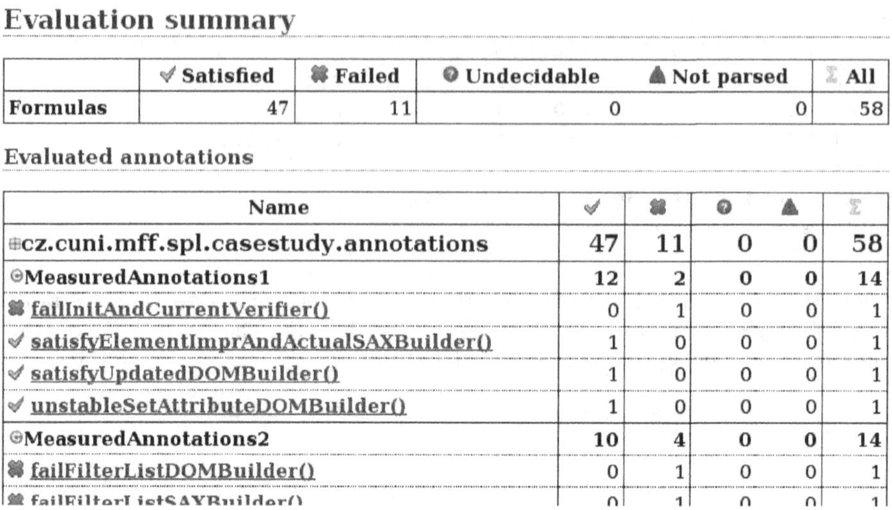

Evaluation summary

Formulas	✔ Satisfied	✇ Failed	⊘ Undecidable	▲ Not parsed	∑ All
Formulas	47	11	0	0	58

Evaluated annotations

Name	✔	✇	⊘	▲	∑
⊞**cz.cuni.mff.spl.casestudy.annotations**	**47**	**11**	**0**	**0**	**58**
⊖MeasuredAnnotations1	12	2	0	0	14
✇ failInitAndCurrentVerifier()	0	1	0	0	1
✔ satisfyElementImprAndActualSAXBuilder()	1	0	0	0	1
✔ satisfyUpdatedDOMBuilder()	1	0	0	0	1
✔ unstableSetAttributeDOMBuilder()	1	0	0	0	1
⊖MeasuredAnnotations2	10	4	0	0	14
✇ failFilterListDOMBuilder()	0	1	0	0	1
✇ failFilterListSAXBuilder()	0	1	0	0	1

Fig. 1. Example screenshot of the HTML report

In addition to the core command line utility, we also provide plugins for the Eclipse integrated development environment and the Hudson continuous integration server. The Eclipse plugin provides project configuration, annotation editor with content assist, and interactive results browser (Figure 2) also for results from Hudson.

3   SPL Unit Testing Case Study

In our previous work on expressing performance requirements as relative time limits [2], we have focused on introducing the basic ideas behind the requirements specification formalism. Here, we want to put the ideas to the test by answering practically motivated questions: How portable are the performance tests ? What coverage can be achieved with reasonable testing duration ? What accuracy can be achieved when some underlying test assumptions are not met ? Plus the ultimate question – are the performance tests something the developers care about ?

To answer these questions, we perform a retroactive case study – we pick an existing software project, augment it with tests and evaluate the results. Our project of choice is JDOM, a software package "for accessing, manipulating, and outputting XML data from Java code" [7] – with about 15000 LOC, it is of reasonable size for an experiment that requires frequent compilation and manual code inspection ; with over 1500 commits spread across 13 years of development, it provides ample opportunity to observe performance regressions ; it also has an open source license and a public source code repository [8].

Our performance tests focus on the SAX builder and the DOM converter as two essential high level components of JDOM, and on the Verifier class as a

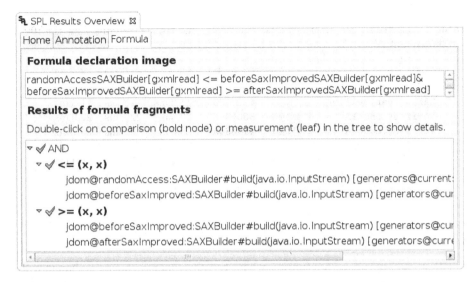

Fig. 2. Example screenshot of the Eclipse plugin

low level component performance critical to JDOM [9]. By looking for keywords such as "performance", "refactor", "improve" or "faster" in the commit log, we have identified commits which the developers consider relevant to performance. We have then written tests that express the developer assumptions about performance, using data from the performance study [9] in the workload generators. In all, we have 103 performance comparisons over 102 measurements in 58 tests across 46 commits. All SPL formulas had the same general form as Example (1), Figure 2 is taken from the case study results.

We report the results collected on an Intel Xeon machine running at 2.33 GHz, 32 kB L1 and 4 MB L2 caches, 8 GB RAM, running 64 bit Fedora 18 with OpenJDK 1.7. Our portability experiments additionally use an Intel Pentium 4 machine running at 2.2 GHz, 8 kB L1 and 512 kB L2 caches, 512 MB RAM, running 32 bit Fedora 18 with OpenJDK 1.7, and an Intel Atom machine running at 1.6 GHz, 24 kB L1 and 512 kB L2 caches, 1 GB RAM, running 32 bit Windows XP Service Pack 2 with Oracle HotSpot 1.7.[1]

In the following sections, we select three examples to illustrate the typical developer assumptions we test. The measurement results for the examples are given in Table 1.

---

[1] Because our tools require Java 7, we have used it to measure even JDOM versions created before Java 7 existed. The differences in the virtual machine could potentially influence measurement results, we have therefore used the Retrotranslator tool [15] to manually measure selected tests with Java 1.5. The results indicate no significant difference.

Table 1. Selected measurement results. The 10% Q and 90% Q columns show the 10% and 90% quantiles.

Method	Commit	Median	10% Q	90% Q
SAXBuilder.build	6a49ef6	9.2 ms	9.1 ms	9.3 ms
SAXBuilder.build	4e27535	11.2 ms	11.1 ms	11.3 ms
Verifier.checkAttributeName	500f9e5	22.5 ms	22.5 ms	22.6 ms
Verifier.checkAttributeName	4ad684a	20.0 ms	19.9 ms	20.1 ms
Verifier.checkAttributeName	e069d4c	21.4 ms	21.3 ms	21.5 ms
Verifier.checkAttributeName	1a05718	25.2 ms	25.2 ms	25.4 ms
Verifier.checkElementName	e069d4c	31.6 ms	28.6 ms	31.7 ms
Verifier.checkElementName	1a05718	42.6 ms	41.3 ms	42.8 ms

3.1   Case I: Negative Improvement

The first example shows a situation where the developers believed a change will improve performance significantly, when the opposite was actually true. The change was introduced with this commit 4e27535 message: "instead of using the slow and broken PartialList to make lists live, we'll be using a *faster and smarter* FilterList mechanism ... it *should be faster* and consume fewer resources to traverse a tree" [8].

Table 1 shows the performance from this commit and the preceding commit 6a49ef6 for the build() method of SAX builder. Instead of the expected performance improvement, the change actually increased the median execution time by 22%.

3.2   Case II: Confirmed Improvement

The second example shows a successful performance improvement confirmed by the performance test. Commit 4ad684a focused on improving performance of the Verifier class after the developers made their own performance evaluation [9]. Comparison with the preceding commit 500f9e5 in Table 1 indicates the method execution time decreased by 11%.

3.3   Case III: Measurement

The last example shows a somewhat creative use of a performance test. We focus on a situation where the developers actually expect a performance problem and want to assess the magnitude. Such situations can arise for example when the code is refactored for readability, possibly assuming that performance optimizations would be applied later, or when more complex code replaces previous implementation.

In the JDOM project, this happened for example between commit e069d4c and commit 1a05718, where modifications bringing better standard conformance were introduced: "bringing the letter/digit checks in line with the spec

... following the BNF productions more closely now" [8]. By adding a test that refers to the execution time of a particular method in both versions, the developers obtain a report that helps assess the magnitude of the performance change. Table 1 shows the execution times of the `checkAttributeName()` and the `checkElementName()` methods, with the median execution time increasing by 18% and 35% respectively. Note that the execution times refer to multiple consecutive invocations, since one method invocation would be too short to measure accurately.

Our experience with these and other examples suggests that unit testing of performance would help the developers confront their assumptions with measurements with relatively little effort. We have observed six cases where the developer assumptions were refuted by the tests, which is about one tenth of all examined assumptions – the retroactive character of our case study does not allow to guess the developer reaction, however, we can still assume the developers would find the feedback helpful. For interested readers, we have made the complete source of our tests and the complete measurement results available on the web at [16].

4   SPL Case Study Lessons

After illustrating how unit testing of performance addresses realistic developer concerns, we look at the technical issues related to the use of performance tests in the case study.

4.1   Platform Portability

Among the features of SPL is the ability to compare performance of multiple functions against each other. This feature is motivated by the need to make the test criteria reasonably portable – while it is generally not possible to make accurate conclusions about performance on one platform from measurements on another, running the same test on similar platforms should ideally lead to similar conclusions. In our case study, we therefore look at how the test results differ between the three different platforms.

We define a metric that describes the relative difference between results of a single test on two different platforms. Assuming a test condition that compares performance of functions M and N on platforms 1 and 2, we compute the ratio $(\bar{M}_1/\bar{N}_1)/(\bar{M}_2/\bar{N}_2)$ or its reciprocal, whichever is greater, where $\bar{X}_i$ denotes the mean execution time of method X on platform i. A perfectly portable test condition would preserve the ratio $\bar{M}/\bar{N}$ on all platforms, giving the portability metric value of one.

Figure 3 shows a histogram of the portability metric values for all test and platform pairs in our case study. Most portability metric values are very close to one, with 96% of values smaller than two and no value greater than five. This leads us to believe most tests in our case study are indeed reasonably portable.

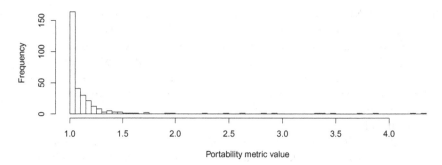

Fig. 3. Histogram of portability metric values

4.2   Accuracy and False Alarms

Inherent to the nature of performance testing are the issues of accuracy. We need tests that are sensitive to small changes in performance, however, we also need to minimize the number of false alarms. The evaluation of SPL formulas is based on statistical testing of hypotheses on collected measurements, we therefore phrase our accuracy requirements in statistical terms – we are interested in the probability that a test fails to spot a performance change due to Type II error and in the probability that a test reports a false alarm due to Type I error.

The need to evaluate the probability of test errors is exacerbated by the fact that we do not meet the statistical test assumptions – the SPL interpretation relies on Welch's t-test [17], which assumes two sets of independent observations of random variables with the same normal distribution. The tests, however, have no control over the execution time of the tested functions, and therefore also no control over meeting the statistical test assumptions. Real measurements are neither normal nor independent.

To investigate the size of execution time changes we can detect, we pick four functions with very different execution time distributions as examples whose testing decidedly breaks the statistical test assumptions. The execution time histograms of the four functions are given on Figure 4 – the distributions are unimodal with a tail, bimodal with small and large coefficient of variation, and quadrimodal. For each of the four functions, we calculate the sensitivity of the performance test to a given change in execution time on a given number of measurements.

Given a set[2] of measurements M of function f, we calculate the sensitivity to a change of scale $s > 1$ on n measurements as follows:

1. We use random sampling to split M in halves M_X and M_Y, $M = M_X \uplus M_Y$.
2. We use random sampling with replacement to create sets of measurements X and Y of size n, $x \in X \Rightarrow x \in M_X$, $y \in Y \Rightarrow y \in M_Y$.
3. We scale one of the sets of measurements by s, $Z = \{y \cdot s : y \in Y\}$.

---

[2] Strictly speaking, measurements are discrete, hence M is multiset.

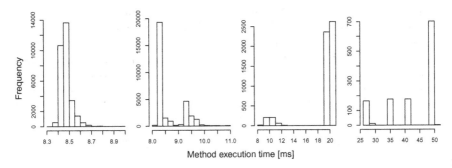

Fig. 4. Execution times of the four example functions

4. We see whether one sided Welch's t-tests reject the null hypothesis $\bar{X} = \bar{Z}$ in favor of the alternative $\bar{X} > \bar{Z}$ and the alternative $\bar{Z} > \bar{X}$ with significance $\alpha = 0.01$.

The sets X and Z represent hypothetical measurements of f before and after a change of scale s in execution time. We repeat the steps enough times to estimate the probability that the tests correctly favor $\bar{Z} > \bar{X}$ and the probability that the tests incorrectly favor $\bar{X} > \bar{Z}$, which together characterize the test sensitivity.

Figure 5 plots the test sensitivity, expressed as the two probabilities, for $s = 1.01$. The results indicate that for the four functions, mere hundreds of measurements are enough to keep the probability of incorrectly concluding $\bar{X} > \bar{Z}$ close to zero, and tens of thousands of measurements are enough to make the probability of correctly concluding $\bar{Z} > \bar{X}$ reasonably high. To save space, we do not show results for other values of s. These results indicate a test would require an unreasonably high number of measurements to detect changes of 0.1%, while changes of 10% are easily detected even from a small number of measurements.

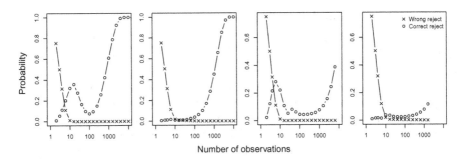

Fig. 5. Sensitivity to 1% execution time change on the four example functions

Robustness of statistical hypothesis testing on measurements that fail test assumptions is but one element of accuracy achievable in practice. As explained in [11], measurements collected in one execution of a program are not necessarily representative of the overall performance of that program – operations that happen once per execution, such as certain program memory allocations, can exert systematic influence over all measurements collected in that execution. In another execution of the same program, this influence can be different, leading to systematically different measurement results. Figure 6 illustrates this effect by showing measurements collected in multiple executions of the SAX builder unit test on the same revision and platform.

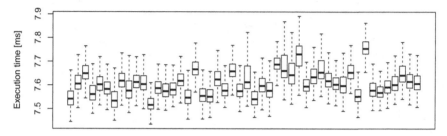

Fig. 6. Measurements from multiple executions of the SAX builder unit test. The outliers are not shown, whiskers are at 1.5 of inter-quartile range.

A robust solution to this effect requires multiple executions for each test [12], something that can increase the test duration by an order of magnitude and is therefore not practical in the unit testing context. A workable alternative is to relax the tests so that the effect is ignored, an easy step given that the tests should already include leeway for portability. In our case study, the magnitude of the effect was about 5%, we would therefore relax the tests by the same amount. Figure 7 shows the points in the project development history where the SAX builder unit test would detect increase in execution time when ignoring changes below 5%.

4.3   Test Duration and Coverage

An important issue in the unit testing context is the test duration. To test a function, a performance test requires more invocations than a functional test. A performance test therefore runs for much longer than a functional test of the same code coverage ; for the sensitivity levels considered in our case study this can be several orders of magnitude longer. In our case study, we have used performance tests that cover about 18% of the code, in contrast with the functional tests that cover almost 90% of the code, as reported by the Eclemma tool in Eclipse. This yielded an average duration of 27 minutes for a checkout, build and test of a single commit, compared to 58 seconds for a checkout and a build where performance is not evaluated.

Another concern related to test duration is the accumulation of tests. If new functions with new tests were added continuously throughout project development, we would soon reach a point where the time needed to collect measurements and evaluate performance would become much too long. Our environment

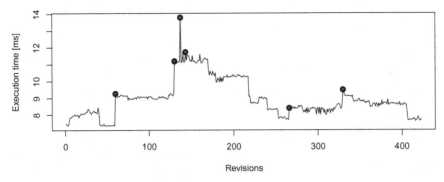

Fig. 7. Execution times of SAX builder with detected regressions marked. The markers denote where tests detect a performance regression over 5%. Data comes from over 400 commits over the entire history, at most one commit per day.

helps alleviate this problem by caching past measurements – the cache records the host used for measurement and the function and revision measured, preventing repeated measurement of baseline functions from past revisions.

Besides measurement caching, we use simple guidelines for constructing performance tests that help minimize the number of measurements needed by each commit:

1. Performance unit tests should be written only for functions that are crucial to the overall performance. Such functions can be identified for example by profiling or other performance analysis tools. While it is recommended to write a functional unit test for every function, writing a performance test for every function is not reasonable.
2. Only very few performance unit tests – preferably those focused on the overall performance – should refer to functions without restricting revision. Other tests should refer to specific revisions where possible, reducing the number of tests per revision and making the past measurement cache effective.
3. Performance unit tests should be arranged in groups to allow manually enabling or disabling test groups as necessary.

The experience collected in our case study indicates adhering to these guidelines maintains balance between test duration and coverage that is acceptable for unit testing during software development. More comprehensive performance measurements can be delegated to separate testing procedures.

5 Related Work

Related to our work are projects aimed at continuous testing. Among those, the Skoll project [14] is a decentralized distributed platform for continuous quality assurance. The execution is feedback-driven: each quality assurance activity is represented by a task that is executed and once its results are analyzed, other tasks are scheduled as necessary. Multiple strategies for executing dependent tasks are used to isolate individual problems.

The DataMill project [13] offers a heterogeneous environment for running tests on different operating systems or on different hardware platforms. No analysis is integrated in DataMill, instead, the goal is to allow testing software on different platforms. This makes DataMill an important complement to many performance testing approaches to resolve the issues related to repeatability of performance measurements, researched in [12].

On system level, Foo et al. [4] stress the need for automated approach to performance regression testing at system level. The proposed approach is based on monitoring a set of performance metrics, such as the system load, and comparing the measurements across different releases. Data-mining and machine-learning techniques are used to correlate the collected metrics, creating performance patterns that can indicate performance regressions.

Also on system level, Ghaith et al. [5] propose to use transaction profiles to identify performance regressions. The profiles are constructed from resource utilization and do not depend on workload. Comparison of transaction profiles reveals the regression. In contrast, our approach captures workload dependent performance, expecting the developers to provide application specific workload generators.

The problem of identifying the change that caused a performance regression is tackled in [6]. The authors use functional unit tests as a basic for monitoring performance regressions. Commit history bisection is used to identify a particular revision, measurement on individual levels of the call tree are used to locate the regression in code. It is not yet clear to what extent the methodology can be automated.

Among the tools targeted at performance unit testing, JUnitPerf [3] and ContiPerf [1] are notable extensions of the JUnit [10] functional unit testing framework. Both tools use absolute time limits to specify performance constraints evaluated by the tests. Both JUnitPerf and ContiPerf support execution of the function under test by multiple threads in parallel. Due to integration with JUnit, both tools are also supported by environments that support JUnit itself, including Eclipse and Hudson.

6   Conclusion

The focus of our paper is the use of performance unit testing in an open source project. We have introduced the concept of testing with relative time constraints and described a tool suite that facilitates such testing, with the constraints expressed using the Stochastic Performance Logic.

In a case study, we have used the tool suite to apply performance unit testing to the JDOM open source project. We have extended the project with tests that evaluate developer assumptions about performance expressed in the project commit logs, showing that about one tenth of these assumptions was wrong. We have also used the results to investigate the important questions of portability, sensitivity to execution time changes and overall test duration. We have shown that changes in the range of tens of percent can be detected reliably even with relatively short tests. We have also shown that relative time constraints detecting such changes are reasonably portable between platforms. Finally, we have outlined guidelines to applying performance unit testing that balance test duration and coverage.

The tool suite used in our case study, as well as all supplementary material, is available at [16].

Acknowledgments. This work has been supported by EU project 257414 ASCENS, GACR project P202/10/J042 FERDINAND and by Charles University institutional funding SVV-2013-267312.

References

1. Bergmann, V.: ContiPerf 2 (2013), http://databene.org/contiperf.html
2. Bulej, L., Bures, T., Keznikl, J., Koubkova, A., Podzimek, A., Tuma, P.: Capturing Performance Assumptions using Stochastic Performance Logic. In: Proc. ICPE 2012. ACM (2012)
3. Clark, M.: JUnitPerf (2013), http://www.clarkware.com/software/JUnitPerf
4. Foo, K., Jiang, Z.M., Adams, B., Hassan, A., Zou, Y., Flora, P.: Mining performance regression testing repositories for automated performance analysis. In: Proc. QSIC 2010. IEEE (2010)
5. Ghaith, S., Wang, M., Perry, P., Murphy, J.: Profile-based, load-independent anomaly detection and analysis in performance regression testing of software systems. In: Proc. CSMR 2013. IEEE (2013)
6. Heger, C., Happe, J., Farahbod, R.: Automated root cause isolation of performance regressions during software development. In: Proc. ICPE 2013. ACM (2013)
7. JDOM (2013), http://www.jdom.org
8. hunterhacker/jdom [Git] (2013), https://github.com/hunterhacker/jdom
9. hunterhacker/jdom: Verifier performance (2013), https://github.com/hunterhacker/jdom/wiki/Verifier-Performance
10. JUnit (April 2013), http://junit.org
11. Kalibera, T., Bulej, L., Tůma, P.: Benchmark Precision and Random Initial State. In: Proc. SPECTS 2005. SCS (2005)
12. Kalibera, T., Tůma, P.: Precise Regression Benchmarking with Random Effects: Improving Mono Benchmark Results. In: Horváth, A., Telek, M. (eds.) EPEW 2006. LNCS, vol. 4054, pp. 63–77. Springer, Heidelberg (2006)
13. Oliveira, A., Petkovich, J.-C., Reidemeister, T., Fischmeister, S.: Datamill: Rigorous performance evaluation made easy. In: Proc. ICPE 2013. ACM (2013)
14. Porter, A., Yilmaz, C., Memon, A.M., Schmidt, D.C., Natarajan, B.: Skoll: A process and infrastructure for distributed continuous quality assurance. IEEE Trans. Softw. Eng. 33(8), 510–525 (2007)
15. Puchko, T.: Retrotranslator (2013), http://retrotranslator.sourceforge.net
16. SPL Tools (2013), http://d3s.mff.cuni.cz/software/spl-java
17. Welch, B.L.: The Generalization of Student's Problem when Several Different Population Variances are Involved. Biometrika 34(1/2), 28–35 (1947)

Phase-Type Fitting Using HyperStar

Philipp Reinecke, Tilman Krauß, and Katinkà Wolter

Freie Universität Berlin
Institut für Informatik
Takustraße 9
14195 Berlin, Germany
{philipp.reinecke,tilman.krauss,katinka.wolter}@fu-berlin.de

Abstract. In this paper we provide a hands-on discussion of the use of
the HyperStar phase-type fitting tool in common application scenarios.
HyperStar allows fitting Hyper-Erlang distributions to empirical data,
using a variety of algorithms and operation modes. We describe simple
cluster-based fitting, a new graphical method for refining the density
approximation, a new command-line interface, and the integration of
HyperStar with a Mathematica implementation of a fitting algorithm.
Furthermore, we describe the use of Hyper-Erlang distributions in simulation. Throughout our discussion we illustrate the concepts on a data
set which has been shown to be difficult to fit with a PH distribution.

Keywords: Phase-type fitting, Tool description, Case-study.

1 Introduction

Phase-type (PH) distributions [1] are a very flexible class of distributions for
modelling e.g. failure times or response times. As PH distributions have Markovian representation, they can be used in analytical as well as in simulation approaches to system evaluation.

Phase-type distributions are typically applied to approximate empirical data
sets. In recent years several tools have been developed to help with the task of
fitting PH distributions to data: EMPHT [2] is a command-line tool that can
fit arbitrary phase-type distributions. PhFit [3] fits acyclic phase-type distributions (both discrete and continuous), offering both a graphical user-interface and
command-line tools. G-FIT [4] fits Hyper-Erlang distributions and runs on the
command-line.

In [5] we proposed a cluster-based fitting approach for fitting mixtures of
distributions, and in [6] we presented the HyperStar tool that implements this
approach. HyperStar complements the above set of tools in that its intuitive
user-interface helps domain-experts to apply PH distributions for data fitting;
furthermore, its user-interface can also be applied to existing tools and proto-
types, thus fostering the development of new fitting approaches. HyperStar is
implemented in Java and is available for download at [7].

M.S. Balsamo, W.J. Knottenbelt, and A. Marin (Eds.): EPEW 2013, LNCS 8168, pp. 164–175, 2013.
© Springer-Verlag Berlin Heidelberg 2013

In this paper we provide a hands-on discussion of the use of HyperStar in common fitting tasks. HyperStar implements several varieties of the fitting algorithm described in [5] and also offers several operation modes. Our focus here will be on illustrating the application of HyperStar in typical scenarios. We will therefore focus on the simple mode and on the command-line mode, as these are probably the modes that are used most of the time. Expert mode offers a high degree of flexibility in parameterising different variants of the clustering algorithm, and also supports the inclusion of existing tools, such as PhFit and G-FIT for fitting the branch distributions. Although this allows the expert to configure HyperStar in great detail when fitting, we have observed that in typical examples there are only minor improvements. We will therefore only describe the Mathematica interface, as this interface has proved to be helpful in evaluating new fitting algorithms. With the Mathematica interface, the user only has to implement the functionality of the fitting algorithm, which then seamlessly integrates with the dataset manipulation and display of results of HyperStar. Throughout the paper we first discuss the application and then provide some details on the underlying algorithms.

The paper is structured as follows: In Section 2 we briefly introduce some properties of phase-type distributions. We then describe the data set that we use throughout this paper. In Section 4 we describe the simple mode of using HyperStar. This mode enables the user to fit a HyperErlang distribution without requiring expert knowledge of PH distributions. Section 5 describes the new peak-adjustment feature that allows the adjustment of the shape of the fitted density using purely graphical means. In Section 6 we introduce the new command-line mode, which automatically detects peaks before applying cluster-based fitting. In Section 7 we give an example of how HyperStar can be integrated with a Mathematica implementation of a PH-fitting algorithm using the Mathematica interface of the expert mode. We complement our discussion of phase-type fitting by a description of how to use Hyper-Erlang distributions in simulation tools in Section 8, before concluding the paper with an outlook on future work.

2   Phase-Type Distributions

Continuous phase-type (PH) distributions are defined as the distribution of time to absorption in a Continuous-Time Markov Chain (CTMC) with one absorbing state [1]. PH distributions are commonly represented by a vector-matrix tuple $(\boldsymbol{\alpha}, \mathbf{Q})$, where

$$\boldsymbol{\alpha} = (\alpha_1, \ldots, \alpha_n) \in \mathbb{R}^n \text{ and } \mathbf{Q} = \begin{pmatrix} -\lambda_{11} & \cdots & \lambda_{1n} \\ \vdots & \ddots & \vdots \\ \lambda_{n1} & \cdots & -\lambda_{nn} \end{pmatrix} \in \mathbb{R}^{n \times n} \qquad (1)$$

with $\lambda_{ij} \geq 0, \lambda_{ii} > 0, \mathbf{Q}\mathbb{1} \leq \mathbf{0}$, $\mathbf{Q}$ is non-singular, and $\boldsymbol{\alpha}\mathbb{1} = 1$, where $\mathbb{1}$ is the column vector of ones of the appropriate size. $\boldsymbol{\alpha}$ is referred to as the initial probability vector, and $\mathbf{Q}$ is the sub-generator matrix of the phase-type distribution.

Definition 1. *If* $(\alpha, \mathbf{Q})$ *is the representation of a phase-type distribution, then the* probability density function (PDF), cumulative distribution function (CDF), *and kth* moment, *respectively, are given by [1,3,8]:*

$$f(t) = \alpha e^{\mathbf{Q}t}(-\mathbf{Q}\mathbb{1}), \tag{2}$$

$$F(t) = 1 - \alpha e^{\mathbf{Q}t}\mathbb{1}, \tag{3}$$

$$E\left[X^k\right] = k!\alpha(-\mathbf{Q})^{-k}\mathbb{1}. \tag{4}$$

HyperStar fits mixtures of m phase-type distributions, that is, the distributions created by HyperStar have branch structure. Each branch has a sub-generator matrix $\mathbf{Q}_1, \ldots, \mathbf{Q}_m$ and an initial probability vector $\alpha_1, \ldots, \alpha_m$. The mixture is then given by

$$\mathbf{Q} = \begin{pmatrix} \mathbf{Q}_1 & \mathbf{0} \\ & \ddots & \ddots \\ & & \mathbf{0} \\ & & & \mathbf{Q}_m \end{pmatrix} \text{ and } \alpha = (\alpha_1, \ldots, \alpha_m). \tag{5}$$

HyperStar is most commonly used to fit Hyper-Erlang distributions, i.e. mixtures of Erlang distributions [4]. With Hyper-Erlang distributions, all block matrices $\mathbf{Q}_1, \ldots, \mathbf{Q}_m$ in (5) are of the form

$$\mathbf{Q}_i = \begin{pmatrix} -\lambda_i & \lambda_i \\ & \ddots & \ddots \\ & & & \lambda_i \\ & & & -\lambda_i \end{pmatrix}, \tag{6}$$

and only the first element in each initial probability vector $\alpha_i, i = 1, \ldots, m$ is non-zero.

3   The Data Set

Throughout this paper we use the data set shown in Figure 1. This data set contains samples of the packet-delivery ratio in the DES testbed, a testbed for wireless mesh networks deployed in different buildings across the campus of Freie Universität Berlin [9]. Since the data is for packet-delivery ratios, which are in the interval $[0, 1]$, the density is 0 for samples outside this interval. The histogram of the density shows three peaks, at 0, 0.75, and 1. Note that this data set is very difficult to fit using a phase-type distribution; in particular, the density of 0 for PDR values larger than 1 cannot be fitted exactly with any phase-type distribution. We use this data set as an extreme example for showing the potential of HyperStar for fitting difficult-to-fit data sets. For a more in-depth evaluation and comparison to other fitting tools we refer the reader to [5].

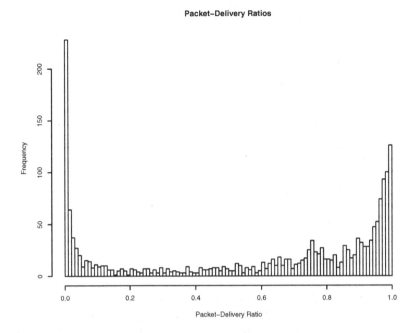

Fig. 1. Histogram of the DES data set

4   Fitting a Data Set in Simple Mode

When started without parameters, HyperStar shows the user interface for simple mode. Simple mode is probably the most commonly used mode of HyperStar and allows the user to quickly and accurately fit a Hyper-Erlang distribution to a data set.

The user interface for simple mode is shown in Figure 2: The left-hand panel displays the histogram and empirical CDF for the data set and, after fitting, the fitted PDF and CDF. Furthermore, this panel also serves to control the fitting algorithm. The panel on the top right guides the user through the steps necessary to fit a PH distribution. The panel on the bottom right shows default quality measures for the fitted distribution, as defined in [10].

In order to fit a PH distribution, we first have to load the data set from a file. HyperStar expects an ASCII file with one sample per line, given in a common numerical format. In the next step we can adjust the number of bars in the histogram, in order to get a better understanding of the shape of the density. In this example we set the number of bars to 100, and we observe the peaks at $0, 0.75$, and 1. We can then mark these peaks by clicking on them. In doing so, we create new clusters for the clustering algorithm and define the initial cluster centres to be at the location of the marker. Each cluster corresponds to an Erlang branch in the final distribution, and thus the choice of cluster centres determines the number of

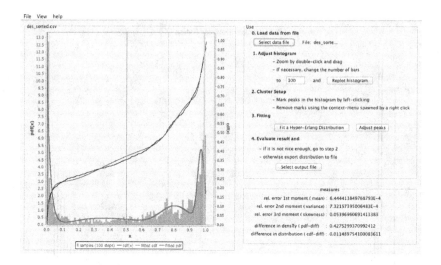

Fig. 2. User interface in Simple Mode, with fitted distribution

branches in the result. We then start the fitting algorithm by clicking on the 'Fit' button. The resulting PDF and CDF are displayed in the left-hand panel, and the bottom right panel shows various quality measures. The distribution can be further refined by adding or removing clusters or by shifting peaks (see Section 5). Once we are satisfied with the results, we save the distribution in a file. In simple mode HyperStar exports the distribution in G-FIT output format, which is a simple text file that is both human-readable and easily parsable for further use [4]. G-FIT files specify the number of branches, the branch lengths, the rates, and the initial branch probabilities, one value per line.

4.1   Algorithm

Simple mode uses the clustering algorithm with probabilistic re-assignment, as described in [5] for fitting Hyper-Erlang distributions. In the first step, the samples in the data set are clustered using the k-means algorithm [11], starting with the cluster centres specified by the user. Clustering aggregates similar samples in the same cluster and thereby identifies the samples that correspond to individual peaks of the density. The algorithm then fits each cluster's samples with an Erlang distribution. The assignment of samples to clusters is refined iteratively until either convergence is reached or a maximum number of 100 rounds has elapsed.

5   Refinement Using Peak Adjustment

Simple mode usually produces a PH distribution whose density is very close to the empirical density. In some cases, however, the peaks of the fitted distribution are not located exactly on the peaks of the empirical distribution. Then, the user

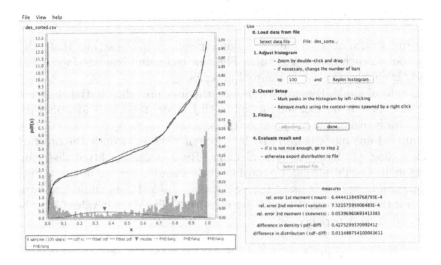

Fig. 3. User interface in Peak-Adjustment Mode

can try to improve the result by manually adjusting the branch distributions to better fit the peaks.

Manual adjustment is performed by switching to 'Peak Adjustment' mode after fitting. In this mode, HyperStar displays individual branch densities and their modes, marked by a triangle atop the mode. By clicking on a triangle and dragging the mouse to a different location, we can move the mode of this branch distribution to a different location, typically to a peak nearby. The density is adjusted accordingly, and a second click places the mode at the new location.

It should be noted that relocating the peaks of the distribution can lead to a worse fit than the automatic fitting, according to the quality measures displayed in the bottom right panel. On the other hand, iterative application of peak adjustment and fitting can improve the results. Furthermore, peak adjustment can be used to explore the impact of changes in the measurements. For instance, with our data set we may be interested not only in a distribution that fits the current peak placement well, but also in the effect of moving the middle peak from 0.75 to other values. In this case, we would relocate this peak in the fitted distribution and use the result in our evaluation.

5.1 Algorithm

After the user has moved the peak, the new mode of the distribution is read from the graphical interface and a new rate λ is computed from the mode, $\frac{1}{\lambda}(k-1)$, as follows:

1. Let x be the new mode of the Erlang distribution with length k and rate λ.
2. Let $\lambda' = \max\left\{\frac{(k-1)}{x}, 1\right\}$
3. Return (k, λ')

6   The Command-Line Interface

For fitting several data sets at once, one typically employs scripts that call the fitting tool on each data set in turn. The new command-line interface (CLI) to HyperStar enables the use of the tool in scripting.

In graphical mode, HyperStar relies on the user providing initial cluster centres. Since there is no user interaction in CLI mode, this mode identifies peaks automatically, using one of two algorithms.

Command-line mode is initiated by specifying the `-cli` option upon startup and providing `-f`, followed by a filename. By default, the fitted distribution is written in G-FIT format to the file `cbhe-result.txt`. A different output filename can be specified using the `-of` option. Table 1 lists additional options to control the behaviour of the fitting algorithm. The default values have been chosen based on experience.

Table 1. Parameters for command-line mode

Parameter	Description (default value)
`-cli`	Use command-line interface
`-f`	Select input file
`-of`	Select output file (`cbhe-result.txt`)
`-bn`	Number of branches to be fitted (10)
`-ip`	Initial Erlang lengths (10)
`-lc`	Convergence threshold (10^{-10})
`-mi`	Maximum number of iterations (10)
`-qu`	Compute quality measures and append them to the output file
`-pd`	Peak-detection algorithm, either `simple` or `hist` (`simple`)
`-b`	Number of bars for `hist` peak detection.

6.1   Algorithm

Since there is no user interaction, the command-line mode requires a different approach for finding initial cluster centres. Cluster centres should ideally be close to peaks in the empirical density. Therefore, CLI mode first detects peaks and then uses their locations as initial cluster centres.

We implemented two algorithms for peak detection. The first one, `simple`, operates directly on the samples:

1. Let $S = \{s_1, \ldots, s_N\}$ be the set of samples, sorted in increasing order.
2. Let m be the number of branches.
3. $d := \frac{N}{m+1}$
4. Return initial cluster centres $s_d, s_{2d}, \ldots, s_{rd}$.

The algorithm simply places equidistant peaks on the sorted data set. If there are peaks in the empirical density, these are characterised by long stretches of similar values and are likely to receive a cluster centre.

Our second approach explicitly detects peaks in the histogram:

1. Let h_i, c_i $(i = 1, \ldots, M)$ be the height and centre of the ith bucket in the histogram with M buckets.
2. Let m be the number of branches.
3. $s_0 := 2h_0 - h_1$
4. $s_{m-1} := 2h_{M-1} - h_{M-2}$
5. for $i = 1, \ldots, M - 2$: assign $s_i := 2h_i - h_{i-1} - h_{i+1}$.
6. Pick the m highest values of all of the s_i, and let $i_1, \ldots, i_m$ be their indices.
7. Return initial cluster centres $c_{i_1}, c_{i_2}, \ldots, c_{i_m}$.

The basic assumption underlying this method is that a peak appears in the histogram as a tall bucket surrounded by buckets of much smaller height. For each bucket the algorithm computes the height difference to the surroundings and then picks the buckets with the largest height differences.

There are clearly two application domains of these methods. If nothing is known about the data, the `simple` method is more suitable. Observe that the method does not yield good results if the number of branches m is small. With a high value of m, the probability of guessing a value, which is near to a peak in density, is high. If the dataset is well-known and one can easily detect peaks in the histogram, it is likely that the same peaks are chosen by the `hist` approach.

7   The Mathematica Interface

So far, we have discussed modes of operation that aim at quickly fitting a phase-type distribution to data. The Mathematica interface to HyperStar differs from these in that its goal is mainly to support algorithm development, prototyping and evaluation. It is often beneficial to first implement new PH-fitting algorithms in Mathematica, before writing a dedicated tool, since Mathematica has higher numerical stability and provides a large library of dedicated mathematical functions, which typically leads to more elegant programs than possible in general-purpose languages. With the HyperStar Mathematica integration, the HyperStar GUI can be used as a front-end to such implementations. The user can then focus on the algorithm itself and evaluate the fitting quality using HyperStar's interface. In this mode, HyperStar does not apply clustering; instead, it only forwards data into Mathematica and displays the results.

Mathematica integration requires the implementation of the following three methods in the Mathematica script:

`fit[Samples_]` : Fits a distribution to the sample set contained in the array `Samples`. This function must return a compact representation of the phase-type distribution (e.g. as fixed list of rules) that can be parsed by the `parameters[]` function.

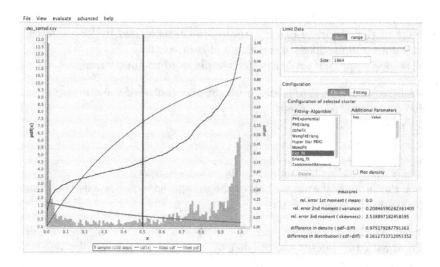

Fig. 4. User interface in Mathematica interface mode

parameters[D_] : This method is invoked with the return value of **fit**, in order
to convert the representation in **D** (which could be an arbitrary representation
used in the fitting algorithm) to a list of key-value pairs. The returned value
is the textual representation of the PH distribution.

ph[D_] : Returns the (α, A) representation of the phase-type distribution in the
arbitrary description **D**. All methods (like moment- or density-computation)
within HyperStar use this representation. This method should return a list of
two rules, where α yields the vector-representation of the initial distribution
and **Q** yields the sub-generator matrix. Note that this method must return
a valid ph-distribution.

HyperStar redirects all output of the **Print** statement in Mathematica to the
standard output, in order to help with debugging the Mathematica code.

The following Mathematica code illustrates how to implement these functions
for a very simple fitting algorithm:

```
fit[Samples_] := lambda->1/Mean[Samples];
parameters[D_] := {{"lambda", lambda}} /. D;
ph[D_] := {alpha->{1.0}, A->{{-lambda}}}/. D;
```

The algorithm simply fits the mean of the data set using an exponential distribution (i.e. a phase-type distribution of size 1). The result is shown in Figure 4.
As expected, the mean is fitted well, while the all other measures and the shapes
of the distribution and the density show large errors. For practical application,
the reader might want to implement a more sophisticated algorithm.

7.1 Technical Configuration

In order to configure HyperStar to use Mathematica mode, the following steps have to be taken:

1. The `KernelCommand` entry in the file `config.prop` must be set to the full path to the `MathKernel` executable. `MathKernel` is typically located in Mathematica's root folder or in one of its sub-folders, depending on the operating system.
2. The `JLink.jar` file must be added to the classpath for HyperStar.
3. The Mathematica script containing the algorithm must be made known to HyperStar, as follows:
   (a) Append the algorithm name (e.g. `exp_fit`) to the property `Algorithms`.
   (b) Introduce three new properties for the functions `fit`, `ph` and `parameters` (e.g. `exp_fit.fit`), which point to the respective functions in the script
   (c) Include the filename by setting the property `[algorithm].source` (e.g. `exp_fit.source`) to the full path of the Mathematica script.

HyperStar can then be started with the `-c` option. When started with this option, HyperStar will also test the configured algorithms with a fixed trace before displaying the graphical user interface.

8 Simulation

The Hyper-Erlang distributions created with HyperStar are especially useful to introduce phenomena of real systems in simulations without modelling the underlying systems in detail. Unfortunately, common simulation tools such as OMNeT++ or NS-2 [12,13] do not support Hyper-Erlang distributions as part of their toolkits for random variates. In this section we describe the Libherd library for generating random variates from Hyper-Erlang distributions.

The Libherd library has been developed as a simpler alternative to the Libphprng library in the Butools package [14,15]. It provides the same mechanisms to interface to simulation tools, but is focussed on Hyper-Erlang distributions. In contrast to Libphprng, Libherd does not support other classes of phase-type distributions and does not provide the advanced techniques for optimising phase-type distributions for efficient random-variate generation that are implemented in Libphprng. These restrictions to the functionality resulted in a very small codebase, which is often easier to integrate with specific simulation tools than Libphprng.

Libherd is implemented in C++ as a shared library that must be linked to the simulation framework, e.g. OMNeT++ or NS-2. The library provides the class `HerdGen`. Each instance of this class generates random variates from one Hyper-Erlang distribution specified by the user. In order to generate random variates, the class requires a source of uniform random numbers in the range $(0, 1)$. Libherd uses the random-number generators that are provided by the simulation tool. This requires the user to write a class implementing the

`RandomSourceWrapper` interface and registering an instance of this class with
the `HerdGen` instance. The `Libherd` distribution includes wrappers for several
simulation frameworks and is available from the main HyperStar page [7].

In the following we illustrate how Libherd can be used to apply Hyper-Erlang
distributions fitted with HyperStar in discrete-event simulation. We assume that
we have fitted a Hyper-Erlang distribution to the DES data set and saved it in
the file `des.gfit`. We want to use this distribution to generate links with typical
packet-delivery ratios in a large network.

This requires the following steps:

1. Creation of a new `HerdGen` instance to store the distribution:
   ```
   PhGen * prng = new HerdGen("des.gfit");
   ```
2. Creation of a wrapper object for the random-number stream from the simulation. Assuming that we have a wrapper class called `RSWrapper`, we create
   an instance of this class as
   ```
   RSWrapper * ursw = new RSWrapper();
   ```
3. Registration of the uniform random number stream with the `HerdGen` object:
   ```
   prng->setUniformRandomSource(ursw);
   ```
4. Drawing of random variates from the distribution:
   ```
   double x;
   while ((x = prng->getVariate()) > 1) {};
   ```
   Note that with our example we need to ensure that the packet-delivery ratios
   stay within the range $[0, 1]$, and therefore we truncate the distribution to this
   range.

9 Conclusion

In this paper we have illustrated the application of HyperStar in common fitting
tasks. We have introduced the manual peak adjustment and the command-line
interface as new features for HyperStar. These features required new algorithms
for the adjustment of the peaks and for the automatic detection of peaks in a
data set. Although HyperStar already gives good results in many cases, further
improvement of the fitting algorithms is certainly possible and will be studied
as part of future work. Furthermore, we are exploring the use of HyperStar, or
a similar approach, in fitting other stochastic processes.

Acknowledgements. We would like to thank Chris Guenther for his valuable
reports on various bugs and usability issues with HyperStar.

References

1. Neuts, M.F.: Matrix-Geometric Solutions in Stochastic Models. An Algorithmic
   Approach. Dover Publications, Inc., New York (1981)
2. Asmussen, S., Nerman, O., Olsson, M.: Fitting Phase-Type Distribution Via the
   EM Algorithm. Scand. J. Statist. 23, 419–441 (1996)

3. Horváth, A., Telek, M.: PhFit: A General Phase-Type Fitting Tool. In: Field, T., Harrison, P.G., Bradley, J., Harder, U. (eds.) TOOLS 2002. LNCS, vol. 2324, pp. 82–91. Springer, Heidelberg (2002)
4. Thümmler, A., Buchholz, P., Telek, M.: A Novel Approach for Phase-Type Fitting with the EM Algorithm. IEEE Trans. Dependable Secur. Comput. 3(3), 245–258 (2006)
5. Reinecke, P., Krauß, T., Wolter, K.: Cluster-based fitting of phase-type distributions to empirical data. Computers & Mathematics with Applications 64(12), 3840–3851 (2012); Special Issue on Theory and Practice of Stochastic Modeling
6. Reinecke, P., Krauß, T., Wolter, K.: HyperStar: Phase-Type Fitting Made Easy. In: 9th International Conference on the Quantitative Evaluation of Systems (QEST) 2012, pp. 201–202 (September 2012); Tool Presentation
7. Reinecke, P., Wolter, K., Krauß, T.: HyperStar Homepage (2013), http://www.mi.fu-berlin.de/inf/groups/ag-tech/projects/HyperStar
8. Telek, M., Heindl, A.: Matching Moments for Acyclic Discrete and Continous Phase-Type Distributions of Second Order. International Journal of Simulation Systems, Science & Technology 3(3-4), 47–57 (2002)
9. Blywis, B., Günes, M., Juraschek, F., Hahm, O., Schmittberger, N.: Properties and Topology of the DES-Testbed (2nd Extended Revision). Technical Report TR-B-11-04, Freie Universität Berlin (July 2011)
10. Lang, A., Arthur, J.: Parameter Approximation for Phase-Type Distributions. Matrix-Analytic Methods in Stocastic Modells 183, 151–206 (1996)
11. Lloyd, S.P.: Least squares quantization in pcm. IEEE Transactions on Information Theory 28(2), 129–136 (1982)
12. Varga, A.: The OMNeT++ Discrete Event Simulation System. In: Proceedings of the European Simulation Multiconference, ESM 2001 (June 2001)
13. Various contributors: The Network Simulator ns-2, http://www.isi.edu/nsnam/ns/ (last seen May 11, 2010)
14. Reinecke, P., Horváth, G.: Phase-type Distributions for Realistic Modelling in Discrete-Event Simulation. In: Proceedings of the 5th International ICST Conference on Simulation Tools and Techniques, SIMUTOOLS 2012, Brussels, Belgium, ICST (Institute for Computer Sciences, Social-Informatics and Telecommunications Engineering), pp. 283–290 (2012)
15. Bodrog, L., Buchholz, P., Heindl, A., Horváth, A., Horváth, G., Kolossváry, I., Németh, Z., Reinecke, P., Telek, M., Vécsei, M.: Butools: Program packages for computations with PH, ME distributions and MAP, RAP processes (October 2011), http://webspn.hit.bme.hu/~butools

Towards the Quantitative Evaluation of Phased Maintenance Procedures Using Non-Markovian Regenerative Analysis

Laura Carnevali[1], Marco Paolieri[1], Kumiko Tadano[2], and Enrico Vicario[1]

[1] Dipartimento di Ingegneria dell'Informazione, Università di Firenze, Italy
{laura.carnevali,marco.paolieri,enrico.vicario}@unifi.it
[2] Service Platforms Research Laboratories, NEC Corporation, Kawasaki, Japan
k-tadano@bq.jp.nec.com

Abstract. The concept of Phased Mission Systems (PMS) can be used to describe maintenance procedures made of sequential actions that use a set of resources and may severely affect them, for instance operations that require outage of hardware and/or software components to recover from a failure or to perform upgrades, tests, and configuration changes. We propose an approach for modeling and evaluation of this class of maintenance procedures, notably addressing the case of actions with non-exponential and firmly bounded duration. This yields stochastic models that underlie a Markov Regenerative Process (MRP) with multiple concurrent timed events having a general (GEN) distribution over a bounded support, which can be effectively analyzed through the method of stochastic state classes. The approach allows evaluation of transient availability measures, which can be exploited to support the selection of a rejuvenation plan of system resources and the choice among different feasible orderings of actions. The experiments were performed through a new release of the Oris tool based on the Sirio framework.

Keywords: Phased mission systems, maintenance-induced failures, transient availability measures, Markov regenerative processes, stochastic state classes.

1 Introduction

Phased Mission Systems (PMS) perform multiple tasks with possibly different requirements during non-overlapping phases of operation, typically achieving the mission success only if each phase is completed without failure [8]. The abstraction of PMS is fit by several critical applications, which notably include: aircrafts flights comprising distinct steps from take-off to landing, command sequences executed by aerospace systems, recovery operations performed to bring back automated systems from the breakdown state to a recovery point, and maintenance procedures requiring the safe shutdown and restart of hardware (HW) and software (SW) subsystems [27,14,30].

Reliability analysis of PMS faces challenges concerned with the evaluation of the success probability and the distribution of the completion time, for the

M.S. Balsamo, W.J. Knottenbelt, and A. Marin (Eds.): EPEW 2013, LNCS 8168, pp. 176–190, 2013.

overall mission or for intermediate phases. This often conflicts with the possible failure and recovery of resources supporting the different steps. Steady state analysis is usually applied to evaluate the system availability in the presence of recurrent phased procedures, while transient analysis is more appropriate in the case of one-shot operations where the focus is rather on the probability that the procedure is completed within a given deadline.

Various modeling approaches have been proposed in the literature, and in particular different causes of failure and policies for error detection, rejuvenation, and repair have been addressed. Methods based on state-space analysis address PMS with complex behaviors deriving from fixed or random phase sequence, deterministic or random phase duration, permanent or transient components failures, and dependencies among components. Notable examples include: the approach of [15], which leverages Markovian analysis to support the reliability evaluation of PMS with deterministic sojourn time in each phase; the method proposed in [18], where the Markov Renewal Theory [13,1,2] is tailored to the evaluation of PMS with random phase sequence and duration, forcing a repetition or a premature completion of unfinished repair works at each phase end to guarantee that phase completion times are regeneration points for the underlying stochastic process; the methodology of [6] for performance evaluation of composed web services, which derives steady state and transient measures through WebSPN [5] by relying on the approximation of GEN timers with discrete phase type distributions over unbounded supports.

If the events order does not affect the mission outcome, the problem of state-space explosion can be circumvented by applying combinatorial solution techniques, which achieve a lower computational complexity at the expense of reducing the modeling expressivity. In this area, several approaches have been developed on the structure of Binary Decision Diagrams (BDD) [31,28], also encompassing phase uncovered failures that cause a mission failure [29]. More recently, approaches that integrate methods based on state-space analysis and combinatorial techniques have been proposed. The joint probability method of [19] combines results obtained by independently solving static and dynamic system components through BDD and Markovian analysis, respectively. In [26], a hierarchical approach is presented which addresses PMS with repairable components, modeling their aging process as a Continuous Time Markov Chain (CTMC). The modular technique developed in [21] also encompasses the case of unordered and ordered component states.

When the overall process duration is much shorter than the mean time between failures of used resources, concentrated failure or error probabilities induced by the usage itself become more relevant in the evaluation of the overall reliability. This is for instance the case of system level maintenance procedures, where HW and SW resources are subject to operations exposed to various types of faults, such as disk failures at shutdown and restart, or erroneous restoration of exposed services in infrastructural SW components.

In this paper, we model such classes of phased missions as a sequence of non-concurrent actions that may affect and downgrade a set of resources, evaluating the impact that the operations may have on the system availability in the transient regime. According to a two-mode failure scheme, resources may reach an error state before incurring a breakdown. While quite onerous repair actions are necessary to restore failed resources, lighter rejuvenation operations can be performed to prevent failures of already flawed resources. Actions are subject to a timeout mechanism that limits their repetitions due to subsequent resource failures and to precedence constraints that restrain their feasible orderings.

As a salient trait of the contribution, we face the representation and analysis of steps with non-exponential and firmly bounded duration, which may take relevance in the synchronization of events. To this end, we leverage the method of stochastic state classes [25,9,17], which supports the analysis of models with multiple concurrent timed events having a non-Markovian distribution over a possibly bounded support. This enables evaluation of transient availability measures that can be used to support the choice among the possible orderings of actions and the selection of a rejuvenation plan. Computational experience is reported on a case of real complexity to show the potentialities of the approach. The experiments have been performed through a new release of the Oris tool based on the Sirio framework [10,12,7].

The rest of the paper is organized as follows. In Section 2, we illustrate the proposed modeling framework of maintenance procedures and we introduce a running case study. In Section 3, we present an extension of stochastic Time Petri Nets (sTPNs) that leaves unchanged their analysis complexity while largely enhancing their modeling convenience, and we discuss the structure of the sTPN model of maintenance procedures with reference to the running case study. In Section 4, we briefly recall the main results of the solution technique of [17] for transient analysis of non-Markovian models and we discuss the conditions that must be satisfied to guarantee its applicability, referring the reader to [17] for more details. In Section 5, we present the experimental results. Conclusions are finally sketched in Section 6.

2   Problem Formulation

We address sequential maintenance procedures performing potentially critical operations that require usage of system resources and may affect their status (Section 2.1). This fits the class of PMS provided that adequate assumptions are made to guarantee that the executed operations do not overlap. A running example illustrates model specification (Section 2.2).

2.1   A General Class of Phased Maintenance Procedures: Stylized Facts

We consider phased mission procedures intended to perform non-overlapping operations that may severely affect a set of system resources. When the procedure duration is much shorter than the mean time between age-related failures, then the probability of maintenance-induced failures turns out to be prevailing for

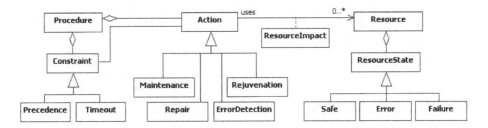

Fig. 1. An UML class diagram representing the maintenance procedure model

the purposes of the evaluation of transient availability measures and can be well accounted by concentrated failures or error probabilities. This in particular fits the case of maintenance procedures requiring outage of HW and/or SW components, for instance to recover from a failure or to perform upgrades, tests, and configuration changes. Figure 1 illustrates involved concepts.

Actions and Resources. A procedure is a sequence of non-concurrent *actions* subject to *precedence* constraints that restrict their possible orderings. An action may need to *use* one or more system *resources* to perform its assigned task and its execution may *impact* on some of them, possibly causing errors or failures.

Resource Failures. At the beginning of a procedure, all resources are in a *safe* state. During the execution of a maintenance action, a resource may reach an *error* state (from a safe state) or a *failure* state (either from an error state or directly from a safe state). The switch probabilities that represent the state transitions of resources may vary from action to action. While a resource is being used by an action, if the resource reaches an error state then the action is nevertheless successfully completed, whereas if the resource reaches a failure state then the action also fails. The execution time of an action may vary depending on whether the resources in use become flawed or failed. A resource can be recovered from a failure through a *repair* operation.

Failure Management. If a resource fails while it is used by an action, then the action is interrupted and a repair operation is started. When the resource has been repaired, the action is restored. Repetitions of the same action due to subsequent failures of its requested resources occur according to the Preemptive Repeat Different (PRD) semantics , i.e., no memory is carried across repetitions. Repetitions are also limited by a *timeout*, which is activated when the action is started for the first time. When the timeout elapses, the action is stopped and the overall procedure is restarted, possibly waiting for ongoing repair operations to be completed. In a variant of this policy, when the timeout of an action expires, the procedure is restarted from that action.

Policy at Action Completion. At the end of each action, a procedure waits for the completion of ongoing repair operations and possibly performs a *rejuvenation* of system resources. Specifically, an *error detection* operation can be executed to identify the flawed resources and a rejuvenation activity of failed resources can be started to bring them back to the safe state. This can be performed according to various schemes, e.g., every n executed actions or at the end of selected actions. In a variant of this policy, the rejuvenation of flawed resources that are not used by the remaining actions is avoided and performed only if the procedure is repeated due to the failure of other resources.

2.2   An Example

A maintenance procedure can be specified by detailing its actions according to the procedure model shown in Figure 1. As a running example, we consider a procedure made of a sequence of 10 maintenance actions a_1, a_2, ..., a_{10} which may affect a system resource r_1. Table 1 shows a fragment of the specification of such procedure, which pertains to the maintenance action a_1 and to the repair, error detection, and rejuvenation actions performed on r_1. Action a_1 may affect r_1 while performing its requested task. When a_1 is in execution, if r_1 is in a safe state then it remains safe, reaches an error state, or fails with probability 0.75, 0.23, and 0.02, respectively, and the execution time of a_1 is uniformly distributed over $[8, 10]$, $[8, 10]$, and $[2, 5]$ min, respectively. Conversely, if r_1 is in an error state, then it remains flawed or fails with probability 0.75 and 0.25, respectively, and the time spent in the execution of a_1 has a uniform distribution over $[8, 10]$ and $[2, 5]$ min, respectively. The repair of r_1 requires a uniformly distributed time over $[30, 45]$ min. Error detection is performed on r_1 at the completion of a_1 and a_6, triggering a subsequent rejuvenation if r_1 is in an error state. The error detection time and the rejuvenation time have a uniform distribution supported over $[0, 1]$ minutes and $[12, 15]$ minutes, respectively.

Table 1. A fragment of the specification of a procedure (times expressed in minutes)

Maintenance actions								
Act.	Time Out	Res.	Safe2Safe Ex. time	Safe2Err Ex. time	Safe2Fail Ex. time	Err2Err Ex. time	Err2Fail Ex. time	Fail2Fail Ex. time
a_1	60	r_1	$p = 0.75$ $[8, 10]$, unif	$p = 0.23$ $[8, 10]$, unif	$p = 0.02$ $[2, 5]$, unif	$p = 0.75$ $[8, 10]$, unif	$p = 0.25$ $[2, 5]$, unif	$p = 1$ $[2, 5]$, unif

Repair actions			
Action	Res.	Execution time	Triggering condition
rep_1	r_1	$[30, 45]$, unif	r_1 failed

Error detection actions			
Act.	Res.	Execution time	Triggering condition
$errd_1$	r_1	$[0, 1]$, unif	a_1 completed $\|$ a_6 completed

Rejuvenation actions			
Act.	Res.	Execution time	Triggering condition
rej_1	r_1	$[12, 15]$, unif	r_1 error detected

3   Modeling

The specification of a maintenance procedure can be translated into a formal model that supports the deployment of a theory of analysis. We formulate the model as an extension of *stochastic Time Petri Nets* (sTPN) [25,9] with enabling and flush functions, which change the enabling condition of transitions and the rule according to which tokens are moved after each firing (Section 3.1). This augments the modeling convenience by facilitating the representation of dependent actions and decision-making activities, without restricting the model expressivity or impacting on the subsequent analysis (Section 3.2). The proposed sTPN extension is basically equivalent to SRNs [23].

3.1   An Extension of Stochastic Time Petri Nets

Syntax. An sTPN is a tuple $\langle P; T; A^-; A^+; A^{\cdot}; m_0; EFT^s; LFT^s; \mathcal{F}; \mathcal{C}; E; L \rangle$.

The first ten elements are the model of *stochastic Time Petri Nets* (sTPN) [25,9]. Specifically, P is a set of places; T is a set of transitions disjoint from P; $A^- \subseteq P \times T$, $A^+ \subseteq T \times P$, and $A^{\cdot} \subseteq P \times T$ are the sets of precondition, postcondition, and inhibitor arcs; $m_0 : P \to \mathbb{N}$ is the initial marking associating each place with an initial non-negative number of tokens; $EFT^s : T \to \mathbb{Q}_0^+$ and $LFT^s : T \to \mathbb{Q}_0^+ \cup \{\infty\}$ associate each transition with a *static Earliest Firing Time* and a (possibly infinite) static *Latest Firing Time*, respectively ($EFT^s(t) \leq LFT^s(t) \; \forall \; t \in T$); $\mathcal{C} : T \to \mathbb{R}^+$ associates each transition with a weight; $\mathcal{F} : T \to F_t^s$ associates each transition with a static Cumulative Distribution Function (CDF) supported over its static firing interval $[EFT^s(t), LFT^s(t)]$.

As usual in Petri Nets, a place p is said to be an *input*, an *output*, or an *inhibitor* place for a transition t if $\langle p, t \rangle \in A^-$, $\langle t, p \rangle \in A^+$, or $\langle p, t \rangle \in A^{\cdot}$, respectively. As typical in Stochastic Petri Nets, a transition t is called *immediate* (IMM) if $[EFT^s(t), LFT^s(t)] = [0, 0]$ and *timed* otherwise. A timed transition t is called *exponential* (EXP) if $F_t^s(x) = 1 - e^{\lambda x}$ over $[0, \infty]$ for some rate $\lambda \in \mathbb{R}_0^+$ and *general* (GEN) otherwise. A GEN transition t is called *deterministic* (DET) if $EFT^s(t) = LFT^s(t) > 0$ and *distributed* otherwise (i.e., $EFT^s(t) \neq LFT^s(t)$). For each distributed transition t, we assume that F_t^s is absolutely continuous over its support $[EFT^s(t), LFT^s(t)]$ and, thus, that there exists a Probability Density Function (PDF) f_t^s such that $F_t^s(x) = \int_0^x f_t^s(y) dy$.

E and L extend the model of sTPN with enabling and flush functions, respectively. $E : T \to \{true, false\}^{\mathbb{N}^P}$ associates each transition $t \in T$ with an *enabling function* $E(t) : \mathbb{N}^P \to \{true, false\}$ that, in turn, associates each marking $m : P \to \mathbb{N}$ with a boolean value; $L : T \to \mathcal{P}(P)^{\mathbb{N}^P}$ associates each transition $t \in T$ with a *flush function* $L(t) : \mathbb{N}^P \to \mathcal{P}(P)$ that, in turn, associates each marking $m : P \to \mathbb{N}$ with a subset of P, i.e., an element of the power set of P.

Semantics. The *state* of an sTPN is a pair $\langle m, \tau \rangle$, where $m : P \to \mathbb{N}$ is a marking that associates each place with a non-negative number of tokens and $\tau : T \to \mathbb{R}_0^+$ associates each transition with a (dynamic) real-valued time-to-fire.

A transition t is *enabled* by marking m if: *i)* each of its input places contains at least one token (i.e., $m(p) \geq 1 \; \forall \; \langle p, t \rangle \in A^-$), *ii)* none of its inhibitor places contains any token (i.e., $m(p) = 0 \; \forall \; \langle p, t \rangle \in A^{\cdot}$), and *iii)* its enabling function evaluates to true in marking m (i.e., $E(t)(m) = true$). An enabled transition t is *firable* in state $s = \langle m, \tau \rangle$ if its time-to-fire is not higher than that of any other transition enabled by marking m (i.e., $\tau(t) \leq \tau(t') \; \forall \; t' \in T^e(m)$, where $T^e(m)$ is the set of transitions that are enabled by m). When multiple transitions are firable, one of them is selected as the firing transition according to the random switch determined by $\mathcal{C}$. Specifically, $Prob\{t$ is selected$\} = \mathcal{C}(t) / \sum_{t_i \in T^f(s)} \mathcal{C}(t_i)$, where $T^f(s)$ is the set of transitions that are firable in s.

The state of an sTPN evolves depending on the times-to-fire sampled by transitions and the resolution of random switches according to the weights of transitions. Specifically, when a transition t fires, the state $s = \langle m, \tau \rangle$ is replaced by a new state $s' = \langle m', \tau' \rangle$. Marking m' is derived from marking m by: *i)* removing a token from each input place of t and assigning zero tokens to the places belonging to the subset $L(t)(m)$ of P (identified by the value of the flush function of t in m), which yields an intermediate marking m_{tmp}, *ii)* adding a token to each output place of t, which finally yields m'. Transitions that are enabled both by m_{tmp} and by m' are said *persistent*, while those that are enabled by m' but not by m_{tmp} or m are said *newly-enabled*. If the fired transition t is still enabled after its own firing, it is always regarded as newly enabled [4,24]. For any transition t_p that is persistent after the firing of t, the time-to-fire is reduced by the time elapsed in the previous state s (which is equal to the time-to-fire of t measured at the entrance in s), i.e., $\tau'(t_p) = \tau(t_p) - \tau(t)$. For any transition t_n that is newly-enabled after the firing of t, the time-to-fire takes a random value sampled in the static firing interval according to the static CDF $F^s_{t_n}$, i.e., $EFT^s(t_n) \leq \tau'(t_n) \leq LFT^s(t_n)$, with $Prob\{\tau'(t_n) \leq x\} = F^s_{t_n}(x)$.

3.2   Deriving an sTPN Model of Maintenance Procedures

The specification of a maintenance procedure can be translated into a corresponding sTPN model, which is made of a submodel for each action and a submodel for each resource that the actions may affect. The sTPN shown in Figure 2 is a model fragment of the procedure introduced in Section 2.2, specifically corresponding to action a_1 and resource r_1 specified in Table 1.

The IMM transition *start* models the outset of the overall procedure and its output place is chained with the IMM transition $a1start$ representing the beginning of action a_1. When $a1start$ fires, a token arrives in $a1timeout\_start$, enabling the DET transition $a1timeout$ which models the timeout of 60 minutes associated with a_1. The firing of $a1start$ also deposits a token in $a1switch$, which is an input place for the 6 IMM transitions that model the concentrated probabilities of error/failure affecting r_1 as a consequence of the usage by a_1. Specifically, if r_1 is safe, then it may remain safe or become either flawed or failed with probability 0.75, 0.23, and 0.02, respectively. This is modeled by the random switch among the IMM transitions $a1r1safe2safe$, $a1r1safe2err$, and

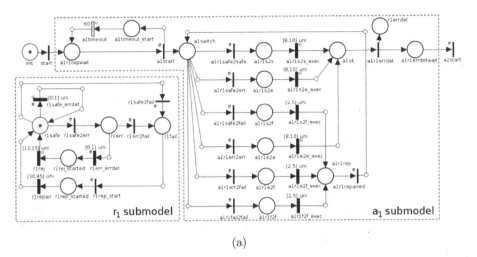

(a)

Transition	Enabling function	Flush function	Weight
a1start	r1rep_started==0	-	1
a1r1safe2safe	r1safe>0	-	75
a1r1safe2err	r1safe>0	-	23
a1r1safe2fail	r1safe>0	-	2
a1r1err2err	r1err>0	-	75
a1r1err2fail	r1err>0	-	25
a1r1fail2fail	r1fail>0	-	1
a1r1s2s_exec	-	{a1_timeout}	1
a1r1s2e_exec	-	{a1_timeout}	1
a1r1e2e_exec	-	{a1_timeout}	1
a1r1_repaired	r1safe>0	-	1
a1timeout	-	{a1_switch, safe2safe, safe2err, safe2fail, err2err, err2fail, a1_r1repaired}	1
a2start	r1errdet==0	-	1
r1safe2err	safe2err>0	-	1
r1err2fail	err2fail>0	-	1
r1safe2fail	safe2fail>0	-	1
r1repstart	a1r1rep>0	-	1
r1safe_errdet	r1_errdet==1	{r1_errdet}	1
r1err_errdet	r1_errdet==1	-	1
r1rej	-	{r1_errdet}	1

(b)

Fig. 2. An sTPN fragment of the example procedure of Section 2.2, representing the action a_1 and the resource r_1 specified in Table 1 (a). A table that details the enabling functions, the flush functions, and the weights of the transitions that appear in the model fragment (b). The entire model of the procedure integrates the r_1 submodel and 10 action submodels like the a_1 submodel.

$a1r1safe2fail$, which are actually enabled if $r1safe$ contains a token and have a weight equal to 75, 23, and 2, respectively. In a similar manner, if r_1 is flawed, then it may remain flawed or become failed, which is represented by the random switch between $a1r1err2err$ and $a1r1err2fail$. Conversely, if r_1 is failed, then the only enabled transition of the 6 mentioned IMM transitions is $a1r1fail2fail$, which models the fact that r_1 remains failed until a repair operation is started.

When the outcome of the random switch in the a_1 submodel corresponds to an r_1 state transition, then the corresponding IMM transition in the r_1 submodel becomes firable. Specifically, if $a1r1safe2err$, $a1r1safe2fail$, or $a1r1err2fail$ fires, then a token arrives in $a1r1s2e$, $a1r1s2f$, or $a1r1e2f$, respectively, thus making $r1safe2err$, $r1safe2fail$, or $r1err2fail$ fireable, respectively.

The firing of $a1r1safe2safe$, $a1r1safe2err$, and $a1r1err2err$ enables $a1r1s2s\_exec$, $a1r1s2e\_exec$, and $a1r1e2e\_exec$, respectively, which model the execution time of a_1 in the cases of successful completion. When one of the latter transitions fires, a token is removed from $a1timeout\_start$ (i.e., the timeout is stopped) and a token is added to $a1ok$. This enables $a1r1errdet$ which triggers an error detection operation on r_1. Specifically, when a token arrives in $r1errdet$, either $r1safe\_errdet$ or $r1err\_errdet$ (in the r_1 submodel) becomes enabled depending on whether r_1 is safe or flawed, respectively: *i)* If r_1 is safe, the firing of $r1safe\_errdet$ simultaneously removes and adds a token to $r1safe$ (in the r_1 submodel) and removes a token from $r1errdet$ (in the a_1 submodel), thus enabling $a1start$ which models the beginning of the subsequent action. *ii)* If r_1 is flawed, the firing of $r1err\_errdet$ removes a token from $r1err$ and deposits a token in $r1rej\_started$ (in the r_1 submodel), enabling $r1rej$ which models a rejuvenation. The firing of $r1rej$ adds a token to $r1safe$ (in the r_1 submodel) and removes a token from $r1errdet$ (in the a_1 submodel), thus enabling $a2start$.

The firing of $a1r1safe2fail$, $a1r1err2fail$, and $a1r1fail2fail$ enables $a1r1s2f\_exec$, $a1r1e2f\_exec$, and $a1r1f2f\_exec$, respectively, which model the execution time of a_1 in the cases of unsuccessful completion. The firing of one of the latter transitions adds a token to $a1r1rep$ enabling $r1rep\_start$ (in the r_1 submodel), whose firing in turn enables $r1repair$ which models a repair operation performed on r_1. When $r1repair$ fires, a token is moved in $r1safe$, enabling $a1r1repaired$ (in the a_1 submodel) whose firing brings a token back to $a1switch$ so that a_1 is repeated.

If $a1timeout$ fires before a token arrives in $a1ok$, then all the tokens in the a_1 submodel are removed, a token is deposited in $a1repwait$, and $a1start$ becomes fireable as soon as $r1repstarted$ contains no tokens (i.e., if the timeout elapses before the successful completion of a_1, then a_1 is restarted, possibly waiting for an on-going repair of r_1 to be completed).

4   Quantitative Analysis

We discuss the conditions that guarantee the applicability of the solution technique of [17] to the analysis of procedure models that underlie a Generalized Semi-Markov Process (GSMP) [20,1] (Section 4.1) or a Markov Regenerative Process (MRP) [13,1,2] (Section 4.2). The approach is efficiently implemented in the new release of the Oris tool based on the Sirio framework [10,12,7] under the assumption that all timed transitions have expolynomial PDF. For space limitations, the reader is referred to [17] for the details on the analysis technique.

4.1   Transient Analysis

The sTPN model derived in Section 3.2 includes multiple concurrent GEN transitions with bounded support, e.g., a repair action enabled together with the timeout associated with a maintenance action. According to this, the model underlies a GSMP [20,1] with equal-speed timers, for which a viable approach to transient analysis within any given time bound is the solution technique of [17]. The approach samples the state of the underlying GSMP after each transition firing, maintaining a timer τ_{age} that accounts for the absolute time elapsed since the entrance in the initial state. This identifies an embedded Discrete Time Markov Chain (DTMC) called *transient stochastic graph*. A state in the embedded DTMC is named *transient stochastic state class* (transient class for short) and provides the marking of the sTPN plus the joint support and PDF of τ_{age} and the times-to-fire of the enabled transitions. The marginal PDF of τ_{age} permits to derive the PDF of the absolute time at which the transient class can be entered. This enables evaluation of continuous-time transient probabilities of reachable markings within a given time horizon, provided that either the number of transient classes that can be reached within that time interval is bounded (*exact analysis*) or it can be truncated under the assumption of some approximation threshold on the total unallocated probability (*approximated analysis*).

The number of transient classes enumerated within a given time bound is guaranteed to be finite by Lemma 3.4 of [17] provided that the state class graph of the underlying TPN model is finite and does not include a cycle that can be executed in zero time. The state class graph of the underlying TPN model can be regarded as a non-deterministic projection of the transient stochastic class graph and its finiteness is assured under fairly general conditions by Lemma 3.2 of [17], which is not addressed here for the shortness of discussion.

If the state class graph of the underlying TPN model includes cycles that can be executed in zero time, then the number of transient classes enumerated within a given time bound is not finite. In this case, termination can be guaranteed in probability by Lemma 3.5 of [17] if cycles that must be executed in zero time are not allowed. This permits to stop the enumeration when the total probability of reaching one of the discarded successor transient classes within a given time bound is lower than a predefined threshold. In particular, approximated analysis can be leveraged also when the number of transient classes enumerated within a given time bound is theoretically finite but practically too large to afford the enumeration within a reasonable computation time.

The complexity of the analysis actually grows with the number of enumerated transient classes and, thus, with the time horizon. In the experiments performed in this paper, approximated analysis turned out to be feasible with a computation time lower than 5 minutes up to procedures made of 4-5 maintenance actions.

4.2   Transient Analysis of Markov Regenerative Processes

The issue of complexity can be overcome for models that underlie an MRP that within a finite number of steps always reaches a regeneration point, which is a state where the future behavior of the stochastic process is independent from the past behavior through which the state has been reached. In the approach of [17], regeneration points can be identified as the transient classes where all times-to-fire are either *i)* newly-enabled, or *ii)* exponentially distributed, or *iii)* deterministic, or *iv)* bounded to take a deterministic delay with respect to a time-to-fire satisfying any of the previous conditions. According to this, the sTPN model derived in Section 3.2 is guaranteed to reach a regeneration point at the completion of each action, since the subsequent action is not started until any ongoing repair is completed. When the underlying stochastic process satisfies this condition, the solution technique of [17] can be limited to the first regeneration epoch and repeated from every regenerative point. This supports the derivation of the local and global kernels that characterize the behavior of the MRP [13,1,2] and enables the evaluation of the transient probabilities of reachable markings at any time through the numerical integration of generalized Markov renewal equations (*regenerative exact analysis*). Termination is guaranteed if the number of transient classes reached within the first regeneration epoch is bounded. This is assured by Lemma 4.1 of [17] if the state class graph of the underlying TPN model is finite and every cycle that it contains visits at least one state class that is a (non-deterministic) projection of a regenerative transient class. If the number of transient classes reached within the first regeneration epoch is not finite or practically too large, termination can be guaranteed in probability by Lemma 3.5 of [17] under the assumption of a time bound and an approximation threshold on the total unallocated probability (*approximated regenerative analysis*).

In the experiments performed in this paper, regenerative analysis permitted to afford cases of real complexity concerning procedure made of 10 or more maintenance actions, and it seems to be a solid ground for future developments.

5   Computational Experience

We consider the procedure introduced in Section 2.2, which is made of 10 maintenance actions a_1, a_2, ..., a_{10} that use and may affect a resource r_1. For the simplicity of interpretation of experimental results, we adopt for each maintenance action the specification given in Table 1. According to this, the sTPN model of such procedure is a composition of the r_1 submodel shown in Figure 2 with 10 action submodels equal to the a_1 submodel shown in Figure 2. The switch probabilities and the supports of the temporal parameters appearing in Table 1 were selected according to general experience at NEC Corporation [22], with the aim of experimenting the approach on plausible data. The way how experimental data are acquired and interpreted to derive not only the expected min-max duration of temporal parameters but also their distribution is still matter of study. In such cases, the principle of insufficient reason, or maximum entropy can be advocated to motivate the assumption of a uniform distribution [3].

To illustrate the potentialities of the approach, the experimentation is finalized to evaluate, for each maintenance action a_i, the transient probability that a_i is completed and the subsequent action a_{i+i} (if any) is still ongoing. Specifically, this measure of interest is derived as the sum of the transient probabilities of any marking such that: *i)* the submodel of any action that precedes a_i or follows a_{i+1} (if any) contains no tokens, and *ii)* *aiok* in the a_i submodel contains a token, or *aiok* and *air1errdet* in the a_{i+1} submodel contain no tokens. This permits to derive the time at which a given action or the overall procedure has been successfully completed with an assigned probability or, vice-versa, the probability that a given action or the overall procedure has been successfully completed within a given time bound. The considered performance measures also permit to evaluate different strategies for error detection and rejuvenation, also with respect to different feasible orderings of the maintenance actions.

The experiments were performed through the new release of the Oris tool based on the Sirio framework [10,12,7]. Regenerative analysis with approximation threshold equal to 0.01 and time bound equal to 300 minutes was repeated for four different policies of error detection and rejuvenation. In all the cases, the analysis took 1 s to enumerate transient classes and less than 4 minutes to solve Markov renewal equations.

Error Detection and Rejuvenation Never Performed. Figure 3a shows that the probability of successful completion of the overall procedure within 125, 150, and 175 minutes is nearly 0.29, 0.35, and 0.74, respectively, while the time by which the procedure has been successfully completed with probability higher than 0.99 is 293 minutes.

Error Detection and Rejuvenation Performed Every 5 Actions. Figure 3b shows that rejuvenation improves the probability of successful completion of the overall procedure within 150 and 175 minutes to nearly 0.48 and 0.78, respectively, while decreasing the probability of successful completion within 125 minutes to 0.136134. The time by which the procedure has been successfully completed with probability higher than 0.99 is 269 minutes.

Error Detection and Rejuvenation Performed Every 3 Actions. Figure 3c shows that the probability of successful completion of the overall procedure within 150 minutes is increased to nearly 0.54, while the probability of successful completion within 125 minutes is further decreased to 0.11 and the probability of successful completion within 175 minutes is slightly reduced to nearly 0.77. The time by which the procedure has been successfully completed with probability higher than 0.99 is 267 minutes.

Error Detection and Rejuvenation Performed after Each Action. Figure 3d shows that the probability of successful completion of the overall procedure within 125 minutes is nearly halved and it is equal to 0.06; the probability of successful completion within 150 minutes is decreased to nearly 0.47, while the probability of successful completion within 175 minutes is increased to 0.79. The time by which the procedure has been successfully completed with probability higher than 0.99 is 258 minutes.

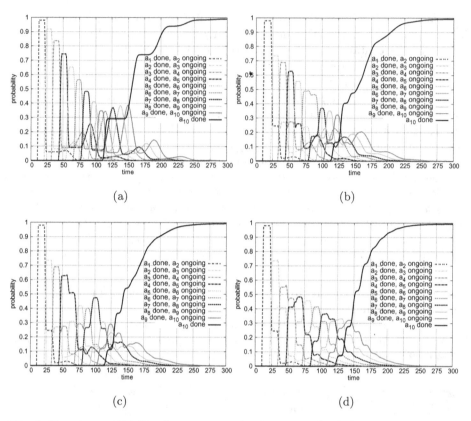

Fig. 3. Transient probability that a_i is completed and a_{i+i} (if any) is ongoing for each action a_i of the procedure specified in Section 2.2, under the assumption that error detection and rejuvenation are: never performed **a)**, performed every 5 actions **b)**, performed every 3 actions **c)**, and performed after each action (except a_{10}) **d)**

6   Conclusions

We experimented with the approach of stochastic state classes [17] in quantitative evaluation of maintenance procedures that may induce errors or failures of system resources. To this end, we considered a general modeling framework, including precedence and timeout constraints on maintenance actions, repair operations of system resources, and strategies for error detection and rejuvenation of resources. As a relevant aspect, the execution times of such actions may have a non-Markovian distribution over a bounded support. This yields models that underlie an MRP with multiple concurrently enabled GEN timers, which can be effectively solved through the regenerative approach to transient analysis developed in [17]. The method permits to derive transient availability measures, which can be used to support the selection of a rejuvenation plan and the choice among feasible orderings of actions. Computational experience addresses a relatively challenging case study that is able to fit the complexities of reality beyond the enabling restriction. In so doing, a major contribution of this paper consists in a proof of the applicability of the solution technique of [17], which seems to be extremely promising for the analysis of models of higher complexity and size. While applied to the solution of a specific problem pertaining to the evaluation of critical maintenance procedures, the proposed approach is formulated as a method for modeling and analysis of a more general class of critical applications referred to the abstraction of PMS.

The proposed approach is amenable to integration within a model driven development process where the results of quantitative analysis can be used to support iterative feedback cycles [11,16]. Specifically, the temporal parameters with unknown distribution are initially associated with a uniform distribution or with a distribution guessed by analogy with previous implementations. Then, they are progressively refined on the basis of quantitative measures and the results of a profiling technique for the estimation of execution times.

Acknowledgments. We kindly thank Stefano Ballerini for his support in the experimentation stage.

References

1. Ciardo, G., German, R., Lindemann, C.: A characterization of the stochastic process underlying a stochastic Petri net. IEEE Trans. SW Eng. 20(7), 506–515 (1994)
2. Bobbio, A., Telek, M.: Markov regenerative SPN with non-overlapping activity cycles. In: Int. Comp. Perf. and Dependability Symp. - IPDS 1995, pp. 124–133 (1995)
3. Bernardi, S., Campos, J., Merseguer, J.: Timing-failure risk assessment of UML design using time Petri net bound techniques. IEEE Transactions on Industrial Informatics 7(1), 90–104 (2011)
4. Berthomieu, B., Diaz, M.: Modeling and verification of time dependent systems using time Petri nets. IEEE Trans. on SW Eng. 17(3), 259–273 (1991)
5. Bobbio, A., Puliafito, A., Scarpa, M., Telek, M.: WebSPN: a web-accessible Petri net tool. In: Proc. Conf on Web-based Modeling and Simulation (1998)
6. Bruneo, D., Distefano, S., Longo, F., Scarpa, M.: Stochastic evaluation of QoS in service-based systems. IEEE Trans. on Parallel and Distributed Systems (2012)
7. Bucci, G., Carnevali, L., Ridi, L., Vicario, E.: Oris: a tool for modeling, verification and evaluation of real-time systems. Int. Journal of SW Tools for Technology Transfer 12(5), 391–403 (2010)
8. Burdick, L., Fussell, J.B., Rasmuson, D., Wilson, J.: Phased mission analysis: a review of new developments and an application. IEEE Trans. on Rel. 26(1), 43–49 (1977)
9. Carnevali, L., Grassi, L., Vicario, E.: State-density functions over DBM domains in the analysis of non-Markovian models. IEEE Trans. on SW Eng. 35(2), 178–194 (2009)
10. Carnevali, L., Ridi, L., Vicario, E.: A framework for simulation and symbolic state space analysis of non-Markovian models. In: Flammini, F., Bologna, S., Vittorini, V. (eds.) SAFECOMP 2011. LNCS, vol. 6894, pp. 409–422. Springer, Heidelberg (2011)
11. Carnevali, L., Ridi, L., Vicario, E.: Putting preemptive time Petri nets to work in a V-model SW life cycle. IEEE Trans. on SW Eng. 37(6) (November/December 2011)

12. Carnevali, L., Ridi, L., Vicario, E.: Sirio: A framework for simulation and symbolic state space analysis of non-Markovian models. In: 8th Int. Conf. on Quantitative Evaluation of Systems (QEST 2011), pp. 153–154 (2011)

13. Choi, H., Kulkarni, V.G., Trivedi, K.S.: Markov regenerative stochastic Petri nets. Perform. Eval. 20(1-3), 337–357 (1994)

14. Combacau, M., Berruet, P., Zamai, E., Charbonnaud, P., Khatab, A.: Supervision and monitoring of production systems. In: Proc. IFAC Conf. on Management and Control of Production and Logistics (2000)

15. Dugan, J.B.: Automated analysis of phased-mission reliability. IEEE Trans. on Reliability 40(1), 45–52 (1991)

16. Dugan, J.B.: Galileo: A tool for dynamic fault tree analysis. In: Haverkort, B.R., Bohnenkamp, H.C., Smith, C.U. (eds.) TOOLS 2000. LNCS, vol. 1786, pp. 328–331. Springer, Heidelberg (2000)

17. Horváth, A., Paolieri, M., Ridi, L., Vicario, E.: Transient analysis of non-Markovian models using stochastic state classes. Perf. Eval. 69(7-8), 315–335 (2012)

18. Mura, I., Bondavalli, A.: Markov regenerative stochastic Petri nets to model and evaluate phased mission systems dependability. IEEE Trans. Comput. 50(12), 1337–1351 (2001)

19. Ou, Y., Dugan, J.B.: Modular solution of dynamic multi-phase systems. IEEE Transactions on Reliability 53(4), 499–508 (2004)

20. Glynn, P.W.: A GSMP formalism for discrete-event systems. Proceedings of the IEEE 77, 14–23 (1989)

21. Shrestha, A., Xing, L., Dai, Y.: Reliability analysis of multistate phased-mission systems with unordered and ordered states. IEEE Transactions on Systems, Man and Cybernetics, Part A: Systems and Humans 41(4), 625–636 (2011)

22. Tadano, K., Xiang, J., Kawato, M., Maeno, Y.: Automatic synthesis of SRN models from system operation templates for availability analysis. In: Flammini, F., Bologna, S., Vittorini, V. (eds.) SAFECOMP 2011. LNCS, vol. 6894, pp. 296–309. Springer, Heidelberg (2011)

23. Trivedi, K.S.: Probability and statistics with reliability, queuing, and computer science applications. John Wiley and Sons, New York (2001)

24. Vicario, E.: Static analysis and dynamic steering of time dependent systems using time Petri nets. IEEE Trans. on SW Eng. 27(1), 728–748 (2001)

25. Vicario, E., Sassoli, L., Carnevali, L.: Using stochastic state classes in quantitative evaluation of dense-time reactive systems. IEEE Trans. on SW Eng. 35(5), 703–719 (2009)

26. Wang, D., Trivedi, K.S.: Reliability analysis of phased-mission system with independent component repairs. IEEE Trans. on Reliability 56(3), 540–551 (2007)

27. Weiss, K.A., Leveson, N., Lundqvist, K., Farid, N., Stringfellow, M.: An analysis of causation in aerospace accidents. In: Digital Avionics Systems Conference (DASC), vol. 1, pp. 4A3–4A1. IEEE (2001)

28. Xing, L., Dugan, J.B.: Analysis of generalized phased-mission system reliability, performance, and sensitivity. IEEE Trans. on Reliability 51(2), 199–211 (2002)

29. Xing, L., Dugan, J.B.: A separable ternary decision diagram based analysis of generalized phased-mission reliability. IEEE Trans. on Rel. 53(2), 174–184 (2004)

30. Yam, R., Tse, P., Li, L., Tu, P.: Intelligent predictive decision support system for condition-based maintenance. Int. Journal of Advanced Manufacturing Technology 17(5), 383–391 (2001)

31. Zang, X., Sun, N., Trivedi, K.S.: A BDD-based algorithm for reliability analysis of phased-mission systems. IEEE Transactions on Reliability 48(1), 50–60 (1999)

Performance Enhancement by Means of Task Replication

Peter G. Harrison and Zhan Qiu

Department of Computing, Imperial College London
Huxley Building, 180 Queen's Gate, London SW7 2AZ, UK
{pgh,zq11}@doc.ic.ac.uk

Abstract. In order for systems in which tasks may fail to be fault-tolerant, traditional methods deploy multiple servers as replicas to perform the same task. Further, in real time systems, computations have to meet strict time-constraints, a delayed output being unacceptable, even if correct. The effectiveness of sending task-replicas to multiple servers simultaneously, and using the results from whichever one responds first, is considered in this paper as a means of reducing response time and improving fault-tolerance. Once a request completes execution in one server successfully, it immediately cancels (kills) its replicas that remain at other servers. We assume a Markovian system and use the generating function method to determine the Laplace transform of the response time probability distribution, jointly with the probability that not all replicas fail, in the case of two replicas. When the failure rate of each task is greater than the service rate of the server, we make the approximation that the queues are independent, each with geometric queue length probability distributions at equilibrium. We compare our approximation with simulation results as well as with the exact solution in a truncated state space and find that for failure rates in that region, the approximation is generally good. At lower failure rates, the method of spectral expansion provides an excellent approximation in a truncated, multi-mode, two-dimensional Markov process.

Keywords: Fault-tolerance, reliability, response time.

1 Introduction

Fault-tolerance has for long been a requirement of real-time (and other) systems and is now particularly important in web services since the failure of a task may have a serious impact on system performance and reliability. Web services usually perform well when failure-rate is low and response time is fast and consistent. However, in reality, the reliability of web services is uncertain and the performance of the Internet is also unpredictable. Many performance metrics relating to quality of service (QoS) are not attained consistently – often violating SLA limits – such as long latency, high failure-rate and excessive energy consumption [11]. Task completion is the fundamental usability metric of a website:

M.S. Balsamo, W.J. Knottenbelt, and A. Marin (Eds.): EPEW 2013, LNCS 8168, pp. 191–205, 2013.

if users can't accomplish what they are trying to do, it's unlikely they will return or refer their friends favourably [10].

If redundancy in time (i.e. retrying) is not acceptable for meeting dependability requirements, or if the delay is unacceptable, replicas may be used in systems that deploy multiple servers to perform the same task [2]; for example, active replication and backup/restart schemes [3]. For the active replication scheme, several processors are scheduled simultaneously, and a task will succeed if at least one of its replicas does not encounter a failure [7]. In real time systems, outputs have to meet strict time-constraints, a delayed output being unacceptable even if correct. For instance, a delayed braking signal in the cruise control system of a car may cause an accident and a delayed output in an industrial application may lead to economic losses, environmental damage or even personal injury [8]. Active replication facilitates a faster response to user actions.

It is mentioned in [4] that "A simple way to curb latency variability is to issue the same request to multiple replicas and use the results from whichever replica responds first". This approach is equally applicable to response time reduction and enhancement of system-dependability. This is precisely the replication scheme described above. In order to reduce unnecessary workload, servers communicate updates on the status of their copies to each other. When a request completes execution, it immediately cancels (kills) its replicas that remain at other servers. Systems using this approach are more likely to meet their SLA requirements by ensuring high availability and low latency in time-critical applications, by using the results from whichever replica responds first.

We consider the situation where a task may encounter a failure during service, such as in a parallel database search or in a system with mirroring, for example. In this case, on a failure, only the task itself is lost, the server continues processing the next task in its queue. The failure of a task during service can arise for various reasons, such as an item being searched for not being found, software error or a faulty disk sector.

2   Conditional Task-Response Time Distribution

We consider a pair of FCFS queues, each having independent and identical exponential service times with parameter μ, and a single Poisson arrival process of rate λ that sends a task to both queues at an arrival instant. In addition, the task in service is subject to failure, where its time to failure, once in service, is also an exponential random variable with parameter α. When a task completes service, it "kills" (removes) it's partner-task (that was inserted in the other queue at their arrival instant) if it is still there, including when it is currently being served, defining a "join-operation" to match the "fork" at the arrival instant. However, it may be that the partner-task had already failed, in which case no action is taken on the service completion.

In conventional queueing terminology, we seek the joint probability that the two customers in a tagged pair are not both killed, i.e. one completes service in one of the queues, and that its response time W does not exceed a positive real value t, conditioned on the numbers of customers ahead of each of the tagged pair, A_1 and A_2, in each queue initially – e.g. at the tagged pair's arrival instant. If the tagged customers are both killed, $W > t$ for all $t > 0$, so that $W = \infty$ with probability one. For integers $m, n \geq 0$, we define $F_{mn}(t) = \mathbb{P}(W \leq t \mid A_1 = m, A_2 = n)$ and obtain a recurrence formula for $F_{mn}(t)$, which we solve via a generating function of its Laplace transform. We then decondition against the joint stationary distribution of A_1 and A_2 at the arrival instant of the tagged pair. In section 3 we assume that A_1 and A_2 are distributed as the equilibrium queue length random variables by appeal to the random observer property of the Poisson process. Let $f_{mn}(t)$ be the derivative of $F_{mn}(t)$ with respect to t and $L_{mn}(s) = (\mathcal{L}F)(s)$ be the Laplace transform of $F_{mn}(t)$ – not the Laplace-Stieltjes transform (LST) of $F_{mn}(t)$, which is the Laplace transform of $f_{mn}(t)$.

Noting that, $F_{mn}(t) = F_{nm}(t)$ and $L_{mn}(s) = L_{nm}(s)$ for all $m, n \geq 0$ by the symmetry of the two queues, let $G_k(x) = \sum_{n=1}^{\infty} L_{n+k,n} x^n = \sum_{n=1}^{\infty} L_{n,n+k} x^n$ for $k \geq 0$ and $G_{-k}(x) = \sum_{n=1}^{\infty} L_{n,n+k}(s) x^n = G_k(x)$ for notational convenience. We now define:

$$G(x,y) = \sum_{n=1}^{\infty} \sum_{k=1}^{\infty} L_{n+k,n} x^n y^k = \sum_{n=1}^{\infty} \sum_{k=1}^{\infty} L_{n,n+k} x^n y^k = \sum_{k=1}^{\infty} G_k(x) y^k$$

$G(x,y)$ encodes all the information we need to obtain the Laplace transforms of the required conditional response time distribution; and hence also unconditional distributions once the initial queue length probabilities are known. Of course, if these were to be geometric, the required result would follow by evaluating $G(x,y)$ at the values of the geometric parameters, as we shall see. We determine $G(x,y)$ through a series of lemmas and propositions below.

When one of the tagged pair of customers has been killed, the problem reduces to a single queue and we define $F_{m,-1}(t) = F_{-1,m}(t) = \mathbb{P}(W' \leq t \mid A_1 = m)$ for $m \geq 0$, where W' is the response time random variable of queue 1 considered in isolation when there are m customers ahead of a single tagged customer on its arrival. Similarly to the previous notation, $f_{m,-1}(t) = F'_{m,-1}(t)$ and $L_{m,-1} = \mathcal{L}F_{m,-1}$. We define the corresponding one-parameter generating functions:

$$H_0(y) = \sum_{m=1}^{\infty} L_{m0} y^m, \quad H_{-1}(y) = \sum_{m=1}^{\infty} L_{m,-1} y^m \tag{1}$$

Assuming that the tagged pair arrives at time 0, let $A_1(t), A_2(t)$ be the numbers of customers ahead of the tagged customers in queue 1 and queue 2 respectively at time t. Then we have:

$$F_{mn}(t+h) = \mathbb{P}(W \leq t + h \mid A_1(0) = m, A_2(0) = n)$$

$$= \sum_{i,j=0}^{\infty} \mathbb{P}(W \leq t + h \mid A_1(0) = m, A_2(0) = n, A_1(h) = i, A_2(h) = j)$$

$$\times \mathbb{P}(A_1(h) = i, A_2(h) = j \mid A_1(0) = m, A_2(0) = n)$$

by the law of total probability. The terms $IP(A_1(h) = i, A_2(h) = j \mid A_1(0) = m, A_2(0) = n)$ correspond to the possible events that can occur during the interval $(0, h]$ for $h > 0$, which we take to be infinitesimal.

Proposition 1. *For* $|x| < 1, |y| < 1$,

$$G(x, y) = \frac{(\alpha x y^{-1} + \mu x)H_0(y) + (\alpha + \mu)yG_0(x) - \alpha x G_1(x) - \alpha x L_{1,0}}{2\mu + 2\alpha + s - \mu x - (\alpha + \mu)y - \alpha x y^{-1}} \quad (2)$$

Proof. When $m > n > 0$, e.g. $m = n + k$ with $k \geq 1, n \geq 1$, the possible events in the interval $(0, h]$ have the following probabilities, by the memoryless property of the exponential random variable:

- a departure of the customer in service in queue 1, with probability $\mu h + o(h)$ if $i = m - 1, j = n$;
- a departure of the customer in service in queue 2, with probability $\mu h + o(h)$ if $i = m - 1, j = n - 1$, since the departure of the customer in the shorter queue will kill its partner-task in the longer queue;
- a failure of the customer in service in queue 1, with probability $\alpha h + o(h)$ if $i = m - 1, j = n$;
- a failure of the customer in service in queue 2, with probability $\alpha h + o(h)$ if $i = m, j = n - 1$;
- no change to the states of the queues with probability $1 - 2\alpha h - 2\mu h + o(h)$ if $i = m, j = n$.

All other values of i and j give a second-order contribution as more than one event in the interval $(0, h]$ would be required. Thus, $F_{mn}(t + h)$ satisfies:

$$
\begin{aligned}
F_{mn}(t + h) = \\
\mu h IP(W \leq t + h \mid A_1(0) = m, A_2(0) = n, A_1(h) = m - 1, A_2(h) = n) \\
+ \mu h IP(W \leq t + h \mid A_1(0) = m, A_2(0) = n, A_1(h) = m - 1, A_2(h) = n - 1) \\
+ \alpha h IP(W \leq t + h \mid A_1(0) = m, A_2(0) = n, A_1(h) = m - 1, A_2(h) = n) \\
+ \alpha h IP(W \leq t + h \mid A_1(0) = m, A_2(0) = n, A_1(h) = m, A_2(h) = n - 1) \\
+ (1 - 2\mu h - 2\alpha h)IP(W \leq t + h \mid A_1(0) = A_1(h) = m, A_2(0) = A_2(h) = n) \\
+ o(h)
\end{aligned}
$$

By the Markov property applied at time h and the residual life property of exponential random variables, the remaining response time of the tagged pair after time h, $W_h = W - h$ say, is distributed as the full response time of a hypothetical arrival-pair at time h conditioned on there being $A_1(h)$ and $A_2(h)$ customers ahead in queues 1 and 2 respectively, c.f. [6]. The last conditional probability (for instance) then simplifies to

$$IP(W_h \leq t \mid A_h = m, B_h = n) = IP(W \leq t \mid A_0 = m, B_0 = n) = F_{mn}(t)$$

Thus we have

$$
\begin{aligned}
F_{mn}(t + h) = \mu h F_{m-1,n}(t) + \mu h F_{m-1,n-1}(t) + \alpha h F_{m-1,n}(t) + \alpha h F_{m,n-1}(t) \\
+ (1 - 2\mu h - 2\alpha h)F_{mn}(t) + o(h)
\end{aligned}
$$

Rearranging, dividing by h, taking the limit $h \to 0$ and omitting the argument t for brevity, we obtain

$$f_{mn} = \mu F_{m-1,n} + \mu F_{m-1,n-1} + \alpha F_{m-1,n} + \alpha F_{m,n-1} - (2\mu + 2\alpha)F_{mn}$$

Taking the Laplace transform, noting that $(\mathcal{L}f_{mn})(s) = sL_{mn}(s)$ and writing $n+k$ for m, we obtain

$$(2\mu + 2\alpha + s)L_{n+k,n} = (\alpha + \mu)L_{n+k-1,n} + \alpha L_{n+k,n-1} + \mu L_{n+k-1,n-1} \quad (3)$$

Multiplying by x^n and summing from $n=1$ to ∞, we find

$$(2\mu + 2\alpha + s - \mu x)G_k(x) = (\alpha + \mu)G_{k-1}(x) + \alpha x G_{k+1}(x) + \alpha x L_{k+1,0} + \mu x L_{k,0}$$

Multiplying by y^k, summing from $k=1$ to ∞ and rearranging now gives

$$G(x,y) = \frac{(\alpha x y^{-1} + \mu x)H_0(y) + (\alpha + \mu)yG_0(x) - \alpha x G_1(x) - \alpha x L_{1,0}}{2\mu + 2\alpha + s - \mu x - (\alpha + \mu)y - \alpha x y^{-1}}$$

Lemma 1

$$L_{0,-1} = \frac{\mu}{s(s + \mu + \alpha)} \quad (4)$$

Proof. Proceeding as in the proof of Proposition 1, for $m=0, n=-1$, we have

$$F_{0,-1} = \mu h \cdot 1 + \alpha h F_{-1,-1}(t) + (1 - \mu h - \alpha h)F_{0,-1}(t) + o(h)$$

The term $\mu h \cdot 1$ corresponds to the tagged customer completing service in queue 1. The term $F_{-1,-1}(t) = 0$ corresponds to the failure of the tagged customer in both queues, with zero probability of completing service in less than time t for any $t > 0$. Then we obtain $L_{0,-1}$, proceeding analogusly to the proof of Proposition 1.

Lemma 2

$$L_{0,0} = \frac{2\mu s + 2\mu^2 + 4\alpha\mu}{s(s + \mu + \alpha)(s + 2\mu + 2\alpha)} \quad (5)$$

Proof. For $m=0, n=0$, we have, similarly to above,

$$(2\mu + 2\alpha + s)L_{0,0} = \alpha L_{-1,0} + \alpha L_{0,-1} + 2\mu/s = 2\alpha L_{0,-1} + 2\mu/s \quad (6)$$

The result follows by substituting Equation 4 into Equation 6.

Lemma 3. *For $|y| < 1$,*

$$H_{-1}(y) = \frac{\mu y(\mu + \alpha)}{s((\mu + \alpha + s) - y(\mu + \alpha))(\mu + \alpha + s)} \quad (7)$$

Proof. For $m > 0, n = -1$, we have

$$(\mu + \alpha + s)L_{m,-1} = (\alpha + \mu)L_{m-1,-1} \quad (8)$$

Multiplying by y^m, summing from $m=1$ to ∞ now gives

$$(\mu + \alpha + s)H_{-1}(y) = (\alpha + \mu)y(H_{-1}(y) + L_{0,-1})$$

The result now follows from Lemma 1.

Lemma 4. *For* $|y| < 1$,

$$H_0(y) = \frac{(\alpha + \mu)yL_{0,0} + \alpha H_{-1}(y) + \mu y(s(1 - y))^{-1}}{s + 2\mu + 2\alpha - (\mu + \alpha)y} \tag{9}$$

Proof. For $m > 0, n = 0$, we have, following the previous proof method:

$$F_{m0} = \mu h F_{m-1,0}(t) + \mu h \cdot 1 + \alpha h F_{m-1,0}(t) + \alpha h F_{m,-1}(t)$$
$$+ (1 - 2\mu h - 2\alpha h)F_{m0}(t) + o(h)$$

Similar steps to before yield,

$$(2\mu + 2\alpha + s)L_{k,0} = (\alpha + \mu)L_{k-1,0} + \alpha L_{k,-1} + \mu/s \tag{10}$$

so that

$$(2\mu + 2\alpha + s)H_0(y) = (\alpha + \mu)yH_0(y) + (\alpha + \mu)yL_{0,0} + \alpha H_{-1}(y) + \frac{\mu y}{s(1 - y)}$$

and the result follows from Lemma 2 and Lemma 3.

Proposition 2. *For* $|x| < 1$,

$$G_0(x) = \frac{(\alpha xy_0(x)^{-1} + \mu x)H_0(y_0(x)) + \mu x L_{0,0}}{s/2 + (\alpha + \mu)(1 - y_0(x)) - \mu x}, \tag{11}$$

where $y_0(x) = \frac{s+2\alpha+2\mu-\mu x-\sqrt{(s+2\alpha+2\mu-\mu x)^2-4\alpha x(\alpha+\mu)}}{2(\alpha+\mu)}.$

Proof. For $m = n > 0$, i.e., $k = 0, n \geq 1$, we have:

$$(2\mu + 2\alpha + s)L_{n,n} = \alpha L_{n-1,n} + \alpha L_{n,n-1} + 2\mu L_{n-1,n-1} \tag{12}$$

Multiplying by x^n, summing from $n = 1$ to ∞ then gives

$$(2\mu + 2\alpha + s)G_0(x) = 2\alpha x(G_1(x) + L_{1,0}) + 2\mu x(G_0(x) + L_{0,0}) \tag{13}$$

Now consider the expression for $G(x, y)$ in equation 2. Since it is analytic in the unit disks of both x and y, the numerator must vanish wherever the denominator is equal to 0. The zeros of the denominator are those of the quadratic

$$\text{Den} \equiv (\alpha + \mu)y^2 - (s + 2\mu + 2\alpha - \mu x)y + \alpha x = 0$$

When $y = 0$, Den $= \alpha x > 0$ and when $y = 1$, Den $= -(\alpha + \mu)(1 - x) - s < 0$ for $0 < x < 1$. When $y \to +\infty$, Den > 0 since the equation is dominated by y^2. Thus this equation has one (smaller) root ininterval $(0, 1)$ and another in $(1, \infty)$. Given some $x \in (0, 1)$, let the smaller root for y be $y_0(x) \in (0, 1)$, namely:

$$y_0(x) = \frac{s + 2\alpha + 2\mu - \mu x - \sqrt{(s + 2\alpha + 2\mu - \mu x)^2 - 4\alpha x(\alpha + \mu)}}{2(\alpha + \mu)}. \tag{14}$$

To make $G(x, y)$ analytic, the pair $(x, y_0(x))$ must also be a root of the numerator of Equation 2, i.e. we must have

$$(\alpha x y_0(x)^{-1} + \mu x) H_0(y_0(x)) + (\alpha + \mu) y_0(x) G_0(x) - \alpha x G_1(x) - \alpha x L_{1,0} = 0 \quad (15)$$

Furthermore, from equation 13, we find

$$\alpha x (G_1(x) + L_{1,0}) = (s/2 + \mu + \alpha) G_0(x) - \mu x (G_0(x) + L_{0,0}) \quad (16)$$

Thus, for all $x \in (0, 1)$,

$$(\alpha x y_0(x)^{-1} + \mu x) H_0(y_0(x)) + (\alpha + \mu) y_0(x) G_0(x)$$
$$= (s/2 + \mu + \alpha) G_0(x) - \mu x (G_0(x) + L_{0,0})$$

Substituting into Equation 15, we have

$$G_0(x) = \frac{(\alpha x y_0(x)^{-1} + \mu x) H_0(y_0(x)) + \mu x L_{0,0}}{s/2 + (\alpha + \mu)(1 - y_0(x)) - \mu x}, \qquad \forall x \in (0, 1). \quad (17)$$

Taking the above lemmas and propositions together, we arrive at the main result of this paper.

Theorem 1. *For $|x| < 1, |y| < 1$,*

$$G(x, y) = \frac{(\alpha x y^{-1} + \mu x) H_0(y) + \mu x L_{0,0} + G_0(x) \left[\mu x - (\alpha + \mu)(1 - y) - s/2 \right]}{2\mu + 2\alpha + s - \mu x - (\alpha + \mu) y - \alpha x y^{-1}}$$
$$(18)$$

Proof. Substitute the expression for $\alpha x (G_1(x) + L_{1,0})$ given by equation 13 in equation 2.

3   Initial Equilibrium State-Probabilities

Under FCFS discipline, the unconditional probability distribution of response time at equilibrium, $W(t)$, is $W(t) = P(W \le t) = \sum_{n \ge 0} \sum_{m \ge 0} \pi_{mn} F_{mn}(t)$, which has Laplace transform $W^*(s) = \sum_{n \ge 0} \sum_{m \ge 0} \pi_{mn} L_{mn}(s)$, where π_{mn} is the steady state probability that the joint state of the queues is (m, n). There is no closed form for π_{mn} and so we proceed in two ways in the following subsections: (a) direct calculation of π_{mn} and L_{mn} in a truncated state space; and (b) approximation of π_{mn} by a product-form and use of the generating function G.

Notice that the probability that a positive customer completes service at either of the servers is the marginal probability $W(\infty) = s W^*(s)|_{s=0}$.

3.1   Direct Solution in a Truncated Space

The equilibrium probabilities π_{mn} are estimated, to any degree of accuracy in a stable underlying Markov process, by solving directly the Kolmogorov equations restricted to a finite state space, i.e. in which the queues have finite capacity C and the equilibrium probability that either queue is at full capacity is negligible. Let the generator matrix of the Markov process in our model be $A = (a_{ij;mn}), (i, j, m, n \geq 0)$. Then $\{\pi_{mn} \mid 0 \leq m, n \leq C\}$ is the unique, normalised solution of the balance equations

$$\sum_{i=0}^{C}\sum_{j=0}^{C} \pi_{ij}a_{ij;mn} = 0, \quad \text{for } 0 \leq m, n \leq C$$

The instantaneous rates a_{ij} are simply read off from the problem specification, for example $a_{ij;i+1,j+1} = \lambda$ for $0 \leq i, j < C$. The capacity C is chosen by guessing and repeatedly increasing it until the values computed for $\{\pi_{mC} \mid m \geq 0\} \cup \{\pi_{Cn} \mid n \geq 0\}$ are negligible.

The corresponding conditional Laplace transforms L_{mn}, L_{nm} can be obtained recursively from Equation 3, 4, 5, 8, 10 and 12, then we make the estimate:

$$W(s) = \sum_{m=0}^{C}\sum_{n=0}^{C} \pi_{mn}L_{mn} \tag{19}$$

In fact we found that $C = 50$ was an appropriate capacity at which to truncate the state space when computing the exact equilibrium probabilities numerically.

3.2   Product-Form Equilibrium Probabilities

The procedure of the previous section is inefficient and at high utilisations, the capacity $C = 50$ would be far too small. Notice too that the generating function G was not necessary, the coefficients L_{mn} being calculated directly. However, in the event that the queues are approximately independent, each with geometric queue length probability distributions with parameter $\pi_{mn} = (1 - \rho)^2\rho^{m+n}$. Then by the symmetry between m and n, the Laplace transform of $W(t)$ is

$$W(s) = \sum_{n\geq 0}\left[\sum_{m>n} \pi_{mn}L_{mn} + \sum_{m<n} \pi_{mn}L_{mn} + \sum_{m=n} \pi_{mn}L_{mn}\right]$$

$$= 2\sum_{n\geq 0}\sum_{m>n} \pi_{mn}L_{mn} + \sum_{n=0}^{\infty} \pi_{nn}L_{nn}$$

When $\pi_{mn} = (1 - \rho)^2\rho^{m+n}$, the first term becomes

$$2\left[\sum_{n\geq 1}\sum_{k\geq 1} \pi_{n+k,n}L_{n+k,n} + \sum_{k\geq 1} \pi_{k,0}L_{k,0}\right] = 2(1 - \rho)^2\left[G(\rho^2, \rho) + H_0(\rho)\right]$$

and the second $(1-\rho)^2 \sum_{n=0}^{\infty} \rho^{2n} L_{nn} = (1-\rho)^2 \left[G_0(\rho^2) + L_{0,0} \right]$. Thus

$$W(s) = (1-\rho)^2 \left[2G(\rho^2, \rho) + 2H_0(\rho) + G_0(\rho^2) + L_{0,0} \right] \qquad (20)$$

In the case that $\alpha \gg \mu$, the two queues are less synchronised and we might expect the product-form to give a good approximation. This is investigated in the next section. We now need to find the value of ρ, which we do by considering the pair of queues as a G-network [5], in which a customer that completes service at one node either kills (removes) a customer from another node – in our case, its partner – with probability p^- or just leaves the network with probability $1 - p^-$ without killing. p^- is the probability that the partner is still waiting in the other queue or is being served [1,5], i.e. it is the probability that the queue length at the other node is less than that of the completing customer's queue at the instant of departure. This is a function of the current queue length and does not admit a geometric probability distribution.

We therefore further approximate by assigning to p^- its mean value at equilibrium. The average killing rate of queue 2, say, given that the queue length of queue 1 is m, is $\mu \mathbb{P}(1 \le N \le m) = \mu(1 - \mathbb{P}(N > m) - \mathbb{P}(N = 0)) = \mu \rho(1 - \rho^m)$. The average rate of killing when the queue length of queue 1 is greater than 0 is therefore

$$\frac{\mu}{1 - \pi_0} \sum_{m=1}^{\infty} \pi_m \rho(1 - \rho^m) = \mu(1 - \rho) \sum_{m=1}^{\infty} (\rho^m - \rho^{2m}) = \frac{\mu \rho}{\rho + 1} \qquad (21)$$

We therefore define the killing probabilty $p^- = \rho/(\rho + 1)$. Since the two queues are symmetric, the traffic equations are:

$$\lambda^+ = \lambda, \qquad \lambda^- = \alpha + \mu \rho p^- = \alpha + (\mu \rho^2)/(\rho + 1) \qquad (22)$$

where $\rho = \lambda^+/(\mu + \lambda^-)$ and λ^+, λ^- are the positive and negative arrival rates respectively in a single G-queue. Then the utilization ρ is the root of the following equation that lies in the interval $(0, 1)$:

$$\mu \rho^3 + (\mu + \alpha)\rho^2 + (\mu + \alpha - \lambda)\rho - \lambda = 0 \qquad (23)$$

Since the left hand side is negative at $\rho = 0$ and positive at $\rho = 1$ when the stability condition $\lambda < \mu + \alpha + \mu \rho^2/(\rho + 1)$, such a root does exist.

3.3 Numerical Comparisons

The various tables and graphs presented in this section assume that $\mu = 1$ and vary the input rate λ and failure rate α. The mean value and standard deviation of response time, conditional on a customer not being killed, are obtained from the first two derivatives of the Laplace transform at 0, divided by $W(\infty)$, and tabulated in Tables 1 and 2 for $\alpha = 1, 10, 100, 1000$ and ratio $\lambda/(\alpha + \mu) = 0.1, 0.5, 0.9$. The simulations in this paper were run 10,000 times, giving 95% confidence bands. For larger arrival rates λ, the exact truncated values are noticeably lower than the simulation values, since we ignore queue lengths bigger than 50. We see that as α increases, the approximation becomes more accurate.

Table 1. Comparison of mean response times with $\mu = 1$: simulation, exact truncated values and product-form approximation

α	λ	Simulation[95%]	Exact Truncated	Prod. Form App/%err
	1.1	0.0980 ±0.0002	0.0979	0.0986/0.72
10	5.5	0.1670 ±0.0002	0.1672	0.1737/3.89
	9.9	0.5830 ±0.0008	0.5805	0.6609/13.36
	10.1	0.0109 ±0.0001	0.0110	0.0110/0.00
100	50.5	0.0196 ±0.0001	0.0196	0.0197/0.51
	90.9	0.0922 ±0.0004	0.0912	0.0950/3.04
	100.1	0.0011 ±0.0000	0.0011	0.0011/0.00
1000	500.5	0.0020 ±0.0000	0.0020	0.0020/0.00
	900.9	0.0100 ±0.0001	0.0096	0.0099/1.00

For $\alpha = 0.1, 1, 10, 100$ and ratio $\lambda/(\alpha + \mu) = 0.5$, we also computed the CDF of response time using the approximation. This is shown in Figure 2, where it is compared with the corresponding result computed exactly up to state-space truncation. The agreement is good when α is large and improves with increasing α. However, for small α, the approximation is much poorer, especially for $\alpha <$ 0.5. We therefore examined the accuracy of the product-form approximation.

Table 2. Comparison of standard deviation of response times with $\mu = 1$: simulation, exact truncated values and product-form approximation

α	λ	Simulation[95%]	Exact Truncated	Prod. Form App/%err
	1.1	0.0990 ±0.0001	0.0989	0.0997/0.81
10	5.5	0.1672 ±0.0002	0.1673	0.1755/4.90
	9.9	0.5641 ±0.0005	0.5577	0.6683/18.47
α	λ	Simulation	Exact Truncated	Prod. Form App/%err
	10.1	0.0109 ±0.0001	0.0110	0.0110/0.00
100	50.5	0.0196 ±0.0001	0.0196	0.0197/0.51
	90.9	0.0917 ±0.0003	0.0878	0.0951/3.71
α	λ	Simulation	Exact Truncated	Prod. Form App/%err
	100.1	0.0011 ±0.0000	0.0011	0.0011/0.00
1000	500.5	0.0020 ±0.0000	0.0020	0.0020/0.00
	900.9	0.0100 ±0.0001	0.0091	0.0099/1.00

3.4   Approximate Marginal and Joint Probabilities

To check the accuracy of the approximate, geometric marginal stationary probabilities, we set $\alpha = 0.1, 10, 100$ and $\lambda/(\alpha+\mu) = 0.1, 0.5, 0.9$, as shown in figure 1. We see that as α increases, the approximation becomes more accurate. However, increasing the ratio $\lambda/(\alpha + \mu)$ makes it less accurate.

For the joint stationary probabilities, we set $\alpha = 0, 1, 100$ respectively. Figure 3 shows the comparison of the joint probability of exact truncated values with the approximation using $\lambda/(\alpha + \mu) = 0.5$. Again it is seen that with the increasing of α, the approximation becomes more accurate. However, near the point $(0, 0)$, there is a significant discrepancy in the joint probability, arising from the dependence between the two queues.

4   Formulation Based on Difference-Modes

Instead of defining the state as the pair of queue lengths, we instead use the shorter queue length, n, and the difference between the queue lengths, d, which we call the *mode*, exploiting the symmetry of the model. We then essentially use the mode to modulate the Markov process followed by the shorter queue length, first approximately and then exactly by the Spectral Analysis Method (SEM). For example, mode 4 means the queue lengths are $(4 + n, n)$ or $(n, 4 + n)$, where $n \geq 0$ is the length of the shorter queue. To avoid confusion, we denote the equilibrium probabilities with primes, e.g. $\pi'_{d,n} = \pi_{n,n+d} + \pi_{n+d,n}$.

4.1   Approximation

Whilst the mode remains fixed, the shorter queue length can increase by 1, due to an arrival (to both queues), and can decrease by 1 when the task at the front of the shorter queue departs and then kills its partner. Thus, we make the approximation, for $n \geq 0$, that $\pi'_{0,n} = p_0(1 - \lambda/2\mu)(\lambda/2\mu)^n$ and $\pi_{d,n} = p_d(1 - \lambda/\mu)(\lambda/\mu)^n$, for $d > 0$, where p_d is the equilibrium marginal mode-probability considered next.

We further approximate regarding mode-transitions since the transition rates depend on the individual queue lengths. For example, no mode-transition is possible in the empty system with state $(0, 0)$. We therefore use average rates, with respect to the above shorter queue length probabilities. The transition from mode 0 to mode 1 is therefore approximated by $2\alpha\lambda/2\mu = \alpha\lambda/\mu$, since a task at the front of either queue can only fail when one is present. For the mode-transition $d \to d + 1, (d > 0)$, the task at the front of the shorter queue can fail only when that queue is non-empty, so we use the averaged rate $\alpha\lambda/\mu$. For the transition $d + 1 \to d, (d \geq 0)$, the rate is $\alpha + \mu$, due to the departure or failure of the task at the front of the longer queue. This gives equilibrium mode-probabilities:

$$p_0 = \frac{\mu(\mu + \alpha) - \alpha\lambda}{\mu(\mu + \alpha)}, \qquad p_d = \frac{\mu(\mu + \alpha) - \alpha\lambda}{\mu(\mu + \alpha)} \left(\frac{\alpha\lambda}{\mu(\mu + \alpha)} \right)^d \quad (d > 0),$$

giving Laplace transform

$$W^*(s) = \sum_{n \geq 0} \sum_{m \geq 0} \pi_{mn} L_{mn}(s) = p_0 \sum_{n \geq 0} \pi'_{0,n} L_{n,n} + \sum_{d > 0} p_d \sum_{n \geq 0} \pi'_{d,n} L_{d+n,n}(s)$$

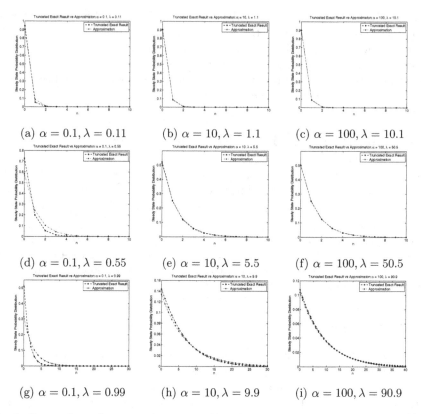

(a) $\alpha = 0.1, \lambda = 0.11$ (b) $\alpha = 10, \lambda = 1.1$ (c) $\alpha = 100, \lambda = 10.1$

(d) $\alpha = 0.1, \lambda = 0.55$ (e) $\alpha = 10, \lambda = 5.5$ (f) $\alpha = 100, \lambda = 50.5$

(g) $\alpha = 0.1, \lambda = 0.99$ (h) $\alpha = 10, \lambda = 9.9$ (i) $\alpha = 100, \lambda = 90.9$

Fig. 1. Comparison of truncated exact result with approximaton with the ratio $\lambda/(\alpha + \mu) = 0.1, 0.5, 0.9$

Combining Equation 5,9,18, we obtain

$$
W^*(s) = \frac{(2\mu - \lambda)(\mu\alpha + \mu^2 - \lambda\alpha)}{2\mu^2(\alpha + \mu)} \left[L_{00} + G_0\left(\frac{\lambda}{2\mu}\right) \right]
$$
$$
+ \frac{(\mu - \lambda)(\mu\alpha + \mu^2 - \lambda\alpha)}{\mu^2(\alpha + \mu)} \left[H_0\left(\frac{\lambda\alpha}{\mu(\alpha + \mu)}\right) + G\left(\frac{\lambda}{\mu}, \frac{\lambda\alpha}{\mu(\alpha + \mu)}\right) \right] \tag{24}
$$

This approximation is very fast and works well at low α but deteriorates as λ increases, i.e. at higher utilisations. We therefore seek a more accurate numerical approximation of the exact result in the next section.

4.2   Spectral Expansion Method

The spectral expansion method (SEM) of [9] is ideally suited to calculating the joint equilibrium probabilities in the difference-mode formulation, in which the

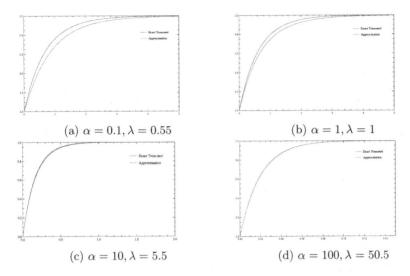

Fig. 2. CDF: approximation vs. exact truncated result

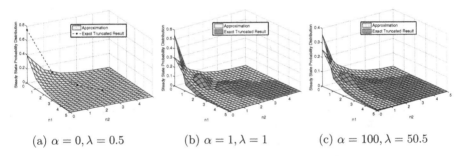

Fig. 3. Joint queue length probabilities: exact truncated result vs. approximation with the ratio $\lambda/(\alpha + \mu) = 0.5$

system state is described by a pair of random variables, (K, X); K is a control variable that determines the transition rates in the Markov process followed by X. Here, K is the mode (difference between the queue lengths) and X is the length of the shorter queue. The random variable K must be finite and so again we truncate the state space, but even at high utilisations the probability of large differences between the queue lengths should be small; a truncation at maximum mode 5 was found sufficient. In the SEM, above a threshold $X = M$, the transition rates on X must be independent of K; here the threshold $M = 1$. Following the SEM, let the eigenvalue-eigenvector pairs of the characteristic equation be denoted (α_ℓ, v_ℓ), with $|\alpha_\ell| < 1, 1 \le \ell \le N + 1$, where N is the

Table 3. Mean response times with $\mu = 1$: simulation, exact truncated, product-form approximation, difference-modes approximation and SEM

α	λ	Simulation[95%]	Exact Truncated	Prod. Form/%err	Diff-Modes/%err	SEM/%err
0.001	0.1	0.5270 ±0.0003	0.5268	0.5531/4.99	0.5268/0.00	0.5268/0.00
	0.5	0.6669 ±0.0004	0.6671	0.8449/26.65	0.6674/0.04	0.6671/0.00
	0.9	0.9091 ±0.0004	0.9095	1.4837/63.13	0.9135/0.44	0.9095/0.00
0.01	0.1	0.5310 ±0.0003	0.5312	0.5574/4.93	0.5312/0.00	0.5310/0.04
	0.5	0.6707 ±0.0005	0.6708	0.8483/26.46	0.6740/0.48	0.6708/0.00
	0.9	0.9121 ±0.0005	0.9127	1.4797/62.12	0.9529/4.40	0.9127/0.00
0.1	0.1	0.5558 ±0.0004	0.5555	0.5810/4.59	0.5583/0.50	0.5555/0.00
	0.5	0.6906 ±0.0005	0.6901	0.8563/ 24.08	0.7207/4.43	0.6901/0.00
	0.9	0.9236 ±0.0006	0.9223	1.4100/52.88	1.2931/40.20	0.9223/0.00
	0.99	0.9987 ±0.0007	0.9993	/	/	0.9997/0.04
0.5	0.1	0.5204 ±0.0004	0.5203	0.5349/2.81	0.5315/2.15	0.5203/0.00
	0.5	0.6242 ±0.0005	0.6236	0.7145/14.58	0.7407/18.78	0.6236/0.00
	0.9	0.7852 ±0.0005	0.7857	1.0115/28.74	2.0558/161.65	0.7857/0.00
	1.35	1.1347 ±0.0007	1.1359	/	/	1.1359/0.00
1	0.2	0.4470 ±0.0004	0.4469	0.4617/3.31	0.4844/8.39	0.4469/0.00
	1.0	0.6351 ±0.0005	0.6352	0.7521/18.40	0.7762/22.20	0.6352/0.00
	1.8	1.1446 ±0.0008	1.1467	/	/	1.1468/0.01

Table 4. Standard deviation of response times with $\mu = 1$: simulation, exact truncated, product-form approximation, difference-modes approximation and SEM

α	λ	Simulation[95%]	Exact Truncated	Prod. Form/%err	Diff-Modes/%err	SEM/%err
0.001	0.1	0.5279 ±0.0002	0.5277	0.5522/4.64	0.5277/0.00	0.5277/0.00
	0.5	0.6674 ±0.0004	0.6677	0.8164/22.27	0.6682/0.07	0.6677/0.00
	0.9	0.9101 ±0.0004	0.9098	1.3980/53.66	0.9319/2.43	0.9098/0.00
0.01	0.1	0.5394 ±0.0002	0.5395	0.5656/4.80	0.5397/0.00	0.5395/0.00
	0.5	0.6762 ±0.0003	0.6763	0.8348/23.44	0.6810/0.70	0.6763/0.00
	0.9	0.9151 ±0.0004	0.9155	1.4217/55.29	1.1137/21.65	0.9155/0.00
0.1	0.1	0.6042 ±0.0002	0.6037	0.6362/5.38	0.6062/0.41	0.6037/0.00
	0.5	0.7243 ±0.0004	0.7234	0.9187/27.00	0.7623/5.38	0.7234/0.00
	0.9	0.9409 ±0.0004	0.9392	1.4896/58.60	2.0947/123.03	0.9392/0.00
	0.99	1.0115 ±0.0004	1.0128	/	/	1.0128/0.00
0.5	0.1	0.5711 ±0.0004	0.5711	0.5909/3.47	0.5814/1.80	0.5711/0.00
	0.5	0.6647 ±0.0003	0.6636	0.7833/18.04	0.7934/19.56	0.6636/0.00
	0.9	0.8076 ±0.0004	0.8087	1.1019/32.26	3.1574/290.43	0.8087/0.00
	1.35	1.1260 ±0.0005	1.1288	/	/	1.1288/0.00
1	0.2	0.4469 ±0.0002	0.4772	0.4968/4.06	0.5143/7.73	0.4773/0.02
	1.0	0.6514 ±0.0003	0.6515	0.8032/23.28	0.7812/19.91	0.6514/0.02
	1.8	1.1165 ±0.0006	1.1201	/	/	1.1202/0.01

truncation value chosen for the mode. These values can be computed numerically by standard algorithms. We then obtain

$$
W^*(s) = \sum_{k=0}^{N}\sum_{n\geq 0} \pi_{k+n,n} L_{k+n,n}(s) = \sum_{n\geq 0} \pi_{n,n} L_{n,n}(s) + \sum_{k=1}^{N}\sum_{n\geq 0} \pi_{k+n,n} L_{k+n,n}(s)
$$

$$
= \sum_{\ell=1}^{N+1} \alpha_\ell/x_\ell \left[v_{\ell 0}(G_0(x_\ell) + L_{00}) + \sum_{k=1}^{N} v_{\ell k}(L_{k0} + G_k(x_\ell)) \right],
$$

(25)

where $L_{k,0}$ and $G_k(x)$ are obtained iteratively from equations 10 and 4.

If the number of eigenvalues obtained in the unit disk is other than $N + 1$, a steady-state distribution does not exist, so we increase N. The SEM results for mean and standard deviation of response time are shown and compared with simulation and exact truncated values in table 4, which reveals a high degree of accuracy at all parameterisations of the model.

5   Conclusion

We have made a start in analysing the effectiveness of replication schemes by considering the case of two replicas. Exact solution is not practical because of the lack of a product-form solution for the equilibrium state, and so we had to find approximations and bounds on the exact result that do have product-form. Based on this analysis, we next intend to investigate the corresponding scheme with $n \geq 2$ replicas by approximate methods, for example by considering successively a set of r replicas together with a further single replica for $r = 1$ (the base case), 2 (as in this paper), ..., n.

References

1. Artalejo, J.R.: G-networks: A versatile approach for work removal in queueing networks. European Journal of Operational Research 126(2), 233–249 (2000)
2. Chan, P., Lyu, M.R., Malek, M.: Reliableweb services: Methodology, experiment and modeling. In: IEEE International Conference on Web Services, ICWS 2007, pp. 679–686. IEEE (2007)
3. Dabrowski, C.: Reliability in grid computing systems. Concurrency and Computation: Practice and Experience 21(8), 927–959 (2009)
4. Dean, J., Barroso, L.A.: The tail at scale. Communications of the ACM 56(2), 74–80 (2013)
5. Gelenbe, E.: Product-form queueing networks with negative and positive customers. Journal of Applied Probability, 656–663 (1991)
6. Harrison, P.G., Pitel, E.: Sojourn times in single-server queues with negative customers. Journal of Applied Probability, 943–963 (1993)
7. Koren, I., Krishna, C.M.: Fault-tolerant systems. Morgan Kaufmann (2010)
8. Maxion, R.A., Siewiorek, D.P., Elkind, S.A.: Techniques and architectures for fault-tolerant computing. Annual Review of Computer Science 2(1), 469–520 (1987)
9. Mitrani, I.: Spectral expansion solutions for markov-modulated queues. In: Calzarossa, M.C., Tucci, S. (eds.) Performance 2002. LNCS, vol. 2459, pp. 17–35. Springer, Heidelberg (2002)
10. Sauro, J.: The high cost of task failure on websites (2012),
    http://www.measuringusability.com/blog/cost-task-failure.php
11. Tang, C., Li, Q., Hua, B., Liu, A.: Developing reliable web services using independent replicas. In: Fifth International Conference on Semantics, Knowledge and Grid, SKG 2009, pp. 330–333. IEEE (2009)

Improving and Assessing the Efficiency of the MC4CSL^{TA} Model Checker

Elvio Gilberto Amparore and Susanna Donatelli

University of Torino, Corso Svizzera 187, Torino, Italy
{amparore,susi}@di.unito.it

Abstract. CSL^{TA} is a stochastic logic which is able to express properties on the behavior of a CTMC, in particular in terms of the possible executions of the CTMC (like the probability that the set of paths that exhibits a certain behavior is above/below a certain threshold). This paper presents the new version of the the stochastic model checker MC4CSL^{TA}, which verifies CSL^{TA} formulas against a Continuous Time Markov Chain, possibly expressed as a Generalized Stochastic Petri Net. With respect to the first version of the model checker presented in [1], version 2 features a totally new solution algorithm, which is able to verify complex, nested formulas based on the timed automaton, while, at the same time, is capable of reaching a time and space complexity similar to that of the CSL model checkers when the automaton specifies a neXt or an Until formulas. In particular, the goal of this paper is to present a new way of generating the MRP, which, together with the new MRP solution method presented in [2] provides the two cornerstone results which are at the basis of the current version. The model checker has been evaluated and validated against PRISM [3] (for whose CSL^{TA} formulas which can be expressed in CSL) and against the statistical model checker Cosmos[4] (for all types of formulas).

1 Introduction

System verification is a topic whose relevance increases with the increase of the dependency of everyday life from software systems. The more our society relies on computer-based systems, more critical is the demand for system reliability. Model checking of temporal logics has represented an important milestone in the computer science approach to verification, allowing the exhaustive check of systems with billions of states and more. Temporal logics allows to express invariant properties, like "in all states variable x is positive", as well as path-dependent properties, like "it exists a system execution (a path) in which variable x is always incremented after a decrement of variable y". When the system at hand includes timing aspects, temporal logic can be extended to include constraints over time intervals, like "on all paths the lift door will open within 2 seconds after the lift reaches the target floor". Finally, when the system description includes also probabilistic aspects, its evaluation and verification can be based on stochastic logics that allows properties like: "with probability greater than α the lift door will open within 2 seconds after the lift reaches the target floor".

M.S. Balsamo, W.J. Knottenbelt, and A. Marin (Eds.): EPEW 2013, LNCS 8168, pp. 206–220, 2013.

The most well known stochastic logic is CSL [5], for which various verification engines (model-checkers) exists, like Prism [3], MRMC [6] and Marcie [7], to verify behaviour of DTMC or CTMC, possibly generated from higher level languages, like the guarded command language of Prism or the stochastic Petri nets of Marcie. CSL has a predefined set of operators to specify the paths of interest (called neXt and Until), and this might constitute a limitation. This restriction is nevertheless well motivated by the fact that the verification of these formulas only requires transient and steady-state solution of the chain.

CSL^{TA} [8] represents a step forward, as it allows to specify the paths of interest as the set of paths accepted by a single clock timed automaton [9], where the restriction to single clock is the key to allow the verification of CSL^{TA} formulas in terms of the steady-state solution of a Markov Regenerative Process (MRP). A multi clock CSL^{TA} has been defined in [10], but the gain in formula expressiveness is paid in solution terms, as the underlying process becomes a piece-wise deterministic process (PDP). In terms of model checkers, single clock CSL^{TA} formulas can be verified using MC4CSL^{TA} [1], and single and multiple clock formulas using Codemoc [11]. More recently the statistical model checker Cosmos [4] has been delivered. The tool uses simulation to verify formulas specified through timed (and even hybrid) automata [12], for a stochastic model that is a Stochastic Petri Net extended to arbitrary distributions for the transition firing.

This paper concentrates on CSL^{TA} and presents the new version of the model checker MC4CSL^{TA}. Version 2 solves a few inefficiencies of the first version, as will be explained in the next section, and introduces a totally new solution engine. As we shall see, the translation into Deterministic Stochastic Petri Net (DSPN) has been removed; to allow the evaluation of nested formulas the implementation now includes forward and backward solution; different MRP solution methods can now be employed (in particular the efficient component-based approach described in [2]), and non useful computations are removed thanks to a pre-analysis of the timed automata of the formula. This theory behind the pre-analysis and an assessment of the correctness and efficiency of MC4CSL^{TA} version 2 are the main contributions of this paper. Most of the work presented in this paper is the result of the PhD work of the first author [13].

2 Background and Motivations

In this section we review the basic literature in CSL and CSL^{TA} and related tools and discuss the status of the MC4CSL^{TA} model checker, version 1 and the limits that the tool has shown in verifying "large" systems. The focus will be on the solution algorithms employed. It is important to recall that "large" in the stochastic context is never as large as in the qualitative model checking, since, unless approximate techniques are applied, the limit in size is given by the size and the number of vectors required by the solution process. In this paper we have considered systems with up to 10 millions states.

CSL and Prism. Prism allows to model check CSL formula in a very efficient way. The most complex operator, apart from steady state, is the evaluation of the probability of the set of paths that verify an Until formula of the type $\mathcal{P}_{\bowtie\lambda}(\Phi \, \mathcal{U}^{[t,t']}\Psi)$ for a CTMC $\mathcal{M}$, where Φ and Ψ are boolean functions over the set AP of atomic propositions associated to the states of $\mathcal{M}$, $\bowtie \in \{<, \leq, \geq, >\}$ is a comparison operator, $\lambda \in \mathbb{R}_{[0,1]}$ is interpreted as a probability, and $0 \leq t \leq t'$ is a time interval. The probability of the paths that satisfy the Until formula can be computed by the (transient) solution of one or two CTMCs (depending on the time interval $[t, t']$). These CTMCs are derived from the original model $\mathcal{M}$ by making certain states absorbing, and we shall term $\mathcal{M}[\Phi]$ the CTMC obtained from $\mathcal{M}$ by making all the states that satisfy Φ in $\mathcal{M}$ absorbing. When $t \neq t'$ the model checking algorithm requires the transient solution of two modified CTMCs: the chain $\pi^{\mathcal{M}[\neg\Phi]}$ is solved for time t, assuming we start in s at time 0, the resulting probability vector is then used as initial probability for the solution at time $t' - t$ of the chain $\pi^{\mathcal{M}[\neg\Phi\vee\Psi]}$, where the result of the first computation are filtered out to put to zero the probability of all states which are not Φ states. The elements of the second transient solution vector that satisfy Ψ are then summed-up to obtain the probability of the set of paths starting from the initial state s and that satisfy the Until. A comparison with λ allows to define whether s satisfies the formula or not.

Prism allows also an hybrid solution engine, in which the CTMC, and the modified CTMCs required in the computation, are stored efficiently using decision diagrams, while the solution vector is stored in full. Moreover, although the above description is fully forward, from time 0 to time t', the model checking works backward (as explained later) from the states that satisfy Ψ to the set of states that satisfies the full formula. This allows to compute, through two transient solutions only, the full set of states that satisfy the formula. Other model checkers like Marcie and MRMC apply the same solution approach.

CSL^{TA} *and* $MC4CSL^{TA}$, *version 1* CSL^{TA} (single clock) uses timed automata (TA) to specify (timed) accepted path and the model checker goal is to compute the probability of the set of accepted paths. To avoid the introduction of non-determinism the TA is required to be "deterministic" (DTA): for each path in the automaton there is at most one path in the TA that accepts it. A DTA $\mathcal{A}$ is made of a set of *locations* and a set of *edges*. Each DTA is equipped with a *clock*, usually named x, that runs constantly and whose value increases linearly over time. Edges describe the transition relation and can be labeled with a *clock constraint*. The DTA of Figure 1(A) has three locations l_0, l_1, l_2. Location l_0 is initial, and l_2 is final.

An edge with a constraint in the form $x = c_1$ is a *Boundary* edge (marked with a ♯), and is triggered by the elapse of time. An edge with a constraint $c_1 < x < c_2$ is an *Inner* edge (as the l_0, l_1) edge) and is triggered by a transition firing in the GSPN (or by a transition in the CTMC). Each edge can have an associated reset of the clock x. *Inner* edges can have an associated set of actions (transition names of a GSPN or action names of a decorated CTMC), and locations can have an associated boolean formula (the atomic propositions Φ and Ψ in the example).

(A) A simple DTA that describes which CTMC paths are accepted.

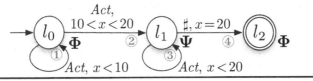

(B) State space of the cross product of any CTMC with the DTA (A).

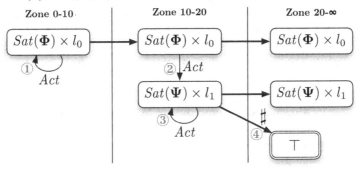

Fig. 1. An example of DTA

With reference to GSPN, we can say that a transition in the underlying CTMC from marking m to marking m' due to the firing of transition a is accepted by the DTA in location l through the edge (l, l') if, assuming that m satisfies the boolean condition associated to l, the transition a is in the set of actions associated to the (l, l') edge, the current value of x satisfies the edge constraint, and m' satisfies the boolean condition of l'. The DTA of the example accepts CTMC paths that stay in a Φ state for at least 10 unit time, then moves to a Ψ state at any time between 10 and 20, with any CTMC move in the Act set, and at time 20 is found in a state that satisfies Φ. Note that all edges in the DTA are *Inner* edges, but the one between l_1 and l_2. For each DTA is possible to define $C = \{c_i\}$, the ordered set of clock values that label $\mathcal{A}$ clock constraints, with the addition of 0 and ∞. For the example in Figure 1(A), $C = \{0, 10, 20, \infty\}$ A state of a (D)TA is then given by a pair (l, c) where l is a location and c is a clock value in C.

CSL^{TA} is a variation of CSL in which the $\mathcal{P}_{\bowtie\lambda}(\varphi)$ operator (with φ being either a timed neXt or a a timed Until operator) is substituted by a $\mathcal{P}_{\bowtie\lambda}(\mathcal{A})$. CSL^{TA} is more expressive than CSL [8], and this comes at the price of a more complex model checking algorithm: verifying a formula requires the steady state solution of an (absorbing) Markov Regenerative Process (MRP) obtained as the cross-product of the Markov chain with the DTA. If s is the state of a CTMC and (l, c) is the state of the DTA, a state in the cross-product is the triple (s, l, c), or one of the two states $\top$ or $\bot$ The cross-product is built in such a way that all and only the paths of the CTMC that take the DTA to a final location end up in a $\top$ state. A state s of a CTMC $\mathcal{M}$ satisfies the formula $\mathcal{P}_{\bowtie\lambda}(A)$ if in the cross-product MRP $\mathcal{M} \times \mathcal{A}$ the probability of reaching $\top$ from (s, l_0, c_0) is $\bowtie \lambda$. Fig. 1(B) shows the general cross-product induced by the DTA (A) on any CTMC, where the rectangles are set of CTMC states that satisfies the DTA's state propositions.

As depicted in the upper part of Figure 2, model checking of CSL^{TA} requires two steps: building the MRP $\mathcal{M} \times \mathcal{A}$ and then solving it. In the first version of MC4CSL^{TA} the cross product algorithm produces a DSPN whose underlying process is isomorphic to the $\mathcal{M} \times \mathcal{A}$, so that the solution step can be left to existing DSPN tools. This approach is inspired by software reuse, but it is highly inefficient, since even the starting CTMC has to be translated into a DSPN, moreover the use of existing tools, not specifically designed for model-checking, allows to use only the much less efficient forward approach.

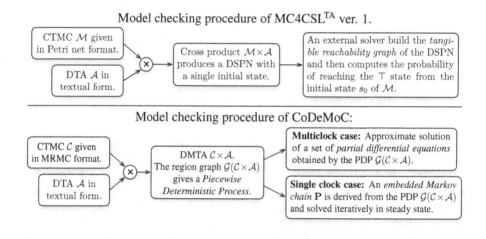

Fig. 2. Working structures of the MC4CSL^{TA} and Codemoc model checkers

MRP solution methods There is a large degree of variation in the solution approaches for MRP. When applied to CSL^{TA} the classical approach builds the embedded Markov chain $\mathbf{P}$ and solves it to compute the probability of the renewal state $\top$. This approach suffers from the *fill-in* approach: P is usually a very dense matrix and only small states spaces can be solved. A matrix-free approach has been defined in [14], which computes the probability of renewal states without ever building and storing P. This approach has been extended in [15] to deal with non ergodic MRPs, as required by CSL^{TA}. More recently a component-based approach [2] has been defined for non-ergodic MRPs, which can significantly reduce the space and time complexity of model-checking CSL^{TA}. In particular it was shown in the same paper that the algorithm, when applied for DTAs that are Until formulas, reduces to the computation of the transient solution of two CTMC, although the space complexity is not the same since the

$\mathcal{M} \times \mathcal{A}$ includes both the two CTMCs that have to be solved, while a CSL model checker can build and solve the one at a time.

CSL^{TA} *and Codemoc* The work in [10] considers the model checking of paths specified by DTAs with multiple clocks. It actually changes also the semantics of how the DTA reads a path in the CTMC, so, even for the single clock case it might not be trivial to specify a CSL^{TA} properties using the DTAs in [10]. The lower part of Figure 2 shows the algorithm used in the Codemoc tool [11] to model check CSL^{TA} with multiple clocks: the cross product is built and then a *region graph* (a classical construction in multi-clock timed automata) is computed, which identifies a *Piece-wise Deterministic process*, that is then solved through the numerical solution of a set of differential partial equations. Codemoc has a specific procedure for the case of single clock DTAs (since in this case the stochastic process reduces to an MRP) , which builds and solves the embedded DTMC of the MRP. This last solution does not work very well and we could not use it in our comparison part.

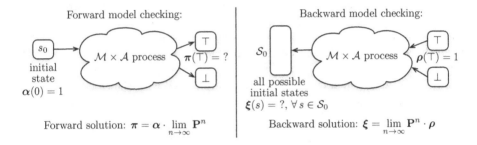

Fig. 3. Forward and backward model checking

Forward vs, backward approaches. Forward and backward model checking refers to the two different ways of formulating the system of linear equations to compute the $\mathcal{P}()$ operator. Figure 3 shows the different approaches and the solution equations. The forward method starts with the probability vector α at time 0, and computes the limiting probability π of reaching the $\top$ state. Backward probability instead starts with a reward ρ of 1 in the $\top$ state in the long run, and computes, for each state, the probability of reaching the $\top$ state, at the same cost as the computation of the forward probability from a *single* initial state. Note that, despite its name, even in the backward approach the $\mathcal{M} \times \mathcal{A}$ state space is built forward, starting from one or more initial states, and it is only the numerical solution that works backward.

Overdimensioning of the state space In some cases, the $\mathcal{M} \times \mathcal{A}$ process contains more states than it is needed. This is very clearly indicated by considering the cross-product between a generic CTMC $\mathcal{M}$ and the DTA of Figure 1(A) depicted in (B). The $\mathcal{M} \times \mathcal{A}$ is represented in compact form (putting together all states with the same (l, c) pair. It is clear from the picture that the two sets of states in the rightmost zone $(20, \infty)$ are useless, since the objective is to compute the probability of reaching $\top$, a computation that can be correctly performed even if the two sets are substituted by a single $\bot$ state. Since any of the two sets can be as big as the whole state space, the substitution with a single state can be particularly interesting.

3 The Zoned-DTA Technique

To avoid the construction of non useful states in the cross-product we propose to expand the DTA automaton $\mathcal{A}$ into its *zoned transition system* (ZDTA) $\mathcal{Z}(\mathcal{A})$, where each state is a pair (location, clock zone). This new structure is then analyzed to collapse into a single $\bot$ state each pair for which there is no path that leads to an accepting location, before building the cross-product $\mathcal{M} \times \mathcal{Z}(\mathcal{A})$.

Zoned DTA. Let us recall that C is the ordered set of clock values that label the $\mathcal{A}$ clock constraints, with the addition of 0 and ∞, and we write $C = \{c_0, c_1, \ldots, c_m\}$, with $c_0 = 0$, $c_{i+1} > c_i$ $\forall i \in [0, m)$ and $c_m = \infty$. Then two clock values $a, b \in \mathcal{R}_{\geq 0}$ are in the same *equivalence class* if, for all edges e, the evaluation of the clock constraint of e is unchanged. A zone automaton $\mathcal{R}(\mathcal{A})$ records the smallest set of *equivalence classes* of clock values, denoted as *zones*. Since $\mathcal{A}$ has a single clock x, classes in $\mathcal{R}(\mathcal{A})$ have form $[x = c]$ or $(c < x < c')$, for all the values $c \in C$. Therefore, the construction of $\mathcal{R}(\mathcal{A})$ is a straightforward partitioning of $\mathbb{R}_{\geq 0}$, as in [9]. From the above we can build a Zoned DTA $\mathcal{Z}(\mathcal{A})$ for any DTA $\mathcal{A}$, in which the locations of $\mathcal{A}$ are paired with the clock zones. We first define the set of *immediate zones* $\dot{C}$ and the set of *timed zones* $\overline{C}$.

$$\dot{C} \stackrel{\text{def}}{=} \left\{ [c] \mid c \in C \right\} \qquad \text{and} \qquad \overline{C} \stackrel{\text{def}}{=} \left\{ (c, \text{next}(c)) \mid c \in C \right\}$$

Starting from the initial location $(l_0, [c_0])$ we can generate all possible reachable pairs $(l_0, [c])$, or $(l, (c, \text{next}(c)))$ through a set of rules that can be found in [13].

Figure 4 illustrates the zoned DTAs of two sample DTAs. Each location in (c) and (d) reports the location $z \in Z$, the state proposition of l (that holds also in each $z = \langle l, c \rangle$), and, on the second line, the DTA location and the clock zone. Immediate and timed locations are drawn with a dotted and a solid border, respectively, while final locations have a double border. The set of locations that cannot reach a final location are colored in gray. Edges are marked as χ if they are generated from a *Boundary* edge of the DTA, δ (let time elapse) otherwise. The timed reachability of some locations (for instance z_8 and z_9 in (d)) represents an information that is not directly available in the DTA $\mathcal{A}$. These locations are irrelevant for the computation of the path probability, and can be discarded, since they will never reach a final location. Observe also that the construction of (d) could be modified to avoid the construction of the edge $z_2 \stackrel{\delta}{\longrightarrow} z_3$: indeed the *Boundary* edges ② and ③ in the DTA have priority over the ① edge and the process will take for sure one of the first two edges, since the logic condition for remaining in l_0 in $[\alpha]$ is: $\Phi_1 \wedge \neg(\Phi_2 \vee (\Phi_1 \wedge \neg\Phi_2))$ which always evaluates to false, for any CTMC. If z_3 is unreachable, also z_4 and z_5 are so they could be removed. This condition can be evaluated for any χ edge, to remove those locations that

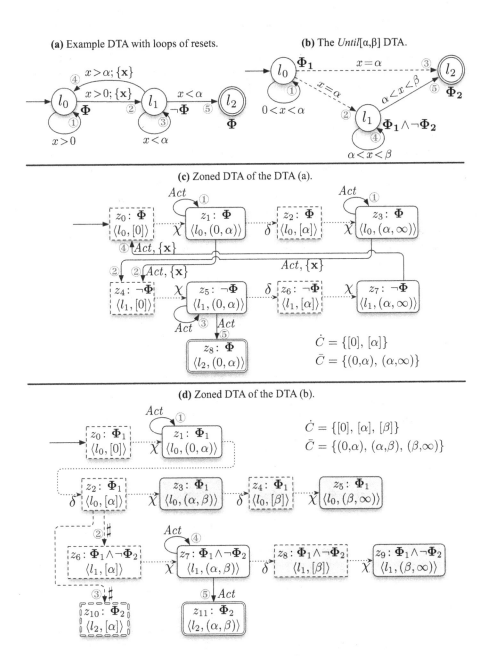

(a) Example DTA with loops of resets.

(b) The *Until*[α,β] DTA.

(c) Zoned DTA of the DTA (a).

$\dot{C} = \{[0], [\alpha]\}$

$\bar{C} = \{(0,\alpha), (\alpha,\infty)\}$

(d) Zoned DTA of the DTA (b).

$\dot{C} = \{[0], [\alpha], [\beta]\}$

$\bar{C} = \{(0,\alpha), (\alpha,\beta), (\beta,\infty)\}$

Fig. 4. Two sample DTAs with their associated zoned DTAs

are logically unreachable. Each location $\langle l, c \rangle$ of Fig. 4(c,d) is labeled with the state proposition expressions of l. The presence of immediate zones can make the construction of the $\mathcal{M} \times \mathcal{Z}(\mathcal{A})$ process more complex and we prefer to define the concept of *tangible zoned DTA*, where only timed locations are kept, and boundary locations are collapsed with a transitive closure. The firing of a sequence of DTA *Boundary* edges $l_0 \xrightarrow{\gamma_1, \sharp, r_1} l_1 \xrightarrow{\gamma_2, \sharp, r_2} \ldots \xrightarrow{\gamma_n, \sharp, r_n} l_n$ may happen only if all the state proposition expressions $\Lambda(l_0), \Lambda(l_1), \ldots, \Lambda(l_n)$ are satisfied by the destination CTMC state s'. A transitive closure of *Boundary* firings is more easily expressed by moving the state proposition onto the edge, which give rise to the Tangible Zoned DTA $\mathcal{T}(\mathcal{A})$ of $\mathcal{A}$.

A TZDTA edge (z, z') has a logical condition λ which is the logical *and* of satisfying the destination location condition $\Lambda(z')$, as well as all the intermediate location conditions $\Lambda(\dot{z}_i), 1 \le i \le n$, and in the last immediate location every other *Boundary* edge must not be satisfied. Given $\mathcal{Z}(\mathcal{A})$, the corresponding $\mathcal{T}(\mathcal{A})$ is constructed by taking all the timed locations and *Inner* edges, and by applying the closure rule on all *Boundary* edges. The ZDTA edges are not marked as either δ or χ since all edges are from tangible to tangible locations.

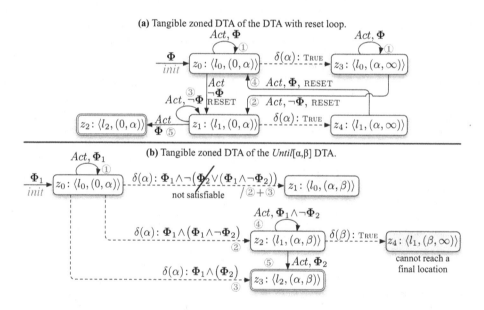

(a) Tangible zoned DTA of the DTA with reset loop.

(b) Tangible zoned DTA of the *Until*[α, β] DTA.

Fig. 5. Tangible zoned DTA of the two DTAs of Fig. 4

Figure 5 shows the *tangible* closure of the two ZDTA of Fig. 4. Boundary edges are all collapsed into δ edges, which are labeled with a state proposition expression that is the transitive closure of all the s.p.e. that must be satisfied to follow that edge. In the tangible ZDTA of the *Until*[t, t'], location z_1 is unreachable because the condition associated to the edge is false. Location z_4 is irrelevant for the computation of the probability of reaching a final state, since any path that reaches this location will certainly be rejected. The advantage of collapsing the state proposition expression of the closure of *Boundary* edges is that it becomes clear whether an edge has an unsatisfiable condition. Each edge is also labelled with the sequence of DTA edges that represents (with circled numbers), and which DTA edges are not satified by the transitive closure (written after a '/'). The structure of Fig. 5(b) shows that there are at most three tangible zones for an $Until[\alpha, \beta]$, while the other two zones can be discarded. This allows to optimize the $\mathcal{M} \times \mathcal{A}$ cross product, by removing irrelevant states in advance.

4   The MC4CSL^TA Tool, Version 2: Features and Assessment

The MC4CSL^TA tool, version 1, presented in [1], based on the theoretical results defined in [16], was meant as a prototype implementation to show the feasibility of model-checking CSL^TA, but it had many drawbacks that make it an unpractical tool to use even on small to medium size examples (around ten thousand states). The main problem was the use of DSPN, as explained above, and the limited set of numerical methods available for matrix-free solution of DSPN solver (as the explicit MRP solution method is never a realistic option). The dependency from DSPN has been solved by implementing directly the $\mathcal{M} \times \mathcal{A}$ construction, which leads to an MRP for which several solution techniques can then be applied, techniques that implement the theoretical advancements in [15] and [2]. The backward solution approach has been implemented for both the matrix-free approach (which is rather straightforward despite the fact that the embedded DTMC **P** is never built or stored) and the component-based method (which can be less intuitive). A full discussion of the topic and the precise formulation of the backward solution process can be found in [13], and it is implemented in version 2. Another issue that has been solved in version 2 is the presence of significant number of states in the $\mathcal{M} \times \mathcal{A}$ process that never lead to the $\top$ state, since the implementation now is based on a cross product of the Markov chain with the tangible zoned DTA.

Figure 6 shows the structure of MC4CSL^TA version 2, available through [17]. The tool takes in input a model, which can be either a Generalized Stochastic

Model checking procedure of MC4CSL^TA ver. 2.

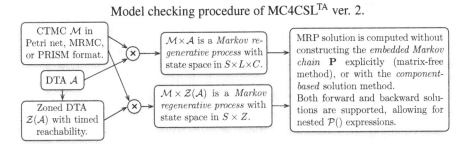

Fig. 6. Structure of MC4CSL^TA version 2

Petri Net in GreatSPN [18] format, or a CTMC in MRMC/Prism format, and a formula specification, which consists of a single clock DTA in textual form. When the input language is a Petri net, the atomic proposition associated with the locations of the timed automaton are expressions over the Petri net marking, while the actions associated to the edges are sets of transitions' names. There are two ways of generating the underlying MRP, according to the two different ways of computing the cross-product: either as $\mathcal{M} \times \mathcal{A}$ or as $\mathcal{M} \times \mathcal{Z}(\mathcal{A})$. We now evaluate the tool correctness and efficiency against Prism and Cosmos. No comparison with version 1 is reported since it would hardly solve the first instances of the proposed models.

Cell cycle control. This first test considers a probabilistic model of the cell replication control in eukaryotes. This biological model is taken from [19], and originally specified in [20]. This model describes the molecular machinery used by eukaryotic cells in order to control their replication. The control mechanism is made by an antagonistic interaction between two proteins, CDK and APC, the first extinguishing the activity of the second and viceversa. The cell replication cycle is controlled by the binding of CDK with its activator cyclin. The state of the model is described by the quantities of the proteins involved in the biochemical interaction, and transitions represent the reactions. The tool directly imports the CTMC produced by Prism.

Table 1 shows three CSL queries asking for the probability of having all the CDK proteins bound by their cyclin activator in a given time window - where N is the quantity of CDK proteins in the system. For the first and second queries, the probability is set at time 10 and in the time interval (10-20). In the third case, the time interval is (0-5), with the condition that the initial state must have a probability of having all the CDK molecules bounded within 1 second.

The table shows the overall model checking time of both tools. For Prism, both the hybrid (default) engine and the sparse engine are used. For MC4CSL^{TA} the timings for the explicit, matrix-free and component-based (SCC) methods are shown. The data reflect the theoretical result of [2], which ensures that the sparse engine of Prism and the SCC method have the same asymptotical cost. The Table also reports, for the (A) and (B) cases, the state space of the MRP produced using the DTA $\mathcal{A}$ or the tangible zoned DTA $\mathcal{T}(\mathcal{A})$ introduced in this paper, which shows the advantage of the method. The time reported are for the tangible ZDTA case. In all the tests, Prism performs better than MC4CSL^{TA}, which is not surprising since the CSL model checking algorithm works with a predefined structure of the formulas and requires fewer steps than that of CSL^{TA}. All tests were run on a Xeon 2.13 GHz single-core of a multicore machine with $128G$ bytes of available memory.

Workflow model. In this second sample we compare the MC4CSL^{TA} tool against the simulator Cosmos [4], which has an input modeling language that is a superset of CSL^{TA} DTAs [12].

Figure 7 shows the (Generalized Stochastic) Petri net of the model [21] which describes an order-handling company. The net illustrates the flow of an order, which involves two separate tasks: preparing and sending the bill to the client, and

Table 1. Performance comparison of Prism 4.1 and MC4CSL^{TA}

(**A**) CSL Until with a single time interval. Durations are expressed in seconds.

N	States	Trns.	Prism 4.1		MC4CSL^{TA}				
			hybrid	sparse	explicit (1 smc)	matrix-free	SCC (1 comp)	$\mathcal{M}$x$\mathcal{A}$ (no zdta)	$\mathcal{M}$x$\mathcal{T}(\mathcal{A})$ (zdta)
2	4666	18342	0.1	0.1	0.1	0.2	0.1	8524	4668
3	57667	305502	1.5	0.7	3.2	11.6	2.8	109148	57667
4	431101	2742012	37.3	14.0	39.7	157.9	38.0	830119	431103
5	2326666	16778785	277.8	144.6	306.3	1277.3	307.7	4525426	2326668
6	9960861	78768799	nc	nc	2267.5	9108.0	2050.9	19495025	9960863

CSL: P=? [true U[10,10] *cyclin_bound*=N]

CSL^{TA}: PROB=? until_AA (10 | | True, (#*cyclin_bound*=N))

(**B**) CSL Until with (t, t') time interval.

N	States	Trns.	Prism 4.1		MC4CSL^{TA}					
			hybrid	sparse	explicit	smc	matrix-free	SCC (2 comp)	$\mathcal{M}$x$\mathcal{A}$ (no zdta)	$\mathcal{M}$x$\mathcal{T}(\mathcal{A})$ (zdta)
2	4666	18342	0.5	0.1	78.61	3827	0.6	0.1	12380	8524
3	57667	305502	2.8	1.5	~29 hours	51394	26.0	5.7	160627	109148
4	431101	2742012	54.3	26.0	-	-	354.3	73.0	1229135	830119
5	2326666	16778785	502.2	234.5	-	-	3814.4	690.6	6724184	4525426
6	9960861	78768799	nc	nc	-	-	21004.2	4646.8	29029187	19495025

CSL: P=? [true U[10,20] *cyclin_bound*=N]

CSL^{TA}: PROB=? until_AB (10, 20 | | True, (#*cyclin_bound*=N))

(**A**) Nested CSL query.

N	States	Trns.	Prism 4.1		MC4CSL^{TA}	
			hybrid	sparse	matrix-free	SCC
2	4666	18342	0.1	0.1	0.1	0.1
3	57667	305502	0.7	0.5	5.7	2.0
4	431101	2742012	17.2	9.6	79.6	25.1
5	2326666	16778785	159.1	78.3	608.9	192.0
6	9960861	78768799	nc	nc	3356.6	1123.6

CSL: P=? [P>0.5 [true U<1 *cdk_cat*=2] U<5 *cyclin_bound*=2]

CSL^{TA}: PROB=? until_0B(5 | | PROB>0.5 until_0B (1 | | True, #*cdk_cat*=2), #*cyclin_bound*=2)

to ship the requested goods. The company reckons on three types of employees: those who manage accounting (F), logistics (L) and generic employees (E). Different tasks are carried out by different employees. The Petri net is made of some subnets consisting of an immediate transition (thin bar), a place and an exponentially distributed timed transition (white box). Such subnets first allocate one of these staff resources, execute the specified task and then release the resource. The staff is represented by three places *finance*, *logistics* and *employees*. Arrows from and to these three places are drawn only for the case of the activity represented by the *register_E* transition, and omitted in the picture for the other subnets whose transitions have labels with suffixes "_E", "_F" and "_L".

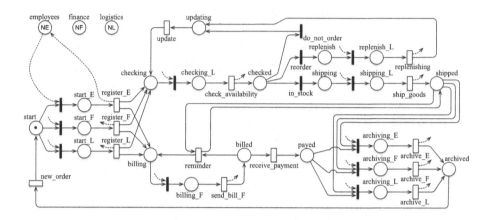

Fig. 7. Petri net of the workflow model

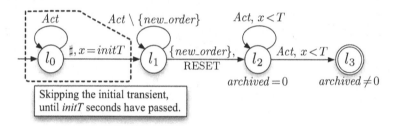

Skipping the initial transient, until *initT* seconds have passed.

Fig. 8. Property tested in the workflow model with Cosmos and MC4CSL^{TA}

The DTA of the measured property is depicted in figure 8. A path starts in the initial state and skips *initT* time units, as an initial transient. Then the DTA waits for the arrival of a *new_order* event, which signals the beginning of the ordering cycle. The path is accepted if the order is *archived* in less than T time units. This DTA can be converted in the input language of Cosmos, allowing for a cross validation of the MC4CSL^{TA} tool for non-CSL queries.

Table 2. Performance comparison of Cosmos and MC4CSL^{TA}

| | | | Cosmos | | | | MC4CSL^{TA} | |
| | | | width=0.001 | | width=0.0001 | | matrix-free | SCC |
N	States	Trns	paths	Time	paths	Time	MC	MC
1	44	81	7000	19.95	63000	58.68	0.75	0.02
2	1811	6408	7000	26.25	62000	177.58	330.64	2.12
3	68942	349980	7000	45.64	67000	413.19	-	210.23
4	2440192	15827904	8000	91.03	75000	669.82	-	~5 hours
5	81M	633M	9000	108.53	85000	1072.15	-	-

The probabilities computed with MC4CSL^{TA} are in accordance with that computed with Cosmos available in [22]. The comparison with Cosmos, on this and on other models, proved to be very useful in detecting errors in MC4CSL^{TA}. Table 2 shows a performance comparison of the simulator Cosmos with the numerical solution of MC4CSL^{TA}, with the timings set to $initT = 100$ and $T = 50$. Simulations were run at a 99% of precision with the confidence interval width reported in the Table. As expected, simulator scales better for large state spaces. The chosen timings of the GSPN transitions and of the DTA queries have been chosen so as to require very long uniformization sequences, thus putting MC4CSL^{TA} in its worst possible conditions, a case in which the advantage of the component-based solution over the matrix-free one is very evident. Tests were run on a Intel core Duo 2.4GHz with $4G$ bytes of memory.

5 Conclusion

This paper presents the new version of the CSL^{TA} model checker MC4CSL^{TA}, which represents a total innovation with respect to the previous version, since it includes a new solution approach which builds on some recently published results on MRP solution and on the construction of a zoned DTA, presented in this same paper. The tool has been evaluated for correctness and performance against the well-known CSL model checker Prism (on the subset of the DTA which can be equivalently expressed as a CSL property) and with the statistical model checker Cosmos, for whose formulas that go beyond CSL. The reported tests, as well as some other tests reported in [13], suggest that the new version of MC4CSL^{TA} is a mature tool, able to deal with very large state spaces, where, again, large is intended as "large for being a stochastic process".

The construction of the zoned DTA will be the basis for our future work on the tool. In particular the application of the component-based method for MRPs, paired with the analysis of the ZDTA, can lead to an on-the-fly implementation of the tool: the state space is built component by component, only when it is actually needed for the computation of the probability of the success state $\top$.

References

1. Amparore, E.G., Donatelli, S.: MC4CSL^{TA}: an efficient model checking tool for CSL^{TA}. In: International Conference on Quantitative Evaluation of Systems, pp. 153–154. IEEE Computer Society, Los Alamitos (2010)
2. Amparore, E.G., Donatelli, S.: A component-based solution for reducible markov regenerative processes. Performance Evaluation 70, 400–422 (2013)
3. Kwiatkowska, M., Norman, G., Parker, D.: PRISM: Probabilistic Model Checking for Performance and Reliability Analysis. Performance Evaluation 36, 40–45 (2009)
4. Ballarini, P., Djafri, H., Duflot, M., Haddad, S., Pekergin, N.: COSMOS: a statistical model checker for the hybrid automata stochastic logic. In: Proceedings of the 8th International Conference on Quantitative Evaluation of Systems (QEST 2011), pp. 143–144. IEEE Computer Society Press, Aachen (2011)

5. Aziz, A., Sanwal, K., Singhal, V., Brayton, R.: Model-checking continuous-time Markov chains. ACM Transactions on Computational Logic 1, 162–170 (2000)
6. Katoen, J.P., Zapreev, I.S., Hahn, E.M., Hermanns, H., Jansen, D.N.: The ins and outs of the probabilistic model checker MRMC. Performance Evaluation 68, 90–104 (2011)
7. Heiner, M., Rohr, C., Schwarick, M.: Marcie - model checking and reachability analysis done efficiently. In: Colom, J.-M., Desel, J. (eds.) PETRI NETS 2013. LNCS, vol. 7927, pp. 389–399. Springer, Heidelberg (2013)
8. Donatelli, S., Haddad, S., Sproston, J.: Model checking timed and stochastic properties with CSL^{TA}. IEEE Transactions on Software Engineering 35, 224–240 (2009)
9. Alur, R., Dill, D.L.: A theory of timed automata. Theoretical Comp. Science 126, 183–235 (1994)
10. Chen, T., Han, T., Katoen, J.P., Mereacre, A.: Model checking of continuous-time Markov chains against timed automata specifications. Logical Methods in Computer Science 7 (2011)
11. Barbot, B., Chen, T., Han, T., Katoen, J.-P., Mereacre, A.: Efficient ctmc model checking of linear real-time objectives. In: Abdulla, P.A., Leino, K.R.M. (eds.) TACAS 2011. LNCS, vol. 6605, pp. 128–142. Springer, Heidelberg (2011)
12. Ballarini, P., Djafri, H., Duflot, M., Haddad, S., Pekergin, N.: HASL: An expressive language for statistical verification of stochastic models. In: Proceedings of the 5th International Conference on Performance Evaluation Methodologies and Tools (VALUETOOLS 2011), Cachan, France, pp. 306–315 (2011)
13. Amparore, E.G.: States, actions and path properties in Markov chains. PhD thesis, University of Torino, Italy (2013)
14. German, R.: Iterative analysis of Markov regenerative models. Performance Evaluation 44, 51–72 (2001)
15. Amparore, E.G., Donatelli, S.: Revisiting the Iterative Solution of Markov Regenerative Processes. Numerical Linear Algebra with Applications, Special Issue on Numerical Solutions of Markov Chains 18, 1067–1083 (2011)
16. Amparore, E.G., Donatelli, S.: Model Checking CSL^{TA} with Deterministic and Stochastic Petri Nets. In: Proceedings of the 2010 IEEE/IFIP International Conference on Dependable Systems and Networks (DSN). IEEE Computer Society Press (2010); DSN-PDS 2010
17. Amparore, E.G., Donatelli, S.: The $MC4CSL^{TA}$ model checker (2013), http://www.di.unito.it/~amparore/mc4cslta/
18. Baarir, S., Beccuti, M., Cerotti, D., Pierro, M.D., Donatelli, S., Franceschinis, G.: The GreatSPN tool: recent enhancements. SIGMETRICS Performance Evaluation Review 36, 4–9 (2009)
19. Lecca, Priami: Cell Cycle Control in Eukaryotes - Prism case studies (2011), http://www.prismmodelchecker.org/casestudies/cyclin.php
20. Lecca, P., Priami, C.: Cell cycle control in eukaryotes: A BioSpi model. In: Proc. Workshop on Concurrent Models in Molecular Biology (BioConcur 2003). Electronic Notes in Theoretical Computer Science (2003)
21. van der Aalst, W.M.P.: Business process management demystified: A tutorial on models, systems and standards for workflow management. In: Desel, J., Reisig, W., Rozenberg, G. (eds.) ACPN 2003. LNCS, vol. 3098, pp. 1–65. Springer, Heidelberg (2004)
22. Amparore, E.G., Ballarini, P., Beccuti, M., Donatelli, S., Franceschinis, G.: Expressing and Computing Passage Time Measures of GSPN models with HASL. In: Colom, J.-M., Desel, J. (eds.) PETRI NETS 2013. LNCS, vol. 7927, pp. 110–129. Springer, Heidelberg (2013)

End-to-End Performance of Multi-core Systems in Cloud Environments

Davide Cerotti, Marco Gribaudo, Pietro Piazzolla, and Giuseppe Serazzi

Dip. di Elettronica e Informazione, Politecnico di Milano,
via Ponzio 34/5, 20133 Milano, Italy
{cerotti,gribaudo,piazzolla,serazzi}@elet.polimi.it

Abstract. Multi-core systems are widespread in all types of computing systems, from embedded to high-end servers, and are achievable in almost all public cloud providers. The sophistication of the hardware and software architectures make the performance studies of such systems very complicated. Further complexity is introduced by the virtual environments which are the basis of all clouds paradigms. While there have been several studies concerning the performance of multi-core systems considered stand alone, few of them are focused on the end-to-end performance of these systems when accessed through virtualized platforms.

In this paper we describe the results obtained with experiments on both Amazon EC2 and VirtualBox platforms. The experiments are performed with some of the DaCapo benchmarks and with IOzone. The objective is to explore at a high abstraction level how the interference between the characteristics of the applications and those of the architectures impact on the performance that users of multi-core systems experience. We also designed some expressions that, although the high-level of abstraction and the low complexity, have a good precision with regard to the performance prediction of the overall system. We think this is a first step toward understanding the end-to-end performance that a multi-core system is able to provide when accessed through a cloud platform.

1 Introduction

The widespread availability of multi-core systems has brought with it a number of new problems, some of which have yet to be addressed and resolved. Indeed, it soon became clear that the problem of being able to effectively use all the available computational power was very complicated. A number of papers on the performance analysis of stand alone multi-core systems have been published. Most of them are focused on stand alone systems and investigate the impact of different architectural design on some performance indices. For example, multi-threaded design schemes [17], sharing L2 caches between the cores [6], [19], [13] and scheduling [15], [14] for reducing memory and cores contention, optimization algorithms for memory hierarchies[21] are just a few of the studies appeared in the literature. Other papers, like [16], [3] tackle the problem of

M.S. Balsamo, W.J. Knottenbelt, and A. Marin (Eds.): EPEW 2013, LNCS 8168, pp. 221–235, 2013.
© Springer-Verlag Berlin Heidelberg 2013

performance prediction of virtualized multi-core systems using queuing networks models. The computational overhead introduced by virtualization is the subject of other works like [11] and [5]; the computational overhead introduced by a complete cloud environment is investigated in [10].

In this paper, we approach the problem of the evaluation of end-to-end performance provided by multi-core systems that are accessed through a cloud platform. We explore the impact of both the different system's architectural choices and the application characteristics on the end-to-end performance that users experience. To this end, we perform experiments executing some of the DaCapo benchmarks [22] and the IOzone [12] on the Amazon EC2 systems, with up to 8 cores, and on VirtualBox virtual machines executed on a standard x86 quad-core system.

We then propose analytical expressions to approximate the end-to-end response time of the systems at a high level of abstraction, considering both the processors and the I/O resources. This allows us to take into account the interference of the several phenomena that have occurred at the low level of granularity (e.g., the interferences among threads, caches and memory accesses) together with the complexity introduced by the virtualized environments. In this way we can easily estimate the demands D of an application, and then for example use it in performance models like the one in [9] to determine the best consolidation or replication options to match a given performance objective.

The paper is organized as follows. The results obtained from the experiments performed, the measurement environments, the benchmarks used, and the metrics used are presented in Section 2. Section 3 is devoted to evaluate the quality of fitting between the analytical models and the benchmark results. We conclude the paper in Section 4.

2   Experimental Results

In this Section we present the experimental results obtained running a closed workload over different multi-core systems. The goal is to obtain a clear understanding on how the workload characteristics and the multi-core system configuration affects the end-to-end response time. We execute several tests of both CPU-bound and I/O-bound benchmarks increasing the number of concurrently running instances. Firstly we investigate the behavior of single-threaded applications, both CPU-bound and I/O-bound, then we focus on multi-threaded applications and their efficiency when running on multi-core systems.

2.1   Methodology

The focus of this work is to characterize the performance that a user can obtain from a multi-core systems, when running common applications. For this reason we have chosen to use benchmarks that allow the evaluation of user end-to-end completion times of real-life application rather than so called "microbenchmarks". The latter mainly focus on determining very low level features, such as cache miss, spin-locks, and read/write speed. This gives a clear picture on how system resources are utilized, but it does not give sufficient insights on the effective performance that a user may experience when running a real application. In the following we will refer the "end-to-end response time" simply as "response time".

Benchmarks. To test the behavior of CPU-bound applications we use Batik, Sunflow and Xalan from the daCapo[22] suite. The first one produces a number of Scalable Vector Graphics (SVG) images based on the unit tests in Apache Batik, the second renders a set of images using ray tracing, while the last one transforms XML documents into HTML. The three applications are chosen because they represent three different ways to exploit multi-threading. In particular, while the bulk of Batik's work is handled by a single thread, Sunflow and Xalan are able to split the load in several threads. Sunflow is driven by a client thread for each available hardware thread, while Xalan is explicitly driven by the number of hardware threads.

DaCapo benchmarks can be parametrized to best suit the need of the user. In particular we can limit the maximum number of threads spawned by an application to control the usage of the available cores. In most of our tests, we have limited the number of used threads to one, and this should be considered as the default setting of the experiments unless explicitly stated.

To test the performance of I/O-Bound applications, we use IOzone[12]. It is a filesystem benchmark that performs different read-write operations, such as sequential, backward, strided or random access. Parameters such as maximum file size, record size and asynchronicity of I/O operations can be specified. Table 1 summarizes the main features of the used benchmarks.

Table 1. Benchmarks features

Benchmark	Type	Threaded	Parallelism
Batik	Mixed	Single	Low
Sunflow	CPU-bound	Multiple	High
Xalan	CPU-bound	Multiple	Medium
IOzone	I/O-bound	Single	None

Performance Metrics. We compute the response time as the mean time needed to complete a single job in a virtualized environment. As noted in [5] and [7], applications run in such environments are subject to high performance variability. We address this problem in Section 2.4.

2.2 Experimental Setup

Environment. Experiments are run on both a hosted hypervisor and a cloud environment. The hosted hypervisor is a quad-core Asus Intel *i7* [2] laptop with eight physical threads running Windows 8 and *VirtualBox*[18]. For the cloud environment we use the Amazon Elastic Computing Cloud (EC2)[1]: an IaaS cloud computing service that provides on-demand computational and storage power in the form of Virtual Servers. These servers are categorized based on their virtual hardware characteristics into *instances* that can be requested and activated by users. Table 2 summarizes the main features of EC2 instances types.

Table 2. Main characteristics of Amazon EC2 instances (March 2012)

type	Cores	ECU	Approx. core speed	Memory
m1.small	1	1	1 ECU $\sim$ 1.2 GHz	1.7 GB
m1.medium	1	2	2 ECU $\sim$ 2.4 GHz	3.7 GB
m1.large	4	2	2 ECU $\sim$ 2.4 GHz	7.5 GB
m1.xlarge	4	8	2 ECU $\sim$ 2.4 GHz	15.0 GB
m2.xlarge	2	6.5	3.25 ECU $\sim$ 3.9 GHz	17.1 GB
m2.4xlarge	8	26	3.25 ECU $\sim$ 3.9 GHz	68.4 GB
c1.xlarge	8	20	2.5 ECU $\sim$ 3 GHz	7 GB

The tests are run mainly on the *m2.4xlarge* instance type, that is characterized by 8 virtual cores.

Experiments Generation. The Linux distribution we used as guest OS allows to turn off one or more cores using simple bash commands. This feature was exploited to study the behavior of the benchmarks under different core configurations. To execute the full set of experiments, we resort to a bash script able to launch the benchmark applications changing some parameters in each run. For the experiments described in the paper, which require the simulation of a closed system, the bash script manages to keep constant the number of concurrent running benchmark instances. Moreover, it collects the response time of each instance discarding the values that do not satisfy the experiment assumptions. In particular, we remove the initial and final transient of the experiments when the number of concurrent instances is not constant.

2.3   Studies on Virtual CPUs

The first set of experiments investigates the performance of an application running on both a hosted hypervisor and a cloud environment. To this end, we evaluate the response times of the three DaCapo benchmarks run on the local *VirtualBox*[18] installation and on the *m2.4xlarge* EC2 instance type. For what concern the VirtualBox experiments, only 4 out of the 8 available threads have been used to avoid the effects of simultaneous hardware multi-threading. To study a closed workload, during each experiment a constant number of instances of the same benchmark are executed concurrently.

For both EC2 and VirtualBox, we perform a full factorial experiment considering the following parameters: the benchmarks presented in Table 1, the number of cores c and the number of concurrent benchmark instances N ranging from 1 to 10. For each combination of parameters, each experiment is repeated between

40 and 70 times to obtain a statistically significant set of measures. We use an equivalent number of repetitions for the experiments presented in the following Sections.

Each curve in Figure 1 represents the behavior of the selected benchmark executed with a given cores configuration with an increasing number N of concurrent benchmark instances. As expected, the *VirtualBox* VM are faster than the EC2 instances, however both of them show a similar behavior. The two CPU-bound benchmarks, Sunflow and Xalan, maintain a stable response time R as long as N is less than or equal to the number of cores. In such a case, each core handles at most one of the N benchmark instances that, as we impose, it cannot split itself into multiple threads. When N exceeds the number of cores, the response time starts to increase due to the concurrent execution of several instances on the same core. Batik behaves in a similar way, but the response time starts to increase even when N is below the number of cores, in particular around $N = 3$ if the system is 4 cores, around $N = 6$ if the system is 8 cores. Probably this is due to the load characteristics of the benchmark which includes both CPU and I/O operations.

2.4   Performance Variability Analysis

In this Section we study the variability of the response times described in Section 2.3. Several causes of variability in large-scale cloud environment exist: for instance, the geographical location [20] and the architecture of the VMs provided by Amazon [4], the period of time in which the experiments are executed [8]. A detailed analysis of the causes of the variability of the performance is a challenging task and is not the main focus of the present work. In this paper we study the variability due to the application characteristics and the number of cores of the VMs in which the benchmarks run. To reduce the cloud-related sources of variability, we run all the experiments on VMs belonging to the same EU-Ireland (eu-west) availability zone of the Amazon Cloud and in the same period of time.

Figure 2 shows a sub-set of the resulting distributions using *box and whisker plots*[1]: for space constraints we have omitted to show the same type of figures for the other experiments, which however exhibit similar behaviors. Independently on the workload size and the number of cores, the response times of Xalan and Sunflow have quite narrow distributions, however the spread size with respect to the number of cores are different. In particular, in Xalan the spread is greater with a lower number of cores, while in Sunflow the opposite occurs. Disregarding some outliers, the results suggest that the distributions are narrow, and thus that they are well characterized by their mean. Instead, Batik presents a huge

---

[1] The two ends of the box correspond to the first and third quartile, while the two whiskers are respectively the lowest and highest datum inside the 1.5 interquartile range (IQR) below the lower quartile or above the upper. The mean of the distribution is shown with the horizontal line inside the box. Outliers are represented by points outside the whiskers.

VirtualBox   EC2

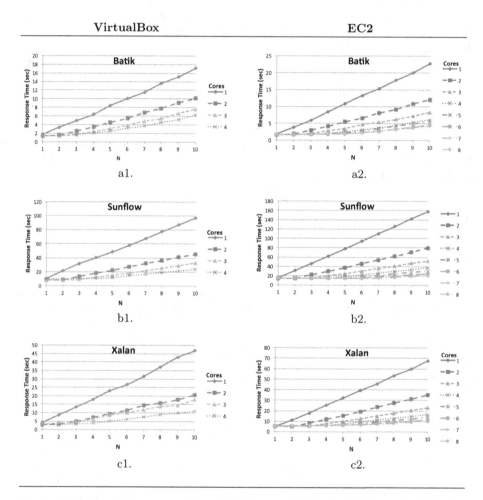

Fig. 1. Response time vs number of instances N of the DaCapo benchmarks. Comparison between single threaded configuration on EC2 and on VirtualBox VMs.

number of outliers independently on number of cores or workload size. This suggests that the response time distributions of Batik could be heavy tail, and that care is needed in characterizing such benchmark only with its mean value. This will also be confirmed by the fitting procedures that will be presented in Section 3.

2.5   I/O-Bound Applications

In this Section we focus on I/O-bound applications. In Figure 3 the behavior of IOzone on Amazon EC2 cloud is shown. In both cases we allocate the same type of EC2 $m1.xlarge$ instance with 4 cores. However, the specific CPU provisioned in the two runs, and thus its computational power, is different. This is due to the allocation policy used by Amazon, where a number of processors with different (but sufficiently similar) computing power may be assigned to satisfy the same instance type request. The impacts on performance of this flexible allocation policy of the CPU was investigated deeply in [4]. In Figure 3a the CPU architecture of the VM provided by Amazon is an Intel $E6545$, while in Figure 3b an $E2 - 2650$ is considered. As it can be seen, the number of active cores does not influence the response time of IOzone directly. Even if each active core can contribute with an extra quantity of caching to the overall capacity, this does not influence the performance of the benchmark. The different power of the two CPU architectures is reflected by the mean response time obtained for different values of the number of concurrent executions N. It is important to note here that the asymptotic behavior is independent of the number of available cores, as expected by an I/O-Bound application. However, the mean response time may vary according to CPU architecture. This outcome extends the validity of the results in [4], obtained for the CPU, also for the I/O.

2.6   Software Multi-threading

A third set of experiments investigates the impact of software multi-threading on the behavior of the DaCapo benchmarks under different core configurations. First, we study how the mean execution time of a single multi-thread run varies as function of the number of cores: in particular, we set the number of threads that benchmark can use equal to the number of available cores. Results are shown in Figure 4. As it can be seen, the one that has the best improvement when increasing the number of cores is Sunflow, since it is the application that can best exploit the parallelization. On the other hand, Batik does not have any improvement, since it is mainly composed by a single thread application. We then focus on Sunflow (since it is the benchmark that can better exploit the parallelization), and we test an increasing number of simultaneous executions, on systems with an increasing number of cores. To this end, we exploit the DaCapo feature that allows to fix the number of threads which Sunflow will be able to use during its execution. The results are show in Figure 5. As it can be seen, an higher number of threads can indeed improve the response time performance of the benchmarks, as long as the system runs a number of instances N less than

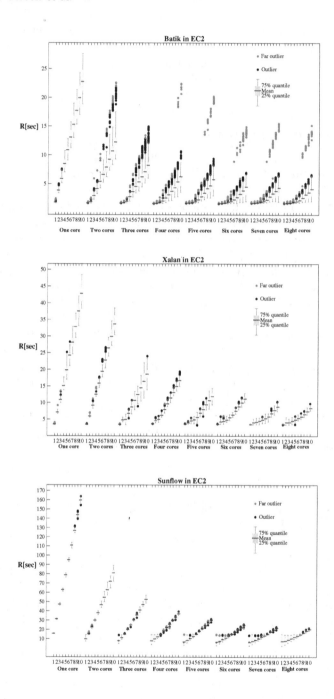

Fig. 2. Response time benchmark distribution. Single threaded configuration with a constant workload size N ranging from 1 to 10 and a number of cores c from 1 to 8.

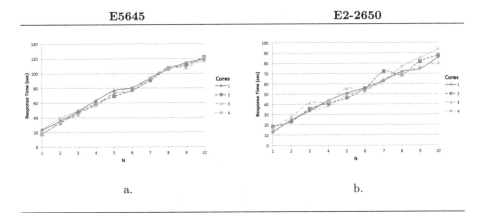

Fig. 3. Response time vs number of instances N of the IOZone benchmarks. Comparison between EC2 architectures E5645 and E2-2650.

or equal to the number of active cores. This also means that multi-threading provides limited advantage when there is a number of instances greater than the number of available cores.

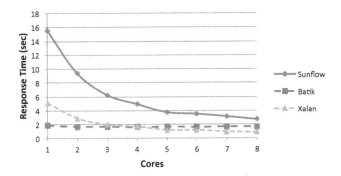

Fig. 4. Response time vs number of cores c of the DaCapo benchmarks on EC2 with a single instance in execution. The number of threads is equal to the number of cores.

2.7 Efficiency

On cloud systems, the provisioning of a single machine with many cores can be more costly than the provisioning of many single-core machines. Thus, when it comes to run several copies of the same application, it can be useful to provide an index that support the user in the choice of running all the instances on a single VM with a large number of cores, or on several single-core VMs. To this end, we propose an index to measure the efficiency of running several instances

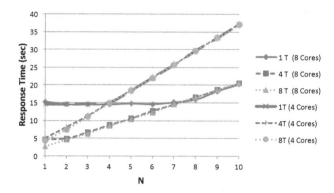

Fig. 5. Response time vs number of instances N of the Sunflow benchmark on EC2 running on 4 or 8 core machines and with different thread configurations.

of an application in a multi-core environment and we run a set of experiments to evaluate it for the considered DaCapo benchmarks. We define the efficiency as:

$$\epsilon = \frac{R(1,1)}{R(n,c)} \tag{1}$$

where $R(n,c)$ is the mean response time obtained when n instances of the selected benchmark run on a c-cores system. The proposed definition is similar to the standard definition of efficiency for parallel applications: speedup divided by number of processors, or $E = T(1)/(n \cdot T(n))$. In multi-core systems $n \cdot T(n)$ is replaced by $R(n,c)$.

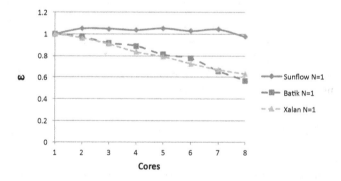

Fig. 6. Efficiency vs number of cores c of the DaCapo benchmarks on EC2 with a single instance in execution

Figure 6 shows how the efficiency decreases as the number of cores increases for both Batik and Xalan: this means that such applications do not have any benefit on running on VMs with a large number of cores, and that it would be a better choice to execute several single application instances on single-core VMs. Sunflow instead exhibits efficiencies greater than one: this means that the common L2 cache architecture, employed by most multi-core systems, reduces the execution times, making thus a better choice to consolidate several instances of the application in a single VM with a larger number of cores.

3   Fitting CPU and I/O Demands in Virtualized Multi-core Systems

3.1   Resource Demand Estimation for Multi-core CPUs

Applying some simplifying assumptions, a multi-core CPU can be seen as a service station of an $M/M/c$ queue, where c represents the number of cores.

The service time required by a complete execution of a job can be characterized by the service demand $D(n, c)$. The response time can be estimated as:

$$R(n, c) = \frac{n}{\min(n, c)} D(n, c) \tag{2}$$

As a first assumption, we assume $D(n, c) = D_{Application}$ constant. The parameter $D_{Application}$ can be estimated from the data using a simple model-parameter fitting procedure. In this work we used the *"GRG solver"* of Microsoft Excel to minimize the squared distance between the response time predicted by the Eq. (2), and the one measured on the real system. The mean relative error of this procedure is reported in column "Application" of Table 3. As it can be seen, the errors are between 10% and 16%. Only Sunflow has a limited error, as shown in Figure 7a.

As a first improvement, we assume the demand $D(n, c)$ depend on the number of jobs n, as long as n is less than or equal to the number of cores c, that is $D(n, c) = D_{Jobs}(\min(n, c))$. The number of parameters to be estimated is equal to the number of cores c. The rationale of this improvement is that a CPU works in the same way independently on the number of cores used: locks and cache misses depends only on the number of concurrent jobs in execution, but only until all the cores are saturated. Column "Jobs" in Table 3 shows that in this case the results are much better, and that the mean error remains high only for Batik, which is the benchmark with the most complex behavior. Figure 7c compares the estimation with the real data for the Xalan benchmark: the ability of making the estimation dependent on the number of jobs, allows the estimated response time to have a variable behavior even when the number of jobs is less than the number of considered cores, a features that has been observed in the measurement.

Another option with c parameters, is to assume the demand dependent on the number of cores, i.e. $D(n, c) = D_{Cores}(c)$. However this extension does not provide great improvement in the results, as it can be seen in Table 3 (column "Cores"). Figure 7b compares the results of the estimation with the real data for the Batik benchmark.

In the most complex scenario, we assume that the demand $D(n, c)$ depend both on the number of jobs n and on the number of cores c, but only until n is less than or equal to the number of cores c. In this case a total of $c(c+1)/2$ parameters is required, and we have $D(n, c) = D_{Full}(\min(n, c), c)$. As expected, this choice provides very good results, even for problematic benchmarks such as Batik, as it can be shown in Table 3 (column "Full") and Figure 7d. Despite being high, the number of parameters is still manageable, (i.e. 10 for a quad-core system, and 36 for an eight core machine).

3.2 Estimating the I/O Demand in Multi-core Environments

As was shown in Figure 3, since the I/O on a multi-core environment cannot be parallelized as the CPU, the behavior of the I/O, is more like an $M/M/1$ queue. Thus, response time can be estimated as:

$$R(n, c) = n \cdot D(n, c) \tag{3}$$

As before, we can fit the measurements by either considering a single demand $D(n, c) = D_{Application}$ for the entire application, or a demand $D(n, c) = D_{Cores}(c)$ that depends on the number of cores (to account for possible speed-up at the OS level that can be achieved by exploiting the multi-core CPU to schedule I/O requests). Both cases produces similar errors, as it can be seen in first two columns of Table 3. A visual comparison of the fitted model (for a single parameter $D_{Application}$) and the measurements is given in Figure 7e.

In order to increase the accuracy, the demand must take into account that the actual service time can vary as function of the number of jobs, due to scheduling and disk optimizations that can be made by the OS when it has to serve a large workload. This however cannot be limited to the number of cores as done for CPU-bound applications, since the OS optimizations takes place for any I/O queue length. As a simplifying assumption, we imagine that the actual demand $D(n, c)$ varies between to levels D_0 and D_1 that represents the speed at which the system can work either when it is under or over-utilized. The same two demands are mixed according to an exponential weight with parameter n_0. In this way, the response time can be estimated as:

$$R(n, c) = n \left[D_0(c) e^{-\frac{n}{n_0(c)}} + D_1(c) \left(1 - e^{-\frac{n}{n_0(c)}} \right) \right] \tag{4}$$

Also in this case, we can consider two cases when either the three parameters depend on the number of cores (the optimization done by the OS can take advantage of an higher number of cores, when present), or not. The two cases have respectively $3 \cdot c$ and 3 parameters, and the results of the fitting are reported in the last two columns of Table 3. As it can be seen in Figure 7f, the ability of varying the demand among a high and a low load, allows the expression to follow precisely the measured behavior. Results further improves when considering a dependency on the number of cores. Despite the increased complexity, also the core dependent expression still maintains a reasonable number of parameters (i.e. 12 for a quad-core, and 24 for an eight core machine).

Table 3. Mean relative fitting errors of the considered demand estimations

Benchmark	Application	Cores	Jobs	Full
Sunflow	3.90%	1.98%	2.20%	0.83%
Batik	16.16%	14.05%	13.93%	4.32%
Xalan	10.87%	10.73%	8.82%	3.19%
IoZone	13.08%	12.75%	5.94%	3.99%

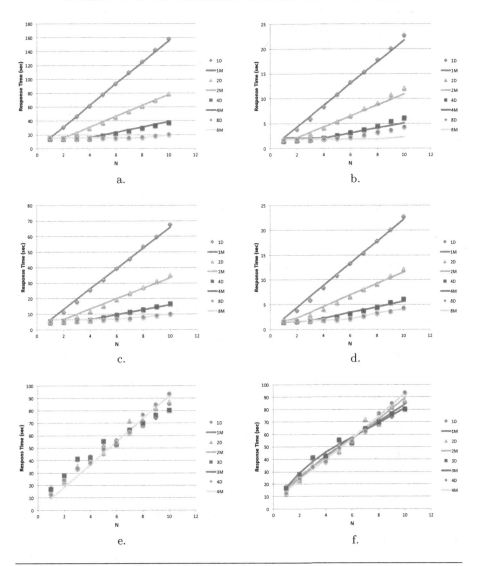

Fig. 7. Fitting of the measured response times against the considered demand models: a - Sunflow, independent; b - Batik, core-dependent; c - Xalan, job-dependent; d - Batik, job and core-dependent; e - IoZone, independent; f - IoZone, job and core-dependent

4   Conclusions

The main contribution of this paper has been measuring the performance and the behavior of benchmark applications in virtualized multi-core environment. The obtained results have been used to define expressions that can provide good estimates of the end-to-end response time, and we have evaluated the distance among the measures and performance indexes. In order to have more accurate parameter estimations, new measurement campaigns, that accounts also for CPU and I/O usage, should be performed: this will lead our future works. Other directions will study transactional workloads, and will consider the effects that can be experienced when considering multiple class of application concurrently running on the same VM.

Acknowledgments. This work has been partially supported by the "AWS in Education research grant" from Amazon, and by the "ForgeSDK" project sponsored by Reply srl.

References

1. Amazon Web Services - Elastic Cloud Computing, http://aws.amazon.com
2. Asus N56VJ specifications, http://www.asus.com/notebooks_ultrabooks/n56vj
3. Benevenuto, F., Fernandes, C., Santos, M., Almeida, V.A.F., Almeida, J.M., Janakiraman, G.J., Santos, J.R.: Performance models for virtualized applications. In: Min, G., Di Martino, B., Yang, L.T., Guo, M., Rünger, G. (eds.) ISPA Workshops 2006. LNCS, vol. 4331, pp. 427–439. Springer, Heidelberg (2006)
4. Cerotti, D., Gribaudo, M., Piazzolla, P., Serazzi, G.: Flexible cpu provisioning in clouds: A new source of performance unpredictability. In: QEST, pp. 230–237 (2012)
5. Cherkasova, L., Gardner, R.: Measuring cpu overhead for i/o processing in the xen virtual machine monitor. In: Proc. of the USENIX Annual Technical Conference, ATEC 2005, pp. 24–24. USENIX Association, Berkeley (2005)
6. Doweck, J.: Microarchitecture and smart memory access (2006), http://software.intel.com/sites/default/files/m/3/4/d/6/3/18374-sma.pdf
7. El-Khamra, Y., Kim, H., Jha, S., Parashar, M.: Exploring the performance fluctuations of hpc workloads on clouds. In: Proceedings of the 2010 IEEE II Intern. Conf. on Cloud Computing Technology and Science, CLOUDCOM 2010, pp. 383–387. IEEE Computer Society, Washington, DC (2010)
8. Ghoshal, D., Canon, R.S., Ramakrishnan, L.: I/o performance of virtualized cloud environments. In: Proceedings of the Second International Workshop on Data Intensive Computing in the Clouds, DataCloud-SC 2011, pp. 71–80. ACM, New York (2011)
9. Gribaudo, M., Piazzolla, P., Serazzi, G.: Consolidation and replication of vms matching performance objectives. In: Al-Begain, K., Fiems, D., Vincent, J.-M. (eds.) ASMTA 2012. LNCS, vol. 7314, pp. 106–120. Springer, Heidelberg (2012)
10. Huber, N., von Quast, M., Hauck, M., Kounev, S.: Evaluating and modeling virtualization performance overhead for cloud environments. In: Leymann, F., Ivanov, I., van Sinderen, M., Shishkov, B. (eds.) CLOSER, pp. 563–573. SciTe Press (2011)

11. Huber, N., von Quast, M., Brosig, F., Kounev, S.: Analysis of the performance-influencing factors of virtualization platforms. In: Meersman, R., Dillon, T., Herrero, P. (eds.) OTM 2010. LNCS, vol. 6427, pp. 811–828. Springer, Heidelberg (2010)
12. IOzone Filesystem Benchmark, http://www.iozone.org
13. Kavadias, S.G., Katevenis, M.G., Zampetakis, M., Nikolopoulos, D.S.: On-chip communication and synchronization mechanisms with cache-integrated network interfaces. In: Proc. of the 7th ACM Int. Conf. on Computing Frontiers, pp. 217–226. ACM, New York (2010)
14. Kim, Y., Han, D., Mutlu, O., Harchol-Balter, M.: Atlas: A scalable and high-performance scheduling algorithm for multiple memory controllers. In: HPCA 2010, pp. 1–12 (January 2010)
15. Liu, F., Jiang, X., Solihin, Y.: Understanding how off-chip memory bandwidth partitioning in chip multiprocessors affects system performance. In: HPCA 2010, pp. 1–12 (January 2010)
16. Menasce', D.A.: Virtualization: Concepts, applications, and performance modeling. In: Proc. of the Computer Measurement Groups 2005 International Conference (2005)
17. Moseley, T., Kihm, J., Connors, D., Grunwald, D.: Methods for modeling resource contention on simultaneous multithreading processors. In: Proceedings of the 2005 IEEE International Conference on Computer Design: VLSI in Computers and Processors, ICCD 2005, pp. 373–380 (2005)
18. Oracle Virtual Box, https://www.virtualbox.org
19. Qureshi, M.K., Patt, Y.N.: Utility-based cache partitioning: A low-overhead, high-performance, runtime mechanism to partition shared caches. In: Proc. of the 39th IEEE/ACM Int. Symp. on Microarchitecture, MICRO 39, pp. 423–432. IEEE Computer Society, Washington, DC (2006)
20. Schad, J., Dittrich, J., Quiané-Ruiz, J.A.: Runtime measurements in the cloud: observing, analyzing, and reducing variance. Proc. VLDB Endow. 3, 460–471 (September 2010), http://dl.acm.org/citation.cfm?id=1920841.1920902
21. Schneider, S., Yeom, J.S., Nikolopoulos, D.: Programming multiprocessors with explicitly managed memory hierarchies. Computer 42(12), 28–34 (2009)
22. The DaCapo Benchmark Suite Website, http://dacapobench.org

Performance Analysis and Formal Verification of Cognitive Wireless Networks

Gian-Luca Dei Rossi, Lucia Gallina, and Sabina Rossi

Università Ca' Foscari, Venezia, Italy
{deirossi,lgallina,srossi}@dais.unive.it

Abstract. Cognitive Networks are a class of communication networks, in which nodes can learn how to adjust their behaviour according to the present and past network conditions. In this paper we introduce a formal probabilistic model for the analysis of wireless networks in which nodes are seen as processes capable of adapting their course of action to the environmental conditions. In particular, we model a network made of mobile nodes using the gossip protocol, and we study how the energy performance of the network varies, according to the topology changes and the transmission power. The stochastic process underlying the model is a discrete time Markov chain. We use the PRISM model checker to obtain, through Monte-Carlo simulation, numerical results for our analysis, which show how the learning-driven dynamic adjustment of transmission power can improve the energy performance while preserving connectivity.

1 Introduction

Cognitive networks [4] are communication networks in which nodes can alter their behaviour according to changes of the environmental conditions. What differentiate this approach from the one of *cognitive radio* [8] networks are that, while in the latter the choices that nodes can take are restricted to radio channel selection, in the former nodes can take complex decisions, taking into account the global goals of the network. Cognitive processes are particularly useful when we have to deal with ad hoc networks, where the absence of a fixed infrastructure and the dynamic nature of the network topology, as well as the limited power capacities of nodes, make the network prone to problems such as link breakages, energy waste and interferences.

Topology Control is a technique aimed at guaranteeing network connectivity, while optimising network performance with respect to several metrics, depending on the specific objective of each single network.

Although several formal models for the analysis of wireless ad hoc and sensor networks and for cognitive radio networks were proposed in the literature (see, e.g., [13,5]), to the best of our knowledge formal models for the analysis of cognitive networks are rare. In [9] the authors discuss the issues concerning the definition of a PEPA model for cognitive networks, although they do not propose any actual model, and thus they do not perform any quantitative or qualitative analysis.

M.S. Balsamo, W.J. Knottenbelt, and A. Marin (Eds.): EPEW 2013, LNCS 8168, pp. 236–250, 2013.

PRISM [10] is a tool for modelling and analysing systems that exhibit a probabilistic behaviour. It supports, among others, the modelling of Markov Decision Processes (MDPs), where nondeterministic and probabilistic aspects coexist. In addition to the traditional model checking, PRISM provides *statistical model checking*, allowing one to compute probabilities of properties' satisfaction. In particular, PRISM also offers a discrete-event simulator, allowing one to generate approximate results for the verification of properties. This approach is particularly useful for very large models, when other approaches to model checking are not feasible, due to the well known problem of state space explosion.

This paper presents a probabilistic model for the analysis of networks exhibiting cognitive behaviours. The model is written in the PRISM language, and supports broadcast communications, node mobility, and the ability of nodes to dynamically adjust the transmission power during their operations.

Paper structure. The paper is organised as follows. In Section 2 we give an introduction to the use of cognitive networks for topology control, Section 3 reviews the basic features of PRISM that we use in the rest of the paper. In Section 4 we introduce a novel model for cognitive networks, and in Section 5 we use the PRISM tool to analyse its behaviour, giving numerical examples. Finally, in Section 6 we give some final remarks, concluding the paper.

2   Topology Control with Cognitive Networks

Topology Control [14] is a technique aimed at guaranteeing the connectivity of a communication network, while limiting other cost factors, such as the level of interference and the energy consumption, thus extending the network lifetime. In the presence of mobility this problem is not trivial, since the network topology continuously changes, causing frequent link breakages and variations in the interference levels. In wireless networks, this can be considered as the problem of finding a trade-off between power saving and network connectivity through the choice of the appropriate transmission power for each node. It is evident that if each node transmits at a low power, then its connectivity level, and potentially the one of the whole network, will be reduced, while if we assign high transmission power to the nodes, we generally enhance the connectivity of the network, but we consume far more energy. This relation is, indeed, not a trivial one, since increasing transmission power, and thus the coverage area of a radio station, can increase the chances of collisions and interferences, decreasing the whole network connectivity. For omni-directional antennas we can reasonably model the coverage radius as a function of the power used by the transmitter, and vice-versa. The function can be arbitrary, but usually the coverage radius is proportional to the square root of the transmission power [12]. Of course connectivity is also influenced by factors independent from the transmission power, such as routing and link-level protocols. However in this paper we focus on energy consumption, leaving all the other factors unchanged. In particular, we assume that the network uses the well-known *gossip* protocol to propagate messages.

In this article we also assume that every node in the network is somewhat smart, and capable of applying some strategies to decide its transmission power, based on the conditions in which it operates. In particular, we assume that, observing the past behaviour of the network, or using some link-level techniques usually employed for interference, collision and congestion detection [17], each node is able to guess how many other stations are present in a given radius. Given that information, the node can perform a very simple decision, i.e.,

- If there is a radius $r < r_{\max}$ for which there are at least n other nodes, use the minimum transmission power capable of transmitting with radius r.
- Use the maximum allowed power, corresponding to radius $r_{\max}$, otherwise.

It is clear that, due to mobility and interferences, the guess of the aforementioned node can be wrong, however this mistake will have an effect on the next retransmissions of the node itself. In this way, we have just defined a *cognitive network* in which nodes are able to learn, from the observed environment, an appropriate behaviour for the net itself.

3   The PRISM Model Checker

PRISM [10] is a probabilistic model checker which supports several types of models, such as *discrete-time Markov chains* (DTMCs), *continuous-time Markov chains* (CTMCs), *Markov decision processes* (MDPs), and Probabilistic Timed Automata (PTA). Models are expressed using PRISM's own language.

This paper deals with models that can be represented by Discrete Time Markov Chains [15], and studies their qualitative and quantitative properties using model checking techniques. In the following we briefly introduce the main aspects of the PRISM language.

3.1   Modules

PRISM models consist of modules, expressed through a simple state-based language. A *module* is specified as:

```
module name
...
endmodule
```

and it is composed of variables and commands. *Variables* are names associated to values. The syntax for variables is:

```
name : [ range ] init initial_value;
```

Commands describe all the possible behaviours of the modules, i.e. all the possible transitions from one state to another. They include *guards*, which indicate the states where the transitions can occur, and the *updates*, which modify the variables in order to reach the arrival states. The syntax for a command is:

```
[action]  guards -> p1:update1 + p2:update2 .. pn:updaten;
```

where $p1, ..., pn$ express the probability of each possible update ($\sum_{i=1}^{n} p_i = 1$), guards is the list of conditions associated to that transitions, and action is the label of the transitions, which is used to synchronise different modules, since two modules can synchronise if they can execute an action with the same label.

3.2   The Property Specification Language

PRISM provides a specification language to express rewards and quantitative properties and it supports the automated analysis of these properties with respect to the probabilistic models. It supports several temporal logics, such as PCTL (Probabilistic Computation Tree Logic) and LTL (Linear Temporal Logic) [7]. In particular, when dealing with DTMCs, the PRISM property specification language enables us to study many important properties, such as the probability to reach a particular state under some conditions.

The **P** operator is used to reason about the probability of the occurrence of an event. Formally, we write:

```
P bound [ pathprop ]
```

which is true if the probability that the path property pathprop is satisfied by the paths reachable from the initial states respects the bound bound.

We can also adopt a quantitative approach, by computing the actual probability that a path property is satisfied. An example is:

```
P =? [pathprop]
```

which computes the probability of satisfying pathprop.

The PRISM property specification language introduces a set of *temporal operators* in order to express the PCTL path formulas or the LTL formulas which can be verified for a single path of a model. Among these operators, the most used are **F**, which expresses the property that the condition will be eventually satisfied by the path, and **G** which expresses the property that the condition is always true (i.e., it expresses the *invariancy* property).

3.3   Costs and Rewards

Reward properties are based on the possibility of defining rewards associated with a given PRISM model. Rewards can assign values, or costs, either to states or transitions. We are interested in transitions rewards, whose syntax is:

```
rewards ''name''
[action_1] constraint_1 : cost_1
[action_2] constraint_2 : cost_2
...
[action_n]constraint_n : cost_n
endrewards
```

where, for each $i \in [1 - n]$ assigns the cost cost_i to the transitions labelled with [action_i] satisfying the constraint constraint_i.

With the PRISM property specification language we can use the **R** operator to compute the expected value of the rewards associated with the model. As for the *reachability properties* (the **P** operator), we can verify if the cost of reaching the states satisfying some particular property respects a certain bound:

```
R bound [ rewardprop ]
```

We can also compute the expected cost of reaching states satisfying a given property:

```
R = ?  [F rewardprop]
```

3.4   Statistical Model Checking

Due to the well-known problem of state space explosion, in addition to the standard model checking techniques, which need to build the entire model for the verification of properties, PRISM also provides a *discrete-event simulator*, which can be used to perform approximate (or statistical) model checking. Approximate results can be obtained by generating a large number of paths through the model, without building the entire state space, evaluating the properties on each run, and using the information to generate approximate results. This technique can be used to analyse both reachability and reward properties, and it is particularly useful to study models with a large number of modules and interactions (see [11]).

4   The Model

We consider a wireless network with both static and mobile devices, where communications are carried on using a basic gossip protocol. Nodes can, through radio-frequency channels, broadcast messages, which are receivable by all the nodes which are inside the sender node's transmission area and are listening to the same channel. We analyse the energy costs of a multi-hop communication between two random network nodes, and we study how the ability of learning and reasoning in the processes behaviour can improve the performance of the network.

In particular, we model 15 mobile nodes, and 10 static nodes, evenly distributed in a network area of 50×100 square meters, as depicted in Figure 1. The static nodes are located at positions $\{7, 9, 17, 19, 27, 29, 37, 39, 47, 49\}$, while the movements for all the other nodes are described by the bidirectional arrows in Figure 1. We model the network area as a grid of 5×10 cells. The distances between cells are determined by considering the centre of each cell and calculating the euclidean distance between each pair of centres (each cell is 10×10 square metres). Moreover, we consider each node as a cognitive process, that can dynamically change the transmission power for its communications, depending on the position of its active neighbours, with the global aim of an efficient topology control. Usually, modern technologies allow the devices to choose among a

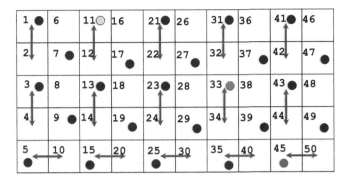

Fig. 1. Topology of the Network

discrete set of possible power levels. In what follows we will use the transmission radius to represent the transmission power, since those quantities are strictly related. As we mentioned in Section 2, usually the power spent for a transmission is proportional to the squared radius. The processes that model nodes listen to the channel and, when they receive a message, they forward it, according to the gossip strategy, i.e., they will forward the message with a certain probability psend, and discard it with probability 1 − psend. We will study the performance of the network, for different gossip strategies, i.e., with the value of the forwarding probability ranging in the set $\{0.65, 0.7, 0.75, 0.8, 0.85, 0.9, 0.95, 1.0\}$.

Several papers, such as [6,1,2,3], already present analysis of gossip-based protocols, comparing modifications which are particularly appropriate for ad hoc and wireless networks. In this paper we analyse how the presence of cognitive processes in the network can strongly improve the performance of these kinds of communication protocols. In our model, each node can choose its transmission radius in the set {10m, 15m, 20m}. Specifically, it will choose the minimum radius which ensure the possibility to receive the message for at least two receivers or, if there are not enough available neighbours in the transmission area, it will transmit with its maximum power (radius = 20m).

As introduced in Section 3, the PRISM model checker supports different model types. Here we model the network as a DTMC, where probabilities are used to model both the possible topology changes, and the behaviour of the processes. In what follows we will give the essential elements of the mapping of the aforementioned model in PRISM's own language. Table 1 shows the representation of a single network node.

Variables. The most important variables of our model mapping are the following:

- $steps_i$ controls the sequentiality of the process executed by the sensor node i. In particular, $steps_i = 2$ means that the node is ready to receive, $steps_i = 1$ means that the node is ready to transmit, and $steps_i = 0$ means that the node has completed a transmission.
- l_i: is the variable containing the actual location of the sensor node i.

Table 1. The PRISM module for a node

```
module P8
steps8 : [0 .. 2] init 2;
18 : [15 .. 20] init 15;

[move] (18 = 15) → 0.8 : (18′ = 20) + 0.8 : (18′ = 15);
[movee] (18 = 20) → 0.8 : (18′ = 15) + 0.8 : (18′ = 20);

//beginning of a new round
[round] no_one_sending → (steps8′ = 2);

//transmission
//[c8] (steps8 = 1) → (steps8′ = 0);

//reception
[c3] (steps8 = 2)& s1p3 & s1p38 → psend : (steps8′ = 1) + (1 − psend) : (steps8′ = 0);
[c3] (steps8 = 2)& s2p3 & s2p38 → psend : (steps8′ = 1) + (1 − psend) : (steps8′ = 0);
[c3] (steps8 = 2)& s3p3 & s3p38 → psend : (steps8′ = 1) + (1 − psend) : (steps8′ = 0);
[c3] (steps8! = 2) |!((s1p3 & s1p38) | (s2p3 & s2p38) | (s3p3 & s3p38)) → (steps8′ = steps8)

[c5] (steps8 = 2)& s2p5 & s2p58 → psend : (steps8′ = 1) + (1 − psend) : (steps8′ = 0);
[c5] (steps8 = 2)& s3p5 & s3p58 → psend : (steps8′ = 1) + (1 − psend) : (steps8′ = 0);
[c5] (steps8! = 2) |!((s2p5 & s2p58) | (s3p5 & s3p58)) → (steps8′ = steps8)

[c7] (steps8 = 2) & s1p7 & s1p78 → psend : (steps8′ = 1) + (1 − psend) : (steps8′ = 0);
[c7] (steps8 = 2) & s2p7 & s2p78 → psend : (steps8′ = 1) + (1 − psend) : (steps8′ = 0);
[c7] (steps8 = 2) & s3p7 & s3p78 → psend : (steps8′ = 1) + (1 − psend) : (steps8′ = 0);
[c7] (steps8! = 2) |!((s1p7 & s1p78) | (s2p7 & s2p78) | (s3p7 & s3p78)) → (steps8′ = steps8)

[c10] (steps8 = 2) & s1p10 & s1p108 → psend : (steps8′ = 1) + (1 − psend) : (steps8′ = 0);
[c10] (steps8 = 2) & s2p10 & s2p108 → psend : (steps8′ = 1) + (1 − psend) : (steps8′ = 0);
[c10] (steps8 = 2) & s3p10 & s3p108 → psend : (steps8′ = 1) + (1 − psend) : (steps8′ = 0);
[c10] (steps8! = 2) |!((s1p10 & s1p108) | (s2p10 & s2p108) | (s3p10 & s3p108)) → (steps8′ = steps8)

[c12] (steps8 = 2)& s2p₁2 & s2p128 → psend : (steps8′ = 1) + (1 − psend) : (steps8′ = 0);
[c12] (steps8 = 2)& s3p₁2 & s3p128 → psend : (steps8′ = 1) + (1 − psend) : (steps8′ = 0);
[c12] (steps8! = 2) |!((s2p₁2 & s2p128) | (s3p₁2 & s3p128)) → (steps8′ = steps8)

[c13] (steps8 = 2)& s1p13 & s1p138 → psend : (steps8′ = 1) + (1 − psend) : (steps8′ = 0);
[c13] (steps8 = 2)& s2p13 & s2p138 → psend : (steps8′ = 1) + (1 − psend) : (steps8′ = 0);
[c13] (steps8 = 2)& s3p13 & s3p138 → psend : (steps8′ = 1) + (1 − psend) : (steps8′ = 0);
[c13] (steps8! = 2) |!((s1p13 & s1p138) | (s2p13 & s2p138) | (s3p13 & s3p138)) → (steps8′ = steps8)

endmodule
```

Modelling the Network Topology. In order to model the level of connectivity of the network, which dynamically changes depending on the positions of the nodes inside the network area, and before defining the modules for the network nodes, we introduce a list of formulas, which allow us to verify the distance between each pair of possible neighbours. In particular, for each pair $i, j \in \{1, ..., 25\}$ and for each $h \in \{2, 3, 4\}$, if the formula shpij is true, it means that the node P_j is actually able to listen to a P_i's transmission with radius $5 \times h$. Moreover, for each $i \in \{1, ..., 25\}$ and for $h \in \{2, 3, 4\}$, if the formula shpi is true, then there exists at least two possible receiver nodes inside the transmission area of the sender, when transmitting with radius $5 \times h$. Table 2 shows the set of formulas modelling the connectivity of P_1. As an example,

$$\text{formula s1p12} = ((\text{steps2} = 2) \& (12 - 11 = 1));$$

is true when node P_2 is ready to receive (steps2 = 1), and the distance between P_1 and P_2 is 1, i.e., looking at Figure 1, is true only when $l1 = 2$ and $l2 = 3$,

Table 2. Connectivity formulas

```
//P1 strategies
formula s1p12 = ((steps2 = 2) & (12 − 11 = 1));
formula s1p14 = ((steps4 = 2) & (14 = 11 − 5));

formula s2p12 = s1p12;
formula s2p14 = (steps4 = 2);
formula s2p15 = ((steps5 = 2) & (15 − 11 = 6));

formula s3p12 = ((steps2 = 2) & (12 − 11 < 3));
formula s3p14 = (steps4 = 2);
formula s3p15 = s2p15;
formula s3p16 = ((steps6 = 2) & (16 − 11 = 10));

formula s1p1 = (s1p12 & s1p14);
formula s2p1 =!s1p1 & ((s2p12 & s2p14) | (s2p12 & s2p15) | (s2p14 & s2p15));
formula s3p1 =!s1p1 & !s2p1;
```

which, since we consider the nodes lying in the centre of each cell, means that
radius 10m guarantees their connection.

Transitions.

- [move]: is the transition modelling the periodic topology changes. Node mobility is expressed in terms of the transition matrix of a discrete time markov
  chain: each entry of the matrix denotes the probability that a sensor node
  moves from a location to another. In particular, static nodes are associated
  with the identity m atrix. When the transition move is performed, a node
  will change location with probability ε, and will remain in the same location
  with probability $1 - \varepsilon$. Here we choose 0.8 as the value for ε.
- [round]: is the transition occurring when no more transmissions are possible.
  At the end all the nodes will be in the reception state ($steps_i = 2$), except
  for the sender node, whose *steps* variable will be set to 1.
- [ci]: is the transition modelling a broadcast trasmission. In particular, if
  a node is in the state *ready to transmit* ($steps_i = 1$), it will execute the
  following transition:

$$[ci] \, (steps_i = 1) \rightarrow (stepsi' = 0);$$

meaning that the node i transmits the message and then transits in a sleeping
phase. If another node P_j is in the state *ready to transmit* ($steps_j = 2$), and
it is inside the transmission area of the sender node (s1pij, s2pij, s3pij), it
will synchronize with the sender node and receive the message. Transition [ci]
($steps_j = 2$)&s1pi&s1pij $\rightarrow$ psend : ($steps_j' = 1$) + (1 − psend):($steps_j' = 0$);
models the basic gossip strategy: the node receiving the message will forward it
with probability psend, and discard it with probability 1 − psend.

Rewards. As introduced in Section 3, PRISM allows us to specify rewards (or costs), associated to both states and transitions. In order to study the energy performance of the networks, we associate a cost to each transition. In particular, for each transition $[ci]$ (meaning that P_i is sending a message) we verify which transmission power has been used for the transmission (s1p1, s2p1 or s3p1), and we use the values 1 for radius 10 m, 1.5 for radius 15m and 2 for radius 20m.

We are interested also in studying how many retransmissions the sender must perform before the communication is successfully completed. In order to do so, we introduce another reward, simply assigning 1 to each transition tagged with [round].

Formally, rewards are written as follows:

```
rewards "rounds"
    [round] true : 1;
endrewards

rewards "costs"
[c1] s1p1 : 1;
[c1] s2p1 : 1.5;
[c1] s3p1 : 2;
[c2] s1p2 : 1;
[c2] s2p2 : 1.5;
[c2] s3p2 : 2;}
[c3] s1p3 : 1;
[c3] s2p3 : 1.5;
[c3] s3p3 : 2;}
. . .
endrewards
```

5   Simulations and Results

In this section we show some numerical results obtained using our model for the analysis of connectivity and performance properties of wireless networks. As usual for large models, we use statistical model checking, using the discrete-event simulator of PRISM.

We show how, using a cognitive process, which is able to dynamically adjust the transmission power of a node depending on the relative positions of the surrounding ones, it is possible to improve the performance of the network, guaranteeing a high level of connectivity, while limiting the energy consumption.

In the following examples, we use the same network that we have seen in Section 4, and we set the node P_{23}, i.e., the red node in Figure 1, as the final destination for the communications, while we change the sender node, in order to study how the performance of the network depend on the relative distance between sender and receiver. In particular we will show numerical results using as sender either the node P_{17} or the node P_6, i.e., the blue and yellow nodes in Figure 1, respectively.

We compare the connectivity and the power consumption of the cognitive network with other networks having exactly the same topology and using the same gossip strategy, but with a fixed transmission power.

5.1   Reachability Property

We first study the reachability properties of the system, i.e., the probability to reach a successful state of the model, which corresponds to the correct reception of a message by the final destination of the network.

In our PRISM representation of the model, since steps23 = 1 means that the node P_{23} has correctly received the message, the formula which represents the success of the communication is

$$\text{formula goal} = (\text{steps}23 = 1);$$

and the property that we are interested in verifying is

P=?[F goal]

which gives us the probability that the sender and the receiver nodes will eventually complete their communication successfully.

As stated before, in order to perform statistical model checking, i.e., to get approximate results for the verification of properties, we use the PRISM simulator, that relies on Monte Carlo simulations. As we expected, since we assume that the sender node may retransmit a possibly infinite number of times, the probability to reach the goal state was correctly computed as 1.0 for all the network configurations, where the confidence interval was $+/-0$, based on a confidence level 95%. This result ensures us that, in our setting , using a fixed transmission power or dynamically changing the transmission power, depending on the surrounding environment, does not affect the network connectivity. Moreover, this result ensures that a message will always reach the destination in a finite number of steps.

Table 3. Results for Energy Costs, Distance = 28,3 m

VariableRadius		FixedRadius = 15	
psend	cost	psend	cost
0.65	26.15733	0.65	25.5838
0.7	23.741	0.7	24.2405
0.75	22.5360	0.75	22.5333
0.8	20.7675	0.8	20.2982
0.85	18.2167	0.85	17.8995
0.9	15.7207	0.9	15.8523
0.95	13.3402	0.95	13.3570
1.0	11.21633	1.0	10.8015

5.2 Energy Cost Properties

As stated before, it is possible to analyse the performance of the network, in terms of energy consumption. As already introduced in Section 4, the transmission radius of a node in a wireless network is usually strictly related to its transmission power. In the literature we can find several formulas to estimate both reception and transmission energy costs (see, e.g., [12], [16]).

Here we abstract from those possible formulas, and we simply assign to each transmission the correspondent transmission radius as a reward. Notice that this is a choice that doesn't affect the complexity of the model or of its analysis. Moreover, we do not consider the energy spent for receiving data or to move, since the former is usually a fixed quantity, which does not depend on the actual activity of the node, and the latter usually come from a different power source, e.g., the legs of the mobile device user.

Again, we analyse the costs using statistical model checking. The reward property that has been studied is:

```
R{``costs''}=?[F goal]
```

As in the previous case, we used a Monte Carlo simulation, and we obtained a maximum confidence interval of $2 - 3\%$ with respect to the averages, based on a confidence level of 95%.

The results for a distance of $28.3m$ are shown in Figure 2.(a).

We notice that, while with a fixed radius of 10 or $20m$, the energy costs of the communications critically increase, especially for small value of the gossip probability psend, using cognitive processes, or a fixed radius of $15m$, the performance is consistently improved. Since the curves for the variable radius and the fixed radius $15m$ almost overlap, Table 3 reports the results in detail.

We analyse the average number of retransmissions, after the first one, that the sender node must perform to complete the communication with the receiver node, since it is useful to better understand the results of the previous reward property verification. Figure 2.(b) shows some results for this kind of analysis. Notice that, by fixing the radius to the maximum value, on average the communication reaches the successful state after less than 1 retransmissions. As an instance, the result for psend $= 0.65$ is 0.67567. Here the energy waste is given by the high power employed for each forwarding, rather than by the number of transmissions to reach the success. Again the curves for the Variable Radius, and the Fixed Radius $15m$ are almost overlapping. This result lead us to the conclusion that, with this particular network configuration, if the processes can dynamically choose their transmission radius, depending on the neighbours' positions, the average radius will be $15m$.

We now perform the same kind of analysis changing the sender. In this case the distance between sender and receiver is $72, 1m$. Figure 3 shows the results for energy consumption: in this case, with a fixed radius of $15m$,the energy performance of the network critically deteriorates. However, the results for a fixed radius $20m$ and a variable radius are similar. Table 4 gives the precise values for each psend. Notice that results for a fixed Radius of $10m$ are not

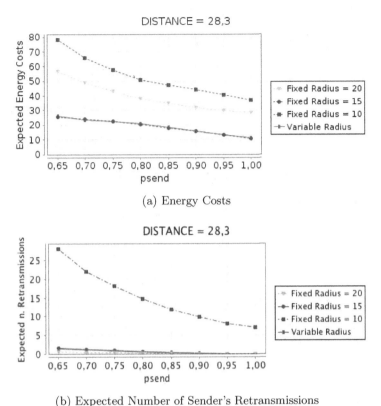

(a) Energy Costs

(b) Expected Number of Sender's Retransmissions

Fig. 2. Distance between sender and receiver: 28,3 m

reported: this is due to the fact taht the power needed for small values of psend is very high and this would have led to an unreadable graph.

Again the analysis of the number of retransmissions by the sender nodes is helpful to understand the behaviour of the network: the curves for a fixed radius and a variable radius are similar. For psend = 0.65 we have, on average, 1.6834 retransmissions for the fixed radius network, and 2.519 for the cognitive networks, while for psend = 1.0 we have 0 on average for both the network configurations), meaning that, for a larger distance a fixed radius 20m is close to the ideal value of the transmission radius to guarantee the energy performance optimisation.

The results prove that, using a fixed radius, the performance of the network strictly depends on the relative positions of the sender and the receiver, while using a variable radius, we always get a power consumption that is closed to the minimum (that is closed to the fixed radius 15m in the first case, and to the fixed radius 20m in the second case).

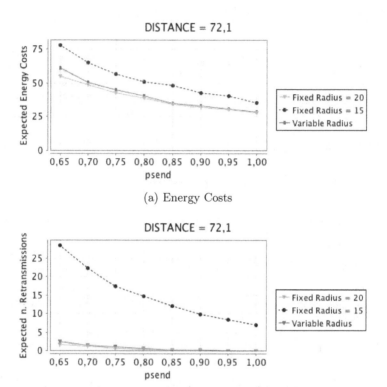

(a) Energy Costs

(b) Expected Number of Sender's Retransmissions

Fig. 3. Distance between sender and receiver: 72,1 m

Table 4. Results for Energy Costs, Distance = 71,2 m

VariableRadius		FixedRadius = 20	
psend	cost	psend	cost
0.65	60.9090	0.65	54.7933
0.7	50.61383	0.7	48.95267
0.75	44.64067	0.75	42.7287
0.8	40.1177	0.8	38.3973
0.85	34.9950	0.85	34.2673
0.9	32.8725	0.9	32.1087
0.95	30.8292	0.95	30.2807
1.0	28.6423	1.0	28.1893

6   Conclusion

In this paper we have presented a probabilistic model for a class of cognitive networks in a wireless setting, in which nodes dynamically choose their transmission power, using data collected from the network itself. We have shown how this model can be encoded in the PRISM language, allowing for the analysis of its performances and for the verification of properties of its behaviour. Moreover, we have used that kind of analysis to compare the energy efficiency of those networks with others based on different strategies, namely ones in which a static transmission power is set. We have given some numerical results about this comparison, and we have concluded that cognitive-networks-based strategies could be effective in the analysed setting.

Future works.   As a further enhancement of our model, we plan to consider more sophisticated routing protocols, and different decision strategies as well. On the other hand, further simplifications of the model could lead to a faster solution, even for models with a greater number of nodes. Moreover, the analysis of different kinds of rewards, such as latencies or throughputs, could, and should, be performed in order to better understand any possible advantage or drawback of a power allocation strategy in wireless settings.

References

1. Dimakis, A.G., Sarwate, A.D., Wainwright, M.J.: Geographic Gossip: Efficient Aggregation for Sensor Networks. In: Proc. of the 5th International Conference on Information Processing in Sensor Networks, pp. 69–76. ACM (2006)
2. Donald, J.S., Yasinac, A.: Dynamic probabilistic retransmission in ad hoc networks. In: Proc. of the Int. Conference on Wireless Networks (ICWN 2004), pp. 158–164. CSREA Press (2004)
3. Fehnker, A., Gao, P.: Formal Verification and Simulation for Performance Analysis for Probabilistic Broadcast Protocols. In: Kunz, T., Ravi, S.S. (eds.) ADHOC-NOW 2006. LNCS, vol. 4104, pp. 128–141. Springer, Heidelberg (2006)
4. Fortuna, C., Mohorcic, M.: Trends in the Development of Communication Networks: Cognitive Networks. Computer Networks 53(9), 1354–1376 (2009)
5. Gelenbe, E., Lent, R.: Power-aware ad hoc cognitive packet networks. Ad Hoc Networks 2(3), 205–216 (2004)
6. Haas, Z.J., Halpern, J.Y., Li, L.: Gossip-based Ad Hoc Routing. IEEE/ACM Trans. Netw. 14(3), 479–491 (2006)
7. Hansson, H., Jonsson, B.: A logic for reasoning about time and reliability. Formal Aspects of Computing 6(5), 512–535 (1994)
8. Mitola III., J.: Cognitive Radio - An Integrated Agent Architecture for Software Defined Radio. PhD thesis, Royal Institute of Technology, Stockholm, Sweden (2000)
9. Guo, L., Wang, J., Zhao, G.: Study on Formal Modeling and Analysis Method Oriented Cognitive Network. In: 2012 Fifth International Symposium on Computational Intelligence and Design (ISCID), vol. 2, pp. 402–405 (2012)
10. Kwiatkowska, M., Norman, G., Parker, D.: Prism 4.0: Verification of probabilistic real-time systems. In: Gopalakrishnan, G., Qadeer, S. (eds.) CAV 2011. LNCS, vol. 6806, pp. 585–591. Springer, Heidelberg (2011)

11. Norman, G., Kwiatkowska, M., Parker, D.: Advances and Challenges of Probabilistic Model Checking. In: 48th Annual Allerton Conference on Communication, Control, and Computing, pp. 1691–1698. IEEE (2010)
12. Madhav, T.V., Sarma, N.V.S.N.: Maximizing Network Lifetime through Varying Transmission Radii with Energy Efficient Cluster Routing Algorithm in Wireless Sensor Networks. International Journal of Information and Electronics Engineering 2(2), 205–209 (2012)
13. Mahmoodi, T.: Energy-aware routing in the cognitive packet network. Performance Evaluation 68(4), 338–346 (2011)
14. Santi, P.: Topology Control in Wireless Ad Hoc and Sensor Networks. ACM Computing Surveys (CSUR) 37(2), 164–194 (2005)
15. Stewart, W.J.: Probability, Markov Chains, Queues, and Simulation. Princeton University Press, UK (2009)
16. Younis, O., Fahmy, S.: HEED: A Hybrid, Energy-Efficient, Distributed Clustering Approach for Ad Hoc Sensor Networks. IEEE Transactions on Mobile Computing 3(4), 366–379 (2004)
17. Zhai, H., Fang, Y.: Physical carrier sensing and spatial reuse in multirate and multihop wireless ad hoc networks. In: Proc. of INFOCOM 2006. 25th IEEE International Conference on Computer Communications, pp. 1–12 (2006)

Sliding Hidden Markov Model for Evaluating Discrete Data

Tiberiu Chis

Department of Computing, Imperial College London,
180 Queen's Gate, London, SW7 2RH, UK
tc207@doc.ic.ac.uk

Abstract. The possibility of handling infrequent, higher density, additional loads, used mainly for on-line characterization of workloads, is considered. This is achieved through a sliding version of a hidden Markov model (SlidHMM). Essentially, a SlidHMM keeps track of processes that change with time and the constant size of the observation set helps reduce the space and time complexity of the Baum-Welch algorithm, which now need only deal with the new observations. Practically, an approximate Baum-Welch algorithm, which is incremental and partly based on the simple moving average technique, is obtained, where new data points are added to an input trace without re-calculating model parameters, whilst simultaneously discarding any outdated points. The success of this technique could cut processing times significantly, making HMMs more efficient and thence synthetic workloads computationally more cost effective. The performance of our SlidHMM is validated in terms of means and standard deviations of observations (e.g. numbers of operations of certain types) taken from the original and synthetic traces.

1 Introduction

The hidden Markov model (HMM) has been relatively popular in workload characterization [3] in recent years. Its parsimony, portability and efficient training, through its expectation maximization algorithm, has made it useful for reproducing representative workload traces for simulating live systems. Research has also complimented these applications through an incremental storage model [9,12], on which quantitative measures were made. This work has proven that computation time for a reliably parameterized model can be significantly reduced, whilst maintaining accuracy of the model. Indeed, the incremental approach, by which a model's parameters are progressively updated rather than periodically re-calculated, has been appealing in terms of run-time performance.

1.1 Background

To achieve an incremental model, one can adapt the standard HMM algorithms used to train the model. These statistical algorithms under investigation are essentially those solving the three fundamental problems associated with HMMs:

M.S. Balsamo, W.J. Knottenbelt, and A. Marin (Eds.): EPEW 2013, LNCS 8168, pp. 251–262, 2013.
© Springer-Verlag Berlin Heidelberg 2013

firstly, obtain $P(O; \lambda)$, or the probability of the observed sequence O given the model λ; secondly, maximize $P(O; \lambda)$ by adjusting the model parameters for a given observation sequence O; thirdly, determine the most likely hidden state sequence for an observed sequence. These three problems are solved by three respective algorithms: using the Forward-Backward algorithm [1], the Baum-Welch algorithm[1] [2] and the Viterbi algorithm [10]. The solutions to the Forward-Backward and Baum-Welch algorithms are presented in the following sections.

1.2   Forward-Backward Algorithm

The Forward-Backward algorithm aims to find $P(O; \lambda)$, which is the probability of the given sequence of observations $O = (O_1, O_2, \ldots, O_T)$ given the model $\lambda = (A, B, \pi)$, where there are T observations, A is the state transition matrix, B is the observation matrix and π is the initial state distribution. This is equivalent to determining the likelihood of the observed sequence O occuring. We use the same format presented in [17], which is based partly on Rabiner's solution [13,14]. Initially, the focus is on the α-pass, which is the "forward" part of the Forward-Backward algorithm. Then, we shift our attention to the corresponding β-pass, aka. the "backward" part of the algorithm.

To begin with, we define $\alpha_t(i)$ as the probability of obtaining the observation sequence up to time t together with the state q_i at time t, given our model λ. Using N as the number of states and T as the number of observations, the mathematical notation is

$$\alpha_t(i) = P(O_1, O_2, \ldots, O_t, s_t = q_i; \lambda) \tag{1}$$

where $i = 1, 2, \ldots, N$, $t = 1, 2, \ldots, T$, and s_t is the state at time t.

Proceeding inductively, we write the solution for $\alpha_t(i)$ as follows:

1. For $i = 1, 2, \ldots, N$,

$$\alpha_1(i) = \pi_i b_i(O_1).$$

2. For $i = 1, 2, \ldots, N$ and $t = 1, 2, \ldots, T-1$,

$$\alpha_{t+1}(i) = [\textstyle\sum_{j=1}^{N} \alpha_t(j) a_{ji}] b_i(O_{t+1})$$

where $\alpha_t(j) a_{ji}$ is the probability of the joint event observing $O_1, O_2, \ldots O_t$ and moving from state q_j at time t to state q_i at time $t + 1$.

3. It follows that,

$$P(O; \lambda) = \textstyle\sum_{i=1}^{N} \alpha_T(i)$$

where $\alpha_T(i) = P(O_1, O_2, \ldots, O_T, s_T = q_i; \lambda)$

---

[1] This algorithm uses the Forward-Backward algorithm iteratively.

The backward variable, $\beta_t(i)$, is defined as the probability of obtaining the observation sequence from time $t+1$ to T, given state q_i at time t and the model λ:

$$\beta_t(i) = P(O_{t+1}, O_{t+2}, \ldots, O_T; s_t = q_i, \lambda) \tag{2}$$

and the solution of $\beta_t(i)$ is given by

1. For $i = 1, 2, \ldots, N$,

$$\beta_T(i) = 1$$

2. For $i = 1, 2, \ldots, N$ and $t = T-1, T-2, \ldots, 1$,

$$\beta_t(i) = \sum_{j=1}^{N} a_{ij} b_j(O_{t+1}) \beta_{t+1}(j)$$

where we note that O_{t+1} can be observed from any state q_j.

1.3   Baum-Welch Algorithm

The Baum-Welch algorithm attempts to maximise $P(O; \lambda)$ by iteratively updating A, B, π, given the model $\lambda = (A, B, \pi)$ and the observation sequence $O = (O_1, O_2, \ldots, O_T)$. We first define the probability of making a transition from state q_i at time t to state q_j at time $t+1$, given O and λ, as

$$\xi_t(i, j) = P(s_t = q_i, s_{t+1} = q_j; O, \lambda) \tag{3}$$

Computing $\xi_t(i, j)$ can be described as a three-step process. Firstly, the observations $O_1, O_2, \ldots, O_t$ finishing in state q_i at time t will be covered by $\alpha_t(i)$. Secondly, the transition from q_i to q_j, where O_{t+1} was observed at time $t+1$, is represented by the term $a_{ij} b_j(O_{t+1})$. Thirdly, the remaining observations $O_{t+2}, O_{t+3} \ldots O_T$ beginning in state q_j at time $t+1$ are covered by β_{t+1}. Putting those together, and dividing by a normalizing term ($P(O; \lambda)$) we have

$$\xi_t(i, j) = \frac{\alpha_t(i) a_{ij} b_j(O_{t+1}) \beta_{t+1}(j)}{P(O; \lambda)} \tag{4}$$

We now sum the terms in (4) over j and notice that this gives the probability of being in state q_i at time t, given the observation sequence O and model λ:

$$\gamma_t(i) = P(s_t = q_i; O, \lambda) = \sum_{j=1}^{N} \xi_t(i, j)$$

Summing $\gamma_t(i)$ over time t up to T, we get the expected visits of state q_i. Similarly, summing up to $T-1$ gives the expected number of transitions from q_i. Thus:

$$\sum_{t=1}^{T} \gamma_t(i) = \text{Expected times state } q_i \text{ is visited.}$$

$$\sum_{t=1}^{T-1} \gamma_t(i) = \text{Expected transitions from } q_i.$$

Similarly, we sum $\xi_t(i,j)$ over t as follows:

$$\sum_{t=1}^{T} \xi_t(i,j) = \text{Expected visits of } q_i \text{ then } q_j.$$

$$\sum_{t=1}^{T-1} \xi_t(i,j) = \text{Expected transitions } q_i \text{ to } q_j.$$

Using these terms, the re-estimation formulas for our HMM parameters are:

$$\pi_i' = \gamma_1(i), \quad a_{ij}' = \frac{\sum_{t=1}^{T-1} \xi_t(i,j)}{\sum_{j=1}^{N} \sum_{t=1}^{T-1} \xi_t(i,j)}, \quad b_j(k)' = \frac{\sum_{t=1, O_t=k}^{T} \gamma_t(j)}{\sum_{t=1}^{T} \gamma_t(j)}$$

Using these re-estimation formulas, we can update our model $\lambda' = (A', B', \pi')$, where $A' = \{a_{ij}'\}$, $B' = \{b_j(k)'\}$ and $\pi' = \{\pi_i'\}$. Our model will have fixed parameters once $P(O; \lambda') > P(O; \lambda)$, when the optimal model λ' is found.

1.4 Incremental Model

The incremental Storage Workload Model (iSWoM) [12] made use of these algorithms with modifications to the mechanisms of the Forward-Backward algorithm (creating a forward-recurrence backward approximation). Therefore, inherently, the Baum-Welch algorithm was adapted to create a model for incremental learning of discrete data. The iSWoM generated workload traces, running on live systems where quantitative measurements were made. These measurements, acting as statistical validation, included means, standard deviations and confidence intervals for both raw and iSWoM-generated traces. Also, comparisons of hidden state sequences, as generated by the Viterbi algorithm, further validated the iSWoM with a standard HMM, and found similar model parameters (A, B, π). Using the incremental approach of the iSWoM, by which a model's parameters are progressively updated rather than periodically re-calculated, was accurate and also appealing in terms of run-time performance. However, the continuous training of new, incoming data points resulted in the accumulation of an increasingly large observation set. As a result, older observation points become outdated after many updates and should not necessarily be included in statistical measurements of traces. Thus, we seek a more efficient on-line characterization method for discrete time analysis than that of the incremental model. Our aim is to create a model with a fixed sliding window to effectively analyse discrete data traces (appropriately discarding the outdated observations) whilst updating its model parameters. In the next section, we build such a model, which is essentially a sliding version of a HMM.

2 Sliding HMM

The sliding HMM (SlidHMM) has a number of benefits over the standard HMM: firstly, handling infrequent, higher density, additional loads mainly for on-line characterization of workloads; secondly, to measure time-variant processes efficiently through updating the observation set at different stages of analysis; thirdly, to reduce the space and time complexity of the Baum-Welch algorithm.

These benefits are also matched by the iSWoM, but where the SlidHMM maintains a fixed window of observations for training, the iSWoM has an observation set that grows continuously over time. This will make the SlidHMM computationally more efficient than the iSWoM for training on large data sets. The SlidHMM allows for effectively comparing different sections of the observation set using its sliding window, a technique which the iSWoM nor the standard HMM can achieve. We employ the simple moving average technique on the SlidHMM, enabling the updating of terms whilst maintaing a fixed size window of analysis.

2.1   Moving Average

A *moving average* [7] or *running average* is a statistical technique where a set of data points is split into subsets and averages are calculated on each of these subsets. Moving averages have seen many applications in industry, such as trend following analysis in finance [5]. For a simple moving average (SMA) [6], we select a fixed subset size (n) and shift along, subtracting old points from the summation as we add new points to it. For example, if we begin with the data points $\{x_1, x_2, \ldots, x_n\}$, then we can work out an average of these points:

$$ave = \frac{x_1 + x_2 + \cdots + x_n}{n} \tag{5}$$

Then, from (5) we can create a SMA when we add one more data point (x_{n+1}):

$$sma = \frac{x_1 + x_2 + \cdots + x_n + x_{n+1} - x_1}{n} = ave + \frac{x_{n+1}}{n} - \frac{x_1}{n}$$

The idea of SMA is applied to HMMs for observation sets with discrete data. New data points are added to the input trace without any unnecessary re-calculations of model parameters, whilst simultaneously discarding any "outdated" observations. We replace the data points x_t by our model recurrence terms such as αs, βs, etc. This process is explained in the following section, where we present a simple algorithm for executing the slide on discrete data.

2.2   Sliding Baum-Welch Algorithm

To perform the slide on an observation set, the Baum-Welch algorithm trains on new data, whilst storing information on the original data set. Therefore, a new technique is required to store existing α and β values (terms worked out from the current observation set) and efficiently calculate α and β values for the new set of observations. For example, if we are given the observation set $\{O_{T+1}, O_{T+2}, \ldots, O_{2T}\}$, having an existing HMM defined on the set $\{O_1, O_2, \ldots, O_T\}$, then the αs for the new observations will be:

For $T \leq t \leq 2T$, we have

$$\alpha_{t+1}(i) = b_i(O_{t+1}) \sum_{j=1}^{N} \alpha_t(j) a_{ji}$$

However, we cannot compute the new β values incrementally for the new set $\{O_{T+1}, O_{T+2}, \ldots, O_{2T}\}$ without working out all β values for the aggregate observation set $\{O_1, O_2, \ldots, O_{2T}\}$. Unlike the α values, the β values define $\beta_{2T}(i) = 1$ for any state i (as O_{2T} is our latest observation) and the remaining β terms are calculated using the backward recurrence formula.

There exists a solution, or rather an approximation, of these unknown β values for the new observation set $\{O_{T+1}, O_{T+2}, \ldots, O_{2T}\}$. The technique used by Stenger et al. in 2001 [11] assumes the following simple approximation:

For $1 \leq i \leq N$, we have

$$\beta_T(i) = \beta_{T+1}(i) = \beta_{T+2}(i) = \cdots = \beta_{2T}(i) = 1 \tag{6}$$

From the knowledge of the traditional backward recurrence formula for the β values, we deduce that the sequence $\beta_{2T}(i), \beta_{2T-1}(i), \ldots, \beta_T(i)$ decreases in value, where $\beta_{2T-1}(i)$ is significantly less than $\beta_{2T}(i)$, etc. Eventually, this decreasing sequence of β values should tend exponentially to zero. Therefore, setting all new β values to one, as seen in (6), is not the most efficient solution. We can attempt a more accurate approximation for the β values by assuming that only $\beta_{2T}(i) = 1$ and then use the normal β recurrence formula to update the terms: $\beta_{2T-1}(i), \beta_{2T-2}(i), \ldots \beta_{T+1}(i)$. Notice the change only for the new observations in terms of β.

So, $\beta_{2T-1}(i)$ is calculated as follows:

$$\beta_{2T-1}(i) = \sum_{j=1}^{N} a_{ij} b_j(O_{2T}) \beta_{2T}(j) = \sum_{j=1}^{N} a_{ij} b_j(O_{2T})$$

Therefore, $\beta_{2T-2}(i)$ is given by:

$$\beta_{2T-2}(i) = \sum_{k=1}^{N} a_{ik} b_k(O_{2T-1}) \beta_{2T-1}(k)$$
$$= \sum_{k=1}^{N} a_{ik} b_k(O_{2T-1}) [\sum_{j=1}^{N} a_{kj} b_j(O_{2T})]$$

We continue in this fashion until we obtain a value for $\beta_{T+1}(i)$ in terms of all new β values. Essentially, this methodology utilizes part of the backward formula, but ignores any "old" β values. Once there is a complete approximation of both α and β sets, we calculate the ξ and γ values for the set $\{O_{T+1}, O_{T+2}, \ldots, O_{2T}\}$:

For $T + 1 \leq t \leq 2T - 1$,

$$\xi_t(i, j) = \frac{\alpha_t(i) a_{ij} b_j(O_{t+1}) \beta_{t+1}(i)}{\sum_{i=1}^{N} \alpha_t(i) \beta_t(i)}$$

and for $T + 1 \leq t \leq 2T$,

$$\gamma_t(i) = \frac{\alpha_t(i) \beta_t(i)}{\sum_{i=1}^{N} \alpha_t(i) \beta_t(i)}$$

However, these points are added incrementally and therefore the Baum-Welch algorithm adds one new term for each observation (in T separate steps). Hence, for each new observation added, the modified re-estimation formulas for $\hat{A}$ and $\hat{B}$, for $i = 1, \ldots, N$, are as follows:

$$\hat{a}_{ij}^{T+1} = \frac{\sum_{t=2}^{T} \xi_t(i,j) + \xi_{T+1}(i,j)}{\sum_{j=1}^{N} \sum_{t=2}^{T} \xi_t(i,j) + \sum_{j=1}^{N} \xi_{T+1}(i,j)}$$

$$= \frac{\sum_{t=2}^{T} \gamma_t(i)}{\sum_{t=2}^{T+1} \gamma_t(i)} \frac{\sum_{t=2}^{T} \xi_t(i,j)}{\sum_{t=2}^{T} \gamma_t(i)} + \frac{\xi_{T+1}(i,j)}{\sum_{t=2}^{T+1} \gamma_t(i)}$$

$$= \frac{\sum_{t=2}^{T} \gamma_t(i)}{\sum_{t=2}^{T+1} \gamma_t(i)} \hat{a}_{ij}^{T} + \frac{\xi_{T+1}(i,j)}{\sum_{t=2}^{T+1} \gamma_t(i)}$$

Thus, only the new $\xi_{T+1}(i,j)$ and $\gamma_{T+1}(i)$ for O_{T+1} need to be calculated.

$$\hat{b}_j(k)^{T+1} = \frac{\sum_{t=2,O_t=k}^{T} \gamma_t(j) + \sum_{t=T+1,O_t=k}^{T+1} \gamma_t(j)}{\sum_{t=2}^{T} \gamma_t(j) + \gamma_{T+1}(j)}$$

$$= \frac{\sum_{t=2}^{T} \gamma_t(j)}{\sum_{t=2}^{T+1} \gamma_t(j)} \hat{b}_j(k)^{T} + \frac{\sum_{t=T+1,O_t=k}^{T+1} \gamma_t(j)}{\sum_{t=2}^{T+1} \gamma_t(j)}$$

where updating $\gamma_{T+1}(j)$ (such that $O_{T+1} = k$) is sufficient.

Under these modified parameters (similar to [11]), a sliding version of the Baum-Welch algorithm is created (referred to as **SlidHMM**). We summarise our sliding methodology, for any discrete observation sets, in four steps:

1. Train HMM on observations $\{O_1, O_2, \ldots, O_T\}$ until convergence.
2. Slide on M new observations $\{O_{T+1}, O_{T+2}, \ldots, O_{T+M}\}$ using SlidHMM.
3. Calculate new α, β, ξ and γ sets for new observations.
4. Update parameters (A, B, π) for SlidHMM and continue to step 2.

Since the SlidHMM requires only a partial computation of the forward and backward variables, it converges to fixed results much quicker than training with the traditional Baum-Welch algorithm. The time steps saved using this "slide" training can be described as follows. We set K to be the number of times that M new observations appear and T is the size of the original observation set. Then, the steps taken to train the HMM (t_1) and SlidHMM (t_2), respectively, are:

$$t_1 = T + (T+M) + \ldots + (T+KM) = T + (KT) + (\tfrac{1}{2}K(K+1))M$$
$$t_2 = T + M + \ldots + M = T + KM$$

Taking the difference between the terms of these two models, we obtain d, the time saved in training using our SlidHMM, given by:

$$d = t_1 - t_2 = KT + \tfrac{1}{2}K^2M - \tfrac{1}{2}KM = K(T + \tfrac{1}{2}M(K\text{-}1))$$

3   Collecting and Processing Traces

To train our SlidHMM on discrete data we process various traces such that they pass as eligible inputs into the Baum-Welch algorithm. Two different traces are used to train the model: first, the NetApp trace with thousands of read and write commands from a server; second, patient arrivals observed at a hospital over several weeks. In the next sections, this "raw" data is transformed into binned traces and finally into discrete observation sets.

3.1   Raw Traces

The raw NetApp data, which contains hundreds of thousands of entries collected from NetApp storage servers, essentially form a CIFS (Common Internet File System) network trace (of about 750 GB). These file servers, located at the NetApp headquarters, were accessed mainly by Windows desktops and laptops using various applications. We denote the aforementioned trace as the "NetApp trace" for the remainder of this paper. The trace used for analysis consisted of I/O commands (single CIFS reads and writes) and a timestamp entry (i.e. the time in seconds when the command was made). The data was transferred from a web page into read and write arrays (in a local Java class) using an *InputStreamReader*.

The data describing patient arrival times is anonymised data characterising patient arrival times at a London hospital between April 2002 and March 2007, as used in the study [16]. We extracted the arrival times for a period of four weeks, resulting in a "Hospital trace" that was output into a csv file, read into a Java class, and stored as an array. With both traces collected, the next stage of the transformation process is assigning "bins" to these traces.

3.2   Binned Traces

We partitioned the entries of the raw traces into uniform bins of a pre-defined size. These bins are essentially fixed-size intervals, dividing the raw data into a discrete time series. For the NetApp trace, each bin contains two values: the number of read entries and the number of write entries (during each time interval). For the Hospital trace, each bin is an interval (i.e. an hour) where a number of patients can arrive at the hospital.

The size of the bin was decided by the timescale required for the modelling exercise. For example, if the raw trace spans a time period of several days, then we expect much larger bin sizes than if we had a raw trace spanning several hours. Also, the level of detail at which the raw trace is operating (e.g. at the Application level) is also an important factor in determining the bin size. After experimenting with the NetApp raw trace, we found the best bin size to be one second. Having tried 100 milliseconds resulted in too many empty time intervals, whilst with a larger time interval (i.e. five seconds), there were issues of missing out low-level, operation sequence characteristics such as mode transitions. Using one second bin sizes allowed us to represent each index in an array as a second. Counting the number of commands occuring each second (separately for reads and writes) resulted in filling our arrays easily. For example, reads[3] = 76 and writes[3] = 23 represented 76 reads and 23 writes in the third second. A vector list, holding a pair of reads and writes was formed from the arrays.

The Hospital trace was binned in a similar fashion, but only contained one entry (i.e. the number of patient arriving every hour). After analysing the frequency of patient arrivals over four weeks, almost one third of cases had no activity. On the other hand, two patients arrived in the same hour about 17% of the time. In fact, on very few occasions were there more than eight patients in one hour. Thus, choosing the one hour bin sizes resulted in an ideal range of values for forming clusters around our data points. In the next section, the NetApp and Hospital traces (acting as vectors with paired and single tuple values, respectively) are inputted into a K-means clustering algorithm to obtain our observation traces.

3.3 K-means Clustering

Apply a clustering algorithm to the binned traces further reduces them to a more manageable format (i.e. the observation trace). We implemented the K-means clustering algorithm, which essentially groups data into K clusters. Each cluster contains either a pair of values (i.e. the mean number of reads and mean number of writes) or single value (i.e. number of patient arrivals) to represent the centroid. Logically, the cluster also contains every data point belonging to that cluster. A Euclidean-distance itervative algorithm calculated the cluster centroids over and over again until they became fixed. As we inputted K manually, we chose a value of seven clusters for the NetApp trace and three clusters for the Hospital trace. These values were not too large (which gives surplus or even empty clusters) nor too small (missing out significant differences among clusters) for our data traces. The NetApp trace was divided into seven clusters, which represented the centroids as vectors consisting of a pair of values (reads and writes). The Hospital trace was bound by five clusters or less because clustering with $K = 6$ returned two empty clusters (i.e. value of 0.0). As we inputted K manually, we chose three clusters, as it gave closer means to the raw data when compared to HMM-generated data. Having performed the K-means clustering on both traces, we obtain observation traces ideal for input into the Baum-Welch algorithm. Essentially, the SlidHMM will train on these observation traces as slides are performed on various sections of observations.

4 Simulation of SlidHMM and Results

To achieve both simulations of the SlidHMM, for both NetApp and Hospital traces, each observation trace is inputted into the Baum-Welch algorithm as a training set of 8000 points. A HMM (with two hidden states) is trained on this set until parameter convergence (i.e. A, B, π become fixed). Afterwards, 2000 new observations are added to this set, evaluating the 2000 points using the sliding technique and the new β approximation from the Forward-Backward algorithm. Thus, a sliding MAP (SlidMAP) with fixed parameters is formed, which stores information on 10000 consecutive observation points. Our SlidMAP then generates its own synthetic NetApp and Hospital traces using its initial state distribution (π), state transition matrix (A) and observation matrix (B). The SlidMAP reproduces the observed values using random generation sampling, which are simulated 1000 times, summarised as means and standard deviations, where 95% intervals are performed on both statistics. We compare SlidHMM-generated results with mean and standard deviation for raw and HMM-generated traces. Note that the HMM-generated trace is a result of a traditional HMM trained on an observation trace of length 10000, with no incremental learning.

After performing the simulation of the SlidHMM on both data traces, the Baum-Welch parameters (A, B, π) converged as expected. From these new parameters, the SlidHMM generated new observation traces for both NetApp and Hospital data. We present the results in tables, first for the NetApp trace. Table 1 presents statistics on Reads/bin and Table 2 represents Writes/bin, where the "bin" is a one-second interval. For example, a "Raw Mean of 111.350 Reads/bin" implies that the raw NetApp trace produces, on average, 111.350 read commands per second. The "SlidHMM Mean" and "SlidHMM Std Dev" are the averages of the SlidHMM-generated trace. The "HMM"-prefixed averages are calculated from a standard HMM-generated trace with no sliding activity.

Table 1. Reads/bin statistics on the raw, HMM and SlidHMM-generated NetApp traces after 1000 simulations

Trace	Mean	Std Dev
Raw	111.350	254.904
HMM	111.26 ± 0.66	254.38 ± 0.65
SlidHMM	113.32 ± 0.60	253.18 ± 0.58

The results in Table 1 show very similar results between raw and HMM-generated means and standard deviations. The SlidHMM produces a mean of 113.32 with a 95% confidence interval of 0.6, which is pleasing after 1000 simulations, but this mean is less accurate than the traditional HMM. The standard deviation of the SlidHMM-generated trace (253.18) matches the raw trace well, but again is outperformed slightly by the value of the HMM trace.

Table 2. Writes/bin statistics on the raw, HMM and SlidHMM-generated NetApp traces after 1000 simulations

Trace	Mean	Std Dev
Raw	0.382	0.208
HMM	0.38 ± 0.0005	0.21 ± 0.001
SlidHMM	0.392 ± 0.0005	0.23 ± 0.001

Table 2 shows good results for the SlidHMM-generated mean and standard deviation, which slightly underperform the values produced by the HMM trace. The Hospital observation trace is also generated by the SlidHMM, with means and standard deviations presented in similar fashion. Table 3 shows bin-means that match well, and more pleasingly, the standard deviations are even closer to raw values. We can conclude, from these statistics alone, that our SlidHMM faithfully reproduces meaningful representations of patient arrival times.

Table 3. Arrivals/bin statistics on the raw, HMM and SlidHMM-generated Hospital traces after 1000 simulations

Trace	Mean	Std Dev
Raw	1.483	1.565
HMM	1.461 ± 0.003	1.551 ± 0.001
SlidHMM	1.474 ± 0.002	1.572 ± 0.001

5   Conclusion and Future Work

HMMs, combined with the supporting clustering analysis and appropriate choice of bins, is able to provide a concise, parsimonious and portable synthetic workload. This has already been established, in [3] for example, but the deficiency of such models is their heavy computing resource requirement, which essentially precludes them from any form of on-line analysis. The sliding HMM developed in this paper has a vastly reduced computing requirement making it ideal for modelling workload data in real-time. In fact, with the availability of new data, the SlidHMM avoids re-training on "old data" like the traditional HMM. Additionally, compared with both the resource-costly HMM and raw traces, the SlidHMM provides excellent accuracy of training data. In comparison to the previously mentioned iSWoM [12], the SlidHMM will handle fast-growing observation sets more efficiently, as it slides and trains on different parts of the data. Where the iSWoM increases its observation set after every training session, the SlidHMM also discards outdated data points using its sliding window.

Such mathematical descriptions of workloads and arrivals should be measured quantitatively against independent data (i.e. traces not used in model construction) that they represent, and more extensive tests are planned for our sliding model. Nonetheless, the SlidHMM β approximation has been successful after statistical comparisons between raw and SlidHMM-generated traces (on two independent traces). Analysing current work in this field, for example, the incremental model from [4] used a backward formula in its learning that was not recursive in terms of previous β values. The SlidHMM backward formula, however, stores all information in the β set, unlike the formula in [11], where all βs were set to one and accuracy was lost over Baum-Welch iterations.

There are a few extensions which follow from the SlidHMM. Firstly, another way to approximate the β values is to use the backward formula from [12]. The result would be an incremental model (namely the forward-recurrence updating of the βs) with a "sliding window" learning technique. As this paper illustrates, SlidHMM applies to discrete time series, in fact on two different traces. The next step is to derive a sliding model for continuous time, which requires a continuous Baum-Welch algorithm [8]. The time intervals would not be discrete observation points, but rather a sliding window along continuous time series. Therefore, a degree of accuracy is needed in choosing these time intervals for the SlidHMM, perhaps in terms of timescale of workload traces.

References

1. Baum, L.E., Petrie, T.: Stastical Inference for Probabilistic Functions of Finite Markov Chains. The Annals of Mathematical Statistics 37, 1554–1563 (1966)
2. Baum, L.E., Petrie, T., Soules, G., Weiss, N.: A maximization technique occurring in the statistical analysis of probabilistic functions of Markov chains. The Annals of Mathematical Statistics 41, 164–171 (1970)
3. Harrison, P.G., Harrison, S.K., Patel, N.M., Zertal, S.: Storage Workload Modelling by Hidden Markov Models: Application to Flash Memory. Performance Evaluation 69, 17–40 (2012)
4. Florez-Larrahondo, G., Bridges, S., Hansen, E.A.: Incremental Estimation of Discrete Hidden Markov Models on a New Backward Procedure, Department of Computer Science and Engineering, Mississippi State University, Mississippi, USA (2005)
5. Burghardt, G., Duncan, R., Liu, L.: What You Should Expect From Trend Following (2004)
6. Chou, Y.: Statistical Analysis. In: Holt International, 17.9 (1975)
7. Whittle, P.: Hypothesis Testing in Time Series Analysis, Almquist and Wicksell (1951)
8. Zraiaa, M.: Hidden Markov Models: A Continuous-Time Version of the Baum-Welch Algorithm, Department of Computing, Imperial College London, London (2010)
9. Chis, T., Harrison, P.G.: Incremental HMM with an improved Baum-Welch Algorithm. In: Proceedings of Imperial College Computing Student Workshop (2012)
10. Viterbi, A.J.: Error bounds for convolutional codes and an asymptotically optimum decoding algorithm. IEEE Transactions on Information Theory 13, 260–269 (1967)
11. Stenger, B., Ramesh, V., Paragois, N., Coetzee, F., Buhmann, J.M.: Topology free Hidden Markov Models: Application to background modeling. In: Proceedings of the International Conference on Computer Vision, pp. 297–301 (2001)
12. Chis, T., Harrison, P.G.: iSWoM: An Incremental Storage Workload Model using Hidden Markov Models, Department of Computing, Imperial College London (to be published, 2013)
13. Rabiner, L.R., Juang, B.H.: An Introduction to Hidden Markov Models. IEEE ASSP Magazine 3, 4–16 (1986)
14. Rabiner, L.R.: A Tutorial on Hidden Markov Models and Selected Applications in Speech Recognition. IEEE 77, 257–286 (1989)
15. Zhai, C.X.: A Brief Note on the Hidden Markov Models (HMMs), Department of Computer Science, University of Illinois at Urbana-Champaign, IL, USA (2003)
16. Au-Yeung, S.W.M., Harder, U., McCoy, E., Knottenbelt, W.J.: Predicting patient arrivals to an accident and emergency department. Emergency Medicine Journal 26, 241–244 (2009)
17. Chis, T.: Hidden Markov Models: Applications to Flash Memory Data and Hospital Arrival Times, Department of Computing, Imperial College London (2011)

Using Queuing Models for Large System Migration Scenarios – An Industrial Case Study with IBM System z

Robert Vaupel[1], Qais Noorshams[2], Samuel Kounev[2], and Ralf Reussner[2]

[1] IBM R&D GmbH, Böblingen, Germany
vaupel@de.ibm.com
[2] Karlsruhe Institute of Technology, Germany
{noorshams,kounev,reussner}@kit.edu

Abstract. Large IT organizations exchange their computer infrastructure on a regular time basis. When planning such an environment exchange, it is required to explicitly consider the impact on the Quality-of-Service of the applications to avoid violations of Service Level Agreements. In current practice, however, using explicit performance models for such estimations is frequently avoided due to scepticism towards their practical usability and benefits for complex environments. In this paper, we present a real-world case study to demonstrate that a queuing model-based approach can be effectively used to predict performance impact when migrating to a new environment in an industrial context. We first present a general modeling methodology and explain how we apply it for system migration scenarios. Then, we present a real-world industrial case study and show how the performance models can be used. The migration is planned for a System z environment running a large scale banking application. Finally, we validate the performance models after the system has been migrated, evaluate the prediction accuracy, and discuss possible limitations. Overall, the measurements show very high agreement with the prediction results.

Keywords: Business Transactions, Performance, Prediction.

1 Introduction

Large IT companies use their IT systems for a limited period of time. Typically, the main computing infrastructure is exchanged every two to three years and replaced with newer versions of the same computing architecture. These system upgrades are very expensive and require a thorough planning explicitly considering the performance implications on the existing applications and (business) transactions.

When planning such an environment exchange, i.e., a system migration, multiple questions arise as for instance: *i) What capacity is required to maintain comparable Quality-of-Service (QoS)? ii) How does the QoS of the main applications change in the migrated environment? iii) How does the QoS of the main applications change under higher workload intensity?* Moreover, there are multiple aspects that need to be considered posing further challenges: There

M.S. Balsamo, W.J. Knottenbelt, and A. Marin (Eds.): EPEW 2013, LNCS 8168, pp. 263–275, 2013.
© Springer-Verlag Berlin Heidelberg 2013

can be many alternatives to choose from with regard to single processor speed and overall system capacity. Systems with higher processor speed require fewer processors to maintain the same total capacity. The higher speed of the processors might improve the transaction response times at a lower system utilization level, however, the response times might increase more drastically with increasing workload intensity. Furthermore, a system migration might initially target a system with lower capacity with the possibility of a stepwise capacity increase (as supported by many system architectures) if required.

In current practice, however, using explicit performance models to answer typical capacity planning questions is usually avoided. The main obstacle is the still existing scepticism in industry towards the practical usability, benefits, and return-on-investment of classical queuing models in the context of complex real-world scenarios.

To this end, in this paper, we present a real-world case study demonstrating the practicality and effectiveness of using queuing models to predict the performance impact when migrating to a new system environment in an industrial context. More specifically, we first present a general queuing model approach and explain how it is applied in system migration scenarios. Then, we present an industrial case-study and use our approach to plan a migration of a business transaction workload of a banking institute in an IBM System z server environment. We evaluate the queuing model and validate the results with real-world production workloads after the migration has been completed. The evaluation of the approach shows very high agreement with the predictions. Finally, we discuss practical challenges and possible limitations that need to be considered when applying our queuing model approach and under which conditions it can be used.

In summary, the contribution of this paper is a real-world case study in industrial context to show how a queuing model-based approach can be effectively used to project transaction response times for large business environments. Furthermore, we discuss limitations of the modeling approach and identify conditions that need to be considered when using such methodologies in real-world scenarios.

The remainder of this paper is organized as follows: Section 2 gives an overview of our modeling approach. In Section 3, we present our case study. Section 4 discusses limitations when using the modeling approach in complex scenarios. Finally, Section 5 summarizes and concludes the paper.

2   Modeling Approach

To evaluate system migration decisions providing capacity management support, we employ a queuing model-based approach to predict the performance after migrating to another system environment. Our methodology is based on established work [1,2] and comprises the following steps:

1. *System Environment Analysis*:
   We analyze the structure of the environment and, more specifically, we identify the important partitions that need to be analyzed in case of a virtualized environment.

2. *Workload Characterization*:
   We identify and characterize the main workloads for the system migration as well as possible workloads running in parallel affecting the main workloads.
3. *Metrics Measurements and Estimation*:
   We measure performance metrics for both the workload and the system infrastructure, e.g., the workload response time and the system utilization. Furthermore, we estimate the metrics that cannot be measured directly.
4. *Performance Modeling*:
   Finally, we model the transaction processing in a queuing model enabling to project and predict the response time as well as the system utilization of the target system environment depending on the workload.

After migrating the system infrastructure, the results can be evaluated and compared with new measurements to validate the predictions or to refine the approach and include further performance influences for future studies.

2.1 System Environment Analysis

In general, our approach is not limited to specific environments. In this paper, we apply our approach to *System z* mainframe computers. System z environments are state-of-the-art virtualized environments with logically partitioned, shared resources. The main operating system used by large organizations is predominantly the mainframe operating system *z/OS* hosting applications and databases.

Depending on the organization, the partition structure on System z mainframes may vary significantly. On the one hand, many large IT organizations – especially financial institutes – typically use a few partitions to host their applications. Such systems use many processors, large I/O subsystems and big memory environments. On the other hand, the system can be used for up to 60 partitions with few resources allocated for each partition. Such environments are mostly used by organizations hosting systems for other companies. The partition and resource characteristics employed in such environments are very different and need to be identified in the analysis.

2.2 Workload Characterization

Most z/OS-based production systems deploy *batch* and *online transaction processing (OLTP)* workloads. Usually, such workloads run in parallel, where either workload dominates in certain time periods. In some environments, the batch and the OLTP workloads are deployed in separate partitions. For the considered environment, we first identify the main workload and the respective performance characteristics of interest. Since the workload intensity varies over time, we then choose a representative time period in which the workload is running to parameterize the performance model.

The main workload may be a batch workload or an OLTP workload. For a batch workload, the total runtime and throughput (TP) are significant. Single request response times (RT) or the system utilization are usually less important, since the system is usually fully utilized during the batch runtime. For an OLTP workload, the transaction response times and throughput as well as the system utilization are significant. Moreover, the correlation between transaction throughput and system utilization is relevant as an indicator for resource efficiency and CPU cost per transaction.

Since the transaction response times are usually part of the *Service Level Agreements* with end users, our approach is specifically targeted at modeling and predicting the performance of the OLTP workload after system migration.

2.3   Metrics Measurements and Estimation

As previously mentioned, we focus on i) the transaction response time comprised by several components, ii) the transaction throughput describing the workload intensity, and iii) the total system utilization including load generated by workloads running in parallel. These metrics are measured in the existing environment. In general, the transaction response time is comprised of the following components, which are estimated on the existing system by measuring the execution states of the transactions and calculating their proportions of the total response time: i) CPU Processing Time, ii) CPU Wait Time, iii) I/O Data Transfer Time, iv) I/O Wait Time, and v) Other Time (e.g., due to software locking).

2.4   Performance Modeling

In this section, we model the system performance for transactional workloads. More specifically, we model the transaction response times by projecting the CPU processing times from the existing environment to the target environment. We assume that the general CPU processor architecture is the same for the existing and the target system. Furthermore, we assume that the I/O and Other components of the response time are not affected significantly by the migration. The assumption is reasonable for I/O if only the computing system is replaced. For the Other wait times, it is a simplifying assumption that needs to be validated after the migration. Overall, our performance modeling methodology is comprised of *Model Creation*, *Model Calibration*, and *Model Projection*.

Model Creation. To model the CPU service demand, we use an open multi-server queuing model with general interarrival and service time, i.e., a G/G/C queuing model, to cover a wide range of modeling scenarios with arbitrary interarrival and service times, which are obtained by parameterization from real-world measurement data. The model is solved using the *Allen-Cunneen Approximation* [3] shown in Equation (1), where k is the Allen-Cunneen factor, U is the CPU utilization of the system, C is the number of servers (i.e., CPUs) and S is the service time. Furthermore, $P_W(U, C)$ is the probability for waiting in a system with C servers and utilization U expressed by the *Erlang-C formula* [4].

$$W = k \cdot \frac{P_W(U,C)}{C(1-U)} \cdot S, \quad P_W(U,C) = \frac{\frac{(UC)^C}{C!}}{\frac{(UC)^C}{C!} + (1-U) \cdot \sum_{i=0}^{C-1} \frac{(UC)^i}{i!}} \quad (1)$$

The Allen-Cunneen factor k is determined as

$$k = \frac{c_a^2 + c_s^2}{2}, \text{ where} \tag{2}$$

c_a = *coefficient of variation* of the interarrival time distribution,

c_s = *coefficient of variation* of the service time distribution.

Model Calibration. For model calibration, the Allen-Cunneen factor k is either determined based on measurements or estimated. Typically, a value of 1 assuming a M/M/C queuing environment is a reasonable assumption. The CPU processing time S is estimated based on measured transaction response time and observed execution states as

$$S = \frac{\text{CPU Processing States}}{\text{All States}} \cdot RT, \tag{3}$$

where RT is the transaction response time.

Model Projection. To predict the performance in the target environment, we project the transaction processing times of the existing environment to the target environment. Generally, this can be done by determining the relative CPU capacity of the two systems, e.g., using MIPS[1] comparison or CPU benchmarks.

In System z environments, the Large System Performance Reference (LSPR) [5] value is used to determine the capacity of the target system. In LSPR, the capacity of all systems is expressed as a multiple or a fraction of a base system. The capacity also depends on the considered workload and the system layout. IBM performs for each system generation a set of performance benchmarks covering batch workloads and different types of OLTP workloads as well as mixes of them. These benchmarks are used to obtain five performance values that characterize the systems when running different workloads. The values cover aspects from memory to I/O intensive workloads, batch environments and environments with very high transaction volumes. For many real-world environments, the mean or *Average* value of the performance numbers can be used as a representative value. This average value is also used when System z performance is expressed in MIPS. For a given environment, the exact LSPR value can be obtained using a tool called zPCR [6]. Thus, we project the CPU processing time of the existing system S to the CPU processing time in the target system S^* using the relative CPU capacity α as

$$S^* = \phi(S) = \alpha \cdot S, \ \alpha \in \mathbb{R}^+. \tag{4}$$

The system utilization in the target environment U^* is predicted using the *Utilization Law*

$$U^* = S^* \cdot TP, \tag{5}$$

where, in steady state, the arrival rate (or *transaction rate*) equals the throughput TP. The transaction response time in the target environment RT^* is

---

[1] Million Instructions Per Second

predicted by using the CPU processing time S^* from Equation (4) and the number of CPUs in the target environment C^* and applying Equation (1) to obtain W^*, thus

$$RT^* = S^* + k \cdot \frac{P_{W^*}(U^*, C^*)}{C^*(1 - U^*)} \cdot S^* \tag{6}$$
$$+ \text{I/O Processing Time} + \text{I/O Wait Time}$$
$$+ \text{Other Time}$$

3 Case Study

In this section, we present a real-world migration study for a banking institute performed in 2012 with the following requirements of the installation:

- An existing System z10 with 33 processors should be upgraded to a target System zEC12. The I/O subsystem remains unchanged.
- The initial capacity of the target system should be *below* the existing system to allow incremental capacity upgrades if necessary. Moreover, the initial transaction rates were not expected to be that high to require the full capacity.

To support the migration, appropriate System zEC12 configurations, i.e., number of CPUs, should be identified with the following two prediction objectives:

- Prediction of the *transaction response times* of the main application on the target system as well as their *development upon increase in transaction rates*.
- Prediction of the *utilization of the target system* and, especially, the *increase in utilization* due to the migration to a system with less capacity.

3.1 System Environment Analysis

The existing System z10, i.e., the *base system*, hosts two large partitions that process identical types of workload. For our analysis we summarize the data from both partitions. The operating system on both partitions is z/OS. The data collection is performed with a standard monitoring tool *Resource Measurement Facility* (RMF). The collected data is written to log files, which are managed by the z/OS component *Systems Management Facility* (SMF). The data analysis is performed using a set of tools created by the authors of this paper.

3.2 Workload Characterization

The workload analysis encompasses a three day period. Figure 1 depicts the total workload utilization summarized across both z/OS systems for the System z10. The main OLTP workload is produced by a banking application accessing DB2 databases. In addition, other transaction and batch processing workloads run on the system. We observe that most batch processing takes place during night

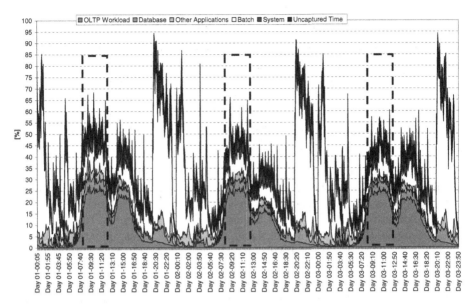

Fig. 1. Total Workload Utilization for Base Environment

Table 1. Measured Input Data of Base System

	Total CPU Utilization	Average Transaction Rate	Average Response Time (s)
Day 1	52%	320	0.096
Day 2	48%	343	0.087
Day 3	45%	336	0.087
Average	48%	333	0.090

time and OLTP during day time. Thus, the batch workload shows the highest utilization periods during night time[2]. For our analysis, we focus on the OLTP workload produced by the banking application and, more specifically, we focus on the period between 8:00 and 12:00 since it is the most critical period having the highest utilization for that workload, cf. dashed lines in Figure 1.

3.3 Metrics Measurements and Estimation

For our analysis, we summarize the system utilization and transaction rates. Furthermore, we calculate the average transaction response time (weighted over the number of transactions per day). Table 1 shows the measured input data for the specified time period for each day and the average values for all three days. We use the total utilization for the system, because we must consider the influence of the other workloads on the OLTP application. Even lower priority work (e.g., a parallel batch workload) shows influence. One main reason is that

---

[2] The analysis for the batch window has been omitted due to space constraints.

Table 2. Analysis of Execution States of Base System

Execution	Number of Samples			Corresponding Time Value (s)			
State	Day 1	Day 2	Day 3	Day 1	Day 2	Day 3	Average
CPU Using	10145	9919	9552	0.029	0.026	0.026	0.027
CPU Wait	2350	2251	2127	0.007	0.006	0.006	0.006
I/O Using	11248	10862	10422	0.032	0.029	0.028	0.030
I/O Wait	734	702	618	0.002	0.002	0.002	0.002
Other	9306	9302	9292	0.026	0.025	0.025	0.025

two partitions are used and the workloads running in different partitions are equally prioritized. Another reason is that the other workloads use the same cache structures and influence the execution of the considered workload.

The information shown in Table 1 can be measured directly. To obtain the CPU processing time for our model, we use execution state samples to apportion the measured response time. RMF samples execution states of all workloads in the system. These samples are taken every second and detect whether an execution unit is i) using CPU, ii) waiting on CPU, iii) using I/O, iv) waiting on I/O, or v) whether the execution unit is in a state not known to the operating system, e.g., waiting on a database lock. We summarize the samples of the OLTP workload and use them to apportion the response time so that we can calculate the CPU processing time. Table 2 shows the sample breakdown for the time frame from 08:00 to 12:00 of the three days being analyzed.

We will also use the sample states of Table 2 later when we compare the results of our model with data from the target system. We then evaluate whether our assumption that the influence of the I/O subsystem has not changed and that the I/O load is the same is correct. The same applies for the *Other* samples.

3.4   Performance Modeling

Model Creation, Calibration, and Projection. The next step is to select the possible target system configurations. Thus, we calibrate the model with the results from the previous section and project it using the relative capacity of the base and target systems. The relative capacity of each possible target system is taken from LSPR as described in Section 2.4. For our analysis we use the *Average* value, which applies to most installations. We also performed the analysis with the values obtained from the zPCR tool, which provide a slightly more accurate relative capacity, but in order to simplify the study we omit this step. Also, the results showed no significant difference.

Our base system has 33 processors. The target system is supposed to have less capacity and we compare five zEC12 that provide from 85% of the base system capacity up to a slightly higher capacity. The target system configurations have between 14 and 18 processors. The single processor speed of the target systems is nearly twice as fast as for the base system. As described in Section 2.4, for our model we use the number of processors and the relative capacity of the base and target system configurations. In addition, initially we assume an Allen-Cunneen

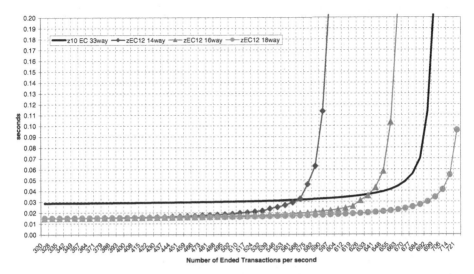

Fig. 2. Change in CPU Response Time

factor of one and later modify the model explicitly with factors of two and four to provide different estimations.

Prediction Results. We model the base system and, as example, three of the possible target system with 14, 16, and 18 processors. The interesting question is how the CPU processing time will change when the transaction rate is increased and how many transactions can be processed before the capacity of any of the target systems is exceeded. Figure 2 depicts the change in CPU processing time for the base system and the three possible target system configurations. On the z10 base system, 320 to 350 transactions per second are processed on average. With the same rate, no negative impact can be expected on any of the target systems, because the overall utilization on the base system is well below 60% as shown in Figure 1. Furthermore, Figure 1 shows that even peak utilizations are always below 70% during the main online processing time from 08:00 to 12:00.

More interesting is the question how many transactions can be processed before the CPU response time shows a significant increase. We define the threshold for a significant increase as two times the measured or projected CPU processing time. We choose two times, because this means that the CPU wait time at this point equals approximately the CPU processing time. At this point, we can expect that a slight change on the system can cause significant queuing and a high disturbance of transaction response times. We also take into account that the total system utilization includes other workloads being processed on the system, which may increase as well.

The base system is able to process at least 680 transactions per second before the CPU wait time has the same magnitude as the CPU processing time. The target system with 14 processors will be able to process 570 transactions per

Table 3. Maximum Capacity in Number of Transactions

Allen Cunneen	z10	zEC12		
Factor	33 CPUs	14 CPUs	16 CPUs	18 CPUs
1	680	570	630	690
2	660	530	610	665
4	605	500	550	610

Table 4. Measurement Data for New System with 14 Processors

	Total CPU Utilization	Average Transaction Rate	Average Response Time	Workload CPU Processing Time
Day 4	59%	370	0.075	0.014
Day 5	59%	364	0.093	0.017
Day 6	63%	382	0.075	0.014
Average Measured	60%	372	0.081	0.015
Modeling Results	62%	—	0.080	0.015

Table 5. Analysis of Execution States of New System

	Number of Samples			Corresponding Time Value			
State	Day 4	Day 5	Day 6	Day 4	Day 5	Day 6	Average
CPU Using	5114	5249	5462	0.014	0.017	0.014	0.015
CPU Wait	787	870	864	0.002	0.003	0.002	0.002
I/O Using	12328	12558	13208	0.033	0.041	0.034	0.036
I/O Wait	580	589	621	0.002	0.002	0.002	0.002
Other	9271	9469	9460	0.025	0.031	0.024	0.027

second. Table 3 shows the influence of different interarrival and service time distributions on the maximum number of transactions that can be processed on the considered systems.

The utilization law shown in Equation (5) allows us to predict the change of the total CPU Utilization on the target system when the number of transaction increases. When we use the results in the first row of Table 3 assuming an exponentially distributed transaction rate, we can determine that the maximum number of transactions corresponds to a system utilization of around 95%.

Finally, based on the modeling results we can recommend that for the OLTP workload, a target system with 14 CPUs should replace the existing system. We previously mentioned that another analysis was performed to estimate the total execution time of the batch workloads running during night time (cf. Figure 1). This analysis also suggested that a 14 CPU system was initially sufficient to accommodate the workload.

3.5   Evaluation

We took another set of measurements for a three day period after replacing the 33 processor system with the newer 14 processor zEC12 system. The measurement results are now compared to the modeling results in order to evaluate whether the model predictions were accurate. The measurement were taken for the same time period from 08:00 to 12:00 and summarized in Table 4.

Table 4 also shows the modeling results when we assume around 370 transactions for the new system. A comparison of the measurement data between Table 1 and Table 4 shows that around 11% more transactions were processed on the new system for our evaluation period than on the previous z10 system. Based on the utilization law we can determine that 360 to 380 processed transactions will cause a CPU utilization between 61% and 63%. Our measurements show a CPU utilization between 59% and 63%. Figure 2 shows that for 360 to 380 transactions the CPU processing time is around 0.015s, which also agrees with the measurements.

Finally, Table 5 depicts the processing states on the new system, which we compare with Table 2 from the previous system. We observe that the number of *Other* states has not changed, which means that the processing time for non-OS-related resources has not changed. I/O processing is slightly higher by 13%, however, we also observed 11% more transactions.

4   Discussion

Next, we discuss encountered caveats and practical challenges when using the proposed modeling and analysis approach.

CPU Parking. When we take a look at Table 2 and Table 5, we observe that the CPU wait samples and CPU wait times are higher for the 33 processor system compared to the 14 processor system. This is surprising and in general the times look too high for systems that are utilized by less than 70%. It is also not possible to model these waiting times in Table 2 with the existing queuing formula readily. In fact, the relatively high CPU queuing times result from an optimization for System z. The queuing formula assumes that the processors are always active and ready to process work, however, in the real environment, this is not the case. Many processors are placed in a parking state especially when the system is not too highly utilized. As a result, the system is optimized to reduce cache conflicts and, thus, the CPU processing time decreases and exhibits lower variability. The CPU wait time, however, is slightly higher, because the CPU dispatcher queues are longer than expected on a highly parallel system. In the end, this optimization provides much better throughput, however, the effect diminishes when the system utilization approaches 90% and can be ignored for our purposes.

Secondary Workload. It is difficult to use the model for subordinated workloads that typically run with lower priorities than the main workload. Especially when the transaction rates of the subordinate workloads are low compared to the main workload, the results may become questionable.

Virtualization. Another limitation arises from the environment setup. Our case study showed a fairly simple virtualized environment consisting of two partitions running identical workloads. This is not always the case. Especially many small partitions that process different types of workloads can be very disturbing and cause that no reliable results can be derived from the queuing model.

Clusters. In our case study, we used the methodology to replace a single hardware system. In many large IT installations, the target workload does not only run on a single system, but is spread across a cluster of systems. There are various difficulties arising from clusters to predict transaction response times and utilization of the systems. The most disturbing factors are that the workload distribution is often unequal between the systems and that the systems are configured differently. A different configuration means both that the hardware can be different, for example, that the systems have different number of processors, as well as that the number of partitions executed on the systems is different. Such influencing factors can cause inaccuracies when applying the modeling approach. For such environments, the queuing model needs to be extended to a queuing network modeling both the workload scheduler and the cluster systems.

5   Conclusion

We presented an industrial migration case study for a banking institute in a real-world environment based on IBM System z server technology. Our general goal in this paper was to show how a queuing model-based approach can be effectively used in a complex state-of-the-art real-world context.

In the study, an existing System z10 should be replaced with a newer System zEC12 model. Our approach was used to determine the appropriate number of processors to support the main OLTP workload even during peak periods. We used an open multi-server queuing model with general interarrival and service time distributions calibrating the service times with measurements on the existing system. The service times were projected to the new system using relative capacity information to predict the workload performance in the new environment. With this model, the recommended number of processors was determined. After the system migration, the prediction accuracy was evaluated by comparing the model predictions against measurements with a real-world production workload. Both the average response time and the total system utilization exhibited very high agreement with the predictions.

Finally, we discussed practical challenges and the conditions under which the queuing model would be inaccurate or require a more fine-grained extension to provide reliable predictions. Such challenges typically arise when there are system-specific optimizations, e.g., CPU parking, when the workload is running under low priority, or when the environment is highly distributed and heterogeneous, e.g., in large-scale virtualized and cluster environments.

Acknowledgements. This work was partially supported by the German Research Foundation (DFG) under grant No. RE 1674/5-1 and KO 3445/6-1.

References

1. Menascé, D., Almeida, V., Dowdy, L., Dowdy, L.: Performance by Design: Computer Capacity Planning by Example. Prentice Hall science explorer. Prentice Hall (2004)
2. Bolch, G., Greiner, S., de Meer, H., Trivedi, K.: Queueing Networks and Markov Chains: Modeling and Performance Evaluation with Computer Science Applications. Wiley (2006)
3. Allen, A.O.: Probability, Statistics, and Queueing Theory with Computer Science Applications. Academic Press (September 1978)
4. Kleinrock, L.: Queueing Systems: Theory. In: Queueing Systems. Wiley (1975)
5. IBM: Large Systems Performance Reference for IBM System z, https://www-304.ibm.com/servers/resourcelink/lib03060.nsf/pages/lsprindex
6. Shaw, J., Walsh, K.: J.F.: zPCR, IBM's Processor Capacity Reference. IBM, http://www-03.ibm.com/support/techdocs/atsmastr.nsf/WebIndex/PRS1381

Performance Evaluation for Collision Prevention Based on a Domain Specific Language*

Freek van den Berg[1], Anne Remke[1], Arjan Mooij[2], and Boudewijn Haverkort[1]

[1] DACS, University of Twente, Enschede, The Netherlands
[2] Embedded Systems Innovation by TNO, Eindhoven, The Netherlands
{f.g.b.vandenberg,a.k.i.remke,b.r.h.m.haverkort}@utwente.nl,
arjan.mooij@tno.nl

Abstract. The increasing complexity of embedded systems requires performance evaluation early in the design phase. We introduce a generic way of generating performance models based on a system description given in a domain-specific language (DSL). We provide a transformation from a DSL to a performance model in the Parallel Object-Oriented Specification Language (POOSL). A case study shows the feasibility of the approach in a complex interventional X-ray system, which requires appropriate measurement data on a prototype. Since distance computations are an integral part of the system, performance profiles of our chosen distance package, Proximity Query Package, have been created. The overall model has been successfully validated by comparing its outcomes with real measurements.

1 Introduction

Model-based and model-driven design methods have been proposed to improve the complex design process for embedded systems [7, 12, 17], but addressing the performance aspects remains difficult. Particularly, predicting performance early-in-design is hard, since the real system does not exist yet [4, 18]. This paper addresses early-in-design performance evaluation using a Domain Specific Language (DSL).

We report about an industrial study at Philips Healthcare aimed at redesigning collision prevention components used in their interventional X-ray (iXR) machines. Collision prevention strategies vary across product configurations and medical applications. To enhance reuseability across product configurations a prototype domain specific language (DSL, [16, 22]) for collision prevention was developed in collaboration with Philips. A DSL instance is a formal system specification, from which executable code is generated; see Figure 1 (left). Early in the study, distance computations were identified as performance critical. In the

---

* This research was supported as part of the Dutch national program COMMIT, and carried out as part of the Allegio project under the responsibility of the Embedded Systems Innovation group of TNO, with Philips Medical Systems B.V. as the carrying industrial partner.

M.S. Balsamo, W.J. Knottenbelt, and A. Marin (Eds.): EPEW 2013, LNCS 8168, pp. 276–287, 2013.
© Springer-Verlag Berlin Heidelberg 2013

context of robotics, various contributions [3, 15] about the use of the Proximity Query Package (PQP, [14]) for distance computations exist. Hence, we decided to use PQP to illustrate our approach.

This paper introduces DSL-based performance evaluation in the design phase (Figure 1, right). Formal specification mechanisms that allow reasoning about product families and enable design space exploration exist [19, 23]. DSL-based performance evaluation requires an automatic transformation from DSL-instances to performance models. We used the Parallel Object-Oriented Specification Language (POOSL, [6, 20]) as modelling language and derive functional flows of executable functions from DSL-instances. To gain insight in the execution times, we used PQP-profiles and use cases as additional model parameters.

Related Work. A variety of techniques exist for the performance evaluation of embedded software, both from the more traditional field of queueing theory, as from the field of embedded system design. A good overview using a model-based approach is provided in [1]. We address a few recent cases below, without attempting to be exhaustive. Process algebra models, in particular PEPA, have been used for the

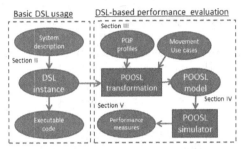

Fig. 1. Basic DSL usage (left), extended with DSL performance evaluation (right)

evaluation of an industrial production cell [8], whereas [2] uses PEPA to specify active badge models to compute so-called passage times. Petri nets, data flow graphs (SDF) and timed automata (UPPAAL) were compared for the evaluation of an image processing pipeline [9]. The Petri net approach provided the most expressive modelling framework, UPPAAL was most adequate in finding schedules and SDF appeared to be most scalable. [10] describes the evaluation of a printer datapath, where UPPAAL is used to compute worst-case completion times. Using PRISM, a CTMC model of an embedded system is evaluated and shutdown probabilities are obtained [13]. POOSL [6] has been used for a production cell model [11] and an in-car navigation system model [21]. In the current case study, a soft real-time system in which consecutive distance query functions need to be executed is modelled. A worst-case analysis seems less appropriate here, as this assumes the extremely unlikely case that all functionality under-performs at the same time. We therefore turn our attention to discrete-event simulations, supported by the tool POOSL, which provide us with useful statistical results.

Paper Outline. This paper is further organised according to Figure 1. Section 2 describes the case study system. Section 3 specifies the PQP-query profiling. Section 4 presents the POOSL model. Section 5 validates the POOSL performance-model. Section 6 concludes the paper.

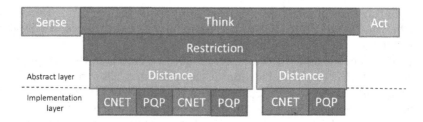

Fig. 2. The structure (GANNT-chart) of the functions of the movement-control loop

2   System Description

iXR systems obtain patient images with X-ray technology. They consist of large and heavy objects (Figure 3) that move based on user-input. Collision prevention is vital for the safety of the patient and implemented by a movement control loop. We focus on a collision prevention technique based on 3D-models which frequently computes the shortest distance between two 3D-objects.

The movement control loop intervenes when two objects are getting too close to each other by overriding user speed-requests. It demands stable and low response times to ensure timely and correct actions. The movement control loop executes in a single-threaded, sequential and non-preemptive manner. At its highest abstraction level, it can be decomposed in three functions: **Sense**, **Think** and **Act** (Figure 2). They are responsible for reading geometric sensor positions, decision taking, and sending object speed-requests. **Sense** and **Act** are atomic functions by design. The more complex function **Think** has recently been re-

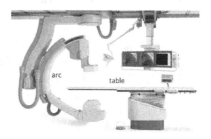

Fig. 3. iXR system with a "table" that can move in several dimensions, and an "arc" that rotates around the table in various ways, at relatively high speeds

designed using a DSL prototype. It is of utmost importance that the redesigned function executes fast enough to ensure safety, at all times.

Think consists of several so-called **restrictions**. The DSL implements restrictions by a conditional collision-danger clause (yielding true if it applies to the currently sensed situation) and a (translational or rotational) speed limit. Both the collision-danger clause and the speed limit may contain distance queries.

At the lowest abstraction level, distance queries are executed, implemented using the Proximity Query Package (PQP [14]). Distance queries are performed for a pair of geometrical objects in a specific model. They comprise one or more PQP calls (due to object decomposition), each preceded by one preparatory CNET operation. Compared to PQP, CNET operates fast and in constant time.

3   PQP Profiling

We create a PQP performance profile by measuring execution times in a variety of circumstances, using a 3D-model of a real iXR system. The resulting empirical cumulative density functions are used for simulations (Section 4). PQP-queries require two sets of triangles as input and execute an heuristic algorithm that selects one triangle per set, to minimize the distance between triangles. PQP returns an exact distance even though the algorithm is heuristic. PQP uses bounded volumes [14] as an abstraction mechanism for objects. This makes PQP faster than the $O(nm)$ theoretical worst-case (with n and m the number of triangles per object), however, results in variable execution-times that are hard to determine a priori.

Experimental profiling conveyed that both the complexity of the input objects and their relative geometric positions affect the performance of PQP significantly. To take this into account, we first classify PQP queries on the basis of input object-pairs to account for run-time variations resulting from different object complexities. Hence, we do not compare PQP queries that are performed on different objects. Second, we perform PQP queries for a large amount of relative geometric positions to diminish the effect relative positions have. The effect the relative positions have on the performance of PQP is caused by the heuristic way PQP looks for the distance-defining triangles. PQP operates in a 3-dimensional space in which objects can be translated and/or rotated using 12 dimensions with $\geq 10^{35}$ positions. Due to the immense size of this space, we use four profiling methods to take a representative sample from the immense search space, named 2D, 3D, 9D-grid, and 9D-random.

2D and 3D profiling cover positions that match so-called test cases, that represent realistic scenarios that include positions in which objects are near each other. As will turn out, PQP generally performs worse when object distances are small. Profiling using 2D or 3D allows for small step sizes, but is restricted to a small part of the sample space. In con-

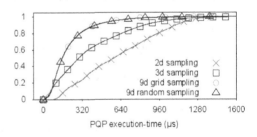

Fig. 4. The execution-time CDFs for PQP_1

trast, the 9D-grid method varies in 3 or 4 positions in 9 dimensions, while the 9D-random selects geometric positions with uniform probability in 9 dimensions. Both cover a large part of the search-space, but local maxima and minima may be missed. Note that the 2D and 3D methods sample in a biased way and the 9D methods in a unbiased way.

We took 13467 (2D), 137417 (3D), 88671 (9D-grid) and 90012 (9D-random) geometric positions on which we performed eleven PQP distance queries. PQP-queries were classified for eleven object pairs and four profiling methods, resulting in 44 kinds of PQP-queries. We constructed 44 empirical CDFs, as follows:

$$\hat{F}_j(t) = \frac{1}{n_j} \sum_{i=1}^{n_j} \mathbf{1}\{x_i^j \le t\}, \quad j = 1, \cdots, 44,$$

where n_j is the sample size, and x_i^j the execution-time of sample i for case j. The results for the most complex PQP-query in terms of both object complexities and execution-time illustrate the difference between the different profiling methods. As shown in Figure 4, the execution times of the 2D and 3D methods are higher than their 9D counterparts. This is a result of using biased test cases with 'difficult' geometric positions versus unbiased positions in 9d sampling.

4   POOSL-Performance Model

We present a performance model of the Think-component, by far the most time-consuming part of the movement control loop. The model is automatically generated from a DSL instance using a model transformation. It is specified in POOSL [6, 20], which enables fast-simulation using the Rotalumis engine [5].

4.1   POOSL Model Outline

The POOSL model (Figure 5) contains five components, i.e., Think, Cache, Distance Query, PQP and Use case. It is initialized using three parameters: the DSL instance, PQP profiles and Use case characteristics. Loops, conditional code executions and functions are assumed independent to keep the model simple without sacrificing accuracy too much.

The POOSL-model corresponds to the Think-part of the movement control loop. It is triggered by an incoming message at its start-port, after which it delegates work, via the components Cache and Distance_query, to the PQP component, by triggering the respective start-ports. In return, messages go all the way back through the finished-ports to confirm successful executions. This mechanism yields a single-threaded model, in accordance with the real Think-component. The model components have specific responsibilities: Think generates distance queries to be performed and forwards them to the Cache. The Use case determines which conditional distance queries are executed. The Cache filters out redundant distance queries to ensure consistent distance values and to enhance performance. PQP simulates PQP-executions according to a given profile by taking samples from the corresponding CDF. Simulating the Think-component requires three parameters named DSL-instances, use cases and PQP profiles, respectively. First, a DSL-instance is transformed into a sequence of (conditional) distance queries that repeats indefinitely. For each distance query in Think, the Use case-component is accessed to decide whether it should be executed. The Use case-component is initialized with the use-case parameter, which comprises a set of use case characteristics, i.e., the conditional distance queries in the Think-component and the probability of execution. Distance queries in the Think-component that have no cache-hit become PQP-queries. The CDFs of PQP's execution-times (the third parameter) are used for

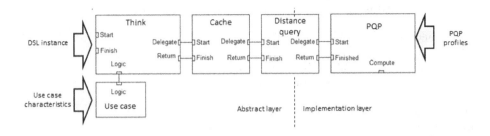

Fig. 5. POOSL performance-model of the movement control

sampling execution-times using random numbers. The object pair of the PQP-query determines which CDF is used, while geometric positions are implicitly considered by the variation the CDF provides.

4.2   The DSL-Instance

A prototypical DSL with a tailored grammar has been designed that specifies safe object movements by keeping track of object distances and speeds. In practice, DSL-instances are automatically transformed to executable code. They declare models and objects that form the basis of distance queries. Restrictions impose a speed limit on an object when an activation condition is met. The condition generally contains distance queries to check whether objects are far enough apart. The speed limit can be constant or may depend on object distances and potentially overrides higher user requests.

We have also constructed a second transformation from DSL-instances to POOSL-model **Think**-components that can be applied to all DSL-instances (Figure 1, right). It generates a POOSL **Think**-component with a fixed amount of distance queries. However, distance queries (may) execute conditionally for two reasons. First, binary boolean connectors are frequently implemented using lazy evaluation, making the evaluation of the right operand conditional. Consequently, distance queries in the right operand might not be performed. Second, when the activation evaluates to false, distance queries that are in the effect are not performed. The transformation accounts for both aspects by enclosing conditional POOSL-code fragments with if-statements, the so-called use-case characteristics.

In our case study, we use a DSL-instance with four pairs of restrictions of which we show two in Table 1. They prevent collisions between the TableTop and the Beam object. The remaining pairs are similar, but apply to other object pairs. The **ApproachingTableTopBeam** clause (lines 6-11) activates when the objects are within a certain distance (line 8) and approach each other (line 9). If so, the speed limit is lowered, using a monotone break pattern (line 11). The **CloseTableTopBeam** clause (lines 13-18) results in an emergency stop for very small distances (line 18). We provide pseudo-code of the **Think**-component (Table 2) derived from the DSL-instance in Table 1, with seven distance queries. Both restrictions start with an unconditional distance query (Table 2, lines 1

Table 1. A DSL-instance example with two restrictions

```
 1 supervisor
 2
 3 object TableBase, TableTop, Beam, Detector
 4 model Now, Future, NowHyst, FutureHyst
 5
 6 restriction ApproachingTableTopBeam
 7 activation
 8    Distance[FutureHyst](TableTop, Beam) <18 + 125 &&
 9    Distance[Future](TableTop, Beam) <Distance[Now](TableTop, Beam) - 0.3
10 effect
11    limit Beam[Rotation] at ((Distance[Future](TableTop,Beam) - 25) / 100))
12
13 restriction CloseTableTopBeam
14 activation
15    Distance[NowHyst](TableTop, Beam) <17.5 &&
16    Distance[Future](TableTop, Beam) <Distance[Now](TableTop, Beam) + 0.3
17 effect
18    limit TableTop[Translation] at 0
```

and 9), since the left operands of the &&-operators execute each loop (Table 1, lines 8 and 15). Next, two queries per restriction are conditional (Table 2, lines 3,4,11 and 12), since the right operands of the &&-operators are lazy-evaluation susceptible (Table 2, lines 9 and 16). Finally, the first restriction has a fourth distance query (Table 2, line 6). It only executes when both operands of the &&-operators yield true, because it is in the effect clause (Table 1, line 11).

4.3 Use Cases

The requirements of iXR-systems depend on the use-case at hand. We define a use-case as a set of labels that refer to fragments of code and an execution probability for each label. Table 3 displays, for three use cases, the probabilities for each label (with "other" the probability for all other labels). A label is decomposed into a fixed prefix "r", restriction number (1 to 8) and restriction part (activation or limit) in line with the pseudo code (Table 1). The values represent the probabilities that the corresponding fragments of conditional code are executed. For instance, the value 0.29 for r2a in Use case 1, indicates that in restriction 2, distance queries 2 and 3 (Table 2, lines 11 and 12) are executed in 29% of the cases.

4.4 PQP Profiles

We created PQP-profiles (Section 3) to enable the sampling of execution-times for simulation. For this purpose, the profiles are injected into the PQP-component of the POOSL-model, which simulates the execution of a CNET-operation (converting objects to triangles), followed by a PQP-query based on a distance pair.

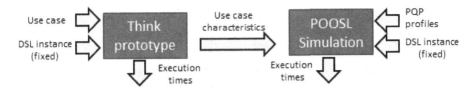

Fig. 6. The experimental setup; compare simulations with `Think`-prototype executions

The execution of CNET took 517 μs on average with a 58 μs standard deviation. We model this as an uniform distribution U(459,575), for each distant pair. The PQP-component receives distance queries (with an object pair parameter) from `Think`. PQP selects the CDF of the object-pair, draws a sample from this CDF and simulates a CNET-operation followed by a PQP-query (using a POOSL delay). While sampling from these CDFs during simulation, we choose to not use interpolation. Instead, we "round" to the first higher sample, hence, only return values that have actually been observed during profiling.

5   Validating the Movement-Control Performance Model

We assess the validity of the performance model by providing the experimental set-up, results per use case and additional measurements. We use the DSL-instance (Table 1) for all experiments and three use cases (Table 3). We simulate for four different profiling methods (Section 3).

We performed one real-time execution on the `Think`-prototype machine (Figure 6) with different user inputs, for 278, 284 and 301 seconds, respectively. We performed simulations, for 4 profiling methods and 3 use cases, covering 125488, 144178 and 140618 cycles, respectively. Finally, we generated distributions of simulation and execution results per use case. We used one PC (i5-2400, QuadCPU@3.10Ghz, 3Gb RAM) for executions and another PC (AMD A6-3400m, QuadCPU@1.4Ghz, 6Gb RAM) for simulations.

Table 2. Pseudo code of Think component for two restrictions

Restriction 1
ApproachingTableTopBeam
1 $Distance[FutureHyst]$
2 if (r1a){
3    $Distance[Future]$
4    $Distance[Now]$
5   if (r1lim) {
6      $Distance[Future]$ } }

Restriction 2
CloseTableTopBeam
9 $Distance[NowHyst]$
10 if (r2a) {
11   $Distance[Future]$
12   $Distance[Now]$ }

Use Case 1. The `Arc`-object has been rotated in various ways around and towards the `Table`-object, while the `Table` remained motionless. As shown in Figure 7 (left-top) simulations based on 2D and 3D profiling are pessimistic, whereas those based on 9D-profiling match the execution slightly better. This is due to 2D and 3D-based profiling overestimating the most complex query PQP_1.

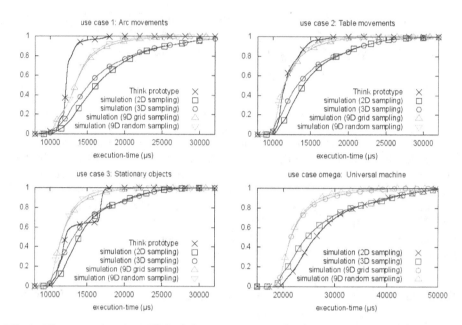

Fig. 7. The execution-time CDFs for use case 1 and 2 (top), use case 3 and Ω (bottom)

Use Case 2. The `Table`-object has been moved towards and away from the `Arc` mimicking situations in which patients enter and leave iXR systems. Figure 7 (right-top) shows that 9D-simulations match the prototype execution reasonably

Table 3. Use case 1,2,3: characteristics

Label	r2a	r2lim	r3a	r4a	r4lim	other
UC1	0.29	0.99	0.02	0.11	0.71	0
UC2	0.07	0.04	0	0	0	0
UC3	0.01	0.79	0.01	0.12	0.62	0

well. Therefore, replacing unknown PQP-queries with similar ones and using assumptions to keep the model simple, has not affected the results much. 2D and 3D simulations overestimate execution-times, which is again contributed to the PQP_1 profile. Both 9D-simulations underestimate for low execution-times.

Use Case 3. Stationary behaviour that is common for iXR machines, has been performed. Nevertheless, computations took place with objects close to each other. All stationary positions resemble those in previous use cases. Figure 7 (left-bottom) displays the results for Use case 3. The curve of the `Think`-prototype contains three points of inflection. The results are concentrated around two values, namely 11 and 16 ms. We contribute this to spending a large amount of time in a few number of positions, opposed to changing between positions gradually. On average, the outcomes of simulations match the execution well for non-dependent use case characteristics. Again, simulations based on 2D and 3D profiles are more pessimistic than their 9D-counterparts.

Use Case Ω. In addition to the three use cases, we constructed a fourth one in which all conditional code executes, i.e., all use case characteristics have value 1. We have simulated this use case for all profiling methods (Figure 7, right-bottom), but did not execute it on the Think-prototype. The use case Ω represents the worst use case. Use case Ω illustrates the proportion of conditional code for the specific DSL instance.

Table 4 shows the Kolmogorov distances K between the Think-prototype F and corresponding simulations G, per use case and profiling method, computed as $K = \sup_x |F(x) - G(x)|$. A small distance indicates a high similarity. The results indicate that profiling methods that cover many dimensions have lower Kolmogorov distances. Since both 9D-simulations have similar CDFs, their Kolmogorov distances are small. We conclude that for the current geometrical domain the 9D grid and 9D random method yield equal results. Although the simulation and exectuion CDFs differ much for Use case 3, their Kolmogorov distances are low.

To determine how quickly simulations converge we have also computed the Kolmogorov distance between short and long simulations runs. 2D and 3D-simulations converged within a second, while the 9D-ones needed 15 seconds. Therefore, the presented simulations are of sufficient length.

We have computed the ratios of simulation and prototype execution times as a measure of how much the simulations overestimate the Think-prototype. The ratio R is derived as $R = \sup_{x>0 \wedge y>0} \{x/y \mid F(x) = G(y)\}$. The results (Table 5) indicate that 2D and 3D-simulations lead to higher ratios than both 9D-simulations. This is due to higher expected executions-times for 2D and 3D-profiling. Use case 1 contains the highest ratios of 2.02 (2D) and 2.03 (3D). They correspond to the large distances shown in Figure 7 (left-top). In general, low execution-times correlate with low ratios. Hence, simulation results have a higher variance than Think-prototype results and are particularly overestimating at peak execution-times. The highest observed ratio of 2.03 indicates that the amount of overestimation is bounded.

Table 4. Kolmogorov distances per use case and profiling method

	2D	3D	9Dg	9Dr
UC1	0.67	0.58	0.41	0.41
UC2	0.42	0.30	0.16	0.16
UC3	0.29	0.18	0.27	0.30

Table 5. Maximum execution-time ratios per use case and profiling method

	2D	3D	9Dg	9Dr
UC1	2.02	2.03	1.53	1.68
UC2	1.79	1.79	1.54	1.72
UC3	1.81	1.81	1.55	1.58

We draw three conclusions from the experiments. First, applying use cases saves dramatically on hardware resources and determining the use case characteristics is a delicate procedure that can lead to underestimating execution-times. Second, the execution-time ratio between use case Ω and others is DSL-dependent, since it depends on the proportional amount of conditional code. Third, we conclude that simulations yield higher execution-times than the Think-prototype. 2D and 3D sampling showed higher execution-times then 9D sampling, as a result of test case-based profiling. Overestimation is desirable to some extend, since underestimation might lead to non-safe machines in the very end. However, over-dimensioned hardware literally has its price. Finally, simulations of various lengths have confirmed that the simulations of the experiment are of sufficient length.

6   Conclusion and Future Work

We have constructed a DSL-based POOSL-performance model for interventional X-ray systems. Additionally, we have profiled PQP distance queries and introduced use cases to make the models more situation specific. We evaluated the validity of our model by comparing POOSL-simulation results with Think-prototype executions. In the worst case, the model over-estimated the execution-times of the Think-prototype with a factor 2.03. Simulations converged within 15 seconds. When comparing our approach that uses a transformation from DSL to a performance model with one in which the performance model is made manually, we observe the following. Our DSL-based approach better connects the roles of the domain expert (building the DSL model) and the performance analysis expert, building the transformation. Also, the DSL-transformation makes it possible to easily generate multiple performance model instances based on different DSL-instances. A manual low-level approach would be much more labour intensive. Compared to a manually constructed performance model, DSLs make the switch to other performance techniques easier. Furthermore, a DSL-instance can, using multiple transformations, be the source of different artefacts at the same time, such as true code, models, and documentation.

In future work, we will investigate the use of analytical methods, such as data flow diagrams, process algebra and queuing networks to explore a wide range of scenarios and to get insight in the underlying system characteristics, at even lower costs than with simulation. Based on our experiences so far, we foresee DSLs to be an integral aspect while applying these methods.

References

1. Balsamo, S., Di Marco, A., Inverardi, P., Simeoni, M.: Model-based performance prediction in software development: A survey. IEEE Transactions on Software Engineering 30(5), 295–310 (2004)
2. Bradley, J., Dingle, N., Gilmore, S., Knottenbelt, W.: Extracting passage times from PEPA models with the HYDRA tool: A case study. In: Proc. of the 19th Annual UK Performance Engineering Workshop, pp. 79–90 (2003)
3. Carpin, S., Mirolo, C., Pagello, E.: A performance comparison of three algorithms for proximity queries relative to convex polyhedra. In: Proc. of Int. Conference on Robotics and Automation, pp. 3023–3028. IEEE (2006)
4. de Gooijer, T., Jansen, A., Koziolek, H., Koziolek, A.: An industrial case study of performance and cost design space exploration. In: Proc. of the 3rd Int. Conference on Performance Engineering, WOSP/SIPEW, pp. 205–216. ACM (2012)
5. Eindhoven University of Technology. Software/Hardware Engineering - High-Speed Simulation of POOSL Models with Rotalumis,
   http://www.es.ele.tue.nl/she/index.php?select=42

6. Eindhoven University of Technology. Software/Hardware Engineering - Parallel Object-Oriented Specification Language (POOSL), http://www.es.ele.tue.nl/poosl/
7. Henzinger, T., Sifakis, J.: The discipline of embedded systems design. IEEE Computer 40(10), 32–40 (2007)
8. Holton, D.: A PEPA specification of an industrial production cell. The Computer Journal 38(7), 542–551 (1995)
9. Igna, G., Kannan, V., Yang, Y., Basten, T., Geilen, M., Vaandrager, F.W., Voorhoeve, M., de Smet, S., Somers, L.: Formal modeling and scheduling of datapaths of digital document printers. In: Cassez, F., Jard, C. (eds.) FORMATS 2008. LNCS, vol. 5215, pp. 170–187. Springer, Heidelberg (2008)
10. Igna, G., Vaandrager, F.: Verification of printer datapaths using timed automata. In: Margaria, T., Steffen, B. (eds.) ISoLA 2010, Part II. LNCS, vol. 6416, pp. 412–423. Springer, Heidelberg (2010)
11. Jinfeng, H., Voeten, J., Groothuis, M., Broenink, J., Corporaal, H.: A model-driven design approach for mechatronic systems. In: 7th Int. Conference on Application of Concurrency to System Design, pp. 127–136. IEEE (2007)
12. Karsai, G., Sztipanovits, J., Ledeczi, A., Bapty, T.: Model-integrated development of embedded software. Proc. of the IEEE 91(1), 145–164 (2003)
13. Kwiatkowska, M., Norman, G., Parker, D.: Controller dependability analysis by probabilistic model checking. Control Engineering Practice 15(11), 1427–1434 (2007)
14. Larsen, E., Gottschalk, S., Lin, M., Manocha, D.: Fast distance queries with rectangular swept sphere volumes. In: Proc. of Int. Conference on Robotics and Automation, vol. 4, pp. 3719–3726. IEEE (2000)
15. Lingelbach, F., Aarno, D., Kragic, D.: Constrained path planning for mobile manipulators. In: Proc. of the 3rd Swedish Workshop on Autonomous Robotics (2005)
16. Mernik, M., Heering, J., Sloane, A.: When and how to develop domain-specific languages. ACM Computing Surveys 37(4), 316–344 (2005)
17. Schätz, B., Pretschner, A., Huber, F., Philipps, J.: Model-based development of embedded systems. In: Bruel, J.-M., Bellahsène, Z. (eds.) OOIS 2002. LNCS, vol. 2426, pp. 298–311. Springer, Heidelberg (2002)
18. Sharma, V., Trivedi, K.: Architecture based analysis of performance, reliability and security of software systems. In: Proc. of the 5th Int. workshop on Software and Performance, pp. 217–227. ACM (2005)
19. Tawhid, R., Petriu, D.: User-friendly approach for handling performance parameters during predictive software performance engineering. In: Proc. of the 3rd Int. Conference on Performance Engineering, WOSP/SIPEW, pp. 109–120. ACM (2012)
20. Theelen, B., Florescu, O., Geilen, M., Huang, J., van der Putten, P., Voeten, J.: Software/hardware engineering with the parallel object-oriented specification language. In: Proc. of Formal Methods and Models for Codesign, pp. 139–148. IEEE (2007)
21. Theelen, B., Voeten, J., Kramer, R.: Performance modelling of a network processor using poosl. Computer Networks 41(5), 667–684 (2003)
22. van Deursen, A., Klint, P., Visser, J.: Domain-specific languages: an annotated bibliography. ACM SIGPLAN Notices 35(6), 26–36 (2000)
23. Wang, S., Shin, K.: Early-stage performance modeling and its application for integrated embedded control software design. ACM Software Engineering Notes 29(1), 110–114 (2004)

An Approximate Mean Value Analysis Approach for System Management and Overload Control

Vittoria De Nitto Personé and Andrea Di Lonardo

University of Rome Tor Vergata, Italy
denitto@info.uniroma2.it

Abstract. Blocking is the phenomenon where a service request is momentarily stopped, but not lost, until the service becomes available again. Despite its importance, blocking is a difficult phenomenon to model analytically, because it creates strong inter-dependencies in the systems components. Mean Value Analysis (MVA) is one of the most appealing evaluation methodology since its low computational cost and easy of use. In this paper, an approximate MVA for Bloking After Service is presented that greatly outperforms previous results. The new algorithm is obtained by analyzing the inter-dependencies due to the blocking mechanism and by consequently modifying the MVA equations. The proposed algorithm is tested and then applied to a capacity planning and admission control study of a web server system.

Keywords: blocking, modeling techniques, performance, system management, overload control, multi-tiered systems.

1 Introduction

Blocking is the phenomenon where a service request is momentarily stopped, but not lost, until the service becomes available again. This service unavailability can stem from a physical limit (e.g., memory, connectivity or concurrency constraints) or it can even relate to a system management decision in order to overcome an overload period and to guarantee QoS requirements. Consequently, blocking can affect system performance significantly. We point the interested reader to [3,10,11,12] for an extensive bibliography of different blocking mechanisms that model distinct behaviors of real systems. A lot of applications of blocking models can be found from recent literature including computer systems [7], communication systems and networks [6], software architectures [2], multi-tier applications [9] and also in the emerging area of health care systems [8].

Despite its importance, blocking is a difficult phenomenon to model analytically, because it results in strong dependencies in the behavior of the system components. As is known, the most results for blocking queueing networks are limited to tandem or cyclic topologies. Differently, in this paper, we consider general topology networks. Among the analytical techniques for general topologies, Mean Value Analysis [13] still plays an important role, since its simplicity and efficiency, as this is proved by its recent use in different application fields [4,5,16,17,20]. To the best of our knowledge, in the literature there are very few results for general topology networks and extensions of MVA were presented for Repetitive Service (RS) blocking in [14] and for Blocking

M.S. Balsamo, W.J. Knottenbelt, and A. Marin (Eds.): EPEW 2013, LNCS 8168, pp. 288–299, 2013.
© Springer-Verlag Berlin Heidelberg 2013

After Service (BAS) blocking in [1,19]. The interested reader can refer to [19] for other references for cyclic networks. In particular, in [14] a class of product form (PF) networks is considered. It is worth noting that in that case the interdependencies among the nodes due to blocking are "neutralized" by the separability property of PF networks. Moreover, RS blocking is the simplest blocking model. Indeed, according to its definition, the queue is not blocked at all, but the service is repeated until the destination queue becomes "available" again. In both papers [1,19], non-PF networks with BAS blocking are considered. In [19], the proposed extension, called EMVA, is obtained by means of load dependent servers and queue length distribution. As for standard MVA, in this case the method suffers of instability as more pronounced as the population grows. The MVABLO algorithm tries to modify the arrival theorem [13] to include the blocking behavior without resorting to the queue length distribution. In some cases, the results are quite good to provide the throughput, but are not so reliable for the other performance measures. In particular, the proposed approximation shows the worst results for cyclic networks.

On the basis of these considerations, in this paper an iterative version of MVA for BAS blocking is proposed that greatly improves the previous results. The method is called MVABAS and is obtained by an in-depth analysis of the inter-dependencies due to the blocking mechanism and by consequently modifying the MVA equations. MVABAS shows good results for general topology networks and improves significantly the approximation for cyclic networks. In all cases, the convergence speed is fast. This is the main contribution of the paper. The proposed method is applied to a capacity planning study for a web server system under two different workloads. The aim is to investigate among different system management strategies to meet a Service Level Objective (SLO) defined as the average session response time. The model parameters are set depending on both the workload and the architecture characteristics. Some guidelines are derived from the results. We chose this case study to further emphasize the importance of an efficient and low-cost modelling technique to investigate and correctly drive the system management decision process.

The rest of the paper is organized as follows. Section 2 present the model and the analysis of the MVABLO algorithm and its weak points. In Section 3, we define our MVABAS algorithm and compare the results with MVABLO. Section 4 presents the case study. Finally, Section 5 concludes the paper.

2   MVABLO Analysis

We consider a single-class closed queueing network with routing matrix P such that jobs departing from queue i are directed to queue j with probability p_{ij}. The queue service time s_i is assumed exponentially distributed for each queue i. If the capacity of queue j is B_j and n_j denotes the current population at queue j, then when $n_j = B_j$ queue j is *full* and does not accept in its waiting buffer any *new* job before a departure occurs. Queue i can become *blocked*. Note that deadlock can occur in presence of blocking. In the following, we assume that the network population value is such that the deadlock prevention is guaranteed [3]. The time of blocking, the unblocking rule and the behavior of the job possibly in execution in i at the blocking time are defined by the blocking mechanism.

Blocking After Service (BAS) is one of the most used blocking mechanisms and is defined as follows: a queue i, if not empty, processes a job regardless of the job population at its destination j. When node i completes service and node j is full, node i suspends any activity (i.e., it is blocked) and the completed job waits until a departure occurs from node j. At that moment two simultaneous transitions take place: the completed/blocked job moves from i to j (since j can now accept a job, i "unblocks") and the job that leaves j (which effectively "unblocks" server i). In a general network topology where more than one queue compete for sending a job towards a full queue j, a policy regulating the order in which queues unblock has to be defined. Usually, the First Blocked First Unblocked (FBFU) policy is considered fair: first unblock the queue that was blocked first. BAS mechanism is also used to model production systems and disk I/O subsystems [18].

Despite the complexity of the queues behavior, due to their dependences and simultaneous transitions that can involve more than two queues, in the following section we show an approximate iterative MVA that shows good results. We focus just on the mean residence time equation, since this is the modified equation in respect of classical MVA. According to [1], the mean residence time of queue j can be computed as follows:

$$E[t_j(k)] = E[s_j](z_j(k) + E[n_j(k-1)]) + BT_j(k) \qquad (1)$$

where k is the network population, $z_j(k) = 1$ or $z_j(k) = 0$ represents the job arrived to queue j when this is not full or full respectively, while $BT_j(k) \geq 0$ represents the increment of residence time of queue j due to blocking, as described below. Note that when $z_j(k) = 1$ and $BT_j(k) = 0$ equation (1) coincides with the standard MVA equation. On the contrary, when blocking occurs the original arrival theorem does not hold and the idea behind the proposed solution is as follows:

- when the mean length of queue j exceeds its capacity B_j (called "violation"), the job cannot be enqueued and the arrival theorem equation has to be corrected setting $z_j(k) = 0$; the algorithm continues to iterate until the violation is removed;
- on the other hand, when the queue j is blocked by a queue i, its residence time is increased by the remaining mean service time $E[s_{rest_i}]$ of queue i, and assuming exponential service time distribution, $E[s_{rest_i}] = E[s_i]$, so the increment is the blocking time $BT_j(k) = E[s_i]p_{ji}e_j/e_i$, where e_j is the relative throughput obtained as a solution of the system $e = eP$.

First, note that the proposed solution does not consider the delay centers. Indeed, all the experiments in [1] exclude delay centers. Moreover, as we introduced in the previous section, MVABLO does not yield a so good approximation. In particular, as soon as the congestion grows the results worse, especially for residence times and mean queue lengths. Moreover, the results fluctuate between overestimating and underestimating the performance metrics, so returning difficult error estimate. Cyclic networks show the worst results. An error cause is identified by the author himself in [1] and resides in the "method" to recognize a saturation condition. Indeed, using the *mean* queue lengths is not enough to capture the blocking condition: a blocking condition can appear even when the mean queue length is less than the node capacity. In fact, it is enough that the total network population N is greater than B_j to produce blocking conditions in the sending nodes of node j. On the other hand, by growing N values the blocking will occur more frequently. In our opinion, this is not the main error cause, but we envisage the following most important error cause: the "effective intensity" of the blocking is not captured and the correction is operated always in the same measure using an "all or nothing" rule, that is simply canceling the arriving job ($z_j(k) = 0$). On the contrary, it is worth noting that the blocked job cannot disappear from the network, but it has to wait in the sending node, accordingly to BAS blocking. We think cyclic topologies represent one critical case for this reason: sequence of full queues are possible and simultaneous transitions can involve more than two queues. Moreover, we define a factor depending on the network population of the current iteration and on the node finite capacity B_j, thus capturing the effective incidence of the blocking phenomenon as the network population grows at each iteration step. As we show in the following section, this seems to partially overtake the limit of the *mean* analysis of MVA.

3   The MVABAS Algorithm

The MVA algorithm [13] is based on iteration on the network population and, for each step, the queue mean performance indices are computed. In MVABLO, as explained in the previous section, the blocking condition is detected when the mean queue length $E[n_j(k)]$ violates the queue capacity B_j. In this case, the two corrections are produced both on the queue j itself and on its possibly sending nodes i. This corrections are lacking in two aspects: 1. the correction is too "drastic": the "blocked job" is canceled from the network; 2. the corrections are applied without regulating their intensity. This is against the main characteristic of MVA that is based on mean values. As a consequence, the detected violation cannot capture the different intensities of the blocking phenomenon on the different queues. Finally, the MVABLO does not consider delay centers. On the contrary, this kind of servers are very important to model different aspects of systems, e.g. sessions in multi-tier applications [17] or access networks.

For these reasons, we define the mean residence time $E[t_j(k)]$ as follows:

$$E[t_j(k)] = \begin{cases} E[s_j] + \dfrac{BT_j(k)}{k} & \text{delay center} \\ E[s_j](z_j(k) + E[n_j(k-1)]) + BT_j(k) & \text{single server center} \end{cases} \qquad (2)$$

where k is the network population at the given iteration step, $BT_j(k)$ is defined as in Section 2 and initially set to 0; $z_j(k)$ is initially set to 1 and is updated when a blocking condition is detected, i.e. $E[n_j(k)] > B_j$, as follows:

$$z_j(k) = z_j(k) - \beta_j(k) * z_j(k) \qquad (3)$$

for the blocking queue j

$$z_i(k) = z_i(k) + \beta_j(k) * p_{ij} * z_j(k) \qquad (4)$$

for each sending nodes i. In both equations (3) and (4), $\beta_j(k)$ is a a *blocking intensity* factor defined as follows:

$$\beta_j(k) = \begin{cases} 1 - \dfrac{B_j}{k} & \text{if } k > B_j \\ 0 & \text{otherwise} \end{cases} \tag{5}$$

As explained above, the ratio of the proposed solution is that the blocked job cannot disappear from the network. On the other hand, given the use of mean measures, the incidence of the blocked job on j is reduced according to the blocking intensity factor $\beta_j(k)$ (see eq.((3)). Moreover, this population removed from j, is "redistributed" on all its sending node i, according to their "connectivity weight" p_{ij} (see eq.((4)), thus correcting the "all or nothing" approach in MVABLO. Finally, note that for delay centers, according to BAS blocking, the blocking time is divided by the number of servers, that is k (see eq.(2)). The Figure 1 shows the main steps of the proposed algorithm.

To the best of our knowledge just two papers [1,19] consider general topologies with BAS blocking. We implemented EMVA [19] and conducted a broad experimentation that reveals instability, in particular when the population grows and the node characteristics are unbalanced, as frequently happens in a blocking network. As a consequence, we limit our comparison to the method in [1]. We compare the results obtained by the proposed MVABAS algorithm with the MVABLO and the exact results [3] for over 50 queueing networks, different in topology and parameters so to verify the algorithm on networks that are both "balanced" and "unbalanced" from the point of view of bottlenecks and blocking incidence. We consider cyclic topology with 3, 4 and 5 nodes, double ring topology and central server topology with 3 nodes. In all cases we observed very fast convergence speed. The error is drastically reduced and also the erratic behavior is corrected. We note that, according to intuition, the error grows as the blocking phenomenon grows in the networks. To this aim, we compute the blocking probability pb_j, for each node j, by exact analysis. It is easy to be convinced that the error is not so affected by the number of nodes, but by how many nodes can be blocked and with which frequency, given by pb_j. Due to lack of space we just show the results for two critical cases. In both cases, we show the residence time, since this is the most critical measure to predict [1].

First, we consider a five nodes cyclic network with the queue parameters as in Table 1 (a). The performance behavior of the network is analyzed as the population grows until the maximum admissible value ($N = 17$) for deadlock prevention [3]. The last column of the Table shows the blocking probability pb_j computed by exact results when $N = 17$.

Note that this is a critical case: all queues can be blocked and two neighboring queues (4 and 5) can be both simultaneously full as soon as the population exceeds the value 6 ($B_5 + B_1$). As the results in Fig. 2 indicate, as soon as the population enters in the critical region $N > 6$, the performance measures significantly deviate from the exact results. The Fig. 2 (a) shows the mean residence time for queue 1. Even though queue 1 is practically never blocked, its residence time cannot be accurately predicted by MVABLO. On the contrary, with the proposed MVABAS the prediction is quite accurate and the mean relative error decreases from 27.82% of MVABLO to 7.72% of

```
for ( k = 1; k <= N; + + k )
do
    repeat = 0;
    for ( j = 0; j < M; + + j ) {
        if ( j is delay center )
```
$$E[t_j(k)] = E[s_j] + \frac{BT_j(k)}{k}$$
```
        else
```
$$E[t_j(k)] = E[s_j] * (z_j(k) + E[n_j(k-1)]) + BT_j(k);$$
```
    }
    for ( j = 0; j < M; + + j ) {
        temp = 0
        for ( i = 0; i < M; i + +)
            temp+ = E[t_i(k)] * e_i/e_j
```
$$E[X_j(k)] = \frac{k}{temp}$$
```
    }
    for ( j = 0; j < M; + + j ) {
        E[n_j(k)] = E[t_j(k)] * E[X_j(k)]
        if ( E[n_j(k)] > B_j ) {   // check for violation
            repeat = 1
            for ( i = 0; i < M; + + i ) {
                if (E[n_i(k)] < B_i ) {
                    z_i(k)+ = β_j(k) * p_{ij} * z_j(k)
```
$$BT_i(k)+ = \frac{p_{ij}e_i}{e_j} * E[s_j]$$
```
                }
            }
            z_j(k)- = β_j(k) * z_j(k)
        }
    }
}
while( repeat );   // repeat until no more violation are detected
```

Fig. 1. *MVABAS* algorithm

MVABAS. It is worth noting that we evaluate the mean relative error by averaging the traditional relative error for a given population value k [1] on all the population values that can determine blocking (i.e. $k \geq min\{B_j\}+1$). On the other hand, for $N = 17$ the relative error decreases from 44.47% of **MVABLO** to 0.18% of **MVABAS**. Moreover, **MVABLO** converges in 200 steps, while **MVABAS** converges in 85 steps. Note that we measure the convergence speed as the number of detected violations.

As a second critical case, we consider a central server topology with the parameters as in Table 1 (b). Again, the population grows until the maximum admissible value ($N = 39$) for deadlock prevention. The routing probabilities from the central server are balanced, that is $p_{1j} = 0.5$ for $j = 2, 3$. On the contrary, it is easy to be convinced that the other parameters values are quite unbalanced. Indeed, for $N = 39$, queue 1 is almost always blocked $pb_0 = 0.966667$, while the other two queues are never blocked.

Table 1. Networks characteristics

(a) Cyclic network				(b) Central server network			
queue	B_j	$E[s_j]$	pb_j	queue	B_j	$E[s_j]$	pb_j
1	4	20.1	0.073476	1	35	0.1	0.966667
2	3	2.0	0.907808	2	20	2.5	0.000000
3	5	10.0	0.539043	3	5	6.0	0.000003
4	4	2.1	0.903199				
5	2	5	0.769521				

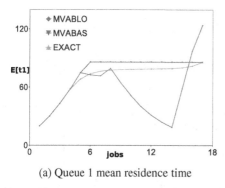

(a) Queue 1 mean residence time

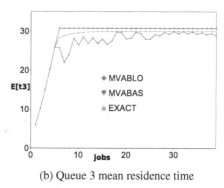

(b) Queue 3 mean residence time

Fig. 2. Mean performance indices for the cyclic network (a) and the central server (b)

Fig. 2 (b) shows the mean residence time of the bottleneck queue 3. The results obtained by MVABLO show a trend quite erratic that makes them practically unusable. On the contrary, the results obtained by MVABAS correct well the erratic behavior and reduce the mean relative error from 5.3% of MVABLO to 2.97%. In this case, the convergence speed are practically the same, that is 16 steps for MVABLO and 17 steps for MVABAS.

4   The Case Study

In this section, we apply the MVABAS method on capacity planning for a web server system. The objective of the study is to investigate about different system configurations and management mechanisms to satisfy QoS requirements. The performance of web server systems are affected by a lot of aspects related both to the system configuration and to the load characteristics. As a consequence, simulation studies could be too much expensive in terms of efforts and time and it is also well known that simulation offers poor trade-off evaluation. On the contrary, the MVA algorithm is the best candidate to conduct a broad alternatives evaluation, since its low computational cost and its easy of use, that make it one of the most well accepted approach in industrial environment.

Let us consider a system that provides web services and which is built according to the widely used multi-tiered paradigm. Typically, access to a web service occurs in the form of a session consisting of many individual requests. For example, for e-commerce

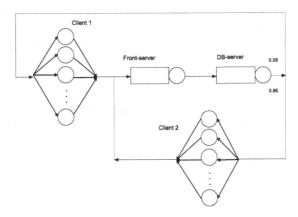

Fig. 3. The baseline system model

systems, placing an order through the web site involves further requests relating to selecting a product, providing shipping information, arranging payment agreement and finally receiving a confirmation. For a customer trying to place an order, or a retailer trying to make a sale, the real measure of a web server performance is its ability to process the entire sequence of requests needed to complete a transaction. To this aim, we model the web system as illustrated in Fig. 3. The job flow is modeled at single request level and we include two client centers, Client 1 and Client 2, to distinguish between the first request of a session (jobs leaving Client 1) called new request, and the successive requests of an already accepted sessions (jobs leaving Client 2) called online requests. Note that in this model, we don't consider caching effects and assume that each request makes one visit to front-server and to DB-server before to come back to the client. This assumption has been taken into account in the parametrization.

To model the workload of a web service system, we use the results obtained by the TPC-W benchmark, which simulates the operations of an online bookstore [15] . The TPC-W defines 14 transactions, each of which can be generally classified as browsing or ordering. In this paper, we use two different traffic mixes: the *ordering mix*, that consists of 50% browsing and 50% ordering transactions, and the *shopping mix* consisting of 80% browsing and 20% ordering transactions. Note that since the model is single-class we use the mixes separately. Mean request service times at the servers are derived by the utilization law from the results in [20], where the authors use a one-visit model as explained above. We obtain the following parameters: for the ordering mix 0.015 sec and 0.0066 sec for the front- and DB- server respectively; for the shopping mix 0.019 sec and 0.012 sec respectively. For both mixes, the mean think time is set to 7 sec [15]. Moreover, as stated above, each session consists of a sequence of requests that is uniformly distributed with parameters 5 and 35, that is with expected mean equal to 20. Hence, we define the routing probabilities from the DB-server as 0.05 and 0.95 towards clients 1 and 2 respectively.

We assume that the QoS requirement is to minimize the average response time of the whole session, in other words the response time in respect of Client 1. In the following, we investigate on the effectiveness of the following changes in meeting the SLO: 1.

server replication; 2. admission control mechanisms 3. dedicated servers 4. possible combinations of some of these.

First, we consider the baseline system when the workload N grows from 0 to 1500 sessions. Note that, according to MVA analysis, we are considering steady state results. We evaluate the average response time for the system without any congestion control and with an admission control mechanism: the mechanism is modeled by means of finite capacities at both front- and DB-servers of value 80 requests. In all the following experiments, when we consider admission control we assume queue finite capacity of value 80 on all servers. The results show a modest improvement of the response time which reaches about the 3% for both the ordering and the shopping mixes. Due to lack of space, we omit the figures for this first set of experiments. We evaluate also the mean queue lengths on both front- and DB- servers. For both mixes, the bottleneck is the front-server that shows a rapid growth (linear) as soon as the workload is about 400 sessions. It is worth noting that the front-server shows a worse congestion under the shopping mix. This suggests the use of front-end replica to meet SLO.

Let us consider the three configuration systems with replication: system CS1 with two replicas FS1 and FS2 for the front-end server; system CS2 with three replicas for the front-end server, FS1, FS2 and FS3; system CS3 with two replicas for the front-end, FS1 and FS2, and two replicas for the back-end server DB1 and DB2. In case of replication, a dispatcher is usually responsible for balancing load across replicas. Note that we are assuming unbalanced load between replicas. In practise, as remarked in [17], perfect load balancing is difficult to achieve for the *affinity* principle according to which, if a session is stateful, successive requests will need to be serviced by the same stateful server. Moreover, if caching is employed by a tier, a session and its requests may be preferentially forwarded to a replica where a response is likely to be cached. To set the routing probabilities towards the replicas, in all the considered configurations, we use the results in [17]. In particular, we define the routing probabilities for both clients $j = 1, 2$ as follows:

- system CS1: $p_{Clj,FS1} = 0.57, p_{Clj,FS2} = 0.43$;
- system CS2: $p_{Clj,FS1} = 0.25, p_{Clj,FS2} = 0.32, p_{Clj,FS3} = 0.43$;
- system CS3: $p_{Clj,FS1} = 0.57, p_{Clj,FS2} = 0.43$ and $p_{FSi,DB1} = 0.57, p_{FSi,DB2} = 0.43$ for both front-end server $i = 1, 2$.

Figure 4 shows the session average response time. For the ordering mix, the figure (a) compares the baseline system with the system CS1 both without admission control. As one can expect, the session response time is generally improved by replication: the response time starts to increase for higher load and the gain is about of 43%. In this case, the admission control mechanism on the CS1 system still gives a further small improvement of about the 2% only for high load ($N > 800$). On the contrary, despite of expectations, the investment in further replicas as in CS2 and in CS3, is not more effective and the improvement is practically negligible. On the other hand, the results show that the effect of admission control depends on the load characteristics. Indeed, the shopping mix seems to be not beneficial of the replication at first tier. To this aim, we observe the mean queue lengths for each server and note that replication changes the system bottleneck: while for the ordering mix the bottleneck still remains on the front-server, for the shopping mix the replica on the first-tier switches the bottleneck to

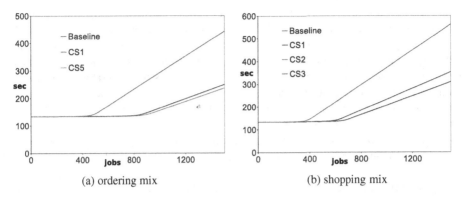

(a) ordering mix   (b) shopping mix

Fig. 4. Session response time for the system with replication

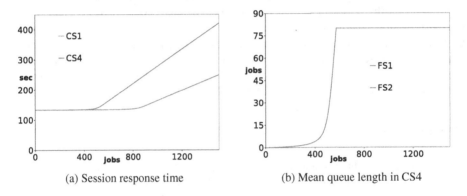

(a) Session response time   (b) Mean queue length in CS4

Fig. 5. Dedicated replicas: ordering mix

the DB-server. This also confirm the results in Fig. 4 (b): further replicas on the first tier and admission control are not enough to improve SLO in case of the shopping mix load. Indeed, the system CS2 does not yield better performance than the system CS1 and the response times are practically overlapped. On the contrary, if a replica is used also at the second tier as in the system CS3 the average session response time show an improvement using admission control on each server.

Given the inefficacy of system with three replicas on the first tier for both mixes, we conjecture that the third replica has a negative effect due to more new requests entering the system. To investigate on this conjecture, we consider a new system configuration CS4: a replica at the front tier is completely dedicated to the new requests $p_{Cl1,FS1} = 1$, while the second replica is dedicated exclusively to the online requests $p_{Cl2,FS2} = 1$. In this experiment, we consider the ordering mix since it showed to be more beneficial of the replicas on the first tier. The Figure 5 (a) compares the session response time for the system CS4 with admission control with the system CS1 without admission control. In spite of both the replication and the admission control, for the system CS4 the average session response time significantly grows even for low load. As contro-intuitive results, in Figure 5 (b) we show the mean queue lengths for this case. As soon as the number of sessions exceed the value of 400, the online requests explodes to the limit value of 80. Indeed, for a medium value of 800 sessions, the response time grows from 136.71 sec of the CS1 system to 221 sec for the CS4 case, that is an increment of about the 62%. It is easy to be convinced that this sudden worsening is due to the fact that each new request corresponds to a new session and each new session generates many online requests. This seems to argue our conjecture: to reach better results the online requests have to be privileged in obtaining service access with respect to the new ones. This will favor the session completions instead to overload the system with new arriving sessions. In this direction, in the last experiment we consider the system CS5 with one front-server dedicated to only online requests $p_{Cl2,FS1} = 0.57$, while the least loaded replica FS2 is shared by the new and online requests $p_{Cl1,FS2} = 1$, $p_{Cl2,FS2} = 0.43$. In Fig. 4, curve CS5 shows a performance improvement of about the 5% starting from 800 sessions.

In conclusion, the following points can be stated: i. the workload characteristics have great effect on the performance; an intuitive management choice can be good for a workload profile, but can be bad for another one, as we show for the replication case. So the model parametrization is an important step. ii. Sometimes, system enhancements can lead even worse performance, as we show for the shopping mix. iii. Different management mechanisms, like dedicated servers, can be successful. iv. An investigation and trade-off analysis needs of efficient solution methods.

5   Conclusions

We have considered the problem of providing an efficient solution for general topology queueing networks with blocking. In this paper, we have defined an approximate MVA for queueing networks with BAS blocking (MVABAS), that greatly outperform the previous results. Moreover, we have extended the algorithm to include delay centers. We have tested our algorithm on over 50 different networks. In all cases, the convergence is fast. We have applied the proposed MVABAS to a capacity planning study for a web system. In this contest, blocking is used to model admission control in order to overcome an overload period and to guarantee QoS requirements. Since the versatility and the low computational cost of the proposed algorithm, we have investigated on different directions: use of replicas, admission control and dedicated servers. The results of the case study confirm the importance of an efficient and low-cost modelling technique to investigate and correctly drive the system management decision process. As future work, the algorithm should be further improved and also extended to include different blocking mechanisms and workload burstiness [5].

Acknowledgments. The authors are grateful to the anonymous referees for their useful comments that greatly improved the readability of the paper. The authors thank Massimiliano Macchia for a previous version of MVABAS in his master degree thesis.

References

1. Akyildiz, I.F.: Mean value analysis of blocking queueing networks. IEEE Trans. on Software Eng. 14 (1988)
2. Balsamo, S., De Nitto Personé, V., Inverardi, P.: A review on Queueing Network Models with finite capacity queues for Software Architectures performance prediction. Perform. Eval. 51(2-4), 269–288 (2003)
3. Balsamo, S., De Nitto Personé, V., Onvural, R.: Analysis of Queueing Networks with Blocking. Kluwer Academic (2001)
4. Bogrdi-Mszly, A., Levendovszky, T.: A novel algorithm for performance prediction of web-based software systems. Perform. Eval. 68(1), 45–57 (2011)
5. Casale, G., Smirni, E.: MAP-AMVA: Approximate mean value analysis of bursty systems. In: IEEE/IFIP International Conference on Dependable Systems and Networks (2009)
6. Daduna, H., Holst, M.: Customer Oriented Performance Measures for Packet Transmission in a Ring Network with Blocking. In: Proc. of 14th GI/ITG Conf. On Measurement, Modeling and Evaluation of Computer and Comm. Systems (2008)
7. De Almeida, D., Kellert, P.: Markovian and analytical models for multiple bus multiprocessor systems with memory blockings. Journal of Systems Architecture 46, 455–477 (2000)
8. Koizumi, N., Kuno, E., Smith, T.E.: Modeling patient flows using a queuing network with blocking. Health Care Management Science 8(1), 49–60 (2005)
9. Lu, L., Cherkasova, L., de Nitto Personè, V., Mi, N., Smirni, E.: AWAIT: Efficient Overload Management for Busy Multi-tier Web Services under Bursty Workloads. In: Benatallah, B., Casati, F., Kappel, G., Rossi, G. (eds.) ICWE 2010. LNCS, vol. 6189, pp. 81–97. Springer, Heidelberg (2010)
10. Onvural, R.O.: Survey of Closed Queueing Networks with Blocking. ACM Computing Surveys 22(2), 83–121 (1990)
11. Onvural, R.O.: Special Issue on Queueing Networks with Finite Capacity. Perform. Eval. 17(3) (1993)
12. Perros, H.G.: Queueing networks with blocking. Oxford University Press (1994)
13. Reiser, M., Lavenberg, S.S.: Mean value analysis of closed multichain queueing networks. J. ACM 27(2), 313–322 (1980)
14. Sereno, M.: Mean value analysis of product form solution queueing networks with repetitive service blocking. Perform. Eval. 36-37, 19–33 (1999)
15. TPC-W Benchmark, http://www.tpc.org
16. Tribastone, M.: Approximate Mean Value Analysis of Process Algebra Models. In: Proc. of IEEE19th International Symposium on Modeling, Analysis and Simulation of Computer and Telecommunication Systems, MASCOTS (2011)
17. Urgaonkar, B., Pacifici, G., Shenoy, P., Spreitzer, M., Tantawi, A.: An Analytical Model for Multi-tier Internet Services and its Applications. In: Proc. of the ACM SIGMETRICS 2005, Banff, Canada, pp. 291–302 (June 2005)
18. Yamadaa, T., Mizuharab, N., Yamamotoc, H., Matsuib, M.: A performance evaluation of disassembly systems with reverse blocking. Computers & Industrial Engineering Intelligent Manufacturing and Logistics 56(3), 1113–1125 (2009)
19. Yuzukirmizi, M.: Performance Evaluation of Closed Queueing Networks with Limited Capacities. Turkish J. Eng. Env. Sci. 30, 269–283 (2006)
20. Zhang, Q., Cherkasova, L., Smirni, E.: A regression-based analytic model for dynamic resource provisioning of multitier applications. In: Proc. of the 4th ICAC Conference, p. 27 (2007)

Modeling and Timing Simulation
of Agilla Agents for WSN Applications
in Executable UML*

Luca Berardinelli[1], Antinisca Di Marco[1], Stefano Pace[1], Stefano Marchesani[2],
and Luigi Pomante[2]

[1] Dipartimento di Ingegneria e Scienze dell'Informazione, e Matematica, L'Aquila
[2] DEWS Center of Excellence, Università degli Studi dell'Aquila, Italy
{name.surname}@univaq.it

Abstract. Wireless Sensor Networks are becoming one of the most successful choices for the development and deployment of a wide range of applications, from intelligent homes to environment monitoring. In response to the growing demand for fast development of WSN applications, we extend an existing UML-based approach for the design and code generation of Agilla applications with functional simulation and timing analysis capabilities through executable UML models. The proposed approach makes use of both a UML profile and an executable model library for Agilla. Execution times, annotated on Agilla instructions and patterns in the library, are given as additional input parameters during the model execution to carry out a timing analysis of the simulated Agilla applications. Modeling and simulation activities rely on MagicDraw©️ and Cameo Simulation Toolkit©️. A running case study is provided to show the approach and the supporting tools at work.

Keywords: Software Performance Engineering, Wireless Sensor Network, Code Generation, Agilla.

1 Introduction

A Wireless Sensor Network (WSN) consists of spatially distributed autonomous sensors that cooperate in order to accomplish a task. Sensors have unique *characteristics*: they are small, low-cost, wireless and battery-powered devices. They can be easily deployed to monitor different environmental parameters and they create large-scale flexible architectures. Sensors can be distributed on roads, vehicles, buildings, people and they enable different applications such as domotics, disaster relief and environmental monitoring.

The unique *characteristics* of sensors also complicate the development of applications, mainly because the quality of the services they provide is influenced by factors like network availability, battery level of the motes, and so on. Despite

---

* This work is partially supported by the EU-funded VISION ERC project (ERC-240555), and by PRESTO ARTEMIS project (GA n. 269362).

M.S. Balsamo, W.J. Knottenbelt, and A. Marin (Eds.): EPEW 2013, LNCS 8168, pp. 300–311, 2013.

this, a WSN must continue providing its services as long as possible, and with the best effort trying to guarantee network longevity. Traditionally, WSN applications have been developed by programming each sensor with the use of low level primitives. Although different programming abstractions and middlewares have been proposed, various research challenges are still open [17].

Agilla [10] is an agent-based middleware for WSNs, based on TinyOS [18]. It allows creating the agents, substituted and destroyed at run-time, without stopping the execution of the code. The agents are written in a bytecode-like language, that is interpreted by the corresponding virtual machine.

In order to help WSN application developers and to provide more abstract modeling instruments, we proposed in [7] a model-driven approach that permitted to model Agilla agents [3] using the Unified Modeling Language (UML) [15] combined with our Agilla UML profile. Then, an Acceleo [2] Model-to-Code (M2C) transformation was implemented to automatically transform the UML designed models into executable Agilla agents' code. This paper is the continuation of the work in [7] and the new contributions are the following:

- We performed measurements of the execution time of each Agilla instruction on the Memsic MicaZ mote [12]. These measurements were made by modifying/extending the Agilla platform with additional NesC code;
- We extended the Agilla UML Profile proposed in [7] to allow the annotation of the models with non-functional information and to permit the modeling of the timing characteristics of Agilla agents using the UML MARTE profile [1]. This extension introduces a distinct predefined UML behavioral unit (e.g., an action) for the whole Agilla instruction set and, beyond the name, it includes the annotation of the measured execution time.
- We extended the Agilla Profile with a model library that makes the Agilla behavioral units (e.g., each single instruction, patterns) ready to be directly executed as part of executable UML Models for sake of functional simulation and timing analysis.

The rest of the paper is organized as follows. In Section 2, we detail the model-driven approach we use. Section 3 introduces the case study used to show the approach at work. Section 4 explains the approach we follow to measure the execution times of the instructions on Memsic MicaZ mote. Section 5 presents the Agilla Modeling Framework by recalling the Agilla UML profile characteristics published in [7] and presenting the new modeling features; moreover, it shows the modeling of the case study that follows the proposed approach. Section 6, instead, explains the devised analysis technique and shows it at work on the proposed case study. Finally, Section 7 reviews related works and Section 8 concludes the paper outlining future research directions.

2 Model-Driven Approach to Agilla Agent Modeling, Timing Analysis and Code Generation

In this section, we describe the UML-based model-driven approach we follow. It supports Agilla-based WSN application modeling, timing analysis and code

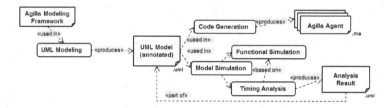

Fig. 1. Our UML-based Model-Driven approach

generation to ease the development of a WSN application to non-expert of Agilla. Agilla structures an application in terms of one or more mobile agents, which are special processes that can explicitly migrate or clone from node to node while maintaining their state. Figure 1 sketches the proposed approach, where boxes represent artifacts whereas rounded boxes represent operational steps.

The approach is composed by five operational steps:

UML Modeling. A developer models the agents of the WSN application using the devised Agilla Modeling Framework (AMF). AMF specifies the modeling rules for an Agilla-based WSN application. The framework leverages UML enriched with Agilla [7] and MARTE (Modeling and Analysis of Real-Time and Embedded Systems) [1] profiles. An agent is modeled through UML Activities (i.e., Actions, Control/Object Flows) and displayed on Activity Diagrams. During the modeling, the developer might use the library of Agilla patterns we provide to speed up the modeling process. The Agilla patterns are themselves UML models annotated through the Agilla and MARTE profiles. A suitably annotated UML Model is then taken as input from both the Code Generation and Model Simulation steps. In this paper, we extend the modeling approach proposed in [7] to annotate the models with non-functional information (Section 5).

Code Generation. This step takes as input the UML Model of an agent and generates the corresponding Agilla code. It is implemented as a M2C transformation using the Acceleo technology [2]. The annotated UML Model, serialized into the Eclipse UML file format *.uml*, is imported into the Acceleo Eclipse plug-in, where the transformation automatically generates the agents' code saving it in a *.ma* file. More details on this step are given in [7].

Model Simulation. On the annotated UML Model, Functional Simulation and Timing Analysis can be performed. The former simulates Agilla through Cameo Simulation Toolkit, plug in of MagicDraw. The AMF relies on these two tools and extends their capabilities with Timing Analysis of Agilla applications. The Timing Analysis results are stored within the annotated UML Model itself.

3   Case Study

In this section, we describe the Wildfire Tracking Application (WTA) that we selected to show the modeling and the simulation steps at work. The WTA example can be found in the Agilla project (in the `agents/case_studies` sub-directory). Figure 2 shows the high-level behavior of the application. WTA is deployed on a WSN distributed into a region that is prone to forest fires. It must detect a fire and determine its perimeter. When a fire starts, its movements are unpredictable and WTA is implemented to continuously reprogram itself, by using mobile agents.

In particular, WTA is composed by three Agilla agents. The *temp_reading* agent runs on all the WSN nodes and is programmed to sense the temperature at regular time intervals. The readings are sent to the base station (BS).

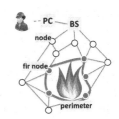

A *temp_forwarder* agent runs on all the WSN nodes and the BS. This agent forwards the sensed values up to the PC, where the temperature level is evaluated. If the value is greater than a previ-

Fig. 2. The WTA application

ously fixed threshold, a tuple containing the position and a "fir" string is saved on the node (i.e., the *fir nodes* in Figure 2). After notifying the alarm, the agents on fir nodes release the used resources. Once notified by fir nodes, the BS can transmit an alarm to the firemen[1].

Once a fire has been detected by fir nodes, a *tracker* agent is injected from the PC into the BS. The tracker begins to expand from BS into the network, by cloning itself to random neighbors where, of course, the "fir" tuple is not present. The tracker agents collect real-time information about the precise position of the fire. The life cycle of a tracker agent ends when a "fir" tuple is inserted into the tuple space of the node where it runs, killing the agent itself.

In order to dynamically determine the perimeter of the fire, the tracker agents continuously verify whether the neighbor nodes are in an alarm state (i.e., contains the fir tuple). If not, the tracker agents migrate to a randomly chosen neighbor. This step is repeated until the tracker agents run on all the neighbors of the fir nodes. In this way, they swarm around the fire forming a *perimeter* and they dynamically adjust it according with the movements of the fire.

WTA shows real-time requirements, in particular it must be fast in determining the fire perimeter and in readapting it on the basis of the fire movements and network dimension. In Section 6, we determine the execution time of a single tracker on the reference platform, while (i) the time WTA needs to distribute the tracker on a set of automatically generated WSN and (ii) the timing analysis of fire perimeter re-adaptation are left for the future.

4   Experimental Measurement of Agilla ISA Execution Times

In order to execute the timing analysis of Agilla-based WSN applications, we measure the execution times of each Agilla instruction. The experimental approach we define for this purpose, together with some details about the adopted

---

[1] Note that this part of the system is not included in the considered version of WTA.

experimental setup, is described in the following. The obtained results are used to annotate each instruction in the AMF.

In the proposed experimental approach, the execution time of an Agilla instruction is evaluated by means of timestamps caught by instrumenting the original nesC Agilla code in proper points of measurements. Such timestamps have been caught by using the *SysTimeM* component of TinyOS1.x while running ad-hoc agents (one at a time) on two Memsic MicaZ nodes [12].

The first node, acting as Agilla BS node connected to a PC via the UART interface, has been used to measure the time of Agilla instructions that is not related to the radio communications operations. The second node, programmed with the Agilla middleware and in direct radio visibility with the first one, has been used to measure the time of radio-related Agilla instructions.

The *SysTimeM* component implements the *SysTime* interface that returns the value of a free running timer. On the adopted platform and configuration, such a timer is running at a frequency of 921,600 KHz.

The nesC Agilla code has been thoroughly analyzed in order to identify the best points to catch timestamps. The results of this analysis shows that, even though each Agilla instruction is characterized by its own execution path throughout different nesC components, all these paths share a common starting point. So, timestamps have been taken at the beginning of each execution path.

At a first analysis, it seemed enough to catch a couple of timestamps at the beginning and at the end of each execute command. However, since some instructions could involve a more complex execution path (e.g., by posting background tasks or by means of split-phase operations), this approach could give rise to under measures. Instructions like them are, for example, *sense* and others related to agent migration, or that access to the remote tuple space. In order to overcome this problem and to avoid the detailed analysis of each different execution path, timestamps have been taken only at the beginning of each execution path.

Such timestamps are then stored in a buffer (in the *AgillaEngimeM* component) and sent to an external PC by means of the UART interfaces, at the end of the agent execution. In this way, since an Agilla instruction is never executed before the end of the previous one, the execution time of an Agilla instruction is simply the difference of sequential timestamps. Since the collected timestamps are sent to the PC at the end of the agent execution, the timestamps collection overhead is negligible (i.e. the measurement process does not affect the results). It is worth noting that this approach is correct when considering only one agent running on the node. This is exactly the situation that arose in the adopted experimental setup. In addition, with such a "very basic" experimental setup, we have collected times that are deterministic since they are not affected by the underlying low-level operations like, the events related to radio protocol management, the packets overhearing, the overall system state/load, the position of the node in the topology, etc. So, the collected timing data could be considered as constants (for the selected platform) that represent the best-case situation. This is very important since the evaluation of both network and system overheads could be then completely performed at simulation time while taking into account proper network architecture and topology, and the overall system state/load.

5   The Agilla Modeling Framework

In this section, we present the AMF the proposed approach is based on. Figure 3 shows such a framework that is an extension of [7], whose primary goal was the generation of Agilla code, to address simulation and timing analysis capabilities.

Fig. 3. The Agilla Profile extended with MARTE and the InstructionSet and Patterns executable model libraries

5.1   Modeling for Code Generation

The AMF in [7] includes an Agilla Profile (see Figure 3) that defines three stereotypes: *AgillaAgent, AgillaTask*, and *AgillaInstruction*. They are used to define a hierarchy of Activities as shown Figures 4(a,b) and 5(a,b) for the WTA temp_forwarder and tracker agents, respectively. The Code Generation step takes as input such Activities and produces the corresponding Agilla code by means of M2C transformations implemented in Acceleo [2] (see Figure 4(c) and 5(c)).

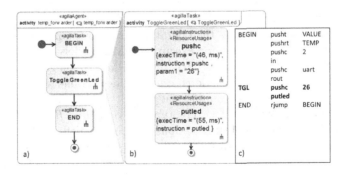

Fig. 4. The temp_forwarder: a) the agillaAgent, b) the ToggleGreenLed agillaTask from Patterns and c) the corresponding code

An AgillaAgent corresponds to a *top-level, compound* Activity whose actions are stereotyped as AgillaTasks (Figure 5a). Each AgillaTask represents a *middle-level, compound* Activity which groups a flow of ActivityNode stereotyped as AgillaInstructions (Figures 4(b) and 5(b)). The action names act as indentifiers of the corresponding blocks within the agent's code (e.g., BEGIN in Figure 4(c)). An AgillaInstruction is a *basic, atomic* behavioral unit of an Agilla agent. In [7], we modeled the instruction set of Agilla as a UML Enumeration of string-based values (*instrEnum*) to be assigned to the *instruction* property[2] of the containing stereotype, as shown for the Agilla task in Figure 4. Finally, we also provided a set of already stereotyped UML Activities corresponding to common recurring tasks in Agilla applications as toggling a led on sensor nodes. For example, the ToggleGreenLed AgillaTask and the corresponding code, in bold, are shown in Figure 4(b) and (c), respectively. We collected this and similar Activities in the Patterns model library in Figure 3.

5.2   Modeling for Simulation

The AMF framework described so far has been suitably extended to support the model simulation as well as its subsequent steps shown in Figure 1.

We realize two extensions that allow (i) the annotation of the measured execution times of Agilla instructions and (ii) the model simulation and analysis.

The first extension is realized by integrating the MARTE profile [1] to annotate the execution times measured in Section 4. For this purpose, we choose the execTime property of the MARTE's ResourceUsage stereotype as shown for the Agilla instructions of the ToggleGreenLed pattern in Figure 4(b). Thanks to the predefined annotation of all the instructions as well as patterns within the respective model libraries of the AMF, the annotation process of any Agilla application is quicker and less error-prone.

The second extension makes any UML Model of an Agilla application, once modeled with our framework, directly executable and analyzable in UML, without the need of any model transformation towards an external analysis notation. In 2011, the Object Management Group published the Foundational UML (fUML) standard [16]. It defines the operational semantics of a subset of UML and provides a virtual machine for executing UML models compliant to this subset. The fUML subset contains parts of the UML language (Classes, Common Behaviors, Activities, and Actions) and provides actions to manipulate the UML model at run time. For example, the Activity shown in Figures 5(b) and (c) include several fUML-specific stereotyped actions like *ReadSelf* or *Value-Specification*. The semantics of these actions was already defined in [15] but only with fUML [16] they have been concretely implemented as part of the fUML VM. Similar actions are used to manipulate them in UML model at run-time, in particular, to access the runtime object (ReadSelf) and to create values like String o Integer (ValueSpecification), enabling the execution of UML Activities.

---

[2] It is worth noting that action names cannot be used for this purpose since they should be unique within the same Activity.

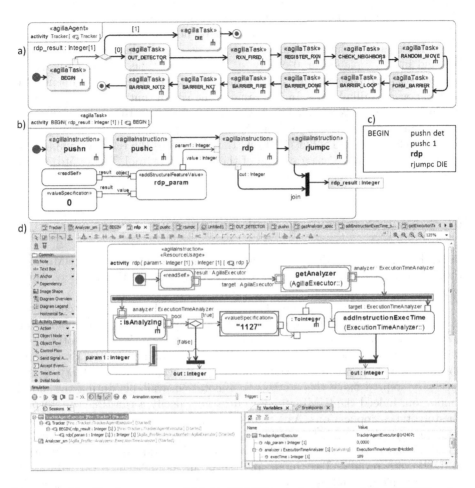

Fig. 5. a) The Tracker agent and b) its BEGIN task Activities, c) the BEGIN code and d) the rdp instruction Activity running within Cameo Simulation Toolkit

Following the fUML standard, we represent any AgillaInstruction, previously modeled as structural elements by means of string-valued entries of a UML Enumeration, for back compatibility with work done in [7] with a distinct UML Activity. These new activities, grouped together in the InstructionSet library in Figure 3, remain hidden from and are given as reusable modeling elements to the users of our framework. The advantage is that any basic, atomic AgillaInstruction can now be executed by the fUML VM, as well as their combinations in compound behavioral units (agents, tasks and patterns).

Figure 5(d) shows an example of such new, fUML-compliant Activities for the **rdp** *AgillaInstruction* that, in turn, is part of the BEGIN AgillaTask (Figure 5(b)) of the tracker AgillaAgent (Figure 5(a)). We modeled the remaining agents of WTA application (i.e., temp_reading and temp_forwarder) in a similar way[3]. The behavior of the AgillaInstructions can be now detailed and simulated in UML. For example, the `rdp` Agilla instruction returns 1 whether a certain tuple is found in the tuple space, 0 otherwise [10]. At run time, this value is stored in a *rdp_result::Integer* (Figure 5(d)) that, in turn, can be used to influence the control flow of AgillaAgents. In this respect, the `rdp` output is used to halt (DIE AgillaTask) the tracker AgillaAgent if already running on the node.

The functional simulation of UML Models of Agilla applications is supported by Cameo Simulation Toolkit (CST) [6] that integrates the reference implementation of the fUML VM as a plug in of the MagicDraw tool. Figure 5(d) shows a screenshot during the simulation of the `rdp` Agilla instruction.

6   Timing Analysis by Model Simulation

In AMF, the timing analysis algorithm is directly implemented in fUML and, then, relies on CST to perform the Timing Analysis of UML Models of Agilla applications (see Figure 1).

In particular, we use Activities like those shown in Figure 5(d) to collect the execution time of each AgillaInstruction. The execution times, previously annotated through the execTime property of the ResourceUsage stereotype (see Figure 4), are now modeled through ValueSpecification actions [16]. It is worth noting that this is not a redundant modeling choice. On the contrary, it is a necessary step to make this stereotype annotation available during the model simulation. Indeed the fUML standard does not specify a run-time counterpart for stereotypes applications. As a consequence, the fUML VM treats them like a common compiler does with comments in programming languages: they are ignored. In [5], we propose a systematic approach that addresses the combination of fUML with profiles. The timing analysis of an AgillaAgent is carried out by an ExecutionTimeAnalyzer that is itself a fUML-compliant model as shown in Figure 6. It is part of the InstructionSet library and it is linked to any Agilla agent under analysis through an AgentExecutor class. The TrackerAgentExecutor, that appears in Figure 6, is a user defined UML Class that contains the AgillaAgent and AgillaTask stereotyped UML Activities as those shown in Figures 4 and 5. Therefore, during the simulation of an Agilla UML Model, a distinct instance of the ExecutionTimeAnalyzer is concurrently executed with the corresponding agent-specific AgillaExecutor by the fUML VM. The former sums the execTimes of the simulated AgillaInstructions, following the simulation workflow of its constituting AgillaTasks. Figure 5(d) shows a snapshot of the execution of the *rdp* AgillaInstruction within the BEGIN AgillaTask of the Tracker agent. The timing analysis results are then collected by the agent-specific ExecutionTimeAnalyzer as shown in the variable panel on the bottom right corner of the figure. The execTime run-time variable contains the sum of the execution times

---

[3] The complete model is available on the project web site
https://code.google.com/a/eclipselabs.org/p/agilla-modeling-framework/

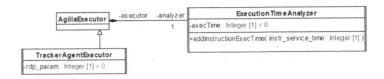

Fig. 6. The TrackerAgentExecutor and the ExecutionTimeAnalyzer

of the AgillaInstructions (189 milliseconds) that precede the *rdp* instruction that requires 1127 milliseconds for its own execution.

Finally, the results can be saved as slot values of the execTime property in the agent-specific instance of the ExecutionTimeAnalyzer. As suggested by France et al. in [11], AMF then realizes the integration of the analysis algorithms directly with the modeling language, in this case UML, used in systems development.

7   Related Works

In [7], we started our approach, whose continuation led us to this work. We developed the Agilla UML Profile, that we have now extended, and we took the direction of code generation, via M2C transformation. The analysis part was missing, so now we have integrated it for a more complete approach.

In [13], the authors present a model-driven framework in which an application developer can model a WSN application by using Stateflow constructs and then the model can be transformed into platform-specific application code or used to perform multi-platform Hardware-In-the-Loop simulation. The modeling and analysis framework is based on MathWorks tools. Our approach is more generic since it considers as starting notation UML, a de facto modeling standard. It targets Agilla code that, being interpreted opens the approach to dynamic software adaptation. Further, our simulation technique is UML-based too.

In [4], the authors investigate the possibility to adapt an existing model-based approach that exploits such techniques to combine the modeling and performance analysis of software for WSN. They introduce a UML-based framework where a system model (i) is extended with a new profile for representing NesC application along with the supporting hardware platform, and (ii) is annotated with performance parameters defined in the standard UML MARTE profile. Thereafter they apply a set of transformations to this enhanced UML model that targets a Queueing Network performance model.

In [14], the authors generate SystemC code from UML statecharts for simulation purposes. Different from our approach, [14] does not generate executable code that can be directly run on the sensor nodes. Further, its approach allows to obtain a simulation model that permits to evaluate the scalability and the performance of the modeled WSN application, while our approach is actually used for timing and functional simulations.

In [9], the model-driven approach is used to model separately the software architecture of the WSN, the low-level hardware specification of the WSN nodes and the physical environment where nodes are deployed in. The framework can use these models to generate executable code to analyze the energy consumption of the modeled application. The last three approaches have the aim of evaluating the quality of the WSN application (that is its performance for the first two and energy consumption for the last one). Instead our approach wants to generate executable code, ready to be deployed and run on a node. We plan to extend it in the future to allow the quality analysis of the modeled application.

In [19], the OMNeT++ simulation environment is presented. It's a complete environment capable of simulating various kind of networks, including WSNs. Even if OMNeT++ is a complete environment, it's difficult to use and instead of directly providing simulation components for computer networks, queuing networks or other domains, it provides the basic machinery and tools to write such simulations. Further, the Omnet++ models are created with a specific description language or with a graphical editor, while our models and simulation environment are all UML based, shortening the beginners' learning curve.

8   Conclusion

We developed a Model-driven approach that allows the modeling of software for WSN nodes running the Agilla mobile agents-based middleware. With our approach, we simplify the design, analysis and the implementation of WSN software for non-expert programmers. The proposed approach provides: *i)* the Agilla Modeling Framework that allows the UML modelling of Agilla-based WSN application; *ii)* the generation of agents' code from models, using M2C transformations; *iii)* the timing and functional analysis of the models conform to the Agilla Modeling Framework. We show the modeling framework and the timing analysis at work on the WTA case study.

Several research directions can be considered in the future. As short-term goals, we are working on the timing analysis of WTA to determine the average time needed to the tracker to distribute on a WSN and to readapt the fire perimeter to fire movements. For this scope we need to extend the existing AMF with further executable UML model libraries[4] to support network-level timing analysis. Moreover, we are working on removing the gap between the modeling for code generation and for simulation to remove extra effort in modeling Agilla-based WSN applications. We are measuring the energy consumption on the reference hardware platform [12] of each Agilla instruction to extend the proposed approach to the analysis of energy consumption. Finally, we plan to target other quality attributes such as performance and reliability by enriching the AMF and providing M2C transformations generating analysis models.

As mid-term goals, we will deeply investigate the usage of the presented approach in run-time adaptation to provide a middleware able to monitor the WSN motes, to capture context, resources or requirement changes, to trigger

---

[4] For sake of supporting network level analysis we already extended the modeled library with a random network generator.

the adaptation by deciding how to adapt the application by changing its models and reflect this change in the running system, similar to what defined in [8].

References

1. UML Profile for MARTE, Version 1.1 (2011), http://www.omg.org/spec/MARTE/
2. Acceleo Eclipse Plug-in, http://www.eclipse.org/acceleo/
3. Agilla Insstruction Set, http://mobilab.cse.wustl.edu/projects/agilla/isa.html
4. Berardinelli, L., Cortellessa, V., Pace, S.: Modeling and analyzing performance of software for wireless sensor networks. In: Proc. of the 2nd Workshop on Software Engineering for Sensor Network Applications, pp. 13–18. ACM (2011)
5. Berardinelli, L., Langer, P., Mayerhofer, T.: Combining fUML and Profiles for Non-Functional Analysis Based on Model Execution Traces. In: Ninth International ACM Conference on the Quality of Software Architectures (2013)
6. Cameo Simulation Toolkit, http://www.nomagic.com/products/magicdraw-addons/cameo-simulation-toolkit.html
7. Di Marco, A., Pace, S.: Model-driven approach to agilla agent generation. In: IWCMC 2013 Conference - Wireless Sensor Networks Symposium (July 2013)
8. Di Marco, A., Pace, S., Marchesani, S., Pomante, L.: Model-driven agent generation approach for adaptable and resource-aware sensor node. In: Software Engineering for Sensor Network Applications
9. Doddapaneni, K., Ever, E., Gemikonakli, O., Malavolta, I., Mostarda, L., Muccini, H.: A model-driven engineering framework for architecting and analysing wireless sensor networks. In: Software Engineering for Sensor Network Applications
10. Fok, C.-L., Roman, G.-C., Lu, C.: Agilla: A mobile agent middleware for self-adaptive wireless sensor networks. ACM Transactions on Autonomous and Adaptive Systems 4(3), 16 (2009)
11. France, R.B., Rumpe, B.: Model-driven development of complex software: A research roadmap. In: Proc. of the Workshop on the Future of Software Engineering, pp. 37–54 (2007)
12. Memsic MicaZ mote, http://www.memsic.com/wireless-sensor-networks/
13. Mozumdar, M.M.R., Lavagno, L., Vanzago, L., Sangiovanni-Vincentelli, A.L.: Hilac: A framework for hardware in the loop simulation and multi-platform automatic code generation of wsn applications. In: Symposium on Industrial Embedded Systems (SIES), pp. 88–97. IEEE (2010)
14. Mura, M., Sami, M.G.: Code generation from statecharts: Simulation of wireless sensor networks. In: Digital System Design Architectures, Methods and Tools, pp. 525–532. IEEE (2008)
15. Object Management Group. OMG Unified Modeling Language, Superstructure, Version 2.4.1 (2011), http://www.omg.org/spec/UML/2.4.1
16. Object Management Group. Semantics of a foundational subset for executable UML models (fUML), version 1.0 (February 2011)
17. Stankovic, J.A.: Research challenges for wireless sensor networks. ACM SIGBED Review 1(2), 9–12 (2004)
18. TinyOS Operating System for WSNs, http://www.tinyos.net/
19. Varga, A., Hornig, R.: An overview of the omnet++ simulation environment. In: Proc. of the 1st ICST Conference, p. 60 (2008)

Applying Model Differences to Automate Performance-Driven Refactoring of Software Models

Davide Arcelli, Vittorio Cortellessa, and Davide Di Ruscio

Dipartimento di Ingegneria e Scienze dell'Informazione e Matematica
Università degli Studi dell'Aquila
67100 L'Aquila, Italy
{davide.arcelli,vittorio.cortellessa,davide.diruscio}@univaq.it

Abstract. Identifying and removing the causes of poor performance in software systems are complex problems, and these issues are usually tackled after software deployment only with human-based means. Performance antipatterns can be used to harness these problems since they capture design patterns that are known leading to performance problems, and they suggest refactoring actions that can solve the problems. This paper introduces an approach to automate software model refactoring based on performance antipatterns. A Role-Based Modeling Language is used to model antipattern problems as Source Role Models (SRMs), and antipattern solutions as Target Role Models (TRMs). Each (SRM, TRM) pair is represented by a difference model that encodes refactoring actions to be operated on a software model to remove the corresponding antipattern. Differences are applied to software models through a model transformation automatically generated by a higher-order transformation. The approach is shown at work on an example in the e-commerce domain.

1 Introduction

Identifying and removing the causes of poor performance in software systems are complex problems due to a variety of factors to take into account. Similarly to other non-functional properties, performance results from interactions among software components, underlying platforms, users and contexts [24]. Current approaches to these problems are mostly based on the skills and experience of software developers or, in the best cases, the ones of performance analysts. Profiling tools have been introduced for performance monitoring of running applications [20], but it is well-known that the cost of solving performance problems at runtime is orders of magnitude larger than the one at early phases of the software lifecycle. Hence, instruments that help to identify and remove causes of performance problems early in the lifecycle would be very beneficial.

In the last two decades the concept of performance antipattern has been used for "codifying" knowledge and experience of analysts. Smith et al. [21] have ultimately specified 14 performance antipatterns. A performance antipattern identifies a *problem*, i.e. a bad practice that negatively affects software performance, and a *solution*, i.e. a set of refactoring actions that can be carried out to remove it. We have based our recent research work on this repository of knowledge with the aim of making it a cornerstone

M.S. Balsamo, W.J. Knottenbelt, and A. Marin (Eds.): EPEW 2013, LNCS 8168, pp. 312–324, 2013.

in identifying and removing performance problems. We have first tackled the problem of providing a less ambiguous antipatterns representation, in respect with their original definition in natural language [7]. However, performance antipatterns are very complex (as compared to other software patterns) because they are founded on different characteristics of software systems, and they additionally include values of performance indices. This high complexity requires multi-view representations. Thereafter, we have introduced several techniques aimed at detecting performance antipatters in software models [7]. More recently we undertook the problem of removing performance antipatterns detected in a software model by introducing a role-based approach that allows to formalize the refactoring of the latter [3].

In this paper we build up on previous results and move a further step ahead. We work on introducing automation in refactoring of software models that show unsatisfactory performance indices. In particular, we present an innovative approach that uses model differencing to represent and apply actions that remove performance antipatterns from

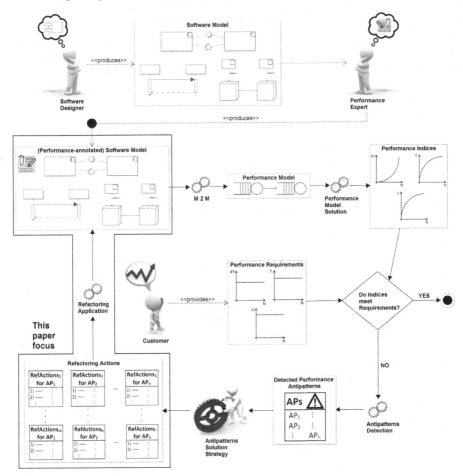

Fig. 1. Software model refactoring based on antipattern detection

software models. Goal of the paper is to introduce mechanisms that enable developers to analyze automatically generated solutions to performance problems, instead of looking for them only on the basis of experience.

Figure 1 shows the process envisaged to address this problem. Human roles are explicitly shown. Rectangles represent artifacts; gears represent automated activities.

The process starts with a *Software Model* produced by a software designer. A performance expert[1] annotates the software model with performance characteristics (i.e. workload, resource demands, etc.), and a round-trip performance engineering process starts in order to meet performance requirements provided by the customer. At each process iteration the *(Performance-annotated) Software Model* is transformed into a *Performance Model* (i.e. a queueing network) that, once solved, provides *Performance Indices* (i.e. response time (RT), throughput (T), and utilization (U)) [9]. If the indices do not meet performance requirements, then the backward path of the round-trip process is executed. A detection step produces a list of *Detected Performance Antipatterns* (APs) occurring in the software model [7]. Then, with the help of heuristic strategies, the development team can identify critical antipatterns [8] and *Refactoring Actions* ($Ref Actions_j$) that allow to remove them [3]. The final step of the process consists to apply refactoring actions to the *(Performance-annotated) Software Model*, thus producing a refactored software model where the antipatterns have been removed. The focus of this paper is the specification and automated application of refactoring actions, i.e. *Refactoring Actions* and *Refactoring Application* items in Figure 1.

The paper is organized as follows: Section 2 provides background on antipatterns and role models; Section 3 describes our approach for antipattern-based software model refactoring; Section 4 shows the approach at work on an e-commerce case study; Section 5 presents related work, and finally Section 6 concludes the paper.

2   Role Modeling for Antipatterns Definition and Solution

In this section we provide a background on performance antipatterns through the role-based description of the Empty Semi Trucks (EST) antipattern [21].

The concept of role has been introduced in the last years in many contexts to express the possibility to assign different functions to the same entity in different settings. We have used a Role-Based Modeling Language (RBML) to annotate model entities involved in performance antipatterns, and to track these entities for applying refactoring actions that remove antipatterns. In particular, we have ported RBML, that was introduced in [12] to assign roles to UML elements for applying design patterns, into the performance antipattern domain. In order to do this, we have first replaced the original UML elements on which RBML was defined with notation-independent ModelElements[2]. They represent a vocabulary, called SML+ [22], used for specifying performance

---

[1] Note that software designer and performance expert are not necessarily distinct.

[2] Since we assume to have multi-view software models annotated with performance-related data that concur to the antipattern definition, ModelElements can appear in *static*, *dynamic* and *deployment* views.

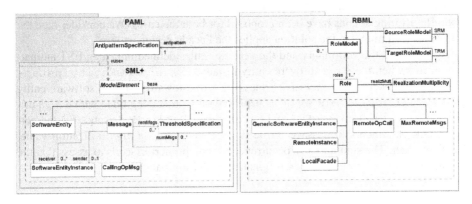

Fig. 2. Role-Based Modeling Language applied to performance antipatterns

antipatterns within a metamodel called PAML (*Performance Antipattern Modeling Language*)[3]. The left-hand side of Figure 2 shows an excerpt of PAML/SML+.

The right-hand side of Figure 2 shows an excerpt of our RBML reference metamodel and the relationships that we have defined with PAML [3]. Topmost boxes represent the RBML concepts we have inherited from [12], that are: `RoleModel`, `Role` and `RealizationMultiplicity`. A `RoleModel` contains a set of `Roles`, where each role annotates (is played by) a certain number of **ModelElements**. A `RealizationMultiplicity` specifies the number of elements playing a certain role. Furthermore, we have introduced the concepts of `SourceRoleModels` and `TargetRoleModels` (as specializations of `RoleModel`) in order to describe antipattern problems and solutions as pairs of `RoleModels`, where a `SourceRoleModel` (SRM) represents (part of) a problem and a `TargetRoleModel` (TRM) represents the corresponding solution. The set of **ModelElement** specializations in SML+ represents target elements (i.e. the `bases`) that should play the `Roles` (specializations) defined in RBML, thus enabling the role-annotation of software model elements. Bases and roles have been detailed in SML+ and RBML but not reported in Figure 2 for sake of readability. Note that dashed boxes in Figure 2 are not complete, as other **ModelElement**s and `Roles` have been defined up to now and can be defined in future.

Different refactoring actions can be applied to solve a performance antipattern, hence different (SRM, TRM) pairs can be associated to the same antipattern. We have used RBML to build several (SRM, TRM) pairs. Our repository of `RoleModels` [2] currently contains: three pairs for the *Blob* antipattern, one pair for the *Concurrent Processing Systems* antipattern, one pair for the *Empty Semi Trucks*, and two pairs for the *Pipe and Filter*. We recall that Smith et al. have specified 14 performance antipatterns [21], hence we cover 4/14 performance antipatterns as a starting point for our work.

---

[3] In the following we use subsequent notation: with a `typewritten` font we refer RBML elements, whereas with a **sans-serif** we refer PAML/SML+ elements.

EST may be due to inefficient use of available bandwidth, an inefficient interface, or both. Refactoring actions have been proposed for both the cases. We consider here the latter one, assuming that the solution applies the Facade design pattern[4].

According to the vocabulary and the detection rules defined in [7], an EST antipattern occurs when there is a software entity instance (`GenericSwEntityInstan-ce`) that: (i) generates an *excessive* [5] message traffic towards another software entity instance (`RemoteInstance`), (ii) is deployed on a processing node with a *high* utilization value, i.e. `GenericSwEntityInstanceDeployNode`, and (iii) the network link on which the message traffic is generated shows a *high* utilization value, i.e. `Network`. The simultaneous occurrence of such properties leads to assess that the `GenericSwEntityInstance` originates an EST antipattern.

3   Model Differencing for Model Refactoring

In this section we propose our approach based on model differencing of (SRM, TRM) pairs and model-to-model transformations for automating the application of refactorings aimed at removing antipatterns from software models. Figure 3 maps the concept of refactoring actions to the metamodeling view of our approach in the MDE domain.

In the conceptual domain, we want to apply a set of refactoring actions $RefActions_j(AP_i)$ to a software model that contains a certain antipattern instance $AP_i problem$, in order to produce a new software model where an $AP_i solution$ has been applied. In the MDE domain, $RefActions_j(AP_i)$ are represented by their corresponding difference model $DiffModel_j(AP_i)$. This model is the output of a model transformation $DiffCalculation$ that takes as input a $(SRM_j(AP_i), TRM_j(AP_i))$ pair describing $AP_i problem$ and $AP_i solution$. Finally, as illustrated in the bottom part of the MDE domain, refactoring actions are applied by means of the model transformation $DiffApplication$ that produces the *(Role-annotated) Refactored Software Model* starting from the original *(Role-annotated) Software Model* [6]. Topmost half of the MDE domain box of Figure 3 describes the metamodels to which models conform and their relationships (level *M2* in a MDE hierarchy). *Software Model*s conform to SML+. $DiffModel_j(AP_i)$ conforms to RBMLDIFF, i.e. a difference metamodel corresponding to RBML. RBMLDIFF is automatically generated by means of the $MM2MMDIFF$ model-to-model transformation we have defined basing on the metamodel-independent approach for differences representation proposed in [6]. RBMLDIFF contains modeling constructs able to manage all the refactoring actions that can be operated on models conforming to RBML and can be grouped as *add*, *delete*, *change*, and *keep-as-is* actions (see Section 2).

By exploiting a "once-defined" higher-order transformation (HOT) $MMDIFF$-$2DiffApplication$, it is possible to automatically generate the $DiffApplication$

---

[4] http://developer.java.sun.com/developer/restricted/
patterns/SessionFacade.html

[5] The characterization of antipattern parameters related to system characteristics (e.g. *excessive* message traffic) or to performance results (e.g. *high*, *low* utilization) is based on thresholds [7].

[6] Note that *Software Model*s are "Role-annotated" because we need to properly assign roles to their elements to reflect the refactoring defined by the $(SRM_j(AP_i), TRM_j(AP_i))$ pair.

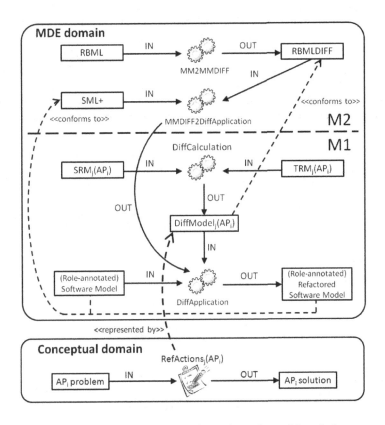

Fig. 3. Meta-modeling view and model transformations of the solution step

transformation. Recall that the latter is able to concretely refactor a *(Role-Annotated)*
Software Model by means of a set of refactoring actions represented by
$DiffModel_j(AP_i)$ and induced by the $(SRM_j(AP_i), TRM_j(AP_i))$ pair. In this paper, $DiffModel_j(AP_i)$ difference models are manually defined, but we might adopt
model comparison techniques [13] in order to automatically generate them, as similarly
done in [5,19].

In the remaining of this section, the implementation of our approach[7] is detailed. It
uses EMF [8] as modeling platform, and ATL[9] as model transformation language.

3.1 RBML Difference Model

The $MM2MMDIFF$ transformation is based on the metamodel-independent ap-
proach for differences representation proposed in [6]. In particular, for each metaclass
MC of the RBML metamodel, the metaclasses AddedMC, DeletedMC and Changed-
MC are added in the generated difference metamodel to enable the representation of

---

[7] http://www.di.univaq.it/cortelle/docs/ModelRefactoring.rar
[8] http://www.eclipse.org/modeling/emf/
[9] http://www.eclipse.org/atl/

additions, deletions, and changes, respectively. For instance, the metaclass
`GenericSwEntityInstance` of RBML induces the generation of the
`AddedGenericSwEntityInstance`, `DeletedGenericSwEntityInstan-`
`ce`, and `ChangedGenericSwEntityInstance` metaclasses. As better explained
later in the paper, in order to represent additions, deletions, and changes of structural features (in the elements of the considered software model), RBMLDIFF contains
also the metaclasses `AddedFeature`, `DeletedFeature`, and `ChangedFeatu-`
`re`, respectively.

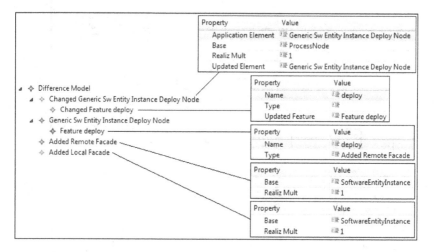

Fig. 4. Sample difference model

Figure 4 shows an excerpt of the difference model for the $(SRM_1(EST), TRM_1\text{-}$
$(EST))$ pair of the EST antipattern discussed in the previous section. The model represents *i)* the addition of new `LocalFacade` and `RemoteFacade` roles and *ii)* changes
of the `GenericSwEntityInstanceDeployNode` element. On the right-hand side
of the figure, some properties have been represented. In particular, the metaclass `Chan-`
`gedGenericSwEntityInstanceDeployNode` represents the changes which
have been operated on the **ProcessNode** (see the *base* attribute) where the `Gene-`
`ricSwEntityInstance` is deployed. In particular, the `RemoteFacade` element
is deployed on it. In fact, according to the properties shown on the right-hand side of the
figure, the `deploy` feature of `ChangedGenericSwEntityInstanceDeploy-`
`Node` is changed (see the `ChangedFeature` element named *deploy*, which refers to
the updated *deploy* feature whose type is `AddedRemoteFacade`).

3.2 Applying Differences for Model Refactoring

A fragment of the ATL implementation of the $Diff Application$ model transformation
is shown in Listing 1.1. The transformation implements the rules for applying on the
source software model (referred by `softwareModel` in the code) the additions, deletions, and changes specified in the difference model (referred by `delta` in the code). In
particular, for each metaclass `MC` of RBML, the following rules are provided:

– `AddedMC`: it manages the difference model elements that conform to the `AddedMC` metaclass of RBMLDIFF. For each element, the rule creates a new element conforming to the metaclass of the SML+ metamodel referred by the feature *base* of the considered `AddedMC` role. For instance, lines 3-15 of Listing 1.1 are related to the management of `AddedRemoteFacade` elements. For each of them, a corresponding **SoftwareEntityInstance** element is created. By considering the difference model in Figure 4, the rule is applied on the represented added `RemoteFacade` having **SoftwareEntityInstance** as base element;

– `ChangedMC`: according to the modifications specified in the difference model by means of instances of the metaclass `ChangedMC`, the rule generates refactored elements of the SML+ metamodel that play the MC role. For instance, lines 16-29 of Listing 1.1 contain the transformation rule managing the `ChangedGenericSwEntityInstanceDeployNodes`. For each of them a target **ProcessNode** element is generated, and to set the changed structural features, dedicated helpers are exploited. In particular, to specify the value of the reference `deploy` for referring to the node where the changed process node is deployed the `getChanged_deploy` helper is used (see lines 23 and 31-35). By considering the changed process node the helper retrieves all the deploy elements that have kept unchanged and those that have been added (e.g., see the software entity instance role named `RemoteFacade` represented in Figure 4);

Listing 1.1. Fragment of the *DiffApplication* ATL transformation

```
1 module deltaApplication;
2 create refSwModel : SML from swModel : SML, srm : RBML, delta : RBMLDIFF;
3 rule AddedRemoteFacade {
4     from
5         s: ROLEPROFILEDIFF!AddedRemoteFacade (
6         s.base.oclIsTypeOf('SML!SoftwareEntityInstance'))
7     to
8         t : SML!SoftwareEntityInstance (
9             name <- s.name,
10            ...
11        )
12    do {
13        thisModule.generatedStaticView.subviews->first().modelElements <- t;
14    }
15 }
16 rule ChangedGenericSwEntityInstanceDeployNode {
17     from
18         s : ROLEPROFILEDIFF!ChangedGenericSwEntityInstanceDeployNode (
19         s.base.oclIsTypeOf('SML!ProcessNode'))
20     to
21         t: SML!ProcessNode (
22             name <- s.applicationElement.getDiscoveredProcessNode().name,
23             deploy <- s.getChanged_deploy(),
24             ...
25         )
26     do {
27         thisModule.generatedDeploymentView.subviews->first().modelElements <- t;
28     }
29 }
30 ...
31 helper context ROLEPROFILEDIFF!ChangedGenericSwEntityInstanceDeployNode def:
        getChanged_deploy() : Sequence(SML!SoftwareEntityInstance) =
32     self.applicationElement.getDiscoveredProcessNode().deploy
33         ->union(ROLEPROFILEDIFF!ChangedFeature.allInstances()
34         ->select(cf | cf.owner = self and cf.name = 'deploy')
35         ->first().updatedFeature.type->collect(e|thisModule.resolveTemp(e ,'t')))
        ;
```

Concerning the management of deleted role elements (i.e., instances of the metaclass `DeletedMC` of RBMLDIFF), no rules are provided for them, because they do not contribute to the generation of any target model element. Contrariwise, additional rules are provided to manage the unchanged elements of the source software model. In this respect, for each metaclass `MC` in the SML+ metamodel a corresponding `CopyMC` rule is generated. Such rule copies the unmodified model elements playing the `MC` role.

A higher-order transformation $MMDIFF2DiffApplication$ has been defined to generate the $DiffApplication$ transformation.

4   Application Example

In this section we present a case study in the e-commerce domain as an application example of our approach. We first describe the (Performance-Annotated) Software Model of the E-Commerce System (ECS), on which the process in Figure 1 is stepwise applied. Finally, the obtained numerical results are discussed.

ECS is a web-based system that manages business data related to generic products. Among all provided services, we focus in this paper on the customer registration scenario, namely *Register* service (see [2] for a complete figure of ECS).

A performance requirement has been defined on the average response time of *Register*: it has to be completed in 1.4 seconds under workloads of 1, 100 and 200 users.

The performance analysis has been conducted by transforming the software model into a Queueing Network (QN) model [9], and by solving the latter with JMT [4].

Table 1. Response times of the *Register* service

Software Model	Number of users	RT($Register$) $<=$ 1.4 sec
	1	1.55992 sec
ECS	100	1.56769 sec
	200	1.65494 sec
	1	0.9199 sec
$ECS\backslash$	100	0.9514 sec
$\{EST - TRM_1\}$	200	1.584 sec

Table 1 reports the response times of the *Register* service. The first row contains data of the original ECS model (i.e. without any refactoring). The service shows response times that do not fulfill the required one for all considered workloads.

The antipatterns detection sub-process [7] reported four performance antipattern occurrences: Blob, Concurrent Processing Systems (CPS), Empty Semi Trucks (EST), and Pipe and Filter (P&F). For sake of space, in the following we only discuss EST [2].

Figure 5 shows the (Role-Annotated) Software Model. The EST antipattern occurrence in the ECS can be described as follows: *UserController* originates the EST, since it sends to the *Database* more than two (see ThresholdSpecification in Figure 5) remote messages, and the communicating instances are remotely deployed.

Figure 6 shows the (Role-annotated) refactored ECS software model after the refactoring transformation induced by the corresponding $DiffModel_1(EST)$ is applied. In agreement with $TRM_1(EST)$: (i) two new software entity instances have been added, i.e. *RemoteFacade* and *LocalFacade* (see Figure 6(a)); (ii) the communication has been

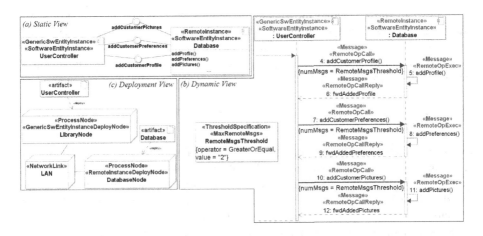

Fig. 5. ECS case study - (Role-Annotated) Software Model restricted to the EST occurrence

refactored and local messages have replaced remote ones (see Figure 6(b)); (iii) *RemoteFacade* and *LocalFacade* have been deployed on *LibraryNode* and *DatabaseNode*, respectively (see Figure 6(c)). This refactoring removes the EST occurrence.

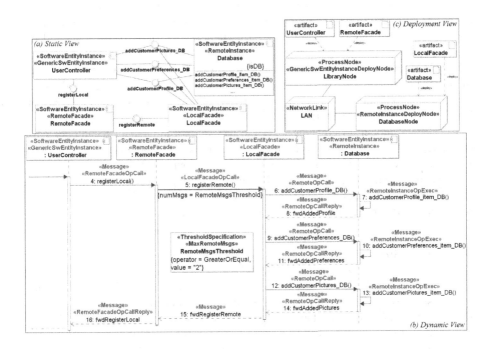

Fig. 6. ECS case study - Refactored Software Model restricted to the EST occurrence

In order to check whether the refactoring actions are effective, the second row of Table 1 reports response times of the refactored ECS. Refactoring actions are beneficial for populations of 1 and 100 users, whose new response times become lower than the required one. Instead, for a population of 200 users the *Register* service maintains a response time higher than the required one, probably due to some other antipattern.

5   Related Work

An extensive overview of existing research in the field of software refactoring is provided in [17]. In literature many approaches often apply the refactoring to the program itself (i.e. the source code), but it is difficult to maintain consistency between the refactored code and the other software artifacts. Hence, processes and tools that address refactoring in a more consistent, generic, scalable and flexible way are needed.

In general, there has been a significant effort in the area of refactoring software design patterns. For example, UML-based design patterns have been specified in [12] in terms of UML metamodel concepts. However, differently from patterns, antipatterns look as bad design practices in software systems, and describe commonly occurring solutions to solve them [21,15].

Performance antipatterns have been documented and discussed in different papers: *technology-independent* antipatterns have been defined in [21] and they represent the main reference in our work; *technology-specific* antipatterns have been specified in [11]. Nevertheless, few model-based approaches for automated performance diagnosis and improvement have been introduced up today in the software modeling domain [14,18].

In [25] performance problems are identified before the implementation of the software systems, but they are based only on bottlenecks and long paths, identified by means of performance analysis on Layered Queueing Network (LQN) models.

In [1] we have discussed pros and cons of refactoring either software or performance models, by comparing two approaches we have recently introduced: one based on detection and solution of performance antipatterns on software models, and another one based on bidirectional transformations between software and performance models.

Concerning model differencing, over the last years a number of techniques have been adopted for managing different activities in software development and evolution. For instance, to support transformation testing [16], coupled evolution of metamodel and models [5], data migration [23], and to support the upgrade of open source systems [10]. However, the adoption of model differencing in the area of software refactoring based on performance analysis is a novelty of this paper.

6   Conclusions

In our previous work [3], we have introduced a first definition of role-based language to represent (SRM, TRM) pairs of performance antipatterns. In this paper, we have refined its definition and introduced an approach to refactor software models basing on results of performance analysis. This result has been achieved by using sophisticated model-driven techniques, i.e. model differencing.

Our experience represents a first promising step towards the automation of this type of refactoring. In fact, by means of a HOT (which is written only once) we can automatically generate a transformation that applies refactorings described by (SRM, TRM) pairs. This allows to avoid writing an ad-hoc transformation for each of the latter.

Several aspects of this approach still need more investigation: (i) an extension of the (SRM, TRM) pairs repository would allow more extensive validation of the approach; (ii) model view consistency has to be taken into account for allowing automated propagation of changes among views; (iii) the refactoring transformation generated by model differences could contain ambiguities, due to the application order of refactoring steps, thus it is our intent to study these ambiguities; (iv) in this paper difference models are manually built, as conforming to the difference metamodel, but in future we aim at using automated model-driven techniques for generating a difference model starting from a (SRM, TRM) pair (e.g., see [5,19]); this step would allow to achieve a full automation of our process.

Acknowledgments. This work has been supported by EOARD, Grant no. FA8655-11-1-3055 on "Consistent evolution of software artifacts and non-functional models".

References

1. Arcelli, D., Cortellessa, V.: Software model refactoring based on performance analysis: better working on software or performance side? In: Buhnova, B., Happe, L., Kofron, J. (eds.) FESCA. EPTCS, vol. 108, pp. 33–47 (2013)
2. Arcelli, D., Cortellessa, V., Trubiani, C.: A repository of Source and Target Role Models for software performance antipatterns. Technical report (2011),
   http://www.di.univaq.it/cortelle/docs/005-2011-report.pdf
3. Arcelli, D., Cortellessa, V., Trubiani, C.: Antipattern-based model refactoring for software performance improvement. In: Proceedings of the 12th QoSA (2012)
4. Casale, G., Serazzi, G.: Quantitative system evaluation with java modeling tools. In: ICPE, pp. 449–454 (2011)
5. Cicchetti, A., Di Ruscio, D., Iovino, L., Pierantonio, A.: Managing the evolution of data-intensive web applications by model-driven techniques. Software and Systems Modeling 12(1), 53–83 (2013)
6. Cicchetti, A., Di Ruscio, D., Pierantonio, A.: A Metamodel Independent Approach to Difference Representation. Journal of Object Technology 6(9), 165–185 (2007)
7. Cortellessa, V., Di Marco, A., Trubiani, C.: An approach for modeling and detecting software performance antipatterns based on first-order logics. Journal of Software and Systems Modeling (2012), doi:10.1007/s10270-012-0246-z.
8. Cortellessa, V., Martens, A., Reussner, R., Trubiani, C.: A process to effectively identify "Guilty" performance antipatterns. In: Rosenblum, D.S., Taentzer, G. (eds.) FASE 2010. LNCS, vol. 6013, pp. 368–382. Springer, Heidelberg (2010)
9. Cortellessa, V., Mirandola, R.: PRIMA-UML: a performance validation incremental methodology on early UML diagrams. Sci. Comput. Program. 44(1), 101–129 (2002)
10. Di Cosmo, R., Di Ruscio, D., Pelliccione, P., Pierantonio, A., Zacchiroli, S.: Supporting software evolution in component-based foss systems. Science of Computer Programming 76(12), 1144–1160 (2011), http://dx.doi.org/10.1016/j.scico.2010.11.001
11. Dudney, B., Asbury, S., Krozak, J.K., Wittkopf, K.: J2EE Antipatterns. Wiley (2003)

12. France, R.B., Kim, D.-K., Ghosh, S., Song, E.: A UML-Based Pattern Specification Technique. IEEE Trans. Software Eng. 30(3), 193–206 (2004)

13. Kolovos, D.S., Di Ruscio, D., Paige, R.F., Pierantonio, A.: Different models for model matching: An analysis of approaches to support model differencing. In: CVSM at ICSE (2009)

14. Koziolek, A., Koziolek, H., Reussner, R.: Peropteryx: automated application of tactics in multi-objective software architecture optimization. In: QoSA/ISARCS, pp. 33–42 (2011)

15. Laplante, P.A., Neill, C.J.: AntiPatterns: Identification, Refactoring and Management. Auerbach (2005)

16. Lin, Y., Zhang, J., Gray, J.: A testing framework for model transformations. Model-Driven Software Development (2005)

17. Mens, T., Taentzer, G.: Model-driven software refactoring. In: Dig, D. (ed.) WRT, pp. 25–27 (2007)

18. Parsons, T., Murphy, J.: Detecting performance antipatterns in component based enterprise systems. Journal of Object Technology 7(3), 55–90 (2008)

19. Pierantonio, A., Iovino, L., Di Rocco, J.: Bridging state-based differencing and co-evolution. In: Models and Evolution Workshop at MODELS (September 2012)

20. Ramachandran, K., Fathi, K., Rao, B.: Recent trends in systems performance monitoring & failure diagnosis. In: IEEM, pp. 2193–2200 (2010)

21. Smith, C.U., Williams, L.G.: More new software antipatterns: Even more ways to shoot yourself in the foot. In: CMG Conference, pp. 717–725 (2003)

22. Trubiani, C.: A model-based framework for software performance feedback. In: Dingel, J., Solberg, A. (eds.) MODELS 2010. LNCS, vol. 6627, pp. 19–34. Springer, Heidelberg (2011)

23. Vermolen, S., Visser, E.: Heterogeneous Coupled Evolution of Software Languages. In: Czarnecki, K., Ober, I., Bruel, J.-M., Uhl, A., Völter, M. (eds.) MODELS 2008. LNCS, vol. 5301, pp. 630–644. Springer, Heidelberg (2008)

24. Woodside, C.M., Franks, G., Petriu, D.C.: The future of software performance engineering. In: Workshop on the Future of Software Engineering (FOSE), pp. 171–187 (2007)

25. Xu, J.: Rule-based automatic software performance diagnosis and improvement. In: Workshop on Software and Performance (WOSP), pp. 1–12 (2008)

Reduction of Subtask Dispersion
in Fork-Join Systems

Iryna Tsimashenka and William J. Knottenbelt

Imperial College London, 180 Queen's Gate,
London SW7 2AZ, United Kingdom
{it09,wjk}@doc.ic.ac.uk

Abstract. Fork-join and split-merge queueing systems are well-known abstractions of parallel systems in which each incoming task splits into subtasks that are processed by a set of parallel servers. A task exits the system when all of its subtasks have completed service. Two key metrics of interest in such systems are task response time and subtask dispersion. This paper presents a technique applicable to a class of fork-join systems with heterogeneous exponentially distributed service times that is able to reduce subtask dispersion with only a marginal increase in task response time. Achieving this is challenging since the unsynchronised operation of fork-join systems naturally militates against low subtask dispersion. Our approach builds on our earlier research examining subtask dispersion and response time in split-merge systems, and involves the frequent application and updating of delays to the subtasks at the head of the parallel service queues. Numerical results show the ability to reduce dispersion in fork-join systems to levels comparable with or below that observed in all varieties of split-merge systems while retaining the response time and throughput benefits of a fork-join system.

Keywords: Fork-Join System, Subtask Dispersion, Task Response Time.

1 Introduction

Nowadays parallel systems are becoming more prevalent than ever, with large automated warehouses, concurrent computing systems and distributed storage systems taking centre stage in the world of industry. Despite the fact that performance and operational efficiency are primary concerns in these systems, there are significant challenges from a modelling perspective in predicting and optimising their dynamic behaviour.

Queueing network models are natural abstractions for representing the flow and processing of tasks in parallel systems in which high-level tasks split into subtasks which are concurrently processed by a set of (heterogeneous) parallel servers. This paper focuses on two subclasses of queueing network models for parallel systems, namely *fork-join* and *split-merge* systems [3]. Definitions and operational characteristics of each of these two kinds of system are presented in the next section.

Two performance metrics of interest in these systems are *task response time* – that is the time taken from the entry of a task into the system until its exit – and *subtask dispersion* – that is the difference in time between the service completions of the first and last subtasks originating from a given task. Since subtasks in a fork-join system

M.S. Balsamo, W.J. Knottenbelt, and A. Marin (Eds.): EPEW 2013, LNCS 8168, pp. 325–336, 2013.

are subject to less synchronisation than those in a split-merge system, the structure of a fork-join system naturally yields lower response times but higher subtask dispersion when compared to a split-merge system with similar parallel service time distributions.

In this paper we present an online technique for applying judiciously-chosen delays to subtask processing times in elementary fork-join systems with heterogeneous exponential service times. The technique reduces subtask dispersion significantly with only a marginal impact on task response time. Our method assumes non-preemptive scheduling; that is, once subtasks begin service they are executed to completion. Although preemption gives more flexibility for scheduling from a theoretical perspective, preemptive scheduling can lead to considerable overhead when applied in practice [12].

This paper makes the following specific contributions over our previous work exploring subtask dispersion and task response time in parallel systems [15, 24–26]:

1. We extend our modelling capability to fork-join systems, rather than split-merge systems. Since fork-join systems are more widely deployed in practice owing to their greater efficiency, this means our present technique is more applicable to the realistic modelling of modern parallel systems.
2. In contrast to our previous algorithms which were static, the method we present here is a dynamic online one that is sensitive to the current state of the system. Not only is it to be expected that a dynamic method will outperform any static one – at least in the absence of significant scheduling overhead (see e.g. [13, 16, 19, 21]), but also our dynamic method can support non-stationary workloads.

The remainder of the paper is organised as follows. Section 2 presents relevant preliminaries including details of the parallel processing systems considered and the theory of homogeneous and heterogenous order statistics (subsequently applied in computing state-dependent subtask delays). Section 3 elaborates on the two performance metrics we consider and recaps important results from the literature related to each metric and the trade-off between them. Section 4 describes our method for the online control of subtask dispersion. Section 5 presents numerical results showing the ability of our methodology to simultaneously achieve low subtask dispersion (better even that than achieved by the best static algorithm for reducing subtask dispersion in split-merge systems), and low response time (only slightly higher than a fork-join system without subtask delays). Section 6 concludes.

2 Preliminaries

2.1 Parallel Processing Systems

Fork-Join. An *elementary fork-join system* (see Fig. 1) is composed of N parallel heterogeneous FCFS service queues, fork and join points and join queues (join buffers) for completed subtasks [3]. When a task arrives in the system (usually assumed to happen according to a Poisson process with mean rate λ) it instantaneously enters the fork point, where it forks into N independent subtasks. Each subtask enters the queue of its corresponding parallel server. Here we assume parallel server i processes its queue of subtasks according to an exponential service time distribution with mean service time

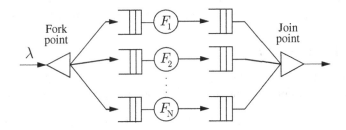

Fig. 1. Fork–Join queueing model

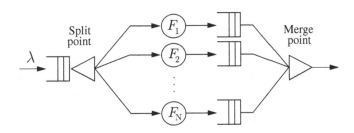

Fig. 2. Split–Merge queueing model

$1/\mu_i, i = 1, \ldots, N$. After service, a subtask enters a join queue. Only when all subtasks (of a particular task) are present in the join queues does the original task instantaneously exit the system via the join point.

Split-Merge. A more synchronised type of parallel system is the *split-merge system* (see Fig. 2), where the system processes only one task at a time. A split-merge system consists of split and merge points, a FCFS queue before the split point (split queue) and several heterogeneous parallel servers with queueing capability after service (merge buffers). When a task arrives in the system (usually assumed to happen according to a Poisson process with mean rate λ) it joins the split queue. Whenever all servers are idle and the split queue is not empty, a task is taken from the head of the split queue and is injected into the system, splitting into N subtasks at the split point. Each subtask enters the queue of its corresponding parallel server (where it is served according to a service time distribution with mean time $1/\mu_i$, $i = 1, \ldots, N$). After service, a subtask enters a merge buffer. Only when all subtasks (of a particular task) are present in the merge buffers does the original task instantaneously exit the system via the merge point.

Join and Merge Buffers. We note that in many real-life applications the join/merge buffers are managed as a single shared physical space set aside for the storage of partially completed subtasks. In such cases we term this space the *output buffer*. Careful management of the arrival times of subtasks into the output buffer is vital especially in circumstances where it occupies limited physical space and/or where it is highly utilised. One way to achieve this is to maintain low levels of subtask dispersion.

2.2 Theory of Order Statistics

Ordinary (homogeneous) order statistics [6] enable reasoning about *sorted* samples drawn from independent random variables having the same underlying distribution.

Definition 1. *If iid random variables $X_1, X_2, \ldots, X_n$ each having distribution $F(x)$ are arranged in the increasing order $X_{(1)} \leq X_{(2)} \leq \ldots \leq X_{(n)}$, then $X_{(i)}$ is the ith order statistic $(1 \leq i \leq n)$.*

The extremes are given by $X_{(1)}$ (the minimum order statistic), and $X_{(n)}$ (the maximum order statistic). $X_{(n)} - X_{(1)}$ is the range.

2.3 Theory of Heterogeneous Order Statistics

Heterogeneous order statistics [7] enable reasoning about sorted samples drawn from independent, but not necessarily identically distributed (inid) random variables.

Definition 2. *If inid random variables $X_1, X_2, \ldots, X_n$ each having distribution $F_i(x)$, are arranged in the increasing order $X_{(1)} \leq X_{(2)} \leq X_{(3)} \leq \ldots \leq X_{(n)}$, then $X_{(k)}$ is the kth heterogeneous order statistic having corresponding cdf $F_{(k)}(x)$ $(1 \leq k \leq n)$.*

The cumulative distribution functions of the minimum and maximum heterogeneous order statistics are:

$$F_{(1)}(t) = \Pr\{X_{(1)} \leq t\} = 1 - \prod_{i=1}^{n}[1 - F_i(t)],$$

and

$$F_{(n)}(t) = \Pr\{X_{(n)} \leq t\} = \prod_{i=1}^{n} F_i(t).$$

The cumulative distribution function of the range $X_{(n)} - X_{(1)}$ is [26]:

$$F_{range}(t) = \sum_{i=1}^{n} \int_{-\infty}^{\infty} f_i(x) \prod_{j=1, j \neq i}^{n} [F_j(x + t) - F_j(x)] \, dx \tag{1}$$

3   Metrics

There are two important metrics in fork-join and split-merge systems:

- **Task response time**, that is the time taken from the entry of a task into the system until its exit. This has been the primary focus of research effort over many decades (see e.g. [1, 2, 4, 5, 8–11, 14, 17, 18, 20, 22, 23, 27–30]). The vast majority of this work targets the mean (and rarely higher moments) of task response time and/or the stationary distribution of the number of tasks queued at parallel servers.

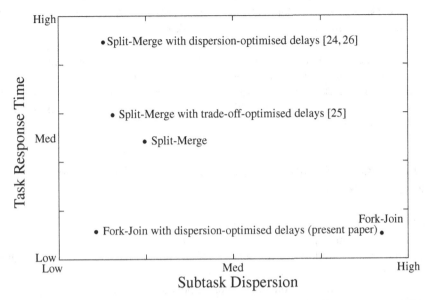

Fig. 3. Task response time vs. subtask dispersion of fork-join and split-merge queues with and without optimised subtask delays

– **Subtask Dispersion**, that is the difference in time between the service completions of the first and last subtasks of a given task. This is an especially important metric in the context of automated warehouses which process orders made up of multiple items. In such systems the first arrival of a subtask in the output buffer triggers reservation of physical space for that subtask and its siblings. Only when the final subtask belonging to a task has arrived in the output buffer can the space be freed. Efficient management of the output buffer space therefore requires the times of arrival of a subtask and its siblings in the output buffer to be clustered as close together as possible. It is also a consideration in other environments like full service restaurants, where customer satisfaction requires that the food for each course ordered by each table arrives at nearly the same time, and that each dish is hot (if appropriate) and freshly prepared. Research interest in this metric is relatively recent, see e.g. [24–26].

As illustrated in Fig. 3 these metrics are in tension in the sense that taking action to reduce one usually results in an increase in another; this is especially the case for high-intensity workloads. Unmodified fork-join systems yield low task response times (and therefore higher maximum sustainable system throughput), but subtask dispersion is high under load. Conversely, unmodified split-merge systems are characterised by low to moderate subtask dispersion, but can suffer from higher task response times (and therefore reduced maximum sustainable system throughput) under load. As we have shown in our previous work, adding delays to subtask processing times in split-merge systems can help to reduce mean subtask dispersion [24] and/or percentiles of subtask dispersion [26], but the sole focus on subtask dispersion only serves to exacerbate the problem of poor task response times under load. One solution is to apply load-dependent subtask delays which minimise the product of expected task response time and expected subtask dispersion [25]. This is highly effective at achieving a balance between the metrics; however, maximum sustainable system throughput is still limited to that achievable under an unmodified split-merge system. Our goal in the present work is to find a way to reduce dispersion in fork-join systems to levels comparable with or *below* that observed in all varieties of split-merge systems while retaining the response time and throughput benefits of a fork-join system.

4   On Online Technique for Reducing Subtask Dispersion in Fork-Join Systems

In the following we consider a fork-join system with N parallel heterogeneous servers, the ith of which has an exponential service time distribution with rate parameter μ_i, i.e. $F_i(x) = 1 - e^{-\mu_i x}$. To describe the state of the system at time t let $n_i(t)$ denote the number subtasks present in parallel server queue i; as such $N(\max_i n_i(t)) - \sum_i n_i(t)$ subtasks will be present in the join queues (or output buffer) at time t.

Our strategy is to let the system operate in its normal fork-join fashion, but to delay the start of service of certain of the subtasks that are at the head of the parallel service queues. In particular, at *every* time instant at which a *hitherto-unserviced* subtask S reaches the front of a parallel queue, we take the following control actions:

1. If any of the siblings of S have already completed service then the best mean subtask dispersion and task response time with respect to S's task are simultaneously achieved by immediately beginning service of S and also of any of its siblings that are at the front of their parallel queue.

2. Otherwise all siblings are still present in the parallel queues and we apply delays to S and its siblings that are at the front of their parallel queues and which have not yet entered service. We choose appropriate delays (which may include zero delays) by observing that, from the point of view of subtask S and its siblings, the system at that instant is equivalent to an N-server split-merge system in which parallel server i has service time distribution Erlang$(q_i(t) + 1, \mu_i)$, where $q_i(t)$ is a number of subtasks in front of S or its sibling subtask in parallel queue i at time t. The $q_i(t)$ form vector $\mathbf{q}(t) = (q_1(t), q_2(t), \ldots, q_N(t))$. We can then exploit the optimisation method we developed in our previous work [24–26] to determine a vector of (near-)optimal deterministic subtask delays $\mathbf{d} = (d_1, d_2, \ldots, d_N)$. Here element d_i denotes the deterministic delay which should notionally be applied to parallel server i. In fact we only adopt the delays corresponding to S and its siblings that are at the front of their parallel queues and which have not yet entered service (note this may involve overwriting a currently pending delay).

Similarly at time instants at which a subtask S enters a join queue (or output buffer) then we immediately begin service of any of the siblings of S that are at the front of their parallel queues.

The objective function of the optimisation is mean subtask dispersion, computed as the difference between the maximum and minimum heterogeneous order statistics of the split-merge-equivalent system with delays. Utilising the linearity property of the expectation operator over dependent variables, we have:

$$
\begin{aligned}
\mathbb{E}[D_{\mathbf{d}}] &= \left(\mathbb{E}[X_{(N)}^{\mathbf{d}} - X_{(1)}^{\mathbf{d}}] \right) \\
&= \left(\mathbb{E}[X_{(N)}^{\mathbf{d}}] - \mathbb{E}[X_{(1)}^{\mathbf{d}}] \right) \\
&= \int_0^\infty \left(1 - \prod_{i=1}^N F_i(x - d_i) \right) dx - \\
&\quad \int_0^\infty \left(1 - \left(1 - \prod_{i=1}^N (1 - F_i(x - d_i)) \right) \right) dx
\end{aligned}
\tag{2}
$$

where $F_i(x - d_i)$ is a shifted Erlang$(q_i(t) + 1, \mu_i)$ cumulative distribution function.

When optimising, we solve for:

$$
\mathbf{d}_{\min} = \arg\min_{\mathbf{d}} \mathbb{E}[D_{\mathbf{d}}]
\tag{3}
$$

while additionally applying the constraint ($\prod_i d_i = 0$) to avoid the addition of superfluous delays to bottleneck queues.

The optimisation procedure itself is based on Newton's method. Practically, it utilises numerical integration to evaluate the objective function and exploits a disk-based memoisation technique to dramatically reduce the time cost of computing optimised delay vectors for system states that have already been encountered in the current execution or in some previous execution.

5   Numerical Results

In this section we present results from C++ simulations of fork-join and split-merge queueing systems that employ the dynamic optimisation of the present paper for fork-join systems and the static optimisation techniques developed in our previous work [24,25] for split-merge systems. The simulations collect a range of performance-related statistics, e.g. mean task response time, mean subtask dispersion, mean output utilisation of join/merge buffers, task throughput and distributions of subtask dispersion. The simulations were performed on a 3.5GHz Intel Core-i5 workstation with 8GB RAM. Each simulation run is made up of 10 replicas, and each replica consists of a warm-up period of the processing of 250 000 tasks followed by an measurement period of the processing of 250 000 tasks. For the static optimisation techniques, it requires approximately one second to run each replica, and for the dynamic optimisation of fork-join simulator it takes around 7.5 minutes for each replica. The replicas are used to put 95% confidence intervals (CIs) on all measures. Results are reported to three decimal places.

As our case study, consider a parallel system with Poisson arrivals with rate parameter $\lambda = 0.78$ tasks/time unit and 3 parallel service nodes with exponential service time density functions: $Exp(1)$, $Exp(5)$, $Exp(10)$.

In this context, we compute measures of subtask dispersion and of task response time of five different types of fork-join and split-merge queueing systems:

1. A fork-join queueing system (without subtask delays). Here the mean task response time is $\mathbb{E}[R_{d=0}] = 4.553$ (95% CI $[4.504, 4.602]$) time units and mean subtask dispersion $\mathbb{E}[D_{d=0}] = 4.490$ (95% CI $[4.429, 4.54]$) time units. The mean number of subtasks in the output buffer is 6.862 (95% CI $[6.79, 6.93]$).

2. A fork-join queueing system utilising our dynamic online algorithm for reducing mean subtask dispersion. Here mean task response time is $\mathbb{E}[R_{d_{min}}] = 4.703$ (95% CI $[4.586, 4.819]$) time units and mean subtask dispersion is $\mathbb{E}[D_{d_{min}}] = 0.752$ (95% CI $[0.745, 0.759]$) time units. The mean number of subtasks in the output buffer is 1.081 (95% CI $[1.071, 1.091]$). When compared with the fork-join system without subtask delays, we observe mean task response time increased very slightly by 3.3% but mean subtask dispersion dropped very dramatically by 83%. Similarly, the mean number of subtasks in the output buffer decreased by 84%.

3. A split-merge queueing system (without subtask delays). Mean task response time is $\mathbb{E}[R_{d=0, \lambda=0.78}] = 5.212$ (95% CI $[5.1526, 5.271]$) time units and mean subtask dispersion is $\mathbb{E}[D_{d=0}] = 0.976$ (95% CI $[0.975, 0.977]$) time units. The mean number of subtasks in the output buffer is 1.416 (95% CI $[1.415, 1.418]$). This method is thus completely dominated by our dynamic online algorithm for each of these metrics, by factors of 11%, 30% and 31% respectively.

4. A split-merge queueing system with delays applied to reduce mean subtask disperstion [24]. The vector of optimised delays is:

$$d_{min} = (0, 0.553, 0.617)$$

Mean task response time is $\mathbb{E}[R_{d_{min}, \lambda=0.78}] = 63.02$ (95% CI $[58.21, 67.83]$) time units and mean subtask dispersion is $\mathbb{E}[D_{d_{min}}] = 0.783$ (95% CI $[0.780, 0.785]$) time units. The mean number of subtasks in the output buffer is 1.029 (95% CI $[1.027, 1.031]$). This method is dominated by our dynamic online algorithm with respect to the mean task response time and mean subtask dispersion metrics, by factors of 1240% and 4% respectively. There is however a 5% improvement with respect to the mean number of subtasks in the output buffer.

5. A split-merge queueing system with delays applied to optimise the product of mean task response time and mean subtask dispersion [25]. The vector of optimised delays is:

$$d_{min} = (0.0, 0.0398, 0.0673)$$

Mean task response time is $\mathbb{E}[R_{d_{min}, \lambda=0.78}] = 5.329$ (95% CI $[5.272, 5.385]$) time units and mean subtask dispersion is $\mathbb{E}[D_{d_{min}}] = 0.9343$ (95% CI $[0.9336, 0.9349]$) time units. The mean number of subtasks in the output buffer is 1.355 (95% CI $[1.353, 1.357]$). While improving dramatically on the mean task response of the previous case, the method is completely dominated by our dynamic online algorithm for each metric, by factors of 13%, 24% and 25% respectively.

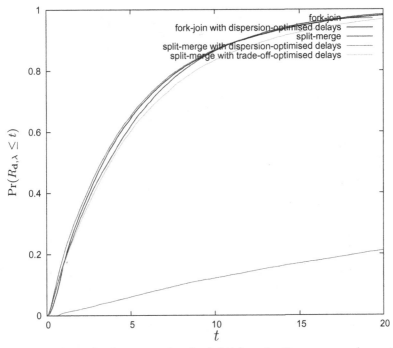

Fig. 4. Distributions of task response time for fork-join and split-merge queueing systems with and without optimised subtask delays. $\lambda = 0.78$

Turning now to distributions of task response time, Fig. 4 demonstrates that the task response time cdf of the fork-join system with dispersion-optimised delays is very close to that of the fork-join system without subtask delays. Here, the response time cdf of the split-merge system without subtask delays is marginally worse than that of the fork-join system, but after applying dispersion-optimised delays response time suffers heavily. Applying delays optimised for the subtask dispersion–task response time trade-off impacts only marginally on task response time.

Fig. 5 shows the corresponding distributions of subtask dispersion. The poor subtask dispersion of the fork-join system·without subtask delays is evident. Applying subtask delays optimised for the subtask dispersion–task response time trade-off yields a similar subtask dispersion profile to that of the split-merge system without delays. The subtask dispersion profile of the fork-join system with dispersion-optimised delays is competitive with that of the split-merge system with dispersion-optimised delays, and even dominates it for percentiles of subtask dispersion below 70%.

Fig. 6 shows how mean task response time varies with various task arrival rates under the various policies. We observe the split-merge system with dispersion-optimised delays has the lowest maximum sustainable system throughput, followed by the split-merge system with delays optimised for the subtask dispersion–task response time trade-off, and then the split-merge system without delays. The highest maximum sustainable system throughput is provided by the fork-join system utilising dispersion-optimised subtask delays and the fork-join system without subtask delays.

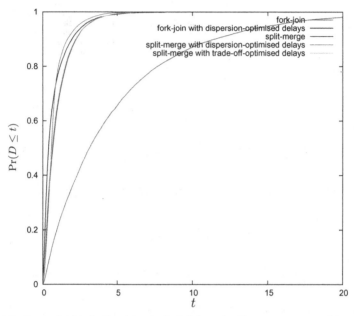

Fig. 5. Distributions of subtask dispersion in fork-join and split-merge queues with and without optimised subtask delays. $\lambda = 0.78$

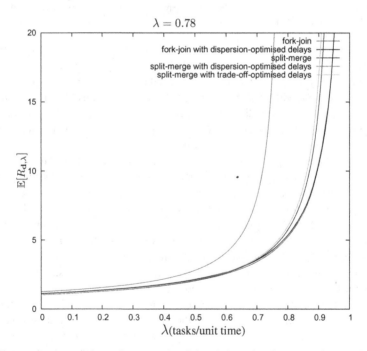

Fig. 6. Expected response time of case study of fork-join and split-merge systems for various customer arrival rates

6   Conclusion

In this paper we considered the problem of reducing subtask dispersion in elementary fork-join queueing systems. To control this metric, we derived an online algorithm which dynamically computes and applies state-dependent delays to subtasks and their siblings at various time instants.

We demonstrated our algorithm on a case study parallel system subjected to five different kinds of split-merge and fork-join queueing policies. The results show how the technique proposed in the present paper is able to deliver low subtask dispersion competitive with split-merge-based systems while simultaneously delivering low task response times competitive with fork-join-based systems.

Our current research can no doubt be extended to apply to fork-join systems with non-exponential services times. Certainly extension to Erlang and phase-type service time distributions is likely to be straightforward given appropriate extensions to the system state vector.

References

1. Baccelli, F., Makowski, A.M., Shwartz, A.: The fork-join queue and related systems with synchronization constraints: Stochastic ordering and computable bounds. Advances in Applied Probability 21(3), 629–660 (1989)
2. Baccelli, F., Massey, W.A., Towsley, D.: Acyclic fork-join queuing networks. Journal of ACM 36(3), 615–642 (1989)
3. Bolch, G., et al.: Queueing Networks and Markov Chains. J. Wiley & Sons, Inc. (2006)
4. Chen, R.J.: A hybrid solution of fork/join synchronization in parallel queues. IEEE Transactions on Parallel and Distributed Systems 12(8), 829–845 (2001)
5. Chen, R.J.: An upper bound solution for homogeneous fork/join queuing systems. IEEE Transactions on Parallel and Distributed Systems 22(5), 874–878 (2011)
6. David, H.A.: Order Statistics. Wiley Series in Probability and Mathematical Statistics. John Wiley (1980)
7. David, H.A., Nagaraja, H.N.: Order Statistics, 3rd edn. Wiley Series in Probability and Mathematical Statistics. John Wiley (2003)
8. Flatto, L.: Two parallel queues created by arrivals with two demands II. SIAM Journal on Applied Mathematics 45(5), 861–878 (1985)
9. Flatto, L., Hahn, S.: Two parallel queues created by arrivals with two demands I. SIAM Journal on Applied Mathematics 44(5), 1041–1053 (1984)
10. Harrison, P.G., Zertal, S.: Queueing models of RAID systems with maxima of waiting times. Performance Evaluation 64(7-8), 664–689 (2007)
11. Heidelberger, P., Trivedi, K.S.: Analytic queueing models for programs with internal concurrency. IEEE Transactions on Computers C-32(1), 73–82 (1983)
12. Jeffay, K., Stanat, D.F., Martel, C.U.: On non-preemptive scheduling of periodic and sporadic tasks. In: Proc. 12th Real-Time Systems Symposium, pp. 129–139 (1991)
13. Kameda, H., Li, J., Kim, C., Zhang, Y.: A comparison of static and dynamic load balancing. In: Optimal Load Balancing in Distributed Computer Systems. Telecommunication Networks and Computer Systems, pp. 225–240. Springer (1997)
14. Kim, C., Agrawala, A.K.: Analysis of the fork-join queue. IEEE Transactions on Computers 38(2), 250–255 (1989)

15. Knottenbelt, W.J., Tsimashenka, I.: Reducing subtask dispersion in parallel systems. In: Trends in Parallel, Distributed, Grid and Cloud Computing for Engineering, ch. 9, pp. 203–227. Saxe-Coburg Publications (April 2013)

16. Kwok, Y., Ahmad, I.: Static scheduling algorithms for allocating directed task graphs to multiprocessors. ACM Computing Surveys 31(4), 406–471 (1999)

17. Lebrecht, A., Knottenbelt, W.J.: Response Time Approximations in Fork-Join Queues. In: 23rd Annual UK Performance Engineering Workshop, UKPEW 2007 (July 2007)

18. Lui, J.C.S., Muntz, R.R., Towsley, D.: Computing performance bounds of fork-join parallel programs under a multiprocessing environment. IEEE Transactions on Parallel Distributed Systems 9(3), 295–311 (1998)

19. Mitrani, I.: Management of server farms for performance and profit. Computer Journal 53(7), 1038–1044 (2010)

20. Nelson, R., Tantawi, A.N.: Approximate analysis of fork/join synchronization in parallel queues. IEEE Transactions on Computers 37(6), 739–743 (1988)

21. Slegers, J., Mitrani, I., Thomas, N.: Static and dynamic server allocation in systems with on/off sources. Annals of Operations Research 170, 251–263 (2009)

22. Sun, J., Peterson, G.D.: An effective execution time approximation method for parallel computing. IEEE Transactions on Parallel and Distributed Systems 23(11), 2024–2032 (2012)

23. Towsley, D., Rommel, C.G., Stankovic, J.A.: Analysis of fork-join program response times on multiprocessors. IEEE Transactions on Parallel and Distributed Systems 1(3), 286–303 (1990)

24. Tsimashenka, I., Knottenbelt, W.J.: Reduction of Variability in Split-Merge Systems. In: Imperial College Computing Student Workshop (ICCSW 2011), pp. 101–107 (2011)

25. Tsimashenka, I., Knottenbelt, W.J.: Trading off subtask dispersion and response time in split-merge systems. In: Dudin, A., De Turck, K. (eds.) ASMTA 2013. LNCS, vol. 7984, pp. 431–442. Springer, Heidelberg (2013)

26. Tsimashenka, I., Knottenbelt, W., Harrison, P.: Controlling variability in split-merge systems. In: Al-Begain, K., Fiems, D., Vincent, J.-M. (eds.) ASMTA 2012. LNCS, vol. 7314, pp. 165–177. Springer, Heidelberg (2012)

27. Varki, E.: Response time analysis of parallel computer and storage systems. IEEE Transactions on Parallel and Distributed Systems 12(11), 1146–1161 (2001)

28. Varma, S., Makowski, A.M.: Interpolation approximations for symmetric fork-join queues. Performance Evaluation 20(1-3), 245–265 (1994)

29. Yang, A.T., Gerasoulis: DSC: Scheduling parallel tasks on an unbounded number of processors. IEEE Transactions on Parallel and Distributed Systems 5(9), 951–967 (1994)

30. Zhao, H., Xia, C.H., Liu, Z., Towsley, D.: A unified modeling framework for distributed resource allocation of general fork and join processing networks. In: Proc. ACM SIGMETRICS International Conference on Measurement and Modeling of Computer Systems (SIGMETRICS 2010), pp. 299–310. ACM, New York (2010)

SAT-Based Bounded Model Checking for RTECTL and Simply-Timed Systems*

Bożena Woźna-Szcześniak, Agnieszka Zbrzezny, and Andrzej Zbrzezny

IMCS, Jan Długosz University. Al. Armii Krajowej 13/15,
42-200 Częstochowa, Poland
{b.wozna,a.zbrzezny,agnieszka.zbrzezny}@ajd.czest.pl

Abstract. We report on a SAT-based bounded model checking (BMC) method for simply-timed systems (i.e., Kripke models where transitions carry a duration, which is an arbitrary natural number) generated by simply-timed automata with discrete data, and properties expressed in the existential fragment of a soft real-time temporal logic (RTECTL). In particular, since in BMC both the system model and the checked property are translated into a Boolean formula to be analysed by a SAT-solver, we introduce a new Boolean encoding of the RTECTL formulae that is particularly optimized for managing quantitative metric temporal operators, typically found in properties of soft real-time systems (simply-timed systems). The proposed BMC algorithm is implemented as a new module of VerICS, and evaluated by means of two scalable scenarios.

1 Introduction

Soft real-time systems can be defined as systems in which the total correctness of a computation depends not only on its logical correctness, but also on a certain subset of deadlines in which it is performed. To verify such systems several models and model checking techniques [2, 9] have been proposed. Popular models of such systems include timed automata [1] and time Petri nets [14], for which plethora of model checking techniques have been proposed and implemented [3–5, 11]. However, soft real-time systems do not always have to be modelled with timed automata or time Petri nets, whose Kripke models are not so simple from the state space symbolic encoding point of view. Namely, if one is interested in verification of soft real-time systems whose time deadlines can be measured by integer values, the standard Kripke models (i.e., transition systems where each transition takes one time unit) can be used as models, and either RTCTL model checking [7, 21] or discrete MTL (or metric LTL) model checking [10, 17, 20] can be applied. Since RTCTL and discrete MTL model checking are not harder than CTL [7] and LTL [10] model checking, respectively, these model checking techniques can enjoy the power of both the OBDD-based symbolic state space representations and translations to SAT. However their limitation is the restricted expressive power of standard Kripke models.

* Partly supported by National Science Centre under the grant No. 2011/01/B/ST6/05317

M.S. Balsamo, W.J. Knottenbelt, and A. Marin (Eds.): EPEW 2013, LNCS 8168, pp. 337–349, 2013.

To increase the expressive power of the standard Kripke models and simultaneously to be able to enjoy the power of OBDD-based symbolic model checking techniques, Markey and Schnoebelen [12] have proposed simply-timed systems (STSs), i.e., Kripke models where each transition holds a duration, which can be any integer value (including zero). Thus the difference between standard Kripke models and STSs is that it is not assumed that each transition takes one and only one time unit. Markey and Schnoebelen have also proposed an OBDD-based symbolic verification algorithm for model checking RTCTL properties over STSs generated by the NuSMV (http://nusmv.fbk.eu/) programs. They implemented this algorithm on the top of NuSMV, and they called it TSMV (http://www.lsv.ens-cachan.fr/~markey/TSMV/).

There are three main reasons why it is interesting to consider STSs instead of standard Kripke models. First, STSs allow for transitions that take a long time, e.g. 100 time units. Such transitions could be simulated in standard Kripke models by inserting 99 intermediate states. But this increases the size of the model, and so it makes the model checking process more difficult. Second, STSs allow transitions to have zero duration. This is very convenient in models where some steps are described indirectly, as a short succession of micro-steps. Third, the transitions with the zero duration allow for counting specific events only and thus omitting the irrelevant ones from the model checking point of view.

SAT-based bounded model checking (BMC) [8, 16, 21] is a verification technique whose basic idea is to consider only prefixes of executions whose length are bounded by some integer k, and which may be counterexamples to an universal property (or equivalently, witnesses to an existential property). If no error is found, then one increases k until either an error is found, or the problem becomes intractable. The usefulness of SAT-based BMC for error tracking and complementarity to the BDD-based symbolic model checking have already been proven in several works, e.g., [6, 13].

The original contribution of this paper consists in defining a SAT-based BMC method for the existential fragment of RTCTL (RTECTL) interpreted over simply-timed systems generated by simply-timed automata with discrete data. We implemented our SAT-based BMC algorithm as a new module of VerICS [11], an existing model checker for timed and multi-agent systems, and we compared it with the BDD-based model checking method for RTCTL and STSs that is implemented in TSMV, the only available model checker for STSs. For a constructive evaluation of our BMC method we have used two scalable scenarios: a modified *bridge-crossing problem* [18] and a modified *generic pipeline paradigm* [15]. Experimental results have shown that our BMC method performs well in practice, and unlike TSMV, our method is insensitive to scaling up the timing parameters (durations).

The rest of the paper is organised as follows. We begin in Section 2 by introducing simply-timed automata with discrete data, simply-timed systems, and we present the syntax and semantics of RTECTL over simply-timed systems. In Section 3 we present our SAT-based BMC method for RTECTL and simply-timed systems. In Section 4 we discuss our experimental results. In the last section we conclude the paper.

2 Preliminaries

Let $\mathbb{Z}$ be the set of integer numbers, $\mathcal{Z}$ a finite set of integer variables, $c \in \mathbb{Z}$, $z \in \mathcal{Z}$, and $\oplus \in \{+, -, *, mod, div\}$. Then, the set $Expr(\mathcal{Z})$ of all the *arithmetic expressions* over $\mathcal{Z}$ is defined by the following grammar:

$$expr ::= c \mid z \mid expr \oplus expr \mid -expr \mid (expr)$$

For $expr \in Expr(\mathcal{Z})$ and $\sim \in \{=, \neq, <, \leq, \geq, >\}$, the set $BoE(\mathcal{Z})$ of all the *Boolean expressions* over $\mathcal{Z}$ is defined by the following grammar:

$$\beta ::= true \mid expr \sim expr \mid \beta \wedge \beta \mid \beta \vee \beta \mid \neg\beta \mid (\beta)$$

For $z \in \mathcal{Z}$, $expr \in Expr(\mathcal{Z})$, ϵ denoting the empty sequence, and ";" denoting composition, the set $Ins(\mathcal{Z})$ of all the *instructions* over $\mathcal{Z}$ is defined as:

$$\alpha ::= \epsilon \mid z := expr \mid \alpha; \alpha$$

We further assume that $Ins^\Diamond(\mathcal{Z})$ denotes the set consisting of all these $\alpha \in Ins(\mathcal{Z})$ in which any $z \in \mathcal{Z}$ appears on the left-hand side of ":=" at most once.

By a *variables valuation* we mean a total mapping $\mathbf{v} : \mathcal{Z} \to \mathbb{Z}$. We extend this mapping to expressions of $Expr(\mathcal{Z})$ in the usual way. Moreover, we assume that a domain of values for each variable is finite. Satisfiability of a Boolean expression $\beta \in BoE(\mathcal{Z})$ by a valuation $\mathbf{v}$, denoted $\mathbf{v} \models \beta$, is defined inductively as follows: $\mathbf{v} \models true$, $\mathbf{v} \models expr_1 \sim expr_2$ iff $\mathbf{v}(expr_1) \sim \mathbf{v}(expr_2)$, $\mathbf{v} \models \beta_1 \wedge \beta_2$ iff $\mathbf{v} \models \beta_1$ and $\mathbf{v} \models \beta_2$, $\mathbf{v} \models \beta_1 \vee \beta_2$ iff $\mathbf{v} \models \beta_1$ or $\mathbf{v} \models \beta_2$, $\mathbf{v} \models \neg\beta$ iff $\mathbf{v} \not\models \beta$, $\mathbf{v} \models (\beta)$ iff $(\mathbf{v} \models \beta)$. Given a variables valuation $\mathbf{v}$ and an instruction $\alpha \in Ins(\mathcal{Z})$, we denote by $\mathbf{v}(\alpha)$ a valuation $\mathbf{v}'$ such that: if $\alpha = \epsilon$, then $\mathbf{v}' = \mathbf{v}$; if $\alpha = (z := expr)$, then for all $z' \in \mathcal{Z}$ it holds $\mathbf{v}'(z') = \mathbf{v}(expr)$ if $z' = z$, and $\mathbf{v}'(z') = \mathbf{v}(z')$ otherwise; if $\alpha = \alpha_1; \alpha_2$ then $\mathbf{v}' = (\mathbf{v}(\alpha_1))(\alpha_2)$.

Definition 1. *Let $\mathcal{PV}$ be a set of atomic propositions. A* simply-timed automaton with discrete data *(STADD) is a tuple $\mathcal{A} = (\Sigma, L, l^0, \mathcal{Z}, E, d, \mathcal{V}_A)$, where Σ is a finite set of actions, L is a finite set of locations, l^0 is an initial location, $\mathcal{Z}$ is a finite set of integer variables, $E \subseteq L \times \Sigma \times BoE(\mathcal{Z}) \times Ins^\Diamond(\mathcal{Z}) \times L$ is a transition relation, $d : \Sigma \to \mathbb{N}$ is a duration function, and $\mathcal{V}_A : L \to 2^{\mathcal{PV}}$ is a valuation function that assigns to each location a set of propositional variables that are assumed to be true at that location.*

Note that the STADD is a simplified versions of a timed automaton with discrete data [23] augmented to include a duration function. Each element $e = (\ell, \sigma, \beta, \alpha, \ell') \in E$ represents a transition from the location ℓ to the location ℓ', where σ is the action of the transition e, β defines the enabling condition for e, and α is the instruction to be performed.

Typically, concurrent (soft) real-time systems are modelled as a set of communicating processes. Thus to verify them, it is reasonable to model communicating processes by a network of STADDs that run in parallel, communicate with each other via shared actions and perform transitions with shared actions synchronously. For a formal definition of such a parallel composition of STADD we refer to [23].

The semantics of the STADD is defined by associating to it a *simply-timed system* as defined below.

Definition 2. *Let $\mathcal{PV}$ be a set of atomic propositions, $\mathbf{v}^0 : \mathcal{Z} \to \mathbb{Z}$ an initial variables valuation, and $\mathcal{A} = (\Sigma, L, \ell^0, \mathcal{Z}, E, d, \mathcal{V}_\mathcal{A})$ a simply-timed automaton with discrete data. A* simply-timed system *(or a model) for $\mathcal{A}$ is a tuple $M = (\Sigma, S, \iota, T, d, \mathcal{V})$, where Σ is a finite set of actions of $\mathcal{A}$, $S = L \times \mathbb{Z}^{|\mathcal{Z}|}$ is a set of states, $\iota = (\ell^0, \mathbf{v}^0) \in S$ is the initial state, $T \subseteq S \times \Sigma \times S$ is the smallest simply-timed transition relation defined as:*

- *for $\sigma \in \Sigma$, $(\ell, \mathbf{v}) \xrightarrow{\sigma} (\ell', \mathbf{v}')$ iff there exists a transition $(\ell, \sigma, \beta, \alpha, \ell') \in E$ such that $\mathbf{v} \models \beta$, $\mathbf{v}' = \mathbf{v}(\alpha)$. We assume that the relation T is total, i.e., for any $s \in S$ there exists $s' \in S$ and $\sigma \in \Sigma$ s.t. $(s, \sigma, s') \in T$ (or $s \xrightarrow{\sigma} s'$),*

$d : \Sigma \to \mathbb{N}$ is the duration function of $\mathcal{A}$, and $\mathcal{V} : S \to 2^{\mathcal{PV}}$ is a valuation function defined as $\mathcal{V}((\ell, \mathbf{v})) = \mathcal{V}_\mathcal{A}(\ell)$.

A *path* in M is an infinite sequence $\pi = s_0 \xrightarrow{\sigma_1} s_1 \xrightarrow{\sigma_2} s_2 \xrightarrow{\sigma_3} \ldots$ of transitions. For such a path, and for $m \in \mathbb{N}$, by $\pi(m)$ we denote the m-th state s_m. For $j \leq m \in \mathbb{N}$, $\pi[j..m]$ denotes the finite sequence $s_j \xrightarrow{\sigma_{j+1}} s_{j+1} \xrightarrow{\sigma_{j+2}} \ldots s_m$ with $m - j$ transitions and $m - j + 1$ states. The (cumulative) duration $D\pi[j..m]$ of such a finite sequence is $d(\sigma_{j+1}) + \ldots + d(\sigma_m)$ (hence 0 when $j = m$). By $\Pi(s)$ we denote the set of all paths starting at $s \in S$.

RTECTL: An Existential Fragment of a Soft Real-Time Temporal Logic. In the syntax of RTECTL we assume the following: $p \in \mathcal{PV}$ is an atomic proposition, and I is an interval in $\mathbb{N} = \{0, 1, 2, \ldots\}$ of the form: $[a, b)$ or $[a, \infty)$, for $a, b \in \mathbb{N}$ and $a \neq b$. Moreover, hereafter, by $right(I)$ we denote the right end of the interval I. The RTECTL formulae are defined by the following grammar:

$$\varphi ::= \mathbf{true} \mid \mathbf{false} \mid p \mid \neg p \mid \varphi \wedge \varphi \mid \varphi \vee \varphi \mid \mathrm{EX}\varphi \mid \mathrm{E}(\varphi \mathrm{U}_I \varphi) \mid \mathrm{E}(\varphi \mathrm{R}_I \varphi)$$

Intuitively, we have an existential path quantifier E, and the symbols X, U_I, and R_I that are the temporal operators for "neXt time", "bounded until", and "bounded release", respectively. The formula $\mathrm{E}(\alpha \mathrm{U}_I \beta)$ means that it is possible to reach a state satisfying β via a finite path whose cumulative duration is in I, and always earlier α holds. The formula $\mathrm{E}(\alpha \mathrm{R}_I \beta)$ means that either it is possible to reach a state satisfying α and β via a finite path whose cumulative duration is in I, and always earlier β holds, or there is a path along which β holds at all states with cumulative duration being in I. The formulae for the "bounded eventually", and "bounded always" are defined as standard: $\mathrm{EF}_I\varphi \stackrel{def}{=} \mathrm{E}(\mathbf{true}\mathrm{U}_I\varphi)$, $\mathrm{EG}_I\varphi \stackrel{def}{=} \mathrm{E}(\mathbf{false}\mathrm{R}_I\varphi)$.

An RTECTL formula φ is *true* in the model M (in symbols $M \models \varphi$) iff $M, \iota \models \varphi$ (i.e., φ is true at the initial state of the model M). For every $s \in S$ the relation $\models$ is defined inductively as follows:

$M, s \models \mathbf{true}$, $M, s \not\models \mathbf{false}$, $M, s \models p$ iff $p \in \mathcal{V}(s)$, $M, s \models \neg p$ iff $p \notin \mathcal{V}(s)$,

$$M, s \models \alpha \wedge \beta \quad \text{iff} \quad M, s \models \alpha \text{ and } M, s \models \beta,$$

$$M, s \models \alpha \vee \beta \quad \text{iff} \quad M, s \models \alpha \text{ or } M, s \models \beta,$$

$$M, s \models \mathrm{EX}\alpha \quad \text{iff} \quad (\exists \pi \in \Pi(s))(M, \pi(1) \models \alpha),$$

$$M, s \models \mathrm{E}(\alpha \mathrm{U}_I \beta) \quad \text{iff} \quad (\exists \pi \in \Pi(s))(\exists m \geq 0)(D\pi[0..m] \in I \text{ and } M, \pi(m) \models \beta$$
$$\text{and } (\forall j < m)M, \pi(j) \models \alpha),$$

$$M, s \models \mathrm{E}(\alpha \mathrm{R}_I \beta) \quad \text{iff} \quad (\exists \pi \in \Pi(s))\big((\exists m \geq 0)(D\pi[0..m] \in I \text{ and } M, \pi(m) \models \alpha$$
$$\text{and } (\forall j \leq m)M, \pi(j) \models \beta) \text{ or } (\forall m \geq 0)(D\pi[0..m] \in I$$
$$\text{implies } M, \pi(m) \models \beta)\big).$$

3   Bounded Model Checking for RTECTL

Bounded semantics is the backbone of each SAT-based bounded model checking (BMC) method, whose basic idea is to consider only finite prefixes of paths that may be witnessed to an existential model checking problem. A crucial observation is that, though the prefix of a path is finite, it still might represent an infinite path if it is a loop. If the prefix is not a loop, then it does not say anything about the infinite behavior of the path beyond its last state.

Let M be a model, and $k \in \mathbb{N}$ a bound. A *k-path* π_k in M is a finite sequence $s_0 \xrightarrow{\sigma_1} s_1 \xrightarrow{\sigma_2} \ldots \xrightarrow{\sigma_k} s_k$ of transitions (i.e., $\pi_k = \pi[0..k]$). $\Pi_k(s)$ denotes the set of all k-paths of M that start at s. A k-path π_k is a *(k, l)-loop* (or *loop*) iff $\pi_k(l) = \pi_k(k)$ for some $0 \leq l < k$. Note that if a k-path π_k is a loop, then it represents the infinite path of the form uv^ω, where $u = (s_0 \xrightarrow{\sigma_1} s_1 \xrightarrow{\sigma_2} \ldots \xrightarrow{\sigma_l} s_l)$ and $v = (s_{l+1} \xrightarrow{\sigma_{l+2}} \ldots \xrightarrow{\sigma_k} s_k)$. Moreover, since in the bounded semantics we consider finite prefixes of paths only, the duality between G_I and F_I (i.e., $\neg F_I \alpha \equiv G_I \neg \alpha$) no longer holds. Therefore, the satisfiability of the R_I operator depends on whether a considered k-path is a loop. Thus, as customary, we introduce a function $loop : \bigcup_{s \in S} \Pi_k(s) \to 2^{\mathbb{N}}$, which identifies those k-paths that are loops. The function is defined as: $loop(\pi_k) = \{l \mid 0 \leq l < k \text{ and } \pi_k(l) = \pi_k(k)\}$.

Bounded Semantics for RTECTL. Let M be a model, $k \geq 0$ a bound, φ an RTECTL formula, and $M, s \models_k \varphi$ denote that φ is k-true at the state s of M. The formula φ is k-true in M (in symbols $M \models_k \varphi$) iff $M, \iota \models_k \varphi$ (i.e., φ is k-true at the initial state of the model M). For every $s \in S$, the relation $\models_k$ (the bounded semantics) is defined inductively as follows:

$M, s \models_k \mathbf{true}$, $\quad\quad\quad\quad\quad M, s \not\models_k \mathbf{false}$,

$M, s \models_k p$ iff $p \in \mathcal{V}(s)$, $\quad M, s \models_k \neg p$ iff $p \notin \mathcal{V}(s)$,

$$M, s \models_k \alpha \vee \beta \quad \text{iff} \quad M, s \models_k \alpha \text{ or } M, s \models_k \beta,$$

$$M, s \models_k \alpha \wedge \beta \quad \text{iff} \quad M, s \models_k \alpha \text{ and } M, s \models_k \beta,$$

$$M, s \models_k \mathrm{EX}\alpha \quad \text{iff} \quad k > 0 \text{ and } (\exists \pi \in \Pi_k(s))M, \pi(1) \models_k \alpha,$$

$$M, s \models_k \mathrm{E}(\alpha \mathrm{U}_I \beta) \quad \text{iff} \quad (\exists \pi \in \Pi_k(s))(\exists 0 \leq m \leq k)(D\pi[0..m] \in I \text{ and }$$
$$M, \pi(m) \models_k \beta \text{ and } (\forall 0 \leq j < m)M, \pi(j) \models_k \alpha),$$

$M, s \models_k E(\alpha R_I \beta)$ iff $(\exists \pi \in \Pi_k(s))((\exists 0 \leq m \leq k)(D\pi[0..m] \in I$ and
$M, \pi(m) \models_k \alpha$ and $(\forall 0 \leq j \leq m)M, \pi(j) \models_k \beta)$ or
$(D\pi[0..k] \geq right(I)$ and $(\forall 0 \leq j \leq k)(D\pi[0..j] \in I$
implies $M, \pi(j) \models_k \beta))$ or $(D\pi[0..k] < right(I)$ and
$(\exists l \in loop(\pi))((\forall 0 \leq j < k)(D\pi[0..j] \in I$ implies
$M, \pi(j) \models_k \beta)$ and $(\forall l \leq j < k)(D\pi[0..k] + D\pi[l..j+1] \in I$
implies $M, \pi(j+1) \models_k \beta))))$.

The *bounded model checking problem* asks whether there exists $k \in \mathbb{N}$ such
that $M \models_k \varphi$. The following theorem states that for a given model and an
RTECTL formula there exists a bound k such that the model checking problem
$(M \models \varphi)$ can be reduced to the bounded model checking problem $(M \models_k \varphi)$.
The theorem can be proven by induction on the length of the formula φ.

Theorem 1. *Let M be a model and φ an RTECTL formula. Then, the following
equivalence holds: $M \models \varphi$ iff there exists $k \geq 0$ such that $M \models_k \varphi$.*

Translation to SAT. Let M be a simply-timed model, φ an RTECTL formula,
and $k \geq 0$ a bound. In BMC, in general, we define the propositional formula

$$[M, \varphi]_k := [M^{\varphi, \iota}]_k \wedge [\varphi]_{M,k} \tag{1}$$

that is satisfiable if and only if the underlying model M is the valid model for
the property φ. Namely, Formula (1) is satisfiable if and only if $M \models_k \varphi$ holds.

The definition of the formula $[M^{\varphi, \iota}]_k$ assumes that states of the model M are
encoded in a symbolic way. Such a symbolic encoding is possible, since the set
of states of M is finite. In particular, each state s can be represented by a vector
$w = (w_1, \ldots, w_r)$ (called a *symbolic state*) of propositional variables (called *state
variables*) whose length r depends on the number of locations in each STADD
automaton and the possible maximal value of integer variables.

Further, since the formula $[M^{\varphi, \iota}]_k$ defines the unfolding of the transition relation of the model M to the depth k, we need to represent k-paths in a symbolic
way. This representation is usually called a *j-th symbolic k-path π_j*. Moreover,
we have to know how many symbolic k-paths should be considered in the propositional encoding. The number of k-paths that is sufficient to translate formulae
of RTECTL is given by the function $f_k : \text{RTECTL} \to \mathbb{N}$, introduced in [16] and
applied to RTECTL (interpreted over standard Kripke models) in [19], that is
defined as follows: $f_k(\mathbf{true}) = f_k(\mathbf{false}) = f_k(p) = f_k(\neg p) = 0$, where $p \in \mathcal{PV}$;
$f_k(\alpha \wedge \beta) = f_k(\alpha) + f_k(\beta)$; $f_k(\alpha \vee \beta) = max\{f_k(\alpha), f_k(\beta)\}$; $f_k(EX\alpha) = f_k(\alpha) + 1$;
$f_k(E(\alpha U_I \beta)) = k \cdot f_k(\alpha) + f_k(\beta) + 1$; $f_k(E(\alpha R_I \beta)) = (k+1) \cdot f_k(\beta) + f_k(\alpha) + 1$.

Given the above, the j-th symbolic k-path π_j is defined as the following
sequence $((d_{0,j}, w_{0,j}), \ldots, (d_{k,j}, w_{k,j}))$, where $w_{i,j}$ are symbolic states and $d_{i,j}$
are *symbolic durations*, for $0 \leq i \leq k$ and $0 \leq j < f_k(\varphi)$. The *symbolic duration*
$d_{i,j}$ is a vector $d_{i,j} = (d_{1,j}, \ldots, d_{x,j})$ of propositional variables (called *duration
variables*), whose length x equals to $\lceil log_2(d_{max}) \rceil$, where d_{max} is a maximal
durations appearing in the system under consideration.

Let w and w' (resp., d and d') be two different symbolic states (resp., durations). We assume definitions of the following auxiliary propositional formulae:

$I_\iota(w)$ - encodes the initial state of the model M, $\mathcal{T}((d, w), (d'w'))$ - encodes the transition relation of M, $p(w)$ - encodes the set of states of M in which $p \in \mathcal{PV}$ holds, $H(w, w')$ - encodes equality of two global states, $\mathcal{B}_k^I(\boldsymbol{\pi}_n)$ - encodes that the duration time represented by the sequence $d_{1,n}, \ldots, d_{k,n}$ of symbolic durations is less than $right(I)$, $\mathcal{D}_j^I(\boldsymbol{\pi}_n)$ - encodes that the duration time represented by the sequence $d_{1,n}, \ldots, d_{j,n}$ of symbolic durations belongs to the interval I, $\mathcal{D}_{k;l,m}^I(\boldsymbol{\pi}_n)$ for $l \leq m$ - encodes that the duration time represented by the sequences $d_{1,n}, \ldots, d_{k,n}$ and $d_{l+1,n}, \ldots, d_{m,n}$ of symbolic durations belongs to the interval I.

The formula $[M^{\varphi,\iota}]_k$ encoding the unfolding of the transition relation of the model M $f_k(\varphi)$-times to the depth k is defined as follows:

$$[M^{\varphi,\iota}]_k \quad := I_\iota(w_{0,0}) \wedge \bigwedge_{j=0}^{f_k(\varphi)-1} \bigwedge_{i=0}^{k-1} \mathcal{T}((d_{i,j}, w_{i,j}), (d_{i+1,j}, w_{i+1,j})) \quad (2)$$

For every RTECTL formula φ the function f_k determines how many symbolic k-paths are needed for translating the formula φ. Given a formula φ and a set A of k-paths such that $|A| = f_k(\varphi)$, we divide the set A into subsets needed for translating the subformulae of φ. To accomplish this goal we need some auxiliary functions that were defined in [22]. We recall the definitions of these functions, but for more details see the paper [22].

The relation $\prec$ is defined on the power set of $\mathbb{N}$ as follows: $A \prec B$ iff for all natural numbers x and y, if $x \in A$ and $y \in B$, then $x < y$ (e.g., $\{1, 2, 3\} \prec \{5, 6\}$, $\{1, 2, 5\} \nprec \{3, 6\}$). Now, let $A \subset \mathbb{N}$ be a finite nonempty set, and $n, e \in \mathbb{N}$, where $e \leq |A|$. Then,

 - $g_l(A, e)$ denotes the subset B of A such that $|B| = e$ and $B \prec A \setminus B$.
 - $g_r(A, e)$ denotes the subset C of A such that $|C| = e$ and $A \setminus C \prec C$.
 - $g_s(A)$ denotes the set $A \setminus \{min(A)\}$.
 - If n divides $|A| - e - 1$, then $h_n^{\mathrm{U}}(A, e)$ denotes the sequence $(B_0, \ldots, B_n)$ of subsets of $A \setminus \{min(A)\}$ such that $\bigcup_{j=0}^n B_j = A \setminus \{min(A)\}$, $|B_0| = \ldots = |B_{n-1}|$, $|B_n| = e$, and $B_i \prec B_j$ for every $0 \leq i < j \leq n$. If $h_n^{\mathrm{U}}(A, e) = (B_0, \ldots, B_n)$, then $h_n^{\mathrm{U}}(A, e)(j)$ denotes the set B_j, for every $0 \leq j \leq n$.
 - If $n+1$ divides $|A| - e - 1$, then $h_n^{\mathrm{R}}(A, e)$ denotes the sequence $(B_0, \ldots, B_{n+1})$ of subsets of $A \setminus \{min(A)\}$ such that $\bigcup_{j=0}^{n+1} B_j = A \setminus \{min(A)\}$, $|B_0| = \ldots = |B_n|$, $|B_{n+1}| = e$, and $B_i \prec B_j$ for every $0 \leq i < j \leq n + 1$. If $h_n^{\mathrm{R}}(A, e) = (B_0, \ldots, B_{n+1})$, then $h_n^{\mathrm{R}}(A, e)(j)$ denotes the set B_j, for every $0 \leq j \leq n + 1$.

Let φ be an RTECTL formula, M a model, and $k \in \mathbb{N}$ a bound. The propositional formula $[\varphi]_{M,k} := [\varphi]_k^{[0,0,F_k(\varphi)]}$, where $F_k(\varphi) = \{j \in \mathbb{N} \mid 0 \leq j < f_k(\varphi)\}$, encodes the bounded semantics for RTECTL, and it is defined inductively as shown below. Namely, let $0 \leq n < f_k(\varphi)$, $m \leq k$, $n' = min(A)$, $h_k^{\mathrm{U}} = h_k^{\mathrm{U}}(A, f_k(\beta))$, and $h_k^{\mathrm{R}} = h_k^{\mathrm{R}}(A, f_k(\alpha))$, then:

$[\mathbf{true}]_k^{[m,n,A]} := \mathbf{true}, \qquad [\mathbf{false}]_k^{[m,n,A]} := \mathbf{false},$

$[p]_k^{[m,n,A]} := p(w_{m,n}), \qquad [\neg p]_k^{[m,n,A]} := \neg p(w_{m,n}),$

$[\alpha \wedge \beta]_k^{[m,n,A]} \quad := [\alpha]_k^{[m,n,g_l(A,f_k(\alpha))]} \wedge [\beta]_k^{[m,n,g_r(A,f_k(\beta))]},$

$$[\alpha \vee \beta]_k^{[m,n,A]} \quad := [\alpha]_k^{[m,n,g_l(A,f_k(\alpha))]} \vee [\beta]_k^{[m,n,g_l(A,f_k(\beta))]},$$

$$[\mathrm{EX}\alpha]_k^{[m,n,A]} \quad := H(w_{m,n}, w_{0,n'}) \wedge [\alpha]_k^{[1,n',g_s(A)]}, \text{ if } k > 0; \textbf{false}, \text{otherwise},$$

$$[\mathrm{E}(\alpha \mathrm{U}_I \beta)]_k^{[m,n,A]} := H(w_{m,n}, w_{0,n'}) \wedge \bigvee_{i=0}^k ([\beta]_k^{[i,n',h_k^{\mathrm{U}}(k)]} \wedge \mathrm{D}_i^I(\boldsymbol{\pi}_{n'}) \wedge$$
$$\bigwedge_{j=0}^{i-1} [\alpha]_k^{[j,n',h_k^{\mathrm{U}}(j)]}),$$

$$[\mathrm{E}(\alpha \mathrm{R}_I \beta)]_k^{[m,n,A]} := H(w_{m,n}, w_{0,n'}) \wedge (\bigvee_{i=0}^k ([\alpha]_k^{[i,n',h_k^{\mathrm{R}}(k+1)]} \wedge \mathrm{D}_i^I(\boldsymbol{\pi}_{n'}) \wedge \bigwedge_{j=0}^i$$
$$[\beta]_k^{[j,n',h_k^{\mathrm{R}}(j)]}) \vee (\neg \mathcal{B}_k^I(\boldsymbol{\pi}_{n'}) \wedge \bigwedge_{j=0}^k (\mathrm{D}_j^I(\boldsymbol{\pi}_{n'}) \to [\beta]_k^{[j,n',h_k^{\mathrm{R}}(j)]}))$$
$$\vee (\mathcal{B}_k^I(\boldsymbol{\pi}_{n'}) \wedge \bigwedge_{j=0}^k (\mathrm{D}_j^I(\boldsymbol{\pi}_{n'}) \to [\beta]_k^{[j,n',h_k^{\mathrm{R}}(j)]}) \wedge \bigvee_{l=0}^{k-1}$$
$$[H(w_{k,n'}, w_{l,n'}) \wedge \bigwedge_{j=l}^{k-1} (\mathrm{D}_{k;l,j+1}^I(\boldsymbol{\pi}_{n'}) \to [\beta]_k^{[j,n',h_k^{\mathrm{R}}(j)]})]))).$$

The theorem below states the correctness and the completeness of the presented translation. It can be proven by induction on the complexity of the given RTECTL formula.

Theorem 2. *Let M be a model, and φ an RTECTL formula. Then for every $k \in \mathbb{N}$, $M \models_k \varphi$ if, and only if, the propositional formula $[M, \varphi]_k$ is satisfiable.*

4   Experimental Results

For the tests we have used a computer with Intel Core i3-2125 processor, 8 GB of RAM, and running Linux 3.2. We set the timeout to 900 seconds, and memory limit to 8GB. In our BMC technique we use the state of the art SAT-solver MiniSat 2 (http://minisat.se/MiniSat.html). We aimed at comparing our experimental results with other tools, to put them into a wider context. Unfortunately, we had not much choice because the number of comparable tools proved to be limited, and after a careful selection we have identified only the tool TSMV to be suitable with respect to input formalisms and checked properties.

The Bridge-Crossing Problem. (BCP) [18] is a famous mathematical puzzle with time critical aspects. A STADD automata model of BCP is shown in Fig. 1. We have five automata that run in parallel and synchronised on actions LR_i, RL_i, and F_{ij}, for $i \neq j$ and $i, j \in \{1, \ldots, 4\}$. The action LR_i (respectively, RL_i) means that the i-th person goes from the left side of the bridge to its right side (respectively, from the right side of the bridge to its left side) bringing back the lamp. The action F_{ij} with $i < j$ (respectively, F_{ij} with $i > j$) means that the persons i and j cross the bridge together from its left side to its right side (respectively, from its right side to its left side). Four automata (those with states named as Li and Ri, for $1 \leqslant i \leqslant 4$) represent persons, and one represents a lamp (i.e., a coordination process) that keeps track of the position of the lamp, and ensures that at most two persons cross in one move.

Let Min denote the minimum time required to cross the bridge, $N \geqslant 2$ be the number of persons, and $right = (2 \cdot N - 3) \cdot (t_1 + (N - 1) \cdot 3)$. We have tested BCP for $N \geqslant 4$ persons, $t_i = t_1 + (i - 1) \cdot 3$ with $1 \leqslant i \leqslant N$ and $t_1 \geq 10$, on the following RTECTL formulae: $\varphi_{1BCP} = \mathrm{EF}_{[Min, Min+1]}(\bigwedge_{i=1}^N Ri)$ and $\varphi_{2BCP} = \mathrm{EG}_{[0,right)}(\bigvee_{i=1}^N \neg Ri)$; the formulae are true in the model for BCP.

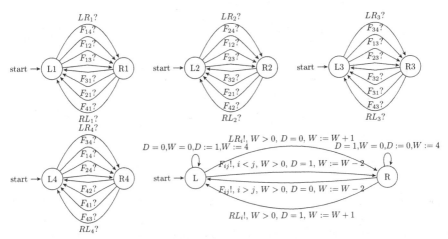

Fig. 1. A network of STADD automata that models BCP for 4 persons. The variable D indicates the crossing direction: $D = 1$ ($D = 0$) means that all the persons cross the bridge from its left side to its right side, (from its right side to its left side). The variable W denotes the number of persons waiting on the left (right) side of the bridge, if $D = 1$ ($D = 0$).

Moreover, we observed that formula $\varphi_{3BCP} = \mathrm{EG}_{[0,right+1)}(\bigvee_{i=1}^{N} \neg R_i)$ is false in the model for BCP. This has been confirmed by TSMV.

Generic Simply-Timed Pipeline Paradigm. We adapted the benchmark scenario of *a generic pipeline paradigm* [15], and we called it the *generic simply-timed pipeline paradigm* (GSPP). The model of GSPP involves Producer producing data, Consumer receiving data, and a chain of n intermediate Nodes that transmit data produced by Producer to Consumer. Producer, Nodes, and Consumer have different producing, sending, processing, and consuming times.

A STADD automata model of GSPP is shown in Fig. 2. We have $n + 2$ automata (n automata representing Nodes, one automaton for Producer, and one automaton for Consumer) that run in parallel and synchronise on actions $Send_i$ ($1 \leqslant i \leqslant n + 1$). Action $Send_i$ ($1 \leqslant i \leqslant n$) means that i-th Node has received data produced by Producer. Action $Send_{n+1}$ means that Consumer has received data produced by Producer. Action $Proc_i$ ($1 \leqslant i \leqslant n$) means that i-th Node processes data. Action *Produce* means that Producer generates data. Action *Consume* means that Consumer consumes data produced by Producer.

Let $1 \leqslant i \leqslant n$. We have tested the GSPP problem with the following basic durations: $d(Produce) = 2$, $d(send_i) = 2$, $d(Proc_i) = 4$, $d(Consume) = 2$, and their multiplications by 50, 100, 150, etc., on the following RTECTL formulae:

$$\varphi_{1GSPP} = \mathrm{EF}_{[Min,Min+1)}ConsReceived$$

$$\varphi_{2GSPP} = \mathrm{EG}_{[0,\infty)}(\neg ProdSend \vee \mathrm{EF}_{[0,Min-d(Produce)+1)}ConsReceived)$$

$$\varphi_{3GSPP} = \mathrm{EG}_{[0,\infty)}(\neg ProdSend \vee \mathrm{EG}_{[0,Min-d(Produce))}ConsReady)$$

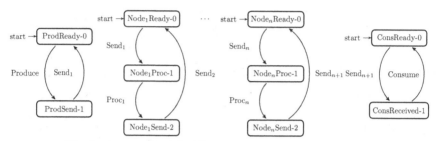

Fig. 2. A network of STADD automata that models GSPP

where Min denotes the minimum time required to receive by Consumer the data produced by Producer. Note that the φ_{2GSPP} and φ_{3GSPP} are properties, respectively, of the type the existential *bounded-response* (asserting that "something good" will happen within a specified amount of time) and existential *bounded-invariance* (asserting that "nothing bad" will happen for a certain amount of time). All the above formulae are true in the model for GSPP.

Performance Evaluation. The experimental results show that our SAT-based BMC method and the BDD-based method (also designed for RTECTL and simply-timed models) implemented in TSMV complement each other. More precisely, on the one hand, our SAT-based BMC is insensitive to scaling up the durations, whereas the computation time and memory consumption of TSMV increases substantially in this case. On the other hand, our method is sensitive to scaling up the size of benchmarks, whereas the TSMV with relatively small durations can handle more components, and it performs much better in terms of the total time and the memory consumption. The inferiority of TSMV in the first case mentioned above probably results from an inefficient encoding of the variable `duration`. The reason that the TSMV performs much better than our method in the second case is that the length of the counterexamples grows with the number of the components and the efficiency of the SAT-based BMC strongly depends on the length of the counterexamples.

We observed that when we scale up the timing parameters of TSMV for both benchmarks and bounded reachability properties (i.e., φ_{1BCP} and φ_{1GSPP}), the computation time grows polynomially and the memory usage grows linearly, regardless of the number of persons or nodes considered. Moreover, for GSPP with 1 node and for BCP with 4 persons, respectively, we managed to increase the timing parameters up to the basic durations multiplied by 30000, and up to the maximal speed of the 1st person equal to 5000. In contrast, the computation time and memory consumption of our SAT-based BMC method are nearly constant, regardless of the value of the timing parameters. To be precise, in order to calculate results for GSPP with 1 node for both the basic durations (bd for short) and the bd multiplied by 1000000, our method uses 6.00 MB and the test lasts 0.05 seconds. To calculate results for BCP with 4 persons for the maximal speeds of the i-th person being of the form (1) $t_i = 10 + (i - 1) \cdot 3$, (2)

$t_i = 5000 + (i - 1) \cdot 3$, and (3) $t_i = 1000000 + (i - 1) \cdot 3$, our method uses 8.00 MB and the test lasts 0.33 (resp. 0.46, 0.30) seconds.

Further, if the value of durations is relatively small, we scale up the size (i.e., the number of nodes/persons) of both benchmarks, and we test formulae φ_{1BCP} and φ_{1GSPP}, then the experimental results show that our SAT-based BMC is inferior to TSMV. Namely, in the set time limit, TSMV can handle GSPP with 350, 300, and 70 nodes, respectively, when we consider the bd, the bd multiplied by 1000, and the bd multiplied by 5000. In case of BCP, TSMV can handle 24 and 23 persons, respectively, for the maximal speeds of the i-th person being of the form $t_i = 10 + (i - 1) \cdot 3$ and $t_i = 100 + (i - 1) \cdot 3$. Our method can handle GSPP with 34 nodes and BCP with 13 persons, regardless of the value of the timing parameters.

The inferiority mentioned above is less of a problem as we increase both the size of benchmarks and the timing parameters. More precisely, if we take BCP with the crossing time of the 1st person equal to 1000 (resp., 3000 and 5000), then TSMV can handle 11 (resp., 5 and 4) persons only. Thus, TSMV becomes inferior to our method. Moreover, TSMV managed to compute 34 and 10 nodes only, respectively, for GSPP with the bd multiplied by 7000 and 10000. In contrast, our method managed to compute 34 nodes for GSPP with the bd multiplied by 1000000 and larger.

For properties φ_{2BCP}, φ_{2GSPP}, and φ_{3GSPP} we have also scaled up both the number of persons/nodes and the timing parameters and we observed the same as for the the bounded reachability properties (see charts in Fig. 3, Fig. 5, Fig. 4).

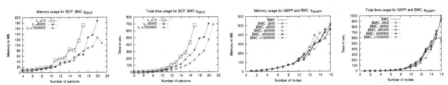

Fig. 3. BMC: Scaling up both the number of persons/nodes and durations

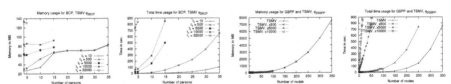

Fig. 4. TSMV: Scaling up both the number of persons/nodes and durations

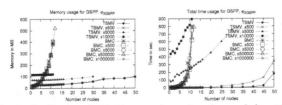

Fig. 5. Scaling up both the number of nodes and durations

5 Conclusions

We proposed SAT-based BMC verification method for model checking RTECTL properties interpreted over the simply-time systems (Kripke structures where transitions carry an arbitrary duration) that are generated for simply-timed automata with discrete data. For the analysis of soft real-time systems, this extends the verification facilities that are offered in VerICS, since our algorithm is implemented as a new module of the tool. Also, to our best knowledge, there is no other BMC technique (SAT- or BDD-based) for RTECTL interpreted over the simply-time systems. Moreover, TSMV, the only existing model checking tool for RTCTL interpreted over the simply-time models, is not being actively developed anymore.

References

1. Alur, R.: Timed automata. In: Halbwachs, N., Peled, D.A. (eds.) CAV 1999. LNCS, vol. 1633, pp. 8–22. Springer, Heidelberg (1999)
2. Alur, R., Courcoubetis, C., Dill, D.: Model checking in dense real-time. Information and Computation 104(1), 2–34 (1993)
3. Behrmann, G., David, A., Larsen, K.G.: A tutorial on UPPAAL. In: Bernardo, M., Corradini, F. (eds.) SFM-RT 2004. LNCS, vol. 3185, pp. 200–236. Springer, Heidelberg (2004)
4. Berthomieu, B., Vernadat, F.: Time petri nets analysis with tina. In: Proceedings of QEST 2006, pp. 123–124. IEEE Computer Society (2006)
5. Beyer, D.: Rabbit: Verification of real-time systems. In: Proceedings of the Workshop on Real-Time Tools (RT-TOOLS 2001), pp. 13–21 (2001)
6. Cabodi, G., Camurati, P., Quer, S.: Can BDDs compete with SAT solvers on bounded model checking? In: Proceedings of DAC 2002, pp. 117–122. ACM (2002)
7. Campos, S., Clarke, E.: Analysis and verification of real-time systems using quantitative symbolic algorithms. International Journal on Software Tools for Technology Transfer 2(3), 260–269 (1999)
8. Clarke, E., Biere, A., Raimi, R., Zhu, Y.: Bounded model checking using satisfiability solving. Formal Methods in System Design 19(1), 7–34 (2001)
9. Clarke, E.M., Grumberg, O., Peled, D.A.: Model Checking. The MIT Press, Cambridge (1999)
10. Furia, C.A., Spoletini, P.: Tomorrow and all our yesterdays: MTL satisfiability over the integers. In: Fitzgerald, J.S., Haxthausen, A.E., Yenigun, H. (eds.) ICTAC 2008. LNCS, vol. 5160, pp. 126–140. Springer, Heidelberg (2008)
11. Kacprzak, M., Nabialek, W., Niewiadomski, A., Penczek, W., Półrola, A., Szreter, M., Woźna, B., Zbrzezny, A.: VerICS 2007 - a model checker for knowledge and real-time. Fundamenta Informaticae 85(1-4), 313–328 (2008)
12. Markey, N., Schnoebelen, P.: Symbolic model checking for simply-timed systems. In: Lakhnech, Y., Yovine, S. (eds.) FORMATS 2004 and FTRTFT 2004. LNCS, vol. 3253, pp. 102–117. Springer, Heidelberg (2004)
13. Męski, A., Penczek, W., Szreter, M., Woźna-Szcześniak, B., Zbrzezny, A.: Two approaches to bounded model checking for linear time logic with knowledge. In: Jezic, G., Kusek, M., Nguyen, N.-T., Howlett, R.J., Jain, L.C. (eds.) KES-AMSTA 2012. LNCS, vol. 7327, pp. 514–523. Springer, Heidelberg (2012)

14. Merlin, P., Farber, D.J.: Recoverability of communication protocols - implication of a theoretical study. IEEE Transaction on Communications 24(9), 1036–1043 (1976)

15. Peled, D.: All from one, one for all: On model checking using representatives. In: Courcoubetis, C. (ed.) CAV 1993. LNCS, vol. 697, pp. 409–423. Springer, Heidelberg (1993)

16. Penczek, W., Woźna, B., Zbrzezny, A.: Bounded model checking for the universal fragment of CTL. Fundamenta Informaticae 51(1-2), 135–156 (2002)

17. Pradella, M., Morzenti, A., San Pietro, P.: A metric encoding for bounded model checking. In: Cavalcanti, A., Dams, D.R. (eds.) FM 2009. LNCS, vol. 5850, pp. 741–756. Springer, Heidelberg (2009)

18. Saul, X., Levmore, E.E.C.: Super Strategies for Puzzles and Games. Doubleday, Garden City (1981)

19. Woźna-Szcześniak, B.: Bounded model checking for the existential part of real-time CTL and knowledge. In: Szmuc, T., Szpyrka, M., Zendulka, J. (eds.) CEE-SET 2009. LNCS, vol. 7054, pp. 164–178. Springer, Heidelberg (2012)

20. Woźna-Szcześniak, B., Zbrzezny, A.: SAT-Based BMC for Deontic Metric Temporal Logic and Deontic Interleaved Interpreted Systems. In: Baldoni, M., Dennis, L., Mascardi, V., Vasconcelos, W. (eds.) DALT 2012. LNCS, vol. 7784, pp. 170–189. Springer, Heidelberg (2013)

21. Woźna-Szcześniak, B., Zbrzezny, A., Zbrzezny, A.: The BMC method for the existential part of RTCTLK and interleaved interpreted systems. In: Antunes, L., Pinto, H.S. (eds.) EPIA 2011. LNCS, vol. 7026, pp. 551–565. Springer, Heidelberg (2011)

22. Zbrzezny, A.: Improving the translation from ECTL to SAT. Fundamenta Informaticae 85(1-4), 513–531 (2008)

23. Zbrzezny, A., Półrola, A.: Sat-based reachability checking for timed automata with discrete data. Fundamenta Informaticae 79(3-4), 579–593 (2007)

Author Index

Aït-Salaht, Farah   13
Aldhalaan, Arwa   28
Amparore, Elvio Gilberto   206
Arcelli, Davide   312

Berardinelli, Luca   300
Bernardo, Marco   104
Brunnert, Andreas   74

Carnevali, Laura   176
Castel-Taleb, Hind   13
Cerotti, Davide   221
Chis, Tiberiu   251
Ciardo, Gianfranco   58
Cortellessa, Vittorio   1, 312

Dei Rossi, Gian-Luca   236
De Nitto Personé, Vittoria   288
Di Lonardo, Andrea   288
Di Marco, Antinisca   300
Di Ruscio, Davide   312
Donatelli, Susanna   206

Fourneau, Jean-Michel   13

Gallina, Lucia   236
Gribaudo, Marco   221

Haas, František   149
Harrison, Peter G.   191
Haverkort, Boudewijn   276
Horký, Vojtěch   149
Horváth, Gábor   119

Knottenbelt, William J.   325
Kotrč, Jaroslav   149
Kounev, Samuel   263
Krauß, Tilman   164
Krcmar, Helmut   74

Lacina, Martin   149
Lladó, Catalina M.   134

Marchesani, Stefano   300
Markovski, Jasen   43
Menascé, Daniel A.   28
Mészáros, András   89
Mooij, Arjan   276

Noorshams, Qais   263

Okamura, Hiroyuki   119

Pace, Stefano   300
Palazzi, Claudio E.   7
Paolieri, Marco   176
Pekergin, Nihal   13
Piazzolla, Pietro   221
Pomante, Luigi   300

Qiu, Zhan   191

Reinecke, Philipp   164
Remke, Anne   276
Reussner, Ralf   263
Rossi, Sabina   236

Serazzi, Giuseppe   221
Smith, Connie U.   134

Tadano, Kumiko   176
Telek, Miklós   89
Tesei, Luca   104
Tsimashenka, Iryna   325
Tůma, Petr   149

van den Berg, Freek   276
Vaupel, Robert   263
Vicario, Enrico   176
Vögele, Christian   74

Wolter, Katinka   164
Woźna-Szcześniak, Bożena   337

Zbrzezny, Agnieszka   337
Zbrzezny, Andrzej   337
Zhao, Yang   58